111

ATMOSPHERIC CHEMISTRY AND
PHYSICS OF AIR POLLUTION

Atmospheric Chemistry and Physics of Air Pollution

JOHN H. SEINFELD

California Institute of Technology
Pasadena, California

A Wiley Interscience Publication

JOHN WILEY & SONS

New York · Chichester · Brisbane · Toronto · Singapore

Copyright © 1986 by John Wiley & Sons, Inc.

All rights reserved. Published simultaneously in Canada.

Reproduction or translation of any part of this work
beyond that permitted by Section 107 or 108 of the
1976 United States Copyright Act without the permission
of the copyright owner is unlawful. Requests for
permission or further information should be addressed to
the Permissions Department, John Wiley & Sons, Inc.

Library of Congress Cataloging in Publication Data:

Seinfeld, John H.
  Atmospheric chemistry and physics of air
pollution.

  "A Wiley-Interscience publication."
  Includes index.
  1. Air–Pollution.   2. Atmospheric chemistry.
3. Environmental chemistry   I. Title.
TD193.S44 1985   628.5′3   85-12251
ISBN 0-471-82857-2

Printed in the United States of America

10 9 8 7 6 5 4 3 2 1

To BRB

Preface

The processes that impact species once they are released into the atmosphere involve a full spectrum of chemistry and physics. While being transported by the motion of the air, a gas molecule may react chemically in the gas phase, may be absorbed into a particle or droplet where it might chemically react, may be transported into the stratosphere, or may be removed by interaction with the earth's surface. An emitted particle may coagulate with other particles, may grow by absorption of vapor molecules, or may be removed at the earth's surface or by incorporation into a water droplet.

The object of this book is to provide a rigorous, comprehensive treatment of the chemistry of air pollutants in the atmosphere, the formation, growth, and dynamics of aerosols, the meteorology of air pollution, and the transport, diffusion, and removal of species in the atmosphere. Each of these elements is covered in detail in the present volume. In each area the central results are developed thoroughly from first principles. In this way, the reader will gain a significant understanding of the science underlying the description of atmospheric processes and will be able to extend theories and results beyond those for which we have space here.

The book assumes that the reader has had introductory courses in thermodynamics, transport phenomena (fluid mechanics and/or heat and mass transfer), and engineering mathematics (differential equations). Thus, the treatment is aimed at the senior or first-year graduate level in typical chemical, mechanical, civil, and environmental engineering curricula as well as in meteorology and atmospheric science programs.

The book is intended to serve as a textbook for a course in the atmospheric aspects of air pollution that might vary in length from one quarter or semester to a full academic year. Aside from its use as a course textbook the book will serve as a comprehensive reference book for air pollution professionals as well as for those from traditional engineering and science disciplines who wish to study air pollution.

Numerous problems are provided to enable the reader to evaluate his or her understanding of the material. In many cases the problems have been chosen to extend the results given in the chapter to new situations.

The book has been divided into six major subject areas:

I.   Air Pollutants, Their Sources and Effects
II.   Air Pollution Chemistry
III.   Aerosols
IV.   Air Pollution Meteorology
V.   Atmospheric Diffusion
VI.   Special Topics

Part I contains three chapters and is intended largely as an introduction to the air pollution problem. Chapter 1 discusses air pollutants, their global behavior, and their typical atmospheric concentration levels. Chapter 2 is a brief survey of effects of air pollution, particularly those on human health. Chapter 3 contains a concise account of sources of air pollutants in combustion processes. (Chapters 2 and 3 are provided as background material for the interested reader and may be skipped.)

Part II is devoted to air pollution chemistry. This section is divided into the two main areas of gas-phase and aqueous-phase atmospheric chemistry. These two chapters are followed by a brief chapter on mass transfer aspects of atmospheric chemistry, a subject that is frequently overlooked in discussions of this subject.

Part III is devoted to four self-contained chapters that cover fundamentals of the mechanics and dynamics of atmospheric aerosols. Particular attention is paid to heat and mass transfer phenomena, aerosol thermodynamics, and the interaction of aerosol populations.

Part IV consists of two chapters on air pollution meteorology. We have selected here only the key material from meteorology relevant to understanding the transport and dispersive properties of the lower atmosphere. Drawing on this material, Part V is devoted to a comprehensive and detailed analysis of atmospheric diffusion. It begins in Chapter 13 with a general discussion of atmospheric diffusion and then proceeds to two chapters that deal with specific types of atmospheric diffusion theories. Chapter 16 deals with atmospheric removal processes and residence times.

Part VI contains special topics in the atmospheric chemistry and physics of air pollution. Chapter 17 concerns air pollution concentration statistics, that is, how one represents the inherently random nature of the atmosphere in terms of statistical distributions of concentrations. The final chapter is devoted to acid rain. In a sense, the acid rain phenomenon combines virtually all the features of the previous chapters of the book, including gas- and aqueous-phase atmospheric chemistry, aerosol properties, transport, dispersion, and removal processes. Thus, while not only a topic of great current focus, acid rain serves as an elegant summarizing problem for the entire field of air pollution chemistry and physics.

Some readers may be familiar with the author's earlier book, *Air Pollution*: *Physical and Chemical Fundamentals* (McGraw-Hill, 1975), now out of print. While the present book is a new and comprehensive treatment of the same subject, those readers will recognize similarities in the level of detail and selection of topics. The present book is appropriate for courses in which the earlier book was used.

JOHN H. SEINFELD

Pasadena, California
October 1985

Acknowledgments

I wish to gratefully acknowledge Mark Cohen, Panos Georgopoulos, Lynn Hildemann, Carol Jones, Sonya Kreidenweis, Liyuan Liang, Chris Pilinis, Toby Shafer, Steve Strand, Dale Warren, Brian Wong, Jin-Jwang Wu, and Fangdong Yin for their assistance with problems and calculations in the book. I am also grateful to Joan Daisey, Fred Gelbard, Michael Hoffmann, William Nazaroff, and Philip Roth for their helpful comments on the manuscript. Finally I thank Pat Houseworth and Chris Conti for typing the manuscript so skillfully.

J.H.S.

Contents

PART FOUR   AIR POLLUTION METEOROLOGY

PART FIVE   ATMOSPHERIC DIFFUSION

ATMOSPHERIC CHEMISTRY AND PHYSICS OF AIR POLLUTION

PART ONE

Air Pollutants, Their Sources and Effects

ONE

Air Pollutants

1.1. AIR POLLUTION SYSTEM

Air pollution may be defined as any atmospheric condition in which substances are present at concentrations high enough above their normal ambient levels to produce a measurable effect on man, animals, vegetation, or materials. By "substances" we mean any natural or man-made chemical elements or compounds capable of being airborne. These substances may exist in the atmosphere as gases, liquid drops, or solid particles. Our definition includes any substance, whether noxious or benign; however, in using the term "measurable effect" we will generally restrict our attention to those substances that cause undesirable effects.

The air pollution problem can be simply depicted as a system consisting of three basic components:

1		2		3
Emission Sources	Pollutants →	Atmosphere	Mixing and chemical transformation →	Receptors

The ultimate aim of a study of this system is to provide an answer to the question: What is the optimum way to abate air pollution? It is quite clear that the abatement of air pollution in the large populated areas of the world will require a substantial economic investment, and perhaps changes in patterns of living and energy use as well. It is unrealistic to speak of no air pollution whatsoever; it is virtually impossible to eliminate entirely all man-made emissions of foreign substances into the atmosphere. It is more sensible to aim toward the reduction of pollutant emissions to a point such that noticeable adverse effects associated with the presence of pollutants in the air are eliminated. Because of the great expenditure of money that will be required, social and political factors will play a major role in meeting this goal.

Efforts to formulate a coherent strategy for air pollution control have been hampered to a large extent by the inability to demonstrate clearly the relationship between emission levels and airborne concentrations and between airborne concentrations and the adverse effects (mainly to human health) of air pollu-

3

tants. In fact, the lack of ability to associate health effects with air pollutant dosages in an unambiguous way has been one of the principal obstacles in gaining public support for air pollution control.

Customarily, air pollution is thought of as a phenomenon characteristic only of large urban centers and industrialized regions, where concentrations may reach values several orders of magnitude greater than ambient background levels. In the broadest sense, however, air pollution is a global problem, since pollutants ultimately become dispersed throughout the entire atmosphere.

Let us consider the elements of an air pollution problem for a particular airshed. Figure 1.1 summarizes in block diagram form the components of the air pollution system.

The genesis of air pollution is an *emission source*. Major emission sources are (1) transportation, (2) electric power generation, (3) refuse burning, (4) industrial and domestic fuel burning, and (5) industrial processes. Associated with emission sources are *source controls*, which are devices or operating procedures that prevent some of the pollutants produced by the emission source from reaching the atmosphere. Typical source controls include the use of gas-cleaning devices, substitution of a fuel that results in lesser emissions for one which results in greater emissions, and modifications of the process itself. Pollutants are emitted to the *atmosphere*, which acts as a medium for transport, dilution, and physical and chemical transformation. Pollutants may subsequently be detected by instruments or by human beings, animals, plants, or materials. Detection by these various "sensors" is manifested by some response, such as an irritation. Finally, as a result of these responses, emission sources and their controls can be modified either through automatic remote sensing of airborne concentrations or through public pressure and subsequent legislation.

In Figure 1.1 we have indicated controls at both the sources and the receptors. Three points in the air pollution system are amenable, at least in

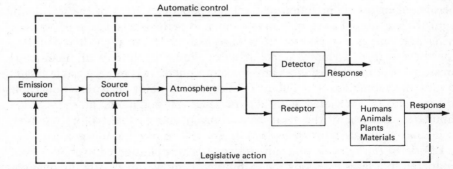

Figure 1.1. Air pollution system. Each block represents a given process in the chain of events from the formation of pollutants at the source to the detection of airborne pollutants by receptors. The dashed lines illustrate means by which responses become a basis for the regulation of emission sources and their controls.

principle, to control action. First, as we have mentioned, control can be exercised at the source of emission, resulting in lower quantities or a different distribution of effluents reaching the atmosphere or an alteration of the spatial and temporal distribution of emissions. Second, control could be directed to the atmosphere, for example by diverting wind flows or by discharging huge quantities of heat to alter the temperature structure of the atmosphere. Finally, control could be reserved for receptors, for example by extensive use of filtered air conditioning systems or, in extremity, use of gas masks. Of the three, control at the emission source is not only the most feasible but also the most practical. In short, the best way to control air pollution is to prevent contaminants from entering the atmosphere in the first place.

In this first chapter we provide an overview of the air pollution problem. We shall spend somewhat more time in this chapter on those aspects that will not be covered subsequently, particularly the global aspects of air pollutants.

1.2. AIR POLLUTANTS

The variety of airborne matter is so great that it can be classified in several different ways. The first classification, and the one that we will use in this section, is according to chemical composition. Virtually every element in the periodic table is found in the atmosphere; however, when classifying air pollutants according to chemical composition, we select a small number of major groupings that prove to be convenient in discussing air pollutants. These groupings are:

1. Sulfur-containing compounds.
2. Nitrogen-containing compounds.
3. Carbon-containing compounds.
4. Halogen-containing compounds.
5. Toxic substances.*
6. Radioactive compounds.[†]

Air pollutants may also be classified according to physical state, that is, gaseous, liquid, or solid. The latter two states imply that the material is present in the atmosphere in particulate form, so the natural division by physical state is either gaseous or particulate in form. In this section we will discuss briefly gaseous air pollutants classified by chemical composition; in Section 1.3 we will consider further those species that are normally present in particulate form.

---

*Toxic substances may clearly encompass compounds in the other classes. Nevertheless, we have devoted a separate section to them—see Section 2.4.5.
[†] Because of their specialized nature, we will not consider radioactive pollutants. The interested reader is referred to Eisenbud (1968).

Air pollutants may also be classed according to the manner in which they reached the atmosphere, namely

1. *Primary Pollutants.*   Those emitted directly from sources.
2. *Secondary Pollutants.*   Those formed in the atmosphere by chemical interactions among primary pollutants and normal atmospheric constituents.

The first recognized type of air pollution was that typified by high concentrations of sulfur compounds (SO_2 and sulfates), and particles, resulting from combustion of coal and high-sulfur-containing fuels. Cities with this characteristic type of air pollution are often in cold climates where electric power generation and domestic heating are major sources of emissions (examples include London, New York, and Chicago). In this case the air pollution consists mainly of the primary pollutant SO_2 and secondary sulfate-containing particles.

A second type of air pollution appeared only with the widespread use of gasoline as a motor fuel. Although automobile exhaust was recognized as a potential air pollutant as early as 1915, it was not until about 1945 that the first urban air pollution problem definitely attributable to automobile emissions appeared in Los Angeles. This type of air pollution, once the exclusive property of Los Angeles, now occurs worldwide in metropolitan areas in which there is a heavy use of automobiles; Tokyo, Athens, and Rome are three examples. Although historically this second type of air pollution has been called "smog" (or "photochemical smog"), presumably borrowed from the English condensation of smoke and fog, it is, in fact, neither smoke nor fog but the reactants and products of a complex series of reactions that take place when sunlight irradiates an atmosphere laden with organic gases and oxides of nitrogen. Photochemical smog occurs with high temperatures, bright sunlight, and low humidity. The main primary pollutants in photochemical smog are nitric oxide and hydrocarbons, which are rapidly converted to secondary pollutants, ozone, organic nitrates, oxidized hydrocarbons, and so-called photochemical aerosol. It is the secondary pollutants that are responsible for effects such as eye irritation and plant damage.

Atmospheric Concentration Units.   Two concentration units that are commonly used in reporting atmospheric species abundances are $\mu g \ m^{-3}$ and parts-per-million by volume (ppm). We develop here the relationship between these two units.

Parts-per-million by volume may be expressed as*

$$\text{concentration of species } i \text{ in ppm} = \frac{c_i}{c} \times 10^6$$

---

*Note that parts-per-million is not really a concentration, but a dimensionless volume fraction. Because of the widespread reference to this unit as a concentration we will retain this usage here.

where c_i and c are moles volume^{-1} of species i and air respectively at p and T. Given a pollutant mass concentration m_i expressed in $\mu g\ m^{-3}$

$$c_i = \frac{10^{-6}m_i}{M_i}$$

where M_i is the molecular weight of species i and $c = p/RT$. Thus

$$\text{concentration of species } i \text{ in ppm} = \frac{RT}{pM_i} \times \text{concentration in } \mu g\ m^{-3}.$$

If T is in K, p in millibars (mb), this relation becomes (where $R = 8.314 \times 10^{-2}\ mb\ m^3\ K^{-1}\ mole^{-1}$, since $1\ mb = 100\ Pa = 100\ N\ m^{-2}$)

$$\text{concentration of species } i \text{ in ppm} = \frac{8.314 \times 10^{-2}T}{pM_i}$$

$$\times \text{concentration in } \mu g\ m^{-3}.$$

We will also have occasion to use the concentration units of parts-per-hundred million by volume (pphm), parts-per-billion by volume (ppb), and parts-per-trillion by volume (ppt). When reporting concentrations of organic (carbon-containing) compounds, the measure parts-per-million of carbon (ppmC) is sometimes used. It is obtained by multiplying the species concentration in ppm by the number of carbon atoms in the molecule.

Units that will be used in this book are summarized in Appendix 1.A.1.

1.2.1. Composition of "Clean" Tropospheric Air

The atmosphere is composed primarily of nitrogen, oxygen, and several noble gases, the concentrations of which have remained remarkably fixed over time. Also present, however, are a number of gases that occur in relatively small and sometimes highly variable amounts. Water vapor, carbon dioxide, and ozone fall in the latter category, and so do the gases considered to be the common urban air pollutants.

In spite of its apparent unchanging nature, the atmosphere is in reality a dynamic system, with its gaseous constituents continuously being exchanged with vegetation, the oceans, and biological organisms. The so-called cycles of the atmospheric gases involve a number of physical and chemical processes. Gases are produced by chemical processes within the atmosphere itself, by biological activity, volcanic exhalation, radioactive decay, and man's industrial activities. Gases are removed from the atmosphere by chemical reactions in the atmosphere, by biological activity, by physical processes in the atmosphere (such as particle formation), and by deposition and uptake by the oceans and earth. The average residence time of a gas molecule introduced into the atmosphere can range from hours to millions of years, depending on the species. Most of the species considered air pollutants (in a region in which their concentrations exceed substantially the normal background levels) have natural as well as man-made sources. Therefore, in order to assess the effect man-made emissions may have on the atmosphere as a whole, it is essential to understand the atmospheric cycles of the pollutant gases, including natural and anthropogenic sources as well as predominant removal mechanisms.

The important atmospheric gases are listed in Table 1.1, arranged according to the nature of their global cycles. The total quantity of a species both in the atmosphere and dissolved in the oceans, say M_g, and that deposited on the earth as sediment, say M_s, must equal that which has been exhaled from the earth's interior over time, M_t. Thus, $M_t = M_g + M_s$. If $M_g > M_s$, most of

TABLE 1.1.   Atmospheric Gases

Gas	Average Concentration ppm	Approximate Residence Time[b]	Cycle	Status
Ar	9340	—		Accumulation
Ne	18	—	No cycle	during earth's
Kr	1.1	—		history
Xe	0.09	—		
N_2	780,840	10^6 yr	Biological and	?
O_2	209,460	10 yr	microbiological	
CH_4	1.65	7 yr	Biogenic and chemical	
CO_2	332	15 yr	Anthropogenic and biogenic	
CO	$0.05–0.2^a$	65 days	Anthropogenic and chemical	
H_2	0.58	10 yr	Biogenic and chemical	
N_2O	0.33	10 yr	Biogenic and chemical	Quasi-steady state or equilibrium (H_2O, CO_2?)
SO_2	$10^{-5}–10^{-4}$	40 days	Anthropogenic and chemical	
NH_3	$10^{-4}–10^{-3}$	20 days	Biogenic, chemical, rainout	
$NO + NO_2$	$10^{-6}–10^{-2}$	1 day	Anthropogenic, chemical, lightning	
O_3	$10^{-2}–10^{-1}$	?	Chemical	
HNO_3	$10^{-5}–10^{-3}$	1 day	Chemical, rainout	
H_2O	Variable	10 days	Physico-chemical	
He	5.2	10 yr		

[a]Species with a range of concentrations indicated are those classed as air pollutants.
[b]Subsequently we will discuss how atmospheric residence times are determined.

the constituent has remained in the atmosphere and, for that reason, it can be called an *accumulative* gas. If, on the other hand, $M_g < M_s$, only a small amount of the gas is in the atmosphere and its concentration level is determined by processes resulting in quasi-steady-state conditions. Such gases can be called nonaccumulative or *equilibrium* gases. The ratio M_g/M_s for the noble gases and N_2 is greater than 1. From CO_2 on down Table 1.1, the ratio $M_g/M_s \leq 10^{-3}$, clearly establishing these species as equilibrium gases.

The processes that govern the abundance of the equilibrium gases vary for different gases. The water composition of the atmosphere is controlled by the variation of the vapor pressure of water with temperature. Ozone abundance is determined, as we shall see, by chemical processes in the upper and lower atmosphere. Methane, hydrogen, nitrous oxide, and carbon monoxide levels are controlled by atmospheric chemical reactions as well as by biological processes. It is estimated that only one one-thousandth of all CO_2 released to the earth's surface by exhalation has remained in the atmosphere–ocean system, with most existing as carbonate sediments on the land and in water. The processes actually governing the atmospheric CO_2 content have not been clearly determined, although it is most likely that these represent a combination of chemical equilibrium with the oceans and geochemical cycles. For oxygen, the estimated range of M_g/M_s lies between $1/50$ and $1/12$. Most of the earth's oxygen is believed to have been produced by photosynthesis. Oxygen is consumed by oxidation of minerals at the earth's surface. Thus, the oxygen concentration in the atmosphere is probably a result of both accumulation and geochemical cycle.

1.2.2. Sulfur-Containing Compounds

The major sulfur-containing compounds in the atmosphere are carbonyl sulfide (COS), carbon disulfide (CS_2), dimethyl sulfide ((CH_3)$_2$S), hydrogen sulfide (H_2S), sulfur dioxide (SO_2), and sulfate (SO_4^{2-}). The sources of atmospheric sulfur compounds are biological decay, combustion of fossil fuels and organic matter, and sea spray. The global sulfur cycle is depicted in Figure 1.2, showing the major reservoirs, pathways, and forms of occurrence of sulfur. Each flux is identified with a number; for example, the anthropogenic flux of SO_2 to the atmosphere is path 5.* Table 1.2 presents estimates from several sources of the sulfur fluxes associated with each of the paths shown in Figure 1.2. We see that anthropogenic emissions of SO_2 are estimated to represent an appreciable fraction of the flux of sulfur to the atmosphere. The variations among the estimates are indicative of the degree of uncertainty involved in estimating the global sulfur cycle.

The major biogenic sulfur species having a clearly defined role in tropospheric chemistry are carbonyl sulfide, carbon disulfide, dimethyl sulfide, and

---

*One metric ton $= 10^3$ kg $= 10^6$ g. One million metric tons (1 MT) $= 10^{12}$ g $= 1$ Tg. These units (MT and Tg) are used interchangeably in discussing global cycles of species.

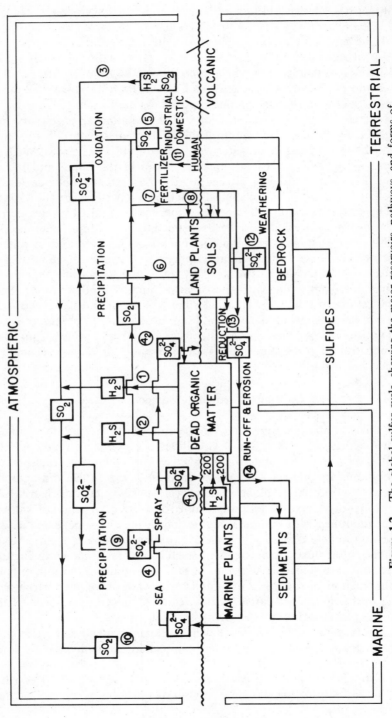

Figure 1.2. The global sulfur cycle, showing the major reservoirs, pathways, and forms of occurrence of sulfur. Figures enclosed in circles refer to the individual fluxes and correspond to figures in column 2, Table 1.2. Flux between marine plants and dead organic matter estimated as 200 Tg yr^{-1}. (Moss, 1978)

TABLE 1.2. Estimates of Annual Fluxes (Tg yr^{-1}) of Environmental Sulfur[a]

Source of Sulfur	Flux Number in Figure	Eriksson (1960, 1963)	Robinson and Robbins (1968, 1970)	Kellogg et al. (1972)	Friend (1973)	Granat et al. (1976)
Biological decay (land)	1	110	68	90	58	5
Biological decay (ocean)	2	170	30		48	27
Volcanic activity	3	—	—	1.5	2	3
Sea spray (total)	4	45	44	47	44	44
To ocean	4$_1$	(40)	—	(43)	(40)	(40)
To land	4$_2$	(5)	—	(4)	(4)	(4)
Anthropogenic	5	40	70	50	65	65
Precipitation (land)	6	65	70	86	86	43
Dry deposition	7	100	20	10	20	28
Absorption (vegetation)	8	75	26	15	15	
Precipitation and deposition (ocean)	9,10	200	96	72	96	73
Total sulfur involved in atmospheric balance		365	212	183	217	144
Atmospheric balance Land → sea		−10	+26	+5	+8	+18
Sea → land		5	4	4	4	17
Fertilizer	11	10	11	—	26	—
Rock weathering	12	15	14	—	42	—
Pedosphere → river runoff	13	55	48	—	89	—
Total river runoff	14	80	73	—	136	122

[a]Source: as cited in each column and, in part, Friend (1973, Table 4). Moss (1978).

hydrogen sulfide. Carbonyl sulfide is the most abundant gaseous sulfur species in the troposphere. Concentrations of COS are approximately 500 ± 50 ppt, with no detectable systematic variations vertically or latitudinally. This uniform concentration suggests an atmospheric lifetime for COS that is at least longer than the characteristic time for mixing throughout the troposphere. The tropospheric abundance and distribution of CS$_2$ are not well known. Available measurements indicate a concentration range from approximately 15 to 30 ppt in surface nonurban air to 100 to 200 ppt in surface level polluted air. The concentration of CS$_2$ appears to decrease rapidly with altitude, indicating ground level sources and a relatively short atmospheric lifetime. Dimethyl sulfide ($(CH_3)_2S$) is the most abundant volatile sulfur compound in seawater, with an average concentration of about 100×10^{-9} g l^{-1}. It is produced by both algae and bacteria. The global sea-to-air flux of sulfur as $(CH_3)_2S$ has been estimated as about 0.1 g S m^{-2} yr^{-1}, which totals to approximately 39 Tg S yr^{-1}. Finally, with respect to H_2S, knowledge of its natural sources is quite incomplete. Preliminary studies have shown that anaerobic, sulfur-rich soils (e.g., coastal soils and sediments) emit H_2S to the atmosphere.

1.2.3.   Nitrogen-Containing Compounds

The important nitrogen-containing compounds in the atmosphere are N_2O, NO, NO_2, NH_3, and salts of NO_3^-, NO_2^-, and NH_4^+. The first of these, nitrous oxide (N_2O), is a colorless gas that is emitted almost totally by natural sources, principally by bacterial action in the soil and by reactions in the upper atmosphere. The gas is employed as an anesthetic and is commonly referred to as "laughing gas." Chemically it is inert at ordinary temperatures and is not considered an air pollutant. The second, nitric oxide (NO), is emitted by both natural and anthropogenic sources. The burning of fuels at high temperatures is the primary anthropogenic source of NO. Nitrogen dioxide (NO_2) is emitted in small quantities along with NO and is also formed in the atmosphere by oxidation of NO. Both NO and NO_2, the sum of which is designated NO_x, are considered air pollutants. Nitric oxide is the major oxide of nitrogen formed during high temperature combustion, resulting from both the interaction of nitrogen in the fuel with oxygen present in the air and the chemical conversion of atmospheric nitrogen and oxygen at the high temperatures of combustion. Other oxides of nitrogen, sometimes expressed as N_xO_y, such as N_2O_3, N_2O_4, NO_3, and N_2O_5, exist in the atmosphere in very low concentrations and are generally not of concern as air pollutants. Ammonia (NH_3) is primarily emitted by natural sources. Finally, nitrate and ammonium salts are not emitted in any significant quantities but result from conversion of NO, NO_2, and NH_3.

TABLE 1.3.   Estimated Rates of Natural and
Anthropogenic Nitrogen Fixation[a]

Source	Process	Rate (Tg N yr^{-1})
Natural	Biological	60
	Atmospheric	7.4
Anthropogenic	Biological	69
	Industrial	40
	Combustion	20

[a] Delwiche (1977).

Nitrogen is an essential nutrient for all living organisms. The primary source of this nitrogen is the atmosphere. However, nitrogen is not useful to most organisms until it is "fixed" or converted to a form that can be chemically utilized by the organisms. The "natural" fixation of nitrogen occurs by two types of processes. One is the action of a comparatively few microorganisms that are capable of converting N_2 to ammonia, ammonium ion, and organic nitrogen compounds. The other natural nitrogen fixation process occurs in the atmosphere by the action of some ionizing phenomena, such as cosmic radiation or lightning, on N_2. This process leads to the formation of nitrogen oxides in the atmosphere, which are ultimately deposited on the earth's surface as biologically useful nitrates.

In addition to natural nitrogen fixation, human activities have led to biological and industrial fixation, and combustion. Humans have increased the cultivation of legumes, which have a symbiotic relationship with certain microorganisms capable of nitrogen fixation. Legumes provide both an in-crease in the soil nitrogen and serve as a valuable food crop. Industrial nitrogen fixation consists primarily of the production of ammonia for fertilizer use. Combustion can also lead to the fixation of nitrogen as NO_x. Table 1.3

TABLE 1.4.   Global Budget for NO_x[a]

Sources	Tg N yr^{-1}
Fossil Fuel Combustion	21
	(14–28)
Biomass Burning	12
	(4–24)
Lightning	8
	(2–20)
Microbial Activity in Soils	8
	(4–16)
Oxidation of Ammonia	0–10
Photolytic or Biological Processes in the Ocean	< 1
Input from the Stratosphere	≈ 0.5
TOTAL	25–99
Sinks	
Precipitation	12–42
Dry Deposition	11–22
TOTAL	23–64

[a] Logan (1983).

presents Delwiche's (1977) estimates of the magnitudes of the rates of these nitrogen fixation processes. On the basis of these estimates, anthropogenic routes to nitrogen fixation are about twice the size of those of natural nitrogen fixation.

Table 1.4 shows the estimated global budget for nitrogen oxides developed by Logan (1983). Each category contains the estimated NO_x flux and the estimated uncertainty bounds. Figure 1.3 depicts the global nitrogen cycle from the point of view of the transformations between nitrogeneous species. Nitrogen oxides are removed from the atmosphere by wet and dry deposition. We will subsequently discuss these removal processes (Chapter 16). At this point we need only note that wet deposition refers to scavenging by liquid drops (or ice) and dry deposition signifies removal by absorption at the surface of the earth.

As in the case of the sulfur cycle, we again note the level of uncertainty involved in attempting to estimate a global cycle from the individual uncertainties in Table 1.4. On the basis of the estimated source strengths and concentrations, the mean tropospheric residence time for gaseous NO_x, including HNO_3,

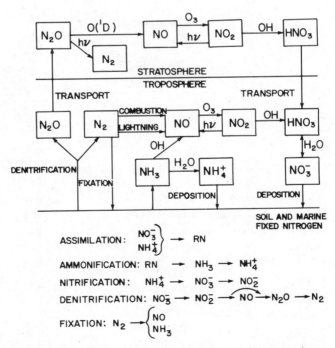

Figure 1.3. Schematic diagram of the processes considered of major importance to the atmospheric cycles of nitrogen compounds (Stedman and Shetter, 1983). A species written over an arrow signifies reaction with the species from which the arrow originates. The chemical reactions shown will be discussed in Chapter 4.

is estimated to be in the range of 1 to 4 days and that for particulate NO_3^-, in the range of 3 to 9 days. Because of these short atmospheric lifetimes, the major effects of emissions of nitrogen oxides are expected to be local or regional rather than global in nature.

Ammonia is the primary basic gas in the atmosphere. The significant sources of NH_3 are animal waste, ammonification of humus followed by emission from soils, losses of NH_3-based fertilizers from soils, and industrial emissions. The other NH_3 sources are due to anthropogenic activities, with the predominant contribution from animal waste. Yearly anthropogenic NH_3 emissions from the United States are estimated to be about 3 Tg N yr^{-1}. Although NH_3 can be oxidized to NO_x in the atmosphere, the gas-phase chemistry of NH_3 is not well understood, and a quantitative estimate of the production rate of NO_x from NH_3 is not available. The ammonium (NH_4^+) ion is an important component of the continental tropospheric aerosol. Because NH_3 is readily absorbed by surfaces such as water and soil, its residence time in the lower atmosphere should be quite short. Wet and dry deposition of NH_3 is probably the main atmospheric removal mechanism for NH_3. In fact, deposition of atmospheric NH_3 and NH_4^+ may represent an important nutrient to the biosphere in some areas. Most of the atmospheric measurements of ammonia-related species are for particulate NH_4^+; gas-phase measurements of NH_3 are very sparse. The most important gas-phase atmospheric reaction for NH_3 is probably oxidation by the hydroxyl (OH) radical,

$$NH_3 + OH\cdot \rightarrow NH_2\cdot + H_2O$$

The subsequent fate of the NH_2 species is unknown. Reaction of NH_3 with HNO_3 to form ammonium nitrate (NH_4NO_3) may be a significant sink for both NH_3 and HNO_3.

TABLE 1.5. Northern Hemisphere Sources of Atmospheric NH_3 and NH_4^{+} [a]

Source	Flux (Tg N yr^{-1})
Wild animal excrement	3[1.8] [b]
Human excrement	1.5[2]
Domestic animals	23[1.4]
Industrial losses and fertilizer evaporation	3.5[1.3]
Burning of coal	< 2
Soil emissions estimated by balancing the annual budget	51 (estimated by difference)
TOTAL	82

[a] Stedman and Shetter (1983).
[b] Estimated uncertainty factor.

There is no set of data on atmospheric concentrations of NH_4^+ or NH_3 adequate to perform an accurate global average. Stedman and Shetter (1983) estimate, with considerable scope for uncertainty, an annual average northern hemispheric inventory of 0.3 Tg N as NH_3 and 0.6 Tg N as NH_4^+, (Stedman et al., 1975). These estimates give sea-level average concentrations of 1 ppb of NH_3 and 1.5 μg m^{-3} NH_4^+. The northern hemispheric sources of NH_3 and NH_4^+ are summarized in Table 1.5.

1.2.4.   Carbon-Containing Compounds

Let us review briefly the classifications of carbon-containing compounds, particularly those of interest in air pollution. The carbon atom has four valence electrons and can therefore share bonds with from one to four other atoms. The nature of the carbon-carbon bonding in a hydrocarbon molecule basically governs the properties (as well as the nomenclature) of the molecule.

In some sense the simplest hydrocarbon molecules are those in which all the carbon bonds are shared with hydrogen atoms except for a minimum number required for carbon-carbon bonds. Molecules of this type are referred to as *alkanes* or, equivalently, as paraffins. The general chemical formula of alkanes is C_nH_{2n+2}. The first four paraffins having a straight chain structure are

$$CH_4 \qquad\qquad \text{methane}$$
$$CH_3—CH_3 \qquad\qquad \text{ethane}$$
$$CH_3—CH_2—CH_3 \qquad\qquad \text{propane}$$
$$CH_3—CH_2—CH_2—CH_3 \qquad\qquad n\text{-butane}$$

Alkanes need not have a straight chain structure. If a side carbon chain exists, the name of the longest continuous chain of carbon atoms is taken as the base name, which is then modified to include the type of group. Typical examples of substituted alkanes are (the numbering system is indicated below the carbon atoms):

$$
\begin{array}{c}
\overset{\displaystyle CH_3}{\underset{|}{}} \qquad \overset{\displaystyle CH_3}{\underset{|}{}}
\end{array}
$$

CH₃—CH—CH₂—CH—CH₂—CH₃   CH₃—CH₂—CH—CH—CH₃
 1   2   3   4   5   6   5   4   3   2   1

       2,4-Dimethyl hexane   2-Bromo-3-chloropentane

Alkanes may also be arranged in a ring structure, in which case the molecule is referred to as a cycloalkane. The name of a cycloalkane is obtained simply by adding the prefix cyclo- to the name of the normal alkane having the same number of carbon atoms as in the ring. Cycloalkanes have the general chemical formula C_nH_{2n}. Examples are

$$
\begin{array}{cccc}
\text{H}_2\text{C} - \text{CH}_2 & \text{H}_2\text{C} - \text{CH}_2 & \text{H}_2\text{C} - \text{CH}_2 & \overset{\text{H}_2}{\text{C}}\cdot \\
\diagdown \diagup & | \quad\quad | & | \quad\quad | & \diagup\quad\diagdown \\
\text{C} & \text{H}_2\text{C} - \text{CH}_2 & \text{H}_2\text{C}\quad\text{CH}_2 & \text{H}_2\text{C}\quad\text{CH}_2 \\
\text{H}_2 & & \diagdown\diagup & | \quad\quad | \\
& & \text{C} & \text{H}_2\text{C}\quad\text{CH}_2 \\
& & \text{H}_2 & \diagdown\diagup \\
& & & \text{C} \\
& & & \text{H}_2
\end{array}
$$

| Cyclopropane | Cyclobutane | Cyclopentane | Cyclohexane |

The alkanes and the cycloalkanes generally react by replacement of a hydrogen atom. Once a hydrogen atom is removed from an alkane, the involved carbon atom has an unpaired electron and the molecule becomes a free radical, in this case an alkyl radical. Examples of alkyl radicals are

$$CH_3\cdot \qquad \text{methyl}$$

$$CH_3CH_2\cdot \qquad \text{ethyl}$$

$$CH_3CH_2CH_2\cdot \qquad \textit{n}\text{-propyl}$$

$$CH_3\dot{C}HCH_3 \qquad \text{isopropyl}$$

$$CH_3CH_2CH_2CH_2\cdot \qquad \textit{n}\text{-butyl}$$

Alkyl radicals are often simply designated $R\cdot$, where R denotes the chemical formula for any member of the alkyl group. The unpaired electron in a free radical makes the species extremely reactive. As we shall see, free radicals play an important role in atmospheric chemistry.

The next class of hyrocarbons of interest in air pollution is the *alkenes*. In this class two neighboring carbon atoms share a pair of electrons, a so-called double bond. Alkenes are also known as alkylenes or olefins. The location of the carbon atom nearest to the end of the molecule that is the first of the two carbon atoms sharing the double bond is often indicated by the number of the carbon atom. Examples of common alkenes are

$$CH_2{=}CH_2 \qquad \text{ethene (ethylene)}$$

$$CH_3CH{=}CH_2 \qquad \text{propene (propylene)}$$

$$CH_3CH_2CH{=}CH_2 \qquad \text{1-butene}$$

$$CH_3CH{=}CHCH_3 \qquad \text{2-butene}$$

Molecules with two double bonds are called *alkadienes*, an example of which is

$$CH_2{=}CH{-}CH{=}CH_2$$

1,3-Butadiene

Molecules with a single triple bond are known as *alkynes*, the first in the series of which is acetylene, $HC{\equiv}CH$.

Double-bonded hydrocarbons may also be arranged in a ring structure. This class of molecules, of which the basic unit is benzene,

is called *aromatics*. Other common aromatics are

| Toluene | Orthoxylene | Metaxylene | Paraxylene | Styrene |

Hydrocarbons may acquire one or more oxygen atoms. Of the oxygenated hydrocarbons, two classes that are of considerable importance in air pollution are *aldehydes* and *ketones*. In each type of molecule, a carbon atom and an oxygen atom are joined by a double bond. Aldehydes have the general form

$$R{-}\overset{\displaystyle O}{\overset{\|}{C}}{-}H$$

whereas ketones have the structure

$$R{-}\overset{\displaystyle O}{\overset{\|}{C}}{-}R$$

TABLE 1.6. Organic Compounds Emitted by Vegetation[a]

Compound	Structure	Comments
Isoprene (C_5H_8)		Emitted by oak, sycamore, willow, balsam, poplar, aspen, spruce, and others.
p-Cymene ($C_{10}H_{14}$)		Emitted by California black sage and from "disturbed" eucalyptus foliage; found in the gum turpentines of scotch pine and loblolly pine.
α-Pinene ($C_{10}H_{16}$)		Emitted by numerous pines, firs, spruce, hemlock, cypress.
β-Pinene ($C_{10}H_{16}$)		Emitted by California black sage, loblolly pine, spruce, and redwood.
d-Limonene ($C_{10}H_{16}$)		Emitted by loblolly pine, California black sage, and "disturbed" eucalyptus, found in the gum turpentines of numerous pines and the essential oils derived from some fruits.
Myrcene ($C_{10}H_{16}$)		Emitted by loblolly pine, California black sage, and redwood, found in the gum turpentines of some pines.
Terpinolene ($C_{10}H_{16}$)		No ambient measurements or emissions reported; however, terpinolene is found in the essential oils of numerous plants and in some pine turpentines.
Δ³-Carene ($C_{10}H_{16}$)		Found in the gum turpentines of some pines and in the essential oils of numerous lower plants.

[a]Arnts and Gay (1979).

Thus, the distinction lies in whether the carbon atom is bonded to one or two alkyl groups. Examples of aldehydes and ketones are

$$
\underset{\text{Formaldehyde}}{\overset{\displaystyle \overset{O}{\|}}{HCH}} \qquad \underset{\text{Acetaldehyde}}{\overset{\displaystyle \overset{O}{\|}}{CH_3CH}} \qquad \underset{\text{Acetone}}{\overset{\displaystyle \overset{O}{\|}}{CH_3CCH_3}}
$$

$$
\underset{\text{Methylethylketone}}{\overset{\displaystyle \overset{O}{\|}}{CH_3CCH_2CH_3}} \qquad \underset{\text{Acrolein}}{\overset{\displaystyle \overset{O}{\|}}{CH_2{=}CHCH}}
$$

Hydrocarbons emitted by vegetation are listed in Table 1.6. Many of these compounds, having the formula $C_{10}H_{16}$, are produced by coniferous trees; the most abundant are α-pinene, β-pinene, and limonene. The principal organic emitted by deciduous vegetation is the compound isoprene.

1.2.5. Halogen Compounds

There has been considerable recent interest in atmospheric halogen compounds because of several atmospheric phenomena, including effects of chlorofluoro-carbons on stratospheric ozone, contributions of HCl to acidic precipitation, atmospheric levels of toxic pesticides, and questions on chemical intermediates in the tropospheric decomposition of chlorinated solvents. Table 1.7 presents a summary of the most important atmospheric halogen-containing species, to-gether with concentrations measured in the northern and southern hemi-spheres.* Also given in Table 1.7 in the column labelled "Source" is an indication of whether the source of each compound is anthropogenic (A) or natural (N). With the exception of CH_3Cl, CH_3Br, and CH_3I, the species listed are all anthropogenic in origin. The major natural source of these three methyl compounds appears to be the oceans. Because of the greater number of anthropogenic sources in the northern hemisphere, a substance released pri-marily from man-made sources will exhibit higher concentrations in the northern than in the southern hemisphere if its atmospheric residence time is short enough so that it is removed before it can be mixed throughout the entire troposphere. (We discuss this point further in Chapter 16.) The principal sink for halocarbons containing labile H atoms or $C{=}C$ double bonds is oxidation by atmospheric OH radicals. For halocarbon species that do not readily react with OH or other tropospheric species, transport to the stratosphere followed by photodissociation at the shorter wavelengths prevalent in the stratosphere is the main atmospheric sink.

*Section 1.4 is devoted to atmospheric concentration levels of air pollutants, and thus in this section we have not been giving concentration levels. Since we will not deal extensively with the halogen species further, their concentration levels are presented here.

TABLE 1.7. Summary of the Average December 1977 Concentrations of Measured Trace Constituents Containing Halogens[a]

Compound	Concentration (ppt)			Source[b]
	N.H. Average	S.H. Average	Global Average	
CCl_2F_2 (F12)[e]	230 (25.5)[c]	210 (25.1)	220	A
CCl_3F (F11)	133 (13.4)	119 (11.7)	126	A
CCl_2FCClF_2 (F113)	19 (3.5)	18 (3.1)	18	A
$CClF_2CClF_2$ (F114)	12 (1.9)	10 (1.3)	11	A
$CHCl_2F$ (F21)	5 (2.6)	4 (1.0)	4	A
SF_6	0.31 (0.04)	0.27 (0.01)	0.29	A
CCl_4	122 (4.9)	119 (4.0)	120	A
CH_3CCl_3[d]	113	75	94	A
CH_3Cl	611 (83.7)	615 (103.0)	613	0.9N + 0.1A
CH_3I	2 (1.0)	2 (1.2)	2	N
$CHCl_3$	14 (7.0)	≤ 3	8	A
CH_2Cl_2	44 (14.0)	20 (4.0)	32	A
C_2HCl_3	16 (8.0)	< 3	8	A
C_2Cl_4	40 (12.0)	12 (3.0)	26	A
CH_3Br	5–20	—	5–20?	N, A
CH_2BrCH_2Br	5	—	5	A

[a] Singh et al. (1978b, 1979) and Cicerone (1981).
[b] A = anthropogenic
   N = natural
[c] Numbers in parentheses are standard deviations.
[d] For those species where significant variations within each hemisphere were observed, the average concentration within each hemisphere is the concentration that, when uniformly mixed in the hemisphere, represents the total burden of the species in that hemisphere.
[e] Chlorofluorocarbons are the collective name given to a series of chemicals with varying numbers of carbon, hydrogen, chlorine, and fluorine atoms. The system of numbering these compounds is that proposed by the American Society of Heating and Refrigeration Engineers in 1957. For the simpler chlorofluorocarbons, the numbering system may be summarized as follows:
  (i) The first digit on the right is the number of fluorine (F) atoms in the compound.
  (ii) The second digit from the right is one more than the number of hydrogen (H) atoms in the compound.
  (iii) The third digit from the right, plus one, is the number of carbon (C) atoms in the compound. When this digit is zero (i.e., only one carbon atom in the compound), it is omitted from the number.
  (iv) The number of chlorine (Cl) atoms in the compound is found by subtracting the sum of the fluorine and hydrogen atoms from the total number of atoms that can be connected to the carbon atoms.

Examples are:

CCl_2F_2 $C_2Cl_2F_4$ $CHClF_2$ CCl_3F
12   114   22   11

TABLE 1.8. Terminology Relating to Atmospheric Particles

Aerosols, aerocolloids, aerodisperse systems	Tiny particles dispersed in gases.
Dusts	Suspensions of solid particles produced by mechanical disintegration of material such as crushing, grinding, and blasting. $D_p > 1.0 \; \mu m$
Fog	A loose term applied to visible aerosols in which the dispersed phase is liquid. Usually, a dispersion of water or ice.
Fume	The solid particles generated by condensation from the vapor state, generally after volatilization from melted substances, and often accompanied by a chemical reaction such as oxidation. Often the material involved is noxious. $D_p < 1 \; \mu m$
Hazes	An aerosol that impedes vision and may consist of a combination of water droplets, pollutants, and dust. $D_p < 1 \; \mu m$
Mists	Liquid, usually water in the form of particles suspended in the atmosphere at or near the surface of the earth; small water droplets floating or falling, approaching the form of rain, and sometimes distinguished from fog as being more transparent or as having particles perceptibly moving downward. $D_p > 1 \; \mu m$
Particle	An aerosol particle may consist of a single continuous unit of solid or liquid containing many molecules held together by intermolecular forces and primarily larger than molecular dimensions ($> 0.001 \; \mu m$). A particle may also be considered to consist of two or more such unit structures held together by interparticle adhesive forces such that it behaves as a single unit in suspension or upon deposit.
Smog	A term derived from smoke and fog, applied to extensive contamination by aerosols. Now sometimes used loosely for any contamination of the air.
Smoke	Small gas-borne particles resulting from incomplete combustion, consisting predominantly of carbon and other combustible material, and present in sufficient quantity to be observable independently of the presence of other solids. $D_p \geq 0.01 \; \mu m$
Soot	Agglomerations of particles of carbon impregnated with "tar," formed in the incomplete combustion of carbonaceous material.

1.3. ATMOSPHERIC PARTICULATE MATTER

By "particulate matter" we refer to any substance, except pure water, that exists as a liquid or solid in the atmosphere under normal conditions and is of microscopic or submicroscopic size but larger than molecular dimensions (about 2 Å). Among atmospheric constituents, particulate matter is unique in its complexity. Airborne particulate matter results not only from direct emissions of particles but also from emissions of certain gases that either condense as particles directly or undergo chemical transformation to a species that condenses as a particle. A full description of atmospheric particles requires specification of not only their concentration but also their size, chemical composition, phase (i.e., liquid or solid), and morphology.

There are a number of ways of expressing particle size. Particle size is usually expressed in terms of actual or equivalent diameters. Nonspherical particles are frequently characterized in terms of equivalent spheres, that is, on the basis of equal volumes, equal masses, or equal settling velocity. We will define the conventional particle size measures used in Chapter 7. For the present we will simply refer to particle size as diameter in micrometers (μm), equal to 10^{-6} m or 10^{-4} cm. Several terms used in conjunction with airborne particulate matter are defined in Table 1.8.

1.3.1. Sizes of Atmospheric Particles

Figure 1.4 shows a classification of the sizes of atmospheric aerosols. Particles less than 2.5 μm in diameter are generally referred to as "fine" and those greater than 2.5 μm diameter as "coarse". Atmospheric aerosols consist of particles ranging in size from a few tens of Ångstroms to several hundred micrometers. Aerosol sources can be classified as primary and secondary. Primary aerosols are those that are emitted in particulate form directly from sources, such as airborne dust as a result of wind or smoke particles emitted from a smokestack. Secondary aerosols refer to particles produced in the atmosphere, for example, from gas-phase chemical reactions that generate condensable species. Although primary sources yield particles of all sizes, secondary sources produce mainly submicron-sized particles.

Once aerosols are in the atmosphere, their size, number, and chemical composition are changed by several mechanisms until ultimately they are removed by natural processes. Some of the physical and chemical processes that affect the "aging" of atmospheric aerosols are more effective in one regime of particle size than another. In spite of the specific processes that affect particulate aging, the usual residence time of particles in the lower atmosphere is of the order of a couple of days to a week. Very close to the ground the main mechanisms for particle removal is settling and impaction on surfaces, whereas at altitudes above about 100 m, wet deposition is the predominant removal mechanism.

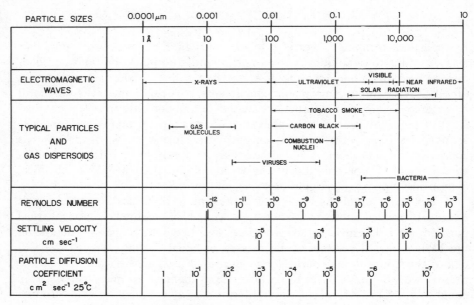

Figure 1.4.   Characteristics of atmospheric particles.

The fine and coarse particle modes, in general, originate separately, are transformed separately, are removed from the atmosphere by different mechanisms, require different control techniques, have different chemical composition, and have different optical properties. Therefore, the distinction between fine and coarse particles is a fundamental one in any discussion of the physics, chemistry, measurement, or air quality standards of aerosols. As we will note in Chapter 2, fine and coarse particles differ significantly in their deposition patterns in the respiratory tract.

The phenomena that influence particle sizes are shown in an idealized schematic in Figure 1.5, which depicts the typical distribution of surface area of an atmospheric aerosol. Fine particles can often be divided roughly into two modes: the nuclei mode and the accumulation mode. The nuclei mode, extending from about 0.005 to 0.1 μm diameter, accounts for the preponderance of particles by number; but because of their small size, these particles rarely account for more than a few percent of the total mass of airborne particles. Particles in the nuclei mode are formed from condensation of hot vapors during combustion processes and from the nucleation of atmospheric species to form fresh particles. The accumulation mode, extending from 0.1 to about 1 μm diameter, usually accounts for most of the aerosol surface area and a substantial part of the aerosol mass. The source of particles in the accumulation mode is the coagulation of particles in the nuclei mode and from condensation of vapors onto existing particles, causing them to grow into this size range. The accumulation mode is so named because particle removal

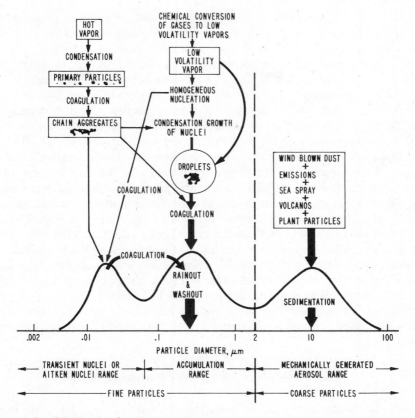

Figure 1.5. Idealized schematic of the distribution of particle surface area of an atmospheric aerosol (Whitby and Cantrell, 1976). The principal modes, sources, and particle formation and removal mechanisms are indicated.

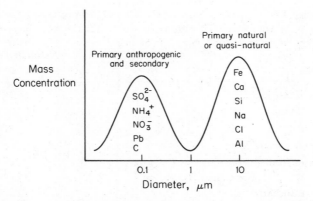

Figure 1.6. Idealized aerosol mass distribution showing a typical segmentation of chemical species into fine and coarse particle fractions.

mechanisms are least efficient in this regime, causing particles to accumulate there. The coarse mode, from 1 to 100 μm diameter, is formed by mechanical processes and usually consists of man-made and natural dust particles.

Whether or not nuclei and accumulation modes are present, the existence of a biomodal distribution with fine and coarse modes has been clearly demonstrated in atmospheric aerosol measurements. Studies in which chemical composition has been determined as a function of particle size also demonstrate the division between fine and coarse modes and show the difference in chemical composition of the two modes. On the basis of such studies, it is possible to divide the major chemical species observed in atmospheric aerosols as shown in Figure 1.6. The major components of the fine fraction of the atmospheric aerosol are sulfate, ammonium, nitrate ions, lead, carbon-containing material including soot and condensed organic matter. In urban areas the fine fraction, as a percent of total suspended particulate matter, varies from 15 to 25% in Denver to 40 to 60% in the Los Angeles and New York–New Jersey urban areas. The percentage of the fine particle fraction that is secondary in nature usually exceeds 50% in these urban areas. Several studies have shown that toxic species, such as polynuclear aromatic compounds, As, Se, Cd, and Zn, are more concentrated in the fine particle fraction. The coarse fraction consists mainly of crustal material, such as Fe, Ca and Si. The major sources are wind erosion products, primary emissions, sea spray, and volcanic eruptions.

1.3.2. Sources of Atmospheric Particulate Matter

Significant natural sources of particles include soil and rock debris (terrestrial dust), volcanic action, sea spray, wild fires, and reactions between natural

TABLE 1.9.   Global Estimate of Particles of Natural Origin Smaller than 20 μm Diameter Emitted to or Formed in the Atmosphere[a]

Source	Estimated Emissions (Tg yr^{-1})
Soil and Rock Debris	50–250
Forest Fires	1–50
Sea Salt	300
Volcanic Debris	25–150
Particles formed from Gaseous Emissions of H_2S, NH_3, NO_x, and HC	345–1100
Total natural particles	721–1850

[a]United Nations (1979).

TABLE 1.10. Estimated Annual Anthropogenic Particulate Matter Emissions in the United States[a]

Source Category	Emissions ($Tg\ yr^{-1}$)
Fuel combustion and industrial processes	10
Industrial process fugitive emissions	3.3
Nonindustrial fugitive emissions	110–370
Transportation	1.3
TOTAL	125–385

[a] U.S. Environmental Protection Agency (1982).

gaseous emissions. Table 1.9 presents a range of emission estimates of particles less than 20 μm diameter generated from natural sources, on a global basis.

Emissions of particulate matter attributable to the activities of humans arise primarily from four source categories, fuel combustion and industrial processes, industrial process fugitive particulate emissions, nonindustrial fugitive sources (roadway dust from paved and unpaved roads, wind erosion of cropland, etc.), and transportation sources (automobiles, etc.). Estimated emissions from these categories for the United States are summarized in Table 1.10.

Process fugitive particles are not emitted from a definable point such as a stack. Industrial fugitive dust emissions result from wind erosion of storage piles and unpaved plant roads and from vehicular traffic over plant roads. Fugitive process emissions result from industry-related operations such as materials handling, loading, and transfer operations. Three broad categories account for nearly all of the potential process fugitive emissions—mineral products, food and agriculture, and primary metals. It has been estimated that for a modern integrated iron and steel plant about 15 percent of total suspended particulate matter (TSP) emissions are from stacks, 25 percent are fugitive process emissions, and 60 percent are fugitive dusts from paved and unpaved roads inside the facility and from storage piles (National Research Council, 1980).

Nonindustrial fugitive particulate emissions, commonly termed *fugitive dust*, are caused by traffic entrainment of dust from public paved and unpaved roads, agricultural operations, construction, and fires. Except for the last, all these sources entail dust entrainment by the interaction of machinery with materials and by the forces of wind on materials. While it is estimated that fugitive dust emissions exceed particulate emissions from stationary point sources in most areas, their impact is limited because the emissions are mostly large particles that settle a short distance from the source, and fugitive dust sources exist mainly in rural areas.

Transportation source emissions occur in two categories, (1) vehicle exhaust, and (2) vehicle-related particles from tire, clutch, and brake wear. In 1978 total transportation source emissions of particles from highway vehicles, aircraft, railroads, and ships were estimated at 1.3×10^6 Tg. About 75 percent of those particulate emissions were from highway vehicles. Engine-related particulate emissions are composed primarily of lead halides, sulfates, and carbonaceous matter and are mostly smaller than 1 μm in diameter. About 40 percent of particles from tire wear are less than 10 μm (about 20 percent are less than 1 μm) and are primarily carbon. Particles from brake linings are less than 1 μm and are composed mainly of asbestos and carbon.

Atmospheric particulate matter samples can be analyzed routinely for more than 40 trace elements. Whereas air quality trace element data are becoming available, the emission sources responsible for the release of these species often are not obvious. Trace element emissions arise from more than 60 different source types in a large urban area (U.S. Environmental Protection Agency, 1977). There are, for example, motor vehicles burning leaded fuel, electric arc steel furnaces, Kraft recovery boilers, and secondary lead smelters. The wide spectrum of sources, together with the fact that trace metals often are only a minor fraction of the mass emissions from each source, obscure the relative importance of the contributors to atmospheric trace element levels.

As with all atmospheric species, trace metal emissions undergo atmospheric transport and dilution before they reach a particular receptor site. Mathematical models can be constructed based on the fundamentals of atmospheric chemistry and physics that will track the contributions from many emission sources as they undergo atmospheric transport. Indeed, the development of such models will receive considerable attention in this book. In the case of particulate emissions, an alternative to the use of physico-chemical air quality models is available. It is possible to attack the source contribution identification problem in reverse order, proceeding from measured particulate concentrations at a receptor site backward to the responsible emission sources. The unique metals content of the emissions from each source type is viewed as a fingerprint for the presence of material from that source in an ambient aerosol sample (Friedlander, 1973). This approach proceeds as follows.

Suppose we know the fraction of chemical species i in the particulate emissions from source j. Call this fraction a_{ij}, and say that there are n species and m sources. Let c_i be the concentration (μg m^{-3}) of element i ($i = 1, 2, \ldots, n$) in the ambient sample at a particular location, and let f_{ij} be a fraction representing any modification to a_{ij} due to atmospheric processes (e.g., gravitational settling) that occur between the source and the receptor point. Then if s_j is the mass concentration (μg m^{-3}) of the material from source j at the receptor site, we can express the concentration of element i at the site as

$$c_i = \sum_{j=1}^{m} f_{ij} a_{ij} s_j \qquad i = 1, 2, \ldots, n$$

Usually f_{ij} is assumed equal to 1, thus neglecting any removal processes or

TABLE 1.11. Average Results of Chemical Element Balances of 130 Samples from Washington, D.C. Area for Summer 1976[a]

Element	Predicted Contributions,[b] ng m^{-3}							Total, ng m^{-3}	
	Soil	Limestone	Coal	Oil	Refuse	Motor Vehicle	Marine	Predicted	Observed[c]
Na[e]	43	0.83	8.3	12	35	—	201	300	300 ± 20
Mg[e]	74	101	27	3.8	5.4	32	26	270	440 ± 30
Al[e]	812	9	517	0.4	6.1	—	< 0.01	1340	1350 ± 110
K[e]	154	6	67	0.4	47	13	7	295	400 ± 20
Ca[e]	66	635	47	8.2	7.1	47	7.6	820	860 ± 40
Sc[e]	0.15	0.002	0.18	0.0002	0.0006	—	< 0.0001	0.33	0.33 ± 0.03
Ti[e]	52	0.83	31	0.03	1.0	—	< 0.0001	85	110 ± 10
V[e]	1.06	0.042	1.6	23	0.013	—	< 0.0001	26	25 ± 2
Cr	0.81	0.023	0.84	0.062	0.21	—	< 0.0001	2.0	14 ± 2
Mn[d,e]	13	2.3	1.6	0.10	0.31	1.3	< 0.0001	18	17 ± 2[d]
Fe[e]	511	8.3	362	2.8	2.8	34	0.0002	920	1000 ± 60
Co[e]	0.22	0.0002	0.25	0.16	0.003	0.05	< 0.0001	0.68	0.83 ± 0.08
Ni	0.46	0.042	1.04	4.0	0.07	0.34	< 0.0001	6.0	17 ± 2
Cu	0.23	0.009	2.2	0.89	0.71	3.0	0.0001	7.1	17 ± 2
Zn[e]	1.14	0.04	2.6	1.6	51	7.3	< 0.0001	64	85 ± 6
Ga[e]	0.38	0.008	0.46	0.0001	—	—	< 0.0001	0.85	1.29 ± 0.17
As[e]	0.061	0.002	3.1	0.028	0.10	—	0.0001	3.32	3.25 ± 0.2
Se	0.0009	0.0002	0.78	0.035	0.016	0.035	0.0001	0.87	2.5 ± 0.2
Br	0.097	0.013	2.1	0.054	0.66	167	1.25	171	136 ± 9
Rb[e]	1.19	0.0064	0.60	0.0001	—	—	0.0023	1.8	2.1 ± 0.2

29

Element									
Sr[e]	3.65	1.29	3.5	0.09	0.027	—	< 0.0001	8.6	10 ± 1
Ag[e]	0.0007	0.0001		0.006	0.23	—	< 0.0001	0.24	0.20 ± 0.01
Cd[e]	0.0011	0.0001	0.0028		0.64	1.03	< 0.0001	1.80	2.4 ± 0.2
In	0.0007	0.0001	0.0023	< 0.0001	0.0024	—	0.0004	0.0059	0.020 ± 0.001
Sb[e]	0.0081	0.0004	0.13	0.007	0.89	0.60	< 0.0001	1.6	2.1 ± 0.2
I	0.058	0.0026	2.1	—	—	1.14		3.3	2.0 ± 0.1
Cs[e]	0.028	0.0011	0.039	0.0005	0.0025	—	< 0.0001	0.07	0.17 ± 0.05
Ba	7.1	0.02	4.7	2.0	0.30	6.4	0.0006	21	19 ± 2
La[e]	0.75	0.014	0.31	0.016	0.0016	—	< 0.0001	1.1	1.5 ± 0.1
Ce[e]	0.98	0.024	0.62	0.014	0.007	—	< 0.0001	1.6	2.0 ± 0.2
Sm[e]	0.068	0.0027	0.057	0.0012	0.0003	—	< 0.0001	0.13	0.20 ± 0.02
Eu[e,f]	0.015	0.0004	0.014	0.0005	0.0002	—	< 0.0001	0.030	0.030 ± 0.003
Yb	0.037	0.0011	0.030	0.0004	0.0009	—	< 0.0001	0.070	0.034 ± 0.003
Lu	0.0067	0.0004	0.0080	0.0001	0.0004	—	< 0.0001	0.016	0.0056 ± 0.0006
Hf[e]	0.031	0.0006	0.022	0.0008	0.0004	—	< 0.0001	0.055	0.10 ± 0.01
Ta[e,f]	0.041	0.0008	0.0077	0.0011	0.0018	—	< 0.0001	0.052	0.036 ± 0.004
W	0.014	0.0013	0.038	0.0004	0.0072	—	< 0.0001	0.061	0.24 ± 0.02
Pb[e]	0.15	0.019	0.39	0.0016	34	428	< 0.0001	465	440 ± 20
Th[e]	0.11	0.0036	0.10	0.0016	0.0008	—	< 0.0001	0.22	0.25 ± 0.02

[a] Kowalczyk et al. (1982).

[b] Contributions designated by "—" indicate that concentration of the element in particles from the source is not known.

[c] Uncertainty is standard deviation of mean value.

[d] For reasons described by Kowalczyk et al. (1982), all observed values reduced by factor of 0.69 prior to fitting.

[e] Element fitted by least-squares procedure.

[f] Actual observed value was 26 ± 3 ng m^{-3}. As noted in Kowalczyk et al. (1982), three observed values were eliminated from fits.

modifications to the signature a_{ij} during atmospheric transport. In this case we simply have

$$c_i = \sum_{j=1}^{m} a_{ij}s_j \qquad i = 1, 2, \ldots, n \qquad (1.1)$$

Thus, the concentration of each chemical element at a receptor site becomes a linear combination of the contributions of each source to the particulate matter at that site. Given the chemical composition of the ambient sample and the source emission signature, Eq. (1.1) may be solved for the source contributions, s_j. When the number of chemical elements exceeds the number of source types, the m-dimensional vector of estimated source contributions s can be determined by least squares inversion of Eq. (1.1),

$$\mathbf{s} = [\mathbf{A}^T\mathbf{W}\mathbf{A}]^{-1}\mathbf{A}\mathbf{W}\mathbf{c} \qquad (1.2)$$

where c is the n-dimensional vector of measured chemical element concentrations, A is the $n \times m$ matrix with elements a_{ij}, and W is a diagonal matrix of weighting factors. The weighting factors are selected to reflect the accuracy with which the concentration of a particular chemical species is measured. A common choice for these weighting factors is $1/\sigma_i^2$, where σ_i is the standard deviation of a single determination of the concentration of species i in an ambient sample. For additional studies using this so-called chemical element balance technique to relate ambient particulate concentrations to sources we refer the reader to Alpert and Hopke (1980), Cass and McRae (1983), and Hopke (1981).

Table 1.11 gives average elemental concentrations in particulate matter observed in the Washington, D.C. area in summer 1976. In developing Table 1.11 Kowalczyk et al. (1982) used the chemical element balance method described above. To obtain the results in Table 1.11, a set of 130 samples from a network of 10 stations were analyzed for about 40 elements. It was assumed that the total composition of the aerosol could be represented as the sum of contributions from seven sources: soil, limestone, coal, oil, refuse incineration, motor vehicles, and sea salt. Nine fingerprint elements were used to characterize these sources: Na for sea salt, V for fuel oil, Pb for motor vehicles, Zn for refuse incineration, Ca for limestone, Al and Fe for the sum of coal and soil, Mn for soil, and As for coal. The source contributions determined by analyzing these nine elements were then used to predict the concentrations of the remainder of the elements as a test of the analysis.

1.3.3. Carbonaceous Particles in the Air

Carbonaceous particles in the atmosphere consist of two major components—graphitic or black carbon (sometimes referred to as elemental or free carbon) and organic material (Novakov, 1982). The latter can be directly emitted from sources or produced from atmospheric reactions involving gaseous organic precursors. Black carbon can be produced only in a combustion process and is therefore solely primary. Soot can be defined as the total primary carbonaceous material; that is, the sum of graphitic carbon and primary organics (Novakov, 1982; Chang and Novakov, 1983). Graphitic carbon particles are thought to be the most abundant light absorbing aerosol species in the atmosphere. Primary particulate carbon emissions to the atmosphere arise from more than fifty classes of mobile and stationary sources (Cass et al., 1982).

A major reason for the study of particulate organic matter has been the possibility that such compounds pose a long-term health hazard (Daisey, 1980). Specifically, certain fractions of particulate organic matter, especially those containing polycyclic aromatic hydrocarbons (PAH), have been shown to be carcinogenic in animals and mutagenic in *in vitro* bioassays. Direct-acting mutagens, that is, compounds that do not require metabolic activation for their effect as do the PAH compounds, have been found to be widely present in organic particulate matter. Organic compounds of relatively low molecular weight and high vapor pressure are distributed between vapor and particulate phases in the atmosphere. At the higher temperatures of combustion sources larger proportions are present in the vapor phase. It has been shown that PAH compounds emitted as vapor from power plant stacks condense on the surface of particulate matter as they cool.

Particulate organic matter is a complex mixture of many classes of compounds. A summary of the classes of compounds that have been identified in urban aerosols and the concentrations at which they have been reported is given in Table 1.12 (Daisey, 1980). Alkanes, alkenes, aromatics, and polycyclic aromatic compounds are primary in nature. The alkanes found in particulate matter generally range from C_{17} to C_{36}. Polycyclic aromatic compounds are among the most widely studied species in the ambient aerosol. Although they comprise only a small fraction by mass of urban particulate matter, they are, as noted above, established carcinogens. Oxidized hydrocarbons, such as acids, aldehydes, ketones, quinones, phenols, and esters, may be emitted directly by combustion sources or may be produced by oxidation reactions in the atmosphere. Nitro derivatives of organic compounds have been identified in urban particulate matter. N-Nitrosamines are potent carcinogens, and thus have attracted interest as atmospheric constituents. Finally, heterocyclic sulfur compounds have recently been identified as present in particulate organic matter.

Wolff et al. (1982) and Mueller et al. (1982) have reported measurements of particulate carbon levels in the United States. Particulate elemental carbon was found to be ubiquitous with mean concentrations ranging from 1.1 μg m^{-3} at a remote site in South Dakota to 13.3 μg m^{-3} in a congested area in New York City, 17.5 μg m^{-3} in Denver, Colorado, and 22.6 μg m^{-3} in Los Angeles. About 80 percent of the elemental carbon mass is associated with particles of diameter less than 2.5 μm. Carbon derived from fossil fuels can be dis-

TABLE 1.12. Classes of Organic Compounds Found in Urban Aerosols[a]

Compound Class	Example	Concentration in Urban Air[b] (ng m^{-3})	Location, Date of Measurement(s)[c]
Alkanes (C_{18}–C_{50})	n-$C_{22}H_{46}$	1000–4000[d]	217 U.S. urban stations, 1966–67
Alkenes	n-$C_{22}H_{44}$	2000[d]	217 U.S. urban stations
Alkylbenzenes		80–680[d]	West Covina, California July 24, 1973
Naphthalenes		40–500[d]	Pasadena, California September 1972
Polycyclic aromatic hydrocarbons		6.6	100 U.S. urban stations, 1958–59
		3.2	32 U.S. urban stations, 1966–67
	(Benzo (a) pyrene)	2.1	32 U.S. urban stations 1970
Aromatic acids		90–380	Pasadena, California September 1972
		8	Average U.S. urban prior to 1965
Cyclic ketones		2–48	U.S. urban site January 1968
Quinones		0.04–0.12[e]	Toronto, Ontario 1972–1973

TABLE 1.12. *Continued*

Compound Class	Example	Concentration in Urban Air[b] (ng m^{-3})	Location, Date of Measurement(s)[c]
Phenols	—OH	~ 0.3	Antwerp, Belgium 1975
Esters	$C-O-C_4H_9$ ... $C-O-C_4H_9$	29–132	Antwerp, Belgium 1976
		2–11	New York City 1975
Aldehydes	$CHO(CH_2)_nCHO$	30–540	Pasadena, California September 1972
Aliphatic carboxylic acid	$C_{15}H_{31}COOH$	220	New York City February 1964
		36.5	Antwerp, Belgium January 1976
Aliphatic dicarboxylic acids	$HOOC(CH_2)_nCOOH$	40–1350	Pasadena, California September 1972
Aza-arenes		0.2	Composite 100 U.S. urban sites, 1963
		0.01	New York City 1976
		~ 0.5	Antwerp, Belgium
N-Nitrosamines	$(CH_3)_2NNO$	$\leq$ 0.03–0.96	Baltimore, Maryland August 1975
		15.6	New York City July 1976
Nitro compounds	$CHO(CH_2)_nCH_2ONO_2$	40–1010	Pasadena, California September 1972

TABLE 1.12. *Continued*

Compound Class	Example	Concentration in Urban Air[b] (ng m^{-3})	Location, Date of Measurement(s)
Nitro compounds		identified	Prague, Czechoslovakia
Sulfur heterocyclic compounds		0.014–0.02	New York City 1976
		identified	Indianapolis and Gary, Indiana
SO_2-adducts		2–18 nmoles m^{-3}	New York City 1976
Alkylhalides	$C_{18}H_{37}Cl$	~ 20–320	Pasadena, California September 1972
Arylhalides		0.5–3	Pasadena, California 1972
Chlorophenols		5.7–7.8	Antwerp, Belgium 1976

[a] Daisey (1980).
[b] Concentration of compound given as example.
[c] References given in Daisey (1980).
[d] Total concentration for class of compounds.
[e] All isomers of given compound.
[f] Speculative.

tinguished from that derived from living organic matter such as wood by measuring the ratio of the radioactive isotope, ^{14}C, to the total carbon mass. Fossil fuels, such as coal and oil, contain none of the isotope, whereas contemporary carbonaceous materials have a ratio that is about the same as that present in the atmosphere.

Lioy and Daisey (1983) have reported the results of a major program aimed at characterizing the atmospheric environment with respect to toxic elements and organic substances at selected locations in New Jersey. Inhalable particulate matter was characterized with respect to organic and inorganic composition and the bacterial mutagenic activity of the organic fraction. There were seasonal shifts in the composition of the aerosol, with wintertime space heating and local motor vehicle traffic appearing to be important factors. The polycyclic aromatic hydrocarbons increased by a factor of two or more during the winter. Similarly, the mutagenic activity of the extractable organic matter increased during the winter.

A research team investigated three main aspects of Denver air pollution for 41 days between November 8 and December 20, 1978 (Countess et al., 1980, 1981). They analyzed the atmosphere's chemical composition, identified the significant visibility-reducing species, and traced these species back to their sources. The unexpected factor uncovered as a result of this study is the importance of wood burning as a contribution to the carbonaceous fraction of the particulate matter. They found that 33 percent of the carbon particulate matter, which corresponds to 18 percent of the visibility reduction, could be attributed to wood burning.

1.4. ATMOSPHERIC POLLUTANT CONCENTRATION LEVELS

We introduced in Section 1.2 the species classified as air pollutants. It is of interest to see the levels of these species that can be attained under polluted conditions. Table 1.13 summarizes ranges of atmospheric concentrations of a number of air pollutant species in both the "clean" troposphere and polluted urban air. We now consider in somewhat more detail the atmospheric concentration levels of pollutant species.

1.4.1. Atmospheric Concentrations of Sulfur Compounds

There exist extensive urban monitoring programs for SO_2 and, to a lesser degree, for sulfates, in the United States and abroad. During particular meteorological conditions, air pollution resulting from major SO_2 source emission areas can extend over distances of 1000 km for periods of several days. For example, atmospheric sulfates frequently accumulate over an area in the northeastern United States stretching from the Ohio River Valley, a major SO_2 source region, to the Atlantic seaboard. Maximum sulfate concentrations

TABLE 1.13. Trace Species Concentrations in the Clean Troposphere and Polluted Urban Air

Species	Concentration, ppb	
	Clean Troposphere	Polluted Air
SO_2	1–10	20–200
CO	120	1000–10,000
NO	0.01–0.05	50–750
NO_2	0.1–0.5	50–250
O_3	20–80	100–500
HNO_3	0.02–0.3	3–50[a,b]
NH_3	1	10–25[b]
HCHO	0.4	20–50[a,b]
HCOOH (formic acid)		1–10[a,b]
HNO_2 (nitrous acid)	0.001	1–8[c]
$CH_3C(O)O_2NO_2$ (peroxyacetyl nitrate (PAN))		5–35[a,b]
NMHC (non-methane hydrocarbons)		500–1200[a,d]

[a] Hanst et al. (1982).
[b] Tuazon et al. (1981).
[c] Harris et al. (1982).
[d] Grosjean and Fung (1984).

routinely occur 100 to 500 km downwind of the major SO_2 source areas. Figure 1.7 shows the frequency distributions of SO_2 and sulfate concentrations measured at nine locations in the northeastern United States from August 1977 through October 1978. The sites in the major SO_2 source area show generally higher SO_2 concentrations, and the differences in SO_2 concentrations are much more distinct than for sulfates. The sulfate concentrations exhibit less variability among locations, although those sites close to the major SO_2 source areas in the Ohio River Valley do exhibit somewhat higher sulfate concentrations than those downwind. Maximum SO_2 and sulfate concentrations were generally observed within a few hundred kilometers of the major SO_2 sources.

Sulfate aerosol, in fact, now comprises the major part of total aerosol mass in sub-micron-sized particles in the nonurban eastern United States and other similarly industrialized regions of the world.

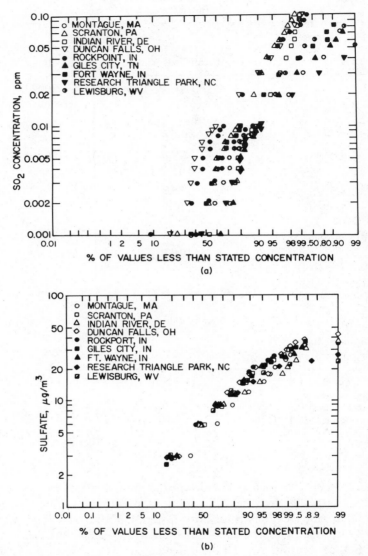

Figure 1.7. Concentrations of sulfur dioxide (*a*) and sulfate (*b*) observed at each of nine stations in the northeastern United States from August 1977 through July 1978. Copyright © 1981, Electric Power Research Institute. EPRI EA-2165-SY-LD, "EPRI Sulfate Regional Experiment: Results and Implications." Reprinted with permission.

1.4.2.   Atmospheric Concentrations of Carbon Monoxide

With the exception of CO_2, carbon monoxide is the most abundant air pollutant in the lower atmosphere. Emissions of CO from anthropogenic sources exceed in quantity the mass of man-made emissions from all other air pollutants combined.

Since the principal source of carbon monoxide in urban areas is motor vehicle exhaust, CO concentrations correlate closely with traffic volume. Virtually all urban areas have CO monitoring capabilities, and there exists an extensive data base of urban CO concentrations. We present here, as an illustration of urban CO levels, some results of the study of Peterson and Allen (1982) in which CO exposures to commuters were determined by measuring CO in three vehicles as they traveled typical commuter routes in Los Angeles.

The cumulative frequency distributions of the data for two of the cars (plotted together) for interior and exterior concentrations are shown in Figure 1.8. The squares and triangles represent the cumulative frequency distribution of one-minute average concentrations, while the circles show the cumulative frequency distribution for 30-minute average concentrations.

The cumulative frequency distribution can be used to estimate the probability of exceeding a given concentration for a specified averaging time. Exterior 30-minute average concentrations, a time more typical of the time spent during a commute, were computed and the cumulative frequency distribution plotted in Figure 1.8. Because of the limited size of the data base it is difficult to construct the upper portion of the frequency distribution confidently. However, for demonstration purposes, if a line is drawn through the upper 50

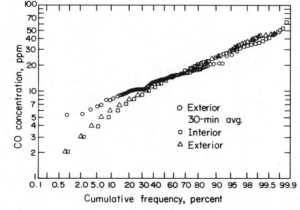

Figure 1.8.   Cumulative frequency distribution of interior and exterior CO concentrations for 1-minute averaging time for two vehicles travelling Los Angeles commuter routes. 30-min average exterior concentrations are plotted as *o*'s (Peterson and Allen, 1982). Reprinted with permission of Journal of the Air Pollution Control Association.

percent of the data a comparison can be made for the 1-minute averages and the 30-minute averages. One would expect to exceed 40 ppm about 1 percent of the time for 1-minute average concentrations, and to exceed 27 ppm about 1 percent of the time for 30-minute average concentrations. Peterson and Allen showed that a spatial or temporal average of fixed site monitors is not a good measure of carbon monoxide exposures to commuters. The ratio of CO exposures to fixed site monitor concentrations ranged from 1.4 to 11.2 with an average of 3.9.

1.4.3.   Atmospheric Concentrations of Nitrogen Oxides

The atmospheric distribution of nitrogen oxides is highly nonuniform. Although about ninety percent of nitrogen oxides in the earth's atmosphere is estimated to be produced by natural bacterial action, localized urban concentrations may far exceed clean air background concentrations. Table 1.13

TABLE 1.14.   Mean Concentrations of Hydrocarbons Observed in
Los Angeles and New York City

	Downtown Los Angeles[a]			Downtown Los Angeles[b]	New York City	
	1963–1965, 0600–0800, 33 Samples ppbC	1971, 0700–0900, 23 Samples ppbC	1973, 0700–0800, 23 Samples ppbC	1976, 0600–0900, 35 Samples ppbC	1969,[c] 0700–0900, 8–13 Samples ppbC	1978,[d] 1030–1100, 4 Samples ppbC
Total Aliphatics[e]	4682	1925	3385	1416	577	486
Acetylene	123	125	178	99	48	20
Ethene	179	61	204	76	53	9
Propene	70	26	49	36	16	10
Σ C$_{4+}$ alkenes	1260	53	84	39	58	21
Σ alkenes	1509	140	337	155	127	40
Butane	300	183	149	119	—	72
Σ C$_4$ paraffins	—	—	—	168	83	166
Isopentane	287	258	193	185	—	103
Σ C$_5$ alkanes	—	—	—	277	135	166
Σ alkanes	3050	1660	2870	1162	402	408
Benzene	229	4	126	46[f]	—	58
Toluene	412	352	156	151	102	111
Σ C$_8$ aromatics	—	—	—	171	142	163

[a]Leonard et al. (1976).   [b]Mayrsohn et al. (1977).   [c]Lonneman et al. (1974).   [d]Altwicker et al. (1980).
[e]Total reported nonmethane aliphatic concentration less ethane; less ethane and propane for Lonneman et al. (1974).
[f]Includes cyclohexane.

indicates the concentration ranges of NO, NO_2, and HNO_3 achieved under polluted urban conditions.

1.4.4. Atmospheric Concentrations of Hydrocarbons

Table 1.14 summarizes a number of hydrocarbon concentration measurements in Los Angeles and New York City. These data provide an indication of the relative distribution of urban atmospheric hydrocarbons among and within hydrocarbon classes.

1.4.5. Atmospheric Concentrations of Particulate Matter

Table 1.15 gives some typical concentrations of atmospheric particulate matter in several locations in the United States. Average particle mass concentrations range from about 20 μg m^{-3} in clean air to values of 60 to 200 μg m^{-3} in

TABLE 1.15. Typical Concentrations of Atmospheric Particulate Matter

Site	Date	Measurement	Concentration μg m^{-3}
New York City[a]	1977 (50 days)	TSP[e]	70.5
		SO_4^{2-}	11.58
		NH_4^+	2.38
		NO_3^-	4.96
South Coast Air Basin, CA[b] (Rubidoux)	1972–3 (24 hr avg)	SO_4^{2-}	10.7
		NO_3^-	31.5
Great Smoky Mountains[c] (Elkmont, TN)	Sept 20–26, 1978	TSP (fine)	24
Washington, D.C.[d]	Summer 1976	TSP	65

[a] Leaderer et al. (1982).
[b] Appel et al. (1978).
[c] Stevens et al. (1980).
[d] The average of 12 TSP values measured during August and September, 1976, by Virginia, Maryland, and Washington, D.C. agencies in the Washington metropolitan area. Kowalczyk et al. (1982).
[e] Total suspended particulate matter.

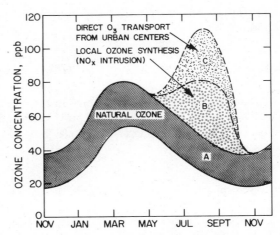

Figure 1.9. A schematic of the idealized ozone variations at remote locations (Singh et al., 1978a).

urban areas. In heavily polluted areas, values as high as 2000 μg m^{-3} have been reported. Number concentrations vary from 10^2 cm^{-3} in very clean air to 10^5 cm^{-3} in polluted air.

1.4.6. Photochemical Smog and Ozone

Photochemical smog is the designation given to the particular mixture of reactants and products that exists when hydrocarbons and oxides of nitrogen occur together in an atmosphere in the presence of sunlight. Hydrocarbons usually occur with oxides of nitrogen in an urban atmosphere since a major fraction of each results from the same type of source, namely motor vehicles. Irradiation of air containing hydrocarbons and oxides of nitrogen leads to (1) oxidation of NO to NO_2, (2) oxidation of hydrocarbons, and (3) formation of ozone.

Ozone is naturally present in the clean, background troposphere at concentrations ranging from 20 to 80 ppb. An idealized schematic of the monthly ozone variations at remote locations is shown in Figure 1.9. The natural variability is due to combinations of tropospheric chemistry and ozone transport into the troposphere from the stratosphere. Also indicated in Figure 1.9 are additions to the natural ozone from local ozone synthesis by chemical processes such as those in photochemical smog and by direct ozone transport from urban centers. Ozone concentrations in urban areas may reach levels as high as 500 ppb, which exceed by a factor of 5 the levels shown in Figure 1.9.

APPENDIX

1.A.1. Units

The units used in this text are more or less those of the cgs metric system. We have chosen not to adhere strictly to the International System of Units (SI) because in several areas of the book the use of SI units would lead to cumbersome and unfamiliar magnitudes of quantities. A book of this type that covers material from a variety of scientific disciplines—chemistry, aerosol physics, meteorology, and chemical and mechanical engineering—has a special problem since the various disciplines tend to use their own sets of units. We have attempted to use a consistent set of units throughout the book while attempting not to deviate markedly from the units commonly used in the particular area. The best compromise seems to us to be the cgs metric system,

TABLE 1.A.1. Units Used in This Book and Basic SI Units

Dimension	Unit in Book	Symbol	SI Unit	Symbol
Length	meter	m	meter	m
Mass	gram	g	kilogram	kg
Time	second	sec	second	s
Electric current	ampere	A	ampere	A
Temperature	degree Kelvin	K	degree Kelvin	K

TABLE 1.A.2. Standard Prefixes

Factor	Prefix	Symbol
10^{-12}	pico	p
10^{-9}	nano	n
10^{-6}	micro	μ
10^{-3}	milli	m
10^{-2}	centi	c
10^{-1}	deci	d
10^{1}	deca	da
10^{2}	hecto	h
10^{3}	kilo	k
10^{6}	mega	M
10^{9}	giga	G
10^{12}	tera	T

TABLE 1.A.3. Units of Some Essential Quantities

Quantity	Name of Unit	Unit Symbol	In Terms of Basic Units
Frequency	hertz (cycle per second)	Hz	sec^{-1}
Density			$g\ cm^{-3}$
Force	newton	N	$kg\ m\ sec^{-2}$
	dyne		$g\ cm\ sec^{-2}$
Surface tension		$dyne\ cm^{-1}$	$g\ sec^{-2}$
Pressure		$N\ m^{-2}$	$kg\ m^{-1}\ sec^{-2}$
		$dyne\ cm^{-2}$	$g\ cm^{-1}\ sec^{-2}$
	atmosphere	atm	[a]
Viscosity	poise	poise	$g\ cm^{-1}\ sec^{-1}$
Energy	joule	J	$kg\ m^2\ sec^{-2}$
	calories	cal	[b]
Power	joule per second, watt	$J\ sec^{-1}$, W	$kg\ m^2\ sec^{-3}$
	horsepower	hp	[c]
Specific heat, gas constant			$cal\ g^{-1}\ °C^{-1}$
Enthalpy			$cal\ g^{-1}$
Entropy			$cal\ g^{-1}\ °C^{-1}$
Thermal conductivity			$cal\ sec^{-1}\ cm^{-1}\ °C^{-1}$
Molecular diffusivity			$cm^2\ sec^{-1}$
Quantity of electricity	coulomb	C	$A\ sec$
Electromotive force	volt	V	$kg\ m^2\ A^{-1}\ sec^{-3}$
Electric field strength		$V\ m^{-1}$	$kg\ m\ A^{-1}\ sec^{-3}$
Electric resistance	ohm	Ω	$kg\ m^2\ A^{-2}\ sec^{-2}$
Electric conductivity			$A^2\ sec^3\ kg^{-1}\ m^{-3}$
Electric capacitance	farad	F	$A^2\ sec^4\ kg^{-1}\ m^{-2}$

[a] $1.0133 \times 10^5\ N\ m^{-2}$.
[b] $4.187\ J/cal$.
[c] $745.8\ W/hp$.

which is largely the unit system in use in most of the disciplines covered in the book and, at the same time, closely related to the SI system.

In this Appendix we will present the units that will be used in the book together with the corresponding SI units for each quantity. The SI system of units consists of a small number of basic units, a set of prefixes to adjust the order of magnitude of the unit, and a set of derived units. The derived units have their own symbols, making their use less cumbersome than always using the basic SI units.

The units used in this book and the basic SI units are given in Table 1.A.1. Standard prefixes are given in Table 1.A.2. For example, 1 cm = 10^{-2} m, 1 mm = 10^{-3} m, 1 μm = 10^{-6} m, 1 nm = 10^{-9} m. Thus, 10^{-4} m can be expressed as 0.1 mm or 100 μm.

Units for quantities that will be used in this book are given in Table 1.A.3. Some of the quantities have special names, whereas others are expressed in terms of the basic units in Table 1.A.1.

REFERENCES

Alpert, D. J., and Hopke, P. K. "A Quantitative Determination of the Sources in the Boston Urban Aerosol," *Atmos. Environ.*, **14**, 1137–1146 (1980).

Altwicker, E. R., Whitby, R. A., and Lioy, P. J. "Specific Non-Methane Hydrocarbons and Their Relationship to Ozone in an Eastern Urban Area, Manhattan," *J. Geophys. Res.*, **85**, 7475–7487 (1980).

Appel, B. R., Kothny, E. L., Hofer, E. M., Hidy, G. M., and Wesolowski, J. J. "Sulfate and Nitrate Data from the California Aerosol Characterization Experiment (ACHEX)," *Environ. Sci. Technol.*, **12**, 418–425 (1978).

Arnts, R. R., and Gay, B. W., Jr. "Photochemistry of Some Naturally Emitted Hydrocarbons," U.S. Environmental Protection Agency Report, EPA-600/3-79-081 (1979).

Cass, G. R., Boone, P. M., and Macias, E. S. "Emissions and Air Quality Relationships for Atmospheric Carbon Particles in Los Angeles," in *Particulate Carbon Atmospheric Life Cycle*, G. T. Wolff and R. L. Klimisch (Eds.), Plenum, New York (1982).

Cass, G. R., and McRae, G. J. "Source-Receptor Reconciliation of Routine Air Monitoring Data for Trace Metals: An Emission Inventory Assisted Approach," *Environ. Sci. Technol.*, **17**, 129–139 (1983).

Chang, S., and Novakov, T. "Role of Carbon Particles in Atmospheric Chemistry," in *Trace Atmospheric Constituents*, S. E. Schwartz (Ed.), Wiley, New York (1983).

Cicerone, R. J. "Halogens in the Atmosphere," *Reviews of Geophysics and Space Physics*, **19**, 123–139 (1981).

Countess, R. J., Wolff, G. T., and Cadle, S. H. "Denver Winter Aerosol: A Comprehensive Chemical Characterization," *J. Air Pollution Control Assoc.*, **30**, 1194–1200 (1980).

Countess, R. J., Cadle, S. H., Groblicki, P. J., and Wolff, G. T. "Chemical Analysis of Size-Segregated Samples of Denver's Ambient Particulate," *J. Air Pollution Control Assoc.*, **31**, 247–252 (1981).

Daisey, J. M. "Organic Compounds in Urban Aerosols," *Annals New York Academy of Sciences*, **338**, 50–69 (1980).

Delwiche, C. C. "Energy Relations in the Global Nitrogen Cycle," *Ambio*, **6**, 106–111 (1977).

Eisenbud, M. "Sources of Radioactive Pollution," in *Air Pollution*, Vol. I, A. C. Stern (Ed.), Academic Press, New York (1968).

Electric Power Research Institute, "EPRI Sulfate Regional Experiment: Results and Implications," Report No. EPRI-EA-2165-SY-LD, Palo Alto, CA (1981).

Ericksson, E. "The Yearly Circulation of Chloride and Sulfur in Nature; Meteorological, Geochemical, and Pedological Implications," *Tellus*, **11**, 375–403 (1960).

Ericksson, E. "The Yearly Circulation of Sulfur in Nature," *J. Geophys. Res.*, **68**, 4001–4008 (1963).

Friedlander, S. K. "Chemical Element Balances and Identification of Air Pollution Sources," *Environ. Sci. Technol.*, **7**, 235–240 (1973).

Friend, J. P. "The Global Sulfur Cycle," in *Chemistry of the Lower Atmosphere*, S. I. Rasool (Ed.), Plenum, New York, 177–201 (1973).

Granat, L., Hallberg, R. O., and Rodhe, H. "The Global Sulfur Cycle," in *Nitrogen, Phosphorus and Sulfur—Global Cycles*, B. H. Svensson and R. Soderlund (Eds.), SCOPE Report 7, *Ecol. Bull.*, **22** (Stockholm), 39–134 (1976).

Grosjean, D., and Fung, K. "Hydrocarbons and Carbonyls in Los Angeles Air," *J. Air Pollution Control Assoc.*, **34**, 537–543 (1984).

Hanst, P. L., Wong, N. W., and Bragin, J. "A Long Path Infra-Red Study of Los Angeles Smog," *Atmos. Environ.*, **16**, 969–981 (1982).

Harris, G. W., Carter, W. P. L., Winer, A. M., Pitts, J. N., Jr., Platt, U., and Perner, D. "Observations of Nitrous Acid in the Los Angeles Atmosphere and Implications for Predictions of Ozone-Precursor Relationships," *Environ. Sci. Technol.*, **16**, 414–419 (1982).

Hopke, P. K. "The Application of Factor Analysis to Urban Aerosol Source Resolution," in *Atmospheric Aerosol: Source/Air Quality Relationships*, E. S. Macias and P. K. Hopke (Eds.), American Chemical Society, Washington, D.C., 21–49 (1981).

Kellogg, W. W., Cadle, R. D., Allen, E. R., Lazrus, A. L., and Martell, E. A. "The Sulfur Cycle," *Science*, **175**, 587–596 (1972).

Kowalczyk, G. S., Gordon, G. E., and Ragingrover, S. W. "Identification of Atmospheric Particulate Sources in Washington, D.C. Using Chemical Element Balances," *Environ. Sci. Technol.*, **16**, 79–90 (1982).

Leaderer, B. P., Tanner, R. L., and Holford, T. R. "Diurnal Variations, Chemical Composition and Relation to Meteorological Variables of the Summer Aerosol in the New York Subregion," *Atmos. Environ.*, **16**, 2075–2088 (1982).

Leonard, M. J., Fisher, E. L., Brunelle, M. F., and Dickson, J. E. "Effects of the Motor Vehicle Control Program on Hydrocarbon Concentrations in Central Los Angeles Atmosphere," *J. Air Pollution Control Assoc.*, **26**, 359–363 (1976).

Lioy, P. J., and Daisey, J. M. "The New Jersey Project on Airborne Toxic Elements and Organic Substances (ATEOS): A Summary of the 1981 Summer and 1982 Winter Studies," *J. Air Pollution Control Assoc.*, **33**, 649–657 (1983).

Logan, J. A. "Nitrogen Oxides in the Troposphere: Global and Regional Budgets," *J. Geophys. Res.*, **88**, 10, 785–807 (1983).

Lonneman, W. A., Kopczynski, S. L., Darly, P. E., and Sutterfield, F. D. "Hydrocarbon Composition of Urban Air," *Environ. Sci. Technol.*, **8**, 229–236 (1974).

Mayrsohn, H., Kuramoto, M., Crabtree, J. H., Southern, R. D., and Mano, S. H. "Atmospheric Hydrocarbon Concentrations, June–September, 1976," State of California Air Resources Board (1977).

Moss, M. R. "Sources of Sulfur in the Environment; The Global Sulfur Cycle," in *Sulfur in the Environment. Part I. The Atmospheric Cycle*, J. O. Nriagu (Ed.), Wiley, New York, 23–50 (1978).

Mueller, P. K., Fung, K. K., Heisler, S. L., Grosjean, D., and Hidy, G. M. "Atmospheric Particulate Carbon Observations in Urban and Rural Areas of the United States," in

Particulate Carbon Atmospheric Life Cycle, G. T. Wolff and R. L. Klimisch (Eds.), Plenum, New York (1982).

National Research Council, "Controlling Airborne Particles," National Academy of Sciences, Washington, D.C. (1980).

Novakov, T., "Soot in the Atmosphere," in *Particulate Carbon Atmospheric Life Cycle*, G. T. Wolff and R. L. Klimisch (Eds.), Plenum, New York (1982).

Peterson, W. B., and Allen, R. "Carbon Monoxide Exposures to Los Angeles Area Commuters," *J. Air Pollution Control Assoc.*, **32**, 826–833 (1982).

Robinson, E., and Robbins, R. C. "Sources, Abundance and Fate of Gaseous Atmospheric Pollutants," SRI Project Report PR-6755, prepared for American Petroleum Institute, New York, (1968).

Robinson, E., and Robbins, R. C. "Gaseous Sulfur Pollutants from Urban and Natural Sources," *J. Air Pollution Control Assoc.*, **20**, 233–235 (1970).

Singh, H. B., Ludwig, F. L., and Johnson, W. B. "Tropospheric Ozone: Concentrations and Variabilities in Clean Remote Atmospheres," *Atmos. Environ.*, **12**, 2185–2196 (1978a).

Singh, H. B., Salas, L. J., Shigeishi, H., and Scribner, E. "Global Distribution of Selected Halocarbons, Hydrocarbons, SF_6 and N_2O," Atmospheric Sciences Laboratory, Stanford Research Institute (1978b).

Singh, H. B., Salas, L. J., Shigeishi, H., and Scribner, E. "Atmospheric Halocarbons, Hydrocarbons, and Sulfur Hexafluoride: Global Distributions, Sources and Sinks," *Science*, **203**, 899–903 (1979).

Stedman, D. H., Chameides, W. L., and Cicerone, R. J. "Vertical Distribution of Soluble Gases in the Troposphere," *Geophys. Res. Letters*, **2**, 333 (1975).

Stedman, D. H., and Shetter, R. E. "The Global Budget of Atmospheric Nitrogen Species," in *Trace Atmospheric Constituents*, S. E. Schwartz (Ed.), Wiley, New York (1983).

Stevens, R. K., Dzubay, T. J., Shaw, R. W., Jr., McClenny, W. A., Lewis, C. W., and Wilson, W. E. "Characterization of the Aerosol in the Great Smoky Mountains," *Environ. Sci. Technol.*, **14**, 1491–1498 (1980).

Tuazon, E. C., Winer, A. M., and Pitts, J. N., Jr. "Trace Pollutant Concentrations in a Multi-Day Smog Episode in the California South Coast Air Basin by Long Path Length Fourier Transform Infra-Red Spectroscopy," *Environ. Sci. Technol.*, **15**, 1232–1236 (1981).

United Nations, *Fine Particulate Pollution*, Pergamon Press, New York (1979).

U.S. Environmental Protection Agency, "Air Quality Criteria for Particulate Matter and Sulfur Oxides," Report No. EPA-600/8-82-029 (1982).

U.S. Environmental Protection Agency, "Compilation of Air Pollutant Emission Factors," Third Edition, AP-42, Research Triangle Park, NC (1977).

Whitby, K. T., and Cantrell, B. "Fine Particles," in International Conference on Environmental Sensing and Assessment, Las Vegas, NV, Institute of Electrical and Electronic Engineers (1976).

Wolff, G. T., Groblicki, P. J., Cadle, S. H., and Countess, R. J. "Particulate Carbon at Various Locations in the United States," in *Particulate Carbon Atmospheric Life Cycle*, G. T. Wolff and R. L. Klimisch (Eds.), Plenum, New York (1982).

PROBLEMS

1.1. Convert a concentration of SO_2 of 0.1 ppm to $\mu g\ m^{-3}$ at T = 298 K and 1 atm. Do the same for 0.1 ppm of NO, NO_2, and O_3.

1.2. Concentrations of aerosol constituents are sometimes expressed as ppb (mole fraction) to enable comparison with gaseous concentrations expressed in ppb. The unit ppb (mole fraction) is evaluated as $RT \times$ concentration of aerosol constituent in nanomoles m^{-3}.

Show that for the nitrate ion, NO_3^-, 1 ppb (mole fraction) is equivalent to 2.14 ppb (mass fraction) or 2.58 $\mu g\ m^{-3}$ at $T = 293$ K and 1 atm.

Show that for the ammonium ion, NH_4^+, 1 ppb (mole fraction) is equivalent to 0.75 $\mu g\ m^{-3}$ at $T = 293$ K and 1 atm.

TWO

Effects of Air Pollution

Substantial evidence has accumulated that air pollution affects the health of human beings and animals, damages vegetation, soils and deteriorates materials, affects climate, reduces visibility and solar radiation, contributes to safety hazards, and generally interferes with the enjoyment of life and property. Although some of these effects are specific and measurable, such as damages to vegetation and materials and reduced visibility, many are difficult to measure, such as health effects on human beings and animals and interference with comfortable living. As a result, there has been disagreement over the quantitative effects of air pollution. Each of the effects mentioned above has been the subject of considerable attention, and a number of comprehensive reviews of the effects of air pollution have been written. In this chapter we shall present a brief summary of some of the most important established effects of air pollution.

2.1. EFFECTS OF AIR POLLUTION ON ATMOSPHERIC PROPERTIES

Air pollutants affect atmospheric properties in the following way:

1. Visibility reduction.
2. Fog formation and precipitation.
3. Solar radiation reduction.
4. Temperature and wind distribution alteration.

In addition, there is much current interest in possible effects of air pollutants, mainly carbon dioxide and particles, on global climate.

Perhaps the most noticeable effect of air pollution on the properties of the atmosphere is the reduction in visibility that frequently accompanies polluted air. Prevailing visibility is defined as the greatest distance in a given direction at which it is just possible to see and identify (1) a prominent dark object in the daytime and (2) an unfocused, moderately intense light source at night; and which is attained or surpassed around at least half the horizon circle but not necessarily in continuous sectors. Visibility is reduced by two effects that gas molecules and particles have on visible radiation: absorption and scattering of light. Absorption of certain wavelengths of light by gas molecules and particles is sometimes responsible for atmospheric colorations. However, light scattering is the more important phenomenon responsible for impairment of visibility. Light scattering refers to the deflection of the direction of travel of light by airborne material. Visibility is reduced when there is significant scattering because particles in the atmosphere between the observer and the object scatter light from the sun and other parts of the sky through the line of sight of the observer. This light decreases the contrast between the object and the background sky, thereby reducing visibility. We will discuss visibility deterioration in Chapter 7.

In addition to reducing visibility, air pollution affects urban climates with respect to increased fog formation and reduced solar radiation.* The frequency of fog formation has been observed to be higher in cities than in the country in spite of the fact that air temperatures tend to be higher and relative humidities tend to be lower in cities as opposed to the country. The explanation for this observation lies in the mechanism of fog formation. With high concentrations of SO_2, sulfuric acid droplets formed by oxidation of SO_2 serve as condensation nuclei for formation of small fog droplets. For example, in determining the correlation between SO_2 concentrations and fog formation in the German cities of Gelsenkirchen and Hamburg, Georgii (1969) found that 80 percent of all cases of high SO_2 concentrations occurred with visibilities below 5 km. In addition to fog formation, increased precipitation has been linked to areas with high particulate concentrations (Changnon, 1968).

Scattering and absorption of both solar and infrared radiation, as well as emission of radiation, occur within the polluted layer. At the ground a reduction in direct and scattered solar radiation is expected because of the blanket of particles over an urban area. The particles are most effective in reducing radiation when the angle of the sun is low, that is, when the path length through the layer is the greatest. Studies in London, for example, have shown that the average duration of bright sunshine in central London (in hours per day) is discernibly less than in the surrounding countryside (Georgii, 1969). In general, the decrease in direct solar radiation due to a polluted layer amounts to 10 to 20 percent.

---

*In discussion of urban climates one must be careful to distinguish between the natural modification of climate due to the concentration of buildings and that directly attributable to air pollution. Climate modifications from air pollution are a result of the "dome" of pollutants existing over a city.

2.2. EFFECTS OF AIR POLLUTION ON MATERIALS

Air pollutants can affect materials by soiling or chemical deterioration. High smoke and particulate levels are associated with soiling of clothing and structures,* and acid or alkaline particles, especially those containing sulfur, corrode materials such as paint, masonry, electrical contacts, and textiles. Ozone is particularly effective in deteriorating rubber. Residents of Los Angeles, where high ozone levels are routinely experienced, must replace automobile tires and windshield wiper blades more frequently than residents in cities where high ozone concentrations are not as common. For a review of the effects of air pollution on materials the reader should consult National Research Council (1979) and the appropriate Air Quality Criteria documents of the U.S. Environmental Protection Agency.

2.3. EFFECTS OF AIR POLLUTION ON VEGETATION

Pollutants that are known phytotoxicants (substances harmful to vegetation) are SO_2, peroxyacetyl nitrate (an oxidation product in photochemical smog), and ethene. Of somewhat lesser severity are chlorine, hydrogen chloride, ammonia, and mercury. In general, the gaseous pollutants enter the plant with air through the stomata in the course of the normal respiration of the plant. Once in the leaf of the plant, pollutants destroy chlorophyll and disrupt photosynthesis. Damage can range from a reduction in growth rate to complete death of the plant. Symptoms of damage are usually manifested in the leaf, and the particular symptoms often provide the evidence for the responsible pollutant. Table 2.1 summarizes the symptoms characteristic of plant damage by several pollutants. For additional information on the effects of air pollution on vegetation, the reader may consult National Research Council (1979) and the appropriate Air Quality Criteria documents of the U.S. Environmental Protection Agency.

2.4. EFFECTS OF AIR POLLUTION ON HUMAN HEALTH

We now come to the most controversial and probably the most important effect of air pollution, that on human health.

Over the years, concentrations of air pollutants in a particular area have, on occasion, reached excessively high levels for periods of several hours to several

---

*For example, in a study of the costs of air pollution (primarily due to soiling) in Steubenville and Uniontown, Ohio, Michelson and Tourin (1966) found that the increased cleaning and maintenance costs which they correlated with particulate concentrations in Steubenville were about 84 dollars per person per year more than the same costs in the similar but less polluted city of Uniontown.

TABLE 2.1.   Summary of Symptoms and Injury Thresholds for
Air Pollution Damage to Vegetation[a]

Pollutant	Symptom	ppm	Sustained Exposure Time
Ozone (O_3)	Fleck, bleaching, bleached spotting, growth suppression. Tips of conifer needles become brown and necrotic.	0.03	4 hr
SO_2	Bleached spots, bleached areas between veins, chlorosis, growth suppression, reduction in yield.	0.03	8 hr
Peroxyacetyl nitrate (PAN)	Glazing, silvering or bronzing on lower surface of leaves.	0.01	6 hr
HF	Tip and margin burn, chlorosis, dwarfing leaf abscission, lower yield.	0.0001	5 weeks
Cl_2	Bleaching between veins, tip and leaf abscission.	0.01	2 hr
Ethene (C_2H_4)	Withering, leaf abnormalities, flower dropping, and failure of flower to open.	0.05	6 hr

[a] Hindawi (1970).

days. The result has been a number of so-called air pollution episodes, the most famous of which are listed in Table 2.2. During an episode, the person most likely to be seriously injured is one who is either elderly or is in questionable health, perhaps already suffering from a respiratory disease.

Although the effects of an air pollution episode can be striking, of equal or greater concern are the chronic effects on a population living in polluted air. One of the most difficult tasks has been to obtain a quantitative link between long-term exposure to air pollution and health effects. To do this, a measured index of pollution (concentrations averaged over a certain period of time), an effect, and a demonstrated relation between the two are needed. The objective, then, is to determine the levels of morbidity (sickness) and mortality for specified diseases that are ascribable to air pollution. The problem in doing this is to separate the effects of air pollution on health from those of personal habits (such as smoking and exercise), diet, living conditions, occupational exposures, and hereditary factors. Because of the great number of factors that play a role in determining a person's health, isolation of the effect of one variable, such as atmospheric pollution, requires data for large populations that presumably differ only in their exposure to air pollutants. The data

TABLE 2.2.　Air Pollution Episodes

Location	Date	Pollutants	Symptoms and Effects
Meuse Valley, Belgium	Dec. 1–5, 1930	SO_2 (9.6–38.4 ppm)	63 excess deaths, chest pain, cough, eye and nasal irritation, all ages affected.
Donora, PA	Oct. 26–31, 1948	SO_2, particles (0.5–2 ppm)	20 excess deaths, chest pain, cough, eye and nasal irritation, older people mainly affected.
Poza Rica, Mexico	Nov. 24, 1950	H_2S	22 excess deaths, 320 hospitalized, all ages affected.
London	Dec. 5–9, 1952	SO_2, particles	4000 excess deaths.
New York	Nov. 24–30, 1966	SO_2, particles	168 excess deaths.

normally available are the rates of morbidity (based on hospital admissions, lost workdays due to sickness, etc.) and mortality for a particular group, usually defined geographically. Unfortunately, many of the above factors, such as smoking and diet, are unknown, so that in the analysis it must be assumed, no doubt incorrectly in many cases, that the factors are roughly the same for groups or that they vary randomly with respect to the level of air pollution.

A classical means of describing the response of an organism to air pollutants is in terms of dose-response relations. Epidemiologists, as well as toxicologists, use this convention. Unfortunately, the problems inherent in establishing dose-response relations that can be applied with confidence to large, diverse groups of individuals are enormous. Epidemiologists face inevitable difficulties in deciding which pollutants to measure, and how to correct for widely different amounts of time spent outdoors, physical activity, or other hazards that may intrude. In spite of ethical and legal constraints, human experimentation continues to provide information critical to the setting of air quality standards. Such experimentation is confined to relatively short exposures to relatively low levels of pollutants. To study possible effects of frequent or long exposures and to obtain guidance in establishing acceptable experimental procedures for human volunteers, the use of animals has been required. Among the important questions addressed by clinical research have been:

What are the dose-response relations for pollutants in human subjects during acute exposures? Do the responses have implications for health or well-being?

Are persons with underlying cardiopulmonary disease more sensitive than healthy persons to the pollutants?

Can otherwise apparently healthy persons who are unusually sensitive to the pollutants be identified? If so, what is the basis for this increased sensitivity, or "hypersensitivity"?

A number of well-documented cases exist that demonstrate that exposures to two or more air pollutants simultaneously or sequentially produce responses not seen with the individual exposures alone. What are the conditions that lead to these enhanced responses, and the mechanisms by which they occur?

Diseases of the respiratory system are generally correlated with air pollution. There are two types of reaction to air pollutants by the respiratory system: acute reaction, such as irritative bronchitis; and chronic reaction, such as chronic bronchitis and pulmonary emphysema.

Bronchitis refers to a condition of inflammation of the bronchial tree. The inflammation is accompanied by increased mucus production and a cough. Airway resistance is increased because of the presence of the thickened mucus layer. Acute bronchitis is generally a short-lasting disease, caused by a virus or foreign material in the lung. Chronic bronchitis, on the other hand, is a sustained inflammation of the bronchial system, leading to an increase in the volume of mucoid bronchial secretion sufficient to cause expectoration. It is frequently accompanied by a cough and shortness of breath. The persistent inflammation leads to swelling of the terminal bronchi and increased airway resistance.

Emphysema is a condition in which the alveoli in the lung become uneven and overdistended due to destruction of the alveolar walls. The disease is accompanied by shortness of breath, particularly following exercise. The destruction of alveoli is progressive, resulting in an increased blood flow necessary to accomplish oxygen transfer and to a decreased ability to eliminate foreign bodies that reach the alveolar region. Emphysema has no known cure and is one of the fastest growing causes of death in the United States.

2.4.1. Carbon Monoxide

The effects of carbon monoxide exposure are reflected in the oxygen-carrying capacity of the blood. In normal functioning, hemoglobin molecules in the red blood cells carry oxygen, which is exchanged for carbon dioxide in the capillaries connecting arteries and veins. Carbon monoxide is relatively insoluble and easily reaches the alveoli along with oxygen. The carbon monoxide diffuses through the alveolar walls and competes with oxygen for one of the four iron sites in the hemoglobin molecule. The affinity of the iron site for CO is about 210 times greater than for O_2, so that this competition is extremely effective. When a hemoglobin molecule acquires a CO molecule it is called

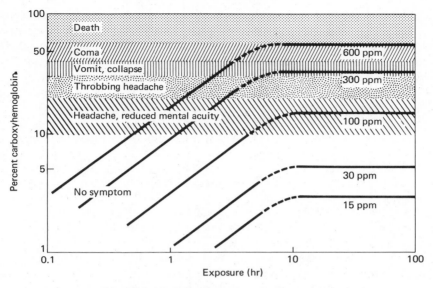

Figure 2.1. Effects of exposure to CO on man.

carboxyhemoglobin (abbreviated COHb). The presence of carboxyhemoglobin decreases the overall capacity of the blood to carry oxygen to the cells. In addition, the presence of CO on one of the iron sites of a hemoglobin molecule not only removes that site as a potential carrier of an O_2 molecule but also causes the other iron sites of the molecule to hold more tightly onto the O_2 molecules they are carrying. Symptoms of CO poisoning depend on the amount of hemoglobin combined with CO. The effects of CO exposure are summarized in Fig. 2.1. Each curve shows the increase of COHb with exposure time for different inhaled concentrations of CO. An equilibrium is reached in each case in about eight hours. The formation of COHb is a reversible process, with a half-life for dissociation after exposure of about two to four hr for low concentrations.

Neural and behaviorial effects of CO have been reported in healthy young adults with COHb (carboxyhemoglobin) levels as low as 5 percent. The observed deficits were in (1) hand-eye coordination (compensatory tracking), (2) vigilance (detection of infrequent events), and (3) visual system sensitivity. Any condition that would reduce oxygen supply to the brain is a reasonable candidate for exacerbating the effects of elevated COHb. A very large subgroup, which is known to have a reduced oxygen supply to the brain, for example, is the aged. Studies of patients with severe coronary artery disease have shown that low concentrations of CO can adversely affect myocardial metabolism. Current air quality standards for CO are based primarily on studies of patients with angina pectoris from coronary artery disease. It is assumed that the development of angina reflects adverse effects on myocardial metabolism. Although ironclad evidence to support the validity of this assumption is lacking, time to develop angina is a measurable outcome that merits further study. An approach that has been proposed to study the effects of CO is to determine whether individuals who are exposed to automotive pollution in large cities have a decrement in exercise tolerance.

As we have noted, the major source of CO in urban areas is automobile exhaust. Levels typical of urban areas range from 5 to 50 ppm. The most serious danger associated with CO may be the exposure of drivers on heavily congested highways to CO levels of the order of 100 ppm (see Section 1.4.2).

2.4.2. Oxides of Sulfur

Sulfur dioxide is highly soluble and consequently is absorbed in the moist passages of the upper respiratory system.* Exposure to SO_2 levels of the order of 1 ppm leads to constriction of the airways in the respiratory tract.

SO_2 causes significant bronchoconstriction in asthmatics at relatively low concentrations (0.25 and 0.50 ppm). While concentration-response studies have been done, and some information on effects at constant SO_2 concentration with different exercise levels is available, knowledge of the relative contributions of SO_2 concentration, exercise level, and time of exposure to the bronchoconstriction response is desirable. While it is known that substantial response to SO_2 does not occur with 5 to 10 minutes of exercise, the effect of exercise continued beyond 10 minutes, and the effects of repeated peak exposures on the same day, needs to be established.

The scientific basis for the 24-hour National Ambient Air Quality Standard of 0.14 ppm (see Section 2.6) stems primarily from epidemiological studies. These studies (Lawther et al., 1970 [analysis of bronchitics]; Martin and Bradley, 1960; Mazumdar et al., 1981; Ware et al., 1981 [analysis of mortality]) do not show evidence of clear thresholds, but rather suggest a continuum of population effects at various concentration levels. The U.S. Environmental Protection Agency has interpreted these studies as suggesting that notable increases in excess mortality occurred in the range of 500 to 1000 μg m^{-3} British Smoke and 0.19 to 0.38 ppm SO_2, and that such effects are most likely when both pollutants exceeded 750 μg m^{-3} (0.29 ppm SO_2). Lawther's study of reported symptoms among bronchitics also suggests that 24-hour averages of 0.19 ppm SO_2 represented a concentration level of the "minimum pollution leading to any significant response." The scientific basis for the development of a one-hour air quality standard for SO_2 rests largely on several major controlled clinical studies that documented measurable changes in respiratory

---

*Sulfur dioxide is highly soluble in water compared with other gaseous pollutants. For example, the solubility of SO_2 at 20°C is 11.3 g/100 ml, as compared with 0.004, 0.006, 0.003, and 0.169 g/100 ml for O_2, NO, CO, and CO_2, respectively.

function of exercising asthmatics at or below concentration levels of 0.50 ppm (Kirkpatrick et al., 1982; Koenig et al., 1982; Linn et al., 1982; Sheppard et al., 1981).

For gases the solubility governs what proportion is absorbed in the upper airway and what proportion reaches the terminal air sacs of the lungs. For example, SO_2 is quite soluble and, consequently, is absorbed early in the airway, leading to airway resistance (swelling) and stimulated mucus secretion. On the other hand, CO, NO_2, and O_3 are relatively insoluble and are able to penetrate deep into the lung to the air sacs. Nitrogen dioxide and ozone cause pulmonary edema (swelling) which inhibits gas transfer to the blood. Carbon monoxide is transported from the air sacs to the blood and combines with hemoglobin as oxygen does.

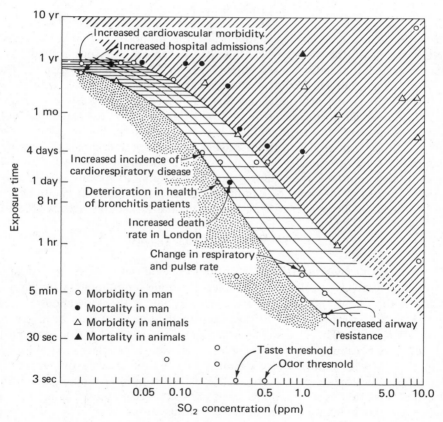

Figure 2.2. Health effects due to various exposures to SO_2. Shaded area represents the range of exposures where excess deaths have been reported. Speckled area represents the range of exposures where health effects are suspected (Williamson, 1973).

It is important to note that more than one pollutant may induce the same effect. For example, sulfur dioxide and formaldehyde both produce irritation and increased airway resistance in the upper respiratory tract, and both CO and NO_2 interfere with oxygen transport by hemoglobin. Several pollutants usually are present at the same time, and, as a result, observed effects may actually be attributable to the combined action of more than one pollutant. For example, high SO_2 levels are often associated with high particulate concentrations. The fact that a three- to fourfold increase in the irritant response to SO_2 is observed in the presence of particulate matter is presumably attributable to the ability of the aerosol particles to transport SO_2 deep into the lung. Figure 2.2 summarizes responses to various dosages of SO_2. For additional information the reader is referred to U.S. Environmental Protection Agency (1982b) and National Research Council (1978, 1979).

2.4.3. Oxides of Nitrogen

There is no available evidence supporting the proposition that nitric oxide (NO) is a health hazard at levels found in urban air. Previous studies have demonstrated that NO_2 causes emphysema in several animal species. The EPA's "Cincinnati Dog Study," which used 0.64 ppm NO_2 in combination with 0.25 ppm NO, also indicated that the effect was progressive during a two-year clean air post-exposure period. Many studies have indicated that NO_2 increases susceptibility to pulmonary bacterial infection. Some studies have shown effects on viral infection, host lung defense mechanisms, and the immune system of animals. Nitrogen dioxide is known to irritate the alveoli, leading to symptoms resembling emphysema upon long-term exposure to concentrations of the order of 1 ppm. For more information on health effects of NO_x we refer the reader to U.S. Environmental Protection Agency (1982a).

2.4.4. Photochemical Oxidants

The term *photochemical oxidants* refers to ozone and other secondary oxidants formed in photochemical smog. The effect of ozone on pulmonary function is still not thoroughly understood. In general, ozone at levels of about 1 ppm produces a narrowing of the airways deep in the lung, resulting in increased airway resistance. The effects of long-term exposure to ozone at levels typical of urban air (about 0.1 to 0.2 ppm) have not been clearly established. Experiments with animals have exhibited irreversible changes in pulmonary function after long-term exposure to levels of 1 ppm. A topic of current speculation is that exposure to low levels of ozone accelerates the aging of lung tissue by the oxidation of certain compounds in proteins. For additional information on health effects of ozone and other oxidants we refer the reader to U.S. Environmental Protection Agency (1978d).

A noticeable effect of photochemical smog is eye irritation. Those compounds in photochemical smog that have been identified as irritants are formaldehyde (HCHO), acrolein (CH_2CHCHO), and members of the family of peroxyacyl nitrates.

2.4.5. Toxic Substances

There is a wide variety of substances in addition to the "common" gaseous air pollutants of Sections 2.4.1 through 2.4.4 that have been demonstrated as or are suspected of being toxic to humans. In many cases the toxicity has been related to the possible carcinogenicity of the substance. Table 2.3 lists several of the more prominent toxic substances, with brief summaries of their uses, their atmospheric fate, and what is currently known concerning their degree of toxicity.

2.5. DEPOSITION OF AEROSOLS IN THE RESPIRATORY TRACT

Pollutants enter the body through the respiratory system, which can be divided into the upper respiratory system, consisting of the nasal cavity and the trachea, and the lower respiratory system, consisting of the bronchial tubes and the lungs. At the entrance to the lungs, the trachea divides into two bronchial trees that consist of a series of branches of successively smaller diameter. The entire bronchial tree consists of over 20 generations of bifurcations, ending in bronchioles of diameters of about 0.05 cm. At the end of the bronchioles are large collections of tiny sacs called alveoli. It is across the alveolar membranes that oxygen and carbon dioxide counterdiffuse. Although an individual alveolus has a diameter of only about 0.02 cm, there are several hundred million alveoli in the entire lung, providing a total surface area for gas transport of roughly 50 m^2. Also, although individual airway diameter in the conducting airways decreases distally, the total cross section for flow increases. As a result, mean air velocity drops from 145 cm sec^{-1} in the trachea to 7 cm sec^{-1} in the terminal bronchioles.

The respiratory system has several levels of defense against invasion by foreign material. Large particles are filtered from the airstream by hairs in the nasal passage and are trapped by the mucus layer lining the nasal cavity and the trachea. In addition, particles may also be scavanged by fine hairlike cilia that line the walls of the entire respiratory system. These cilia continually move mucus and trapped material to the throat where they are removed by swallowing.

Deposition of particles in the respiratory tract is largely determined by characteristics of its regions. There are three regions where particle deposition may occur, the head region, the conductive airway region, and the pulmonary region. Anatomy (airway shape, structure, and diameter), air flow rate, air velocity, and route of entry are properties that have an effect on particle

**TABLE 2.3. Toxic Atmospheric Substances—
Those Confirmed or Strongly Suspected of Being Carcinogenic[a]**

Substance	Discussion	Atmospheric Fate	Carcinogenicity
Arsenic	A	B	C
Asbestos	D	E	F
Benzene	G	H	I
Cadmium	J	K	L
Carbon Tetrachloride (CCl_4)	M	N	O
Chloroform ($CHCl_3$)	P	Q	R
Chromium	S	T	U
1,4-Dioxane 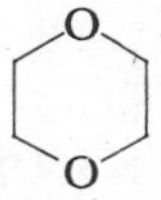	V	W	X
1,2-Dibromoethane ($C_2H_4Br_2$) (Ethylene Dibromide)	Y	Z	AA
1,2-Dichloroethane ($C_2H_4Cl_2$) (Ethylene Dichloride)	BB	CC	DD
Inorganic Lead	EE	FF	GG
Nickel	HH	II	JJ
Nitrosamines 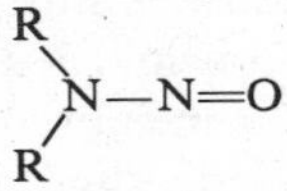	KK	LL	MM
Perchloroethylene (C_2Cl_4)	NN	OO	PP
Polycyclic Aromatic Hydrocarbons	QQ	RR	SS
Vinyl Chloride 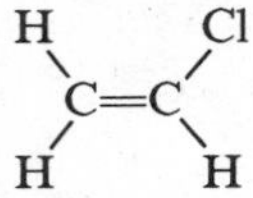	TT	UU	VV

[a]Science Applications, Inc. (1978).

Notes:

A   Although arsenic is used as a metal, as a variety of inorganic oxides and salts, and in several organic forms, only the inorganic oxides and salts have been implicated in carcinogenesis. Arsenic trioxide (As_2O_3) is produced commercially as a byproduct of metal refining operations, and is the feedstock for the production of other arsenicals such as arsenic pentoxide (As_2O_5) and sodium arsenate ($Na_3AsO_412H_2O$). About 5 percent of the arsenic trioxide produced in and imported to the United States is used in the manufacture of pesticides; 9 percent goes to glass and glassware, while industrial chemicals, copper and lead alloys, and pharmaceuticals account for the remaining 10 percent (USBM, 1978). Due to the availability of substitutes and their implication in carcinogenesis, inorganic arsenicals are expected to be used less in the future.

TABLE 2.3 (*Continued*)

B   The question of arsenical mobility and transformation in the atmosphere has not been thoroughly addressed. It is believed that most airborne arsenic particulate material consists of inorganic arsenic (III) compounds (arsenic trioxide, arsenites) and perhaps some pentavalent arsenic (arsenic pentoxide, arsenate) (Braman, 1976). Background concentrations in comparatively nonpolluted locations average about 4 to 6 ng m^{-3} of total arsenic (Braman, 1976). Industrial areas (apart from the immediate vicinity of smelters) may have atmospheric arsenic concentrations of about 20 to 90 ng m^{-3} (NRC, 1976).

C   Arsenic is one of the few substances implicated in human carcinogenesis (IARC, 1978), but not yet convincingly demonstrated to produce cancer in experimental animals (USEPA, 1976).

D   Asbestos is a mineral fiber that has over 2000 individual uses, including: asbestos cement pipe (25%), flooring products (22%), friction products (11%), paper (11%), roofing products (8%), asbestos cement sheet (7%), packing and gaskets (35%), insulation (1%), textiles (1%), and other uses (11%) (Clifton, 1977). Consumption in the United States in 1976 was about 0.63×10^9 kg. Asbestos has been identified as a human carcinogen (IARC, 1978), and a number of major commercial sources of airborne emissions are limited by EPA regulations (USEPA, 1974b, 1975b).

E   Asbestos fibers are extremely resistant to degradation in the environment, usually have negligible gravitational settling properties, and are easily re-entrained at ground surfaces (USEPA, 1978c).

     Asbestos measurements in the ambient air of California have been made in several studies; for example:

Location in California	Number of Fibers m^{-3}	Reference
King City, downwind of a milling plant	6,000 to 1,600,000	John et al. (1976)
King City, upwind of a milling plant	200 to 11,000	John et al. (1976)

F   Asbestos is carcinogenic in humans (IARC, 1978). Cigarette smoking enhances the carcinogenic effect of asbestos.

G   Benzene is a component of gasoline and is widely utilized in the synthesis of organic chemicals. It appears in consumer products principally as a solvent. Benzene has been linked with leukemia in human studies. Large quantities are known to be discharged to the atmosphere and ambient concentrations are commonly measured. U.S. production of benzene in 1976 was 0.45×10^{10} kg (USITC, 1977).

H   With a half-life of roughly four days, benzene is relatively stable in the atmosphere. Recent studies suggest that benzene is converted to phenol in air. Levels in Southern California range between 13 and 360 ppb (Mayrsohn, 1975; Pellizzari, 1977).

I   The IARC has concluded that there is sufficient evidence to classify benzene as a strongly suspected human carcinogen (IARC, 1978).

J   Cadmium and its compounds have many uses, including electroplating (55%), plastics stabilizers (20%), pigments (12%), batteries (5%), and miscellaneous (8%) (USEPA, 1978a). Consumption of cadmium in the United States in 1977 was approximately 4.5×10^6 kg (USBM, 1978). Cadmium and several of its compounds have been identified as animal carcinogens (Christensen et al. 1976) and the Clean Air Act Amendments of 1977 require that the U.S. Environmental Protection Agency determine whether atmospheric emissions of cadmium are hazardous to public health. Cadmium source categories potentially able to cause measurable ambient levels of cadmium were identified as primary zinc, copper, lead, and cadmium smelters; secondary zinc and copper smelters; municipal incinerators; and iron and steel mills (USEPA, 1978a).

TABLE 2.3 (*Continued*)

K	Cadmium is emitted as metallic cadmium vapor from hot processes such as steelmaking and smelting. Cadmium in this form is expected to react quickly to form stable compounds such as the oxide, sulfate, or chloride. Urban concentrations of cadmium are typically 3 ng m^{-3}, ranging from 100 ng m^{-3} to undetectable (USEPA, 1978a). In California, a total of 304 composite quarterly samples were taken at 18 cities from 1970 through 1974. The mean composite quarterly value was 0.015 μg m^{-3}; the maximum value being 0.093 μg m^{-3} (Akland, 1976).
L	Cadmium, its oxides, chloride, sulfate, and other cadmium compounds have been identified as being carcinogenic in mammals (Christensen et al., 1976).
M	Carbon tetrachloride is a high-production chlorinated hydrocarbon used for making fluorocarbon 12 (52%), fluorocarbon 11 (28%), and other applications (20%) (Lowenheim and Moran, 1975). U.S. production in 1976 was 3.9 $\times$ 10^8 kg (USITC, 1977).
N	Carbon tetrachloride is stable in the troposphere and has no degradation products. California rural background levels appear to be roughly 0.11 ppb, while levels in Los Angeles average 0.13 ppb. Atmospheric carbon tetrachloride is thought to be largely or solely anthropogenic in origin (Singh et al., 1977).
O	Carbon tetrachloride is a confirmed animal carcinogen (IARC, 1972a).
P	Chloroform is a chlorinated hydrocarbon with the following uses (Lowenheim and Moran, 1975): fluorocarbon refrigerants and propellants (52%); fluorocarbon resins (41%); miscellaneous and exports (7%). Its U.S. production in 1976 was 1.3 $\times$ 10^8 kg (USITC, 1977).
Q	Chloroform is relatively stable, with a tropospheric half-life of 480 to 770 days, degrading slowly into phosgene, HCl, and chlorine monoxide. The rural background level in California is roughly 0.02 ppb, and urban levels in California average approximately 0.1 ppb. Whether natural sources of chloroform exist is unclear (Singh et al., 1977).
R	In National Cancer Institute tests, chloroform was carcinogenic in rats and mice. However, because of the very high doses given and resulting poor health of the test animals, these tests are controversial (Maugh, 1978).
S	Chromium is used in widely diversified products such as stainless, tool, and alloy steels; heat- and corrosion-resistant materials; special purpose alloys; alloy cast iron; pigments; metal plating; leather tanning; chemicals; and refractories for metallurgical furnaces. These uses are broadly classified as metallurgical, chemical, and refractory (Morning, 1977). The estimated 1976 domestic consumption of chromite ore was 0.9 $\times$ 10^9 kg all of which was imported (USEPA, 1978b). Sodium dichromate is produced from chromite ore and is the principal intermediate in the manufacture of chromium chemicals. The estimated 1976 domestic production of sodium dichromate was 1.4 $\times$ 10^8 kg by four firms. The major derivatives of sodium dichromate are pigments; metal treatment chemicals; leather tanning chemicals, and textile and dye chemicals. Chromium in these chemicals is largely hexavalent (USEPA, 1978b).
T	Chromium cannot be degraded in the air.
U	Chromite, chromium, and several chromium compounds are suspected or confirmed animal carcinogens (Christensen et al., 1976). Hexavalent chromium is suspected of causing lung cancer in dichromate-manufacturing workers (USEPA, 1978b; IARC, 1978).
V	1,4-dioxane is a widely used synthetic organic chemical used mainly as a stabilizer in chlorinated solvents (IARC, 1976). 1,4-dioxane is also found in consumer products such as varnishes, paint and varnish removers, cleaners, detergents, and deodorants (Hawley, 1977). The major use of 1,4-dioxane is as an inhibitor in methyl chloroform used for metal degreasing. The 1976 production was 0.7 $\times$ 10^7 kg (USITC, 1977).
W	1,4-dioxane is unstable in air, forming an explosive perioxide (IARC, 1976). In chamber experiments, 1,4-dioxane was found to have a half-life of 3 to 4 hours in air containing nitric oxide in sunlight (Dilling et al., 1976).
X	1,4-dioxane is carcinogenic in test animals, though administration to mice via inhalation resulted in negative results (IARC, 1976).

TABLE 2.3 (*Continued*)

Y   1,2-dibromoethane (EDB) is a dense, colorless liquid. Almost all ethylene dibromide produced in the United States is used as a scavenger in leaded gasoline preparations. The rest is used as a soil and seed fumigant, as an intermediate in the manufacture of dyes and pharmaceuticals, and as a nonflammable solvent for resins, gums, and waxes (Lowenheim and Moran, 1975).

Z   Ethylene dibromide vapor reacts slowly with oxidizing materials and is subject to photochemical degradation in the atmosphere. Levels near groups of gasoline stations and along highways have been measured to be about 1.4 ppb (Going and Long, 1975).

AA   Ethylene dibromide is carcinogenic in rats and mice after oral administration (IARC, 1977).

BB   A colorless liquid, ethylene dichloride (EDC) is one of the most heavily used chemicals in the United States. Its principal use (almost 80%) is as an intermediate in the production of vinyl chloride; other chemicals for which it is a feedstock include 1,1,1-trichloroethane, trichloroethylene, perchloroethylene, vinylidene chloride, and ethyleneamines. It is also widely used as an extraction solvent, as a lead scavenger in gasoline, as a solvent for textile cleaning and metal degreasing, in adhesives, fumigants, paint remover, soaps and scouring compounds, wetting and penetrating agents, ore flotation, and as a dispersant for nylon, rayon, styrene-butadiene rubber, and other plastics (Bahlman et al., 1978).

CC   EDC is oxidized very slowly in the troposphere and has a half-life of 10^3 to 10^7 days.

DD   Recent tests show that laboratory animals given oral doses of 1,2-dichloroethane experienced a statistically significant excess of cancer as compared with control animals (NCI, 1978).

EE   Lead has many uses but practically all of the lead emitted to the atmosphere is from motor vehicle exhaust. (When emitted after combustion, the lead is in inorganic form.)

FF   Half of the lead emitted from motor vehicle exhaust settles out of the air within 100 m of the roadway, leaving the finer particles to disperse throughout the atmosphere (USEPA, 1983). In 1974, the mean of the annual average lead concentration in 15 California cities was 1.5 μg m^{-3}. The U.S. Environmental Protection Agency has an ambient lead standard of 1.5 μg m^{-3}. Natural background concentrations appear to be roughly 0.001 to 0.03 μg m^{-3} (USEPA, 1983).

GG   The biological basis of lead toxicity is its ability to bind to ligating groups in biomolecular substances crucial to various physiological functions, thereby interfering with these functions by, for example, competing with native essential metals for the sites, inhibiting enzyme activity, and inhibiting or otherwise altering essential ion transport (USEPA, 1983).

HH   U.S. demand for nickel was estimated at 1.9×10^8 kg in 1976, and the use pattern was as follows: chemicals (14.6%), petroleum (8.7%), fabricated metal products (8.7%), transportation (23.2%), electrical goods (12.6%), household appliances (7.1%), machinery (7.6%), construction (9.2%), and other uses (8.3%) (Corrick, 1977).

II   Yearly average nickel levels in California cities in 1974 ranged from 12.8 ng m^{-3} in Santa Ana to 32.1 ng m^{-3} in Torrance (Akland, 1976). In the same year, the national urban arithmetic mean atmospheric nickel concentration was 9 ng m^{-3} (29 ng m^{-3} standard deviation).

JJ   Inorganic nickel has been recognized as carcinogenic in humans (NIOSH, 1977; IARC, 1978).

KK   The three major uses for nitrosamines are rubber processing, organic chemicals manufacturing, and rocket fuel manufacturing. Other potential uses are in the manufacture of rubber, dye-stuffs, gasoline additives, lubricating oils, explosives, insecticides, fungicides, dielectric fluids, acrylonitrile, plasticizers, industrial solvents, and hydrazine. Despite this long list of potential uses, nitrosamines have apparently had relatively little use. Potential or confirmed sources of incidental releases of nitrosamines to the atmosphere include combustion of hydrazine-based rocket fuel, fish meal processing, tobacco smoke, and power plants (USEPA, 1977). The possibility exists that nitrosamines may be formed in the atmosphere in reactions between nitrogen oxides and industrially released amines (Pitts et al., 1978a).

TABLE 2.3 (*Continued*)

LL   Nitrosamines have been detected in industrial urban air, implicating their direct emission or formation from precursor pollutants. Diethylnitrosamine (DEN) can be formed photochemically in chambers from triethylamine and NO_x, and, in opposing photochemical reactions, both dimethylnitrosamine (DMN) and DEN are decomposed in light (Pitts et al., 1978a). Hanst et al. (1977) found that the half-life of DMN under full sunlight was approximately 30 minutes. Those authors concluded that any DMN detected in the air in the afternoon would likely be the result of direct emissions rather than the formation from its immediate precursors.

       Gordon (1977) measured DMN in the ambient air of southern California. In a sampling program around chemical and petroleum plants, three of the samples were positive—0.07, 0.11, and 0.39 μg m^{-3}. Photodecomposition appears to be the single major removal mechanism of nitrosamines.

MM   Nitrosamines, including DEN and DMN, are considered potent and versatile carcinogens in experimental animals (USEPA, 1977) and are suspected of being carcinogenic in humans.

NN   Perchloroethylene is a synthetic organic solvent widely used in dry cleaning (67%), fabric finishing, metal degreasing (15%), and other applications. Nationwide production is 3.2 $\times$ 10^8 kg per year (NIOSH, 1978).

OO   Perchloroethylene has a reported half-life in the troposphere of 100 to 200 days and its degradation products include trichloroacetyl chloride, phosgene, and HCl. The rural background concentration is around 0.04 ppb, and levels in Los Angeles average approximately 0.7 ppb, with high concentrations of 2 ppb (Singh et al., 1977).

PP   Perchloroethylene has recently been confirmed as being carcinogenic in mice (NIOSH, 1978).

QQ   Polycyclic aromatic hydrocarbons (PAH) are multi-ringed compounds usually occurring in particulate form (see Table 1.12). Although benzo(a)pyrene (BaP) is often used as an indicator or surrogate for PAH in general, this class of compounds has hundreds of members. Unfortunately, no direct single-step analytical techniques exist for ambient air measurements of total PAH, although specific compounds or PAH subclasses may be measured by direct or subtractive techniques. In addition, BaP concentrations are not necessarily related to the carcinogenicity of a sample of ambient PAH. Stationary sources account for about 97 percent of the nationwide emissions of BaP (USEPA, 1974a), and include coal refuse fires (34.7%), residential furnaces (33.6%), coke production (19%), vehicle disposal, wood burning, forest and agricultural burning, tire degradation, municipal incineration, petroleum refining, and coal furnaces. Occupational exposure occurs mainly at coke ovens.

RR   Because of the high melting points and low vapor pressures of most PAHs, these compounds are most likely to be present in the atmosphere as pure particulate matter or adsorbed on other particulate matter. Many PAHs oxidize or photodegrade readily under atmospheric conditions. Some may be converted to more mutagenic products; for example, BaP can react with nitric oxide to form 6-nitrobenzo(a)pyrene and a mixture of 1-nitro and 3-nitrobenzo(a)pyrene. Recent experimentation has confirmed that directly active mutagens are formed when PAHs are exposed to simulated atmospheres of photochemical smog (Pitts et al., 1978b). In addition, many PAHs have been found to be sufficiently stable in the atmosphere to travel long distances (Lunde and Bjorseth, 1977). Annual average ambient BaP concentrations in 12 California cities, as measured in the EPA National Air Surveillance Network program, declined from 1.1 to 2.5 ng m^{-3} in 1966 to 0.6 to 1.9 ng m^{-3} in 1970 (USEPA, 1975a). During the same period levels at a rural station decreased from 0.4 to 0.1 ng m^{-3}.

SS   Experimental animals have been exposed to BaP through skin painting, inoculation, oral intake, subcutaneous injection, local implantation, intratracheal inoculation, and inhalation (USEPA, 1975a). In general, PAHs in their parent form do not produce major adverse effects; they must be metabolized by the enzyme systems of the body to produce intermediates capable of inducing cancer. BaP is, through its metabolites, a known animal

TABLE 2.3 (*Continued*)

carcinogen. Studies of inhalation of pure PAHs have largely yielded negative results, and no direct evidence exists that inhalation of ambient levels of PAHs leads to cancer in humans. Epidemiological studies are complicated by the existence of other potential carcinogens in the workplace; the general population would not be exposed to the same "mix" of compounds. However, the IARC (1978) has indicated that soot, tars, and oils are "associated, or strongly suspected to be associated, with cancer induction in humans."

TT   Vinyl chloride (VC), a dense gas at ambient temperature and pressure, is the parent compound of polyvinyl chloride (PVC), a widely-used plastic resin.

UU   The chemical behavior of vinyl chloride in ambient air has not been thoroughly characterized. VC has been shown in laboratory photochemical chamber experiments to react with high concentrations of NO_2, O_3, NO, and hydroxyl radicals; reaction products include carbon monoxide, formaldehyde, formic acid, formyl chloride, and hydrogen chloride (Gay et al., 1976). When potential reactants are at low concentrations or are absent, VC can be quite stable; little potential for autodegradation in sunlight exists.

VV   Vinyl chloride is a known human carcinogen. "The evidence that vinyl chloride causes angiosarcoma of the liver in humans may be considered conclusive" (Milby, 1977). Vinyl chloride is also strongly suspected to induce brain and lung cancer (IARC, 1978).

deposition within each region. Particle size, solubility, and hygroscopicity also affect deposition.

Particles are deposited in the various zones of the respiratory tract by a variety of physical mechanisms:

1. *Interception.* Interception occurs when the trajectory of a particle brings it so close to a surface that the particle hits the surface. The larger and more irregular in shape a particle (e.g., fibrous particles), the greater the chances for interception.

2. *Impaction.* Each time the air stream changes direction, the momentum of a particle tends to keep it on its preestablished trajectory.

3. *Sedimentation.* Particles tend to sediment due to the action of gravity.

4. *Diffusion.* Submicron-sized particles undergo random motion caused by the impact of gas molecules on them, so-called Brownian motion. Brownian motion increases with decreasing particle size.

The head region consists of two sets of airways, the nasal airway and the oral airway. Both airways lead to the larynx in the back of the throat and the top of the trachea. The fraction of total inspired particles deposited in the head region is largely dependent on the route of entry. The nasal path is usually more efficient at removing particles than the oral path, especially at low to moderate flow rates. Air velocity is highest directly after entering the nostril, where passage constriction occurs. As air flows through the nasal cavity a substantial portion of large particles impacts on the surface of the airway walls. High air to surface contact and abrupt changes in cross section and flow direction aid in particle removal. In oral breathing the velocity at any point is less in mouth breathing, and the abrupt changes in cross section that occur in the nasal passage do not occur in quiet oral breathing. Particle deposition in the head region during mouth inhalation occurs on the tongue and at the back wall of the oropharynx. Deposition of aerosols in the head during inhalation via the nose is essentially total for particles of diameter greater than 10 μm at inspiratory flow rates on the order to 30 1 min^{-1}, that is, flow rates corresponding to moderate exercise. During mouth breathing, however, the upper size cutoff for particles penetrating beyond the head increases to about 15 μm.

Inertial impaction is the mechanism primarily responsible for particle removal in the head and conducting airways and is responsible for deposition of the major portion of particles greater than 5 μm (Miller et al., 1979). Each time air changes direction in the nose, mouth, or branching airways, the momentum of the larger particles tends to keep them on their established trajectories, causing them to impact on bends and bifurcations. Impaction is likely to occur in airways where air velocity is high.

Because smaller particles are more likely to stay in the air stream, they are more likely to make it to the deeper parts of the lung, where they will ultimately be deposited by sedimentation or diffusion, or be exhaled. Sedimentation is mostly responsible for the deposition of particles approximately 0.5 μm to 1.0 μm in diameter, and primarily occurs in the bronchioles and alveolar spaces where the airways are small and the air velocity is low. Diffusion is most important for particle sizes below 0.5 μm and occurs in the small airways and alveoli and at airway bifurcations. As particles become smaller in size, their Brownian motion increases, and this becomes an effective mechanism for deposition in the small air spaces.

Total particle deposition measurements quantify the total amount of particles deposited in the overall respiratory tract (head, conducting and pulmonary airways). Regional deposition measurements separately quantify the amount of particles deposited in each individual region of the respiratory tract. The sum of individual regional deposition measurements should equal the total respiratory deposition.

Total deposition data for mouth breathing are given in Figure 2.3. Since mouth breathing bypasses much of the filtration capabilities of the nose and pharyngeal region, mouth breathing data allow a more protective or conservative measure of total deposition. For particles of 0.1 μm to 1.0 μm diameter there is about 20 to 30 percent total deposition in the respiratory system. Total deposition increases more or less linearly from about 50 percent for 2.0 μm diameter particles up to 90 to 100 percent for 10 μm particles (Stahlhofen et al., 1980; Chan and Lippmann, 1980). About 80 to 90 percent of the 8 to 10 μm diameter particles entering the trachea are deposited in the tracheobronchial region. Miller et al. (1979), using the tracheobronchial deposition data of Lippmann (1977) and aerodynamic diameters* computed at a mean flow rate of 30 1 min^{-1}, found that it could be concluded that about 10 percent of

*The aerodynamic diameter of a particle is the diameter of a unit density sphere having the same terminal settling velocity as the particle under study.

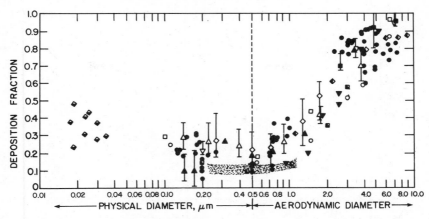

Figure 2.3. Deposition of monodisperse aerosols in the total respiratory tract for mouth breathing as a function of particle diameter. Above 0.5 μm, the diameter refers to aerodynamic diameter (see Chapter 7) and below 0.5 μm to actual physical diameter. The data are individual observations, averages, and ranges as cited by various investigators. (U.S. Environmental Protection Agency, 1982b)

particles as large as 15 μm diameter can enter the tracheobronchial region. Less than 10 percent of the 5 to 10 μm diameter inspired particles are deposited in the pulmonary region (Lippmann and Albert, 1969; Stahlhofen et al., 1980; Chan and Lippmann 1980). Approximately 20 percent of the 1 μm diameter, 30 percent of the 2 μm diameter, and 40 to 50 percent of the 3 to 4 μm diameter particles are deposited in the pulmonary region (Lippmann and Altschuler, 1976) (see Figure 2.4). There is effectively a window in the size range 0.1 to 1.0 μm where the particles are too large to be influenced by Brownian motion but are too small to be removed by impaction in the upper portion of the lung.

Epidemiological data demonstrate that exposure to particulate matter is associated with increased incidence of respiratory illness, chronic bronchitis, bronchoconstriction, decrement in pulmonary function, and increased mortality rates (National Research Council, 1979, and USEPA, 1982b). Among the adverse effects associated with short term exposure to particulate matter are increases in the rate of asthma attacks (Whittemore and Korn, 1980; Cohen et al., 1972). In two investigations conducted 20 years apart, investigators in Great Britain (Martin, 1964) and in the United States (Samet et al., 1981) reported strikingly similar results: a small but statistically significant correlation between particulate matter levels and hospital and emergency room admissions.

Air quality standards for atmospheric particles traditionally have specified limits on the total mass concentration, in μg m⁻³, of total suspended particulate matter (TSP). The potential for adverse health effects depends not only

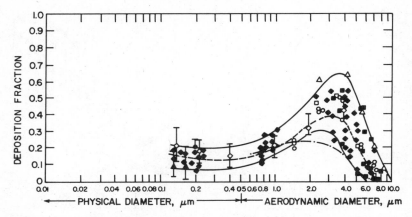

Figure 2.4. Deposition of monodisperse aerosols in the pulmonary region for mouth breathing as a function of particle diameter. Above 0.5 μm, the diameter refers to aerodynamic diameter (see Chapter 7) and below 0.5 μm to the actual physical diameter. The two solid lines represent the approximate ranges of the experimental deposition data. The dashed line is the theoretical deposition model of Yu (1978), and the broken line is an estimate of pulmonary deposition for nose breathing derived by Lippmann (1977). (U.S. Environmental Protection Agency, 1982b)

on the mass concentrations to which people are exposed but also on the physical and chemical properties of the particles. Since removal mechanisms in the head region prevent particles larger than 10 to 15 μm diameter from reaching the lower respiratory tract, and since only particles with diameters less than 2 to 3 μm penetrate to the deepest part of the lung, it is now recognized that particulate air quality standards must include a particle size consideration. The fine particle mode is comprised primarily of sulfates and other secondary material, and it also contains many of the toxic elements. The coarse particle mode is usually dominated by dust. Measurements of TSP tend to be dominated by the coarse particle mode, and measurements of inhalable particulate mass are also likely to contain substantial quantities of dust in sizes from 2 to 15 μm. To monitor airborne particles for purposes of public health protection (and welfare, such as visibility), it is necessary to obtain separate measurements in at least two size ranges, less than about 2 μm diameter and between 2 and 15 μm diameter.

2.6.   AIR QUALITY STANDARDS VERSUS EMISSIONS STANDARDS

The underlying motivation of a study of air pollution is to implement its control and abatement. More specifically, the objective is to control pollutant sources so that ambient pollutant concentrations are reduced to levels considered safe from the standpoint of undesirable effects. To quantify the objectives, it is desirable to know the amount of damage (to all aspects of the environment) caused by each pollutant as a function of exposure to various levels of the pollutant.* As we have seen in the previous section, such information is often difficult to obtain.

The legislative basis for air pollution abatement in the United States is the 1963 Clean Air Act and its amendments. The amendments provide for the establishment of two kinds of national ambient air quality standards. Primary ambient air quality standards are those requisite to protect public health with an adequate margin of safety. Secondary ambient air quality standards specify a level of pollutant concentrations requisite to protect the public welfare from any known or anticipated adverse effects associated with the presence of such air pollutants in the air. Secondary standards are based on damage to crops, vegetation, wildlife, visibility, climate, and on adverse effects to the economy. Thus, an air quality standard is a level to which a pollutant concentration should be reduced to avoid undesirable effects. Air quality standards are not based on technological or economic acceptability; they are dictated solely by the effects of air pollution, not the causes.

Table 2.4 presents the U.S. national primary and secondary ambient air quality standards for photochemical oxidants, carbon monoxide, nitrogen dioxide, sulfur dioxide, suspended particulate matter, and lead.

The Clean Air Act requires each state to adopt a plan that provides for the implementation, maintenance, and enforcement of the national air quality standards. It is, of course, emission reductions that will abate air pollution. Thus, the states' plans must contain legally enforceable emission limitations, schedules, and timetables for compliance with such limitations. The control strategy must consist of a combination of measures designed to achieve the total reduction of emissions necessary for the attainment of the air quality standards. The control strategy may include, for example, such measures as emission limitations, emission charges or taxes, closing or relocation of commercial or industrial facilities, periodic inspection and testing of motor vehicle emission control systems, mandatory installation of control devices on motor vehicles, means to reduce motor vehicle traffic, including such measures as gasoline rationing, parking restrictions, and carpool lanes on freeways, and expansion and promotion of the use of mass transportation facilities.

Each state must also provide a contingency plan to control pollutant sources during periods of air stagnation when air quality is predicted to reach levels that would constitute imminent and substantial endangerment to human health. The contingency plans are to provide for emission reductions based on "warning" and "emergency" episode concentrations. The warning levels indicate that additional control is necessary if meterological conditions can be

---

*In many cases pollutants cannot be considered independently, since their effects are strongly influenced by the presence of other pollutants. Examples include SO_2 and particles and oxides of nitrogen and hydrocarbons.

Effects of Air Pollution

TABLE 2.4. United States National Ambient Air Quality Standards

Air Contaminant	National Standard[a]	Maximum Allowable Annual Mean Concentrations			Maximum Allowable Short-Period Concentrations and Averaging Times[b]			
		AAM[c] μg m^{-3}	AAM[c] ppm	AGM[d] μg m^{-3}	μg m^{-3}	mg m^{-3}	ppm	Averaging Times
Oxidant[e]	Primary				240		0.12	1 hour
(Ozone)	Secondary				240		0.12	1 hour
Carbon	Primary[e]					10	9	8 hours
Monoxide						40	35	1 hour
	Secondary[e]					10	9	8 hours
						40	35	1 hour
Nitrogen	Primary	100	0.05					
Dioxide	Secondary	100	0.05					
Sulfur	Primary	80	0.03		365		0.14	24 hours
Dioxide	Secondary				1300		0.50	3 hours
Particulate	Primary			75	260			24 hours
Matter	Secondary			60	150			24 hours
Lead	Primary					1.5		Quarterly
	Secondary					1.5		Average

[a] National Air Quality Standards as presented in the Code of Federal Regulations, 40, Protection of Environment, Part 50, sec 50.4 to 50.11, July 1, 1974, U.S. Government Printing Office, Washington, D.C., 1974. Primary Standard—Necessary to protect the public health (sec 50.2). Secondary Standard—Necessary to protect the public welfare and the environment from known or anticipated adverse effects of a pollutant (sec 50.2).

[b] Not to be exceeded more than once per year (for ozone, the average number of days per year above the standard must be less than or equal to one).

[c] AAM—Annual Arithmetic Mean.

[d] AGM—Annual Geometric Mean.

[e] Both the eight-hour and one-hour standard must be met.

expected to remain the same for a period of 12 hours. At the emergency levels, the most stringent controls are necessary to ensure that concentrations do not reach levels where imminent and substantial endangerment to the health of any significant portion of the population will occur. Table 2.5 summarizes the national warning, emergency, and significant harm levels.

While air quality standards are based largely on health effects, the question arises: On what are the emissions standards based? In theory, one would like

**TABLE 2.5. United States Environmental Protection Agency
Air Pollution Episode Criteria**

Contaminant	Averaging Time (hr)	Stage 1	Stage 2	Stage 3
Carbon monoxide	8	15 ppm	30 ppm	40 ppm
Nitrogen dioxide	1	0.60 ppm	1.20 ppm	1.60 ppm
	24	0.15 ppm	0.30 ppm	0.40 ppm
Particulate matter	24	$375 \ \mu g \ m^{-3}$	$625 \ \mu g \ m^{-3}$	$875 \ \mu g \ m^{-3}$
Sulfur dioxide/ Particulate matter combined[a]	24	6.5×10^4	2.61×10^5	3.93×10^5

[a] Product of $[SO_2]$ in $\mu g \ m^{-3}$ and particulate matter in $\mu g \ m^{-3}$.

to work backward from air quality standards to determine those emission standards necessary to meet the air quality standards in a particular region. To do this, we need to relate emission rates to air quality, that is, to represent mathematically the "atmosphere" block in Figure 1.1. Because of the great importance in obtaining this relation, we will devote considerable attention in this book to this problem.

REFERENCES

Akland, G. G. "Air Quality Data for Metals, 1970 through 1974, from the National Air Surveillance Networks," U.S. Environmental Protection Agency, Office of Research and Development, EPA-600/4-76-041 (1976).

Bahlman, L. J., Leidel, N. A. et al. "Ethylene Dichloride (1,2-dichloroethane)," *Am. Ind. Hyg. Assoc. J.*, **39**, A35–A43 (1978).

Braman, R. S. "Applications of the Arsine Evolution Methods to Environmental Analyses," presented at the International Conference on Environmental Arsenic, Ft. Lauderdale, FL (1976).

Chan, T. L., and Lippmann, M. "Experimental Measurements and Empirical Modelling of the Regional Deposition of Inhaled Particles in Humans," *Am. Ind. Hyg. Assoc. J.*, **41**, 399–408 (1980).

Changnon, S. A., Jr., "The La Porte Weather Anomaly, Fact or Fiction," *Bull. Am. Meteor. Soc.*, **49**, 4 (1968).

Christensen, H. E., Fairchild, E. F., and Lewis, R. J. "Suspected Carcinogens: A Subfile of the NIOSH Registry of Toxic Effects of Chemical Substances," 2nd ed., National Institute for Occupational Safety and Health, NIOSH 77-149 (1976).

Clifton, R. A. "Asbestos—1977," U.S. Bureau of Mines, Mineral Commodity Profiles, MCP-6 (1977).

Cohen, A. A., Bromberg, S., Buechley, R. W., Heiderescheit, L. T., and Shy, C. M. "Asthma and Air Pollution from a Coal Fueled Power Plant," *Am. J. Public Health*, **62**, 1181–1188 (1972).

Corrick, J. "Nickel—1977," U.S. Bureau of Mines, Mineral Commodity Profiles, MCP-4 (1977).

Dilling, W. L., Bredeweg, C. J., and Tefertiller, N. B. "Organic Photochemistry: Simulated Atmospheric Photodecomposition Rates of Methylene Chloride, 1,1,1-Trichloroethane, Trichloroethylene, Tetrachloroethylene, and Other Compounds," *Environ. Sci. Technol.*, **10**, 351–356 (1976).

Gay, B. W., Jr., Hanst, P. L., Bufalini, J. J., and Noonan, R. C. "Atmospheric Oxidation of Chlorinated Ethylenes," *Environ. Sci. Technol.*, **10**, 58–67 (1976).

Georgii, H. W. "The Effects of Air Pollution on Urban Climates," *Bull. World Health Organ.*, **40**, 624 (1969).

Going, J., and Long, S. "Sampling and Analysis of Selected Toxic Substances: Task II—Ethylene Dibromide," U.S. Environmental Protection Agency, Washington, D.C., EPA-560/6-75-001 (1975).

Gordon, R. J. "Survey for Airborne Nitrosamines in Los Angeles" Quarterly Report Submitted to California Air Resources Board, Contract No. A6-096-30 (1977).

Hanst, P. L., Spence, J. W., and Miller, M. "Atmospheric Chemistry of N-Nitrosodimethylamine," *Environ. Sci. Technol.*, **11**, 403–405 (1977).

Hawley, G. G. *The Condensed Chemical Dictionary*, 9th ed., Van Nostrand Reinhold Co. (1977).

Hindawi, I. J. "Air Pollution Injury to Vegetation," U.S. Dept. of Health, Education and Welfare Publ. AP-71, Raleigh, N.C. (1970).

International Agency for Research on Cancer, "Carbon Tetrachloride," *IARC Monographs on the Evaluation of Carcinogenic Risk of Chemicals to Man*, **1**, 53–60 (1972a).

International Agency for Research on Cancer, "Lead Salts," *IARC Monographs on the Evaluation of Carcinogenic Risk of Chemicals to Man*, **1**, 40–49 (1972b).

International Agency for Research on Cancer, "1,4-Dioxane," *IARC Monographs on the Evaluation of Carcinogenic Risk of Chemicals to Man*, **11**, 247–256 (1976).

International Agency for Research on Cancer, "Ethylene Dibromide," *IARC Monographs on the Evaluation of Carcinogenic Risk of Chemicals to Man*, **15**, 195–209 (1977).

International Agency for Research on Cancer, *Chemicals with Sufficient Evidence of Carcinogenicity in Experimental Animals*, IARC Working Group Report, Lyon, France (1978).

John, H., Berner, A. et al. "Experimental Determination of the Number and Size of Asbestos Fibers in Ambient Air," California Air Resources Board, ARB 3–68 (1976).

Kirkpatrick, M. B., Sheppard, D., Nadel, J. A., and Bonshey, H. A. "Effect of Oronasal Breathing Route on Sulfur Dioxide—Induced Bronchoconstriction in Exercising Asthmatic Subjects," *Am. Rev. Respiratory Disease*, **125**, 627–631 (1982).

Koenig, J. Q., Pierson, W. E., Horike, M., and Frank, R. "Effects of Inhaled Sulfur Dioxide on Pulmonary Function in Healthy Adolescents: Exposure to SO_2 Alone and SO_2 + Sodium Chloride Droplet During Rest and Exercises," *Arch. Environ. Health*, **37**, 5–9 (1982).

Lawther, P. J., Waller, R. E., and Henderson, M. "Air Pollution and Exacerbations of Bronchitis," *Thorax*, **25**, 525–539 (1970).

Linn, W. S., Bailey, R. M., Shamoo, D. A., Venet, J. G., Wightman, L. H., and Hackney, J. D. "Respiratory Response of Young Adult Asthmatics to Sulfur Dioxide Exposure Near Simulated Ambient Exposure Conditions," *Environ. Res.*, **29**, 220–232 (1982).

Lippmann, M., and Albert, R. E. "The Effect of Particle Size on the Regional Deposition of Inhaled Aerosols in the Human Respiratory Tract," *Am. Ind. Hyg. Assoc. J.*, **30**, 257–275 (1969).

Lippmann, M., and Altshuler, B. "Regional Deposition of Aerosols," in *Air Pollution and the Lung*, E. F. Aharonsom, A. Ben David, and M. A. Klingberg (Eds.). Proceedings of the Twentieth Annual OHOLO Biological Conference, Maalot, Israel, Wiley, New York (1976).

Lippmann, M. "Regional Deposition of Particles in the Human Respiratory Tract," in *Handbook of Physiology*, D. H. K. Lee, H. L. Falk, and S. D. Murphy (Eds.). Section 9: Reaction to Environmental Agents, Bethesda, MD, American Physiological Society (1977).

Lowenheim, F. A., and Moran, M. K. (Eds.) *Faith, Keyes and Clark's Industrial Chemicals*, 4th ed., Wiley, New York (1975).

Lunde, G., and Bjorseth, A. "Polycyclic Aromatic Hydrocarbons in Long-Range Transported Aerosols," *Nature*, **268**, 518–519 (1977).

Martin, A. E. "Mortality and Morbidity Statistics and Air Pollution," *Proc. R. Soc. Med.*, **57**, 969–975 (1964).

Martin, A. E., and Bradley, W. H. "Mortality, Fog and Atmospheric Pollution—An Investigation During the Winter of 1958–59," *Monthly Bulletin of the Ministry of Health*, Public Health Laboratory Serv., **19**, 56–72 (1960).

Maugh, T. H. "Chemical Carcinogens: How Dangerous are Low Doses? *Science*, **202**, 37–41 (1978).

Mayrsohn, H. "Atmospheric Hydrocarbon Concentrations," California Air Resources Board, Sacramento (1975).

Mazumdar, S., Schimmel, H., and Higgins, I. "Daily Mortality, Smoke and SO_2 in London, England, 1959–1972," Proceedings of the Specialty Conference on the Proposed SO_2 and Particulate Standard, Air Pollution Control Association, Sept. 16–18, 1980, Pittsburgh, PA, 219–239 (1981).

Michelson, I., and Tourin, B. "Comparative Method for Studying Costs of Air Pollution," *Public Health Report*, **81**, 505 (1966).

Milby, T. H. "Vinyl Chloride," Cancer Control Monograph prepared by Stanford Research Institute for National Cancer Institute and National Institute of Health, Bethesda, MD (1977).

Miller, F. J., Gardner, D. E., Graham, J. A., Lee, R. E., Wilson, W. E., Jr., and Bachmann, J. D. "Size Considerations for Establishing a Standard for Inhalable Particles," *J. Air Pollution Control Assoc.*, **29**, 610–615 (1979).

Morning, J. L. "Chromium—1977," U.S. Bureau of Mines, Mineral Commodity Profiles, MCP-1 (1977).

National Cancer Institute, "Bioassay of 1,2-Dichloroethane for Possible Carcinogenicity," U.S. Department of Health, Education and Welfare, Public Health Service, National Institutes of Health, Carcinogenesis Testing Program, DHEW Publication No. (NIH) 78-1305 (1978).

National Institute for Occupational Safety and Health, "Criteria for a Recommended Standard . . . Occupational Exposure to Inorganic Nickel," (1977).

National Institute for Occupational Safety and Health, "Tetrachloroethylene," NIOSH Current Intelligence Bulletin, **20** (1978).

National Research Council, "Airborne Particles," University Park Press, Baltimore, MD (1979).

National Research Council, "Sulfur Oxides," National Academy of Sciences, Washington, D.C. (1978).

National Research Council, "Arsenic," prepared by Subcommittee on Arsenic, Committee on Medical and Biologic Effects of Environmental Pollutants, Washington, D.C. (1976).

Pellizzari, E. D. "The Measurement of Carcinogenic Vapors in Ambient Atmospheres," U.S. Environmental Protection Agency, EPA-600/7-77-055 (1977).

Pitts, J. N., Jr., Grosjean, D., Van Cauwenberghe, K., Schmid, J. P., and Fitz, D. R. "Photooxidation of Aliphatic Amines Under Simulated Atmospheric Conditions: Formation of Nitrosamines, Nitramines, Amides and Photochemical Oxidant," *Environ. Sci. Technol.*, **12**, 946–958 (1978a).

Pitts, J. N., Jr., Van Cauwenberghe, K. A., Grosjean, D., Schmid, J. P., Fitz, D. R., Belser, W. L., Jr., Knudson, G. B., and Hynds, P. M. "Atmospheric Reactions of Polycyclic Aromatic

Hydrocarbons: Facile Formation of Mutagenic Nitro Derivatives," *Science*, **202**, 515–519 (1978b).

Samet, J. M., Speizer, F. E., Bishop, Y., Spengler, J. D., and Ferris, B. G., Jr. "The Relationship Between Air Pollution and Emergency Room Visits in an Industrial Community," *J. Air Pollution Control Assoc.*, **31**, 236–240 (1981).

Science Applications, Inc. "An Inventory of Carcinogenic Substances Released into the Ambient Air of California," Interim Report to State of California Air Resources Board, Report No. SAI-068-79-530 (1978).

Sheppard, D., Saisho, A., Nadel, J. A., and Boushey, H. A. "Exercise Increases Sulfur Dioxide-Induced Bronchoconstriction in Asthmatic Subjects," *Am. Reviews Respiratory Disease*, **123**, 486–491 (1981).

Singh, H. B., Salas, L., Shigeishi, H., and Crawford, A. "Urban-Nonurban Relationships of Halocarbons, SF_6, N_2O and Other Atmospheric Trace Constituents," *Atmos. Environ.*, **11**, 819–828 (1977).

Stahlhofen, W., Gebhart, J., and Heyder, J. "Experimental Determination of the Regional Deposition of Aerosol Particles in the Human Respiratory Tract," *Am. Ind. Hyg. Assoc. J.*, **41**, 385–398 (1980).

U.S. Bureau of Mines, "Mineral Commodity Summaries," (1978).

U.S. Environmental Protection Agency, "Preferred Standards Path Report for Polycyclic Organic Matter," Office of Air Quality Planning and Standards, Strategies and Air Standards Division, Durham, North Carolina (1974a).

U.S. Environmental Protection Agency, "National Emission Standards for Hazardous Air Pollutants: Asbestos and Mercury," *Federal Register*, **39**, 38064 (1974b).

U.S. Environmental Protection Agency, "Scientific and Technical Assessment Report on Particulate Polycyclic Organic Matter (PPOM)," EPA-600/6-75-001 (1975a).

U.S. Environmental Protection Agency, "National Emission Standards for Hazardous Air Pollutants: Asbestos and Mercury (Amendment)," *Federal Register*, **40**, 48292 (1975b).

U.S. Environmental Protection Agency, "Air Pollutant Assessment Report on Arsenic," Strategies and Air Standards Division, Office of Air Quality Planning and Standards, Office of Air and Waste Management (1976).

U.S. Environmental Protection Agency, "Scientific and Technical Assessment Report on Nitrosamines," Office of Research and Development, EPA-600/6-77-001 (1977).

U.S. Environmental Protection Agency, "Sources of Atmospheric Cadmium," draft report prepared by Energy and Environmental Analysis, Inc., Arlington, Virginia, for Office of Air and Waste Management and Office of Air Quality Planning and Standards (1978a).

U.S. Environmental Protection Agency, "Chromium and Chromium Compounds" Phase I Report, Office of Toxic Substances (1978b).

U.S. Environmental Protection Agency, "Dispersion Model Analysis of the Air Quality Impact of Asbestos Emissions from Iron Ore Beneficiation Plants," Source Receptor Analysis Branch, EPA Contract No. 68-02-2507 (1978c).

U.S. Environmental Protection Agency, "Air Quality Criteria for Ozone and Other Photochemical Oxidants," Report No. EPA-600/8-78-004 (1978d).

U.S. Environmental Protection Agency, "Air Quality Criteria for Oxides of Nitrogen," Report No. EPA-600/8-82-026 (1982a).

U.S. Environmental Protection Agency, "Air Quality Criteria for Particulate Matter and Sulfur Oxides," Report No. EPA-600/8-82-029 (1982b).

U.S. Environmental Protection Agency, "Air Quality Criteria for Lead," Report No. EPA-600/8-83-028 (1983).

U.S. International Trade Commission, "Synthetic Organic Chemicals, United States Production and Sales, 1974," ITC Publication 776 (1976).

U.S. International Trade Commission, "Synthetic Organic Chemicals, United States Production and Sales, 1976," ITC Publication 833 (1977).

Ware, J., Thibodeau, L. A., Speizer, F. E., Colome, S., and Ferris, B. G., Jr. "Assessment of the Health Effects of Atmospheric Sulfur Oxides and Particulate Matter: Analysis of the Exposure-Response Relationship," *Environ. Health Perspectives*, **41**, 255–276 (1981).

Whittemore, A. S., and Korn, E. L. "Asthma and Air Pollution in the Los Angeles Area," *Am. J. Public Health*, **70**, 687–696 (1980).

Williamson, S. *Fundamentals of Air Pollution*, Addison-Wesley, Reading, MA (1973).

Yu, C. P. "A Two Component Theory of Aerosol Deposition in Human Lung Airways," *Bull. Math. Biol.*, **40**, 693–704 (1978).

THREE

Sources of Pollutants in Combustion Processes

Although this is primarily a book on atmospheric processes, it is useful to have an overview of the mechanisms by which air pollutants are formed at the source and of the measures that are used to limit the production of the pollutants. This chapter is devoted, therefore, to a brief discussion of the formation of pollutants in combustion processes and their control.

3.1. POLLUTANT FORMATION IN COMBUSTION

3.1.1. Burning of a Hydrocarbon Fuel

Ideal complete oxidation of hydrocarbon fuel yields only CO_2 and H_2O as combustion products. For a given quantity of fuel, a precise amount of oxygen is required for complete combustion according to

$$C_xH_y + (x + \tfrac{1}{4}y)O_2 \rightarrow xCO_2 + \tfrac{1}{2}yH_2O$$

An air–fuel mixture that is theoretically of the precise ratio to obtain complete combustion, with no excess O_2, is termed a *stoichiometric* mixture. Let us determine the stoichiometric air–fuel ratios for the combustion of *n*-heptane (C_7H_{16}) and isooctane (C_8H_{18}). For these two fuels, based on the above reaction, the stoichiometric quantities of O_2 and N_2 are:

	O_2 (moles)	N_2 (moles)	O_2 (mass)	N_2 (mass)
C_7H_{16}	11	41.36	352	1159.2
C_8H_{18}	12.5	47	400	1316

where N_2 and O_2 are in the molar ratio of 3.76 to 1.

The *air–fuel ratio* is defined as the mass of air per mass of fuel. The molecular weights of C_7H_{16} and C_8H_{18} are 100 and 114, respectively. Thus, the air–fuel ratios for stoichiometric combustion of the two fuels are:

$$C_7H_{16}: \quad \frac{1511}{100} = 15.11$$

$$C_8H_{18}: \quad \frac{1716}{114} = 15.05$$

The stoichiometric air–fuel ratio of a typical gasoline is about 14.6. If the mixture contains less than the stoichiometric amount of air it is said to be *rich*, whereas with excess air the mixture is termed *lean*. A related measure is the so-called *equivalence ratio*, the ratio of the actual fuel–air ratio to the stoichiometric fuel–air ratio (note fuel–air and not air–fuel). The straight air–fuel ratio is more commonly used, although the equivalence ratio has the advantage of indicating exactly the deviation from stoichiometric conditions.

The concentration of unburned hydrocarbons in the exhaust from a combustion process can be estimated by assuming a fraction f of incomplete combustion. We have shown that the complete combustion of 1 mole of a hydrocarbon fuel C_xH_y leads to x moles of CO_2 and $y/2$ moles of H_2O, in addition to the $(x + \frac{1}{4}y)$ 3.76 moles of N_2 assumed to be unaltered during the reaction. Thus, complete combustion of 1 mole of fuel with $F = 4.76 (x + \frac{1}{4}y)$ moles of air yields $M = x + \frac{1}{2}y + 3.76 (x + \frac{1}{4}y)$ moles of products. If a fraction f of the fuel is unburned, then the mole fraction of unburned fuel in the exhaust is $f/[M + f(1 + F - M)]$. The concentration of unburned fuel in the exhaust in parts-per-million by volume is then $10^6 f/[M + f(1 + F - M)]$. A standard blended fuel for the internal combustion engine is indolene, $C_7H_{13.02}$. Let us evaluate the concentration of unburned hydrocarbons in the exhaust from an engine burning indolene for $f = 0.001, 0.01,$ and 0.1:

f	0.001	0.01	0.1
concentration, ppm	19.2	192	1929

This calculation provides us with an estimate for the exhaust concentration level of unburned hydrocarbons in a combustion process.

Aside from unburned hydrocarbons, the second major air pollutant from combustion of hydrocarbon fuel is CO. To estimate the maximum amount of CO that can form at a given combustion temperature, let us calculate the equilibrium mole fraction of CO in the system of CO, CO_2, and O_2 at 1 atm pressure as a function of temperature. The equilibrium is the result of the forward and reverse reactions,

$$CO_2 \rightleftarrows CO + \tfrac{1}{2}O_2$$

The equilibrium constant for this reaction at 1 atm is

$$K = 3 \times 10^4 \exp(-67,000/RT)$$

$$= \frac{x_{CO} x_{O_2}^{1/2}}{x_{CO_2}} \tag{3.1}$$

We consider conditions in which the ratio of the number of oxygen atoms to the number of carbon atoms is 2, 3.125 (stoichiometric combustion of octane), and 5. Using

$$x_{CO_2} + x_{CO} + x_{O_2} = 1 \tag{3.2}$$

$$\frac{2x_{CO_2} + x_{CO} + 2x_{O_2}}{x_{CO} + x_{CO_2}} = \alpha = \frac{\text{moles O}}{\text{moles C}} \tag{3.3}$$

we can obtain K as a function of x_{CO} and α. Choosing T and α then allows us to solve for x_{CO}. The results for $T = 2000K$, $3000K$, and $4000K$ are:

	T, K		
α	2000	3000	4000
2	0.0157	0.383	0.630
3.125	0.0015	0.213	0.448
5	0.00074	0.125	0.302

We see that the equilibrium mole fraction of CO increases with temperature and decreases as the O/C ratio increases. Thus, we expect that CO formation will be favored by high temperature and fuel-rich operation.

3.1.2. Mechanism of Nitrogen Oxides (NO$_x$) Formation

There are two sources of nitrogen oxides, NO and NO_2, in the combustion of conventional fuels. The first is the oxidation of atmospheric molecular N_2 at the high temperatures of combustion. NO_x formed by this route is referred to as *thermal* NO_x. The second source is the oxidation of nitrogen-containing compounds in the fuel. NO_x formed by this path is called *fuel* NO_x.

Since the activation energies of several of the formation reactions involved in thermal NO_x production are high, the rate of formation of thermal NO_x is strongly temperature dependent. Thermal NO_x is formed during the combustion of all fuels in the regions of peak flame temperature.

The mechanism of thermal NO_x production has been studied extensively. The thermal NO_x-forming reactions involve the oxygen-nitrogen system and are effectively decoupled from the combustion process. High temperature and high O_2 concentration favor NO formation, and preventing one or both of the conditions is the basis of most thermal NO_x control technology.

The oxidation of nitrogen compounds chemically bound in the fuel molecules produces fuel NO_x. The amount of fuel nitrogen contained in fossil fuel can vary considerably, with negligible amounts in natural gas, significant amounts found in distillate fuels, and quantities from 0.5 to 3 percent by weight in heavier fuels such as residual oil, coal, and coal-derived and shale-derived fuels. The nitrogen content of U.S. coals varies from about 0.8 percent by weight for anthracite to nearly 2 percent by weight for medium volatile bituminous. As expected, the amount of fuel NO_x produced in combustion processes increases with the nitrogen content of the fuel. Fifty to 90 percent of the total NO_x from the combustion of residual oil and coal is usually fuel-related, even though it has been established that only a fraction of the fuel nitrogen is converted to NO_x, with the remainder forming molecular nitrogen. The main factor affecting the conversion of fuel-bound nitrogen to NO_x is oxygen availability. Because atmospheric nitrogen is extremely stable (bond dissociation energy of 225 kcal mole^{-1}) relative to carbon–nitrogen bonds in fuel molecules (bond dissociation energies from 60 to 150 kcal mole^{-1}), the activation energy required for oxygen to react with nitrogen in the fuel is considerably lower than that required for reacting with molecular nitrogen. Thus, NO formation by oxidation of nitrogen in fuel occurs rapidly and is generally unaffected by changes in combustion temperature.

The chemical mechanism of fuel NO_x formation has not been definitively established. Several qualitative observations have been drawn from experimental studies of fuel NO_x formation. NO formation appears to occur on time scales comparable to the hydrocarbon oxidation. NO yields are sensitive to the fuel-air equivalence ratio, with lean and near stoichiometric conditions resulting in high yields and rich flames resulting in low yields. And, as noted earlier, fuel NO_x yields are not strongly temperature-dependent. The fuel NO_x kinetics relative to thermal NO_x kinetics have the additional complexity of being strongly coupled to the hydrocarbon oxidation process.

3.2. THERMAL NO_x FORMATION

Thermal NO_x results from the reactions that occur when an oxygen-nitrogen mixture is raised to a high temperature. Although thermal NO_x formation during combustion must be analyzed as a kinetic process, a useful starting point is to ask what is the equilibrium composition of an oxygen–nitrogen mixture as a function of temperature. The equilibrium composition provides an estimate for the achievable concentrations of NO and NO_2 corresponding to the temperatures of combustion.

The key chemical reactions in the oxygen-nitrogen system at temperatures below about 4500K are given in Table 3.1. (Dissociation of N_2 into atomic

TABLE 3.1. Rate Constants for Thermal NO_x Production[a]

Reaction	Forward Reaction cm^3 molecule^{-1} sec^{-1} [d]	Reverse Reaction cm^3 molecule^{-1} sec^{-1}
$O_2 + M \rightleftarrows 2O + M$ [c]	$1.876 \times 10^{-6} T^{-1/2} \exp(-118,000/RT)$	2.6×10^{-33} [b]
$O + N_2 \rightleftarrows NO + N$	$1.16 \times 10^{-10} \exp(-75,500/RT)$	2.57×10^{-11}
$N + O_2 \rightleftarrows NO + O$	$2.21 \times 10^{-14} T \exp(-7080/RT)$	$5.3 \times 10^{-15} T \times \exp(-39,100/RT)$

[a] Ammann and Timmins (1966).
[b] Third-order reaction, cm^6 molecule^{-2} sec^{-1}.
[c] M denotes a third body.
[d] For a discussion of the units of chemical reaction rate constants we refer the reader to Appendix 4.A.1.

nitrogen becomes important above 4500 K.) The first reaction is simply the dissociation–recombination reaction of oxygen. The next two are exchange reactions and are those responsible for NO formation. Those reactions having high activation energies will have rates that increase rapidly with increasing temperature. We expect that dissociation of molecular oxygen will not become important until a certain threshold temperature, because of its large activation energy. The forward reaction $O + N_2$ also has a high activation energy, although the reverse reaction $NO + N$ has zero activation energy and is therefore very rapid. The reaction $N + O_2$ has a low activation energy and thus is rapid in the forward direction; its reverse reaction $NO + O$ has a higher activation energy and thus will decrease rapidly with decreasing temperature.

Ammann and Timmins (1966) have presented a calculation of the equilibrium composition of air as a function of temperature over the range 1000 K to 7000 K. The important aspects of the equilibrium calculation are: (1) the maximum NO concentration is obtained at approximately 3500 K; (2) the dissociation of molecular O_2 into the atomic species is extensive above 3000 K; and (3) as noted above, the dissociation of nitrogen becomes important above 4500 K. The maximum NO mole fraction achieved is 0.052.

The qualitative features of the full equilibrium calculation can be elucidated by considering the equilibrium NO concentration that is predicted from the overall reaction,

$$\tfrac{1}{2} N_2 + \tfrac{1}{2} O_2 \rightleftarrows NO$$

with the equilibrium constant,

$$K = 4.69 \exp(-21,600/RT)$$

$$= \frac{x_{NO}}{x_{N_2}^{1/2} x_{O_2}^{1/2}} \tag{3.4}$$

Consider the ratio of nitrogen atoms to oxygen atoms as 4 (approximately air) and 40 (combustion of flue gases at 10 percent excess air). We can use

$$x_{N_2} + x_{O_2} + x_{NO} = 1 \tag{3.5}$$

$$\frac{x_{NO} + 2x_{N_2}}{x_{NO} + 2x_{O_2}} = \beta = \frac{\text{moles N}}{\text{moles O}} \tag{3.6}$$

to obtain K as a function of x_{NO} and β only. The values of NO mole fraction at the same three temperatures at which we determined the equilibrium quantity of CO are:

	T, K		
β	2000	3000	4000
4	0.00785	0.045	0.1
40	0.00295	0.0152	0.029

The equilibrium mole fraction of NO increases with temperature and decreases as the N/O ratio increases. Thus, we expect that conditions of high temperature and high oxygen availability will be most conducive to NO formation.

Following along the same lines, let us estimate the equilibrium mole fraction of NO_2 in a combustion exhaust. For this we need to consider the two reactions,

$$\tfrac{1}{2}N_2 + \tfrac{1}{2}O_2 \rightleftarrows NO \tag{1}$$

$$NO + \tfrac{1}{2}O_2 \rightleftarrows NO_2 \tag{2}$$

with equilibrium constants at 1 atm,

$$K_1 = 4.69 \exp(-21,600/RT)$$

$$= \frac{x_{NO}}{x_{N_2}^{1/2} x_{O_2}^{1/2}} \tag{3.7}$$

$$K_2 = 2.5 \times 10^{-4} \exp(13,720/RT)$$

$$= \frac{x_{NO_2}}{x_{NO} x_{O_2}^{1/2}} \tag{3.8}$$

Using

$$x_{N_2} + x_{O_2} + x_{NO} + x_{NO_2} = 1 \tag{3.9}$$

and

$$\frac{2x_{N_2} + x_{NO} + x_{NO_2}}{2x_{O_2} + x_{NO} + 2x_{NO_2}} = \beta = \frac{\text{moles N}}{\text{moles O}} \qquad (3.10)$$

we can obtain two equations in the two unknowns x_{NO} and x_{NO_2}. This calculation is a bit tedious and can be avoided by assuming that N_2 and O_2 are unchanged as a result of reaction 1. Then taking

$$x_{NO} = K_1 x_{N_2}^{1/2} x_{O_2}^{1/2} \qquad (3.11)$$

we obtain

$$x_{NO_2} = K_1 K_2 x_{N_2}^{1/2} x_{O_2} \qquad (3.12)$$

The values of the NO_2 mole fraction determined in this way will be calculated for air and for a flue gas of composition 3.3 percent O_2 and 76 percent N_2 at $T = 298$ K, 1273 K, and 1873 K:

		T, K	
β	298	1273	1873
4	3.63×10^{-10}	9.69×10^{-6}	2.64×10^{-5}
40	5.59×10^{-11}	1.49×10^{-6}	4.05×10^{-6}

We conclude that virtually all of the NO_x formed in a combustion will exist as NO. (Actually small amounts, about 5 percent, of NO can be converted to NO_2 in the exhaust from a combustion process by the third-order reaction, $2NO + O_2 \rightarrow 2NO_2$. We explore this process in Problem 3.4.)

Up to this point we have focused on calculating the equilibrium quantities of NO and NO_2 in the oxygen-nitrogen system as a function of temperature and the N/O molar ratio. Because of the very short time scales involved in most combustion processes (combustion in the cylinder of an internal combustion engine occurs on the order of milliseconds), thermal NO_x formation must ultimately be considered as a kinetic process. In 1946 Zeldovich proposed the free radical chain reaction mechanism for NO formation from air at high temperature that is given in Table 3.1. That mechanism, which now bears his name, is repeated here for convenience:

$$O_2 + M \underset{-1}{\overset{1}{\rightleftarrows}} 2O + M$$

$$O + N_2 \underset{-2}{\overset{2}{\rightleftarrows}} NO + N$$

$$N + O_2 \underset{-3}{\overset{3}{\rightleftarrows}} NO + O$$

If we now consider these reactions from a kinetic point of view, our object is to derive an expression, a rate equation, for the rate of formation of NO as a result of this set of reactions. If we let R_i denote the rate of reaction i, then the rate of formation of NO is given by

$$\frac{d[NO]}{dt} = R_2 - R_{-2} + R_3 - R_{-3} \tag{3.13}$$

where we will use square brackets to denote the concentration of the species inside the brackets.

To derive an expression for the rate of formation of NO we assume that:

1. Atomic oxygen is at equilibrium from the first reaction.
2. Atomic nitrogen is formed and consumed at equal rates due to the speed of reactions -2 and 3 relative to that of reaction 2.
3. There is excess air.

From assumption (1), the concentration of oxygen atoms obeys

$$[O] = (K_1[O_2])^{1/2} \tag{3.14}$$

where the concentration of the third body M is assumed to be incorporated into K_1. The second assumption states physically that the reactions consuming N are sufficiently rapid so that as soon as an N atom is produced by reaction 2 it is consumed virtually immediately by reactions -2 and 3. When a species behaves in such a way, its concentration is said to obey the pseudo-steady state approximation. We will study this approximation in some detail in the next chapter; suffice it to say here that for N atoms we have the following balance between its formation and consumption reactions:

$$R_2 + R_{-3} - R_{-2} - R_3 = 0 \tag{3.15}$$

or

$$k_2[O][N_2] + k_{-3}[NO][O] - k_{-2}[NO][N] - k_3[N][O_2] = 0 \tag{3.16}$$

Solving for [N], we obtain

$$[N] = \frac{[O](k_2[N_2] + k_{-3}[NO])}{k_{-2}[NO] + k_3[O_2]} \tag{3.17}$$

Finally, the assumption of excess air implies that $k_3[O_2] \gg k_{-2}[NO]$. Combining Eqs. (3.13), (3.14), and (3.17) with this approximation, we obtain the rate of formation of NO as

$$\frac{d[NO]}{dt} = k_f[N_2][O_2]^{1/2} - k_b[NO]^2[O_2]^{-1/2} \tag{3.18}$$

where $k_f = 2K_1^{1/2}k_2$ and $k_b = 2K_1^{1/2}k_{-2}k_{-3}/k_3$. The composite forward and reverse rate constants are $k_f = 1.161 \times 10^3 \exp(-135,000/RT)$ (cm^3 molecule^{-1})$^{1/2}$ sec^{-1} and $k_b = 52.9 \exp(-91,600/RT)$ (cm^3 molecule^{-1})$^{1/2}$ sec^{-1}. The high activation energy for the composite forward reaction is a result of the large activation energies for both O$_2$ dissociation and the O–N$_2$ reaction. Because of this high activation energy we expect thermal NO$_x$ formation to be extremely temperature-dependent. In addition, the large activation energy for the composite reverse reaction indicates that the reverse reaction can be "frozen" by a rapid temperature decrease of the combustion gases.

A picture of the process of thermal NO$_x$ formation in a combustion process can be obtained by considering what the Zeldovich mechanism predicts as hot combustion gases in which an equilibrium amount of NO has formed are rapidly quenched. The forward and reverse reactions 2 and −2 are very rapid, and this reaction is more or less in equilibrium during the quenching process. As the temperature drops, equilibrium for the 2, −2 reaction shifts to the left, resulting in a decrease in NO. The forward rate of reaction 3 is somewhat slower than either rate of reactions 2, −2, but it is about an order of magnitude higher than the reverse rate, −3. Consequently, O$_2$ is depleted by reaction with N and then NO is destroyed by reactions 2, −2. As cooling continues, the N mole fraction decreases rapidly, and a shift in the equilibrium of reaction 2, −2 leads to a marked increase in NO. Thus, as the combustion gases are cooled, NO first decreases then increases. The final NO mole fraction attained may actually be larger than that at the peak combustion temperature, but is smaller than the maximum attainable value. The NO$_x$ quenching process is therefore a complex one, and accurate prediction of final NO levels requires integrating the appropriate rate equations over the time–temperature history of the combustion gases.

In the case of rich combustion conditions the mechanism of thermal NO$_x$ formation becomes more complex than the Zeldovich mechanism. Recent studies suggest that the hydrocarbon oxidation chemistry and NO$_x$ formation chemistry are coupled and that cyanide species are involved in NO$_x$ production.

3.3. FUEL NO$_x$ FORMATION

Figure 3.1 shows the correlation between NO$_x$ emissions and fuel nitrogen content for liquid fuels burned under fuel lean conditions. The lower curve shows the fuel nitrogen conversion as determined by substituting an argon/oxygen mixture for the combustion air. The data for petroleum-, shale-, and coal-derived liquids show the same trend, that is, increasing NO$_x$ with fuel nitrogen content and the fractional conversion decreasing with increasing fuel nitrogen. The difference between the two curves in Figure 3.1 represents the thermal NO$_x$. The consistent trend shown in Figure 3.1 for liquid fuels is not generally observed when one attempts to correlate NO$_x$ production with fuel

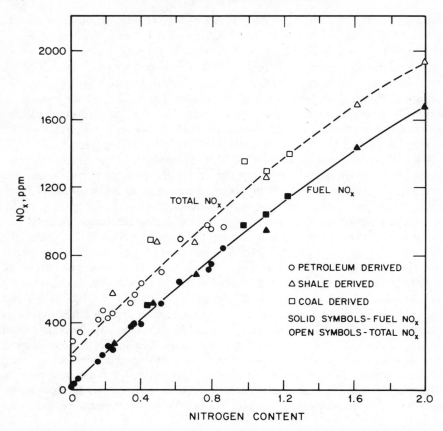

Figure 3.1. NO$_x$ emissions from liquid fuels. Nitrogen content in percent by weight. Combustion carried out at 5% excess O$_2$ (Martin et al., 1979).

nitrogen content for coal (Figure 3.2). While the fuel NO$_x$ levels generally increase with increased fuel nitrogen in coal, there is considerable scatter in the data. The data seem to indicate that the manner in which the nitrogen is bound in the coal affects the fractional conversion to NO$_x$ at a constant operating condition.

3.4. COAL COMBUSTION

Of all the fossil fuels burned, coal not only is the most abundant but also presents the most complex problem of combustion and emission control. Moreover, there is no typical coal; the properties of a coal can vary within the same seam. A general picture of the key pollutant formation mechanisms can be presented by considering the combustion of a single coal particle. In actual

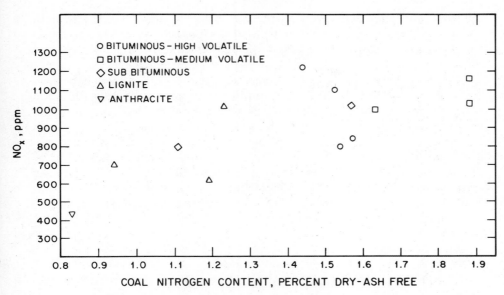

Figure 3.2. Effect of coal nitrogen content on fuel NO_x. Combustion in premixed burner with 5% O_2 in stack (Martin et al., 1979).

coal-fired furnaces, pulverized coal of size about 80 μm is mixed with a fraction of the combustion air, the primary air, and introduced into the furnace through the fuel injector of the burner. The amount of primary air is determined by both the fuel properties and the burner design, and is normally 10 to 30 percent of the air required for stoichiometric combustion.

As the coal particle is heated by radiation and conduction, the volatile portion of the coal begins to evolve. The initial volatile products contain carbon and hydrogen, perhaps from side chains and cross linkages between the ring structures in the coal molecule. These initial volatiles react with the surrounding air and partially deplete the available oxygen. As the temperature increases and the ring structures in the coal begin to fragment, nitrogen-containing intermediates (designated XN) are evolved and begin to react with oxygen to form NO_x. Subsequent reations of XN with NO_x and other species produce molecular N_2. For fuel lean conditions, a substantial fraction of the volatile nitrogen will be converted to NO. For fuel rich conditions, the production of molecular nitrogen increases until an optimum stoichiometry is reached; then, for even richer stoichiometries, the residual nitrogen species (XN) are retained unreacted and burn in leaner secondary combustion zones. During the devolatilization process, inorganic and organic sulfur species are released as sulfur intermediates (designated XS). The XS species are essentially quantitatively converted to sulfur oxides (SO_2 or SO_3) at some point during the combustion process; however, these species may influence other reactions in this devolatilization zone, such as the conversion of XN to NO. Finally, a portion of the mineral matter from the coal is vaporized in the devolatilization zone and subsequently condenses and/or coalesces to form submicron particles.

Following devolatilization, the residual coal matter (called char) is burned. The composition of the char depends on the conditions in the devolatilization zone, although its major components are generally carbon and mineral matter with variable amounts of nitrogen and sulfur species. In the manner in which coal combustion is normally carried out, char combustion occurs under predominantly fuel lean conditions. By design, carbon burnout is intended to be nearly complete, thereby maximizing energy efficiency and minimizing carbonaceous particulate matter. The residual nitrogen species in the char form both NO and N_2 during burnout. The sulfur species are either oxidized to SO_2 or retained with the mineral matter.

3.5.   CONTROL OF NO_x IN STATIONARY COMBUSTION SOURCES

Historically, most stationary-source NO_x air pollution control technology has been concerned primarily with the control of thermal NO_x rather than fuel NO_x. The most effective control of thermal NO_x is achieved by a reduction of the peak temperatures of the flame zone. One approach to lowering the flame temperature is to add an inert diluent to the fuel or air stream. The two most common approaches associated with adding a diluent are flue gas recirculation (the addition of relatively cool combustion gases recycled and mixed with the incoming combustion air) and water injection (addition of water or steam to either the air or fuel stream). Of the two, per unit mass water injection is the more effective in lowering the combustion temperature, due to its latent heat of vaporization. Since inert diluent addition focuses on reducing the flame temperature, it is effective only in reducing thermal NO_x. Using these techniques, 70 to 90 percent reductions in thermal NO_x have been obtained for natural gas and distillate oil combustion. Flue gas recirculation alone or in conjunction with other techniques is used to achieve NO_x emission standards for gas- and oil-fired utility boilers. Water injection is considered the state-of-the-art NO_x control technique for gas turbine engines.

A second approach to NO_x control from stationary combustion is *staged combustion*. Staged combustion involves burning the fuel with insufficient air, followed by adding additional air at a later time to complete the combustion process. Thus, the primary combustion zone is operated in a fuel rich condition to reduce oxygen availability and peak temperature. The reduced oxygen availability in the primary combustion zone leads to lower conversion of fuel nitrogen to fuel NO_x, and the reduction in peak flame temperature leads to a lowering of thermal NO_x. With the subsequent air addition, fuel nitrogen continues to be converted to fuel NO_x, so even though staged combustion can be quite effective in reducing thermal NO_x, it is generally not very effective in reducing fuel NO_x. Although the effectiveness of staged combustion in NO_x control increases significantly as the primary air supplied approaches about 75 percent of the theoretical stoichiometric amount, operational considerations may limit the degree to which primary air can be decreased below stoichiometric. For coal furnaces, for example, to limit slagging and corrosion, the primary combustion zone stoichiometry cannot be reduced below about 95 percent of the stoichiometric air. The maximum NO_x reduction achieved by staged combustion on actual operating coal fired boilers is 30 to 50 percent.

A third approach to stationary source NO_x control is modification of the burner design. The essential elements of a burner are a fuel introduction system and a burner throat to supply combustion air. Design variables used to achieve stable combustion and good fuel conversion efficiency include the fuel injector configuration and the rate of air mixing, controlled by the throat velocity, use of swirl, and design of the flame holder. The fuel and air mix initially in a primary reaction zone that may contain a wide range of stoichiometries from very rich to very lean. The balance of the combustion air is mixed with the primary zone products further downstream and combustion is completed. Also, relatively cool combustion products may recirculate in the combustion chamber and be entrained by the flame, leading to a diluent effect that reduces peak temperature.

Figure 3.3 shows a schematic of such a burner design. The fuel, say coal, is introduced with primary air and the initial combustion takes place at a very rich stoichiometric ratio under which fuel NO_x formation is low. Secondary air is introduced in a manner that provides a gradual leaning out of the reaction zone to a stoichiometry that is still fuel rich. This gradual mixing allows the

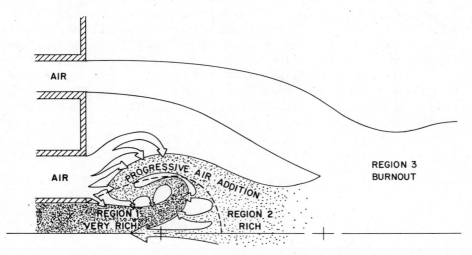

Figure 3.3. Conceptual diagram of low NO_x burner design.

formation of NO_x and a reduction of NO_x to N_2 by fuel nitrogen components still intact. Finally, tertiary air is mixed with the reaction products to give a lean region in which any residual fuel nitrogen species are converted to NO_x, and the remaining fuel is oxidized to give complete combustion. Entrained combustion gas recirculation burners have achieved thermal NO_x reductions in excess of 50 percent for clean fuels such as natural gas and distillate oil. In addition, several studies of advanced burner designs for heavy oil and coal have shown the potential for 65 to 90 percent reduction of thermal NO_x relative to conventional designs.

A new NO_x control technology has been patented by Exxon Research and Engineering Company that selectively removes NO_x from combustion effluents through homogeneous reaction with ammonia and oxygen. This process is distinctly different from other technologies in that it removes NO_x after its formation rather than preventing formation. Thus, the process offers the possibility of removing both thermal NO_x and fuel NO_x. The patent states that the NH_3 must be added to the combustion gases in the amount of 0.4 to 10 moles NH_3 per mole NO and that molecular oxygen must be present in concentrations ranging from 0.1 to 20 volume percent of the effluent gas. The temperature of the effluent gas should be in the range of 1150 to 1375 K. Correct temperature control seems to be critical, since the chemistry is highly temperature-dependent. When the temperature is too low, the NH_3 and NO remain unreacted, and temperatures that are too high result in inefficient consumption of NH_3 and small NO_x reductions. By this process, NO_x reductions of 90 percent have been achieved in the laboratory and 40 to 60 percent in field operating boilers. Due to the need for NH_3 and its associated cost, this technique will probably be used to supplement other combustion control techniques when very low NO_x emissions are required.

Selective catalytic NO_x reduction processes, also employing NH_3, have shown promise as flue gas treatment processes. Although there are several variations, anhydrous NH_3 is usually injected into the flue gas after the boiler, and the resulting mixture is passed over a catalyst. The NH_3 selectively reduces the NO_x in the presence of the catalyst to molecular N_2. A variation of the process can simultaneously remove 90 percent of the NO_x and SO_2 in combustion flue gas. The process uses CuO to absorb the SO_2, and the resulting $CuSO_4$ acts as a catalyst in the reduction of NO to N_2 with NH_3. The $CuSO_4$ is regenerated by reduction with H_2 to produce a concentrated stream of SO_2 that can be used to generate salable byproducts.

3.6. INTERNAL COMBUSTION ENGINE

3.6.1. Operation of the Internal Combustion Engine

There are three common types of internal combustion engines in wide use in the world. The most common is the four-stroke-cycle, spark-ignited internal combustion engine which is used primarily for passenger cars and light-duty

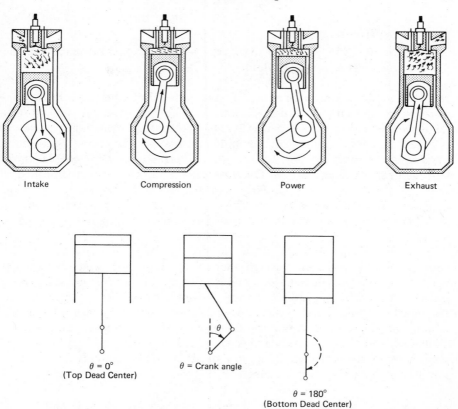

Figure 3.4. Four-stroke-cycle, spark-ignited internal combustion engine: stroke 1, intake; stroke 2, compression; stroke 3, power; stroke 4, exhaust.

trucks. The second most common is the four- and two-stroke-cycle, compression-ignition internal combustion engine, commonly referred to as a diesel engine. This engine is used for large trucks, buses, locomotives, and ships. Finally, the third type of internal combustion engine is the aircraft gas-turbine engine. We will not discuss the operation of the gas-turbine engine here.

The operating cycle of the spark-ignited internal combustion engine is shown in Figure 3.4. The basic principle of operation is that a piston moves up and down within a cylinder, transmitting its motion through a connecting rod to the crankshaft, which drives the vehicle. The four strokes of the spark-ignited internal combustion engine are:

1. *Intake.* The descending piston draws a mixture of gasoline and air in through the open intake valve.

2. *Compression.* The rising piston compresses the fuel–air mixture. Near or at the top of the stroke the spark plug fires, igniting the mixture.

3. *Expansion.* The burning mixture expands, driving the piston down and delivering power.

4. *Exhaust.* The exhaust valve opens as the piston rises, expelling the burned gases from the cylinder.

The fuel–air mixture is prepared in the carburetor. This mixture is characterized by the air–fuel ratio, the weight of air per weight of fuel. Ratios below 9 and above 20 are generally not combustible. Maximum power is obtained at a lower ratio than for minimum fuel consumption. As we have noted, mixtures with low air–fuel ratios are referred to as *rich*, whereas those with high ratios are called *lean*. During acceleration, when power is needed, a richer mixture is required than during cruising. We will return to the question of the air–fuel ratio when we consider pollutant formation, since this ratio is one of the key factors governing the type and quantity of pollutants formed in the cylinder.

In a diesel engine air and fuel are not mixed prior to being passed into the cylinder. Air is drawn in through the intake valve, and while it is being compressed to a high temperature, fuel is injected into the chamber as a spray under high pressure in precise quantities. As the piston nears the top position, the high temperature and pressure of compression cause ignition of the fuel without the aid of a spark. Ignition timing is governed by timing the injection of the fuel, and the power delivered is controlled by the amount of fuel injected in each cycle. The air–fuel mixture in a diesel engine is generally much leaner than that in a spark-ignition engine.

3.6.2. Pollutant Emissions from the Internal Combustion Engine

The type and quantity of exhaust contaminants from an internal combustion engine depend on a number of factors, including the following:

1. Air-fuel ratio.
2. Ignition timing.
3. Compression ratio.
4. Combustion chamber geometry.
5. Engine speed.
6. Type of fuel.

Figure 3.5 shows the relationship of combustion products to air–fuel ratio, the single most important factor in determining emissions. Combustion of rich mixtures leads to CO formation as well as to the presence of residual fuel in the exhaust, either unburned or partially burned. Lean mixtures, on the other hand, produce considerably less CO and unburned hydrocarbons. However, if the mixture is too lean, above an air–fuel ratio of about 17, the mixture may not ignite properly, leading to misfiring and large amounts of fuel passing through unburned.

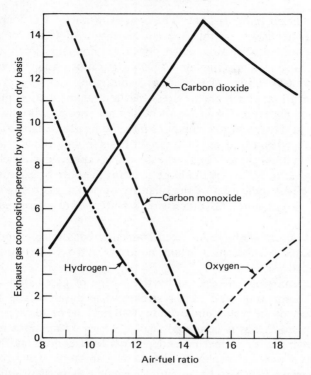

Figure 3.5. Relationship of hydrocarbon combustion products to air-fuel ratio.

The air–fuel ratio is a function of the driving speed, as we described previously. Thus, we expect exhaust emissions to vary depending on the driving mode. Table 3.2 gives typical exhaust gas constituents from an uncontrolled vehicle as a function of driving mode.

During idling, most engines require rich mixtures to compensate for residual combustion products in the cylinder. Thus, CO emissions are high during idling. At deceleration, residual fuel is present in the cylinders, leading to high

TABLE 3.2. Typical Exhaust Gas Constituents as a Function of Driving Mode

Pollutant	Idling	Acceleration	Cruising	Deceleration
Carbon monoxide, percent	4–9	0–8	1–7	2–9
Hydrocarbons (as hexane), ppm	500–1000	50–800	200–800	3000–12,000
Oxides of nitrogen, ppm	10–50	1000–4000	1000–3000	5–50

levels of unburned hydrocarbons. The concentration of CO increases as the air–fuel ratio decreases, so that the concentration of CO is at a maximum during idling and deceleration. High power requirements, such as maximum acceleration, also produce higher CO concentrations than moderate-power cruising where CO emission levels are at a minimum.

It is important at this point to stress that a clear distinction must be made between emissions expressed as a mass rate (g hr^{-1}) or as a fraction of exhaust volume in ppm. Hydrocarbon emissions increase nearly linearly with increased engine air flow when expressed on a weight basis (due to the greater volume of exhaust and fuel consumed) but decrease when expressed on a concentration basis. Clearly, a mass basis is the more relevant measure of exhaust emissions, since it is a direct indication of the quantity of pollutants being emitted. For this reason current automotive emission standards are expressed on a mass basis.

Hydrocarbon emissions result from crankcase emissions, evaporative emissions, and exhaust emissions. Carbon monoxide and NO$_x$ are products of the combustion process.

Crankcase emissions are caused by the escape of gases from the cylinder during the compression and power strokes. The gases escape between the sealing surfaces of the piston and cylinder wall into the crankcase. This leakage around the piston rings is commonly called *blowby*. Emissions increase with increasing engine airflow, that is, under heavy load conditions. The resulting gases emitted from the crankcase consist of a mixture of approximately 85 percent unburned fuel–air charge and 15 percent exhaust products. Because these gases are primarily the carbureted fuel–air mixture, hydrocarbons are the main pollutants. Hydrocarbon concentrations in blowby gases range from 6000 to 15,000 ppm. Blowby emissions increase with engine wear as the seal between the piston and cylinder wall becomes less effective. Blowby was the first source of automotive emissions to be controlled. Beginning with 1963 model year cars, this category of vehicular emissions has been totally controlled in cars made in the United States. The control is accomplished by recycling the blowby gas from the crankcase into the engine air intake to be burned in the cylinders.

Evaporative emissions issue from the fuel tank and the carburetor. Fuel-tank losses result from the evaporation of fuel and the displacement of vapors when fuel is added to the tank. The amount of evaporation depends on the composition of the fuel and its temperature. Obviously, evaporative losses will be high if the fuel tank is exposed to high ambient temperatures for a prolonged period of time. The quantity of vapor expelled when fuel is added to the tank is equal to the volume of the fuel added.

Evaporation of fuel from the carburetor occurs primarily during the period just after the engine is turned off. During operation the carburetor and the fuel in the carburetor remain at about the temperature of the air under the hood. But the airflow ceases when the engine is stopped, and the carburetor bowl absorbs heat from the hot engine, causing fuel temperatures to reach 60 to 70°F above ambient. The vaporized gasoline leaves through the carburetor vents to the atmosphere. This condition is called a *hot soak*. The amount and composition of the vapors depend on the fuel volatility, volume of the bowl, and temperature of the engine prior to shutdown. Roughly 10 g of hydrocarbons may be emitted during a hot soak. Fuel evaporation from both the fuel tank and the carburetor accounts for approximately 20 percent of the hydrocarbon emissions from an uncontrolled automobile.

Gasoline volatility is a primary factor in evaporative losses. The measure of fuel volatility is the empirically determined *Reid vapor pressure*, which is a composite value reflecting the cumulative effect of the individual vapor pressures of the different gasoline constituents. It provides both a measure of how readily a fuel can be vaporized to provide a combustible mixture at low temperatures and an indicator of the tendency of the fuel to vaporize. In a complex mixture of hydrocarbons, such as gasoline, the lowest-molecular-weight molecules have the greatest tendency to vaporize and thus contribute more to the overall vapor pressure than do the higher-molecular-weight constituents. As the fuel is depleted of low-molecular-weight constituents by evaporation, the fuel vapor pressure decreases. The measured vapor pressure of gasoline, therefore, depends on the extent of vaporization during the test. The Reid vapor pressure determination is a standard test at 110°F in which the final ratio of vapor volume to liquid volume is constant (4 : 1) so that the extent of vaporization is always the same. Therefore, the Reid vapor pressure for various fuels can be used as a comparative measure of fuel volatility. The volatility and thus the evaporative loss increase with Reid vapor pressure.

In principle, evaporative emissions can be reduced by reducing gasoline volatility. However, a decrease in fuel volatility below the 8 to 12 Reid vapor pressure range, commonly used in temperate climates, would necessitate modifications in carburetor and intake manifold design, required when low-vapor-pressure fuel is burned. In view of costly carburetion changes associated with reduction of fuel volatility, evaporative emission control techniques have been based on mechanical design changes. Two evaporative emission control methods are the vapor-recovery system and the adsorption-regeneration system. In the vapor-recovery system, the crankcase is used as a storage tank for vapors from the fuel tank and carburetor. In the adsorption-regeneration system, a canister of activated charcoal collects the vapors and retains them until they can be fed back into the intake manifold to be burned.

There are three regions in the combustion chamber of an internal combustion engine where incomplete combustion of the fuel may occur: (1) fuel rich regions in the bulk gas; (2) crevices (e.g., between the piston and cylinder wall); and (3) at the walls. With regard to wall quenching, photographic evidence clearly shows that the luminous flame front does not extend completely to the cylinder wall. Engine emission studies have generally shown increases in exhaust hydrocarbons with increases in the ratio of combustion chamber surface area to volume. Based on this evidence, it had long been theorized that the relatively cool cylinder wall inhibited complete combustion within the layer, thus contributing significantly to exhaust hydrocarbons.

Recent experimental evidence, however, seems to indicate that diffusion of fuel from the wall layer into the flame and free radicals from the flame region to the wall is rapid enough to promote burning in the layer (Blint and Bechtel, 1982). The correlation between increases in the surface-to-volume ratio of the cylinder and increases in exhaust hydrocarbons may, in addition to quenching in the crevices, be attributable to absorption of fuel into the oil film and carbon deposits found on cylinder walls. The absorption would protect the hydrocarbons from burning, and later during the expansion stroke the fuel would be desorbed into the exhaust.

Particulate matter, consisting of carbon, metallic ash, and hydrocarbons, is emitted in the exhaust gases of internal combustion engines. Metal-based particles result from lead antiknock compounds in the fuel, metallic lubricating oil additives, and engine wear particles.* Carbonaceous and hydrocarbon aerosol results from incomplete combustion of fuel and leakage of crankcase oil past the piston rings into the combustion chamber.

Some of the particulate matter in the exhaust is generated during the combustion process and subsequently nucleated in the exhaust system prior to leaving the automobile. On the other hand, a fraction of the particulate matter deposits on the surfaces of the exhaust system to later flake off and become entrained in the exhaust gas. Therefore, the quantity and nature of the exhaust particulate emissions from an automobile at any time are influenced by several different physical and chemical processes, making the complete description of the character of these emissions a very difficult undertaking. Many factors, such as the mode of vehicle operation, the age and mileage of the car, and the type of fuel being burned, influence the composition and total mass emission rate of exhaust particulate matter.

Since NO formation is favored by high temperatures, it is clear that NO is formed primarily in the bulk gases in the cylinder as opposed to within a quench zone near the relatively cold chamber walls.

Figure 3.6 compares actual exhaust NO, CO, and hydrocarbon concentrations as a function of air–fuel ratio for a typical automobile. Actually, as we saw with hydrocarbons and CO, the quantity of NO formed depends markedly on the mode of operation of the vehicle. Emissions of NO under varying driving conditions were shown roughly in Table 3.2. Concentrations are highest during acceleration and cruising, and mass emissions are highest during

---

*Antiknock additives, particularly organometallic compounds, limit the tendency of the fuel–air mixture to autoignite. The most widely used, and effective, of such compounds is tetraethyl lead, $(C_2H_5)_4Pb$. The tendency of a fuel to detonate upon compression is measured by its *octane number*. The octane number of a fuel is defined as the percentage (by volume) of isooctane (2,3,4-trimethyl-pentane) in a mixture of isooctane and *n*-heptane which will just autoignite under the same conditions as the fuel under test. Thus, the addition of tetraethyl lead to a fuel increases its octane number. Tetraethyl lead produces nonvolatile combustion products which accumulate on the spark plugs. However, when ethylene dibromide and ethylene dichloride are also added to the gasoline, the lead compounds formed during combustion are sufficiently volatile to leave with the exhaust gases.

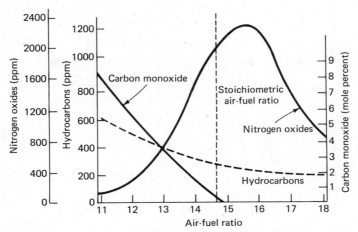

Figure 3.6. Exhaust hydrocarbons, carbon monoxide, and nitric oxide as a function of air–fuel ratio.

acceleration, due to the high volume of exhaust gases produced. At low air–fuel ratios both the amount of available O_2 and the flame temperatures are low, resulting in low NO. As the ratio increases, so do the available O_2, flame temperature, and NO concentrations. However, as the air–fuel ratio is increased beyond about 16, the flame temperature and thus the NO begin to decrease owing to dilution of the combustion mixture with excess air.

In short, experimental data show that modifications in conditions that increase the peak temperature or the oxygen concentration in the combustion gases increase the NO concentration in the exhaust. In addition, NO levels are found to be nearer the equilibrium concentration corresponding to the peak cycle temperature and pressure than to the equilibrium concentration at exhaust conditions.

Nitric oxide concentrations versus crank angle have been computed by Blumberg and Kummer (1971) at three equivalence ratios, as shown in Figures 3.7 to 3.9. For each air–fuel ratio (A/F), both rate calculated and equilibrium NO are shown at three positions in the charge, depending on the first element to burn, the middle element to burn, and the last element to burn. All other parameters are identical for the three cases. In each case, the major contribution to the total NO formed results from the elements that burn first. They experience the highest temperatures and have the longest time in which to react. Under rich conditions considerable decomposition of NO occurs in the first element because of the high temperatures. However, as the first element cools during expansion under rich conditions, the rate of NO decomposition decreases rapidly with temperature so that after about 40 crank angle degrees the equilibrium NO level can no longer be obtained. At this point the NO formed is effectively frozen. Under lean operation the temperature of the first

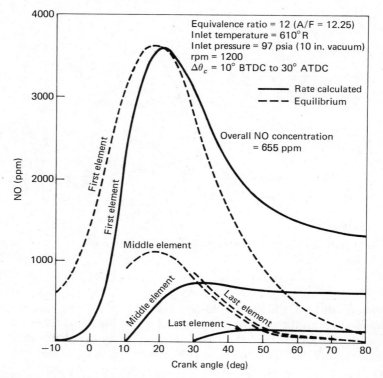

Figure 3.7. Nitric oxide concentration in the burned gas as a function of crank angle for the first, middle, and last element of the charge to burn for a rich charge (A/F = 12.25) (Blumberg and Kummer, 1971). BTDC = before top dead center. ATDC = after top dead center.

element is not as high as under rich operation. Thus, the rate of NO formation is not rapid enough to achieve equilibrium as in the rich-burning case. However, in lean operation there is significantly more oxygen and nitrogen available so that even though equilibrium NO levels are not achieved, the final frozen NO levels are higher than those under rich conditions. Near stoichiometric operation conditions are such that *both* high temperatures and reasonable availability of O_2 and N_2 occur, so that NO levels are largest for this case.

We can now summarize the processes responsible for the production of hydrocarbons and nitric oxide in the internal combustion engine. First, the compressed air–fuel mixture is ignited by the spark plug, and a flame front propagates across the cylinder. As the flame approaches the walls, which are relatively cooler, the flame is quenched, leaving perhaps a very thin layer of unburned or absorbed fuel on the walls and in the crevice between the piston and cylinder wall above the piston ring. During the flame propagation, NO is formed by chemical reactions in the hot just-burned gases. As the piston recedes, the temperatures of the different burned elements drop sharply,

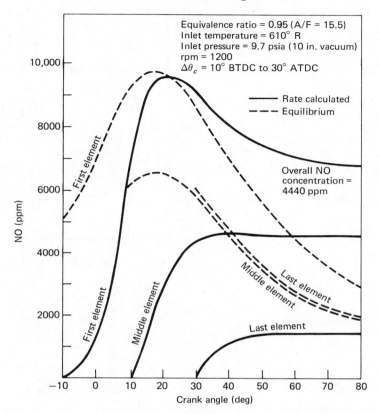

Figure 3.8. Nitric oxide concentration in the burned gas as a function of crank angle for the first, middle, and last element of the charge to burn for a charge near stoichiometric (A/F = 15.5) (Blumberg and Kummer, 1971).

"freezing" the NO (i.e., the chemical reactions which would remove the NO become much slower) at the levels formed during combustion, levels well above those corresponding to equilibrium at exhaust temperatures. As the valve opens on the exhaust stroke, the bulk gases containing the NO exit, entraining the unburned hydrocarbons in the wall layers. It is to these processes that we must devote our attention if we wish to reduce both hydrocarbon and NO formation in the cylinder.

3.6.3. Emission Control for the Internal Combustion Engine

In 1963 the United States government enacted the Clean Air Act, aimed at stimulating state and local air pollution control activity. Amendments to the Clean Air Act in 1965 and 1970 authorized the setting of national standards for emissions from all new motor vehicles commencing with 1968.

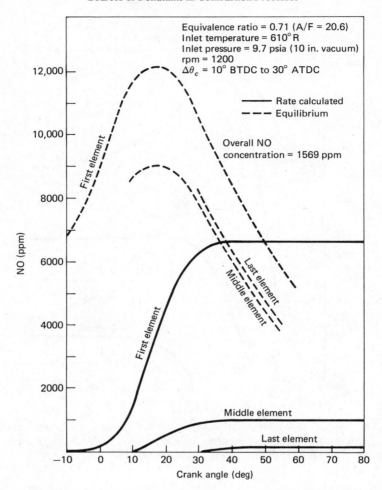

Figure 3.9. Nitric oxide concentration in the burned gas as a function of crank angle for the first, middle, and last element of the charge to burn for a lean charge (A/F = 20.6) (Blumberg and Kummer, 1971).

The magnitude of contaminant emissions from a motor vehicle is a variable in time and is a function of the percentage of time the vehicle is operated in each driving mode (accelerate, cruise, decelerate, idle). The modal split is in turn dependent on the habits of the driver, the type of street on which the vehicle is operated, and the degree of congestion on that street. Also affecting emissions are the presence or absence of an emission control device, the condition of the car, its size, and other factors.

Because of all these factors, measured automobile exhaust emissions depend on the driving condition of the car as well as its make and year. The basic

**TABLE 3.3.   United States Federal Motor Vehicle
Exhaust Emission Standards (g mi^{-1})**

	Light-Duty Automobiles	Light-Duty Trucks	Medium-Duty Trucks
Carbon monoxide	3.4	17	17
Hydrocarbons	0.41	0.9	0.9
Nitrogen oxides (as NO_2)	1.0	2.0	2.0

approach underlying the specification of exhaust emission rates has been the determination of an "average trip," that is, one representative of the average driving habits of the population (usually in an urban area). The trip, usually termed a *driving cycle*, is composed of a series of driving modes (idle, accelerate, cruise, and decelerate) in which a predetermined length of time is spent in each mode. Such a cycle is formulated, in principle, by "tagging" a substantial number of vehicles on a particular day and analyzing their trips according to the sequencing of the different driving modes and the time spent in each. Once the driving cycle has been determined, a standard emission rate for the cycle is determined by running a representative sample of vehicles of varying makes and ages through the cycle in a stationary test (on a chassis dynamometer) and measuring their emissions. Table 3.3 summarizes U.S. federal automotive exhaust emission standards.

There are basically four ways in which exhaust emissions of HC, CO, and NO_x can be reduced in a motor vehicle:

1. Modifications in operation.
2. Modifications in engine design.
3. Modifications in the fuel burned.
4. Exhaust gas treatment.

Modifications in operation of the conventional internal combustion engine comprise those changes which can be instituted without the need for engine redesign. Changes in this category are exemplified by modified air–fuel ratios and ignition timing. Modifications in engine design are considerably more costly to implement than are changes in operating conditions, since they may involve significant changes in parts and, therefore, in assembly-line equipment. Substitution of other hydrocarbon fuels for gasoline constitutes the third general category of control methods. If the new fuel can be used in an unmodified engine, the entire cost of this alternative is related to fuel use. Finally, the fourth class of control methods involves treatment of the exhaust gases (usually together with some modification in operation) by means of reactors placed in the exhaust system of the automobile.

As we saw earlier, and as was illustrated in Figure 3.6, those operating changes, namely adjustment of air–fuel ratio, which result in lower levels of HC and CO, generally lead to higher levels of NO. For example, slightly lean operation minimizes HC and CO formation but favors NO formation. Because of the opposite effect of air–fuel ratio on the three species, it is not possible to reduce all three pollutants solely through modifications in air–fuel ratio and ignition timing.

In order to reduce HC and CO emissions, the engine should be operated on a lean air–fuel mixture, whereas the optimum operation with respect to NO_x is either very rich or very lean combustion (assuming that no exhaust gas treatment is employed). Lean operation is effective as a means of reducing NO formation because the peak cycle temperature decreases as the air–fuel ratio increases. Even though the equilibrium NO levels at the reduced combustion temperatures of lean operation are much higher than desired, the high overall activation energy for NO formation results in a rate of NO formation that declines with temperature much more rapidly than does the equilibrium concentration of NO. As a result, the peak equilibrium NO levels are never attained, as seen in Figure 3.9.

One of the most advantageous means to achieve lean operation is exhaust gas recycle (EGR). The advantages of EGR result mainly from the fact that the air–fuel mixture can be diluted without addition of excess O_2 (from which NO is formed), and that dilution with exhaust gas results in the introduction into the charge of species, such as CO_2 and H_2O, with higher heat capacities than N_2.

A control technique that may not involve engine design changes is the variation of the composition of gasoline or the substitution of alternative fuels for gasoline. The characteristics of fuel amenable to change are hydrocarbon type and additive content. In general, fuels containing large amounts of highly reactive hydrocarbons have exhaust emissions with correspondingly high reactivity. For example, fuels containing the largest concentration of reactive olefins produce the most reactive exhaust hydrocarbon emissions. In general, CO and NO emissions are relatively insensitive to the modifications in the hydrocarbon composition of the gasoline burned. With the replacement of gasoline with suitable low-molecular-weight gaseous hydrocarbon fuels, such as natural gas or petroleum gas,* or methanol/ethanol, hydrocarbon and CO emissions can be reduced over those from conventional gasoline-burning engines.

The fourth mode of reducing HC, CO, and NO_x emissions involves the treatment of exhaust gas in chemical reactors in the exhaust system (Hegedus and Gumbleton, 1980). The basic problem in exhaust gas treatment is that HC and CO must be *oxidized* to CO_2 and H_2O, and NO must be *reduced* to N_2 and O_2, if all three pollutants are to be converted in the system.

---

*Natural gas consists primarily of methane (with small amounts of ethane); petroleum gas contains principally propane and butane. For use in an automobile, both would be stored in liquefied form, called LNG and LPG.

TABLE 3.4. Emission Factors for Sulfur Oxides from Stationary Sources

Source or Process	Emission Factor (SO_2)
1. Fuel combustion	
Coal	19S g kg^{-1} (assumes 5% of sulfur remains in ash)[a]
Natural gas	6.4 kg $(10^6 m^3)^{-1}$
Process gas	45.6C kg $(10^6 m^3)^{-1}$[b]
Fuel oil	19.8S kg $(10^3 l)^{-1}$[a]
Gasoline-powered engine	1.1 kg $(10^3 l)^{-1}$ (assumed sulfur content of 0.07%)
Diesel-powered engine	5 kg $(10^3 l)^{-1}$ (assumed sulfur content of 0.3%)

2. Nonferrous primary smelters

   Several important metallic ores, such as copper, lead, and zinc, occur as sulfides. The natural metal ores are usually mixed with large amounts of worthless rock. The process of removing the worthless rock, concentrating the metallic ore, and finally driving off the sulfur (as SO_2) is called smelting. For example, for copper and lead the important reactions are

$$Cu_2S + O_2 \rightarrow 2Cu + SO_2$$
$$2PbS + 3O_2 \rightarrow 2PbO + 2SO_2$$

   Exit SO_2 concentrations with moderate control are often as high as 8000 ppm.

Copper smelting—primary	625 g kg^{-1} of ore
Lead smelting—primary	330 g kg^{-1} of ore
Lead smelting—secondary cupola	32 g kg^{-1} of metal charged
Lead smelting—secondary reverbatory and sweat furnaces	75 g kg^{-1} of metal charged
Zinc smelting—primary	265 g kg^{-1} of ore

3. Sulfuric acid plants

   Sulfuric acid is essentially made by burning elemental sulfur with a controlled amount of excess air, producing SO_2, and then catalytically oxidizing the SO_2 to SO_3, and finally absorbing SO_3 in water to yield H_2SO_4. The heart of the sulfuric acid plant is the converter in which SO_2 is catalytically converted to SO_3 in a fixed bed. The ultimate SO_2 remaining after the final absorption step (and thus emitted from the plant if uncontrolled)

   Range: 10–35 g kg^{-1} of 100% acid produced

TABLE 3.4. *Continued*

Source or Process	Emission Factor (SO_2)
depends on the operation of the converter. Exit gas concentrations of SO_2 vary from 2000 to 3500 ppm.	

4. Pulp and paper mills

   In pulping, wood is reduced to fiber, bleached, and dried in preparation for making paper at the paper mill. Most pulp mill processes use some type of cooking liquor to dissolve lignins in the wood and free the wood fibers. To make this process economical, spent cooking liquor is recovered, usually by some process involving combustion. It is primarily in recovery processes that particulate matter, odorous sulfur compounds (H_2S and organic sulfides), and SO_2 are produced.

Kraft type—recovery furnace	1.2–6.7 g kg^{-1} of air-dried pulp
Sulfite type—recovery furnace	20 g kg^{-1} of air-dried pulp (assumes 90% recovery of SO_2)

[a]S = percent sulfur by weight.
[b]C = grains of sulfur/100 m^3 of gas.

3.7. STATIONARY SOURCES OF SULFUR OXIDES

Sulfur oxides, primarily SO_2, are generated during combustion of any sulfur-containing fuel and are emitted by industrial processes that consume sulfur-containing raw materials. Because of the relatively high sulfur content of bituminous coals and fuel oils, which are burned in great quantities in the world, fuel combustion accounts for roughly 75 percent of all SO_2 emitted. The major industrial sources of SO_2 are smelting of metallic ores and refining of oil. Table 3.4 summarizes the types of processes, and their SO_2 emission factors, that are important sulfur-contributing emitters.

REFERENCES

Ammann, P. R., and Timmins, R. S. "Chemical Reactions During Rapid Quenching of Oxygen-Nitrogen Mixtures from Very High Temperatures," *AIChE J.*, **12**, 956–963 (1966).

Blint, R. J., and Bechtel, J. H. "Hydrocarbon Combustion Near a Cooled Wall," Society of Automotive Engineers Paper 820063, Society of Automotive Engineers, Warrendale, PA (1982).

Blumberg, P., and Kummer, J. T. "Prediction of NO Formation in Spark-Ignited Engines—an Analysis of Methods of Control," *Combustion Sci. Technol.*, **4**, 73–95 (1971).

Hegedus, L. L., and Gumbleton, J. J. "Catalysts, Computers, and Cars: a Growing Symbiosis," *Chemtech*, **10**, 630–642 (1980).

Martin, G. B., Hall, R. E., and Bowin, J. S. "Nitrogen Oxides Control Technology for Stationary Area and Point Sources and Related Implementation Costs," Technical Symposium on Implications of a Low NO_x Vehicle Emission Standard, U.S. Environmental Protection Agency, Reston, VA, May 2–4, 1979.

PROBLEMS

3.1. The pressure–volume relationships in the four-stroke-cycle internal combustion engine of Figure 3.4 are shown in Figure P3.1. As an idealization of this cycle, one may use the so-called air standard cycle shown in Figure P3.2, in which air is considered as the working fluid and combustion is neglected. In the air standard cycle, compression is followed by heating, then expansion and cooling. The heat added along path *cd* is $q_1 = C_v(T_d - T_c)$, and the heat rejected along path *ef* is $q_2 = C_v(T_e - T_f)$. The thermodynamic efficiency of the cycle is defined by

$$\eta = \frac{q_1 - q_2}{q_1}$$

Show that the efficiency is related to the compression ratio $r = V_f/V_c$ by

$$\eta = 1 - r^{1-\gamma}$$

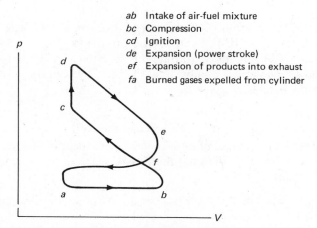

ab	Intake of air-fuel mixture
bc	Compression
cd	Ignition
de	Expansion (power stroke)
ef	Expansion of products into exhaust
fa	Burned gases expelled from cylinder

Figure P3.1. Pressure-volume relationships in the four-stroke-cycle internal combustion engine.

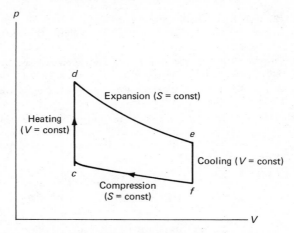

Figure P3.2.   Air standard cycle.

where ideal-gas behavior is assumed and $\gamma = C_p/C_v$, the ratio of specific heats.

3.2.   The precise amount of air required for the complete combustion of a hydrocarbon fuel can be calculated by considering the stoichiometric conversion of the hydrocarbon to CO_2 and H_2O. Determine the stoichiometric air–fuel ratios for combustion of cyclohexane, cyclohexene, and benzene.

3.3.   We have shown that the complete combustion of a hydrocarbon C_xH_y can be expressed chemically as

$$C_xH_y + \left(x + \tfrac{1}{4}y\right)O_2 + \left(x + \tfrac{1}{4}y\right)3.76N_2 \rightarrow$$
$$xCO_2 + \tfrac{1}{2}yH_2O + \left(x + \tfrac{1}{4}y\right)3.76N_2$$

Thus, the combustion of 1 mole of hydrocarbon produces x moles of CO_2 and $\tfrac{1}{2}y$ moles of H_2O, in addition to the $(x + \tfrac{1}{4}y)3.76$ moles of N_2 assumed to be unaltered during the reaction. Show that if f is the fraction of incomplete combustion, the ppm by volume, λ, of unburned fuel in the exhaust is given by

$$\lambda = \frac{10^6 f}{M + f(1 + F - M)}$$

where M is the total number of moles of products resulting from 1 mole of fuel and $1 + F$ is the total number of reacting moles (1 mole of fuel plus F moles of air).

3.4.   Small quantities of NO_2 can be formed in combustion exhaust gases by the third-order reaction

$$2NO + O_2 \overset{k}{\rightarrow} 2NO_2$$

You wish to estimate the amount of NO_2 that can be formed by this route under conditions typical of those in the exhaust of the automobile. Assume that the exhaust system of a car can be represented as a straight pipe through which the exhaust gases flow in so-called plug flow (each element travels through the pipe independently of the other elements). Assume that the concentration of NO at the beginning of the exhaust system is 2000 ppm. For initial O_2 concentrations of 10^2, 10^3, and 10^4 ppm, compute the concentration of NO_2 formed for a residence time of 2 sec if the temperature of the exhaust gases: (1) is constant at 800°C; (2) is constant at 300°C.

The reaction rate constant is $k = 1.066 \times 10^{-5} T^{-2} \exp(530/T)$ $ppm^{-2} min^{-1}$.

PART TWO

Air Pollution Chemistry

FOUR

Gas-Phase Atmospheric Chemistry

Often the most deleterious air pollutants are not those emitted directly by sources but those formed in the atmosphere by chemical reactions, such as sulfuric acid and ozone. In an analysis of air pollution it is therefore essential that the chemical processes taking place in the atmosphere be understood.

The understanding of air pollution chemistry requires identification of the important reactions contributing to the chemical dynamics. Similarly, thorough investigation of a specific reaction is achieved only when the reaction rate constant has been carefully determined and the reaction mechanism properly specified. Because of the large number of important reactions that take place in the atmosphere, the rapid rates of many of them, and the low concentrations of most reactants (e.g., free radicals), the experimental investigation of air pollution chemistry is an enormously large and difficult task. Much has been accomplished, however, in recent years. Our objective in the next two chapters is to elucidate the basic chemical processes that take place in the atmosphere.

With this chapter we begin the study of gas-phase atmospheric chemistry. We will focus largely on the chemistry of three classes of species, oxides of nitrogen, organics, and sulfur dioxide. As we will shortly see, the atmospheric chemistries of each of these classes become interwoven in the atmosphere. The atmosphere is an oxidative medium, and we will see that the tendency in the atmospheric chemistry of species is to continually move them to a more oxidized state. Hydrocarbons are reacted to aldehydes, then to acids, and finally to CO_2. Sulfur-containing compounds go through the chain starting with reduced sulfur compounds, such as H_2S and CH_3SCH_3, which are oxidized to SO_2, and then SO_2 is oxidized to H_2SO_4. In the degradation cycle of nitrogen-containing species, ammonia is oxidized to NO, then NO to NO_2, and finally NO_2 to HNO_3.

Our object in this chapter is to provide a fundamental understanding of the key aspects of gas-phase atmospheric chemistry. References are provided for those readers desiring more detail than is given here.

4.1.   ATMOSPHERIC PHOTOCHEMICAL REACTIONS

Photochemical reactions are initiated by the absorption of a photon by an atom, molecule, free radical, or ion. The primary step of a photochemical reaction may be written

$$A + h\nu \rightarrow A^*$$

where A^* is an excited state of A and $h\nu$ denotes a photon. The excited molecule A^* may subsequently partake in

Dissociation: $A^* \overset{1}{\rightarrow} B_1 + B_2 + \cdots$

Direct Reaction: $A^* + B \overset{2}{\rightarrow} C_1 + C_2 + \cdots$

Fluorescence: $A^* \overset{3}{\rightarrow} A + h\nu$

Collisional Deactivation: $A^* + M \overset{4}{\rightarrow} A + M$

The first two reactions lead to chemical change, whereas the last two return the molecule to its original state.

The quantum yield for a specific process involving A^* is defined as the ratio of the number of molecules of A^* reacting by that process to the number of photons absorbed. Since the total number of A^* molecules formed equals the total number of photons absorbed, the quantum yield ϕ_i for a specific process i, say dissociation, is just the fraction of the A^* molecules that participate in path i. If the four processes above represent all the possible paths for A^*, the sum of the quantum yields for the four processes must equal 1:

$$\sum_{i=1}^{4} \phi_i = 1$$

The rate of formation of A^* is equal to the rate of absorption and can be written

$$\frac{d[A^*]}{dt} = k[A]$$

where $[A]$ denotes the concentration of A, and k, the first-order rate constant, is called the specific absorption rate; k is normally taken to be independent of $[A]$.* The rate of formation of C_1 in step 2 can be expressed as

$$\frac{d[C_1]}{dt} = \phi_2 k[A]$$

where ϕ_2 is the quantum yield of step 2. If we assume that A^* immediately participates in one of the four steps, the total rate of consumption of A^* must equal the total rate of production of A^*, the absorption rate.

---

*The first-order photolysis rate constant of a molecule A is sometimes expressed as J_A. Here we use k to denote all chemical reaction rate constants.

The solar flux, or actinic irradiance, F, in units of photons cm^{-2} sec^{-1}, is the radiation intensity striking a unit area of surface per unit time. This actinic irradiance is related to an actinic irradiance density $I(\lambda)$, such that $dF = I(\lambda)d\lambda$ is the actinic irradiance in the wavelength range $(\lambda, \lambda + d\lambda)$. $I(\lambda)$ thus has units of photons cm^{-3} sec^{-1}.

We will be most interested in photochemical reactions that lead to dissociation. The first-order rate constant for decomposition of a trace atmospheric species by photolysis is given by

$$k_A = \int_{\lambda_1}^{\lambda_2} \sigma_A(\lambda, T)\phi_A(\lambda, T)I(\lambda)\, d\lambda \qquad (4.1)$$

where

$\sigma_A(\lambda, T) =$ the absorption cross section of molecule A at wavelength λ and temperature T (cm^2)

$\phi_A(\lambda, T) =$ the quantum yield or probability that molecule A decomposes on absorbing radiation of wavelength at temperature T

In the troposphere the wavelength range of interest is approximately $\lambda_1 = 280$ nm to $\lambda_2 = 730$ nm, since stratospheric O_2 and O_3 block out most of the uv radiation below 280 nm and because no photochemistry of interest takes place at wavelengths beyond 730 nm. The integral in Eq. (4.1) is usually approximated by a summation over wavelength intervals of 10 to 20 nm,

$$k_A = \sum \bar{\sigma}_A(\lambda_i, T)\bar{\phi}_A(\lambda_i, T)\bar{I}(\lambda_i)\Delta\lambda$$

where the overbar denotes an average over a wavelength interval $\Delta\lambda$ centered at λ_i.

For many species that photodecompose in the troposphere, absorption cross sections and quantum yields have been measured in the laboratory. Figure 4.1 shows absorption cross sections for O_3 and NO_2 and Figure 4.2 shows the primary quantum yield of NO_2 for dissociation to NO. The ground-level actinic irradiance I as function of zenith angle and wavelength for clear sky conditions is given in Table 4.A.4. The major variable that affects atmospheric photochemical reactions is the intensity change that occurs as a function of time of the day, latitude, time of year, and atmospheric state (clouds, aerosols, surface reflection). In the United States the maximum noonday intensity does not vary substantially with latitude during the summer months. In the 300 nm to 400 nm region, the maximum total intensity is about 2×10^{16} photons cm^{-2} sec^{-1} and remains near this value for 4 to 6 hours. In contrast, the winter values vary from 0.7×10^{16} to 1.5×10^{16} as a function of latitude. The time near this maximum is reduced to 2 to 4 hours. The direct solar flux at altitudes of 0 and 15 km is shown as a function of wavelength in Figure 4.3.

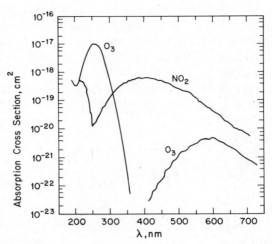

Figure 4.1. Absorption cross sections for O_3 and NO_2 in the uv and visible regions of the spectrum (Luther and Gelinas, 1976).

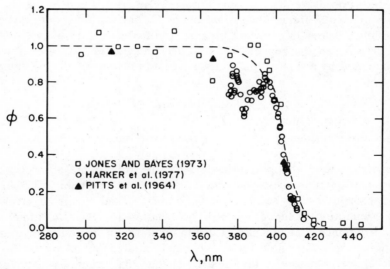

Figure 4.2. Experimental quantum yield data for the production of atomic oxygen (O) from the photolysis of NO_2 as a function of wavelength. The dashed line represents the quantum yields suggested by Demerjian et al. (1980).

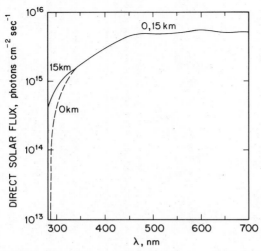

Figure 4.3. Direct solar flux at 0 and 15 km as a function of wavelength (National Center for Atmospheric Research, 1982).

The differences between the fluxes at the two altitudes is a result of absorption by atmospheric ozone for wavelength less than 330 nm.

Since no solar radiation of wavelength shorter than about 280 nm reaches the troposphere, the absorbing species of interest from an air pollution viewpoint are those that absorb in the portion of the spectrum above 280 nm. Table 4.1 lists some of the major photodissociating species in the troposphere.

Nitrogen dioxide is the most important absorbing air pollutant molecule. It absorbs over the entire visible and ultraviolet range of the solar spectrum in the lower atmosphere. Between 300 and 370 nm over 90 percent of the NO_2 molecules absorbing will dissociate into NO and O (see Figure 4.2). Above 370 nm this percentage drops off rapidly, and above about 420 nm dissociation does not occur. The bond energy between O and NO is 73 kcal mole^{-1}. This energy corresponds to the energy contained in wavelengths near 400 nm. At longer wavelengths, there is insufficient energy to promote bond cleavage. The point at which dissociation fails to occur is not sharp because the individual molecules of NO_2 do not possess a precise amount of ground-state energy prior to absorption. The gradual transition area in Figure 4.2 (370 to 420 nm) indicates a variation in ground-state of about 10 kcal mole^{-1}. This transition curve can be shifted slightly to longer wavelengths by increasing the temperature and therefore increasing the ground-state energy of the system.

Ozone photolysis leads to atomic and molecular oxygen, in either ground or excited states. From the point of view of atmospheric chemistry, the oxygen atoms, particularly the excited form, $O(^1D)$, are of importance.

Photochemical dissociation reactions are of importance in air pollution because of the products (mainly free radicals) that result from them. These

TABLE 4.1. Major Photodissociating Species in the Lower Atmosphere

Species	Reactions		Comments
NO_2	$NO_2 + h\nu \rightarrow NO + O$		Because of the atmospheric importance of NO_2 photolysis, considerable research effort has been devoted to its understanding. The literature reviews of Baulch et al. (1982), DeMore et al. (1982), and Atkinson and Lloyd (1984) all recommend the use of the absorption cross-section data of Bass et al. (1976) for the range 290–400 nm and the quantum yield measurements of Harker et al. (1977) in the 375–420 nm region. For shorter wavelengths (295–365 nm) Baulch et al. (1982) and DeMore et al. (1982) suggest the use of the formula $$\phi(\lambda) = 1.0 - 0.0008(\lambda - 275)$$ Atkinson and Lloyd (1984) recommend a slightly different expression $$\phi(\lambda) = 1.0 - 0.0025(\lambda - 295)$$ and Demerjian et al. (1980) use a best fit to a range of different experimental measurements. Atkinson and Lloyd (1984) state that current determinations of $\phi(\lambda)$ and $\sigma(\lambda)$ are accurate to within ± 10–15 percent. The published photolysis rates of Demerjian et al. (1980) provide a suitable basis for establishing NO_2 photolysis rates.
$O_3{}^a$	$O_3 + h\nu \rightarrow O(^3P) + O_2$ $\rightarrow O(^1D) + O_2$	$315 \leq \lambda \leq 1200$ nm $\lambda \leq 315$ nm	Ozone has a bond energy of 26 kcal mole^{-1}. Solar photons having wavelengths between 315 and 1200 nm can dissociate O_3 and produce an oxygen atom in its ground electronic state $O(^3P)$. When O_3 absorbs a photon in the near ultraviolet with wavelengths shorter than 315 nm, an electronically excited oxygen atom, the singlet oxygen atom, $O(^1D)$, is formed. The $O(^1D) \rightarrow O(^3P)$ transition is forbidden, so $O(^1D)$ must react with other species. Information needed to calculate the diurnal variation of O_3 photolysis rate constants is available in Demerjian et al. (1980) and Baulch et al. (1982). Whereas the accuracy of O_3 absorption cross-section data is excellent, there are more uncertainties associated with the wavelength dependence of the O_3 quantum yields for the various photolysis paths, especially those leading to $O(^1D)$ (Atkinson and Lloyd, 1984).
HNO_2	$HNO_2 + h\nu \rightarrow NO + OH$		The photolysis of nitrous acid (HNO_2) is important in atmospheric chemistry because it is a source of hydroxyl (OH) radicals. On the basis of the work by Cox and Derwent (1977), Demerjian et al. (1980), Baulch et al. (1982), and DeMore et al. (1982) all recommend a value

of unity for the quantum yield of the reaction over the wavelength range 300–400 nm. The recommended absorption cross-section measurements are those of Stockwell and Calvert (1978).

The absorption cross sections used by Demerjian et al. (1980) for calculating the H_2O_2 photolysis rates over the range 200–350 nm are based on Molina et al. (1977). These values are slightly higher (5%) than the current recommendations of DeMore et al. (1982). For the purposes of atmospheric calculations the published photolysis rates of Demerjian et al. (1980) are sufficiently accurate.

Recommended values (DeMore et al., 1982): Quantum yield—Magnotta and Johnston (1980); Absorption cross-section—Graham and Johnston (1978).

Formaldehyde photolysis is a significant source of free radicals in the urban atmosphere. The current recommendations of Baulch et al. (1982) for HCHO absorption cross sections are to use an average of the results from Bass et al. (1980) and Moortgat et al. (1980). The relative quantum yields for the production of radicals (H and HCO) and molecular products (H_2 and CO) exhibit a complex variation as a function of wavelength. The peak radical production occurs at 300 nm and path (b) becomes the dominant pathway above 320 nm. Despite these complexities there are only minor variations among the quantum yields recommended by DeMore et al. (1982), Baulch et al. (1982), and Atkinson and Lloyd (1984).

Like HCHO, the photolysis of acetaldehyde is a significant source of free radicals in the urban atmosphere. Recommended Values (Baulch et al., 1982): Quantum Yield—Horowitz and Calvert (1982); Absorption Cross-Section—Calvert and Pitts (1967) and Weaver et al. (1977).

Recommended values (Atkinson and Lloyd, 1984): Quantum yield—$\phi(\lambda) = 0.33$ for acetone $\phi(\lambda) = 1.00$ for methylethylketone; Absorption Cross-section— Calvert and Pitts (1967).

H_2O_2

$$H_2O_2 + h\nu \rightarrow 2OH$$

NO_3

$$NO_3 + h\nu \rightarrow NO + O_2$$
$$\rightarrow NO_2 + O$$

HCHO

$$HCHO + h\nu \begin{array}{l} \overset{a}{\rightarrow} HCO + H \\ \overset{b}{\rightarrow} CO + H_2 \end{array}$$

CH_3CHO

$$CH_3CHO + h\nu \rightarrow CH_3 + HCO$$

$CH_3C(O)CH_3$

$$CH_3C(O)CH_3 + h\nu \rightarrow CH_3 + CH_3CO$$

$CH_3CH_2C(O)CH_3$

$$CH_3CH_2C(O)CH_3 + h\nu \rightarrow C_2H_5 + CH_3CO$$
$$\rightarrow CH_3 + C_2H_5CO$$

[a]Two electronic states of the oxygen atom are important in atmospheric chemistry: the unexcited and first-excited electronic states, triplet-P oxygen atoms $O(^3P)$, and singlet-D oxygen atoms $O(^1D)$, respectively. The dissociation of NO_2 upon light absorption in the wavelength range 290–430 nm yields an oxygen atom in the triplet-P state. It is this form to which our attention will be mainly focused. The singlet-D oxygen atom, which is much more reactive than the ground-state triplet-P oxygen atom, can be formed by ozone photolysis in the wavelength range < 315 nm.

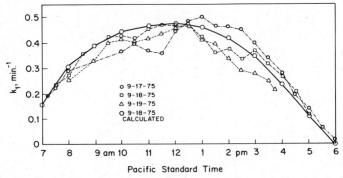

Figure 4.4. Comparison of calculated diurnal variation of NO_2 photolysis rate with experimental measurements of Zafonte et al. (1977) in Los Angeles. Reprinted with permission from Environmental Science and Technology. Copyright (1977). American Chemical Society.

products then initiate or participate in a large number of other reactions responsible for the conversion of primary air pollutants. Note that none of the main primary pollutants, SO_2, NO, CO, and organics (except aldehydes), is an important absorber of radiation at the wavelengths prevalent in the lower atmosphere. Only NO_2, which can be considered both a primary and secondary pollutant, is an important absorber.

The theoretically calculated diurnal variation in the NO_2 photolysis rate in Los Angeles is compared against the experimental observations of Zafonte et al. (1977) for three days in Figure 4.4. Scatter in the experimental measurements was primarily due to the presence of different amounts of clouds on the three days.

4.2. ATMOSPHERIC CHEMISTRY OF THE OXIDES OF NITROGEN

The oxides of nitrogen, NO and NO_2, play an important role in air pollution chemistry. As we know, the principal source of nitrogen oxides in the urban atmosphere is combustion processes. Most of the NO_x formed in combustion is NO. However, NO_2 is formed to some extent from the NO in combustion exhaust gases by

$$2NO + O_2 \rightarrow 2NO_2$$

Even small amounts of NO_2 present in the atmosphere are sufficient to trigger a complex series of reactions involving organics that lead to photochemical smog. The name "photochemical smog" was coined as a result of the discovery by Haagen-Smit (Haagen-Smit, 1952; Haagen-Smit and Fox, 1956) in the early 1950s of the importance of the photolysis of NO_2 in air pollution chemistry. We begin our study of gas-phase atmospheric chemistry with the oxides of nitrogen.

4.2.1.   Basic Photochemical Cycle of NO_2, NO, and O_3

When NO and NO_2 are present in sunlight, ozone formation occurs as a result of the photolysis of NO_2,

$$NO_2 + h\nu \overset{1}{\to} NO + O$$

$$O + O_2 + M \overset{2}{\to} O_3 + M$$

where M represents N_2 or O_2 or another third molecule that absorbs the excess vibrational energy and thereby stabilizes the O_3 molecule formed. There are no significant sources of ozone in the atmosphere other than reaction 2. Once formed, O_3 reacts with NO to regenerate NO_2,

$$O_3 + NO \overset{3}{\to} NO_2 + O_2$$

Let us consider for a moment the dynamics of a system in which only these three reactions are taking place. Let us assume that known initial concentrations of NO and NO_2, $[NO]_0$ and $[NO_2]_0$, in air are placed in a reactor of constant volume at constant temperature and irradiated. The rate of change of the concentration of NO_2 after the irradiation begins is given by

$$\frac{d[NO_2]}{dt} = -k_1[NO_2] + k_3[O_3][NO] \tag{4.2}$$

Treating $[O_2]$ as constant, there are four species in the system: NO_2, NO, O, and O_3. We could write the dynamic equations for NO, O, and O_3 just as we have done for NO_2. For example, the equation for [O] is

$$\frac{d[O]}{dt} = k_1[NO_2] - k_2[O][O_2][M] \tag{4.3}$$

However, if we were to evaluate the right-hand side numerically we would find that it is very close to zero. Physically, this means that the oxygen atom is so reactive that it disappears by reaction 2 virtually as fast as it is formed by reaction 1. In dealing with highly reactive species such as the oxygen atom, it is customary to invoke the pseudo-steady state approximation (PSSA) and thereby assume that the rate of formation is exactly equal to the rate of disappearance, for example,

$$k_1[NO_2] = k_2[O][O_2][M]$$

The steady-state oxygen atom concentration in this system is then given by

$$[O] = \frac{k_1[NO_2]}{k_2[O_2][M]} \tag{4.4}$$

Note that [O] is not constant; rather it varies with $[NO_2]$ in such a way that at any instant a balance is achieved between its rate of production and loss. What this approximation really means is that the oxygen atom concentration adjusts to changes in the NO_2 concentration many orders of magnitude faster than the NO_2 concentration changes. Thus, on a time scale of the NO_2 dynamics, $[O]$ always appears to satisfy Eq. (4.4).

However, from Eqs. (4.2) and (4.3) we see that these three reactions will reach a point where NO_2 is destroyed and reformed so fast that a steady state cycle is maintained. Let us compute the steady-state concentrations of NO, NO_2, and O_3. (The steady-state concentration of oxygen atoms is already given by Eq. (4.4).) The steady-state ozone concentration is given by

$$[O_3] = \frac{k_1[NO_2]}{k_3[NO]} \tag{4.5}$$

This expression, resulting from the steady state analysis of reactions 1 to 3 has been named the *photostationary state relation*. We note that the steady state ozone concentration is proportional to the $[NO_2]/[NO]$ ratio. We now need to compute $[NO_2]$ and $[NO]$. These are obtained from conservation of nitrogen,

$$[NO] + [NO_2] = [NO]_0 + [NO_2]_0$$

and the stoichiometric reaction of O_3 with NO,

$$[O_3]_0 - [O_3] = [NO]_0 - [NO]$$

Solving for $[O_3]$, we obtain the relation for the ozone concentration formed at steady state by irradiating any mixture of NO, NO_2, O_3, and excess O_2 (in which only reactions 1 to 3 are important),

$$[O_3] = -\frac{1}{2}\left([NO]_0 - [O_3]_0 + \frac{k_1}{k_3}\right)$$

$$+ \frac{1}{2}\left\{\left([NO]_0 - [O_3]_0 + \frac{k_1}{k_3}\right)^2 + \frac{4k_1}{k_3}([NO_2]_0 + [O_3]_0)\right\}^{1/2} \tag{4.6}$$

If $[O_3]_0 = [NO]_0 = 0$, (4.6) reduces to

$$[O_3] = \frac{1}{2}\left\{\left[\left(\frac{k_1}{k_3}\right)^2 + \frac{4k_1}{k_3}[NO_2]_0\right]^{1/2} - \frac{k_1}{k_3}\right\} \tag{4.7}$$

We will see later that a typical value of $k_1/k_3 = 0.01$ ppm, so we can compute the ozone concentration attained as a function of the initial concentration of NO_2 with $[O_3]_0 = [NO]_0 = 0$:

$[NO_2]_0$, ppm	$[O_3]$, ppm
0.1	0.027
1.0	0.095

If, on the other hand, $[NO_2]_0 = [O_3]_0 = 0$, then $[O_3] = 0$. This is clear since with no NO_2 there is no means to produce ozone. Thus, the maximum steady-state ozone concentration would be achieved with an initial charge of pure NO_2. The concentrations of ozone attained in urban atmospheres are often greater than those in the sample calculation. However, as we know, most of the NO_x emitted is in the form of NO and not NO_2. Thus, with emissions of principally NO, the concentration of ozone reached, if governed solely by reactions 1 to 3, would be far too low to account for the actual observed concentrations. It must be concluded that reactions other than 1 to 3 are important in urban air in which relatively high ozone concentrations occur. Shortly we will see what those reactions are.

Measurement of the Photolysis Rate of NO_2. The photolysis of NO_2 is a key atmospheric reaction. Its photodissociation rate can be calculated if the solar flux $I(\lambda)$ is known. However, such measurements require specialized apparatus that is complex and expensive. A method that allows one to determine the NO_2 photodissociation rate, k_1, directly circumvents the need for elaborate measurements of the radiation intensity. By exposing a mixture of NO_2 and N_2 to sunlight one can determine the value of k_1 by comparing the measured NO_2 decay as a function of time with that obtained by integration of the rate equations. To integrate the rate equations it is necessary to assume a value for k_1. The desired value of k_1 is that which produces agreement between the observed and predicted NO_2 decay.

In the previous analysis we considered only reactions 1 to 3. There are several other reactions that occur in the NO_x-N_2 system that should be included for a more complete analysis. These are: *

$$O + NO_2 \overset{4}{\rightarrow} NO + O_2$$

$$O + NO_2 \overset{5}{\underset{M}{\rightarrow}} NO_3$$

$$NO + NO_3 \overset{6}{\rightarrow} 2NO_2$$

$$O + NO \overset{7}{\underset{M}{\rightarrow}} NO_2$$

$$NO_2 + NO_3 \overset{8}{\underset{M}{\rightarrow}} N_2O_5$$

$$N_2O_5 \overset{9}{\rightarrow} NO_2 + NO_3$$

We now simply expand our analysis of the NO_x-N_2 system to include these six

*Actually in the presence of sunlight NO_3 photolyzes very rapidly (See Table 4.1) so that we do not expect NO_3 levels to be appreciable. The addition of NO_3 to the mechanism is done at this point largely to illustrate how a somewhat larger mechanism may be analyzed.

reactions. We assume that in addition to oxygen atoms and O_3, NO_3 and N_2O_5 are in steady state. The PSSA applied to these two species yields $R_5 - R_6 = 0$ and $R_8 - R_9 = 0$, respectively. Using these relations and that derived for oxygen atoms, namely $R_1 = R_2 + R_4 + R_5 + R_7$, we obtain,

$$\frac{d[NO_2]}{dt} = -2k_4[O][NO_2] \tag{4.8}$$

Substituting the PSSA relation for [O] into Eq. (4.8) and rearranging, we get

$$\frac{-2k_1}{d \ln[NO_2]/dt} = 1 + \frac{k_5[M]}{k_4} + \frac{k_7[M][NO]}{k_4[NO_2]} + \frac{k_2[M][O_2]}{k_4[NO_2]} \tag{4.9}$$

Equation (4.9) seems complex, but it can be interpreted. In the absence of any reactions except 1 and 4 all oxygen atoms formed would react with NO_2 to form NO and O_2, giving an overall quantum yield of 2; that is, two molecules of NO_2 disappear for each photon absorbed. Thus, in that case

$$-\frac{d \ln[NO_2]}{dt} = 2k_1$$

This result holds if the experiment were run without N_2 at low pressure ($M = 0$). In the actual situation, however, various species compete with NO_2 for the oxygen atoms. The effect of this competition is expressed in the last three terms of Eq. (4.9). These are the ratios of oxygen atom reaction rates by other pathways to the rate of reaction 4.

We can integrate Eq. (4.9) analytically under the assumption that most of the NO_x is either NO_2 or NO,

$$[NO] = [NO]_0 + [NO_2]_0 - [NO_2]$$

The result of the integration is

$$k_1 = \frac{1}{2t}\left[(1 + a_1 - a_2)\ln\frac{[NO_2]_0}{[NO_2]} + a_2\left(\frac{[NO_2]_0}{[NO_2]} - 1\right)\right.$$

$$\left. + (a_2[NO]_0 + a_3[O_2])\frac{[NO_2]_0 - [NO_2]}{[NO_2]_0[NO_2]}\right] \tag{4.10}$$

where

$$a_1 = \frac{k_5[M]}{k_4} \qquad a_2 = \frac{k_7[M]}{k_4} \qquad a_3 = \frac{k_2[M]}{k_4}$$

Equation (4.10) may be simplified if the initial concentrations of NO and O_2

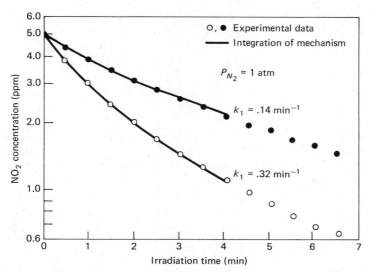

Figure 4.5. Nitrogen dioxide concentration as a function of time in a system initially comprising 5 ppm NO_2 in N_2. Experimental data and the predictions of the mechanism in the text are shown for two light intensities (Holmes et al., 1973).

are zero:

$$k_1 = \frac{1}{2t}\left[(1 + a_1 - a_2)\ln\frac{[NO_2]_0}{[NO_2]} + a_2\left(\frac{[NO_2]_0}{[NO_2]} - 1\right)\right] \qquad (4.11)$$

Equation (4.11) can be used to compute k_1 from the measured $[NO_2]$ versus time data in an irradiated system of NO_2 in N_2 by finding a value of k_1 that produces a fit of the data. Figure 4.5 shows NO_2 concentrations measured as a function of time for two different artificial light intensities. The curves represent Eq. (4.11) using the values of k_1 shown.

4.2.2. Atmospheric Chemistry of Carbon Monoxide and NO_x

We noted that in order to achieve observed ozone levels under polluted conditions it is necessary that reactions other than 1 to 3 must be occurring. For these we must turn to carbon-containing species. In some sense the simplest atmospheric carbon-containing species is CO. Carbon monoxide does not, however, react readily with any of the species present in the NO_x–air system.

We know that ozone photolyzes to produce both ground-state (O) and excited singlet ($O(^1D)$) oxygen atoms,*

$$O_3 + h\nu \overset{4a}{\rightarrow} O + O_2 \qquad \lambda > 315 \text{ nm}$$

$$\overset{4b}{\rightarrow} O(^1D) + O_2 \qquad \lambda < 315 \text{ nm}$$

The ground-state O atom combines rapidly with O_2 by reaction 2 to reform O_3, so reaction $4a$ followed by reaction 2 has no net chemical effect. Subsequently we will neglect path $4a$ and refer to path $4b$ simply as reaction 4. However, when $O(^1D)$ is produced, since the $O(^1D) \rightarrow O$ transition is forbidden, it must react with another atmospheric species. Most often $O(^1D)$ collides with N_2 or O_2, removing the excess energy and quenching $O(^1D)$ to its ground state,

$$O(^1D) + M \overset{5}{\rightarrow} O + M$$

Since the oxygen atom then just reacts with O_2 to replenish O_3, this path consisting of reactions $4b$, 5, and 2 is just another null cycle. Occasionally, however, $O(^1D)$ collides with H_2O and produces two hydroxyl radicals,

$$O(^1D) + H_2O \overset{6}{\rightarrow} 2OH\cdot$$

The key to understanding atmospheric chemistry will turn out to be understanding the reactions of the hydroxyl radical. This radical, unlike many molecular fragments formed from carbon-containing molecules, is unreactive toward oxygen, and it survives to react with most atmospheric trace species, such as hydrocarbons, aldehydes, and carbon monoxide.

Carbon monoxide will react with the hydroxyl radical formed in reaction 6,

$$CO + OH\cdot \overset{7}{\rightarrow} CO_2 + H\cdot$$

and the hydrogen atom formed in reaction 7 combines so quickly with O_2 to form the hydroperoxyl radical HO_2,

$$H\cdot + O_2 + M \rightarrow HO_2\cdot + M$$

that, for all intents and purposes, we can simply write reaction 7 as

$$CO + OH\cdot \overset{7}{\underset{O_2}{\rightarrow}} CO_2 + HO_2\cdot$$

---

*We no longer need the reaction numbering system of the previous example on determination of the NO_2 photolysis rate so we let the O_3 photolysis reaction now be reaction 4. Reactions 1–3 remain the same.

TABLE 4.2.   Atmospheric Chemistry of CO and NO_x

Reaction	Rate Constant[a]
1. $NO_2 + h\nu \rightarrow NO + O$	Depends on light intensity
2. $O + O_2 + M \rightarrow O_3 + M$	$6.0 \times 10^{-34}(T/300)^{-2.3}$ cm^6 molecule^{-2} sec^{-1}
3. $O_3 + NO \rightarrow NO_2 + O_2$	$2.2 \times 10^{-12}\exp(-1430/T)$ cm^3 molecule^{-1} sec^{-1}
4. $O_3 + h\nu \rightarrow O(^1D) + O_2$	$0.0028k_1$
5. $O(^1D) + M \rightarrow O + M$	2.9×10^{-11} cm^3 molecule^{-1} sec^{-1}
6. $O(^1D) + H_2O \rightarrow 2OH\cdot$	2.2×10^{-10} cm^3 molecule^{-1} sec^{-1}
7. $CO + OH\cdot \rightarrow CO_2 + HO_2\cdot$	2.2×10^{-13} cm^3 molecule^{-1} sec$^{-1\,b}$
8. $HO_2\cdot + NO \rightarrow NO_2 + OH\cdot$	$3.7 \times 10^{-12}\exp(240/T)$ cm^3 molecule^{-1} sec^{-1}
9. $OH\cdot + NO_2 \rightarrow HNO_3$	1.1×10^{-11} cm^3 molecule^{-1} sec^{-1}

[a] Baulch et al. (1982).
[b] Atkinson and Lloyd (1984).

The hydroperoxyl radical then reacts with NO to form NO_2 and to regenerate the OH radical,

$$HO_2\cdot + NO \overset{8}{\rightarrow} NO_2 + OH\cdot$$

Finally, OH and NO_2 may react to form nitric acid,

$$OH\cdot + NO_2 \overset{9}{\rightarrow} HNO_3$$

The reaction sequence occurring in the atmospheric system of NO, NO_2, and CO is summarized in Table 4.2

In analyzing this mechanism, the PSSA, as applied to this system, can be represented in terms of the rates of the nine reactions as:

$[O]_{ss}$: $R_1 - R_2 + R_5 = 0$

$$k_1[NO_2] - k_2[O][O_2][M] + k_5[M][O(^1D)] = 0$$

$[O(^1D)]_{ss}$: $R_4 - R_5 - R_6 = 0$

$$k_4[O_3] - k_5[M][O(^1D)] - k_6[H_2O][O(^1D)] = 0$$

$[OH]_{ss}$: $\left.\begin{array}{c} 2R_6 - R_7 + R_8 - R_9 = 0 \\ R_7 - R_8 = 0 \end{array}\right\}$

$[HO_2]_{ss}$:

$$2k_6[H_2O][O(^1D)] - k_9[OH][NO_2] = 0$$

$[O_3]_{ss}$: $R_2 - R_3 - R_4 = 0$

$$k_2[O][O_2][M] - k_3[O_3][NO] - k_4[O_3] = 0$$

We have four equations with four unknowns. ($[HO_2]_{ss}$ was eliminated by using $R_7 - R_8 = 0$ in the $[OH]_{ss}$ equation.) Solving the above equations we obtain,

$$[O]_{ss} = \frac{k_1[NO_2] + k_5[M][O(^1D)]}{k_2[O_2][M]}$$

$$[O(^1D)]_{ss} = \frac{k_4[O_3]}{k_6[H_2O]} a$$

$$[OH]_{ss} = \frac{2k_6[H_2O][O(^1D)]}{k_9[NO_2]} = \frac{2ak_4[O_3]}{k_9[NO_2]}$$

$$[O_3]_{ss} = \frac{k_2[O][O_2][M]}{k_3[NO] + k_4} = \frac{k_1[NO_2]}{k_3[NO] + k_4 a}$$

where

$$a = \frac{1}{1 + \dfrac{k_5[M]}{k_6[H_2O]}}$$

The rate equations for NO_2, NO, and CO are

$$\frac{d[NO_2]}{dt} = -R_1 + R_3 + R_8 - R_9$$

$$\frac{d[NO]}{dt} = R_1 - R_3 - R_8$$

$$\frac{d[CO]}{dt} = -R_7$$

Substituting the expressions for the rates into these equations and using the PSSA results for the free radical concentrations, we obtain

$$\frac{d[NO_2]}{dt} = \frac{k_1 k_4 a[2k_7[CO]/k_9 - 3[NO_2]]}{k_3[NO] + k_4 a}$$

$$\frac{d[NO]}{dt} = \frac{k_1 k_4 a\{[NO_2] - 2k_7[CO]/k_9\}}{k_3[NO] + k_4 a}$$

$$\frac{d[CO]}{dt} = -\frac{2k_1 k_4 k_7 a[CO]/k_9}{k_3[NO] + k_4 a}$$

Before we solve the rate equations let us examine the PSSA relation for ozone

$$[O_3]_{ss} = \frac{k_1[NO_2]}{k_3[NO] + k_4 a}$$

From Figure 4.4 and the rate constant values in Table 4.2, we see that $k_3[NO] \gg k_4 a$ for any atmospherically relevant NO concentration. Thus, $[O_3]_{ss}$ reduces to the photostationary state relation Eq. (4.5).

The qualitative features of the set of CO/NO_x reactions can be described as follows. Photolysis of NO_2 produces NO and O. The O atom immediately combines with an oxygen molecule to form O_3. Ozone then reacts mainly with NO to regenerate NO_2. The cycle of these three reactions can be represented concisely as (where O_2 is not indicated)

$$NO_2 \overset{h\nu}{\rightleftarrows} NO + O_3$$

The characteristic time of this cycle is usually short enough relative to the competing reactions so that a steady state is achieved quickly. The concentration of O_3 at such a steady state condition is given by the photostationary state relation Eq. (4.5). If we now consider the reactions resulting when CO is present, we see that the simple reversible cycle above is modified to be*

$$NO_2 \overset{h\nu}{\rightleftarrows} NO + O_3$$
$$\uparrow \quad HO_2 \quad |$$

The HO_2 radical that converts NO back to NO_2 is converted in the process to OH, which then is available to react with another molecule of CO. Thus, we obtain two interwoven cycles, a "fast" cycle and a "slow" cycle,

$$NO_2 \overset{h\nu}{\rightleftarrows} NO + O_3$$
$$CO + OH \rightarrow HO_2$$

The CO/NO_x reaction mechanism is a chain reaction with OH as the chain carrier. The *chain length* L_c of such a reaction is defined as the number of propagation steps occurring for each termination step,

$$L_c = \frac{R_8}{R_9} = \frac{R_7}{R_9} = \frac{k_7[CO]}{k_9[NO_2]}$$

*The presence of water is also necessary to provide a path for formation of hydroxyl radicals after ozone photolysis to give $O(^1D)$.

The CO–OH cycle is slow enough at typical ambient CO concentrations that the steady state relation for $[O_3]$ is valid. Since the steady state O_3 concentration is proportional to the ratio of $[NO_2]$ to $[NO]$, the effect of the CO cycle is to slowly convert NO to NO_2 and therefore to increase the steady state O_3 concentration. Thus, because of the rapidity of the NO_2/O_3 cycle, an independent path that changes the ratio of $[NO_2]$ to $[NO]$ indirectly controls the ozone concentration.

The basic reaction mechanism of the CO/NO_x system exhibits many of the key features of those involving much more complex organic molecules. In particular, the role of OH as the oxidizing species and the NO to NO_2 conversion by HO_2 are central to virtually every atmospheric organic/NO_x mechanism. It is useful to proceed to a molecule that is somewhat more complicated than CO to see how the similar NO_x mechanism develops. For that purpose, formaldehyde (HCHO) is the ideal molecule to consider.

4.2.3. Atmospheric Chemistry of Formaldehyde and NO_x

Formaldehyde is a primary pollutant and also an oxidation product of hydrocarbons. Thus, the chemistry of formaldehyde is common to virtually all mechanisms of atmospheric chemistry. This subsection serves, therefore, both as a continuation of our discussion of NO_x chemistry as well as an introduction to atmospheric organic chemistry.

Formaldehyde undergoes two primary reactions in the atmosphere, photolysis (recall Table 4.1),

$$HCHO + h\nu \rightarrow H\cdot + HCO\cdot$$

$$\rightarrow H_2 + CO$$

and reaction with OH,

$$HCHO + OH\cdot \rightarrow HCO\cdot + H_2O$$

As we have already noted, the hydrogen atom combines immediately with O_2 to yield HO_2. The formyl radical, HCO, reacts very rapidly with O_2,

$$HCO\cdot + O_2 \rightarrow HO_2\cdot + CO$$

Because of the rapidity of this reaction, the formaldehyde reactions may be written as

$$HCHO + h\nu \rightarrow 2HO_2\cdot + CO$$

$$\rightarrow H_2 + CO$$

$$HCHO + OH\cdot \rightarrow HO_2\cdot + CO + H_2O$$

TABLE 4.3. Atmospheric Reaction Mechanism Involving NO, NO$_2$, and HCHO

Reaction	Rate Constant
1. $NO_2 + h\nu \rightarrow NO + O$	Depends on light intensity
2. $O + O_2 + M \rightarrow O_3 + M$	See Table 4.2
3. $O_3 + NO \rightarrow NO_2 + O_2$	See Table 4.2
4. $HCHO + h\nu \overset{4a}{\rightarrow} 2HO_2\cdot + CO$	Depends on light intensity
$\overset{4b}{\rightarrow} H_2 + CO$	Depends on light intensity
5. $HCHO + OH\cdot \overset{5}{\rightarrow} HO_2\cdot + CO + H_2O$	1.1×10^{-11} cm^3 molecule^{-1} sec^{-1} [a]
6. $HO_2\cdot + NO \overset{6}{\rightarrow} NO_2 + OH\cdot$	See Table 4.2
7. $OH\cdot + NO_2 \overset{7}{\rightarrow} HNO_3$	See Table 4.2

[a] Baulch et al. (1982).

Table 4.3 gives the mechanism for the atmospheric chemistry of HCHO–NO$_x$. We have omitted the CO–OH reaction from Table 4.3 as it is generally slower than those involving HCHO.

Applying the PSSA, we obtain

$$[O_3]_{ss} = \frac{k_1[NO_2]}{k_3[NO]}$$

$$[OH]_{ss} = \frac{2k_{4a}[HCHO]}{k_7[NO_2]}$$

$$[HO_2]_{ss} = 2k_{4a}\left\{1 + \frac{k_5[HCHO]}{k_7[NO_2]}\right\}[HCHO]/k_6[NO]$$

The rate equations for NO$_2$, NO, and HCHO are, as a result,

$$\frac{d[NO_2]}{dt} = \frac{2k_{4a}k_5[HCHO]^2}{k_7[NO_2]} \tag{4.12}$$

$$\frac{d[NO]}{dt} = -2k_{4a}\left\{1 + \frac{k_5[HCHO]}{k_7[NO_2]}\right\}[HCHO] \tag{4.13}$$

$$\frac{d[HCHO]}{dt} = -\left\{k_{4a} + k_{4b} + 2k_{4a}\frac{k_5[HCHO]}{k_7[NO_2]}\right\}[HCHO] \tag{4.14}$$

The chain length of the reaction is given by

$$L_c = \frac{R_6}{R_7}$$

$$= \frac{2R_{4a} + R_5}{R_7}$$

$$= 1 + \frac{k_5[\text{HCHO}]}{k_7[\text{NO}_2]}$$

We see that L_c is always greater than one as long as HCHO is present in the system. Each molecule of HCHO that photolyzes via reaction $4a$ leads to the conversion of two molecules of NO to NO_2 and at the same time generates two OH radicals. The HCHO–OH reaction, on the other hand, leads to one NO to NO_2 conversion and produces a single OH radical.

Let us consider the reaction mechanism in Table 4.3 by integrating the rate equations (4.12) to (4.14) derived from it. We assume that the three photolysis rates are:

$$k_{\text{NO}_2} = 0.533 \text{ min}^{-1}$$

$$k_{\text{HCHO}(4a)} = 1.6 \times 10^{-3} \text{ min}^{-1}$$

$$k_{\text{HCHO}(4b)} = 2.11 \times 10^{-3} \text{ min}^{-1}$$

In general we expect the concentration dynamics to exhibit three regimes of behavior:

1.   If the initial concentrations of NO, NO_2, and O_3 do not conform to the photostationary state, then there is an initial period of short duration during which the concentrations of these species relax to their photostationary state values.

2.   The next phase is characterized by the conversion of NO to NO_2 by the HO_2 radicals generated by HCHO. The conversion of NO to NO_2 is accompanied by the formation of O_3 in accord with the photostationary state. The rate and amount of conversion of NO to NO_2 depend on the initial concentrations of NO, NO_2, and HCHO, since the NO_2–OH reaction continually removes NO_x from the system.

3.   In the final phase, the depletion of HCHO leads to an enhanced importance of the NO_2–OH reaction due to less competition with the HCHO–OH reaction for the OH radical. The NO_2 concentration may begin to decrease as NO_2 is converted to HNO_3.

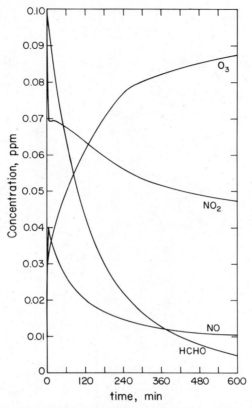

Figure 4.6. Photooxidation of formaldehyde in a mixture of NO, NO_2, and air. Initial concentrations are $[NO_2]_0 = 0.1$ ppm, $[NO]_0 = 0.01$ ppm, and $[HCHO]_0 = 0.1$ ppm.

It is worthwhile to examine the behavior of the system as a function of its initial conditions. Figure 4.6 shows the concentration-time behavior (all concentrations in ppm) for:

$$[NO_2]_0 = 0.1 \qquad [NO]_0 = 0.01 \qquad [HCHO]_0 = 0.1$$

During the first two minutes, the NO, NO_2, and O_3 concentrations relax to their photostationary state values:

$$[NO_2] = 0.069 \qquad [NO] = 0.0405 \qquad [O_3] = 0.032$$

Over the 600 minute period, we see that after the first 20 minutes NO_2

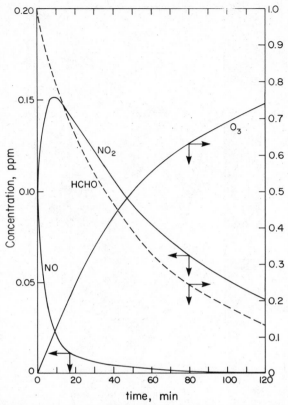

Figure 4.7. Photooxidation of formaldehyde in a mixture of NO, NO$_2$, and air. Initial concentrations are $[NO_2]_0 = 0.1$ ppm, $[NO]_0 = 0.1$ ppm, and $[HCHO]_0 = 1.0$ ppm.

continually decreases, since, even though NO is continually being converted to NO$_2$ by O$_3$, there is such an excess of NO$_2$ that the NO$_2$–OH reaction is removing NO$_2$ to HNO$_3$ at a rate such that it dominates the behavior of NO$_2$.

Figure 4.7 shows the concentrations versus time for the initial conditions:

$$[NO_2]_0 = 0.1 \qquad [NO]_0 = 0.1 \qquad [HCHO]_0 = 1.0$$

In this case there is sufficient initial NO to produce an increase in NO$_2$. Finally, Figure 4.8 shows the concentration-time dynamics for:

$$[NO_2]_0 = 0.1 \qquad [NO]_0 = 1.0 \qquad [HCHO]_0 = 1.0$$

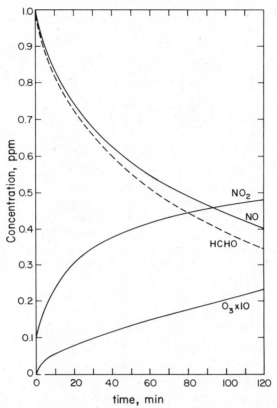

Figure 4.8. Photooxidation of formaldehyde in a mixture of NO, NO_2, and air. Initial concentrations are $[NO_2]_0 = 0.1$ ppm, $[NO]_0 = 1.0$ ppm, and $[HCHO]_0 = 1.0$ ppm.

We see that the conversion of NO to NO_2 takes longer due to the much larger initial NO pool.

The reactivity of the system is controlled by the amount of HCHO. Upon photolysis, HCHO provides two HO_2 radicals on one path and none on the other. Since these paths are roughly comparable in rate, we can say approximately that each HCHO molecule leads to one HO_2 molecule. (It leads to exactly one in the OH reaction.) The conversion of NO to NO_2 and the formation of O_3 are therefore driven by HCHO through its production of HO_2. Thus, the theoretical maximum amount of O_3 that could be produced in this system is

$$[O_3] = [HCHO]_0 + [NO_2]_0$$

When all the NO_x is converted to HNO_3, the system ceases reacting. In a

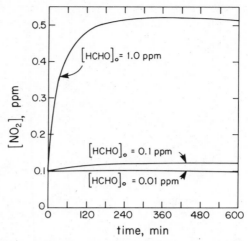

Figure 4.9. Effect of initial concentration of formaldehyde on the dynamics of NO_2 in the photooxidation of a mixture of HCHO, NO, and NO_2 in air. In the three cases shown, $[NO_2]_0 = 0.1$ ppm and $[NO]_0 = 1.0$ ppm.

sense, a given system can be characterized by its ability to produce O_3. The effect of $[HCHO]_0$ on NO_2 dynamics is shown in Figure 4.9.

4.3. CHEMISTRY OF THE BACKGROUND TROPOSPHERE

We are beginning a systematic development of the atmospheric chemistry of organic species and the oxides of nitrogen. We began with carbon monoxide since its atmospheric chemistry is the simplest, while exhibiting some of the essential elements of hydroxyl radical attack, formation of the hydroperoxyl radical, and conversion of NO to NO_2. We then proceeded to formaldehyde, the atmospheric chemistry of which is slightly more complex than that of carbon monoxide. The next logical step would be to consider the simplest alkane, methane (CH_4), and that is in fact what we will now do. It turns out that methane is the key hydrocarbon species in the chemistry of the background (nonpolluted) troposphere. Thus, in studying the atmospheric chemistry of methane we are led naturally to the chemistry of the background troposphere.

Concentration levels of the normal background components of the troposphere are controlled by a series of chemical reactions. The key species involved in these reactions are methane, carbon monoxide, formaldehyde, ozone, NO_x, nitric acid, and hydrogen peroxide (H_2O_2). In this section we review briefly the chemistry of the "clean" troposphere. For additional reading in this area we refer the reader to Chameides and Davis (1982).

The reaction that can be considered to trigger background tropospheric chemistry is the photolysis of ozone to yield the singlet oxygen atom, followed by $O(^1D)$ reaction with H_2O to generate two OH radicals,*

$$O_3 + h\nu \rightarrow O_2 + O(^1D)$$

$$O(^1D) + H_2O \rightarrow 2OH\cdot$$

The hydroxyl radicals react with CH_4 and CO present in the atmosphere (their sources will be discussed shortly),

$$CH_4 + OH\cdot \rightarrow CH_3\cdot + H_2O$$

$$CO + OH\cdot \rightarrow CO_2 + H\cdot$$

The hydrogen atom, as we have already seen, and the methyl radical react instantaneously with O_2 to yield the hydroperoxyl and methylperoxyl radicals,

$$H\cdot + O_2 + M \rightarrow HO_2\cdot + M$$

$$CH_3\cdot + O_2 + M \rightarrow CH_3O_2\cdot + M$$

so that the CH_4- and CO–OH reactions may be written simply as

$$CH_4 + OH\cdot \rightarrow CH_3O_2\cdot + H_2O$$

$$CO + OH\cdot \rightarrow HO_2\cdot + CO_2$$

The peroxy radicals, in turn, participate in a chain-propagating sequence that converts NO to NO_2 and, in the process, produces additional OH and peroxy radical species,

$$CH_3O_2\cdot + NO \rightarrow NO_2 + CH_3O\cdot$$

$$HO_2\cdot + NO \rightarrow NO_2 + OH\cdot$$

$$CH_3O\cdot + O_2 \rightarrow HCHO + HO_2\cdot$$

The major chain terminating steps include nitric acid and hydrogen peroxide formation,

$$OH\cdot + NO_2 \rightarrow HNO_3$$

$$HO_2\cdot + HO_2\cdot \rightarrow H_2O_2 + O_2$$

*Note that photolysis to yield ground state oxygen atoms is followed immediately by $O + O_2 + M \rightarrow O_3 + M$, resulting in a null cycle with no chemical effect.

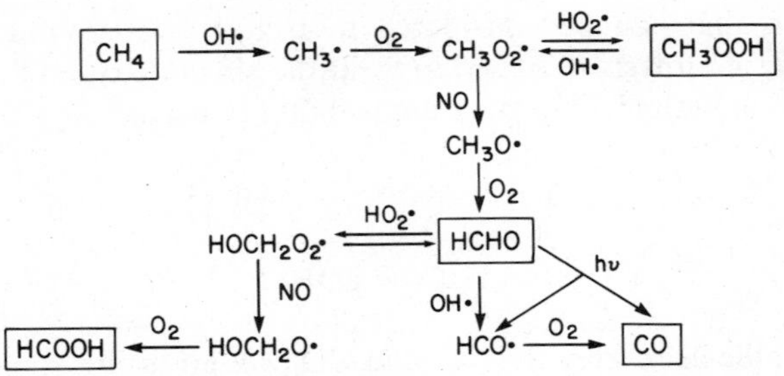

Figure 4.10. Tropospheric methane chemistry.

The formaldehyde produced in the CH_3O-O_2 reaction may photolyze or react with hydroxyl radicals to lead to CO and HO_2 radicals as we have already seen. A small fraction of the hydrogen peroxide formed may be photolyzed (Table 4.1) to again regenerate two OH radicals, thereby serving as a temporary reservoir for OH.

Figure 4.10 shows the atmospheric degradation path for methane. The CH_3O_2 radical can react with either NO or HO_2, the latter reaction being

$$CH_3O_2\cdot + HO_2\cdot \rightarrow CH_3OOH + O_2$$

The two reactions become of equal rates for an $[NO]/[HO_2]$ ratio of about 1.0 at 300 K. At present, the atmospheric fate of CH_3OOH is uncertain; it may be removed heterogeneously or react to give methanol (CH_3OH) and formic acid ($HCOOH$).

Carbon dioxide is the ultimate product of this methane oxidation chain, although CO is a relatively long-lived intermediate. Non-methane hydrocarbons are also oxidized by OH and have oxidation chains leading to CO and CO_2 that are equivalent in principle to that of methane. So-called active nitrogen compounds, such as NO, NO_2, NO_3, N_2O_5, HNO_2, and HNO_3, play a central role in tropospheric chemistry. The $NO-NO_2-O_3$ photochemical cycle, when coupled to the peroxy radical–NO reactions, leads to the production of ozone. Atmospheric active nitrogen compounds are initially produced in the form of NO and NO_2 by soil and ocean processes, combustion, and lightning (see Section 1.2). The major chemical sink for active nitrogen is formation of nitric acid by the $OH-NO_2$ reaction, followed by removal in precipitation.

Even though NO and NO_2 concentrations are less than 0.04 ppb in remote marine and continental areas and from 0.2 to 0.5 ppb in rural continental regions, their relative abundance controls the chemical production of background ozone. In fact, the role of chemistry in controlling the abundance of tropospheric ozone has been a subject of considerable debate.

Current understanding of global tropospheric O_3 recognizes two primary sources of O_3. Stratospheric injection is estimated to contribute a globally averaged annual flux of about 5×10^{10} molecules cm^{-2} sec^{-1}. Photochemical production in the troposphere by the free radical reactions outlined above yields an even larger contribution. Production of O_3 associated with hydrocarbons of natural origin alone is estimated to account for a globally averaged annual rate of about 15×10^{10} molecules cm^{-2} sec^{-1}.

The troposphere can be viewed as a low temperature flame that transforms reduced compounds, released at the surface, to oxidized species that are removed by precipitation, reaction at the surface or upward diffusion to the stratosphere. For tropospheric chemistry it can be said that ozone is the fuel and the hydroxyl radical is the propellor. Although OH is produced at a very significant rate, because of its extreme reactivity its concentration is low and, as a result, the direct measurement of OH has proven to be exceedingly difficult. The term "clean troposphere" might be interpreted as those regions where nonmethane hydrocarbon levels are low enough that the production of OH is dominated by reaction of $O(^1D)$ with H_2O vapor and its destruction is dominated by reaction with CO and CH_4.

By using a full chemical mechanism to simulate tropospheric chemistry, it is possible to estimate the atmospheric concentration of OH. Such calculations suggest a seasonally, diurnally, and globally averaged OH concentration of from 2×10^5 to 10^6 molecules cm^{-3}. Highest OH levels are predicted in the tropics where high humidities and strong actinic fluxes lead to a high rate of OH production from O_3 photolysis to $O(^1D)$. In addition, OH levels are predicted to be about 20 percent higher in the southern hemisphere due to the large amounts of CO produced by human activities in the northern hemisphere. Since direct measurement of atmospheric OH levels is extremely difficult, confirmation of the levels predicted by the chemical mechanisms has been based on budgets of species that are known to be consumed only by OH. For example, Volz et al. (1981) inferred an average tropospheric OH concentration of 6.5×10^5 molecules cm^{-3} from measurements of ^{14}CO. In addition, since methyl chloroform (CH_3CCl_3) is believed to have only an anthropogenic source and since it is removed from the atmosphere by reaction with OH, the concentration of OH determines its mean residence time. From the history of methyl chloroform emission and its present atmospheric level, it is possible to infer its residence time and then to compare the OH level corresponding to that residence time to the level predicted theoretically. At present, such estimates agree within a factor of two or less, providing further tentative support for the correctness of the basic chemical mechanism. Measured and theoretical estimates of [OH] in the troposphere indicate the following ranges:

Daytime (summer)	5–10×10^6 molecules cm^{-3}
Daytime (winter)	1–5×10^6
Nighttime	$\leq 2 \times 10^5$

The atmospheric cycles of CH_4 and CO are thus intimately interwoven through their chemistry. The major sources of atmospheric methane are

TABLE 4.4.   Global Budget of Tropospheric Methane[a]

Sources	Strength, Tg yr^{-1}
Anaerobic fermentation	100–200
Paddy fields	280
Swamps, marshes	190–300
Freshwater sediments	1–25
Tundra	0.3–3
Ocean	1.3–16.6
TOTAL	570–825

Sinks	
$CH_4 + OH$[b]	580
Transport to stratosphere	25–85
Uptake by microorganisms in soil	≤ 1
TOTAL	605–665

[a] The amount of CH_4 present in the troposphere based on an average concentration of 1.55 ppm is 3700 Tg.
[b] Based on assumed OH concentration of 10^6 molecules cm^{-3}.

biogenic, including anaerobic fermentation of organic material in swamps, tropical rain forests, paddies, and in the digestive systems of livestock. It has also been proposed that termites could be an important source of methane (Zimmerman et al., 1982). The major methane sink is reaction with OH. Table 4.4 presents an estimate of the global budget of tropospheric methane. The estimated source and sink strengths are in the same range.

The oxidation of methane by OH leads to a major source of CO. Calculations with chemical mechanisms indicate that CH_4 oxidation produces about 20 to 50 percent of the carbon monoxide in the atmosphere. The remainder is believed to arise from three other processes: the OH oxidation of non-methane hydrocarbons, such as isoprene and terpenes from vegetation, the incomplete combustion of fossil fuels, and the burning of biomass, such as wood, agricultural wastes, and forests. As with methane, the major sink for CO is reaction with OH. Table 4.5 shows an estimate of the global budget of CO.

Carbon monoxide has a chemical lifetime of 30 to 90 days on the global scale of the troposphere. Measurements indicate that there is more CO in the Northern Hemisphere than in the Southern Hemisphere with the maximum values being found near the surface at northern mid-latitudes. In general, the CO concentration decreases with altitude in the Northern Hemisphere to a free tropospheric average value of about 120 ppb near 45°N. In the Southern Hemisphere CO tends to be more nearly uniformly mixed vertically with a

TABLE 4.5. Global Budget of Tropospheric Carbon Monoxide

Sources	Strength, Tg yr^{-1}
Anthropogenic	500–700
CH_4 + OH	70–700
NMHC + OH	20–500
Oceans	60–300
TOTAL	650–2200
Sinks	
CO + OH	1200–1900
Soils	300–500
Transport to Stratosphere	10–60
TOTAL	1500–2500

value of about 60 ppb near 45°S. Seasonal variations have been established to be about ±40 percent about the mean in the Northern Hemisphere and ±20 percent about the mean in the Southern Hemisphere. The maximum concentration is observed to occur during the local spring and the minimum is found during the late summer or early fall.

4.4. ATMOSPHERIC ORGANIC CHEMISTRY

We have up to this point explored the atmospheric chemistry of CO, formaldehyde and methane. Atmospheric organic chemistry is similar in nature to that of HCHO and CH_4, although as the compounds increase in size, the corresponding chemistry increases in complexity. This section is devoted to a brief summary of atmospheric organic chemistry. The material here is based largely on the review of Atkinson and Lloyd (1984). Because extensive rate constant reviews are available (Baulch et al., 1982; Atkinson and Lloyd, 1984), we do not endeavor to provide a thorough summary here. For assistance in carrying out those calculations in the text and in the problems at the end of this chapter, we do provide in Section 4.8 a selected list of rate constants of reactions discussed in this chapter.

4.4.1. Carbonyl Chemistry

We have already discussed the chemistry of formaldehyde, HCHO; in this section we address that of the next two aldehydes, acetaldehyde, CH_3CHO and propionaldehyde, CH_3CH_2CHO, and the first ketone, acetone, $CH_3C(O)CH_3$. Figure 4.11 summarizes the atmospheric oxidation mechanisms of formalde-

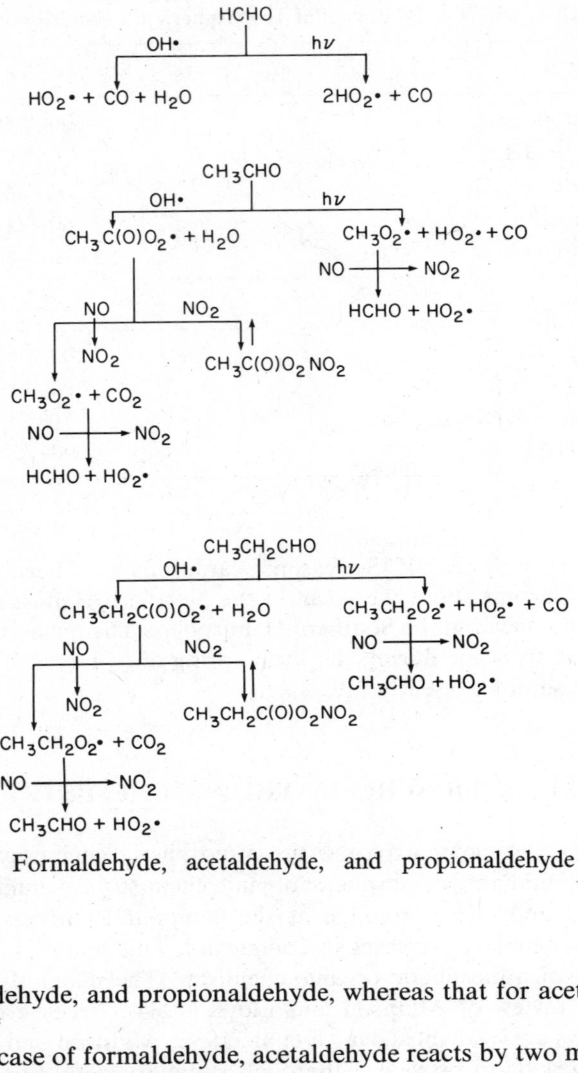

HCHO

OH· $h\nu$

$HO_2\cdot + CO + H_2O$ $2HO_2\cdot + CO$

CH_3CHO

OH· $h\nu$

$CH_3C(O)O_2\cdot + H_2O$ $CH_3O_2\cdot + HO_2\cdot + CO$

NO NO_2 NO $\longrightarrow NO_2$

NO_2 $CH_3C(O)O_2NO_2$ $HCHO + HO_2\cdot$

$CH_3O_2\cdot + CO_2$

NO $\longrightarrow NO_2$

$HCHO + HO_2\cdot$

CH_3CH_2CHO

OH· $h\nu$

$CH_3CH_2C(O)O_2\cdot + H_2O$ $CH_3CH_2O_2\cdot + HO_2\cdot + CO$

NO NO_2 NO $\longrightarrow NO_2$

NO_2 $CH_3CH_2C(O)O_2NO_2$ $CH_3CHO + HO_2\cdot$

$CH_3CH_2O_2\cdot + CO_2$

NO $\longrightarrow NO_2$

$CH_3CHO + HO_2\cdot$

Figure 4.11. Formaldehyde, acetaldehyde, and propionaldehyde photooxidation mechanisms.

hyde, acetaldehyde, and propionaldehyde, whereas that for acetone is given in Figure 4.12.*

As in the case of formaldehyde, acetaldehyde reacts by two major pathways, photolysis and reaction with OH,

$$CH_3CHO + h\nu \rightarrow CH_3\cdot + HCO\cdot$$

$$CH_3CHO + OH\cdot \rightarrow CH_3C(O)\cdot + H_2O$$

*When a reaction is written as $CH_3O_2\cdot \overset{NO}{\underset{NO_2}{\rightsquigarrow}}$ this is a shorthand way of indicating that CH_3O_2 reacts with NO to give NO_2 and the products on the other end of the arrow.

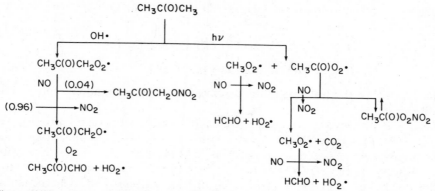

Figure 4.12. Atmospheric photooxidation mechanism for acetone. The initial step is either reaction with the hydroxyl radical or photolysis. After reaction with OH and addition of O_2 (not explicitly shown), the peroxy radical $CH_3C(O)CH_2O_2$ reacts with NO, 4 percent of the reaction leading to $CH_3C(O)CH_2ONO_2$ and 96 percent to NO_2 and $CH_3C(O)CH_2O$.

The methyl and acetyl radicals produced react rapidly as follows:

$$CH_3\cdot + O_2 \rightarrow CH_3O_2\cdot$$

$$CH_3CO\cdot + O_2 \rightarrow CH_3C(O)O_2\cdot$$

Thus, the acetaldehyde reactions are usually written directly as:

$$CH_3CHO + h\nu \rightarrow CH_3O_2\cdot + HO_2\cdot + CO$$

$$CH_3CHO + OH\cdot \rightarrow CH_3C(O)O_2\cdot + H_2O$$

The methylperoxy radical reacts with NO to yield NO_2,

$$CH_3O_2\cdot + NO \rightarrow NO_2 + CH_3O\cdot$$

The methoxy radical reacts rapidly with O_2 to produce formaldehyde and HO_2,

$$CH_3O\cdot + O_2 \rightarrow HCHO + HO_2\cdot$$

The acetylperoxy radical reacts with both NO and NO_2:

$$CH_3C(O)O_2\cdot + NO \rightarrow CH_3C(O)O\cdot + NO_2$$

$$CH_3C(O)O\cdot \xrightarrow{O_2} CH_3O_2\cdot + CO_2$$

$$CH_3C(O)O_2\cdot + NO_2 \rightarrow CH_3C(O)O_2NO_2$$

Because the decomposition of $CH_3C(O)O\cdot$ is rapid, the above three reactions are usually written as

$$CH_3C(O)O_2\cdot + NO \rightarrow CH_3O_2\cdot + NO_2 + CO_2$$

$$CH_3C(O)O_2\cdot + NO_2 \rightleftarrows CH_3C(O)O_2NO_2$$

The product in the last reaction is peroxyacetyl nitrate, commonly referred to as PAN.

Since its discovery in Los Angeles about thirty years ago, peroxyacetyl nitrate (PAN), $CH_3C(O)OONO_2$, has been found to be ubiquitous throughout the troposphere. As seen above, PAN is formed by the reaction of NO_2 with peroxyacetyl ($CH_3C(O)OO\cdot$) radicals, which are themselves produced in the photooxidation of many different types of hydrocarbons and their oxidation products, such as aldehydes and ketones. PAN redissociates to NO_2 and $CH_3C(O)OO$, with a first-order rate constant that is highly temperature-dependent. The lifetime of a PAN molecule is, for example, about 30 min at 300 K, three days at 290 K, and one month at 260 K. The removal of PAN from the atmosphere by processes other than thermal decomposition appears to be slow. Consequently, at the lower temperatures of the middle and upper troposphere PAN is relatively stable and acts as a reservoir for NO_x. When PAN is transported down to the warmer boundary layer it thermally decomposes, releasing NO_x. As we will note shortly, other PAN-type compounds are also expected to be formed in the atmosphere by the NO_2 reaction of the corresponding organic peroxy radicals.

The reactions of propionaldehyde are seen to correspond rather closely to those of acetaldehyde and will not be discussed here.

4.4.2. Alkane Chemistry

We now consider the atmospheric chemistry of alkanes. Hydroxyl radical reaction is the only significant alkane oxidation process in the atmosphere, the general features of which are: first, OH abstraction of a hydrogen atom from a terminal or internal carbon atom, followed by rapid addition of O_2 to form a peroxyalkyl radical, the principal fate of which is reaction with NO to give either NO_2 and an alkoxy radical, RO, or an alkyl nitrate, $RONO_2$.

To elucidate alkane chemistry let us begin with the atmospheric photooxidation of propane:

$$CH_3CH_2CH_3 + OH\cdot \longrightarrow CH_3\dot{C}HCH_3 + H_2O$$

$$CH_3\dot{C}HCH_3 + O_2 \xrightarrow{fast} CH_3CH(O_2\cdot)CH_3$$

$$CH_3CH(O_2\cdot)CH_3 + NO \longrightarrow NO_2 + CH_3CH(O\cdot)CH_3$$

$$CH_3CH(O\cdot)CH_3 + O_2 \xrightarrow{fast} CH_3C(O)CH_3 + HO_2\cdot$$

Internal H–atom abstraction predominates in the initial OH attack. As we have been doing, we can eliminate the fast reactions from the mechanism by combining them with their predecessors. Thus, the above four reactions may be expressed as

$$CH_3CH_2CH_3 + OH\cdot \xrightarrow[O_2]{} CH_3CH(O_2\cdot)CH_3$$

$$CH_3CH(O_2\cdot)CH_3 + NO \xrightarrow[O_2]{} NO_2 + CH_3C(O)CH_3 + HO_2\cdot$$

If we further take the liberty of assuming that the $CH_3CH(O_2\cdot)CH_3$ radical participates only in these two reactions, a good assumption in this case, these two reactions can be written as a single overall reaction,

$$CH_3CH_2CH_3 + OH\cdot \rightarrow NO_2 - NO + CH_3C(O)CH_3 + HO_2\cdot$$

where $NO_2 - NO$ on the product side of the reaction indicates that the reaction converts one molecule of NO to one molecule of NO_2. If we assume further that the sole fate of the HO_2 radical is reaction with NO, we can write this reaction as

$$CH_3CH_2CH_3 + OH\cdot \rightarrow 2NO_2 - 2NO + CH_3C(O)CH_3 + OH\cdot$$

In writing the reaction this way, we can clearly see the net effect of the hydroxyl radical attack on propane, namely the conversion of two molecules of NO to two molecules of NO_2, the production of one molecule of acetone, and the regeneration of the hydroxyl radical. As we already know, the conversion of NO to NO_2 in this way is accompanied by an accumulation of ozone. Acetone itself reacts further by the mechanism given in Figure 4.12. Thus, the photooxidation of propane can be viewed as a chain reaction mechanism in which the active species, the hydroxyl radical, is regenerated. For larger alkanes, such as n-butane, the atmospheric photooxidation mechanisms become more complex, although they continue to exhibit the same essential features of the propane degradation path. Two secondary, but important, issues arise in the reaction mechanisms of the higher alkanes. The first is that some fraction of the peroxyalkyl–NO reactions lead to alkyl nitrates rather than NO_2 and an alkoxy radical. The second is that the larger alkoxy radicals may isomerize as well as react with O_2.

The n-butane–OH reaction leads to the mechanism given in Figure 4.13. Definitive data concerning the relative importance of the two paths of reaction of the sec-butoxy radical, $CH_3CH_2CH(O\cdot)CH_3$, are not currently available, and Atkinson and Lloyd (1984) do not recommend a firm value for the ratio of the rate constants of these two reactions. Consequently, the split is indicated by the unspecified fraction b in the n-butane mechanism.

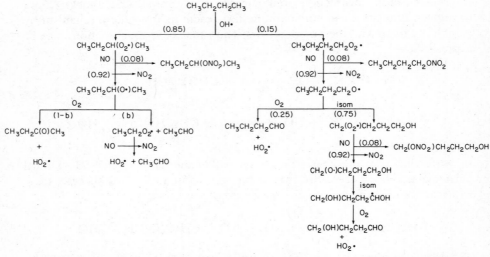

Figure 4.13. Atmospheric photooxidation mechanism for *n*-butane. The only significant reaction of *n*-butane is with the hydroxyl radical. It is estimated that 85 percent of that reaction involves H–atom abstraction from an internal carbon atom and 15 percent from a terminal carbon atom. In the terminal H–atom abstraction path, the $CH_3CH_2CH_2CH_2O$ radical is estimated to react with O_2 25 percent of the time and isomerize 75 percent of the time. The second isomerization is estimated to be a factor of five faster than the first isomerization of the $CH_3CH_2CH_2CH_2O$ radical, so that competition with O_2 reaction is not considered at this step. The predominant fate of α-hydroxy radicals is reaction with O_2. For example, $\cdot CH_2OH + O_2 \rightarrow HCHO + HO_2\cdot$, and $CH_3\dot{C}HOH + O_2 \rightarrow CH_3CHO + HO_2\cdot$. In the *n*-butane mechanism, the α-hydroxy radical, $CH_2(OH)CH_2CH_2\dot{C}HOH$, reacts rapidly with O_2 to form 4-hydroxybutanal, $CH_2(OH)CH_2CH_2CHO$.

Alkyl Nitrate Formation from RO_2–NO Reactions. Alkyl nitrate yields in alkane–NO_x photooxidations suggest that reactions of the type,

$$RO_2\cdot + NO \rightarrow RONO_2$$

are important sources of alkyl nitrates when R contains three or more carbon atoms (Darnall et al., 1976). The basic issue concerning this reaction is determining the fractional split between the two paths,

$$RO_2\cdot + NO \rightarrow NO_2 + RO\cdot$$

$$\rightarrow RONO_2$$

Two new studies are now available that address alkyl nitrate formation from RO_2–NO reactions (Atkinson et al., 1982, 1984).

Alkyl nitrate yields have been determined for the n-alkanes, ethane through n-octane, and monotonically increase from less than about 0.014 for ethane to 0.33 for n-octane (Atkinson et al., 1982). A plot of the yield against carbon number indicates a limiting nitrate yield of about 0.35 for the higher alkanes. All of the evidence currently available concerning alkyl nitrate formation from $RO_2 + NO$ comes from product studies of alkane–NO_x oxidations. The data are totally consistent with a gas-phase mechanism involving $RO_2 + NO$, and, in particular, are inconsistent with their formation from $RO + NO_2$ or from heterogeneous processes. It is important to note that alkyl nitrate formation from the higher alkanes is a significant radical and NO_x loss process that has a marked effect on the conversion of NO to NO_2 by higher alkanes.

4.4.3. Alkene Chemistry

We now proceed to the atmospheric chemistry of alkenes (or olefins). By now we fully expect that alkenes will react with the hydroxyl radical, and that is indeed the case. Because of the double bonded carbon atoms in alkene molecules, they will also react with ozone and atomic oxygen. The reaction with ozone can be an important alkene oxidation path, whereas that with oxygen atoms is generally not due to their extremely low concentration. Let us begin with the hydroxyl radical reaction mechanism and focus on the simplest alkene, ethene (C_2H_4).

Up to this point the initial step in OH attack on a hydrocarbon molecule has been abstraction of a hydrogen atom to form a water molecule and an alkyl radical. In the case of alkenes, OH adds to the double bond rather than abstracting a hydrogen atom. The ethene–OH reaction mechanism is:

$$C_2H_4 + OH\cdot \longrightarrow HOCH_2CH_2\cdot$$

$$HOCH_2CH_2\cdot + O_2 \xrightarrow{\text{fast}} HOCH_2CH_2O_2\cdot$$

$$HOCH_2CH_2O_2\cdot + NO \longrightarrow NO_2 + HOCH_2CH_2O\cdot$$

The $HOCH_2CH_2O$ radical then reacts rapidly with O_2, as we would expect, with the following outcome:

$$HOCH_2CH_2O\cdot + O_2 \xrightarrow{0.72} HCHO + \cdot CH_2OH$$

$$\xrightarrow{0.28} HOCH_2CHO + HO_2\cdot$$

The numbers over the arrows indicate the fraction of the reactions that lead to the indicated products at 298 K. Finally, the CH_2OH radical reacts with O_2 to give

$$\cdot CH_2OH + O_2 \xrightarrow{\text{fast}} HCHO + HO_2\cdot$$

Following our procedure, we can eliminate the fast reactions

$$C_2H_4 + OH\cdot \xrightarrow{O_2} HOCH_2CH_2O_2\cdot$$

$$HOCH_2CH_2O_2\cdot + NO \xrightarrow{2O_2} NO_2 + 0.72(HCHO + HCHO + HO_2\cdot)$$

$$+ 0.28(HOCH_2CHO + HO_2\cdot)$$

Finally, assuming that $HOCH_2CH_2O_2$ participates only in these two reactions, we can write an overall reaction as

$$C_2H_4 + OH\cdot \rightarrow NO_2 - NO + 1.44HCHO + 0.28HOCH_2CHO + HO_2\cdot$$

As we did with propane, we can remove HO_2 assuming that it reacts solely with NO, to give

$$C_2H_4 + OH\cdot \rightarrow 2NO_2 - 2NO + 1.44HCHO + 0.28HOCH_2CHO + OH\cdot$$

We see that the overall result of hydroxyl radical attack on ethene is conversion of two molecules of NO to NO_2, formation of 1.44 molecules of formaldehyde and 0.28 molecules of glycol aldehyde ($HOCH_2CHO$), and regeneration of a hydroxyl radical. By comparing this mechanism to that of propane we see the similarities in the NO to NO_2 conversion and the formation of oxygenated products. As expected, the OH reaction mechanisms of the higher alkenes are more complex than that of ethene. The reaction mechanisms for ethene, propene, and trans-2-butene with OH are given in Figure 4.14.

It is now reasonably well established that the initial step in the alkene-O_3 reaction is the formation of a molozonide that rapidly decomposes to a carbonyl and an energy-rich biradical, called the Criegee intermediate (Martinez et al, 1981; Herron et al., 1982)

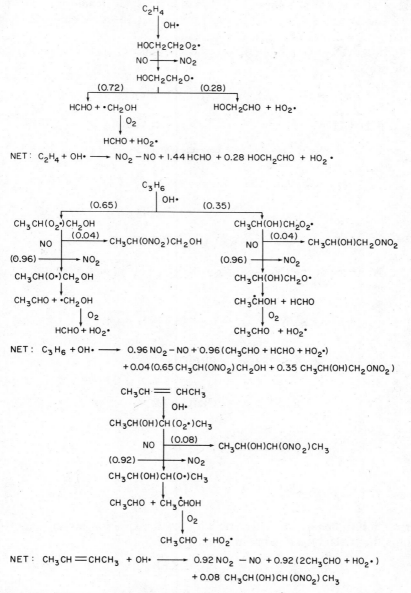

Figure 4.14. OH-reaction mechanisms for ethene, propene, and trans-2-butene. After each mechanism the net reaction is given. The presence of NO_2-NO on the right hand side of the arrow in the net reaction indicates that the OH-reaction is accompanied by the conversion of one molecule of NO to NO_2. If a fractional amount of NO_2 is indicated, the difference between that fraction and 1.0 is the quantity of nitrate formed.

where a 50-50 split between the two paths is usually assumed. The major problem in describing the O_3–alkene reaction lies in establishing the subsequent chemistry of the Criegee intermediate.

The initial O_3 reaction steps for ethene, propene, 1-butene, and trans-2-butene are

$$CH_2 = CH_2 + O_3 \rightarrow HCHO + H_2COO$$

$$CH_3CH = CH_2 + O_3 \rightarrow HCHO + CH_3CHOO$$

$$\rightarrow CH_3CHO + H_2COO$$

$$CH_2 = CHCH_2CH_3 + O_3 \rightarrow HCHO + CH_3CH_2CHOO$$

$$\rightarrow CH_3CH_2CHO + H_2COO$$

$$CH_3CH = CHCH_3 + O_3 \rightarrow CH_3CHO + CH_3CHOO$$

The dynamics of the Criegee intermediate can be analyzed from the general mechanism:

$$ALKENE + O_3 \overset{1}{\rightarrow} CARBONYL + CRIG*$$

$$CRIG* \overset{2}{\rightarrow} PRODUCTS$$

$$CRIG* + M \overset{3}{\rightarrow} CRIG + M$$

$$CRIG \overset{4}{\rightarrow} PRODUCTS$$

$$CRIG + X_i \overset{5i}{\rightarrow} PRODUCTS$$

where CRIG* denotes an energetic form of the Criegee intermediate. If we assume that CRIG* is in a pseudo-steady state, then

$$[CRIG*]_{ss} = \frac{k_1[ALKENE][O_3]}{k_2 + k_3[M]}$$

Thus, the kinetics of the stabilized, or so-called thermalized, Criegee intermediate CRIG are given by

$$\frac{d[CRIG]}{dt} = \frac{k_1[ALKENE][O_3]}{1 + \dfrac{k_2}{k_3[M]}} - \left\{ k_4 + \sum_i k_{5i}[X_i] \right\} [CRIG]$$

and if CRIG is in a pseudo-steady state,

$$[CRIG]_{ss} = \frac{k_1[ALKENE][O_3]}{\left\{1 + \dfrac{k_2}{k_3[M]}\right\}\left\{k_4 + \sum_i k_{5i}[X_i]\right\}}$$

The mechanism above includes two decomposition steps, 2 and 4. If decomposition occurs, it probably does so via reaction 2, so we can assume that $k_4 = 0$. The ratio $k_3[M]/(k_2 + k_3[M])$ is the fraction of the energetic intermediates that is stabilized.

In their review of the chemistry of H_2COO, Atkinson and Lloyd (1984) recommend the following fate of H_2COO^*,

$$H_2COO^* + M \longrightarrow H_2COO + M \qquad\qquad (0.40)$$

$$\longrightarrow CO_2 + H_2 \qquad\qquad (0.12)$$

$$\longrightarrow CO + H_2O \qquad\qquad (0.42)$$

$$\xrightarrow[2O_2]{} CO_2 + 2HO_2 \qquad\qquad (0.06)$$

The thermalized H_2COO biradicals are then available for bimolecular reactions with CO, HCHO, CH_3CHO, and SO_2. The ethene–O_3 reaction can then be written as

$$C_2H_4 + O_3 \rightarrow HCHO + 0.40H_2COO + 0.18CO_2 + 0.42CO$$
$$+ 0.12H_2 + 0.42H_2O + 0.12HO_2$$

For the chemistry of the CH_3CHOO biradical, Atkinson and Lloyd (1984) recommend

$$CH_3CHOO^* + M \longrightarrow CH_3CHOO + M \qquad\qquad (0.40)$$

$$\longrightarrow CH_4 + CO_2 \qquad\qquad (0.12)$$

$$\xrightarrow[O_2]{} CH_3O_2{\cdot} + CO + OH{\cdot} \qquad\qquad (0.192)$$

$$\xrightarrow[2O_2]{} CH_3O_2{\cdot} + CO_2 + HO_2{\cdot} \qquad\qquad (0.192)$$

$$\xrightarrow[O_2]{} HO_2{\cdot} + CO + CH_3O{\cdot} \qquad\qquad (0.048)$$

$$\xrightarrow[2O_2]{} HO_2{\cdot} + CO_2 + CH_3O_2{\cdot} \qquad\qquad (0.048)$$

leading to

$$CH_3CHOO^* \rightarrow 0.40CH_3CHOO + 0.12CH_4 + 0.36CO_2$$

$$+0.24CO + 0.29HO_2\cdot + 0.19OH\cdot + 0.05CH_3O\cdot$$

$$+0.43CH_3O_2\cdot$$

and thus

$$C_3H_6 + O_3 \rightarrow 0.5HCHO + 0.5CH_3CHO + 0.5H_2COO^* + 0.5CH_3CHOO^*$$

followed by the above reactions of H_2COO^* and CH_3CHOO^*.

We note that the radical yields from the ethene–O_3 and propene–O_3 reactions are $0.12HO_2\cdot$ radicals per ethene molecule reacted and $0.205HO_2\cdot +$ $0.095OH\cdot + 0.025CH_3O\cdot + 0.215CH_3O_2\cdot$ per propene molecule reacted.

Finally, for trans-2-butene, we have

$$CH_3CH = CHCH_3 + O_3 \rightarrow CH_3CHO + CH_3CHOO^*$$

followed by the above reactions of CH_3CHOO^*.

The thermalized Criegee intermediates are available to react with other molecules in the system, for example

$$RCHOO + NO \rightarrow NO_2 + RCHO$$

$$+NO_2 \rightarrow NO_3 + RCHO$$

$$+SO_2 \rightarrow SO_3 + RCHO$$

$$+H_2O \rightarrow RCOOH + H_2O$$

4.4.4. Aromatic Chemistry

Aromatic hydrocarbons constitute an appreciable fraction of atmospheric organics. Less is known about the chemistry of aromatics than about that of alkanes, alkenes, and aldehydes. Benzene is not especially reactive with OH, so the next member of the series, toluene, is the aromatic species most frequently studied with respect to its atmospheric chemistry. In this subsection we summarize the current understanding concerning the atmospheric chemistry of toluene.

The only significant chemical reaction of toluene under atmospheric conditions is with the OH radical. The reaction proceeds via two pathways: H atom abstraction from the substituent methyl group and OH radical addition to the ring,

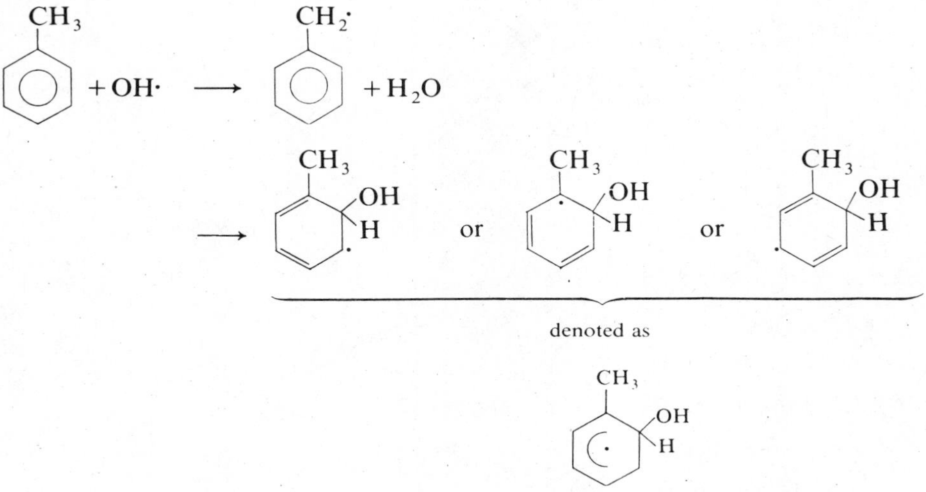

denoted as

Under atmospheric conditions it has been determined that about 90 percent of the toluene–OH reaction proceeds by OH-addition. Although four OH–toluene adducts are possible, experimental product data indicate that the ortho adduct shown above is the primary product. The mechanism for the abstraction pathway is shown in Figure 4.15, the major products being benzaldehyde and benzyl nitrate.

The OH–toluene adduct can react under atmospheric conditions with either O_2 or NO_2. The reaction with O_2 proceeds via two pathways, H atom abstraction to form the cresol or reversible addition to form the peroxy radical,

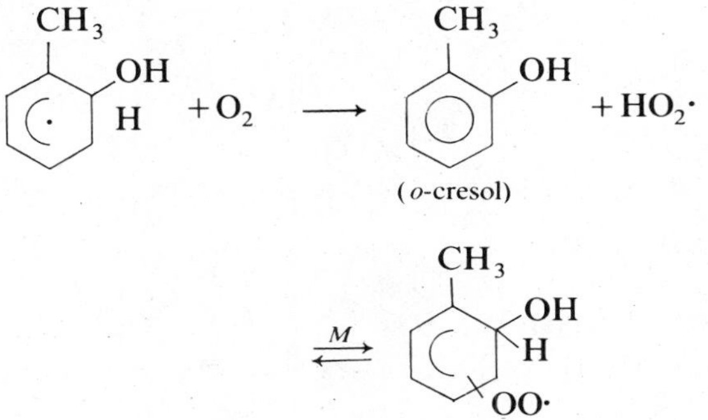

(*o*-cresol)

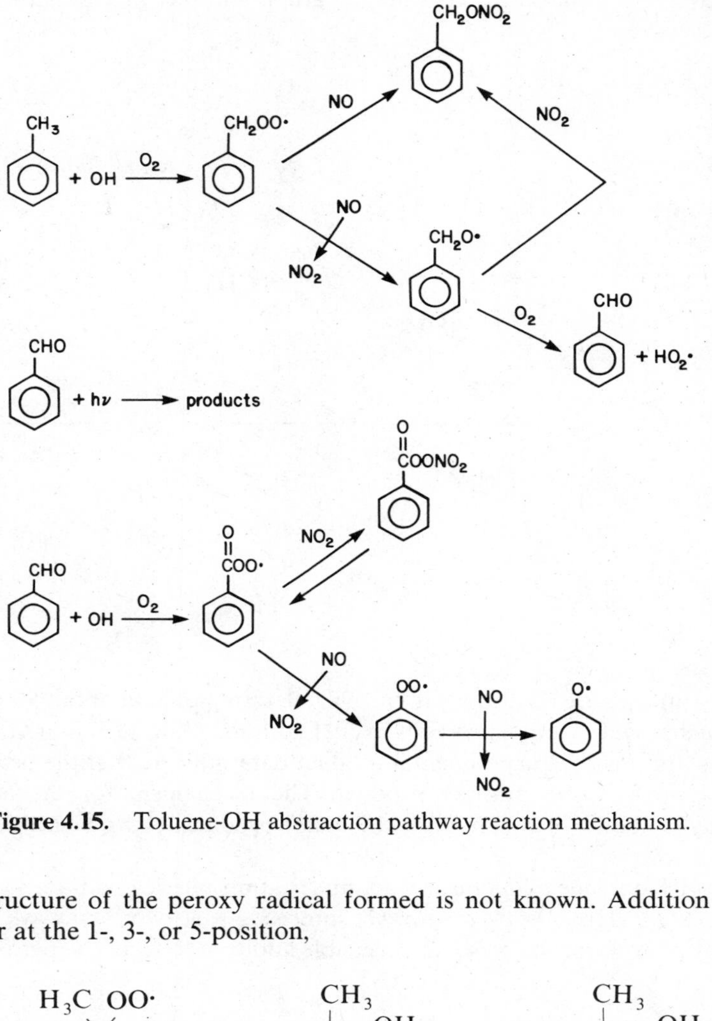

Figure 4.15. Toluene-OH abstraction pathway reaction mechanism.

The structure of the peroxy radical formed is not known. Addition of O_2 may occur at the 1-, 3-, or 5-position,

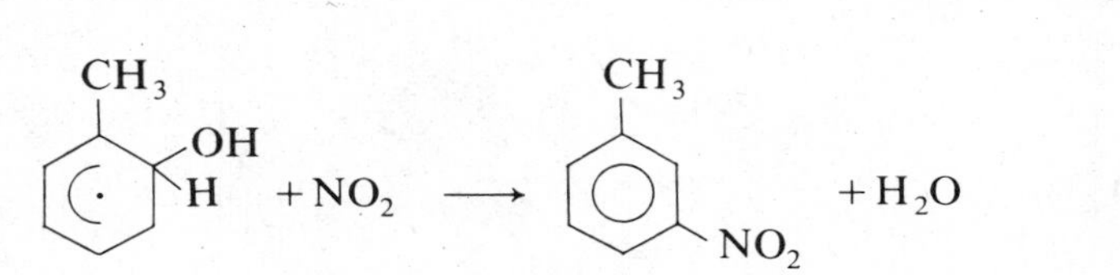

The reaction of the OH–toluene adduct with NO_2 leads to *m*-nitrotoluene,

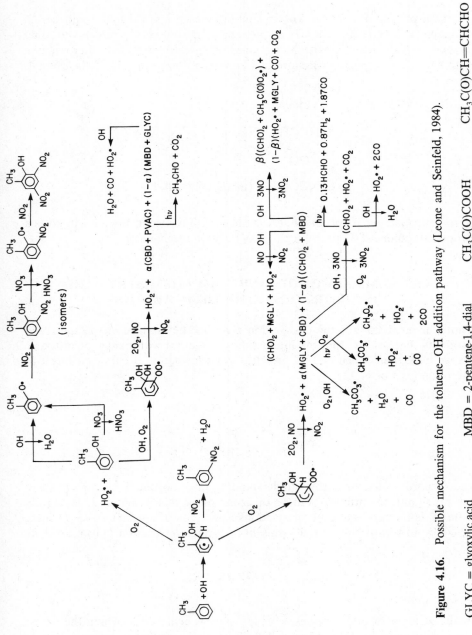

Figure 4.16. Possible mechanism for the toluene–OH addition pathway (Leone and Seinfeld, 1984).

GLYC = glyoxylic acid   MBD = 2-pentene-1,4-dial $CH_3C(O)COOH$ $CH_3C(O)CH=CHCHO$

MGLY = methyl glyoxal   PVAC = pyruvic acid $CHOCH=CHCHO$ $CH_3C(O)CHO$

CBD = cis-2-butene-1,4-dial $CHOCOOH$

At the present time little is known about the reactions of the OH–toluene–O_2 adducts. If the OH–toluene–O_2 adduct reacts in a manner analogous to other peroxy radicals, reaction with NO would be likely, followed by either reaction with O_2 or ring opening. Because of the presence as products of dicarbonyls such as

$$\underset{\text{HCCH}}{\overset{\text{OO}}{\overset{||\,||}{}}} \quad \text{(glyoxal)}$$

$$\underset{\text{CH}_3\text{CCH}}{\overset{\text{OO}}{\overset{||\,||}{}}} \quad \text{(methyl glyoxal)}$$

in toluene systems, it appears that ring opening must occur. Figure 4.16 gives a proposed toluene–OH addition pathway reaction mechanism.

4.5. SUMMARY OF ORGANIC / NO_x CHEMISTRY—THE CHEMISTRY OF PHOTOCHEMICAL SMOG

Photochemical smog is the designation given to the mixture of reactants and products that results from the interaction of organics with oxides of nitrogen. As we have seen, when NO_x is present, ozone formation occurs as a result of the photolysis of NO_2,

$$NO_2 + h\nu \overset{1}{\rightarrow} NO + O$$

$$O + O_2 + M \overset{2}{\rightarrow} O_3 + M$$

and, according to our current understanding of atmospheric chemistry, there are no significant primary sources of ozone other than reaction 2. Relatively little O_3 is formed as a result of reactions 1 and 2 alone since O_3, once formed, reacts rapidly with NO (initially present or formed in reaction 1) to regenerate NO_2,

$$O_3 + NO \overset{3}{\rightarrow} NO_2 + O_2$$

In the absence of other species, a steady state is achieved in which the ozone concentration is given by the so-called photostationary state relation

$$[O_3] = \frac{k_1[NO_2]}{k_3[NO]}$$

The key to understanding atmospheric organic chemistry is the OH radical. Its reaction with many hydrocarbons (RH) leads to peroxyalkyl radicals,

$$RH + OH \cdot \rightarrow R \cdot + H_2O$$

$$R \cdot + O_2 \rightarrow RO_2 \cdot$$

The reaction of OH with aldehydes (RCHO) forms the acyl (RCO·) and acylperoxy ($RC(O)O_2 \cdot$) radicals in similar reactions,

$$RCHO + OH \cdot \rightarrow RCO \cdot + H_2O$$

$$RCO \cdot + O_2 \rightarrow RC(O)O_2 \cdot$$

The peroxy radicals react rapidly with NO to form NO_2 and other free radicals,

$$RO_2 \cdot + NO \rightarrow NO_2 + RO \cdot$$

$$\rightarrow RONO_2$$

$$RC(O)O_2 \cdot + NO \rightarrow NO_2 + RC(O)O \cdot$$

In the case or the HO_2–NO reaction, OH is regenerated, whereas with the RO_2 and $RC(O)O_2$ radicals, alkoxy (RO) and acyloxy (RC(O)O) radicals, respectively, are formed. The most common fate of the smaller alkoxy radicals is reaction with O_2, leading to HO_2 radicals and a carbonyl compound,

$$RO \cdot + O_2 \rightarrow HO_2 \cdot + R'CHO$$

For example, with the simplest alkoxy radical, methoxy (CH_3O), the following reaction occurs,

$$CH_3O \cdot + O_2 \rightarrow HO_2 \cdot + HCHO$$

The RC(O)O· radicals are of short lifetime, decomposing to form an alkyl radical (R·) and CO_2, with the subsequent generation of another peroxyalkyl radical,

$$RC(O)O \cdot \rightarrow R \cdot + CO_2$$

$$R \cdot + O_2 \rightarrow RO_2 \cdot$$

Finally, the hydroperoxyl radicals can react with NO to regenerate OH and complete the cycle,

$$HO_2 \cdot + NO \rightarrow NO_2 + OH \cdot$$

The likely history of typical alkyl and acyl radicals in chain propagation reactions can thus be depicted as

$$RCO \cdot \xrightarrow{O_2} RC(O)O_2 \cdot \xrightarrow{NO} RC(O)O \cdot$$

$$R \cdot \xrightarrow{O_2} RO_2 \cdot \xrightarrow{NO} RO \cdot \xrightarrow{O_2} HO_2 \cdot \xrightarrow{NO} OH \cdot$$

HC

We see that, during the lifetimes of R and RCO, many molecules of NO can be converted to NO_2 (of course, each step in the sequence competes with other propagation and termination reactions). The peroxy radicals (RO_2 and $RC(O)O_2$) efficiently convert NO to NO_2. The key to the chemistry is that one free radical formed, for example, as the result of the reaction of OH with a hydrocarbon will participate in several propagation steps (e.g., the conversion of NO to NO_2) before extinction. This process involving oxygen-containing free radicals provides the path for oxidation of NO to NO_2 not involving O_3 and subsequent accumulation of ozone.

An initial source of free radicals is needed to start the overall process. In the $CO–NO_x$ air system, photolysis of ozone, with subsequent reaction of $O(^1D)$ with water vapor, served as the initial source of OH, whereas in the formaldehyde–NO_x–air system, photolysis of HCHO was the dominant initial source. Photolysis of aldehyde molecules is, in fact, an important source of atmospheric free radicals,

$$RCHO + h\nu \rightarrow R \cdot + HCO \cdot$$

During the course of the chain reaction, the free radical pool is maintained by several sources, but a principal one is photolysis of aldehydes formed from the initial hydrocarbons.

The chemistry of the oxides of nitrogen in a organic-containing atmosphere can be summarized in a general way as follows. The major observed phenomena in the system are conversion of NO to NO_2, formation of a variety of nitrogen-containing species, such as nitric acid and peroxyacyl nitrates, and accumulation of O_3. NO_2 serves both as initiator and terminator of the chain reactions that result in conversion of NO to NO_2 and buildup of O_3. Termination of the chain reactions leads to nitric acid and organic nitrates.

4.5.1. Organic Reactivity

In general, the term *organic reactivity* in atmospheric chemistry refers to the potential of an organic to promote formation of products. Because product formation is manifested in such a variety of ways (e.g., eye irritation, plant damage, ozone formation), it is difficult to find one measure upon which the reactivity of an organic may be expressed that includes all aspects of its atmospheric chemistry. From a chemical standpoint, reactivity may be expressed in terms of reaction rates and product yields; for example:

Reaction Rate Measures

1. Rate of NO$_2$ formation.
2. Rate of organic consumption.
3. Rate of ozone formation.

Product Yield Measures

1. Maximum concentration of ozone achieved.
2. Total ozone dosage over a fixed time of irradiation.
3. Maximum concentration of PAN achieved.

From the standpoint of effects, reactivity may be defined in terms of the amount of eye irritation experienced (say by a panel of judges), the amount of plant damage incurred, or the degree of visibility limitation resulting. Aside from the subjectivity of eye irritation, a major problem in selecting a particular reactivity measure is that the measures are not necessarily interrelatable. Thus, ethene is consumed at a rate much slower than that of tetramethylethene [(CH$_3$)$_2$C$=$C(CH$_3$)$_2$], yet photooxidation of ethene yields formaldehyde, a powerful eye irritant, as its chief end product, and tetramethylethene yields mainly acetone, which is not an eye irritant. Thus, it is clear there does not exist one single reactivity scale that incorporates all the deleterious effects of photochemical smog. Because air quality standards relating to photochemical smog are basically directed toward ozone formation, the reactivity measure that has been most studied is that of the amount of ozone formed upon irradiation of the organic in a mixture of air and NO$_x$.

There are at least four different factors that must be considered in defining reactivity of organics relative to ozone formation:

1.   The rate at which the organic reacts in the atmosphere, particularly with OH radicals, and possibly by photolysis or reaction with O$_3$, determines in part how fast the organic converts NO to NO$_2$ and thus how fast it causes ozone formation.

2. The number of molecules of NO oxidized per molecule of organic reacted determines how much O_3 will be formed by consumption of a given amount of the organic. This number is typically two to three for most organics whose photooxidation mechanisms have been studied (Cox et al., 1980), but can be larger for organics whose intermediate alkoxy radicals undergo extensive isomerization or fragmentation.

3. For organics whose major atmospheric sink is reaction with hydroxyl radicals, the radical levels present also determine how fast the organic will cause O_3 formation. The photooxidation of some organics, for example, aldehydes and aromatics, results in increased radical levels, because either they or their major oxidation products undergo photolysis to form radicals. This enhancement of radical levels causes the rates of ozone formation from *all* organics present to be enhanced. On the other hand, some organics, such as the larger alkanes, depress radical levels by converting radicals to intermediates that undergo termination reactions, and thus the presence of such compounds tends to reduce the O_3 formation rate.

4. Since O_3 formation can occur only as long as NO_x is present, organics whose atmospheric oxidation involves significant NO_x sinks will necessarily allow less O_3 formation under conditions when NO_x is limited. For example, aromatic hydrocarbons such as toluene and the xylenes are highly reactive by criteria 1 and 3 above, yet incremental addition of small amounts of toluene to a surrogate hydrocarbon–NO_x mixture has been observed to depress maximum ozone yields. Thus, the reactivity as measured by the ozone-forming potential of the organic in the absence of other reactive organics may well be quite different from that as determined from ozone yield perturbations resulting from incremental additions of the organic to NO_x–organic–air mixtures.

4.5.2. Analysis of a Generalized Reaction Mechanism for Photochemical Smog

In our discussion of photochemical smog chemistry we outlined a general reaction mechanism, that is reproduced in Table 4.6 with appropriate rate constants. We wish to integrate the rate equations from this mechanism to examine the temporal concentration dynamics of RH, RCHO, NO, NO_2, and O_3 for the three sets of initial concentrations (all in ppm):

	Case 1	Case 2	Case 3
$[RH]_0$	0.1	0.5	2.0
$[RCHO]_0$	0.1	0.5	2.0
$[NO]_0$	0.5	0.5	0.5
$[NO_2]_0$	0.1	0.1	0.1

TABLE 4.6. A Generalized Reaction Mechanism for Photochemical Smog

Reaction	Rate Constant (cm^{-3} molecule-sec units)	Rate Constant (ppm-min units) (298 K)
$NO_2 + h\nu \rightarrow NO + O$	0.533 min^{-1} (assumed)	0.533 min^{-1}
$O + O_2 + M \rightarrow O_3 + M$	$6.0 \times 10^{-34} (T/300)^{-2.3}$ cm^6 molecule^{-2} sec^{-1}	2.183×10^{-5}
$NO + O_3 \rightarrow NO_2 + O_2$	$2.2 \times 10^{-12} \exp(-1430/T)$ cm^3 molecule^{-1} sec^{-1}	26.59
$RH + OH\cdot \rightarrow RO_2\cdot + H_2O$	$1.68 \times 10^{-11} \exp(-559/T)$ cm^3 molecule^{-1} sec^{-1}	3.775×10^3
$RCHO + OH\cdot \rightarrow RC(O)O_2\cdot + H_2O$	$6.9 \times 10^{-12} \exp(250/T)$ cm^3 molecule^{-1} sec^{-1}	2.341×10^4
$RCHO + h\nu \rightarrow RO_2\cdot + HO_2\cdot + CO$	1.91×10^{-4} min^{-1} (assumed)	1.91×10^{-4} min^{-1}
$HO_2\cdot + NO \rightarrow NO_2 + OH\cdot$	$3.7 \times 10^{-12} \exp(240/T)$ cm^3 molecule^{-1} sec^{-1}	1.214×10^4
$RO_2\cdot + NO \rightarrow NO_2 + RCHO + HO_2\cdot$	$4.2 \times 10^{-12} \exp(180/T)$ cm^3 molecule^{-1} sec^{-1}	1.127×10^4
$RC(O)O_2\cdot + NO \rightarrow NO_2 + RO_2\cdot + CO_2$	$4.2 \times 10^{-12} \exp(180/T)$ cm^{-3} molecule^{-1} sec^{-1}	1.127×10^4
$OH\cdot + NO_2 \rightarrow HNO_3$	1.1×10^{-11} cm^{-3} molecule^{-1} sec^{-1}	1.613×10^4
$RC(O)O_2\cdot + NO_2 \rightarrow RC(O)O_2NO_2$	4.7×10^{-12} cm^{-3} molecule^{-1} sec^{-1}	6.893×10^3
$RC(O)O_2NO_2 \rightarrow RC(O)O_2\cdot + NO_2$	$1.95 \times 10^{16} \exp(-13543/T)$ sec^{-1}	2.143×10^{-2} min^{-1}

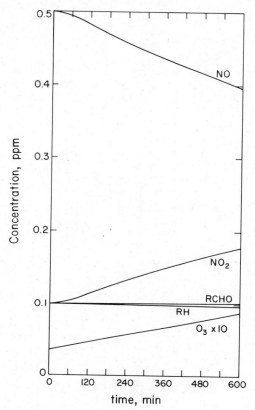

Figure 4.17.   Concentrations predicted by a generalized reaction mechanism for photo-chemical smog. The initial conditions are those of case 1 in Section 4.5.2.

Results of the integration of the rate equations for the three sets of initial concentrations are given in Figures 4.17, 4.18, and 4.19.* The temperature is taken as 298 K and the time period $t = 0$ to $t = 600$ min. is assumed.

In Figure 4.17, showing the results for case 1, we see that little of the initial hydrocarbon RH is consumed, and that the aldehydes RCHO actually increase slightly due to conversion of RH. The conversion of NO to NO_2 is evident. Increasing the organic concentration from 0.2 ppm to 1.0 ppm in going from case 1 to case 2 (Figure 4.18) leads to a more reactive system, including more rapid conversion of NO to NO_2 and increased O_3. Finally, in case 3, when the initial organic concentration is 4.0 ppm, the maximum in the NO_2 concentra-

---

*Although we have made liberal use of the PSSA in analyzing reaction mechanisms, for the purposes of numerical simulation it is generally safer to use an ordinary differential equation solving routine directly on the rate equations for all species, including the free radicals, than to assume the PSSA holds for certain species. This procedure was followed here.

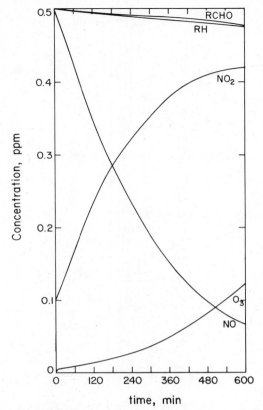

Figure 4.18. Concentrations predicted by a generalized reaction mechanism for photochemical smog. The initial conditions are those of case 2 in Section 4.5.2.

tion is reached at about 120 min with subsequent decay due to formation of nitric acid and PAN. The O$_3$ concentration reaches 0.8 ppm at the end of 600 min. Although the mechanism in Table 4.6 is oversimplified in its representation of photochemical smog chemistry, the qualitative behavior shown in Figures 4.17 to 4.19 is that which is observed in laboratory simulations, atmospheric data, and in computer simulations with more detailed mechanisms.

4.5.3.   The Ozone Isopleth Plot

The chemical features of ozone formation in the photochemical smog system can be represented compactly by plotting isopleths of maximum ozone concentration achieved over a fixed time of irradiation in the plane of initial NO$_x$ concentration $[NO_x]_0 = [NO]_0 + [NO_2]_0$, and initial reactive organic con-

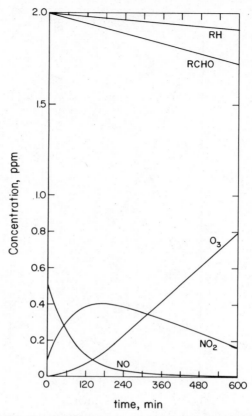

Figure 4.19. Concentrations predicted by a generalized reaction mechanism for photochemical smog. The initial conditions are those of case 3 in Section 4.5.2.

centration, expressed in units of parts-per-million of carbon. Figure 4.20 shows such an ozone isopleth plot. Each point on each curve represents a separate experiment or simulation using a kinetic mechanism. We see that if we fix the initial organic concentration at 1.0 ppmC and reduce $[NO_x]_0$, starting at $[NO_x]_0 = 0.4$, the maximum ozone actually increases, goes through a maximum and then finally decreases as $[NO_x]_0$ gets quite low. This behavior can be explained as follows.

At low $[Organic]_0/[NO_x]_0$ ratios, the order of 1–2, the conversion of NO to NO_2, and the subsequent build-up of O_3, is limited by the limited availability of organics. Thus, sufficient organics are not present to generate enough radicals to effectively convert NO to NO_2. At very high $[Organic]_0/[NO_x]_0$ ratios, on the other hand, the order of 20 or more, O_3 cannot accumulate because either it is consumed by reacting with alkenes, or the NO_2 is removed by reacting with the excess of free radicals present, or radical-radical termina-

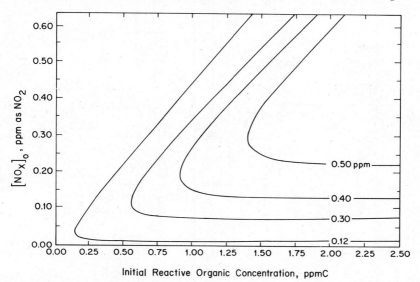

Initial Reactive Organic Concentration, ppmC

Figure 4.20. Ozone isopleth plot. The maximum O$_3$ concentration achieved during a fixed time of irradiation of a mixture whose initial concentrations are [NO$_x$]$_0$ = [NO]$_0$ + [NO$_2$]$_0$ and [Organic]$_0$, where the latter is measured in parts-per-million of carbon (ppmC). Although the general features of this plot are duplicated in virtually all photochemical smog systems, the actual location of the O$_3$ isopleths depends on the specific conditions of the irradiation, such as the particular components of the organic mixture, the light intensity, and so forth.

tion reactions become important. Therefore, at the two extremes of low and high [Organic]$_0$/[NO$_x$]$_0$ ratios little O$_3$ can form, and as one decreases [NO$_x$]$_0$ at constant [Organic]$_0$, an ozone maximum is found. For example, from Figure 4.20 we see that at [Organic]$_0$ = 1.0 ppmC, the maximum O$_3$ achieved is about 0.42 ppm at [NO$_x$]$_0$ ≅ 0.2 ppm, that is, a ratio of 5.

4.5.4. Summary of Atmospheric NO$_x$ Chemistry

Much of this chapter has been devoted to the atmospheric chemistry of the nitrogen oxides. The prominent species in the chemistry of both the natural and the polluted atmosphere are NO, NO$_2$, and HNO$_3$. Figure 4.21 shows an expanded schematic of the atmospheric chemistry of the oxides of nitrogen. The top of the figure indicates four of the organic nitrogen compounds that can form in the presence of organic free radicals. NO$_3$ may be formed by the reaction of NO$_2$ with O or O$_3$, the latter being the more important pathway. The NO$_3$ may react with NO or photolyze to regenerate NO$_2$ or react with an additional NO$_2$ to generate N$_2$O$_5$. Although N$_2$O$_5$ may thermally decompose, it is believed that some fraction of it reacts heterogeneously with H$_2$O, forming

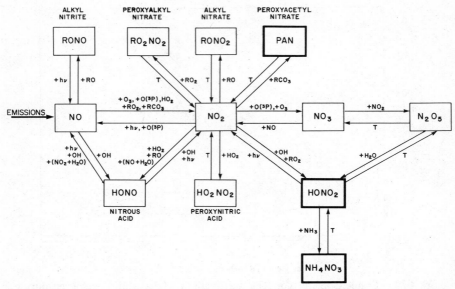

Figure 4.21. Atmospheric nitrogen chemistry (McRae and Russell, 1984).

nitric acid. During daylight hours, the dominant loss process for NO_3 is photolysis (Table 4.1). Under nighttime conditions, the path from NO_2 to NO_3 to N_2O_5 to HNO_3 is predicted to be dominant (Russell et al., 1985; Stockwell and Calvert, 1983).

4.6. CHEMISTRY OF SULFUR DIOXIDE

From a thermodynamic point of view, sulfur dioxide has a strong tendency to react with oxygen in air,

$$2SO_2 + O_2 \xrightarrow{1} 2SO_3$$

The equilibrium concentration ratio of $[SO_3]/[SO_2]$ is about 8×10^{11} in air at 1 atm. and 25°C. However, the rate of reaction 1 is so slow under catalyst-free conditions in the gas phase that it can be totally neglected as a source of SO_3. If formed, SO_3 reacts so rapidly with water vapor to form sulfuric acid,

$$SO_3 + H_2O \xrightarrow{2} H_2SO_4(aq)$$

that any process in which SO_3 is formed in a moist atmosphere can be considered equivalent to the formation of H_2SO_4.

To explain observed atmospheric oxidation of SO_2, one must turn to reactions other than the direct, uncatalyzed reaction of SO_2 and O_2. Sulfur dioxide absorbs light in the ultraviolet region of solar radiation incident in the troposphere, leading to excited states of the SO_2 molecule (Calvert et al., 1978),

$$SO_2 + h\nu \overset{3}{\to} SO_2^*$$

The excited states of SO_2, denoted here simply by SO_2^*, are nondissociative. Only quanta of light at wavelengths below 218 nm, which do not penetrate to the troposphere, provide sufficient energy to allow photodissociation of SO_2. If every molecule of SO_2 that is photoexcited to SO_2^* were oxidized through subsequent reaction with O_2 or other species, then the lifetime of SO_2 in the lower troposphere with overhead sun should be as low as 52 minutes (Sidebottom et al., 1972). We know, however, that the SO_2 lifetime is much longer than this. The reactions of photoexcited SO_2 molecules with other atmospheric species have been studied extensively (Calvert et al., 1978), and quenching of SO_2^* by atmospheric gases is expected to be the dominant process affecting SO_2^*. For example, in air at 1 atm., 298 K, and 50 percent relative humidity, quenching by N_2, O_2, and H_2O will occur 45.7, 41.7, and 12.2 percent of the time, respectively. Thus, we conclude that photooxidation of SO_2 is not an important source of SO_2 oxidation.

We turn next to the reactions of SO_2 with other atmospheric species. Possible reactants include: electronically excited O_2 molecules and reactive molecules and free radicals such as O, O_3, NO_2, NO_3, N_2O_5, OH, HO_2, CH_3O_2, and other peroxyalkyl radicals, $CH_3C(O)O_2$ and other acyl peroxy radicals, and H_2COO and other Criegee intermediates derived from ozone–alkene reactions. The potential candidate reactions are summarized in Table 4.7.

From estimates of the atmospheric concentration of each reactant species X and of the rate constant for its reaction with SO_2, k_x, the importance of the individual reaction can be judged from the estimated rate, $-d[SO_2]/dt = k_x[X][SO_2]$. Such an evaluation is given in Table 4.8 for the reactions of SO_2 with O, OH, HO_2, and CH_3O_2, which are potentially significant sources of SO_2 oxidation.

By far the most important of the gas phase reactions is seen to be

$$OH\cdot + SO_2 \underset{M}{\overset{4}{\to}} HOSO_2\cdot$$

Prevailing evidence indicates that the $HOSO_2$ radical formed in reaction 4 ultimately leads to the formation of H_2SO_4. Recent evidence also suggests that the concentration of OH in photooxidizing mixtures of HNO_2, NO, NO_2, and CO is insensitive to even large additions of SO_2 (Calvert and Stockwell, 1984);

TABLE 4.7. Rate Constants for Potentially Important Reactions of Ground State SO_2 and SO_3 Molecules in the Lower Atmosphere[a]

Reaction	$k,$[b] cm^3 molec^{-1} sec^{-1}
$O_2(^1\Delta_g) + SO_2 \rightarrow SO_4$ (biradical; cyclic) $O_2(^1\Delta_g) + SO_2 \rightarrow SO_3 + O$ $O_2(^1\Delta_g) + SO_2 \rightarrow O_2(^3\Sigma_g^-) + SO_2$	3.9×10^{-20}
$O_2(^1\Sigma_g^+) + SO_2 \rightarrow SO_4$ (biradical; cyclic) $O_2(^1\Sigma_g^+) + SO_2 \rightarrow SO_3 + O$ $O_2(^1\Sigma_g^+) + SO_2 \rightarrow SO_2 + O_2(^1\Delta_g)$	6.6×10^{-16}
$O + SO_2(+M) \rightarrow SO_3(+M)$	5.7×10^{-14}
$O_3 + SO_2 \rightarrow O_2 + SO_3$	$< 8 \times 10^{-24}$
$NO_2 + SO_2 \rightarrow NO + SO_3$	8.8×10^{-30}
$NO_3 + SO_2 \rightarrow NO_2 + SO_3$	$< 7 \times 10^{-21}$
$N_2O_5 + SO_2 \rightarrow N_2O_4 + SO_3$	$< 4 \times 10^{-23}$
$HO_2 + SO_2 \rightarrow OH + SO_3$ $HO_2 + SO_2(+M) \rightarrow HO_2SO_2(+M)$	$< 1 \times 10^{-18}$
$CH_3O_2 + SO_2 \rightarrow CH_3O + SO_3$	$< 1 \times 10^{-18}$
$(CH_3)_3CO_2 + SO_2 \rightarrow (CH_3)_3CO + SO_3$ $(CH_3)_3CO_2 + SO_2 \rightarrow (CH_3)_3CO_2SO_2$	$< 7.3 \times 10^{-19}$
$CH_3C(O)O_2 + SO_2 \rightarrow CH_3CO_2 + SO_3$ $CH_3C(O)O_2 + SO_2 \rightarrow CH_3C(O)O_2SO_2$	$< 7 \times 10^{-19}$
$OH + SO_2(+M) \rightarrow HOSO_2(+M)$	1.1×10^{-12}
$CH_3O + SO_2(+M) \rightarrow CH_3OSO_2(+M)$	5.5×10^{-13}
$RCHOO + SO_2 \xrightarrow{a} RCHO + SO_3$ $RCHOO + H_2O \xrightarrow{b} RCOOH + H_2O$	$k_a/k_b = 6 \times 10^{-5}$ $(R = CH_3)$
$SO_3 + H_2O \rightarrow H_2SO_4$	9.1×10^{-13}

[a] Calvert and Stockwell (1984).
[b] The rate constants are all expressed as second order reactions for 1 atm of air at 298 K.

TABLE 4.8.   Estimated Relative Contributions to
SO$_2$ Oxidation by Gas-Phase Reactions SO$_2$ + X $\xrightarrow{k}$

X	[X], molecule cm^{-3}	k, cm^3 molecule^{-1} sec^{-1}	$k[X]$, sec^{-1}
O	10^6	5.7×10^{-14}	5.7×10^{-8}
OH·	10^7	1.1×10^{-12}	1.1×10^{-5}
HO$_2$·	10^9	$< 1 \times 10^{-18}$	$< 10^{-9}$
CH$_3$O$_2$·	10^9	$< 1 \times 10^{-18}$	$< 10^{-9}$

thus, a mechanism in which OH is regenerated, such as

$$HOSO_2· + O_2 \rightarrow HO_2· + SO_3$$

$$HO_2· + NO \rightarrow NO_2 + OH·$$

$$SO_3 + H_2O \rightarrow H_2SO_4$$

seems favored over one that is chain terminating. The rate-determining step in the sequence is the initial OH–SO$_2$ reaction.

As we saw in Table 4.8, the rate of SO$_2$ oxidation by reaction with the OH radical can be estimated once [OH] has been estimated. In that table we used an urban [OH] estimate of 10^7 molecules cm^{-3}. Using Calvert and Stockwell's (1984) estimate of [OH] of 1.7×10^6 molecules cm^{-3} for the 24-hour average on a typical cloudless summer day in a relatively clean tropospheric air mass, we estimate a 24-hour averaged rate of SO$_2$ oxidation by the OH–SO$_2$ reaction of 0.7 percent hr^{-1} or 16.4 percent per 24-hour period. The wintertime rate is estimated to be lower due to lower [OH].

Chemistry of Reduced Sulfur Species and the Global Sulfur Cycle. Biogenic processes generally release sulfur species in reduced form, such as CS$_2$, H$_2$S, COS, CH$_3$SCH$_3$, and CH$_3$SSCH$_3$. These species are believed to be oxidized to SO$_2$. In the case of H$_2$S and CH$_3$SCH$_3$, the initial oxidation step is most likely reaction with OH, although the subsequent steps that lead to SO$_2$ are still uncertain. Because of large uncertainties in the emission rates and atmospheric abundances of reduced sulfur species, the production rate of SO$_2$ from these species cannot yet be established firmly. Table 4.9 presents a few of the

TABLE 4.9. Reactions of Reduced Sulfur Species: RSH Alkane Thiols, RSR′ Sulfides, RSSR′ Disulfides.

Species	Reaction[a,b]	Rate Constant at 298 K cm^3 molecule^{-1} sec^{-1} [a]	Mean Lifetime Based on $[OH] = 10^6$ molecules cm^{-3}
Hydrogen sulfide	$H_2S + OH\cdot \rightarrow H_2O + HS\cdot$	5.3×10^{-12}	53 hr
Methyl sulfide	$CH_3SH + OH\cdot \rightarrow CH_3S\cdot + H_2O$	$21\text{–}90 \times 10^{-12}$	13–3 hr
Dimethyl sulfide	$CH_3SCH_3 + OH\cdot \rightarrow CH_3SCH_2\cdot + H_2O$ $\rightarrow CH_3\cdot + CH_3SOH$	9.1×10^{-12}	31 hr
Carbon disulfide	$CS_2 + OH\cdot \rightarrow$ Products	$\leq 1.5 \times 10^{-15}$	$\geq 1.8 \times 10^5$ hr
Methyl disulfide	$CH_3SSCH_3 + OH\cdot \rightarrow CH_3SSCH_2\cdot + H_2O$ $\rightarrow CH_3SOH + CH_3S\cdot$	2.2×10^{-10}	1.2 hr
Carbonyl sulfide	$COS + OH\cdot \rightarrow$ Products	$\leq 9 \times 10^{-15}$	$\geq 0.3 \times 10^5$ hr

[a]Baulch et al. (1982).
[b]Grosjean (1984).

reactions of reduced sulfur species. With the exception of the H_2S–OH reaction, there is some uncertainty about the products of these reactions. The atmospheric residence times of these species, based on reaction with OH, are given in Table 4.9 based on an estimated [OH] of 10^6 molecules cm^{-3}. We use the lower OH concentration here since the oxidation of reduced sulfur species occurs predominantly in the free troposphere rather than the polluted urban atmosphere.

4.7. STRATOSPHERIC CHEMISTRY

4.7.1. Stratospheric Ozone

The most important trace constituent of the stratosphere is ozone. Although present only in a few ppm, ozone, nevertheless, is responsible for shielding the earth from ultraviolet (uv) radiation that is harmful to life. Figure 4.22 shows the vertical profile of O_3 in terms of molecules cm^{-3} and parts-per-million by

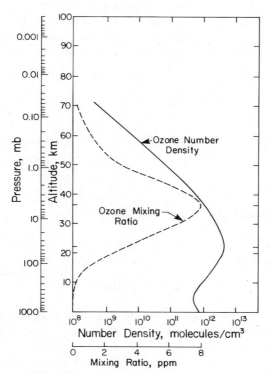

Figure 4.22. Atmospheric ozone concentration profiles. The ozone concentration is shown in terms of both number density and mixing ratio.

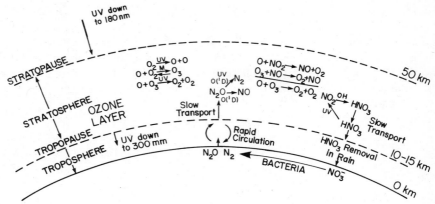

Figure 4.23. Natural stratospheric processes contributing to the formation and destruction of ozone (National Academy of Sciences, 1976).

volume. Because of the decreasing number density of air molecules, the two profiles do not match in shape.

The amount of ozone in the stratosphere is maintained as the result of a dynamic balance between formation and destruction processes. Formation occurs predominantly at altitudes above 30 km (Figure 4.23), where solar uv radiation with wavelengths less than 242 nm slowly dissociates molecular oxygen into oxygen atoms,

$$O_2 + h\nu \overset{1}{\rightarrow} O + O$$

These oxygen atoms rapidly combine with O_2 to form ozone,

$$O + O_2 + M \overset{2}{\rightarrow} O_3 + M$$

the net effect being the conversion of three molecules of O_2 to two molecules of O_3.

As we know, ozone itself absorbs solar radiation strongly in the wavelength region 240 to 320 nm,

$$O_3 + h\nu \rightarrow O_2 + O$$

It is this absorption that, in fact, shields the earth from harmful uv radiation. The photolysis of ozone is not, however, a true destruction mechanism because virtually all of the oxygen atoms produced by this reaction will rapidly combine once again with molecular oxygen to reform ozone. Nevertheless, these two steps do have an important net effect; they convert solar energy into heat, particularly in the upper stratosphere. Thus, besides providing a "shield" against the biologically harmful uv, the presence of ozone in the stratosphere produces the temperature inversion characteristic of that region.

The actual distribution of ozone in the stratosphere is determined to a large extent by transport processes. Ozone is produced mainly in the tropics at altitudes of between 25 and 35 km, but as a result of the motions (and compression) of air masses in the stratosphere, its highest concentrations (in molecules cm^{-3}) are found near the poles at altitudes of about 15 km.

Balancing the formation processes, reactions 1 and 2, are several that destroy ozone. One example is the reaction of ozone and oxygen atoms to produce molecular oxygen,

$$O_3 + O \xrightarrow{3} O_2 + O_2$$

The above scheme, involving only species derived from oxygen, was suggested by Chapman (1930) and has provided the basis for analysis of stratospheric ozone ever since. However, it has been learned over the last 30 years that chemical processes other than reaction 3 destroy large amounts of ozone (Johnston, 1975). The original Chapman scheme given above accounts for about 20 percent of the total natural destruction rate for stratospheric ozone, while transport of ozone to the earth's surface contributes an additional 0.5 percent.

About 10 percent of the destruction is caused by catalytic cycles involving hydrogen-containing species: free hydrogen atoms (H), hydroxyl (OH), and hydroperoxyl (HO_2), which can achieve the same effect as reaction 3 without being themselves removed. For example, reaction 4 followed by reaction 5 is identical in result to reaction 3,

$$O + HO_2\cdot \xrightarrow{4} OH\cdot + O_2$$

$$OH\cdot + O_3 \xrightarrow{5} HO_2\cdot + O_2$$

$$\text{NET:} \quad O + O_3 \rightarrow O_2 + O_2$$

These hydrogen-containing species are produced by the reaction of naturally occurring water vapor and methane with excited oxygen atoms, $O(^1D)$, from O_3 photolysis,*

$$O(^1D) + H_2O \rightarrow 2OH\cdot$$

$$O(^1D) + CH_4 \rightarrow CH_3\cdot + OH\cdot$$

*The mean residence time of CH_4 in the troposphere is sufficiently long so that some CH_4 migrates into the stratosphere.

A catalytic cycle involving NO and NO_2 provides the most important destruction process for ozone. This process accounts for most of the remaining 70 percent of the natural ozone destruction rate; there is also a small contribution from chlorine compounds (natural and man-made), the details of which are given in the next section. For the nitrogen oxides the dominant processes are

$$O + NO_2 \overset{6}{\to} NO + O_2$$

$$NO + O_3 \overset{7}{\to} NO_2 + O_2$$

$$\text{NET:} \quad O + O_3 \to O_2 + O_2$$

These processes again produce the same effect as reaction 3 without the nitrogen oxides being consumed.

The major natural source of NO_x in the stratosphere is provided by the oxidation of nitrous oxide (N_2O), which is produced by bacteria in soil and water. Although almost all of this nitrous oxide is converted by uv light into N_2 and O, about 1 percent reacts with the excited oxygen atoms, $O(^1D)$, formed by the action of uv radiation on ozone, to yield nitric oxide and thereby start the NO_x cycle,

$$O(^1D) + N_2O \to NO + NO$$

The NO_x molecules, in turn, are removed by the formation of nitric acid (HNO_3) by the $OH-NO_2$ reaction which occurs in the lower stratosphere. Just as the atmospheric motions slowly carry N_2O up from the troposphere to the altitudes where it is decomposed, these motions also carry HNO_3 downward from where it is formed to the troposphere, where it is removed by rain.

4.7.2. Chlorofluorocarbons and Stratospheric Ozone

Substances other than HO_x and NO_x can catalyze the destruction of ozone, notably atomic chlorine (Cl) and bromine (Br) and their oxides (ClO and BrO), as indicated by the following cycle:

$$O + ClO \to Cl + O_2$$
$$Cl + O_3 \to ClO + O_2$$
$$\text{NET:} \quad O + O_3 \to O_2 + O_2$$

The possible importance of ClO_x for catalytic destruction of ozone in the stratosphere was only recently recognized (Rowland and Molina, 1975).* There

---

*The term ClO_x is often used to describe both Cl and ClO as in the usage of NO_x for NO and NO_2.

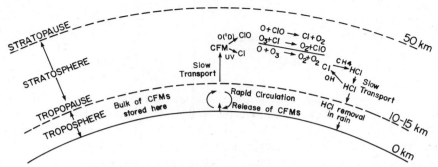

Figure 4.24. Simplified picture of the stratospheric fate of chlorofluoromethanes (CFMs) (National Academy of Sciences, 1976).

are a number of chlorine compounds, from natural as well as human sources, that can serve as sources for the ClO_x. The dominant compounds of chlorine in the troposphere are now known to be methyl chloride (CH_3Cl), very little of which is of industrial origin, the man-made chlorofluoromethanes, $CFCl_3$ (F-11) and CF_2Cl_2 (F-12), and carbon tetrachloride (CCl_4), natural as well as man-made. Human sources of lesser importance include trichloroethylene ($CCl_2{=}CHCl$) and the substances that are replacing it as cleaning agents, methyl chloroform (CH_3CCl_3) and F-113 ($CF_2ClCFCl_2$). The key species from the viewpoint of stratospheric effects are the chlorofluorocarbons $CFCl_3$ (F-11) and CF_2Cl_2 (F-12) whose atmospheric concentrations have increased from 1976 to 1981 by 37 percent (to 187 ppt) and 31 percent (to 325 ppt), respectively. Atmospheric lifetimes for F-11 and F-12 are believed to be about 60 and 110 years, respectively, with measures indicating a minimum lifetime for F-11 of 40 years.

Within a few years after release, these chlorine compounds, like N_2O, are distributed throughout the troposphere where their concentrations tend to become uniform. They rise slowly into the stratosphere (Figure 4.24). The chlorofluorocarbons (F-11, F-12, F-113) are highly inert in the troposphere and lower stratosphere and they will be transported upward in the stratosphere to altitudes of 25 to 50 km. There they are decomposed by uv light at wavelengths around 200 nm, with the production of Cl atoms.

The chlorine atoms then participate in the ClO_x catalytic cycle. This cycle may be be interrupted by conversion of the highly reactive Cl and ClO into inactive forms that do not destroy ozone. Two such processes have been identified. The chlorine atoms are rendered inactive mainly by reaction with methane to form hydrogen chloride

$$Cl + CH_4 \rightarrow HCl + CH_3$$

which acts as a temporary reservoir for active chlorine species in the stratosphere. Chlorine atoms are regenerated from hydrogen chloride by reaction with hydroxyl radicals:

$$OH + HCl \rightarrow H_2O + Cl$$

The destruction and regeneration of the active chlorine species, ClO_x, can occur many times before ultimate removal of the chlorine from the stratosphere. Removal is accomplished largely by net transport of the HCl from the stratosphere into the upper troposphere, where it is washed out by rainfall, as in the case of HNO_3 from the NO_x cycle. The time scale from release of chlorofluorocarbons at ground level to the removal from the atmosphere of its chlorine as HCl in rain is several decades, so that changes in chlorofluorocarbon emission rates are not manifested in the stratosphere for many years.

4.8. SUMMARY OF RATE CONSTANTS FOR GAS-PHASE ATMOSPHERIC REACTIONS

Tables 4.10 and 4.11 summarize a number of rate constants for reactions discussed in this chapter. For additional rate constants we refer the reader to Baulch et al. (1982) and Atkinson and Lloyd (1984).

APPENDIX

4.A.1. Chemical Reaction Rate Constant Units

In the cgs unit system the units of a rate constant k for a second-order chemical reaction,

$$A + B \overset{k}{\rightarrow}$$

are normally expressed as cm^3 molecule^{-1} sec^{-1}. When the concentrations of A and B are expressed in ppm, the appropriate units of k used are ppm^{-1} min^{-1}. The conversion between the two systems can be accomplished as follows. At standard temperature and pressure (STP) condition $p_s = 1$ atm, $T_s = 273$ K, 6.023×10^{23} molecules occupy a volume (V_s) of 22.4 l. A mole of the same gas at any other temperature and pressure occupies a volume V of

$$V = V_s \left(\frac{p_s}{p} \right) \left(\frac{T}{T_s} \right)$$

TABLE 4.10. Rate Constants for Atmospheric Reactions Involving Oxides of Nitrogen

Reaction	Rate Constant[a] cm^3 molecule^{-1} sec^{-1} units
$NO_2 + h\nu \longrightarrow NO + O$	Depends on light intensity
$O + O_2 + M \longrightarrow O_3 + M$	$6.0 \times 10^{-34} \ (T/300)^{-2.3}$[b]
$NO + O_3 \longrightarrow NO_2 + O_2$	$2.2 \times 10^{-12} \exp(-1430/T)$
$O + NO_2 \longrightarrow NO + O_2$	9.3×10^{-12}
$O + NO_2 \xrightarrow{M} NO_3$	2.0×10^{-12}
$NO + NO_3 \longrightarrow 2NO_2$	2.0×10^{-11}
$NO + NO + O_2 \longrightarrow 2NO_2$	$3.3 \times 10^{-39} \exp(530/T)$[b]
$NO_2 + NO_3 \xrightarrow{M} N_2O_5$	$4.7 \times 10^{-13} \exp(259/T)$
$N_2O_5 \longrightarrow NO_2 + NO_3$	$1.96 \times 10^{14} \exp(-10660/T)$[c]
$O_3 + NO_2 \longrightarrow NO_3 + O_2$	$1.2 \times 10^{-13} \exp(-2450/T)$
$O(^1D) + M \longrightarrow O(^3P) + M$	2.9×10^{-11}
$O(^1D) + H_2O \longrightarrow 2OH$	2.2×10^{-10}
$OH + NO \xrightarrow{M} HNO_2$	6.6×10^{-12}
$OH + NO_2 \xrightarrow{M} HNO_3 + M$	1.1×10^{-11}
$NO + NO_2 + H_2O \longrightarrow 2HNO_2$	$\leq 4.4 \times 10^{-40}$[b]
$N_2O_5 + H_2O \longrightarrow 2HNO_3$	$\leq 2 \times 10^{-21}$
$OH + CO \xrightarrow{O_2} HO_2 + CO$	2.2×10^{-13}
$OH + O_3 \longrightarrow HO_2 + O_2$	$1.6 \times 10^{-12} \exp(-940/T)$
$HO_2 + NO \longrightarrow NO_2 + OH$	$3.7 \times 10^{-12} \exp(240/T)$
$HO_2 + NO_2 \xrightarrow{M} HO_2NO_2$	1.4×10^{-12}
$HO_2NO_2 \xrightarrow{M} HO_2 + NO_2$	$1.3 \times 10^{14} \exp(-10418/T)$[c]
$HO_2 + O_3 \longrightarrow OH + 2O_2$	$1.4 \times 10^{-14} \exp(-580/T)$
$HO_2 + HO_2 \xrightarrow{H_2O, M} H_2O_2 + O_2$	$[2.2 \times 10^{-13} \exp(620/T)$ $+ 1.9 \times 10^{-33}[M] \exp(980/T)]$ $\times [1 + 1.4 \times 10^{-21}[H_2O] \exp(2200/T)]$[d]
$OH + H_2O_2 \longrightarrow HO_2 + H_2O$	$3.1 \times 10^{-12} \exp(-187/T)$

[a] Baulch et al. (1982).
[b] Third-order rate constant; units are cm^6 molecule^{-2} sec^{-1}.
[c] First-order rate constant; units are sec^{-1}.
[d] Kircher and Sander (1984).

TABLE 4.11. Rate Constants for RO_x–NO_x Reactions

Reaction	Rate Constant cm^3 molecule^{-1} sec^{-1} units
$CH_3O_2\cdot + NO \rightarrow NO_2 + CH_3O\cdot$	$4.2 \times 10^{-12}exp(180/T)$[a]
$C_2H_5O_2\cdot + NO \rightarrow NO_2 + C_2H_5O\cdot$	$4.2 \times 10^{-12}exp(180/T)$[b]
$CH_3O_2\cdot + NO_2 \rightarrow CH_3O_2NO_2$	4×10^{-12}[c]
$CH_3C(O)O_2\cdot + NO \rightarrow NO_2 + CH_3C(O)O\cdot$	$4.2 \times 10^{-12}exp(180/T)$[a]
$CH_3C(O)O_2\cdot + NO_2 \rightarrow CH_3C(O)O_2NO_2$	4.7×10^{-12}[a]
$CH_3C(O)O_2NO_2 \rightarrow CH_3C(O)O_2\cdot + NO_2$	$1.95 \times 10^{16}exp(-13543/T)$ sec^{-1}[a]
$CH_3O_2NO_2 \rightarrow CH_3O_2\cdot + NO_2$	< 1 sec^{-1}[d]
$CH_3O\cdot + NO \rightarrow CH_3ONO$	3×10^{-11}[a,e]
$\rightarrow HCHO + HNO$	$\leq 1.3 \times 10^{-12}$
$RO\cdot + NO \rightarrow RONO$	3×10^{-11}[e]
$\rightarrow R'R''CO + HNO$	6.6×10^{-12}
$CH_3O\cdot + NO_2 \rightarrow CH_3ONO_2$	1.5×10^{-11}[e]

[a] Baulch et al. (1982).

[b] Atkinson and Lloyd (1984).

[c] Sander and Watson (1980). Values for the rate constants of higher RO_2–NO_2 reactions are not currently available, but they can be inferred by considering the change in rate constant from $HO_2 + NO_2$ to $CH_3O_2 + NO_2$, namely 1×10^{-12} to 4×10^{-12} cm^3 molecule^{-1} sec^{-1}. Until data are available concerning the rate constants of the reactions of the higher peroxy radicals with NO_2, we have no choice but to assume that they all have the same high pressure value as does $CH_3O_2 + NO_2$. Although $CH_3O_2 + NO_2$ does not appear to be at its high pressure limit at atmospheric pressure, it is sufficiently close that it is reasonable to assume that the analogous reactions of the higher peroxy radicals are essentially at the high pressure limit at one atmosphere, and thus that their rate constants can be approximated by the high pressure limit for $CH_3O_2 + NO_2$, which is estimated to be approximately 6×10^{-12} cm^3 molec^{-1} sec^{-1} (Baulch et al., 1982). Thus, we recommend

$$RO_2\cdot + NO_2 \rightarrow RO_2NO_2 \, (R > CH_3) 6 \times 10^{-12} \, cm^3 \, molec^{-1} \, sec^{-1}.$$

[d] It is generally agreed that the thermal decompositions of the peroxynitrates, RO_2NO_2, are sufficiently rapid at normal temperatures that their formation reactions can be ignored. The thermal lifetimes of the alkyl peroxynitrates were originally estimated by Carter et al. (1979), based on semiquantitative data on t-butyl peroxynitrate stabilities; and based on these estimates, formation of alkyl peroxynitrates was estimated to be negligible. Current data support the assumption that the higher alkyl peroxynitrates will have lifetimes comparable to that of $CH_3O_2NO_2$, and hence their formation can be neglected, except perhaps at very low temperatures. In particular, Bahta et al. (1982) obtained

$$CH_3O_2NO_2 \overset{d}{\rightarrow} CH_3O_2\cdot + NO_2 \quad k_d = 2.1 \times 10^{16}exp(-10900/T) \, sec^{-1}$$

the lifetime of which at 291 K and 760 torr is 1 second.

[e] Cox et al. (1980) determined the photolysis rates of CH_3ONO and HNO_2 relative to that for NO_2 as:

$$k(CH_3ONO)/k(NO_2) = 0.47$$
$$k(HNO_2)/k(NO_2) = 0.33$$

Based on the rapid rate of reaction of alkoxy radicals with O_2, by decomposition or isomerization, and based on the relatively rapid photolysis rates of alkyl nitrites, one concludes that alkyl nitrite chemistry should not be important in atmospheric chemistry. In addition, since the rate of the RO–NO_2 reaction is about a factor of two slower than that of the RO–NO reaction, it too can be neglected in mechanisms.

So the number of molecules per cm^3 is given by ($V_s = 22.4$ 1)

$$\frac{\text{molecules}}{\text{cm}^3} = \frac{6.023 \times 10^{23}}{22.4(1/p)(T/273) \times 1000} = 7.34 \times 10^{21}(p/T)$$

The conversion between the two units for rate constants is given by

$$\frac{\text{cm}^3}{\text{molecule sec}} = \frac{60 \text{ sec}}{\text{min}} \times 7.34 \times 10^{21}\left(\frac{p}{T}\right)\frac{\text{molecules}}{\text{cm}^3} \times \frac{1}{10^6 \text{ ppm}}$$

$$= 4.40 \times 10^{17}\left(\frac{p}{T}\right)\frac{1}{\text{ppm min}}$$

Thus,

$$k\left(\text{ppm}^{-1} \text{ min}^{-1}\right) = 4.40 \times 10^{17}\left(\frac{p}{T}\right)k\left(\text{cm}^3 \text{ molecule}^{-1} \text{ s}^{-1}\right)$$

At 298 K, $p = 1$ atm, the conversion factor is 1.47×10^{15}.

The rate constant for a third order reaction

$$A + B + C \xrightarrow{k}$$

is expressed in cgs units as cm^6 molecule^{-2} sec^{-1} and in ppm-min units as ppm^{-2} min^{-1}. The conversion from cm^6 molecule^{-2} sec^{-1} to ppm^{-2} min^{-1} is accomplished as follows,

$$\frac{\text{cm}^6}{\text{molecule}^2 \text{ sec}} \times \frac{60 \text{ sec}}{\text{min}} \times \left[7.34 \times 10^{21}\left(\frac{p}{T}\right)\right]^2 \frac{\text{molecules}^2}{\text{cm}^6} \times \frac{1}{(10^6 \text{ ppm})^2}$$

$$= 3.23 \times 10^{33}\left(\frac{p}{T}\right)^2 \frac{1}{\text{ppm}^2 \text{ min}}$$

Thus,

$$k\left(\text{ppm}^{-2} \text{ min}^{-1}\right) = 3.23 \times 10^{33}\left(\frac{p}{T}\right)^2 k \left(\text{cm}^6 \text{ molecule}^{-2} \text{ s}^{-1}\right)$$

At 298 K, $p = 1$ atm, the conversion factor is 3.64×10^{28}.

The rate constant for a thermal reaction is conventionally written in the Arrhenius form $k = A_0\exp(-E_A/RT)$, where E_A is the activation energy [measured in kilocalories (kcal) per mole,] R is the universal gas constant, and T is the temperature. From the functional dependence of k on T we see that, depending on the value of the activation energy, the rate constant for a reaction has the potential of varying enormously with temperature. Most of the chemical reactions involving air pollutants for which activation energies have been determined have values of E_A less than 5 kcal mole^{-1}. For instance, the $NO-O_3$ reaction, has an activation energy of 2.5 kcal mole^{-1}. Increasing the temperature from 298 to 308 K increases the rate constant from 29.4 to 33.8 ppm^{-1} min^{-1}, a 15 percent change which, by itself, should have only moderate effect on observed atmospheric conversion rates. The activation energy of the NO_2-O_3 reaction, on the other hand, is 7.0 kcal mole^{-1}, and a 10 K in increase in temperature results in a 46 percent increase in the rate constant.

4.A.2. Kinetic Treatment of Combination and Dissociation Reactions

Many atmospheric reactions are of the form

$$A + B + M \rightarrow AB + M$$

where M is a third body, usually N_2 or O_2. The actual elementary processes in this reaction are

$$A + B \underset{-1}{\overset{1}{\rightleftharpoons}} AB^*$$

$$AB^* + M \overset{2}{\rightarrow} AB + M$$

where AB^* is an energetic intermediate whose excess energy must be removed by M to produce a stable AB. The rate of formation of AB is then

$$\frac{d[AB]}{dt} = k_2[AB^*][M]$$

Applying the pseudo-steady state approximation for $[AB^*]$,

$$[AB^*]_{ss} = \frac{k_1[A][B]}{k_{-1} + k_2[M]}$$

Thus,

$$\frac{d[AB]}{dt} = \left[\frac{k_1 k_2[M]}{k_{-1} + k_2[M]}\right][A][B]$$

and if we express the overall rate as

$$\frac{d[AB]}{dt} = k[A][B]$$

then k depends on $[M]$ as indicated above. The so-called low pressure limit is

$$k_0 = \lim_{[M] \to 0} k = \frac{k_1 k_2}{k_{-1}}[M]$$

in which case the overall rate of formation is third-order. The high-pressure limit is

$$k_\infty = \lim_{[M] \to \infty} k = k_1$$

which is independent of $[M]$.

For a combination reaction in the low pressure range, the rate constant is often reported as second-order expressed as the product of a third-order rate constant and the third body concentration (see, for example, Baulch et al., 1982). The transition between the third-order and the second-order range is represented by an expression of k/k_∞ as a function of $k_0/k_\infty = [M]/[M]_c$, where $[M]_c$ indicates the third body concentration for which the extrapolated k_0 would be equal to k_∞. The dependence of k on $[M]$ in general is complicated and has to be analyzed by unimolecular rate theory. For moderately complex molecules at not too high temperatures, the following relationship is used,

$$k = \frac{k_0 k_\infty}{k_0 + k_\infty} F = k_0 \left(\frac{1}{1 + [M]/[M]_c} \right) F$$

$$= k_\infty \left(\frac{[M]/[M]_c}{1 + [M]/[M]_c} \right) F$$

where F is the so-called broadening factor. Expressions for F are discussed by Baulch et al. (1982).

4.A.3. Calculation of Atmospheric Water Vapor Concentration

In carrying out calculations in atmospheric chemistry it is frequently necessary to have the concentration of water vapor in units of either $\mu g\ m^{-3}$ or ppm. For a given ambient temperature T, relative humidity RH is defined as the ratio of the partial pressure of water to its saturation vapor pressure at the same temperature,

$$\text{RH} = 100 \frac{p_{H_2O}}{p_{H_2O}^0}$$

where the factor of 100 is used because RH is usually expressed in percent. Alternatively, RH is the ratio of the actual mole fraction of water vapor y to that at saturation y_s,

$$\text{RH} = 100 \frac{y}{y_s}$$

Since the mole fraction is equivalent to the volume fraction, the water concentration in ppm is given by

$$[H_2O] = 10^6 y = 10^4\ \text{RH}\ y_s\ (\text{ppm})$$

TABLE 4.A.4. Ground Level Actinic Irradiance $I(\lambda_i)\Delta\lambda$ as a Function of Zenith Angle and Wavelength.
(Photons cm^{-2} sec^{-1} $\times$ 10^{-15})

Wavelength Range (nm)	Zenith Angle[a] (Deg)									
	0.0	10.00	20.00	30.00	40.00	50.00	60.00	70.00	78.00	86.00
285–295	0.000	0.000	0.0	0.0	0.0	0.0	0.0	0.0	0.0	0.0
295–305	0.040	0.038	0.033	0.025	0.016	0.007	0.002	0.000	0.0	0.0
305–315	0.439	0.431	0.401	0.351	0.281	0.198	0.110	0.039	0.009	0.001
315–325	0.955	0.944	0.901	0.826	0.717	0.571	0.389	0.194	0.064	0.009
325–335	1.613	1.594	1.538	1.440	1.292	1.083	0.803	0.463	0.203	0.039
335–345	1.713	1.696	1.645	1.555	1.416	1.215	0.936	0.573	0.269	0.061
345–355	1.892	1.875	1.824	1.733	1.591	1.383	1.243	0.684	0.328	0.077
355–365	1.951	1.933	1.885	1.798	1.662	1.459	1.164	0.749	0.363	0.083
365–375	2.397	2.378	2.323	2.224	2.067	1.831	1.480	0.972	0.477	0.107
375–385	2.318	2.301	2.251	2.161	2.019	1.803	1.475	0.988	0.491	0.106
385–395	2.341	2.325	2.279	2.195	2.059	1.852	1.534	1.047	0.529	0.111
395–405	3.174	3.153	3.093	2.984	2.810	2.541	2.125	1.474	0.758	0.156
405–415	3.993	3.968	3.896	3.765	3.556	3.232	2.725	1.919	1.003	0.202
415–425	4.119	4.095	4.025	3.898	3.696	3.378	2.875	2.059	1.097	0.215
425–435	4.222	4.118	4.051	3.390	3.735	3.428	2.938	2.129	1.151	0.223
435–445	4.617	4.512	4.442	4.317	4.113	3.793	3.274	2.402	1.321	0.251
445–455	5.209	5.182	5.101	4.958	4.728	4.366	3.783	2.800	1.559	0.292
455–465	5.615	5.585	5.498	5.344	5.099	4.715	4.099	3.055	1.721	0.319
465–475	5.750	5.721	5.636	5.485	5.242	4.484	4.248	3.193	1.821	0.333
475–485	5.799	5.771	5.688	5.541	5.304	4.918	4.327	3.277	1.887	0.340
485–495	5.784	5.756	5.676	5.533	5.305	4.944	4.352	3.317	1.926	0.342
495–505	5.887	5.857	5.773	5.625	5.390	5.022	4.422	3.377	1.970	0.342
505–515	5.935	5.905	5.818	5.666	5.425	5.053	4.450	3.405	1.994	0.339
515–525	5.932	5.903	5.818	5.669	5.433	5.067	4.472	3.434	2.020	0.338
525–535	5.980	5.950	5.866	5.717	5.482	5.116	4.521	3.476	2.045	0.331
535–545	5.927	5.899	5.816	5.670	5.439	5.080	4.495	3.462	2.040	0.322
545–555	5.910	5.881	5.797	5.650	5.420	5.061	4.479	3.452	2.037	0.315
555–565	5.969	5.940	5.853	5.703	5.467	5.103	4.514	3.479	2.052	0.309
565–575	6.058	6.028	5.941	5.789	5.551	5.183	4.585	3.534	2.081	0.303
575–585	6.174	6.144	6.058	5.905	5.666	5.296	4.714	3.629	2.148	0.311
585–595	6.226	6.197	6.111	5.958	5.722	5.354	4.754	3.686	2.194	0.320
595–605	6.269	6.240	6.152	5.997	5.758	5.387	4.785	3.714	2.218	0.324
605–615	6.312	6.282	6.192	6.036	5.793	5.421	4.815	3.742	2.242	0.327
615–625	6.321	6.292	6.205	5.937	5.638	5.452	4.858	3.798	2.303	0.349
625–635	6.330	6.301	6.217	5.838	5.482	5.482	4.900	3.854	2.363	0.372
635–645	6.421	6.392	6.306	6.039	5.743	5.562	4.979	3.935	2.438	0.400
645–655	6.513	6.483	6.395	6.240	6.004	5.641	5.058	4.015	2.512	0.429

TABLE 4.A.4. (*Continued*)

Wavelength Range (nm)	Zenith Angle[a] (Deg)									
	0.0	10.00	20.00	30.00	40.00	50.00	60.00	70.00	78.00	86.00
655–665	6.594	6.563	6.472	6.314	6.074	5.708	5.122	4.079	2.574	0.455
665–675	6.674	6.643	6.549	6.388	6.144	5.775	5.187	4.142	2.635	0.481
675–685	6.659	6.626	6.537	6.379	6.139	5.777	5.199	4.168	2.671	0.499
685–695	6.643	6.610	6.524	6.369	6.134	5.779	5.211	4.193	2.706	0.518
695–705	6.460	6.450	6.350	6.200	5.980	5.710	5.150	4.090	2.740	0.530
705–715	6.400	6.380	6.290	6.140	5.910	5.650	5.110	4.070	2.750	0.540
715–725	6.340	6.320	6.220	6.080	5.870	5.600	5.050	4.050	2.760	0.560
725–735	6.270	6.250	6.160	6.020	5.800	5.550	5.020	4.040	2.770	0.560
735–745	6.210	6.190	6.100	5.960	5.750	5.490	4.970	4.020	2.780	0.580
745–755	6.140	6.120	6.030	5.900	5.680	5.430	4.920	4.000	2.790	0.590
755–765	6.080	6.060	5.970	5.840	5.640	5.400	4.900	3.990	2.790	0.590
765–775	6.020	6.000	5.910	5.780	5.580	5.340	4.860	3.970	2.790	0.590
775–785	5.950	5.940	5.850	5.720	5.530	5.310	4.840	3.980	2.790	0.600
785–795	5.890	5.880	5.790	5.880	5.470	5.250	4.800	3.940	2.780	0.600
795–805	5.820	5.610	5.730	5.590	5.420	5.220	4.760	5.930	2.780	0.600

[a] The zenith angle is 0° when the sun is directly overhead and 90° at sunrise and sunset. It can be evaluated as a function of the latitude l, the solar declination angle d, and the hour angle h from

$$\cos z = \sin l \sin d + \cos l \cos d \cos h$$

The declination angle d depends on the day of the year and varies from 23°27′ on June 21 to −23°27′ on December 22. At solar noon the hour angle $h = 0$.

This equation can be written in terms of $p^0_{H_2O}$ and the atmospheric pressure p,

$$[H_2O] = 10^4 \, RH \, \frac{p^0_{H_2O}}{p} \, (ppm)$$

In order to evaluate this expression, the saturation vapor pressure must be known. McRae (1980) suggested that the following expression for $p^0_{H_2O}$ due to Richards (1971) be employed because of its ease of use in hand computation:

$$p^0_{H_2O}(T) = p_s \exp[13.3185a - 1.9760a^2 - 0.6445a^3 - 0.1299a^4]$$

$$(4.A.1)$$

where p_s is the standard atmospheric pressure of 1013.25 mb, and the parameter a is defined in terms of the ambient $T(K)$ and the steam temperature $T_s = 373.15$ K at p_s,

$$a = 1 - \frac{T_s}{T} = 1 - \frac{373.15}{T}$$

Equation (4.A.1) is valid to ±0.1 percent over a temperature range of −50 to 140°C.

REFERENCES

Atkinson, R., and Lloyd, A. C. "Evaluation of Kinetic and Mechanistic Data for Modeling of Photochemical Smog," *J. Phys. Chem. Ref. Data*, **13**, 315–444 (1984).

Atkinson, R., Aschmann, S. M., Carter, W. P. L., Winer, A. M., and Pitts, J. N., Jr. "Alkyl Nitrate Formation from the NO_x-Air Photooxidations of C_2–C_8 n-Alkanes," *J. Phys. Chem.*, **86**, 4563–4569 (1982).

Atkinson, R., Carter, W. P. L., and Winer, A. M. "Effects of Temperature and Pressure on Alkyl Nitrate Yields in the NO_x Photooxidations of n-Pentane and n-Heptane," *J. Phys. Chem.*, **87**, 2012–2018 (1983).

Bahta, A., Simonaitis, R., and Heicklen, J. "Thermodecomposition Kinetics of $CH_3O_2NO_2$," *J. Phys. Chem.*, **86**, 1849–1853 (1982).

Bass, A. M., Glasgow, L. C., Miller, C., Jesson, J. P., and Filkin, D. L. "Temperature Dependent Absorption Cross Sections for Formaldehyde (CH_2O): The Effect of Formaldehyde on Stratospheric Chlorine Chemistry," *Plan. Space Sci.*, **28**, 675–679 (1980).

Bass, A. M., Leadfort, A. E., Jr., and Lauffer, A. H. "Extinction Coefficients of NO_2 and N_2O_4," *J. Res. Nat. Bur. Stand.*, **80**, Section A, 143–166 (1976).

Baulch, D. L., Cox, R. A., Crutzen, P. J., Hampson, R. F., Jr., Kerr, F. A., Troe, J., and Watson, R. P. "Evaluated Kinetic and Photochemical Data for Atmospheric Chemistry: Supplement 1." CODATA Task Group on Chemical Kinetics, *J. Phys. Chem. Ref. Data*, **11**, 327–496 (1982).

Calvert, J. G., and Stockwell, W. R. "The Mechanism and Rates of the Gas Phase Oxidations of Sulfur Dioxide and Nitrogen Oxides in the Atmosphere," in *SO_2, NO, and NO_2 Oxidation Mechanisms: Atmospheric Considerations*, J. G. Calvert (Ed.), Butterworth, Boston, 1–62 (1984).

Calvert, J. G., Su, F., Bottenheim, J. W., and Strausz, O. P. "Mechanism of the Homogeneous Oxidation of Sulfur Dioxide in the Troposphere," *Atmos. Environ.*, **12**, 197–226 (1978).

Calvert, J. G., and Pitts, J. N., Jr. *Photochemistry*, Wiley, New York (1967).

Carter, W. P. L., Atkinson, R., Winer, A. M., and Pitts, J. N., Jr. "Evidence for Chamber-Dependent Radical Sources: Impact on Kinetic Computer Models of Air Pollution," *Int. J. Chem. Kinetics*, **13**, 735–740 (1981).

Carter, W. P. L., Atkinson, R., Winer, A. M., and Pitts, J. N., Jr. "An Experimental Investigation of Chamber-Dependent Radical Sources," *Int. J. Chem. Kinetics*, **14**, 1071–1103 (1982).

Carter, W. P. L., Lloyd, A. C., Sprung, J. L., and Pitts, J. N., Jr. "Computer Modeling of Smog Chamber Data: Progress in Validation of a Detailed Mechanism for the Photooxidation of Propene and n-Butane in Photochemical Smog," *Int. J. Chem. Kinetics*, **11**, 45–101 (1979).

Chameides, W. L., and Davis, D. D. "Chemistry in the Troposphere," *Chem. Eng. News.*, **60**, 38–52 (1982).

Chapman, S. "A Theory of Upper-Atmosphere Ozone," *Roy. Meteor. Soc.*, **3**, 103–125 (1930).

Cox, R. A., and Derwent, R. G. "The Ultraviolet Absorption Spectrum of Gaseous Nitrous Acid," *J. Photochem.*, **6**, 23–34 (1977).

Cox, R. A., Derwent, R. G., and Williams, M. R. "Atmospheric Photooxidation Reactions. Rates, Reactivity, and Mechanism for Reaction of Organic Compounds with Hydroxyl Radicals," *Environ. Sci. Technol.*, **14**, 57–61 (1980).

Cox, R. A., Derwent, R. G., Kearsey, S. V., Batt, L., and Patrick, K. G. "Photolysis of Methyl Nitrite: Kinetics of the Reaction of the Methoxy-Radical with O_2," *J. Photochem.*, **13**, 149–163 (1980).

Darnall, K. R., Carter, W. P. L., Winer, A. M., Lloyd, A. C., and Pitts, J. N., Jr. "Importance of RO_2 + NO in Alkyl Nitrate Formation from C_4–C_8 Alkane Photooxidations under Simulated Atmospheric Conditions," *J. Phys. Chem.*, **80**, 1948–1950 (1976).

Demerjian, K. L., Schere, K. L., and Peterson, J. T. "Theoretical Estimates of Actinic (Spherically Integrated) Flux and Photolytic Rate Constants of Atmospheric Species in the Lower Troposphere," *Adv. Environ. Sci. Technol.*, **10**, 369–459 (1980).

DeMore, W. B., Watson, R. T., Howard, C. J., Golden, D. M., Molina, M. J., Hampson, R. F., Kurylo, M., and Ravishankara, A. R. "Chemical Kinetics and Photochemical Data for Use in Stratospheric Modeling," Jet Propulsion Laboratory Publication 82-57, California Institute of Technology, Pasadena (1982).

Graham, R. A., and Johnston, H. S. "The Photochemistry of NO_3 and the Kinetics of the N_2O_5–O_3 System," *J. Phys. Chem.*, **82**, 254–268 (1978).

Grosjean, D. "Gas-Phase Chemistry of Organo-Sulfur Compounds," Conference on Gas-Liquid Chemistry of Natural Waters, Brookhaven National Laboratory, Upton, NY, April 1984.

Haagen-Smit, A. J. "Chemistry and Physiology of Los Angeles Smog," *Ind. Eng. Chem.*, **44**, 1342–1346 (1952).

Haagen-Smit, A. J., and Fox, M. "Ozone Formation in Photochemical Oxidation of Organic Substances," *Ind. Eng. Chem.*, **48**, 1484–1487 (1956).

Harker, A. B., Ho, W., and Ratto, J. J. "Photodissociation Quantum Yield of NO_2 in the Region 375–420 nm," *Chem. Phys. Lett.*, **50**, 394–397 (1977).

Herron, J. T., Martinez, R. I., and Huie, R. E. "Kinetics and Energetics of the Criegee Intermediate in the Gas Phase. I. The Criegee Intermediate in Ozone-Alkene Reactions," *Int. J. Chem. Kinetics*, **14**, 201–224 (1982).

Holmes, J. R., O'Brien, R. J., Crabtree, J. H., Hecht, T. A., and Seinfeld, J. H. "Measurement of Ultraviolet Radiation Intensity in Photochemical Smog Studies," *Environ. Sci. Technol.*, **7**, 519–523 (1973).

Horowitz, A., and Calvert, J. G. "Wavelength Dependence of the Primary Processes in Acetaldehyde Photolysis," *J. Phys. Chem.*, **86**, 3105–3114 (1982).

Johnston, H. S. "Pollution of the Stratosphere," *Ann. Rev. Phys. Chem.*, **26**, 315–338 (1975).

Jones, I. T. N., and Bayes, K. D. "Photolysis of Nitrogen Dioxide," *J. Chem. Phys.*, **59**, 4836–4844 (1973).

Kircher, C. C., and Sander, S. P. "Kinetics and Mechanism of HO_2 and DO_2 Disproportionations," *J. Phys. Chem.*, **88**, 2082–2090 (1984).

Leone, J. A., and Seinfeld, J. H. "Updated Chemical Mechanism for Atmospheric Photooxidation of Toluene," *Int. J. Chem. Kinetics*, **16**, 159–193 (1984).

Luther, F. M., and Gelinas, R. J. "Effects of Molecular Multiple Scattering and Surface Albedo on Atmospheric Photodissociation Rates," *J. Geophys. Res.*, **81**, 1125–1132 (1976).

Magnotta, F., and Johnston, H. S. "Photodissociation Quantum Yields for the NO_3 Free Radical," *Geophys. Res. Lett.*, **7**, 769–772 (1980).

Martinez, R. I., Herron, J. T., and Huie, R. E. "The Mechanism of Ozone-Alkene Reactions in the Gas Phase. A Mass Spectrometric Study of the Reactions of Eight Linear and Branched-Chain Alkenes," *J. Amer. Chem. Soc.*, **103**, 3807–3820 (1981).

McRae, G. J. "A Simple Procedure for Calculating Atmospheric Water Vapor Concentration," *J. Air Pollution Control Assoc.*, **30**, 394–396 (1980).

McRae, G. J., and Russell, A. G. "Dry Deposition of Nitrogen-Containing Species," in *Deposition Both Wet and Dry*, B. B. Hicks (Ed.), Butterworth, Boston, 153–193 (1984).

Molina, L. T., Schinke, S. D., and Molina, M. J. "Ultraviolet Absorption Spectrum of Hydrogen Peroxide Vapor," *Geophys. Res. Lett.*, **4**, 580–582 (1977).

Moortgat, G. K., Klippel, W., Mobius, K. H., Seiler, W., and Warneck, P. "Laboratory Measurements of Photolytic Parameters for Formaldehyde," Federal Aviation Administration Report #FAA-EE-80-47, U.S. Dept. of Transportation, Washington, D.C. (1980).

Moshiri, E., and O'Brien, R. J. "A Concise Hydrocarbon-Specific Photochemical Ozone Model," Division of Environmental Chemistry, American Chemical Society Meeting, St. Louis, MO, April 1984.

National Academy of Sciences, *Halocarbons: Effects on Stratospheric Ozone*, Panel on Atmospheric Chemistry, Washington, D.C., 1976.

National Center for Atmospheric Research, *Regional Acid Deposition: Models and Physical Processes*, Boulder, CO (1982).

Pitts, J. N., Jr., Sharp, J. H., and Chan, S. I. "Effects of Wavelength and Temperature on Primary Processes in the Photolysis of Nitrogen Dioxide and a Spectroscopic-Photochemical Determination of the Dissociation Energy," *J. Chem. Phys.*, **42**, 3655–3662 (1964).

Richards, J. M. "A Simple Expression for the Saturation Vapor Pressure of Water in the Range 50 to 140°C," *British J. Appl. Phys.*, **D4**, L15 (1971).

Rowland, F. S., and Molina, M. J. "Chlorofluoromethanes in the Environment," *Rev. Geophys. Space Phys.*, **13**, 1–35 (1975).

Russell, A. G., McRae, G. J., and Cass, G. R. "The Dynamics of Nitric Acid Production and the Fate of Nitrogen Oxides," *Atmos. Environ.*, **19**, 893–903 (1985).

Sander, S. P., and Watson, R. T. "Kinetics Studies of the Reactions of CH_3O_2 with NO, NO_2, and CH_3O_2 at 298 K," *J. Phys. Chem.*, **84**, 1664–1674 (1980).

Sidebottom, H. W., Badcock, C. C., Jackson, G. E., Calvert, J. G., Reinhardt, G. W., and Damon, E. K. "Photooxidation of Sulfur Dioxide," *Environ. Sci. Technol.*, **6**, 72–79 (1972).

Stockwell, W. R., and Calvert, J. G. "The Near Ultraviolet Absorption Spectrum of Gaseous HONO and N_2O_3," *J. Photochem.*, **8**, 193–208 (1978).

Stockwell, W. R., and Calvert, J. G. "The Mechanism of NO_3 and HONO Formation in the Nighttime Chemistry of the Urban Atmosphere," *J. Geophys. Res.*, **88**, 6673–6682 (1983).

Volz, A., Ehhalt, D. H., and Derwent, R. G. "Seasonal and Latitudinal Variation of ^{14}CO and the Tropospheric Concentration of OH Radicals," *J. Geophys. Res.*, **86**, 5163–5171 (1981).

Weaver, J., Meagher, J., and Heicklen, J. "Photooxidation of CH_3CHO Vapor at 3130A," *J. Photochem.*, **6**, 111–126 (1977).

Zafonte, L., Rieger, E. L., and Holmes, J. R. "Nitrogen Dioxide Photolysis in the Los Angeles Atmosphere," *Environ. Sci. Technol.*, **11**, 483–487 (1977).

Zimmerman, P. R., Greenberg, J. P., Wandiga, S. O., and Crutzen, P. J. "Termites, A Potentially Large Source of Atmospheric Methane, Carbon Dioxide, and Molecular Hydrogen," *Science*, **218**, 563–565 (1982).

PROBLEMS

4.1. Consider the following reaction system:

$$A \overset{1}{\rightarrow} B$$

$$B + M \overset{2}{\rightarrow} C$$

Assume M is present in great excess, so that $[M] \cong$ constant. The concentrations of B and C are zero at $t = 0$.

(a) Derive analytical expressions for the exact dynamic behavior of this system over time. Show mathematically under what conditions the pseudo-steady approximation (PSSA) can be made for $[B]$.

(b) Use the PSSA to derive a simpler set of equations for the concentrations of A, B, and C.

(c) Draw a graph (on log–log paper) that compares the exact behavior of the system to calculations based on the PSSA for the following three sets of conditions. Discuss your results.

Set 1	Set 2	Set 3
$[M] = 10^5$	$[M] = 10^5$	$[M] = 10^5$
$[A]_0 = 10^2$	$[A]_0 = 10^2$	$[A]_0 = 10^2$
$k_1 = 10^{-5}$	$k_1 = 10^{-3}$	$k_1 = 10^{-1}$
$k_2 = 10^{-6}$	$k_2 = 10^{-6}$	$k_2 = 10^{-6}$

4.2. The following is a chemical reaction mechanism for the atmospheric photooxidation of formaldehyde and acetaldehyde:

$$NO_2 + h\nu \xrightarrow{1} NO + O$$

$$O + O_2 + M \xrightarrow{2} O_3 + M$$

$$O_3 + NO \xrightarrow{3} NO_2 + O_2$$

$$HCHO + h\nu \xrightarrow{4a} 2HO_2\cdot + CO$$

$$\xrightarrow{4b} H_2 + CO$$

$$HCHO + OH\cdot \xrightarrow{5} HO_2\cdot + CO + H_2O$$

$$CH_3CHO + h\nu \xrightarrow{6} CH_3O_2\cdot + HO_2\cdot + CO$$

$$CH_3CHO + OH\cdot \xrightarrow{7} CH_3C(O)O_2\cdot + H_2O$$

$$HO_2\cdot + NO \xrightarrow{8} NO_2 + OH\cdot$$

$$CH_3O_2\cdot + NO \xrightarrow{9} NO_2 + HCHO + HO_2\cdot$$

$$CH_3C(O)O_2\cdot + NO \xrightarrow{10} NO_2 + CH_3O_2\cdot + CO_2$$

$$CH_3C(O)O_2\cdot + NO_2 \underset{12}{\overset{11}{\rightleftarrows}} CH_3C(O)O_2NO_2$$

$$OH\cdot + NO_2 \xrightarrow{13} HNO_3$$

Show that by using the PSSA the mechanism can be written as

$$NO_2 + h\nu \underset{3}{\overset{1}{\rightleftarrows}} NO + O_3$$

$$HCHO + h\nu \overset{4a}{\rightarrow} 2NO_2 - 2NO + 2OH\cdot + CO$$

$$\overset{4b}{\rightarrow} H_2 + CO$$

$$HCHO + OH\cdot \overset{5}{\rightarrow} NO_2 - NO + OH\cdot + CO + H_2O$$

$$CH_3CHO + h\nu \overset{6}{\rightarrow} 3NO_2 - 3NO + HCHO + 2OH\cdot + CO$$

$$CH_3CHO + OH\cdot \overset{7}{\rightarrow} CH_3C(O)O_2\cdot + H_2O$$

$$CH_3C(O)O_2\cdot + NO \overset{10}{\rightarrow} 3NO_2 - 2NO + HCHO + OH\cdot + CO_2$$

$$CH_3C(O)O_2\cdot + NO_2 \underset{12}{\overset{11}{\rightleftarrows}} CH_3C(O)O_2NO_2 .$$

$$OH\cdot + NO_2 \overset{13}{\rightarrow} HNO_3$$

and that the chain length of the system is given by

$$L_c = 1 + \frac{k_5[HCHO] + k_7[CH_3CHO]}{k_{13}[NO_2]}$$

4.3. Alkylperoxynitrates, RO_2NO_2, can be presumed to decompose according to the following mechanism,

$$RO_2NO_2 \underset{2}{\overset{1}{\rightleftarrows}} RO_2\cdot + NO_2$$

$$RO_2\cdot + RO_2\cdot \overset{3}{\rightarrow} 2RO\cdot + O_2$$

$$RO\cdot + NO_2 \overset{4}{\rightarrow} RONO_2$$

Let us assume that a sample of RO_2NO_2 decomposes in a reactor and its decay is observed. We desire to estimate k_1 from that rate of disappearance. To analyze the system we assume that both $RO_2\cdot$ and NO_2 are in pseudo-steady state and that $[RO_2] \cong [NO_2]$.

Show that the observed first-order rate constant for RO_2NO_2 decay is related to the fundamental rate constants of the system by

$$k_{obs} = k_1\left\{1 - \frac{k_2}{k_2 + 2k_3}\right\}$$

Thus, given k_{obs} and values for k_2 and k_3, k_1 can be determined.

4.4. In Section 4.2.2 we considered the photooxidation of CO in the presence of NO_x. By invoking the PSSA we derived rate equations for $[NO_2]$, $[NO]$, and $[CO]$. Integrate these equations numerically for the following three sets of conditions and plot $[NO_2]$, $[NO]$, $[CO]$, and $[O_3]$ as a function of time from $t = 0$ to $t = 3000$ hr. Assume $T = 300$ K and RH = 50%.

<table>
<tr><td></td><td colspan="3">Initial conditions (ppm)</td></tr>
<tr><td></td><td>1</td><td>2</td><td>3</td></tr>
<tr><td>$[NO_2]_0$</td><td>0.1</td><td>0.2</td><td>1.0</td></tr>
<tr><td>$[NO]_0$</td><td>0.5</td><td>0.5</td><td>0.5</td></tr>
<tr><td>$[CO]_0$</td><td>10</td><td>10</td><td>10</td></tr>
</table>

In each case you should assume the photolysis rate constant for NO_2 as:

$$k_{NO_2} = 0.533 \text{ min}^{-1}$$

Discuss your results in terms of the conversion of NO to NO_2 and the accumulation of O_3.

4.5. Pitts ["Mechanisms of Photochemical Reactions in Urban Air. Volume I. Chemistry Studies," U.S. Environmental Protection Agency Report EPA-600/3-77-014a, 1977] reported the results of an experiment involving the photooxidation of azomethane $(CH_3N_2CH_3)$ in the presence of NO and air (Figure P4.1). The initial conditions for the experiment were:

$$
\begin{array}{ll}
CH_3N_2CH_3 & 132 \text{ mtorr} \\
O_2 & 2830 \text{ mtorr} \\
NO & 38 \text{ mtorr}
\end{array}
$$

(1 mtorr = 1.316 ppm) and the total pressure in the reactor was 1 atm.

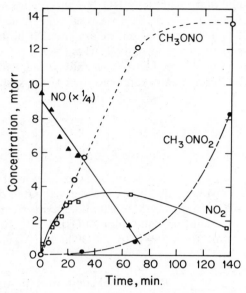

Figure P4.1. Time dependence of CH_3ONO, CH_3ONO_2, NO_2, and NO in the photooxidation of azomethane in the presence of NO (Pitts, 1977).

The following set of reactions has been proposed to describe this system:

$$CH_3N_2CH_3 + h\nu \xrightarrow[2O_2]{1} 2CH_3O_2{\cdot} + N_2$$

$$CH_3O_2{\cdot} + NO \xrightarrow{2} CH_3O{\cdot} + NO_2$$

$$CH_3O_2{\cdot} + NO_2 \underset{3r}{\overset{3f}{\rightleftharpoons}} CH_3O_2NO_2$$

$$CH_3O{\cdot} + NO \xrightarrow{4} CH_3ONO$$

$$CH_3O{\cdot} + NO_2 \xrightarrow{5} CH_3ONO_2$$

$$CH_3O{\cdot} + O_2 \xrightarrow{6} HCHO + HO_2{\cdot}$$

$$HO_2{\cdot} + NO \xrightarrow{7} NO_2 + OH{\cdot}$$

$$OH{\cdot} + NO_2 \xrightarrow{8} HNO_3$$

The spectral distribution and light intensity were not reported, and, therefore, the photolysis rate constant k_1 is unknown. Rate constants for reactions 2 to 8 are given in Chapter 4. (For reaction 6, $k_6 = 1.3 \times 10^{-13}\exp(-1350/T)$ cm^3 molecule^{-1} sec^{-1}.) If k_1 is treated as an adjustable parameter, determine whether the above mechanism is capable of explaining the experimental data.

4.6. Moshiri and O'Brien (1984) have proposed the following simplified mechanism for predicting O_3 formation in photochemical smog systems:

$$HC + OH \overset{1}{\rightarrow} aRO_2 + P \qquad \text{Hydrocarbon loss and}$$
$$\text{product formation}$$

$$P + OH \overset{2}{\rightarrow} bRO_2 + \text{loss} \qquad \text{Product loss}$$

$$P + h\nu \overset{p}{\rightarrow} cRO_2 + \text{loss} \qquad \text{Product photolysis}$$

$$RO_2 + NO \overset{3}{\rightarrow} NO_2 + \text{loss} \qquad \text{NO photooxidation}$$

$$NO_2 + h\nu \overset{4}{\underset{5}{\rightleftarrows}} NO + O_3 \qquad \text{Photostationary state}$$

$$\text{Everything} \overset{d}{\rightarrow} \text{loss} \qquad \text{Dilution}$$

In this mechanism, HO_2 radicals are lumped with RO_2, and, to a first approximation, all RO_2 are assumed to react with NO. This mechanism does not predict the OH concentration, taking instead the quantity $k_1[OH] = m$ as an input hydrocarbon reactivity parameter.

(a) Show that the mechanism can be used to predict the number of net NO photooxidations produced per hydrocarbon consumed,

$$\frac{d([NO]-[O_3])}{d[HC]}$$

$$= \frac{m\left(a[HC] + bk_2/k_1[P]\right) + ck_p[P] + k_d([NO]-[O_3])}{(m + k_d)[HC]}$$

Use of the quantity $[NO]-[O_3]$ as net NO oxidized effectively cancels out the photostationary state; thus, ozone is simply "negative nitric oxide."

(b) To solve the equation in part (a), product concentration $[P]$ must be expressed as a function of parent hydrocarbon concentration $[HC]$. Show that

$$[P] = \frac{mz_1[HC]}{z_2 - z_1^2} + \left(\frac{mz_1[HC]_0}{z_1^2 - z_2}\right)\left(\frac{[HC]}{[HC]_0}\right)^{z_2/z_1^2}$$

where $z_1 = m + k_d$ and $z_2 = (k_2m/k_1 + k_d + k_p)z_1$.

The two equations derived express the ozone-forming ability of any single hydrocarbon in terms of the hydrocarbon's rate parameters, a, b, and k_2/k_1, the overall dilution rate k_d, and the effective hydrocarbon reactivity, $m = k_1[OH]$. Moshiri and O'Brien (1984) illustrate fits of this mechanism to laboratory data by adjusting a, b, and k_2/k_1. The value of m is calculated by subtracting the dilution rate from a semilog plot of HC versus time.

4.7. When nitrogen oxides (NO_x) emissions are reported, they are frequently expressed in terms of equivalent emissions of nitrogen dioxide (NO_2) even though the exhaust NO_x is composed primarily of nitric oxide (NO). Unless the initial NO_2/NO_x ratio is specified from instack measurements it is necessary to establish appropriate fractions for reconstructing the actual emission levels of NO and NO_2. Depending on the source and the characteristics of its combustion process, the fraction can vary from approximately 1 to 10 percent. In addition to the NO_2 formed during combustion, some small quantities can be formed in the exhaust gases by the third-order reaction

$$NO + NO + O_2 \xrightarrow{k} 2NO_2$$

This reaction step is normally ignored in atmospheric reaction mechanisms because of the low ambient levels of NO. The objective of this problem is to develop a simple model that can be used to estimate the fraction of NO that is converted to NO_2 in the vicinity of a source.

(a) If the plume leaving a source can be modeled as a well-mixed reactor of variable volume across each transverse section, then show that the nitric oxide (NO) decay rate in a plume element is given by

$$\frac{d[NO]}{dt} = -2k[NO]^2[O_2] + \frac{1}{D(t)}\frac{dD(t)}{dt}([NO]-[NO]^b)$$

where $D(t)$ is the plume dilution factor, defined as $A_0/A(t)$, the ratio of the initial plume cross-sectional area to that at time t, and $[NO]^b$ is the background concentration of nitric oxide. Show that nitrogen mass constraint enables the direct calculation of $[NO_2]$ from

$$[NO_2] = D(t)[NO_x]_0 + [1 - D(t)][NO_x]^b - [NO]]$$

(b) The reaction rate constant k in air is (Baulch et al., 1982)

$$k = \frac{1.066 \times 10^{-5}}{T^2}\exp(530/T)\ ppm^{-2}\ min^{-1}$$

While entrainment of cool ambient air into the plume causes an increase in the magnitude of $k(T)$, the plume dilution also results in a reduction of NO. This interplay between cooling and dilution can be described by integrating the species rate equation. If the background contribution in the equation for $d[NO]/dt$ is ignored, then show that the NO concentration decay is given by

[NO]

$$= \frac{[NO]_0 D(t)}{1 + 2[NO]_0 \int_0^t k(T)\{D(t)[O_2] + [1 - D(t)][O_2]^b\} D(t)\, dt}$$

where within the plume, the oxygen and temperature distributions are given by

$$[O_2] = [O_2]^b + D(t)\big[[O_2]_0 - [O_2]^b\big]$$

$$T(t) = T^b + D(t)\big[T(0) - T^b\big]$$

(c) Using

$$D(t) = \exp[-0.15t]; \quad t < 30 \text{ sec}$$

given the initial and background conditions for $[NO_x]$, T, and $[O_2]$, solve the system of equations to give the conversion fractions for short travel times. Use an initial $[NO_2]_0/[NO_x]$ ratio of 0.05, $[O_2]_0 = 30000$ ppm, for [NO] varying from 200 to 2000 ppm calculate $[NO_2]$ as a function of travel time from 0 to 30 seconds for $[NO_2]_0 = 25,50,80,105$ ppm. Discuss your results.

4.8. One problem with the use of laboratory reactors to study atmospheric chemistry is the presence of substances that adhere to the walls of the reactor and remain to contaminate future experiments in the vessel. It has been found that this "wall effect" increases the reactivity of the mixture (Carter et al., 1981, 1982). Although the actual species absorbed and dissolved are unknown, the additional reactivity has been attributed to OH radicals being released from the walls.

(a) To estimate the OH present in a reactor, one can irradiate a mixture of NO_x in air with trace levels of two hydrocarbons whose OH-rate constants are known. If reaction with OH is the only significant removal process for the two hydrocarbons, show that the OH concentration can be determined from

$$[OH] = (k_a - k_b)^{-1} \frac{d \ln([B]/[A])}{dt}$$

where k_a and k_b are the rate constants for the reaction of OH radicals with hydrocarbons A and B, respectively.

(b) Let us consider the application of this technique using propane and propene, whose OH rate constants are

propane $6.6 \times 10^6 \, T^{-1}\exp(-680/T)$ $\text{ppm}^{-1} \, \text{min}^{-1}$
propene $1.8 \times 10^6 \, T^{-1}\exp(540/T)$ $\text{ppm}^{-1} \, \text{min}^{-1}$

The reactions of OH with propane and propene can be written as

$$C_3H_8 + OH\cdot \rightarrow 2NO_2 - 2NO + CH_3C(O)CH_3 + H_2O + OH\cdot$$

$$C_3H_6 + OH\cdot \rightarrow 2NO_2 - 2NO + HCHO + CH_3CHO + OH\cdot$$

Consider the following experimental conditions:

EXPT	$T(K)$	$k_1(\text{min}^{-1})$	RH(%)	$[NO]_0$ (ppm)	$[NO_2]_0$ (ppm)
1	303	0.49	0	0.411	0.099
2	303	0.49	50	0.499	0.115
3	303	0.49	100	0.411	0.049

In all experiments, $[C_3H_8]_0 = [C_3H_6]_0 = 10$ ppb.

Assume that the following reactions are taking place:

$$NO_2 + h\nu \overset{1}{\rightarrow} NO + O$$

$$O + O_2 + M \overset{2}{\rightarrow} O_3 + M$$

$$O_3 + NO \overset{3}{\rightarrow} NO_2 + O_2$$

$$O_3 + h\nu \overset{4a}{\rightarrow} O_2 + O \qquad\qquad k_{4a} = 0.068 \, k_1$$

$$\overset{4b}{\rightarrow} O_2 + O(^1D) \qquad\qquad k_{4b} = 0.001 \, k_1$$

$$O(^1D) + M \overset{5}{\rightarrow} O + M$$

$$O(^1D) + H_2O \overset{6}{\rightarrow} 2OH\cdot$$

$$OH\cdot + NO_2 \overset{7}{\rightarrow} HNO_3$$

These reactions establish a steady state OH concentration. When added to this system, propane and propene react with OH to produce no net increase in OH but each converts two molecules of NO to NO_2. (Under the conditions employed, reactions of propene with O and O_3 can be neglected.)

Compare the initial rates of conversion of NO to NO_2 in the absence and presence of propane and propene. Calculate the steady state OH concentration.

(c) The purpose of the experiment is to see how the theoretically predicted OH concentrations compare with those measured by the relative hydrocarbon decay technique. Show that if there is an unknown OH source in the reactor, R_u, its magnitude can be estimated from

$$R_u = k_7[\text{OH·}][\text{NO}_2]$$

where [OH·] is determined as in part (a) and [NO_2] is measured.

FIVE

Aqueous-Phase Atmospheric Chemistry

An important aspect of atmospheric chemistry concerns the reactions that occur in or on atmospheric particles and droplets. Although all atmospheric particles are, by no means, aqueous, the most important particulate phase chemistry involves the presence of liquid water. Thus, we confine our attention in this chapter to aqueous-phase atmospheric chemistry.

Like the gas phase, the aqueous phase encompasses extensive chemical transformations. And, like the gas phase, these chemical transformations are oxidative in their chemical nature. In addition to single-step elementary reactions, there are numerous rapid equilibria in the aqueous phase. Furthermore, aqueous-phase chemistry involves neutral free radicals, free radical ions, nonfree radical ions, and nonradical, nonionic species such as H_2O_2 and O_3.

Reactions occurring within or on atmospheric particles are sometimes referred to as heterogeneous. Normally, a heterogeneous reaction implies one occurring at an interface between two phases (e.g., gas–liquid, gas–solid, or liquid–solid). Reactions occurring within an aqueous droplet are really locally homogeneous but, when viewed from the standpoint of the volume of air in which the droplets reside, might be termed heterogeneous. True heterogeneous reactions may also be of importance in aqueous-phase atmospheric chemistry when certain transition metals that exist in solid form within the aqueous droplet act as catalysts for conversion of a dissolved species. One class of atmospheric heterogeneous reactions that is especially important is that referred to as gas-to-particle conversion. Such reactions involve the transfer of a vapor molecule to an aerosol particle or liquid droplet.

As considered here, particles will range from aerosols having diameters less than a micrometer, to fog and cloud droplets having diameters of 1 to 100 μm, to hydrometeors of diameter of 0.1 to 3 mm. Hydrometeors are composed of water in either the liquid (rain) or ice (snow) phase, and are sufficiently large to have an appreciable fall velocity and move, in part, independently of the surrounding air. Hydrometeors that reach the earth's surface are termed precipitation. Cloud droplets are composed of water in either the liquid or solid phase and are small enough such that they are borne by the atmospheric motions.

The predominant study of aqueous atmospheric chemistry has concerned sulfur conversion, and, consequently, a major portion of the present chapter is devoted to sulfur chemistry. A brief description of the fate of sulfur emissions serves to set the stage for what is to follow in this chapter. Sulfur, as emitted from a smoke stack, is primarily in the form of gaseous SO_2, perhaps with small amounts of SO_3, which, as we already know, will be rapidly converted to sulfuric acid if any water is present. Once in the atmosphere, SO_2 can be oxidized in the gas phase to H_2SO_4 by reacting with OH or other free radical species. The H_2SO_4 molecules produced in this manner will rapidly acquire water vapor and nucleate to form very small H_2SO_4/H_2O particles or condense on existing particles. (We discussed the kinetics of the gas phase SO_2 to H_2SO_4 conversion in Section 4.6; nucleation and condensation will be covered in Chapter 9.) The SO_2 can also be absorbed by dry or moist particles or droplets and then be oxidized to sulfate once in the particulate phase.

We have seen that the gas-phase oxidation of SO_2, predominantly by OH radicals, leads to rates of H_2SO_4 formation that are upwards of one percent per hour. Both laboratory and field observations of rates of SO_2 oxidation, however, exhibit rates of conversion larger than this and hence cannot be explained solely on the basis of gas-phase chemistry. The inescapable supposition is that solution-phase reactions can be important additional sources of sulfate and may, in fact, under certain conditions, dominate those in the gas phase.

A summary of estimated SO_2 oxidation rates based on field measurements in power plant, smelter, and urban plume studies carried out since 1975 is given in Table 5.1. Rates of SO_2 oxidation in industrial plumes range from 0 to 10 percent hr^{-1}, with those in urban plumes reaching values as high as 13 percent hr^{-1}. As might be expected, the highest SO_2 oxidation rates have been observed in daytime in highly polluted atmospheres associated with urban areas, whereas average rates of oxidation reported for long-range transport situations are generally in the range of 0.5 to 2 percent hr^{-1}. In general, SO_2 transformation rates have been estimated by measuring either the increase in submicron particle concentrations, inferred as H_2SO_4 mass, or the actual increase in filtered sulfate mass relative to the total sulfur concentration, or to an inert tracer, such as SF_6. Typical uncertainties in reported rates are 50 percent and may be even greater. The relative contributions of gas-phase and particulate-phase mechanisms to SO_2 oxidation in plumes cannot be determined from the present studies. As noted above, however, the importance of particulate-phase processes is inferred from observed oxidation rates that are too large to be explained on the basis of gas-phase chemistry alone.

Information on the transformations of NO_x to products in industrial and urban plumes is scarce. In measurements downwind of Los Angeles, Spicer et al. (1979) estimated typical rates of NO_x conversion to be 5 to 10 percent hr^{-1}. Other measurements by Spicer et al. (1981) in Boston lead to NO_x conversion

TABLE 5.1.   Field Measurements on the Rates of SO_2 Oxidation in Plumes

Plume Type Location	SO_2 Oxidation Rate (% hr^{-1})	Method	Reference
Power Plant			
Keystone (Pennsylvania)	0–10	$32_S/34_S$ ratio, change with oxidation	Newman et al. (1975)
Labadie (Missouri)	0.41–4.9	Total change in particle volume	Cantrell and Whitby (1978)
Muscle Shoals (Alabama)	0–5	Particulate sulfur to total sulfur ratio	Forrest and Newman (1977a)
Four Corners (New Mexico)	2–8	Cloud condensation nuclei (CCN) production (CCN to SO_2 ratios)	Pueschel and Van Valin (1978)
Labadie (Missouri)	0–4	Particulate sulfur to total sulfur ratio	Gillani (1978) Gillani et al. (1978) Husar et al. (1978)
Cumberland (Tennessee)	0–7	Particulate sulfur to total sulfur ratio	Meagher et al. (1978) Forrest et al. (1981)
Great Canadian Oil Sands (Alberta, Canada)	0–3	Particulate sulfur to total sulfur ratio	Lusis et al. (1978)
Keystone (Pennsylvania)	0–5	Particulate sulfur to total sulfur ratio	Dittenhoefer and dePena (1978)
Central (Washington)	0–6	Total change in particle volume	Hobbs et al. (1979)
Four Corners (New Mexico)	0.15–0.5	CCN production (CCN to SO_2 ratios)	Mamane and Pueschel (1980)
Sherburne County (Minnesota)	0–5.7	Total change in particle volume	Hegg and Hobbs (1980)
Big Brown (Texas)	0.4–14.9	Total change in particle volume; particulate sulfur to total sulfur ratio	Hobbs et al. (1979) Hegg and Hobbs (1980)
Smelter			
INCO Nickel (Copper Cliff, Canada)	0–7	Particulate sulfur to total sulfur ratio	Lusis and Wiebe (1976) Forrest and Newman (1977b) Chan et al. (1980)
Mt. Isa Mines (Mt. Isa, Australia)	0.25[a]	Particulate sulfur to total sulfur ratio	Roberts and Williams (1979)
Urban			
Los Angeles (California)	1.2–13	Particulate sulfur to total sulfur ratio	Roberts and Friedlander (1975)
St. Louis (Missouri)	7–12.5	Particulate sulfur to total sulfur ratio	Alkezweeny and Powell (1977)
St. Louis (Missouri)	3.6–4.2	Particulate sulfur to total sulfur ratio.	Chang (1979)

[a] Diurnal average rate.

rates ranging from 14 to 24 percent hr^{-1}. In contrast to the sulfur situation, it has been found that, in most cases, more than 95 percent of the NO_x conversion can be accounted for by gaseous HNO_3 and PAN, one exception being the Los Angeles area where significant particulate nitrate levels have been observed. We summarize in this chapter the current understanding concerning aqueous-phase NO_x chemistry.

5.1. ABSORPTION EQUILIBRIA AND HENRY'S LAW

Absorption of a species A in water can be represented by either of the reactions,

$$A(g) + H_2O \rightleftarrows A \cdot H_2O$$

$$A(g) \rightleftarrows A(aq)$$

where $A \cdot H_2O$ and $A(aq)$ are simply two different ways of writing A in the dissolved state. We will have occasion to use both forms of notation in this chapter. The equilibrium between gaseous and dissolved A can be expressed either in terms of an absorption equilibrium constant K_A,

$$K_A = \frac{[A \cdot H_2O]}{p_A} \ [\text{mole } l^{-1} \text{ atm}^{-1}]$$

the conventional units of which are indicated, or by a so-called Henry's law coefficient H_A,

$$[A \cdot H_2O] = H_A p_A$$

where p_A is the partial pressure of A in the gas phase and $[A \cdot H_2O]$ is the concentration of the equilibrium amount of dissolved gas A in solution. The customary units of the Henry's law coefficient H_A are $[\text{mole } l^{-1} \text{ atm}^{-1}]$, so we see that K_A and H_A are identical. The unit mole l^{-1} is customarily written as M, a notation that we will use henceforth.

If both gaseous and aqueous concentrations of A are expressed on a molar basis, then we can write

$$\frac{[A \cdot H_2O]}{[A(g)]} = \frac{H_A p_A}{p_A/RT} = H_A RT = \hat{H}_A$$

where $\hat{H}_A$ is a dimensionless form of Henry's law coefficient. In converting between H_A and $\hat{H}_A$, use $R = 0.082$ atm M^{-1} K^{-1}.

TABLE 5.2. Henry's Law Coefficients of Atmospheric Gases Dissolving in Liquid Water[a]

Gas	H, M atm^{-1} (298 K)
O_2	1.3×10^{-3}
NO	1.9×10^{-3}
C_2H_4	4.9×10^{-3}
$O_3{}^d$	9.4×10^{-3}
$NO_2{}^b$	1×10^{-2}
N_2O	2.5×10^{-2}
$CO_2{}^c$	3.4×10^{-2}
$SO_2{}^c$	1.24
$HNO_2{}^c$	49
$NH_3{}^b$	62
HCl	2.5×10^3
HCHO^f	6.3×10^3
H_2O_2	7.1×10^{4e}
$HNO_3{}^c$	2.1×10^5

[a] Adapted from Schwartz (1983) and Martin (1984a).
[b] Physical solubility only. Dissolved NO_2 reacts with liquid water.
[c] Physical solubility only. These species participate in acid-base equilibria that are not reflected in the values of H given.
[d] Ozone is actually a reacting solute in water (Roth and Sullivan, 1981). For our purposes here we will use only the Henry's law coefficient as presented here and as a function of temperature in Table 5.4. The Henry's law coefficient of Roth and Sullivan is presented as $H = 3.84 \times 10^7 [OH^-]^{0.035} \exp(-2428/T)$ [atm mole fraction^{-1}], defined by $p_A = H_A x_A$.
[e] A more recent measurement of the H_2O_2 Henry's law constant is that of Yoshizumi et al. (1984) who report $H_{H_2O_2} = 1.42 \times 10^5$ M atm^{-1} at 293 K.
[f] HCHO exists in solution primarily in the gem-diol form: HCHO + $H_2O \rightleftarrows H_2C(OH)_2$. The Henry's law coefficient given in the table includes both dissolved HCHO and $H_2C(OH)_2$.

Table 5.2 gives the Henry's law coefficients of some atmospheric gases in liquid water at 298 K. The values given reflect only the physical solubility of the gas, that is, only the equilibrium $A(g) + H_2O \rightleftarrows A \cdot H_2O$, regardless of the subsequent fate of $A \cdot H_2O$. Several of the species given in Table 5.2, once dissolved, either undergo acid-base equilibria or react with water. We will consider the effect of these further processes shortly. Those species having large Henry's law coefficients (i.e., $> 10^3$), are essentially completely absorbed by water.

TABLE 5.3. Thermodynamic Data for Henry's Law Coefficients

Gas	ΔH_{298}, kcal mole^{-1}
CO_2	-4.846
NH_3	-8.17
SO_2	-6.247
H_2O_2	-14.5
O_3	-5.04

Sources: Beutier and Renon (1978), Martin et al. (1981), Kirk and Othmer (1981), Liljestrand and Morgan (1981).

The temperature dependence of an equilibrium constant such as a Henry's law coefficient is given by van't Hoff's equation (Denbigh, 1971)

$$\frac{d \ln K}{dT} = \frac{\Delta H}{RT^2}$$

where ΔH is the increase in enthalpy when the reaction takes place from left to right. It is the negative of the heat evolved when the reaction takes place at constant T and p. Over small temperature ranges it may be assumed, as an approximation, that ΔH is independent of temperature and therefore that

$$\ln \frac{K(T_2)}{K(T_1)} = \frac{\Delta H}{R} \left(\frac{1}{T_1} - \frac{1}{T_2} \right)$$

Henry's law coefficients generally increase in value as T decreases, reflecting a greater solubility at lower temperatures. Table 5.3 gives values of ΔH_{298} for several of the gases of interest. The Henry's law constant for O_3 increases from 9.4×10^{-3} to 2.0×10^{-2} as T decreases from 298 K to 273 K, and that for SO_2 from 1.24 to 3.28 over the same temperature range.

5.2. AQUEOUS-PHASE CHEMICAL EQUILIBRIA

The ionization of water is

$$H_2O \rightleftarrows H^+ + OH^-$$

At equilibrium,

$$K_w' = [H^+][OH^-]/[H_2O]$$

where $K_w' = 1.82 \times 10^{-16}$ M at 298 K. The molar concentration of pure water can be incorporated into K_w' to give

$$K_w = [\mathrm{H}^+][\mathrm{OH}^-]$$

with a value of 1.0×10^{-14} M^2 at 298 K. For pure water, $[\mathrm{H}^+] = [\mathrm{OH}^-]$. Thus, at 298 K, $[\mathrm{H}^+] = [\mathrm{OH}^-] = 1.0 \times 10^{-7}$ M. Defining

$$\mathrm{pH} = -\log[\mathrm{H}^+]$$

we see that pH = 7.0 for pure water at 298 K.

5.2.1. Carbon Dioxide / Water Equilibrium

Absorption of CO_2 by water leads to the following equilibria,

$$CO_2(g) + H_2O \rightleftarrows CO_2 \cdot H_2O$$

$$CO_2 \cdot H_2O \rightleftarrows H^+ + HCO_3^-$$

$$HCO_3^- \rightleftarrows H^+ + CO_3^{2-}$$

The equilibrium constants for which are

$$K_{hc} = \frac{[CO_2 \cdot H_2O]}{p_{CO_2}}$$

$$K_{c1} = \frac{[H^+][HCO_3^-]}{[CO_2 \cdot H_2O]}$$

$$K_{c2} = \frac{[H^+][CO_3^{2-}]}{[HCO_3^-]}$$

where K_{hc} is the equilibrium constant for the hydrolysis of CO_2, and K_{c1} and K_{c2} denote the first and second dissociation equilibrium constants for dissolved CO_2. Note that K_{hc} is identical to the Henry's law coefficient H_{CO_2}.

The concentrations of the species in solution are given by

$$[CO_2 \cdot H_2O] = K_{hc} p_{CO_2}$$

$$[HCO_3^-] = \frac{K_{c1}[CO_2 \cdot H_2O]}{[H^+]} = \frac{K_{hc}K_{c1}p_{CO_2}}{[H^+]}$$

$$[CO_3^{2-}] = \frac{K_{c2}[HCO_3^-]}{[H^+]} = \frac{K_{hc}K_{c1}K_{c2}p_{CO_2}}{[H^+]^2}$$

The additional relation among the concentrations of the ions in solution is that of electroneutrality,

$$[H^+] = [OH^-] + [HCO_3^-] + 2[CO_3^{2-}]$$

which, by using the relations for $[OH^-]$, $[HCO_3^-]$ and $[CO_3^{2-}]$ can be placed in the form of an equation for the single unknown $[H^+]$,

$$[H^+] = \frac{K_w}{[H^+]} + \frac{K_{hc}K_{c1}p_{CO_2}}{[H^+]} + \frac{2K_{hc}K_{c1}K_{c2}p_{CO_2}}{[H^+]^2}$$

or

$$[H^+]^3 - (K_w + K_{hc}K_{c1}p_{CO_2})[H^+] - 2K_{hc}K_{c1}K_{c2}p_{CO_2} = 0$$

Given the temperature, which determines the values of K_w, K_{hc}, K_{c1}, and K_{c2}, and p_{CO_2}, $[H^+]$ can be computed from the above equation, from which all other concentrations can be obtained.

Assuming an ambient CO_2 concentration of 330 ppm, it can be shown that at 283 K the solution pH = 5.6. This value is often cited as the pH of "pure" rainwater.

5.2.2. Sulfur Dioxide / Water Equilibrium

Absorption of SO_2 in water results in

$$SO_2(g) + H_2O \rightleftarrows SO_2 \cdot H_2O$$

$$SO_2 \cdot H_2O \rightleftarrows H^+ + HSO_3^-$$

$$HSO_3^- \rightleftarrows H^+ + SO_3^{2-}$$

with

$$K_{hs} = \frac{[SO_2 \cdot H_2O]}{p_{SO_2}}$$

$$K_{s1} = \frac{[H^+][HSO_3^-]}{[SO_2 \cdot H_2O]}$$

$$K_{s2} = \frac{[H^+][SO_3^{2-}]}{[HSO_3^-]}$$

The concentrations of the dissolved species are given by

$$[SO_2 \cdot H_2O] = K_{hs} p_{SO_2}$$

$$[HSO_3^-] = \frac{K_{s1}[SO_2 \cdot H_2O]}{[H^+]} = \frac{K_{hs}K_{s1} p_{SO_2}}{[H^+]}$$

$$[SO_3^{2-}] = \frac{K_{s2}[HSO_3^-]}{[H^+]} = \frac{K_{hs}K_{s1}K_{s2} p_{SO_2}}{[H^+]^2}$$

The electroneutrality relation is

$$[H^+] = [OH^-] + [HSO_3^-] + 2[SO_3^{2-}]$$

which is written in terms of $[H^+]$ as

$$[H^+]^3 - \left(K_w + K_{hs}K_{s1} p_{SO_2}\right)[H^+] - 2K_{hs}K_{s1}K_{s2} p_{SO_2} = 0$$

The total dissolved sulfur in solution in oxidation state 4 is referred to as S(IV). (See Table 5.5 for the definition of oxidation state.)

$$[S(IV)] = [SO_2 \cdot H_2O] + [HSO_3^-] + [SO_3^{2-}]$$

The total dissolved sulfur, [S(IV)], can be related to the partial pressure of SO_2 over the solution by

$$[S(IV)] \doteq K_{hs} p_{SO_2}\left[1 + \frac{K_{s1}}{[H^+]} + \frac{K_{s1}K_{s2}}{[H^+]^2}\right]$$

Noting that K_{hs} is identical to the Henry's law coefficient H_{SO_2}, we can express the above equation in terms of a modified Henry's law coefficient $H^*_{S(IV)}$ as

$$[S(IV)] = H^*_{S(IV)} p_{SO_2}$$

where

$$H^*_{S(IV)} = H_{SO_2}\left[1 + \frac{K_{s1}}{[H^+]} + \frac{K_{s1}K_{s2}}{[H^+]^2}\right]$$

Since $H^*_{S(IV)}$ is always greater than H_{SO_2}, we note that the total amount of dissolved sulfur always exceeds that predicted by Henry's law for SO_2 alone. We also see that the total amount of dissolved S(IV) is quite pH-dependent. Note that similar relations to those for SO_2/H_2O hold for CO_2/H_2O, namely that the total dissolved CO_2 can be expressed in terms of a modified Henry's

TABLE 5.4. Thermodynamic Data for Calculating Temperature Dependence of Aqueous Equilibrium Constants

Equilibrium	ΔH_{298}, kcal mole^{-1}	K at 298 K, M
$H_2O \rightleftarrows H^+ + OH^-$	13.345	1.008×10^{-14}
$CO_2 \cdot H_2O \rightleftarrows H^+ + HCO_3^-$	1.825	4.283×10^{-7}
$HCO_3^- \rightleftarrows H^+ + CO_3^{2-}$	3.55	4.687×10^{-11}
$NH_3 \cdot H_2O \rightleftarrows NH_4^+ + OH^-$	8.65	1.709×10^{-5}
$SO_2 \cdot H_2O \rightleftarrows H^+ + HSO_3^-$ [a]	-4.161	1.29×10^{-2}
$HSO_3^- \rightleftarrows H^+ + SO_3^{2-}$ [a]	-2.23	6.014×10^{-8}

[a] Maahs (1982) has reviewed the data on SO_2/H_2O equilibria and has recommended the following values of K_{hs}, K_{s1}, and K_{s2}:

$$\log K_{hs} = \frac{1376.1}{T} - 4.521$$

$$\log K_{s1} = \frac{853}{T} - 4.74$$

$$\log K_{s2} = \frac{621.9}{T} - 9.278$$

The values of K_{s1} and K_{s2} at 298 K based on these correlations differ slightly from those given in the table: 0.0132 versus 0.0129 and 6.42×10^{-8} versus 6.014×10^{-8}.

law coefficient $H_{CO_2}^*$,

$$H_{CO_2}^* = H_{CO_2}\left[1 + \frac{K_{c1}}{[H^+]} + \frac{K_{c1}K_{c2}}{[H^+]^2}\right]$$

The effect of the acid-base equilibria in each case is to "pull" more material into solution than predicted on the basis of the Henry's law coefficient alone.

Table 5.4 gives values of ΔH at 298 K, together with the equilibrium constants at 298 K for the aqueous CO_2, SO_2, and NH_3 systems.

Let us calculate [S(IV)] as a function of pH for SO_2 concentrations of 0.2 and 200 ppb ($p_{SO_2} = 2 \times 10^{-10}$ atm and 2×10^{-7} atm) over the range pH = 0 to 6 at $T = 273$ K and 298 K. Figure 5.1 shows [S(IV)] as a function of pH for the two SO_2 concentrations at $T = 0°$ (273 K) and 25°C (298 K). Even though [$SO_2 \cdot H_2O$] depends only on p_{SO_2} at a given temperature, and therefore does not change with pH, [S(IV)] increases dramatically as pH increases due to the increased concentrations of HSO_3^- and SO_3^{2-}.

Let us compute the mole fractions of the three sulfur-IV species as a function of solution pH over the pH range of 0 to 12. The mole fractions are

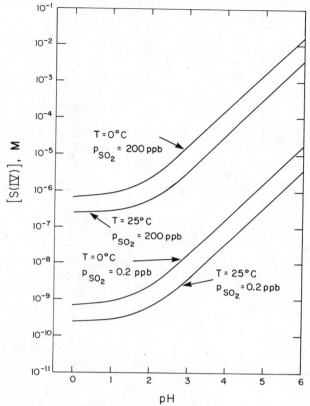

Figure 5.1. Equilibrium dissolved S(IV) as a function of pH, gas-phase partial pressure of SO_2, and temperature.

given by

$$x_{SO_2 \cdot H_2O} = \frac{[SO_2 \cdot H_2O]}{[S(IV)]} = \left[1 + \frac{K_{s1}}{[H^+]} + \frac{K_{s1}K_{s2}}{[H^+]^2} \right]^{-1}$$

$$x_{HSO_3^-} = \frac{[HSO_3^-]}{[S(IV)]} = \left[1 + \frac{[H^+]}{K_{s1}} + \frac{K_{s2}}{[H^+]} \right]^{-1}$$

$$x_{SO_3^{2-}} = \frac{[SO_3^{2-}]}{[S(IV)]} = \left[1 + \frac{[H^+]}{K_{s2}} + \frac{[H^+]^2}{K_{s1}K_{s2}} \right]^{-1}$$

In aquatic chemistry the common notation for these mole fractions is α_0, α_1, and α_2, respectively (Stumm and Morgan, 1981). Figure 5.2 shows these three mole fractions as a function of pH at 25°C, together with [S(IV)] for $p_{SO_2} = 10^{-9}$ atm (1 ppb). At high pH virtually all of the S(IV) is in the form of SO_3^{2-},

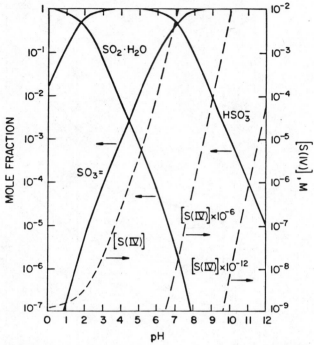

Figure 5.2. Mole fractions and concentrations of the three dissolved S(IV) species, $SO_2 \cdot H_2O$, HSO_3^-, and SO_3^{2-}, as a function of pH at $T = 298$ K, and $p_{SO_2} = 10^{-9}$ atm (1 ppb).

whereas at intermediate pH, all of the S(IV) occurs as HSO_3^-. At low pH, S(IV) is just $SO_2 \cdot H_2O$. Since these different S(IV) species can be expected to have different chemical reactivities, if a chemical reaction occurs in solution involving either HSO_3^- or SO_3^{2-}, we can expect that the rate of the reaction will depend on pH since the concentrations of these species depend on pH.

5.2.3. Ammonia / Water Equilibrium

Absorption of NH_3 in H_2O leads to

$$NH_3(g) + H_2O \rightleftharpoons NH_3 \cdot H_2O$$

$$NH_3 \cdot H_2O \rightleftharpoons NH_4^+ + OH^-$$

with

$$K_{ha} = \frac{[NH_3 \cdot H_2O]}{p_{NH_3}}$$

$$K_{a1} = \frac{[NH_4^+][OH^-]}{[NH_3 \cdot H_2O]}$$

from which we can obtain $[NH_4^+]$ as

$$[NH_4^+] = \frac{K_{a1}[NH_3 \cdot H_2O]}{[OH^-]} = \frac{K_{ha}K_{a1}p_{NH_3}[H^+]}{K_w}$$

If NH_3 is present with CO_2, the electroneutrality equation is

$$[H^+] + [NH_4^+] = [OH^-] + [HCO_3^-] + 2[CO_3^{2-}]$$

which, with the above equation for $[NH_4^+]$, can be reduced as before to an equation in $[H^+]$ only. We noted that the presence of CO_2 in equilibrium with water lowers the pH of the water to about 5.6. However, if NH_3 is present, the H^+ concentration is lowered. (Conversely, $[NH_4^+]$ is increased over that in the absence of CO_2.) At 10°C (283 K) the values of K_{ha} and K_{a1} are (see Tables 5.3 and 5.4)

$$K_{ha} = 126 \ M \ atm^{-1}$$

$$K_{a1} = 1.6 \times 10^{-5} \ M$$

With gas-phase CO_2 and NH_3 concentrations of 330 ppm and 0.004 ppm, respectively, we find that the pH of the solution is about 7.0.

5.2.4.   Aqueous Equilibria of the Nitrogen Oxides

The oxidation states of atmospheric nitrogen species are given in Table 5.5 together with their forms in solution. Nitrite species can be denoted by N(III), whereas nitrate is N(V). When NO and NO_2 are in contact with water, we have the usual absorption equilibria. (We use the notation $A(aq)$ here in place of $A \cdot H_2O$ for conciseness.)

$$NO(g) \rightleftarrows NO(aq)$$

$$NO_2(g) \rightleftarrows NO_2(aq)$$

The dissolved NO and NO_2 then associate to give

$$2NO_2(aq) \rightleftarrows N_2O_4(aq)$$

$$NO(aq) + NO_2(aq) \rightleftarrows N_2O_3(aq)$$

The formation of nitrite and nitrate ions takes place by

$$N_2O_4(aq) \rightleftarrows 2H^+ + NO_2^- + NO_3^-$$

$$N_2O_3(aq) \rightleftarrows 2H^+ + 2NO_2^-$$

TABLE 5.5. Oxidation States of Atmospheric Sulfur and Nitrogen Species[a]

Sulfur Compounds		
Oxidation State	Gas	Molecular/Ionic Forms
$+6$	SO_3, H_2SO_4	H_2SO_4, HSO_4^-
$+5$		
$+4$	SO_2	$SO_2 \cdot H_2O$, HSO_3^-
$+3$		
$+2$	SO	
$+1$		
0		
-1		
-2	H_2S, RSH, RSR′, RSSR′	

Nitrogen Compounds		
Oxidation State	Gas	Molecular/Ionic Forms
$+6$	NO_3	
$+5$	N_2O_5, HNO_3, $R(O)O_2NO_2$	HNO_3, NO_3^-, NO_2^+
$+4$	NO_2, N_2O_4	
$+3$	HNO_2	HNO_2, NO_2^-
$+2$	NO	
$+1$	N_2O	
0	N_2	
-1		
-2		
-3	NH_3, RNH_2, R_2NH, R_3N	NH_4^+, RNH_3

[a]Oxidation state is a convention with the following rules:
1. The oxidation state of an uncombined element as in C, Na, H_2, and so forth, is zero.
2. The sum of the oxidation states of the elements in a compound is zero.
3. The sum of the oxidation states of the elements in an ion is equal to the charge of the ion with sign.
4. The oxidation state of oxygen is -2 in all compounds except peroxides, where it is -1, and superoxides, where it is $-\frac{1}{2}$.
5. The oxidation state of hydrogen is $+1$ in all compounds except a few metal hydrides, where it is -1.
6. Oxidation corresponds to an increase in oxidation state in the positive sense; reduction corresponds to a decrease in oxidation state in the positive sense.
7. The algebraic sum of the changes in oxidation states in the balanced equation for an oxidation-reduction reaction is zero.

TABLE 5.6. **Equilibrium Constants for Aqueous-Phase Nitrogen Oxide Reactions**[a]

Reaction	Equilibrium Constant at 298 K
$NO(g) \rightleftharpoons NO(aq)$	$H_{NO} = 1.93 \times 10^{-3}$ M atm^{-1}
$NO_2(g) \rightleftharpoons NO_2(aq)$	$H_{NO_2} = 1.0 \times 10^{-2}$ M atm^{-1}
$2NO_2(aq) \rightleftharpoons N_2O_4(aq)$	$K_{n1} = 7 \times 10^4$ M^{-1}
$NO(aq) + NO_2(aq) \rightleftharpoons N_2O_3(aq)$	$K_{n2} = 3 \times 10^4$ M^{-1}
$HNO_3(aq) \rightleftharpoons H^+ + NO_3^-$	$K_{n3} = 15.4$ M
$HNO_2(aq) \rightleftharpoons H^+ + NO_2^-$	$K_{n4} = 5.1 \times 10^{-4}$ M
$2NO_2(g) + H_2O \rightleftharpoons 2H^+ + NO_2^- + NO_3^-$	$K_1 = 2.44 \times 10^2$ M^4 atm^{-2}
$NO(g) + NO_2(g) + H_2O \rightleftharpoons 2H^+ + 2NO_2^-$	$K_2 = 3.28 \times 10^{-5}$ M^4 atm^{-2}

[a]Schwartz and White (1981, 1983).

It is possible to combine the last four equilibria to eliminate the $N_2O_4(aq)$ and $N_2O_3(aq)$ species to obtain simply

$$2NO_2(aq) \rightleftharpoons 2H^+ + NO_2^- + NO_3^-$$

$$NO(aq) + NO_2(aq) \rightleftharpoons 2H^+ + 2NO_2^-$$

Thus we see that, upon absorption of NO and NO_2, nitrite and nitrate ion formation occur by two different paths.

Furthermore, we can combine the absorption equilibria with the above two reactions to give two concise equilibria for the $NO-NO_2$ system:

$$2NO_2(g) + H_2O \rightleftharpoons 2H^+ + NO_2^- + NO_3^-$$

$$NO(g) + NO_2(g) + H_2O \rightleftharpoons 2H^+ + 2NO_2^-$$

Equilibrium constants at 298 K for the aqueous phase NO_x system are given in Table 5.6. The ratio of nitrate to nitrite ion at equilibrium in this system is given by

$$\frac{[NO_3^-]}{[NO_2^-]} = \frac{p_{NO_2}}{p_{NO}} \frac{K_1}{K_2}$$

where $K_1/K_2 = 0.74 \times 10^7$ at 298 K.

If p_{NO_2}/p_{NO} is greater than about 10^{-5}, $[NO_3^-] \gg [NO_2^-]$. Thus, except in the total absence of NO_2, nitrate ion will be the preferred state of the dissolved gases at equilibrium. Furthermore, since the electroneutrality equation is

$$[H^+] = [OH^-] + [NO_2^-] + [NO_3^-]$$

an excellent approximation is that $[H^+] \cong [NO_3^-]$.

Let us calculate the dissolved concentrations of nitric and nitrous acids at equilibrium as a function of p_{NO} and p_{NO_2}. We note from the equilibrium constants K_{n3} and K_{n4} in Table 5.6 that HNO_3 is essentially entirely dissociated under most conditions of interest. Nitrous acid is a much weaker acid than HNO_3. For pH $\cong 6$, HNO_2 will be almost entirely dissociated; however, when pH < 4.5, its dissociation equilibrium must be taken into account. The dissolved nitric acid concentration can thus be taken as equivalent to $[NO_3^-]$, whereas that for dissolved nitrous acid must be taken as the sum of $[NO_2^-]$ and $[HNO_2(aq)]$.

Using the fact that $[H^+] \cong [NO_3^-]$, the nitrate ion concentration is given by

$$[NO_3^-] = \left[\frac{K_1^2 p_{NO_2}^3}{K_2 p_{NO}} \right]^{1/4}$$

Very little NO_2^- results from equilibrium (1); most comes from equilibrium (2),

$$[NO_2^-] = \frac{\left(K_2 p_{NO} p_{NO_2} \right)^{1/2}}{[NO_3^-]}$$

Thus, using the expression for $[NO_3^-]$, we have

$$[NO_2^-] = \left[\frac{K_2^3 p_{NO}^3}{K_1^2 p_{NO_2}} \right]^{1/4}$$

The concentration of undissociated nitrous acid is

$$[HNO_2(aq)] = \frac{[H^+][NO_2^-]}{K_{n4}}$$

Using $[H^+] = [NO_3^-]$, this becomes

$$[HNO_2(aq)] = \frac{\left(K_2 p_{NO} p_{NO_2} \right)^{1/2}}{K_{n4}}$$

Figure 5.3 shows the equilibrium concentrations of nitric and nitrous acids as a function of NO and NO_2 partial pressures. We note the overwhelming predominance of nitric over nitrous acid in this system at equilibrium.

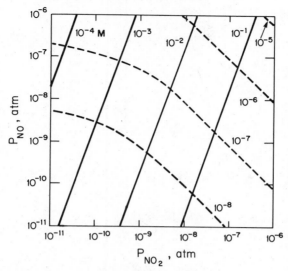

Figure 5.3. Equilibrium concentrations of dissolved nitric acid (solid line) and nitrous acid (broken line) as a function of NO and NO_2 partial pressures (Schwartz, 1984).

Finally, we can summarize the effective Henry's law coefficients for HNO_2 and HNO_3 together with those for NH_3 and SO_2. Figure 5.4 shows these effective coefficients as a function of pH over the range pH = 2–6.

In all the calculations we have carried out to this point it has been implicitly assumed that the equilibria involved are established rapidly enough so that discussion of equilibrium concentration levels has relevance. In the case of the other systems in this section, namely CO_2, SO_2, and NH_3, this supposition will be found to be correct. We will wish to examine the situation with the nitrogen oxides. First, it is known that the aqueous-phase equilibria,

$$2NO_2(aq) \rightleftarrows N_2O_4(aq)$$

$$NO(aq) + NO_2(aq) \rightleftarrows N_2O_3(aq)$$

are established rapidly. The rate of the reaction to form the dissolved acids,

$$2NO_2(aq) \rightarrow 2H^+ + NO_2^- + NO_3^-$$

can be expressed as a first-order reaction involving $N_2O_4(aq)$,

$$N_2O_4(aq) \rightarrow 2H^+ + NO_2^- + NO_3^- \tag{1}$$

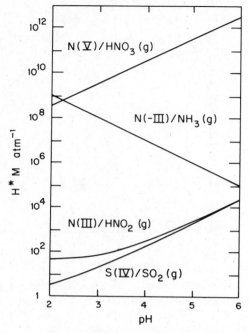

Figure 5.4. Effective Henry's law coefficients for gases that undergo rapid acid-base dissociation reactions in aqueous solution. Buffer capacity of solution is assumed to greatly exceed incremental concentration from uptake of the indicated gas (Schwartz, 1984).

where the rate constants are related through the equilibrium constant K_{n1}. A similar equivalence holds for the reactions

$$NO(aq) + NO_2(aq) \rightarrow 2H^+ + 2NO_2^-$$

$$N_2O_3(aq) \rightarrow 2H^+ + 2NO_2^- \qquad (2)$$

The rate constants for these reactions are given in Table 5.7. Using these values, together with the Henry's law constants for NO and NO_2, we find the

TABLE 5.7.   Rate Constants for Aqueous-Phase Nitrogen Oxide Reactions[a]

Reaction	Rate Expression	Rate Constant, 298 K
$2NO_2(aq) + H_2O \rightarrow 2H^+ + NO_3^- + NO_2^-$	$k[NO_2(aq)]^2$	$k = 0.425 \times 10^8$ M^{-1} sec^{-1}
$NO(aq) + NO_2(aq) + H_2O \rightarrow 2H^+ + 2NO_2^-$	$k[NO(aq)][NO_2(aq)]$	$k = 0.37 \times 10^8$ M^{-1} sec^{-1}
$N_2O_4(aq) + H_2O \rightarrow 2H^+ + NO_3^- + NO_2^-$	$k[N_2O_4(aq)]$	$k = 1.0 \times 10^3$ sec^{-1}
$N_2O_3(aq) + H_2O \rightarrow 2H^+ + 2NO_2^-$	$k[N_2O_3(aq)]$	$k = 1.0 \times 10^3$ sec^{-1}

[a]Schwartz and White (1983).

rates of reactions 1 and 2 at 298 K to be

$$R_1 = 4.25 \times 10^3 p_{NO_2}^2 \text{ M sec}^{-1}$$

$$R_2 = 7 \times 10^2 p_{NO_2} p_{NO} \text{ M sec}^{-1}$$

These rate expressions will be useful subsequently when we consider the reaction kinetics of aqueous nitrogen oxides.

5.3. LIQUID WATER IN THE ATMOSPHERE

The liquid water content of the atmosphere is conveniently expressed either in terms of grams (or cm^3) of water per m^3 of air or as a dimensionless volume fraction L (e.g., m^3 of liquid water per m^3 of air). Values of L for typical situations are:

Clouds $\left(0.1\text{--}1.0 \dfrac{cm^3 \text{ water}}{m^3 \text{ air}}\right)$ $\qquad L = 10^{-7}\text{--}10^{-6}$

Fog $\left(0.05\text{--}0.5 \dfrac{cm^3 \text{ water}}{m^3 \text{ air}}\right)$ $\qquad L = 5 \times 10^{-8}\text{--}5 \times 10^{-7}$

Aerosols $(10\text{--}100 \ \mu g/m^3)$ $\qquad L = 10^{-11}\text{--}10^{-10}$

Table 5.8 gives some properties of aqueous particles and drops in the atmosphere. The distribution of a species A between gas and aqueous phases in, for example, a liquid water cloud can be expressed in terms of the ratio of the concentrations of A in the two phases per unit volume of air,

$$\frac{\text{moles of } A \text{ in solution per liter of air}}{\text{moles of } A \text{ in air per liter of air}} = \frac{H_A p_A L}{p_A/RT} = H_A RTL = \hat{H}_A L$$

(If A participates in additional aqueous phase dissociation equilibria, then H_A is replaced by H_A^*.)

If $H_A RTL \ll 1$, or $H_A \ll (RTL)^{-1}$, species A is present predominantly in the gas phase, whereas if $H_A RTL \gg 1$, A lies mainly in the aqueous phase. For $L = 10^{-6}$, $(RTL)^{-1} \cong 4 \times 10^4$ M atm^{-1}. Thus, if the Henry's law coefficient for a species is much less than 4×10^4 M atm^{-1}, it will exist predominantly in the gas phase. We see from Table 5.2 that, except for the dissociative gases and very highly soluble gases like H_2O_2, the distribution of material lies mainly on the gas side.

For SO_2 at pH = 4, $H_{S(IV)}^* \cong 10^2$, so at $L = 10^{-6}$, $H_{S(IV)}^* \ll (RTL)^{-1}$, so per unit volume of air most S(IV) will be present as SO_2. For HNO_3, as we will

TABLE 5.8. Properties of Atmospheric Aqueous Particles and Drops[a]

Particle or Drop	Radius μm	L, cm^3 m^{-3}	pH	Ionic Strength[b]
Haze	0.03–0.3	10^{-5}–10^{-4}	1–8	≈ 1
Clouds	10	0.1–3	3–6	10^{-3}–10^{-2}
Rain	200–2000	0.1–1	4–5	10^{-4}
Fog	10	0.02–0.2	2–6	10^{-3}–10^{-2}

[a] Martin (1984b).
[b] The ionic strength of a solution is defined by

$$I = \tfrac{1}{2} \sum_i z_i^2 m_i$$

where z_i is the charge on ion i and m_i is the molality of ion i. For dilute solutions the molality and molarity of a dissolved species are virtually identical. Consequently, when dealing with dilute solutions the ionic strength is normally defined in terms of the molarity of each species.

see later, $H^* \cong 10^{10}$, so that nitric acid will be present at equilibrium essentially entirely in solution.

For an extremely soluble gas, the quantity dissolved in solution may have to be determined from mass balance considerations. We can define $[A]_{max}$ as the aqueous-phase concentration that would result if a gas-phase species were to dissolve entirely in the liquid water present in the same unit volume of air. If the partial pressure of A is p_A, then

$$[A]_{max} = \frac{p_A}{RTL}$$

For example, if $p_A = 10^{-9}$ atm (1 ppb) and $L = 10^{-6}$, $[A]_{max} = 4 \times 10^{-5}$ M. Thus, regardless of the value of H_A if A is present at a concentration of 1 ppb and the liquid water content is 10^{-6}, the maximum concentration of A that can be achieved in solution is 4×10^{-5} M.

Consider H_2O_2 equilibrium as a concrete example. $H_{H_2O_2} = 6.1 \times 10^5$ M atm^{-1} at 0°C. A gas-phase concentration of 1 ppb ($p_{H_2O_2} = 10^{-9}$ atm) would lead to an equilibrium concentration predicted by Henry's law of 6.1×10^{-4} M. For a cloud water content of 0.5 g m^{-3}, if all the H_2O_2 goes into solution, the solution concentration would be 8.9×10^{-5} M, less than that predicted on the basis of Henry's law.

There is, however, a mechanism by which concentrations higher than $[A]_{max}$ in the aqueous phase can be achieved. If the liquid water present in a certain physical volume of air such as a cloud has contacted a much larger physical volume of air due to flow of air through the cloud, then concentrations higher than $[A]_{max}$ can be achieved. One might thus define a *potential partial pressure* p_{pot} based on the actual aqueous phase concentration of A (Schwartz, 1984).

$$p_{A_{pot}} = LRT[A(aq)]$$

Shortly we will be discussing rates of reaction of dissolved species. Such rates will generally be expressed in terms of moles per liter of solution per second. It is sometimes useful to express an aqueous-phase reaction rate on the basis of the gas-phase properties, especially when comparing gas- and aqueous-phase reaction rates. In this way both rates are expressed on the same basis.

To place our discussion on a concrete basis, let us say we have a reaction between dissolved S(IV) and some species A,

$$A + S(IV) \xrightarrow{k} \text{Products}$$

the aqueous-phase rate of which is $R_a = k[A(aq)][S(IV)]$, expressed in M sec^{-1}. The rate can be written in terms of gas-phase partial pressures as

$$R_a = kH_A H^*_{S(IV)} p_A p_{SO_2}$$

There are several ways to express the gas-phase reaction rate. By multiplying R_a by the liquid water ratio L, the rate is expressed in terms of moles of

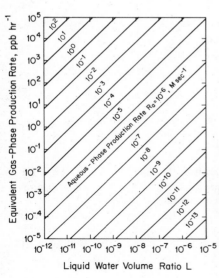

Figure 5.5. Nomogram relating aqueous reaction rates, in M sec^{-1}, to equivalent gas phase reaction rates, in ppb hr^{-1}, at $T = 288$ K, $p = 1$ atm, and given liquid water content L. The diagonal lines are constant aqueous reaction rates (National Center for Atmospheric Research, 1982).

SO_2 per liter of air per second. Then, moles per liter of air can be converted to, say, ppb. Figure 5.5 is a nomogram relating aqueous-phase reaction rates in M sec^{-1} to equivalent gas-phase rates in ppb hr^{-1} at 288 K as a function of L. Reaction rates are sometimes expressed as a fractional rate of conversion, sec^{-1}. Given the rate R_a above, it can be converted to a fractional rate of conversion by

$$\tilde{R}_a = \frac{LR_a}{[SO_2(g)]} = \frac{(LRT)R_a}{p_{SO_2}}[sec^{-1}]$$

The characteristic time for conversion is then $\tau_{SO_2} = \tilde{R}_a^{-1}$.

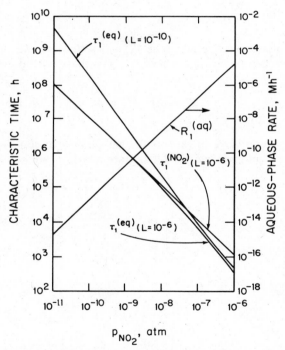

Figure 5.6. Rate and characteristic times of reaction (1), $2NO_2(g) + H_2O(1) \rightarrow 2H^+ + NO_3^- + NO_2^-$, as function of partial pressure of NO_2, $T = 298$ K. $R_1(aq)$ represents reaction rate referred to aqueous-phase concentration of products; $\tau_1^{(NO_2)}$ and $\tau^{(eq)}$ represent characteristic times of removal of $NO_2(g)$ and of establishing equilibrium, respectively. Values of liquid water content $L = 10^{-6}$ and 10^{-10} are representative of liquid-water clouds and clear-air aerosols, respectively (Lee and Schwartz, 1981).

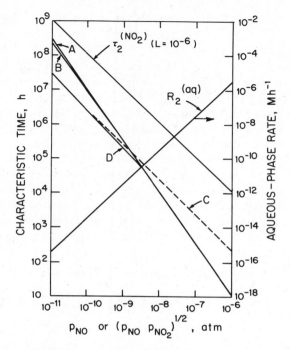

Figure 5.7. Rate and characteristic times of reaction (2), $NO(g) + NO_2(g) + H_2O(l)$ $\rightarrow 2H^+ + 2NO_2^-$; $\tau_2^{(NO_2)}$ represents characteristic time of removal of $NO_2(g)$ as function of p_{NO}. Curves A, B, C, and D show characteristic times of achieving equilibrium, $\tau_2^{(eq)}$ as a function of $(p_{NO}p_{NO_2})^{1/2}$. Curve A, $L = 10^{-10}$; $[H^+] = [NO_2^-]$. Curve B, $L = 10^{-6}$; $[H^+] = [NO_2^-]$. Curve C, $L = 10^{-10}$; $[H^+] = 2.5 \times 10^{-5}$ M (pH = 5.6). Curve D, $L = 10^{-10}$; $[H^+]$ controlled by equilibrium (2) and CO_2 solubility. $R_2^{(aq)}$ represents reaction rate referred to aqueous phase concentration of products, as function of $(p_{NO}p_{NO_2})^{1/2}$ (Lee and Schwartz, 1981).

The characteristic time for removal of NO_2 from the gas phase by reactions (1) and (2) involving NO_2 in the previous section is

$$\tau_{NO_2}^{(i)} = \left(\frac{R_i LRT}{p_{NO_2}} \right)^{-1} \qquad i = 1, 2$$

which can be evaluated as a function of p_{NO_2}. Figures 5.6 and 5.7 show the rates and characteristic times of reactions (1) and (2). These results establish that, despite the high solubility of NO and NO_2 as nitrous and nitric acids at equilibrium, and despite large rate constants for reactions (1) and (2), these two equilibria are not achieved on time scales of atmospheric interest for typical ambient NO and NO_2 levels. The slow rates are a consequence of the second-order dependence of the rate on p_{NO} and p_{NO_2}.

5.4.   REACTION KINETICS OF AQUEOUS SULFUR CHEMISTRY

When SO_2 dissolves in aqueous solution, the three S(IV) species result, $SO_2 \cdot H_2O$, HSO_3^-, and SO_3^{2-}. The conversion of dissolved S(IV) to sulfate, SO_4^{2-}, also referred to as S(VI), since sulfur is in oxidation state 6, is an important route for forming atmospheric sulfate. Several oxidizing species have been identified, including dissolved oxygen, ozone, and hydrogen peroxide. The reaction may be uncatalyzed or catalyzed by certain dissolved metal ions. In spite of their lower gas-phase concentrations, ozone and hydrogen peroxide have significantly higher Henry's law coefficients than O_2, which, combined with their unusual reactivity, make them effective oxidants.

There is a large literature on the reaction kinetics of aqueous sulfur chemistry. We present here only a few of the rate expressions available, largely those that have been recently recommended by Hoffmann and Calvert (1985).

5.4.1.   Uncatalyzed Oxidation of S(IV) by Dissolved Oxygen

In the absence of catalysts the reaction between dissolved O_2 and S(IV) is negligible.

5.4.2.   Oxidation of S(IV) by Dissolved Ozone

Hoffmann (1985) has carried out a detailed evaluation of existing experimental kinetic and mechanistic data on the reaction of S(IV) with dissolved ozone. The rate expression that was found to most appropriately fit all kinetic observations was

$$-\frac{d\,[\text{S(IV)}]}{dt} = (k_0\alpha_0 + k_1\alpha_1 + k_2\alpha_2)[\text{S(IV)}][O_3]$$

where $\alpha_0 = x_{SO_2 \cdot H_2O}$, $\alpha_1 = x_{HSO_3^-}$, and $\alpha_2 = x_{SO_3^{2-}}$. Thus, this rate expression may be written as

$$-\frac{d\,[\text{S(IV)}]}{dt} = (k_0[SO_2 \cdot H_2O] + k_1[HSO_3^-] + k_2[SO_3^{2-}])[O_3]$$

The values of the coefficients recommended by Hoffmann are $k_0 = 2.4 \times 10^4$ $M^{-1}\,sec^{-1}$, $k_1 = 3.7 \times 10^5\ M^{-1}\,sec^{-1}$, and $k_2 = 1.5 \times 10^9\ M^{-1}\,sec^{-1}$.

The ozone—S(IV) reaction proceeds via three independent pathways that involve a nucleophilic attack on ozone by $SO_2 \cdot H_2O$, $HOSO_2^-$, and SO_3^{2-}.

Considerations of nucleophilic reactivity indicate that SO_3^{2-} should react more rapidly with O_3 than HSO_3^- and HSO_3^- should react more rapidly in turn than $SO_2 \cdot H_2O$. This order is reflected in the relative numerical values of k_0, k_1, and k_2.

With a Henry's law coefficient of about 0.01 M atm^{-1} at 298 K, at normal background tropospheric concentrations (30–60 ppb), ozone will exist in equilibrium in solution at concentrations of about $3 - 6 \times 10^{-10}$ M. Since as $[H^+]$ increases the quantity of dissolved S(IV) decreases (Figure 5.2), we expect that the rate of oxidation of S(IV) to S(VI) by ozone will decrease substantially as pH decreases.

5.4.3. Oxidation of S(IV) by Dissolved Hydrogen Peroxide

The reaction of hydrogen peroxide with S(IV) species has been studied in detail (Hoffmann and Edwards, 1975; Penkett et al., 1979; Martin and Damschen, 1981; McArdle and Hoffmann, 1983). The published rates all agree to within experimental error over a wide range of pH (0 to 8). Although there is some question as to whether the reaction involves all S(IV) species in solution or just through the bisulfite ion, the mechanism is generally accepted to be

$$HSO_3^- + H_2O_2 \underset{k_{1b}}{\overset{k_{1f}}{\rightleftharpoons}} \underset{peroxymonosulfurous\ acid}{SO_2OOH^-} + H_2O$$

$$SO_2OOH^- + H^+ \overset{k_2}{\rightarrow} H_2SO_4$$

Peroxymonosulfurous acid reaction to sulfuric acid involves a proton, so that the reaction becomes faster as the medium becomes more acidic. The rate expression has the form

$$\frac{d[SO_4^{2-}]}{dt} = \frac{k_{1f} k_2 [HSO_3^-][H_2O_2][H^+]}{k_{1b} + k_2[H^+]}$$

and specifically is (Hoffmann and Calvert, 1985)

$$-\frac{d[S(IV)]}{dt} = \frac{k[H^+][H_2O_2][S(IV)]\,\alpha_1}{1 + K[H^+]}$$

where $\alpha_1 = x_{HSO_3^-}$, $k = 7.45 \times 10^7$ M^{-1} sec^{-1}, and $K = 13$ M^{-1} at 298 K. For $[H^+] \ll 0.1$ M, the rate of oxidation is independent of pH. Below pH $\cong 1$, the rate decreases as pH decreases.

5.4.4.   Oxidation of S(IV) by Dissolved Oxygen Catalyzed by Iron

Iron is the most abundant transition metal in the atmosphere, with average concentrations ranging from 0.19 to 0.51 $\mu g \, m^{-3}$ in the nonurban atmosphere and from 1.1 to 2.1 $\mu g \, m^{-3}$ in the urban atmosphere (U.S. Environmental Protection Agency, 1979). Important sources of iron containing particulate matter include soil dust, flyash from oil- and coal-fired power plants, particulate emissions from industrial operations, and exhaust from internal combustion engines.

There are several possible modes of interaction between iron and sulfur dioxide in the atmosphere. Physical adsorption can occur on some iron-containing particles. Iron oxide can chemisorb sulfur dioxide, converting it to sulfate at the gas-solid interface.* Iron containing particles could oxidize dissolved S(IV) at the solid–liquid interface in an aerosol consisting of a solid core surrounded by an aqueous shell. This last process can be photoassisted (Faust, 1985; Faust and Hoffmann, 1985). Finally, dissolved iron can catalyze the oxidation of S(IV) by O_2 in aqueous solution.

The homogeneous catalysis of SO_2 oxidation by dissolved iron in aqueous solution has been the subject of many investigations. These can be broadly classified as being either one-phase or two-phase studies, depending on whether solid iron is present in the solution. Detailed kinetic rate expressions have been obtained only from the one-phase (i.e., bulk solution) approach.

In the presence of oxygen, iron in the ferric state, Fe(III) has been conclusively shown to be a catalyst for the oxidation of S(IV) in aqueous solution. The intrinsic rate of the catalytic reaction depends on the concentrations of S(IV) and Fe(III) in solution, pH, ionic strength, and temperature, and can be very sensitive to the presence of certain anions (e.g., SO_4^{2-}) and cations (e.g., Mn^{2+}) in solution.

The equilibria involving iron in the ferric state in aqueous solution are

$$Fe^{3+} + H_2O \rightleftarrows FeOH^{2+} + H^+$$

$$FeOH^{2+} + H_2O \rightleftarrows Fe(OH)_2^+ + H^+$$

$$Fe(OH)_2^+ + H_2O \rightleftarrows Fe(OH)_3(s) + H^+$$

$$2FeOH^{2+} \rightleftarrows Fe_2(OH)_2^{4+}$$

---

*Let us estimate the importance of the adsorption of SO_2 onto Fe_2O_3 in the atmosphere. To give a crude upper estimate for this process, assume that 5 $\mu g \, m^{-3}$ particulate iron is suspended in the form of 0.1 μm spheres. Using the result of Judeikis et al. (1978), we find that the amount of SO_2 adsorbed onto the iron corresponds to 0.0001 ppb in the gas phase. Assuming an average lifetime of these particles of one day, the removal rate of SO_2 due to adsorption onto Fe_2O_3 is 0.02 percent per hour for an atmosphere containing 0.2 ppb SO_2. This does not appear to be significant with respect to other gas to particle conversion pathways for SO_2. The adsorption of sulfur dioxide onto iron could have importance, however, for another reason. Formation of a layer of sulfate material onto an otherwise relatively insoluble particle could enhance its cloud nucleation properties (Parungo et al., 1978). Even at humidities of less than 100 percent, the particle could be "activated" for growth.

Total soluble iron is

$$[Fe]_{soluble} = [Fe^{3+}] + [FeOH^{2+}] + [Fe(OH)_2^+] + [Fe_2(OH)_2^{4+}]$$

whereas the total iron present consists of the solid and soluble forms,

$$[Fe]_{total} = [Fe]_{soluble} + [Fe(OH)_3]$$

The relative amounts of the different forms of iron in aqueous solution are a strong function of pH (Stumm and Morgan, 1981). The overall equilibrium expressing the relationship between solid $Fe(OH)_3$ and Fe^{3+} is

$$Fe(OH)_3 + 3H^+ \rightleftarrows Fe^{3+} + 3H_2O$$

With an equilibrium constant at 298 K of about 10^3,

$$10^3 = \frac{[Fe^{3+}]}{[H^+]^3}$$

we find that at pH = 4.5, $[Fe^{3+}] \approx 3 \times 10^{-11}$ M.

The Fe(III)-catalyzed oxidation of S(IV) by dissolved O_2 in aqueous solution at pH $\leq$ 4 has been studied by several groups, Hoffmann and Calvert (1985) have evaluated the results of these studies and have recommended the rate expression,

$$-\frac{d[S(IV)]}{dt} = k[Fe(III)][S(IV)]\alpha_2$$

where $\alpha_2 = x_{SO_3^{2-}}$ and $k = 1.2 \times 10^6$ M^{-1} sec^{-1} at 293 K.

Oxidation of S(IV) at low pH catalyzed by dissolved Fe(II) has been studied (Huss et al., 1982a, b). An induction period has been observed before the reaction commences, suggesting that Fe(II) must first be oxidized to Fe(III) before oxidation can begin. Above pH = 4.5, the solubility of iron decreases significantly. At pH values above this level, the iron will probably exist as condensed $Fe(OH)_3$ or Fe_2O_3. Martin (1984a) determined the following rate expression at pH = 5:

$$\frac{d[SO_4^{2-}]}{dt} = 5 \times 10^5 [Fe^{3+}(aq)][S(IV)] \text{ M sec}^{-1}$$

Based on the available evidence, the following conclusions can be drawn regarding the catalysis of S(IV) oxidation by dissolved iron in aqueous solution. At low pH, the reaction is roughly first-order in iron concentration and first-order in $[SO_3^{2-}]$. It appears that only Fe(III) catalyzes the S(IV) oxidation reaction, and that when added to a reaction mixture, Fe(II) must first be oxidized to Fe(III) before the reaction commences.

To estimate the rate of iron dissolution in an aqueous aerosol droplet, assume that a 1 μm droplet has formed around a 0.1 μm Fe_2O_3 particle and that the pH is 3 (Waldman et al., 1982). From the result of Brimblecombe and Spedding (1975), who measured the rate of release by iron into aqueous solution from Fe_2O_3 and flyash as a function of pH, the dissolved iron concentration in the aqueous phase grows at a rate of 1.5×10^{-7} M sec^{-1}. After 20 minutes a concentration of 1.8×10^{-4} M has been reached, corresponding to 0.6 percent of the solid iron present initially. This is a higher concentration of dissolved iron than is predicted thermodynamically with Fe_2O_3 as the equilibrium controlling solid phase. As observed by Brimblecombe and Spedding, however, the concentration of dissolved iron resulting from dissolution of Fe_2O_3 can be *highly* supersaturated relative to Fe_2O_3(s). (This may have been microcolloidal iron.) In fact, they observed iron concentrations in excess of 1.8×10^{-4} M at pH 5. Apparently, extensive hydroxide ion complexation of the aqueous phase iron can effectively change the thermodynamically controlling solid phase from Fe_2O_3(s) to $Fe(OH)_3$(s). Although this consideration of iron solubility has been qualitative, it indicates that the dissolution of Fe_2O_3 can lead to significant amounts of dissolved iron at low pH.

5.4.5. Oxidation of S(IV) by Dissolved Oxygen Catalyzed by Manganese

The rate of oxidation of S(IV) by dissolved O_2 catalyzed by dissolved manganese has been summarized by Hoffmann and Calvert (1985)

$$[S(IV)] \leqq 10^{-4} \text{ M}$$

$$[Mn(II)] \leqq 10^{-5} \text{ M}$$

$$-\frac{d[S(IV)]}{dt} = k_2[Mn(II)][S(IV)]\alpha_1$$

$$[S(IV)] > 10^{-4} \text{ M}$$

$$[Mn(II)] > 10^{-5} \text{ M}$$

$$-\frac{d[S(IV)]}{dt} = k_1[Mn^{2+}]^2[H^+]^{-1}\beta_1$$

where $\alpha_1 = x_{HSO_3^-}$, $k_2 = 3.4 \times 10^3$ M^{-1} sec^{-1}, $k_1 = 2 \times 10^9$ M^{-1} sec^{-1}, and

$$\beta_1 = \frac{[Mn_2OH^{3+}][H^+]}{[Mn^{2+}]}$$

with $\log \beta_1 = -9.9$ at 298 K.

TABLE 5.9. Manganese and Iron Concentrations in Aqueous Particles and Drops[a]

Medium	Manganese, M	Iron, M
Haze	10^{-7}–10^{-4}	10^{-4}–10^{-3}
Clouds	10^{-8}–10^{-5}	10^{-7}–10^{-4}
Rain	10^{-8}–10^{-6}	10^{-8}–10^{-5}
Fog	10^{-7}–10^{-5}	10^{-6}–10^{-4}

[a] Martin (1984b).

5.4.6. Oxidation of S(IV) by Dissolved Oxygen Catalyzed by Iron and Manganese

When both Fe^{3+} and Mn^{2+} are present in sulfite solutions, the rate of oxidation is enhanced over that expected from the sum of the Mn^{2+}–S(IV) and Fe^{3+}–S(IV) rates alone. For the combined Fe–Mn system, Martin (1984a) found the rate of sulfate formation to be 3 to 10 times faster than that expected from the sum of the independent rates, with the rate expression,

$$\frac{d\left[SO_4^{2-}\right]}{dt} = 4.7\,[H^+]^{-1}\,[Mn^{2+}]^2 + 0.82\,[H^+]^{-1}\,[Fe^{3+}]\,[S(IV)]$$

$$\times \left\{ 1 + \frac{1.7 \times 10^3\,[Mn^{2+}]^{1.5}}{6.31 \times 10^{-6} + [Fe^{3+}]} \right\}\,[S(IV)] > 10^{-6}\,M$$

Table 5.9 gives the ranges of Mn and Fe concentrations in aqueous particles and drops.

5.4.7. Oxidation of S(IV) by Dissolved HNO₂

Martin et al. (1981) determined the following rate expression for the oxidation of S(IV) by N(III) (i.e., either NO_2^- or HNO_2), at 25°C,

$$\frac{d\left[SO_4^{2-}\right]}{dt} = 142[H^+]^{1/2}[N(III)]\,[S(IV)]\ M\ sec^{-1}$$

Additional study of this reaction has been reported by Oblath et al. (1982).

5.4.8. Oxidation of S(IV) by Dissolved NO₂

Lee and Schwartz (1982) have studied the oxidation of S(IV) by dissolved NO_2 at pH's between 6.4 and 5.8, at $[S(IV)] \cong 10^{-6}\ M$ and at $p_{NO_2} \cong 10^{-7}$ atm (100 ppb). The results were consistent with the reaction stoichiometry,

$$2NO_2 + HSO_3^- + H_2O \rightarrow 2NO_2^- + 3H^+ + SO_4^{2-}$$

TABLE 5.10. Studies on the Carbon-Catalyzed Oxidation of SO$_2$

Authors	T, °C	RH, %	[S(IV)]	pH	Carbon Properties	Comments
Benner et al. (1982)	20–30	NR	$[SO_2] =$ 0.007–222 ppm	3–5	Nuchar SN activated carbon BET surface area(SA) = 1150 m^2 g^{-1}	Fog chamber with particles. Max rate $= 8 \times 10^{-6}$ g SO_4^{2-} g C^{-1} sec^{-1} $$\frac{d[SO_4^{2-}]}{dt} = k[SO_2]^a$$ $[SO_2] = 0.001$–0.5 ppm $a = 0.9$–1.6
Brodzinsky et al. (1980)	20	NA	$[SO_2(aq)] =$ $7 \times 10^{-8} -$ 1×10^{-3} M	1.2–7.5	Nuchar C190 activated carbon BET SA = 550 m^2 g^{-1} $[C_x]$ = 0.02–3.2 g l^{-1}	Batch reactor. Solution $$\frac{d[S(VI)]}{dt} = k[C_x][O_2]^{0.69}$$ $$\times \frac{a[S(IV)]^2}{1 + b[S(IV)] + a[S(IV)]^2}$$ $k = 9.04 \times 10^3$ $\times \exp(-49000/RT)$ $a = 1.5 \times 10^{12}$ M^{-2} $b = 3.06 \times 10^6$ M^{-1}
Rogowski et al. (1982)	23	NA	$[SO_2] =$ 100 ppm	≥ 1.5	Commercial furnace black $[C_x]$ = 100 mg (10 ml)$^{-1}$	Batch reactor. Solution reaction zero order in O$_2$, independent of pH.
Britton and Clark (1980)	20	0–80	$[SO_2] =$ 1–7 ppm	NR	Soot from propane–air diffusion flame BET SA = 24 m^2 g^{-1} $[C_x]$ = 4 mg m^{-3} $\bar{D}_p$ = 0.13 μm	Batch reactor (1 m^3) $$\frac{dW_{SO_3}}{dt} = r_0\left(1 - \frac{W_{SO_3}}{W_{SO_3}^{\infty}}\right)^2$$ W_{SO_3} = weight SO$_3$ g C^{-1} $W_{SO_3}^{\infty}$ = 3.4 mg g C^{-1} $r_0 = 27$–134 μg g^{-1} min^{-1} independent of RH

Reference					
Dlugi et al. (1981)	10–30	28–92	$[SO_2] =$ 0.08–4.3 ppm	3 commercial carbon blacks BET SA = 10, 83, 215 m² g⁻¹	Batch reactor (4.5 m³) $\dfrac{1}{m_{aerosol}}\dfrac{dm_{SO_4^{2-}}}{dt} = a_0\left(1 - \dfrac{m_{SO_4^{2-}}}{m_{SO_4^{2-}}^{\infty}}\right)$ a_0 = funct of (pH, [SO₂])
Dlugi and Jordan (1982)	8–35	25–92	$[SO_2] =$ 0.04–4.35 ppm	2 soots BET SA = 10,215 m² g⁻¹	Batch reactor (4.5 m³) Same rate expression as above with $a_0 = k[SO_2]^m$ $m = \begin{cases} 0.5\text{–}0.8 & \text{low RH} \\ 1 & RH > 75\% \end{cases}$
Baldwin (1982)	25	NR		Commercial charcoal BET SA = 37 m² g⁻¹	Flow reactor $-\dfrac{d[SO_2]}{dt} =$ $0.03\,[SO_2][C]\;sec^{-1}$ [C] in $\mu g\,cm^{-3}$
Cofer et al. (1980)	20–25	0, 65	$[SO_2] =$ 20–80 ppm	Commercial carbon black BET SA = 560 m² g⁻¹	Flow reactor $\dfrac{d[SO_2]}{dt} =$ funct([H₂O],[NO₂]) zero order in [SO₂]. No saturation at 65% RH
Judeikis et al. (1978)	20–30	0–95	$[SO_2] =$ 3–100 ppm	Charcoal BET SA = 40.7 m² g⁻¹	Tubular reactor with coated inner wall. $-\dfrac{d\ln[SO_2]}{dt} = 0.36 \times 10^{-5}$ sec^{-1}
Liberti et al. (1978)	20	35–76	$[SO_2] =$ 8.6 ppm	100 mg atmospheric dust sample[a] BET SA = 0.6–19 m² g⁻¹	Flow reactor. Capacities = 0.08–0.35 mg SO₂ g dust⁻¹ Absorbed SO₂ increases with RH

[a]Dusts used were urban particulate matter and stack emissions. Mn and Al are minor components. A few had high Fe content. Urban dusts desorbed all of the absorbed SO₂. The stack dusts tended not to desorb even on heating.

225

Difficulty was encountered in measuring a rate constant free of mass transfer limitations. As a tentative rate, they suggested

$$\frac{d\left[SO_4^{2-}\right]}{dt} = 2 \times 10^6 \left[S(IV)\right]\left[NO_2(aq)\right]$$

5.4.9. Carbon-Catalyzed Oxidation of S(IV)

A number of studies of the carbon-catalyzed oxidation of SO_2 exist. In the other subsections of Section 5.4 we have not attempted to review past studies, and have selected one rate expression reflecting the latest available work. In contrast to the earlier subsections, we present in Table 5.10 rate expressions for the carbon-catalyzed oxidation of SO_2, along with a brief explanation of the conditions under which the rate was determined. Basically there have been two types of experiments—those done with "dry" carbon particles in a mildly humid atmosphere, and those using aqueous carbon particle suspensions into which SO_2 and O_2 dissolve and react. There is no general agreement among either the dry or aqueous rate expressions, only that in general no saturation effects are observed in the strictly aqueous systems, whereas saturation is observed for dry carbon particles.

There is large disagreement among the rate expressions and the validity of extrapolating them to extreme, polluted conditions is questionable. Carbon-catalyzed SO_2 oxidation is possibly an important mechanism, although due to the great uncertainty in rate expressions, we will not include this mechanism in calculations to follow.

5.4.10. Comparison of Aqueous-Phase SO₂ Oxidation Paths

We will now compare the different routes for SO_2 oxidation in aqueous solution as a function of pH and temperature. In doing so, we will set the pH at a given value and calculate the instantaneous rate of S(IV) oxidation at that pH. The rate expressions used and the parameters in the rate expressions are given in Table 5.11. Figure 5.8 shows the oxidation rates in M sec^{-1} for the different paths at 298 K for the conditions.

$$[SO_2(g)] = 5 \text{ ppb} \qquad [HNO_2(g)] = 2 \text{ ppb}$$

$$[H_2O_2(g)] = 1 \text{ ppb} \qquad [NO_2(g)] = 1 \text{ ppb}$$

$$[O_3(g)] = 50 \text{ ppb}$$

$$[Fe^{3+}(aq)] = 3 \times 10^{-7} \text{ M}$$

$$[Mn^{2+}(aq)] = 3 \times 10^{-8} \text{ M}$$

Oxidant	Rate Expression, $-\dfrac{d[S(IV)]}{dt}$	
O_3	$(k_0[SO_2 \cdot H_2O] + k_1[HSO_3^-] + k_2[SO_3^{2-}])[O_3(aq)]$	Hoffmann and Calvert (1985)
	$k_0 = 2.4 \times 10^4$ M^{-1} sec^{-1} at 298 K	
	$k_1 = 3.7 \times 10^5$ M^{-1} sec^{-1}	
	$k_2 = 1.5 \times 10^9$ M^{-1} sec^{-1}	
H_2O_2	$\dfrac{k[H^+][HSO_3^-][H_2O_2(aq)]}{1 + K[H^+]}$	Hoffmann and Calvert (1985)
	$k = 7.45 \times 10^7$ M^{-1} sec^{-1} at 298 K	
	$k = 13$ M^{-1}	
Fe(III)	$k[\text{Fe(III)}][SO_3^{2-}]$	Hoffmann and Calvert (1985)
	$k = 1.2 \times 10^6$ M^{-1} sec^{-1} at 293 K pH ≤ 5	
Mn(II)	$k_2[\text{Mn(II)}][HSO_3^-]$	Hoffmann and Calvert (1985)
	$k_2 = 3.4 \times 10^3$ M^{-1} sec^{-1} at 298 K	
	$[S(IV)] \leq 10^{-4}$ M	
	$[\text{Mn(II)}] \leq 10^{-5}$ M	
	$k_1[\text{Mn}^{2+}][H^+]^{-1}\beta_1$	
	$k_1 = 2 \times 10^9$ M^{-1} sec^{-1}	
	$\beta_1 = \dfrac{[\text{Mn}_2\text{OH}^{3+}][H^+]}{[\text{Mn}^{2+}]}$	
	$\beta_1 = 10^{-9.9}$ at 298 K	
N(III)[a]	$k[H^+]^{1/2}H_{HNO_2}H^*_{S(IV)}\,p_{HNO_2}\,p_{SO_2}\left(1 + \dfrac{K_{n4}}{[H^+]}\right)$	Lee and Schwartz (1982)
	$k = 142$ M$^{-3/2}$ sec^{-1} at 298 K	
NO_2	$kH_{NO_2}H^*_{S(IV)}\,p_{NO_2}\,p_{SO_2}$	Lee and Schwartz (1982)
	$k = 2 \times 10^6$ M^{-1} sec^{-1} at 298 K	

[a] $[N(III)] = [HNO_2(aq)] + [NO_2^-]$. Based on

$$HNO_2(g) \rightleftarrows HNO_2(aq) \quad H_{HNO_2}$$

$$HNO_2(aq) \rightleftarrows H^+ + NO_2^- \quad K_{n4}$$

we obtain

$$[N(III)] = H_{NO_2}\,p_{HNO_2}[1 + K_{n4}/[H^+]]$$

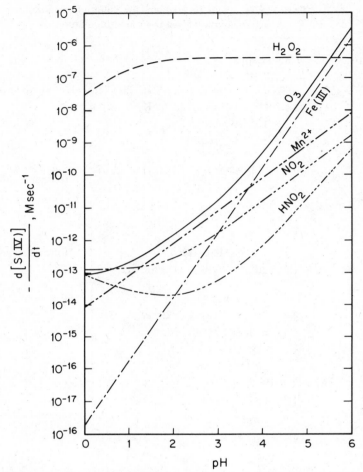

Figure 5.8. Comparison of aqueous-phase SO_2 oxidation paths. The rate of conversion of S(IV) to S(VI) as a function of pH. Conditions assumed are: $[SO_2(g)] = 5$ ppb; $[HNO_2(g)] = 2$ ppb; $[H_2O_2(g)] = 1$ ppb; $[NO_2(g)] = 1$ ppb; $[O_3(g)] = 50$ ppb; $[Fe^{3+}(aq)] = 3 \times 10^{-7}$ M; $[Mn^{2+}(aq)] = 3 \times 10^{-8}$ M.

We see that oxidation by dissolved H_2O_2 is the predominant pathway for sulfate formation at pH values less than roughly 4 or 5. At pH $\cong$ 5 and greater, oxidation by O_3 is 10 times faster than that by H_2O_2. Also, oxidation of S(IV) by O_2 catalyzed by Fe and Mn may be important at high pH, but uncertainties in the rate expressions at high pH preclude a definitive conclusion. Oxidation of S(IV) by NO_2 and $HNO_2(NO_2^-)$ are unimportant at all pH for the concentration levels studied.

The inhibition of most oxidation mechanisms at low pH results mainly from the lower overall solubility of SO_2 with increasing acidity. H_2O_2 is the only identified oxidant for which the rate is virtually independent of pH. The rates of the transition metal catalyzed reactions increase with increasing pH, although this increase is, in the case of Fe, moderated by limitations on solubility as pH increases.

Note that even though we have presented estimates of the rate of S(IV) oxidation by NO_2, the rate expression in Section 5.4.8 is only tentative, and even then, valid only around pH 6.

The effect of temperature on oxidation rates is a result of two competing factors. First, at lower temperatures, higher concentrations of gases are dissolved at equilibrium, which will lead to higher reaction rates. On the other hand, rate constants in the rate expressions generally decrease as temperature decreases. The two effects therefore act in opposite directions. Except for Fe and Mn-catalyzed oxidation, the increased solubility effect dominates and the rate increases with decreasing temperature. In the transition–metal catalyzed reaction, the consequence of the large activation energy is that as temperature decreases the rate of sulfate formation decreases. Also, the Fe and Mn concentrations do not change with temperature, as do the "Henry's law" gases.

As we have noted, it is often useful to express aqueous-phase oxidation rates in terms of a fractional rate of conversion of sulfur. Assuming cloud conditions with 1 g m^{-3} of liquid water, we find that the rate of oxidation by H_2O_2 can exceed 100 percent hr^{-1}. The Fe and Mn-catalyzed rates are below 1 percent hr^{-1} for solutions of pH < 4.5.

5.5. REACTION KINETICS OF AQUEOUS NITROGEN CHEMISTRY

At the end of Section 5.2.4 we derived rate expressions for the forward reactions,

$$2NO_2(aq) \rightarrow 2H^+ + NO_2^- + NO_3^- \tag{1}$$

$$NO(aq) + NO_2(aq) \rightarrow 2H^+ + 2NO_2^- \tag{2}$$

Although the calculations presented in that section presumed equilibrium to exist, we noted that we needed to examine the rates of the above forward reactions. Let us therefore begin this section with an analysis of the rates of formation of nitrite and nitrate ions by these two reactions.

Because of the interconversion that exists between NO_2^- and HNO_2 in solution, when dealing with nitrite it is more appropriate to consider the rates of formation and destruction of N(III) rather than of NO_2^- and HNO_2 separately. We thus write reaction (1) as

$$NO_2(aq) + NO_2(aq) \rightarrow N(III) + NO_3^-$$

Since the equilibrium,

$$HNO_2 \rightleftarrows H^+ + NO_2^-$$

is assumed to hold, we can write that

$$\frac{d[NO_2^-]}{dt} = \frac{K_{n4}}{[H^+]} \frac{d[HNO_2]}{dt}$$

However, we must be careful how we compute these rates.

Consider a reaction that produces NO_2^- whose rate is given by R. Suppose also that the equilibrium, $HNO_2 \rightleftarrows H^+ + NO_2^-$, holds. At high pH, virtually all of the N(III) exists as NO_2^-, in which case the actual rate of NO_2^- formation is equal to R. Also,

$$\frac{d[HNO_2]}{dt} = \frac{[H^+]}{K_{n4}} R$$

We note that "high pH" means that $[H^+]/K_{n4} \ll 1$. At low pH (i.e. $[H^+]/K_{n4} \gg 1$), all N(III) exists as HNO_2, and as soon as NO_2^- is produced by the NO_2–NO reaction, it is immediately transformed to HNO_2 by the equilibrium. In that case,

$$\frac{d[HNO_2]}{dt} = R$$

and

$$\frac{d[NO_2^-]}{dt} = \frac{K_{n4}}{[H^+]} R$$

For this system we can thus write the general rates,

$$\frac{d[NO_2^-]}{dt} = \frac{[NO_2^-]}{[N(III)]} R = \frac{R}{1 + \dfrac{K_{n4}}{[H^+]}}$$

$$\frac{d[HNO_2]}{dt} = \frac{[HNO_2]}{[N(III)]} R = \frac{R}{1 + \dfrac{[H^+]}{K_{n4}}}$$

and that

$$\frac{d[N(III)]}{dt} = R$$

TABLE 5.12. Reactions and Rate Expressions for Aqueous-Phase Nitrite and Nitrate Forming Reactions at 298 K

Reaction	Rate Expression, M sec^{-1}	Reference
$NO_2^- + O_3(aq) \rightarrow NO_3^- + O_2(aq)$	$200[H^+]^{-1}[NO_2^-][O_3(aq)]$	Martin et al. (1981)
$NO_2^- + H_2O_2(aq) \rightarrow NO_3^- + H_2O$	$4.6 \times 10^3[H^+][NO_2^-][H_2O_2(aq)]$	Martin et al. (1981)
$NO_2(aq) + Fe^{2+} \rightarrow NO_2^- + Fe^{3+}$	$5 \times 10^4[Fe^{2+}][NO_2(aq)]$	Schwartz and White (1983)(1983)

The following additional reactions have been identified as nitrite- and nitrate-forming paths in aqueous solution:

$$NO_2^- + O_3(aq) \rightarrow NO_3^- + O_2(aq)$$

$$NO_2^- + H_2O_2(aq) \rightarrow NO_3^- + H_2O$$

$$NO_2(aq) + Fe^{2+}(aq) \rightarrow NO_2^- + Fe^{3+}$$

Rate expressions for these three reactions at 298 K are given in Table 5.12.

Let us now compute the rates of formation of N(III) and N(V) when reactions (1) and (2), together with the three in Table 5.12, are occurring.

Figure 5.9 shows the rates of formation of N(V) as a function of pH up to pH = 7, for various values of p_{NO_2} and $p_{HNO_2} = 10^{-10}$ atm, $p_{O_3} = 5 \times 10^{-8}$ atm, $[H_2O_2(aq)] = 10^{-5}$ M and $[Fe^{2+}(aq)] = 10^{-5}$ M. The rate of N(III) production is shown in Figure 5.10 for comparable conditions. The formation rate of N(V) can be written as

$$\frac{d[N(V)]}{dt} = A + \frac{B}{[H^+]^2} + 4250 p_{NO_2}^2$$

where $A = 1.1 \times 10^{-13}$ and $B = 3.2 \times 10^{-19}$. Based on this expression, we can construct Figure 5.11, illustrating the regions where different formation reactions are important. N(III) production can be similarly represented in Figure 5.12. At a critical pH value, N(III) changes from being produced to being consumed. This pH is found at 298 K from

$$p_{NO_2}\left(4250 p_{NO_2} + 3.1 \times 10^{-3} + 1400 p_{NO}\right) = 1.1 \times 10^{-13}$$

$$+ 3.2 \times 10^{-19}[H^+]^{-2}$$

For a given pH we can construct the locus of NO and NO$_2$ partial pressures at which there is the transition from N(III) formation to consumption. These loci

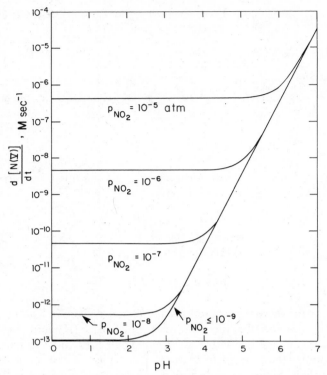

Figure 5.9. Rate of formation of N(V) as a function of pH and p_{NO_2}. For $p_{NO_2} > 5 \times 10^{-9}$ atm, along the horizontal portion of the curve the reaction $NO_2 + NO_2 \rightarrow$ N(III) + N(V) is the dominant mode of N(V) production. For $p_{NO_2} < 5 \times 10^{-9}$ atm and low pH, H_2O_2 reaction is the dominant mode. The curved part of the line indicates the transition between the NO_2–NO_2 reaction and the NO_2–O_3 reaction as the dominant N(V)-producing mechanism. The line at the high pH end represents the rate of formation of N(V) by the $NO_2^- + O_3$ reaction.

are given in Figure 5.13, where, in the regions above the line N(III) is formed and below N(III) is consumed.

We see that at values of p_{NO_2} typical of moderately polluted conditions, nitrate formation is dominated by H_2O_2 at pH ≤ 3 and by O_3 at pH ≥ 3. We can use the results in Figure 5.9 together with the nomogram, Figure 5.5, to place these aqueous-phase rates on a gas-phase basis. For $L = 10^{-10}$, corresponding to aqueous aerosols, we see that the aqueous-phase rate must exceed 10^{-4} M sec^{-1} for the corresponding gas-phase rate to exceed 1 ppb hr^{-1}. The reactions considered here do not lead to rates of this magnitude. Under cloud conditions, (e.g., $L = 10^{-6}$), the aqueous-phase rate must exceed 10^{-8} M sec^{-1} to give a gas-phase rate of 1 ppb hr^{-1}. Only the O_3–NO_2^- and NO_2(aq)–NO_2(aq) reactions might be able to generate such a rate, but only if the pH is greater than about 5 and p_{NO_2} is greater than 10^{-6} atm (1 ppm).

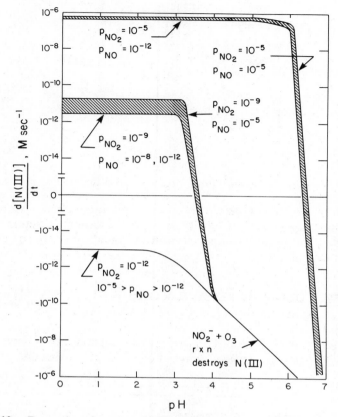

Figure 5.10. Dynamics of aqueous N(III) production as a function of pH, p_{NO} and p_{NO_2}. $T = 298$ K.

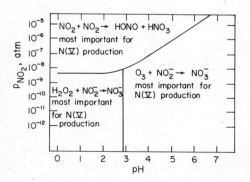

Figure 5.11. Reactions that contribute to N(V) production.

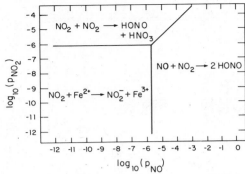

Figure 5.12.   Regions of aqueous nitrogen reactions as a function of p_{NO_2} and p_{NO}.

Such conditions are not expected to occur in the atmosphere. We conclude, therefore, that aqueous-phase nitrite and nitrate-forming reactions are expected to be of only minor importance in the atmosphere except under the most extreme conditions.

5.6.   DYNAMIC BEHAVIOR OF SOLUTIONS WITH AQUEOUS-PHASE CHEMICAL REACTIONS

To compare the rates of various aqueous-phase reaction mechanisms we have been calculating the instantaneous rates of conversion as a function of solution

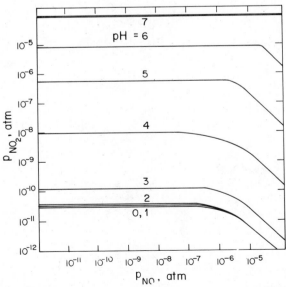

Figure 5.13.   Locus of NO–NO$_2$ partial pressures at critical pH from pH = 0 to 7. Above lines, N(III) is formed. Below lines, N(III) is destroyed, on an overall basis.

pH. In the atmosphere a droplet is formed, usually by nucleation around a particle, and is subsequently exposed to an environment containing reactive gases. Gases are absorbed establishing an initial pH and composition. If aqueous-phase reactions then ensue, the composition and pH will change with time. In this section we consider the calculation of that time evolution. We neglect any changes in droplet size that might result; for dilute solutions such as those considered here, this is a good assumption. We focus on sulfur chemistry here because of its importance in acid deposition (see Chapter 18).

In our calculations up to this point we have simply assumed values for the gas-phase partial pressure. When the process occurs over time, we must consider what is occurring in the gas-phase. Two assumptions can be made concerning the gas phase:

1. *Open System.* Gas phase partial pressures are maintained at constant values, presumably by continuous infusion of new air. (This situation might hold if a cloud is "processing" many volumes of air.)

2. *Closed System.* Gas phase partial pressures decrease with time as material is depleted from the gas phase. (This situation holds if the air and the cloud occupy the same physical volume of space, and gaseous species are not replenished.)

5.6.1. Closed System

The basic assumption in the closed system is that the total quantity of each species is fixed. Consider, as an example, H_2O_2 in a closed system containing liquid water. Let the total concentration of H_2O_2 per unit physical volume of air be $[H_2O_2]_{total}$. Then this total H_2O_2 is distributed between gas and aqueous phases by

$$[H_2O_2]_{total} = \frac{p_{H_2O_2}}{RT} + [H_2O_2(aq)] L \tag{5.1}$$

If, in addition, Henry's law is assumed to hold,

$$[H_2O_2(aq)] = H_{H_2O_2} p_{H_2O_2} \tag{5.2}$$

The fraction of the total quantity of H_2O_2 that resides in the liquid phase is given by

$$\frac{H_{H_2O_2} L}{1/RT + H_{H_2O_2} L}$$

We can evaluate this expression to calculate the aqueous-phase fraction of H_2O_2 at 298 K as a function of $L (H_{H_2O_2} = 7.1 \times 10^4$ M atm^{-1}). As a comparison we can use the same expression to calculate the aqueous-phase fraction of ozone at 298 K as a function of $L(H_{O_3} = 9.4 \times 10^{-3})$:

L	10^{-5}	10^{-6}	10^{-7}
aqueous fraction H_2O_2	0.95	0.63	0.15
aqueous fraction O_3	2.3×10^{-6}	2.3×10^{-7}	2.3×10^{-8}

We can see that a species like H_2O_2 with a large Henry's law coefficient will have a significant fraction of a fixed total quantity in the aqueous phase. As L increases, more liquid is available to accommodate the gas and the aqueous fraction increases.

Figure 5.14 shows $[H_2O_2(aq)]$ as a function of L for $[H_2O_2]_{total}$ equivalent to 1 and 5 ppb (1 ppb = 4.063×10^{-11} M.* The aqueous-phase H_2O_2 concentration increase as L decreases reflecting the decrease in the amount of liquid water available to accommodate the H_2O_2.

The same type of calculation can be carried out for a dissociating species, such as HNO_3. We have[†]

$$[HNO_3]_{total} = \frac{p_{HNO_3}}{RT} + ([HNO_3(aq)] + [NO_3^-])L \qquad (5.3)$$

where Henry's law gives

$$[HNO_3(aq)] = H_{HNO_3} p_{HNO_3} \qquad (5.4)$$

and dissociation equilibrium is

$$K_{n1} = \frac{[H^+][NO_3^-]}{[HNO_3(aq)]} \qquad (5.5)$$

Solving Eqs. (5.3), (5.4), and (5.5) simultaneously,

$$[HNO_3(aq)] = \frac{H_{HNO_3}RT}{1 + LH^*_{HNO_3}RT}[HNO_3]_{total}$$

$$[NO_3^-] = \frac{K_{n1}}{[H^+]}\frac{H_{HNO_3}RT}{1 + LH^*_{HNO_3}RT}[HNO_3]_{total}$$

---

*Richards et al. (1983) measured H_2O_2 levels in Los Angeles cloud water and found values ranging from 0.9×10^{-6} M to 88×10^{-6} M.

[†] In theory nitric acid exists in aqueous solution as both undissociated HNO_3 and $H^+ + NO_3^-$. For this reason we express Eq. (5.3) in terms of both $[HNO_3(aq)]$ and $[NO_3^-]$. Since pK_a of $HNO_3 = -1.2$, the pH would have to be 1.2, or $[H^+] \cong 15.4$ M, for substantial undissociated HNO_3 to exist.

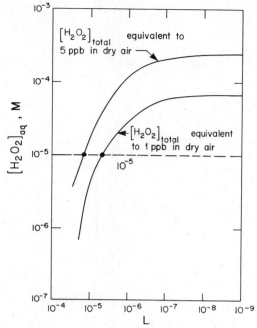

Figure 5.14. Aqueous-phase H_2O_2 as a function of liquid water content L for 1 and 5 ppb H_2O_2.

where

$$H^*_{HNO_3} = \frac{[HNO_3(aq)] + [NO_3^-]}{p_{HNO_3}}$$

5.6.2. Calculation of Concentration Changes in a Droplet with Aqueous-Phase Reactions

Let us consider a droplet that at $t = 0$ is immersed in air containing SO_2, NH_3, H_2O_2, O_3, and HNO_3. Equilibrium is immediately established between the gas and aqueous phases. As the aqueous-phase oxidation of S(IV) to S(VI) proceeds, the concentrations of all the ions adjust so as to satisfy electroneutrality at all times,

$$[H^+] + [NH_4^+] = [OH^-] + [HSO_3^-] + 2[SO_3^{2-}]$$

$$+ 2[SO_4^{2-}] + [HSO_4^-] + [NO_3^-]$$

The concentrations of each ion except $[SO_4^{2-}]$ can be expressed in terms of $[H^+]$ using the equilibrium constant expressions,

$$[NH_4^+] = \frac{K_{ha}K_{a1}}{K_w} p_{NH_3}[H^+]$$

$$[OH^-] = \frac{K_w}{[H^+]}$$

$$[HSO_3^-] = \frac{K_{hs}K_{s1}}{[H^+]} p_{SO_2}$$

$$[SO_3^{2-}] = \frac{K_{hs}K_{s1}K_{s2}}{[H^+]^2} p_{SO_2}$$

$$[NO_3^-] = \frac{K_{hn}K_{n3}p_{HNO_3}}{[H^+]}$$

If we define $[S(VI)] = [SO_4^{2-}] + [HSO_4^-] + [H_2SO_4(aq)]$, then

$$[HSO_4^-] = \frac{[S(VI)]}{\dfrac{[H^+]}{K_{s3}} + 1 + \dfrac{K_{s4}}{[H^+]}}$$

$$[SO_4^{2-}] = \frac{[S(VI)]}{\dfrac{[H^+]^2}{K_{s3}K_{s4}} + \dfrac{[H^+]}{K_{s4}} + 1}$$

where K_{s3} and K_{s4} are the equilibrium constants for the reaction,

$$H_2SO_4(aq) \rightleftarrows H^+ + HSO_4^-$$

$$HSO_4^- \rightleftarrows H^+ + SO_4^{2-}$$

respectively. For all practical purposes K_{s3} may be considered to be infinite since virtually no undissociated sulfuric acid will exist in solution, and $K_{s4} = 1.2 \times 10^{-2}$ M at 298 K.

The concentration changes are computed as follows. At $t = 0$, if no S(VI) is present, the electroneutrality equation is solved to determine $[H^+]$ and, thereby, the concentrations of all the dissolved species. If an open system is assumed, then the gas-phase partial pressures will remain constant with time. For a closed system, the partial pressures change with time as outlined above. The concentration changes are computed over small time increments of length Δt. The sulfate present at any time t is equal to that at time $t - \Delta t$ plus that formed in the interval Δt,

$$[SO_4^{2-}]_t = [SO_4^{2-}]_{t-\Delta t} + \left(\frac{d[SO_4^{2-}]}{dt}\right)_{t-\Delta t} \Delta t$$

The value of $[SO_4^{2-}]$ at time t is then substituted into the electroneutrality equation to obtain the new $[H^+]$ and the concentrations of other dissolved species. This process is then just repeated over the time interval of interest.

Let us compare the evolution of open and closed systems for an identical set of starting conditions. We choose the following conditions at $t = 0$:

$$[S(IV)]_{total} = 5 \text{ ppb} \qquad pH = 6.17$$
$$[HNO_3]_{total} = 1 \text{ ppb} \qquad L = 10^{-6}$$
$$[NH_3]_{total} = 5 \text{ ppb}$$
$$[O_3]_{total} = 5 \text{ ppb}$$
$$[H_2O_2]_{total} = 1 \text{ ppb}$$

For the closed system, there is no replenishment, whereas in the open system the partial pressures of all species in the gas phase are maintained constant at their initial values and aqueous-phase concentrations are determined by equilibrium. The initial gas-phase concentrations in both cases are:

$$p_{SO_2} = 3.03 \text{ ppb} \qquad\qquad p_{O_3} = 5 \text{ ppb}$$
$$p_{NH_3} = 1.87 \text{ ppb} \qquad\qquad p_{H_2O_2} = 0.465 \text{ ppb}$$
$$p_{HNO_3} = 8.54 \times 10^{-9} \text{ ppb}$$

In the open system these partial pressures remain constant throughout the simulation, whereas in the closed system they may be depleted. A comment concerning the choice of O_3 concentration is in order. We selected the uncharacteristically low value of 5 ppb so as to be able to show the interplay possible between both the H_2O_2 and O_3 oxidation rates and, in the closed system, the role of depletion as the reaction proceeds. However, even at O_3 of 50 ppb the dynamics of the system are dominated by the great reduction in O_3 oxidation of S(IV) as pH drops and by the depletion of H_2O_2 in the closed system.

Figures 5.15 and 5.16 show the sulfate concentration and pH, respectively, in the open and closed systems over a 60-minute period.

More sulfate is produced in the open system than in the closed system, but the pH decrease is less in the open system. This behavior is a result of several

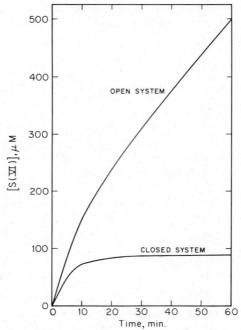

Figure 5.15. Aqueous sulfate concentration as a function of time for both open and closed systems. The conditions for the simulation are: [S(IV)]total = 5 ppb; [NH$_3$]total = 5 ppb; [HNO$_3$]total = 1 ppb; [O$_3$]total = 5 ppb; [H$_2$O$_2$]total = 1 ppb; $L = 10^{-6}$; pH$_0$ = 6.17.

factors:

1. Sulfate production due to H$_2$O$_2$ and O$_3$ is less in the closed system due to depletion of H$_2$O$_2$ and O$_3$.

2. Continued replenishment of NH$_3$ provides more neutralization in the open system.

3. The low pH in the closed system drives S(IV) from solution.

4. The lower pH in the closed system depresses the rate of sulfate formation by O$_3$.

5. S(IV) is continually depleted in the closed system.

6. Total HNO$_3$ *decreases* in the open system due to the decrease in pH.

In the open system the importance of H$_2$O$_2$ in sulfate formation grows significantly, from less than 20 percent to over 80 percent, whereas in the closed system the increasing importance of H$_2$O$_2$ is enhanced at lower pH but suppressed by the depletion of H$_2$O$_2$. The depletion effect predominates so that after about 30 min sulfate formation ceases in the closed system. The fractions of SO$_2$, O$_3$, and H$_2$O$_2$ reacted in the closed system at 60 min are

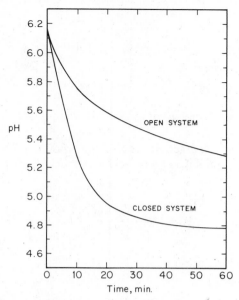

Figure 5.16. pH as a function of time for both open and closed systems. Same conditions as Figure 5.15.

0.432, 0.233, and 0.997, respectively, and the fractions of sulfate production due to O_3 are 0.444 and 0.539 in the open and closed systems, respectively.

5.7. NONIDEAL SOLUTION THERMODYNAMICS

By writing equilibrium constants in terms of concentrations rather than activities, we have in this chapter presumed the solutions to be ideal. In this section, we will examine that assumption and show how it might be relaxed. Equilibrium constants relate the activities of components in solution, and activities can be equated to concentrations only when the ionic strength of the solution is low. At higher ionic strengths, activities and concentrations are not equivalent but are related by activity coefficients. To see this, consider the equilibrium,

$$MX \rightleftarrows M^+ + X^-$$

The equilibrium constant for this reaction is defined by

$$K = \frac{a_{M+}a_{X-}}{a_{MX}} = \frac{(\gamma_{M+}m_{M+})(\gamma_{X-}m_{X-})}{\gamma_{MX}m_{MX}}$$

where

$$a_{M+}, a_{X-}, a_{MX} = \text{activities of } M^+ \text{ and } X^-, \text{ and } MX \text{ in solution}$$

$$\gamma_{M+}, \gamma_{X-}, \gamma_{MX} = \text{activity coefficients of } M^+, X^-, MX$$

$$m_{M+}, m_{X-}, m_{MX} = \text{molalities of } M^+, X^-, \text{ and } MX \, (\text{mole kg}^{-1})$$

It is customary to express the activity coefficient product $\gamma_{M+}\gamma_{X-}$ as $\gamma_{\pm}^2$, where $\gamma_{\pm}$ is called the mean molal activity coefficient of M^+X^-. Thus, the equilibrium expression becomes

$$K = \frac{\gamma_{\pm}^2}{\gamma_{MX}} \frac{m_{M+}m_{X-}}{m_{MX}}$$

The ionic strength of a solution is defined by

$$I = \tfrac{1}{2}\sum_i z_i^2 m_i$$

where z_i is the charge on ion i. For ionic strengths below 0.5, molalities and molarities are virtually identical, so the molalities in the above equation for K can be replaced by the usual molarities. Thus, we have in this case

$$K = \frac{\gamma_{\pm}^2}{\gamma_{MX}} \frac{[M^+][X^-]}{[MX]}$$

For ionic strengths $I < 0.5$ the activity coefficient for ion i can be calculated by the so-called Davies equation,

$$\log \gamma_i = -Az_i^2\left(\frac{I^{1/2}}{1 + I^{1/2}} - 0.2I\right)$$

where $A = 0.5085$ for water.

The use of a correlation such as this assumes that the mean molal activity coefficient of any electrolyte in a multicomponent solution at a given ionic strength is the same as that for pure solution at the same ionic strength. This is the simplest method of estimating activity coefficients in mixed electrolyte solutions and is based on the ionic strength principle of Lewis and Randall. It is a reasonable approximation for most situations that will be encountered in atmospheric chemistry. A notable exception occurs in highly concentrated aerosols where ionic strengths may be as high as 20 (Stelson and Seinfeld,

1981). Modifications of this theory have been developed for this case (Stelson and Seinfeld, 1982a, b, c; Stelson et al., 1984).

For calculations involving cloud and rain drops, the concentrations of dissolved species are sufficiently dilute that all activity coefficients are unity and molalities and molarities are equivalent. Thus, nonideality effects have been neglected in all calculations presented in this chapter.

REFERENCES

Alkezweeny, A. J., and Powell, D. C. "Estimation of Transformation Rate of SO_2 to SO_4 from Atmospheric Concentration Data," *Atmos. Environ.*, **11**, 179–182 (1977).

Baldwin, A. C. "Heterogeneous Reactions of Sulfur Dioxide with Carbonaceous Particles," *Int. J. Chem. Kinetics*, **14**, 269–277 (1982).

Benner, W. H., Brodzinsky, R., and Novakov, T. "Oxidation of SO_2 in Droplets Which Contain Soot Particles," *Atmos. Environ.*, **16**, 1333–1339 (1982).

Beutier, D., and Renon, H. "Representation of NH_3–H_2S–H_2O, NH_3–CO_2–H_2O, and NH_3–SO_2–H_2O Vapor-Liquid Equilibria," *Ind. Eng. Chem. Process Des. Dev.*, **17**, 220–230 (1978).

Brimblecombe, P., and Spedding, D. J. "The Dissolution of Iron from Ferric Oxide and Pulverized Fuel Ash," *Atmos. Environ.*, **9**, 835–838 (1975).

Britton, L. G., and Clarke, A. G. "Heterogeneous Reactions of Sulfur Dioxide and SO_2/NO_2 Mixtures with a Carbon Soot Aerosol," *Atmos. Environ.*, **14**, 829–839 (1980).

Brodzinsky, R., Chang, S. G., Markowitz, S. S., and Novakov, T. "Kinetics and Mechanism for the Catalytic Oxidation of Sulfur Dioxide on Carbon in Aqueous Suspensions," *J. Phys. Chem.*, **84**, 3354–3358 (1980).

Cantrell, B. K., and Whitby, K. T. "Aerosol Size Distributions and Aerosol Volume Formation for a Coal-Fired Power Plant Plume," *Atmos. Environ.*, **12**, 323–334 (1978).

Chan, W. H., Vet, R. J., Lusis, M. A., Hunt, J. E., and Stevens, R. D. S. "Airborne Sulfur Dioxide to Sulfate Oxidation Studies of the INCO 381 m Chimney Plume," *Atmos. Environ.*, **14**, 1159–1170 (1980).

Chang, T. Y. "Estimate of the Conversion Rate of SO_2 to SO_4 from the DaVinci Flight Data," *Atmos. Environ.*, **13**, 1663–1664 (1979).

Cofer, W. R., Schryer, D. R., and Rogowski, R. S. "The Enhanced Oxidation of SO_2 by NO_2 on Carbon Particulates," *Atmos. Environ.*, **14**, 571–575 (1980).

Denbigh, K. G. *The Principles of Chemical Equilibrium*, 3rd ed., Cambridge University Press (1971).

Dittenhoefer, A. C., and dePena, R. G. "Study of Production and Growth of Sulfate Particles in Plumes from a Coal-Fired Power Plant," *Atmos. Environ.*, **12**, 297–306 (1978).

Dlugi, R., Jordan, S., and Lindemann, E. "The Heterogeneous Formation of Sulfate Aerosols in the Atmosphere," *J. Aero. Sci.*, **12**, 185–197 (1981).

Dlugi, R., and Jordan, S. "Heterogeneous SO_2-Oxidation: Its Contribution to the Cloud Condensation Nuclei Formation Process," *J. Hungarian Meteor. Service*, **86**, 82–88 (1982).

Faust, B. C. "Photo-Induced Reductive Dissolution of Hematite (α-Fe_2O_3) by S(IV) Oxyanions," Ph.D. Thesis, California Institute of Technology, Pasadena, CA (1984).

Faust, B., and Hoffmann, M. R. "Photo-Assisted Oxidation of S(IV) by Oxygen in Aqueous Hematite (α-Fe_2O_3) Suspensions," American Chemical Society, 189th National Meeting, Miami, FL (1985).

Forrest, J., and Newman, L. "Further Studies on the Oxidation of Sulfur Dioxide in Coal-Fired Power Plant Plumes," *Atmos. Environ.*, **11**, 465–474 (1977a).

Forrest, J., and Newman, L. "Oxidation of Sulfur Dioxide in the Sudbury Smelter Plume," *Atmos. Environ.*, **11**, 517–520 (1977b).

Forrest, J., Garber, R., and Newman, L. "Conversion Rates in Power Plant Plumes Based on Filter Pack Data—Part I: The Coal-Fired Cumberland Plume," *Atmos. Environ.*, **15**, 2273–2282 (1981).

Gillani, N. V. "Project MISTT: Mesoscale Plume Modeling of the Dispersion, Transformation and Ground Removal of SO_2," *Atmos. Environ.*, **12**, 569–588 (1978).

Gillani, N. V., Husar, R. B., Patterson, D. E., and Wilson, W. E. "Project MISTT: Kinetics of Particulate Sulfur Formation in a Power Plant Plume Out to 300 km," *Atmos. Environ.*, **12**, 589–598 (1978).

Hegg, D. A., and Hobbs, P. V. "Measurements of Gas-to-Particle Conversion in the Plumes from Five Coal-Fired Electric Power Plants," *Atmos. Environ.*, **14**, 99–116 (1980).

Hobbs, P. V., Hegg, D. A., Eltgroth, M. W., and Radke, L. F. "Evolution of Particles in the Plumes of Coal-Fired Electric Power Plants," *Atmos. Environ.*, **13**, 935–951 (1979).

Hoffmann, M. R. "On the Kinetics and Mechanism of Oxidation of Aquated Sulfur Dioxide by Ozone," *Atmos. Environ.*, **19**, in press (1985).

Hoffmann, M. R., and Calvert, J. G. "Chemical Transformation Modules for Eulerian Acid Deposition Models. Volume II. The Aqueous-Phase Chemistry," National Center for Atmospheric Research, Boulder, CO (1985).

Hoffmann, M. R., and Edwards, J. O. "Kinetics of the Oxidation of Sulfite by Hydrogen Peroxide in Acidic Solution," *J. Phys. Chem.*, **79**, 2096–2098 (1975).

Hoffmann, M. R., and Jacob, D. J. "Kinetics and Mechanisms of the Catalytic Oxidation of Dissolved Sulfur Dioxide in Aqueous Solution: An Application to Nighttime Fog Water Chemistry," in SO_2, *NO and NO_2 Oxidation Mechanisms: Atmospheric Considerations*, J. G. Calvert (Ed.), Butterworth, Boston, 101–172 (1984).

Husar, R. B., Patterson, D. E., Husar, J. D., Gillani, N. V., and Wilson, W. E. "Sulfur Budget of a Power Plant Plume," *Atmos. Environ.*, **12**, 549–568 (1978).

Huss, A., Jr., Lim, P. K., and Eckert, C. A. "Oxidation of Aqueous SO_2. 1. Homogeneous Manganese(II) and Iron(II) Catalysis at Low pH," *J. Phys. Chem.*, **86**, 4224–4228 (1982a).

Huss, A., Jr., Lim, P. K., and Eckert, C. A. "Oxidation of Aqueous SO_2. 2. High Pressure Studies and Proposed Reaction Mechanisms," *J. Phys. Chem.*, **86**, 4229–4233 (1982b).

Judeikis, H. S., Steward, T. B., and Wren, A. G. "Laboratory Studies of Heterogeneous Reactions of SO_2," *Atmos. Environ.*, **12**, 1633–1641 (1978).

Kirk, R. E., and Othmer, D. E. (Eds.), *Encyclopedia of Chemical Technology*, Interscience Encyclopedia, New York (1981).

Lee, Y. N., and Schwartz, S. E. "Evaluation of the Rate of Uptake of Nitrogen Dioxide by Atmospheric and Surface Liquid Water," *J. Geophys. Res.*, **86**, 11971–11983 (1981).

Lee, Y. N., and Schwartz, S. E. "Kinetics of Oxidation of Aqueous Sulfur(IV) by Nitrogen Dioxide," Fourth International Conference on Precipitation Scavenging, Dry Deposition and Resuspension, Santa Monica, California (1982).

Liberti, A., Brocco, D., and Possanzini, M. "Adsorption and Oxidation of Sulfur Dioxide on Particles," *Atmos. Environ.*, **12**, 255–261 (1978).

Liljestrand, H. M., and Morgan, J. J. "Spatial Variations of Acid Precipitation in Southern California," *Environ. Sci. Technol.*, **15**, 333–338 (1981).

Lusis, M. A., Anlauf, K. G., Barrie, L. A., and Wiebe, H. A. "Plume Chemistry Studies at a Northern Alberta Power Plant," *Atmos. Environ.*, **12**, 2429–2438 (1978).

Lusis, M. A., and Wiebe, H. A. "The Rate of Oxidation of Sulfur Dioxide in the Plume of a Nickel Smelter Stack," *Atmos. Environ.*, **10**, 793–798 (1976).

Maahs, H. G. "Sulfur Dioxide/Water Equilibria Between 0° and 50°C. An Examination of Data at Low Concentrations," in *Heterogeneous Atmospheric Chemistry*, D. R. Schryer (Ed.), Am. Geophys. Union, 187–195 (1982).

Mamane, Y., and Pueschel, R. F. "Formation of Sulfate Particles in the Plume of the Four Corners Power Plant," *J. Appl. Meteor.*, **19**, 779–790 (1980).

Martin, L. R. "Kinetic Studies of Sulfite Oxidation in Aqueous Solution," in: *SO₂, NO, NO₂ Oxidation Mechanisms: Atmospheric Considerations*, J. G. Calvert (Ed.), Butterworth, Boston, 63–100 (1984a).

Martin, L. R. "Atmospheric Liquid Water as a Reaction Medium," Conference on Gas-Liquid Chemistry of Natural Waters, Brookhaven National Laboratory, Upton, NY, April 1984b.

Martin, L. R., and Damschen, D. E. "Aqueous Oxidation of Sulfur Dioxide by Hydrogen Peroxide at Low pH," *Atmos. Environ.*, **15**, 1615–1622 (1981).

Martin, L. R., Damschen, D. E., and Judeikis, H. S. "The Reactions of Nitrogen Oxides with SO₂ in Aqueous Aerosols," *Atmos. Environ.*, **15**, 191–195 (1981).

Meagher, J. F., Stockburger, L., Bailey, E. M., and Huff, O. "The Oxidation of Sulfur Dioxide to Sulfate Aerosols in the Plume of a Coal-Fired Power Plant," *Atmos. Environ.*, **12**, 2197–2203 (1978).

McArdle, J. V., and Hoffmann, M. R. "Kinetics and Mechanism of the Oxidation of Aquated Sulfur Dioxide by Hydrogen Peroxide at Low pH," *J. Phys. Chem.*, **87**, 5425–5429 (1983).

National Center for Atmospheric Research, *Regional Acid Deposition: Models and Physical Processes*, Boulder, CO (1982).

Newman, L., Forrest, J., and Manowitz, B. "The Application of an Isotopic Ratio Technique to a Study of the Atmospheric Oxidation of Sulfur Dioxide in the Plume from a Coal-Fired Power Plant," *Atmos. Environ.*, **9**, 969–977 (1975).

Oblath, S. B., Markowitz, S. S., Novakov, T. and Chang, S. G. "Kinetics of the Initial Reaction of Nitrite Ion in Bisulfite Solutions," *J. Phys. Chem.*, **86**, 4853–4857 (1982).

Parungo, F., Ackerman, E., Proulx, H., and Pueschel, R. "Nucleation Properties of Fly Ash in a Coal-Fired Power-Plant Plume," *Atmos. Environ.*, **12**, 929–935 (1978).

Penkett, S. A., Jones, B. M. R., Brice, K. A., and Eggleton, A. E. J. "The Importance of Atmospheric Ozone and Hydrogen Peroxide in Oxidizing Sulphur Dioxide in Cloud and Rain Water," *Atmos. Environ.*, **13**, 123–137 (1979).

Pueschel, R. V., and Van Valin, C. C. "Cloud Nucleus Formation in a Power Plant Plume," *Atmos. Environ.*, **12**, 307–312 (1978).

Richards, L. W., Anderson, J. A., Blumenthal, D. L., McDonald, J. A., Kok, J. L., and Lazrus, A. L. "Hydrogen Peroxide and Sulfur (IV) in Los Angeles Cloud Water," *Atmos. Environ.*, **17**, 911–914 (1983).

Roberts, P. T., and Friedlander, S. K. "Conversion of SO₂ to Sulfur Particulate in the Los Angeles Atmosphere," *Environ. Health Persp.*, **10**, 103–108 (1975).

Roberts, D. B., and Williams, D. J. "The Kinetics of Oxidation of Sulfur Dioxide within the Plume from a Sulfide Smelter in a Remote Region," *Atmos. Environ.*, **13**, 1485–1499 (1979).

Rogowski, R. S., Schryer, D. R., Cofer, W. R., and Edahl, R. A., Jr. "Oxidation of SO₂ by NO₂ and Air in an Aqueous Suspension of Carbon," in *Heterogeneous Atmospheric Chemistry*, D. R. Schryer (Ed.), Am. Geophys. Union, Washington, D.C., 174–177 (1982).

Roth, J. A., and Sullivan, D. E. "Solubility of Ozone in Water," *Ind. Eng. Chem. Fund.*, **20**, 137–140 (1981).

Schwartz, S. E., and White, W. H. "Solubility Equilibria of the Nitrogen Oxides and Oxy-Acids in Dilute Aqueous Solution," *Adv. Environ. Sci. Tech.*, **4**, 1–45 (1981).

Schwartz, S. E., and White, W. H. "Kinetics of Reactive Dissolution of Nitrogen Oxides into Aqueous Solution," *Adv. Environ. Sci. Tech.*, **12**, 1–116 (1983).

Schwartz, S. E. "Gas Aqueous Reactions of Sulfur and Nitrogen Oxides in Liquid Water Clouds," in *SO₂, NO, and NO₂ Oxidation Mechanisms: Atmospheric Considerations*, J. G. Calvert (Ed.), Butterworth, Boston, 173–208 (1984).

Spicer, C. W., Joseph, D. W., Sticksel, P. R., Sverdrup, G. M., and Ward, G. F. "Reactions and Transport of Nitrogen Oxides and Ozone in the Atmosphere," Battelle-Columbus Report to EPA (1979).

Spicer, C. W., Koetz, J. R., Keigley, G. W., Sverdrup, G. M., and Ward, G. F. "A Study of Nitrogen Oxides Reactions Within Urban Plumes Transported Over the Ocean," U.S. Environmental Protection Agency, Research Triangle Park, NC (1981).

Stelson, A. W., and Seinfeld, J. H. "Chemical Mass Accounting of Urban Aerosol," *Environ. Sci. Tech.*, **15**, 671–679 (1981).

Stelson, A. W., and Seinfeld, J. H. "Relative Humidity and Temperature Dependence of the Ammonium Nitrate Dissociation Constant," *Atmos. Environ.*, **16**, 983–992 (1982a).

Stelson, A. W., and Seinfeld, J. H. "Relative Humidity and pH Dependence of the Vapor Pressure of Ammonium Nitrate-Nitric Acid Solutions at 25°C," *Atmos. Environ.*, **16**, 993–1000 (1982b).

Stelson, A. W., and Seinfeld, J. H. "Thermodynamic Prediction of the Water Activity, NH_4NO_3 Dissociation Constant, Density and Refractive Index in the $NH_4NO_3-(NH_4)_2SO_4-H_2O$ System at 25°C," *Atmos. Environ.*, **16**, 2507–2514 (1982c).

Stelson, A. W., Bassett, M., and Seinfeld, J. H. "Thermodynamic Equilibrium Properties of Aqueous Solutions of Nitrate, Sulfate, and Ammonium," in *Chemistry of Particles, Fogs and Rain*, J. L. Durham (Ed.), Butterworth, Boston, 1–52 (1984).

Stumm, W., and Morgan, J. J. *Aquatic Chemistry*, Wiley, New York (1981).

U.S. Environmental Protection Agency, *Air Quality Data for Metals from the National Air Surveillance Network*, EPA-600/4-79-054 (1979).

Waldman, J. M., Munger, J. W., Jacob, D. J., Flagan, R. C., Morgan, J. J., and Hoffmann, M. R. "Chemical Composition of Acid Fog," *Science*, **218**, 677–679 (1982).

Yoshizumi, K., Aoki, K., Nouchi, I., Okita, T., Kobayashi, T., Kamakura, S., and Tajima, M. "Measurements of the Concentration in Rainwater and of the Henry's Law Constant of Hydrogen Peroxide," *Atmos. Environ.*, **18**, 395–401 (1984).

PROBLEMS

5.1. Calculate the pH of water in equilibrium with 330 ppm of CO as a function of temperature from 0 to 30°C.

5.2. We wish to compute the total dissolved S(IV) and the pH of a solution exposed to gaseous SO_2 when an initial source of ions is present. Assume that an aqueous solution contains an initial concentration [Ex] of univalent ions from a strong acid or base (e.g., HCl, NaOH). Thus, before exposure to SO_2,

$$[H^+]_0 = [Ex] + [OH^-]_0$$

where

$$[Ex]\begin{cases} > 0 & \text{strong acid} \\ < 0 & \text{strong base} \end{cases}$$

Thus,

$$[Ex] = [H^+]_0 - K_w/[H^+]_0$$

For a strong acid, $[H^+]_0 \gg K_w/[H^+]_0$, so $[Ex] \cong [H^+]_0$.

Calculate [S(IV)] and $[H^+]$ as a function of p_{SO_2} with pH_0 as a parameter. Consider p_{SO_2} values from 1 to 10^3 ppb and pH_0 values from 4 to 10.

5.3. Given an aqueous-phase reaction rate R_a (M sec^{-1}) show that with a liquid water content L, the comparable gas-phase rate in ppb hr^{-1} is

$$R_g(\text{ppb hr}^{-1}) = 2.95 \times 10^{11} LTR_a/p$$

and expressed in % hr^{-1} is

$$R_g(\% \text{ hr}^{-1}) = 2.95 \times 10^{13} LTR_a/pX$$

where X is the total (gas + aqueous) equivalent gas-phase mixing ratio of the reactant species.

(a) We would like to know the rate of sulfate formation through an aqueous S(IV)–O$_3$ reaction in a haze aerosol of $L = 10^{-10}$. Assume $T = 298$ K, pH $= 5.6$, and $p_{O_3} = 5 \times 10^{-8}$ atm (50 ppb). If the total sulfur concentrations (gas + aqueous) is 5 ppb, calculate the rate of sulfate formation in ppb hr^{-1} and R_g in % hr^{-1}.

(b) If a rate of SO$_2$ to sulfate conversion is observed to be 10% hr^{-1}, then if $p_{SO_2} = 5 \times 10^{-9}$ atm (5 ppb), $T = 298$ K, pH $= 5.6$, and $p_{O_3} = 5 \times 10^{-8}$ atm and if $L = 10^{-6}$, are reactions with O$_3$, H$_2$O$_2$, and gaseous OH capable of generating this rate?

(c) What minimum aqueous H$_2$O$_2$ concentration is needed to account for a 1% hr^{-1} conversion of SO$_2$ to sulfate when pH $= 3$, $L = 10^{-11}$ and $T = 298$ K?

5.4. Consider the surface-catalyzed oxidation of SO$_2$ on solid particles. Let us assume that the process consists of absorption of SO$_2$ gas on the surface followed by reaction with O$_2$ and H$_2$O to produce a molecule of H$_2$SO$_4$ adsorbed on the surface. The rate of the process is controlled by the rate of diffusion of SO$_2$ to the particle, but stops when the surface of the particle is covered with sulfuric acid molecules. We assume that one molecule of H$_2$SO$_4$ occupies 30 Å^2 of area. With these assumptions, determine the total concentration of sulfate (as μg m^{-3} of sulfur) that is possible under the following sets of conditions: Note that the total volume of particles should be held constant; only the surface area changes.

	A	B
N_0, total particles cm^{-3}	10^6	10^3
$\overline{D}_p$, mean particle diam., μm	0.1	1.0

5.5. If the liquid water content of a cloud is 1 g m^{-3}, and if the dissolved concentration of SO_2 is 10^3 times that in the air, what must the rate of conversion in the liquid phase be to achieve an overall rate of oxidation of 1% hr^{-1}?

5.6. The importance of dissolved iron catalyzing the oxidation of S(IV) to sulfate within aqueous droplets in the atmosphere is unknown. If we assume, for the purposes of a conservative estimate, that 0.1% of the total iron in the atmosphere is soluble and that iron is present at a level of 1 μg m^{-3}, that a phase volume ratio of $L = 10^{-10}$ exists, at a pH of 4 and an ambient SO_2 level of 5 ppb, calculate the rate of SO_2 oxidation that would result, in % hr^{-1}.

5.7. We want to estimate the rate of H_2SO_4 formation in cloud droplets under the following two sets of conditions:

	A	B
p_{SO_2}, ppb	50	5
T	298 K	298 K
Liquid water content, g m^{-3}	0.1	1
pH	3.5–4.5	4.5–6.0
p_{O_3}, ppb	100	40
[H_2O_2(aq)], M	4.7×10^{-5}	5.9×10^{-6}
[Mn^{2+}], M	10^{-6}	2×10^{-9}
[Fe^{3+}], M	10^{-6}	3.3×10^{-8}

Condition A represents a polluted cloud whereas B is for a cloud in continental background conditions. Plot the H_2SO_4 production rate in M sec^{-1} as a function of pH for each of the two sets of conditions showing the individual contributions of each oxidation mechanism.

5.8. Repeat the open and closed system calculations of Section 5.6 using $p_{O_3} = 5 \times 10^{-8}$ atm (50 ppb). Discuss your results.

5.9. We consider here a chemical model for the acidification of fog droplets (Hoffmann and Jacob, 1984). Fog droplets are assumed to form around activated cloud condensation nuclei (ACCN) such as NaCl. At time $t = 0$ droplets are assumed to condense suddenly in an atmospheric "closed box" containing ACCN and the trace gases CO_2, SO_2, NH_3, HNO_3, H_2O_2, and O_3. As soon as the droplets form, they receive an initial chemical loading from the water-soluble fraction of the ACCN and immediately establish the Henry's law equilibria. The concentrations of the dissolved species at equilibrium are obtained by solving the electroneutrality equation,

$$[H^+] + [NH_4^+] + [Na^+] + 3[Fe^{3+}] + 2[Mn^{2+}]$$

$$= [OH^-] + [HCO_3^-] + 2[CO_3^{2-}] + [HSO_3^-]$$

$$+ 2[SO_3^{2-}] + 2[SO_4^{2-}] + [NO_3^-] + [Cl^-]$$

where we have assumed the ACCN to be $NaCl$, $FeCl_3$, and $MnCl_3$.

Calculate the formation of S(VI) in the liquid phase over a period of 4 hours by numerically integrating the appropriate rate equations. In your numerical integration use $\Delta t = 0.001$ min during the first 10 minutes and $\Delta t = 0.01$ min. thereafter. The following initial concentrations are assumed:

$$[CO_2(g)] = 330 \text{ ppm} \qquad [O_3(g)] = 10 \text{ ppb}$$
$$[NH_3(g)] = 5 \text{ ppb} \qquad [H_2O_2(g)] = 1 \text{ ppb}$$
$$[HNO_3(g)] = 3 \text{ ppb} \qquad [Fe^{3+}] = 3.33 \times 10^{-5} \text{ M}$$
$$[SO_2(g)] = 20 \text{ ppb} \qquad [Mn^{2+}] = 2.5 \times 10^{-6} \text{ M}$$

Plot the sulfate formed, the pH and the total aqueous-phase S(IV) and S(VI) as a function of time. Discuss your results in terms of the mechanisms contributing to S(IV) oxidation over the course of the 4-hour period.

SIX

Mass Transfer Aspects of Atmospheric Chemistry

In order for an aqueous-phase reaction to occur in an atmospheric particle or droplet several mass transfer steps must take place:

1. Diffusion of gaseous species from the bulk gas to the surface of the droplet.
2. Transfer across the gas-liquid interface.
3. Ionization of the species, if it occurs.
4. Diffusion of the dissolved species in the aqueous phase.
5. Chemical reaction.

The rate of the last step is referred to as the intrinsic reaction rate, and is, for example, the rate discussed in Sections 5.4 and 5.5. These processes occur in series, and thus the overall rate of reaction of a dissolving, reacting species is controlled by the slowest of these steps.

When calculating the rate of conversion in an aqueous-phase chemical reaction it is important to estimate the characteristic times associated with each of these processes in order to determine which of the steps may be controlling the rate of the overall process. The characteristic time of the gas-phase diffusion is the time it takes to establish a steady-state concentration profile of the species in the gas phase surrounding the particle. The characteristic time of the interfacial transfer process is the time it takes to establish the local solubility (Henry's law) equilibrium at the interface. The characteristic time of the ionization is that needed to achieve equilibrium of any dissociation reactions involving the dissolved species. The characteristic time of the liquid-phase diffusion is the time it takes for the dissolved species to diffuse throughout the entire droplet to produce a relatively uniform liquid-phase concentration in the droplet. Finally, the characteristic time of the chemical reaction is the time needed to convert $1/e$ of the reactants to products.

If the characteristic time of the chemical reaction is slow compared to all the other characteristic times, then the rate of conversion of dissolving species will equal the rate of the intrinsic chemical reaction. On the other hand, if the characteristic times of one or more of the other steps are longer than that of the reaction, then steady state or equilibrium conditions will not be achieved in those steps and the observed rate of conversion will be smaller than the intrinsic rate.

The purpose of this chapter is to develop the theory needed to estimate the characteristic times of the steps involved in aqueous-phase atmospheric chemistry. In our application of the theory we will pay special attention to aqueous sulfur chemistry. Much of this chapter is based on the work of Schwartz, particularly Schwartz (1984), Schwartz and Freiberg (1981), and Freiberg and Schwartz (1981).

6.1. CHARACTERISTIC TIME OF GAS-PHASE DIFFUSION TO A DROPLET

The unsteady state diffusion of species A to the surface of a stationary droplet of radius R_p is described by*

$$\frac{\partial c}{\partial t} = D_g \left(\frac{\partial^2 c}{\partial r^2} + \frac{2}{r} \frac{\partial c}{\partial r} \right) \tag{6.1}$$

$$c(r, 0) = c_\infty \quad r > R_p \tag{6.2}$$

$$c(r, t) = c_\infty \quad r \to \infty \tag{6.3}$$

$$c(R_p, t) = c_s(t) \tag{6.4}$$

where $c(r, t)$ = gas phase concentration of A, D_g = molecular diffusivity of A in air, c_∞ = concentration of A far from the droplet, and $c_s(t)$ = concentration of A in the gas phase at the droplet surface. By defining a dimensionless radius equal to r/R_p, we obtain a dimensionless time in Eq. (6.1) equal to $R_p^2 t/D_g$. Thus, we know that the characteristic time for gas-phase diffusion will be proportional to R_p^2/D_g.

We can obtain a precise expression for the characteristic time of this diffusion process by solving Eqs. (6.1) to (6.4). The maximum rate of diffusion is obtained for so-called perfect absorption; that is, $c_s(t) = 0$. The solution of

*In this chapter we confine our attention to particles and droplets of size larger than a micron so that continuum diffusion theories may be employed. We consider diffusion to smaller particles in Chapter 8. Also the transport of species A to or from a particle in a background gas of species B (say air) gives rise to a net flow of vapor to or from the particle which is called a Stefan flow. If the mixture of A and B is sufficiently dilute in A, then the Stefan flow contribution that appears as a convective term in Eq. (6.1) can be neglected. We neglect this effect in this chapter.

Eq. (6.1) subject to Eqs. (6.2) to (6.4) is for $c_s = 0$ (Appendix 6.A.1),

$$\frac{c(r,t)}{c_\infty} = 1 - \frac{R_p}{r} + \frac{2R_p}{r\sqrt{\pi}} \int_0^{(r-R_p)/2\sqrt{D_g t}} e^{-\xi^2} d\xi \qquad (6.5)$$

Because of the form of the solution we see that the response of the concentration at radial position r to a change at $r = R_p$ depends on terms of the form $\exp[-(r - R_p)^2/4D_g t]$. Thus, the characteristic time for relaxation of the concentration profile increases with r. However, with increasing r, the influence of a change in conditions at $r = R_p$ increasingly diminishes so that one has a smaller and smaller response occurring more and more slowly as the distance from the particle increases. The characteristic time for the concentration profile to relax to the steady state value close to the surface of the particle is thus

$$\tau_{dg} = \frac{R_p^2}{4D_g} \qquad (6.6)$$

where the subscript dg refers to diffusion in the gas-phase. This characteristic time can be evaluated for a typical molecular diffusivity of $D_g = 0.1$ cm^2 sec^{-1} as a function of R_p:

R_p, cm	0.1	0.01	0.001
τ_{dg}, sec	0.025	2.5×10^{-4}	2.5×10^{-6}

We conclude that the characteristic time for gas-phase diffusion to attain a steady-state profile is the order of 10^{-3} sec or smaller for all particles of atmospheric interest.

Transient Absorption of SO$_2$ by a Droplet.   Let us consider the transient absorption of SO$_2$ by a droplet initially free of any dissolved S(IV). We can use the transient solution just presented if we define the SO$_2$ gas-phase concentration just above the drop surface as $c_s = c_\infty(1 - a)$, where a will be a function of the drop composition and time. The general solution for the diffusion problem is (see Appendix 6.A.1)

$$u(\eta) = A + B \int_0^\eta e^{-\xi^2} d\xi \qquad (6.7)$$

The new boundary conditions are

$$u(0) = a \qquad \eta = 0 \qquad (6.8)$$

$$u = 0 \qquad \eta \to \infty \qquad (6.9)$$

where we note that

$$u = \frac{r}{R_p}\left[\frac{c_\infty - c}{c_\infty}\right] \tag{6.10}$$

Previously $u = 1$ at $r = R_p$ ($\eta = 0$). Now since $c(R_p, t) > 0$, $u = a$, $0 \le a \le 1$, at $r = R_p$. The concentration profile is thus

$$\frac{c(r,t)}{c_\infty} = 1 - a\left(\frac{R_p}{r} - \frac{2R_p}{r\sqrt{\pi}}\int_0^{(r-R_p)/2\sqrt{D_g t}} e^{-\xi^2}\, d\xi\right) \tag{6.11}$$

From Henry's law

$$c_s = \frac{[SO_2 \cdot H_2O]}{HRT} \tag{6.12}$$

Since the moles of SO_2 diffusing up to time t must equal the total moles of S(IV) produced,

$$[SO_2 \cdot H_2O] = \frac{M(t)x_{SO_2 \cdot H_2O}}{\frac{4}{3}\pi R_p^3} \tag{6.13}$$

where $M(t)$ is the total quantity of SO_2 that has entered the drop, and $x_{SO_2 \cdot H_2O}$ is the mole fraction of the liquid phase form of SO_2 that offers an SO_2 vapor pressure over the drop. We have that

$$\frac{dM(t)}{dt} = 4\pi R_p^2 D_g\left(\frac{\partial c}{\partial r}\right)_{R_p}$$

$$= 4\pi R_p^2 c_\infty D_g a\left(\frac{1}{R_p} + \frac{1}{\sqrt{\pi D_g t}}\right) \tag{6.14}$$

Thus,

$$c_s = \frac{3M(t)x_{SO_2 \cdot H_2O}}{4\pi R_p^3 HRT} \tag{6.15}$$

or

$$a = 1 - \frac{3M(t)x_{SO_2 \cdot H_2O}}{4\pi R_p^3 HRTc_\infty} \tag{6.16}$$

Then

$$\frac{dM(t)}{dt} = 4\pi R_p^2 c_\infty D_g \left(1 - \frac{3M(t)x_{SO_2 \cdot H_2O}}{4\pi R_p^3 HRTc_\infty}\right)\left(\frac{1}{R_p} + \frac{1}{\sqrt{\pi D_g t}}\right) \quad (6.17)$$

$$M(0) = 0 \quad (6.18)$$

Solving

$$M(t) = \frac{4\pi R_p^3 Hc_\infty RT}{3x_{SO_2 \cdot H_2O}}$$

$$\times \left\{1 - \exp\left[\left(-\frac{3D_g x_{SO_2 \cdot H_2O}}{R_p^2 HRT}\right)\left(t + \frac{2R_p\sqrt{t}}{\sqrt{\pi D_g}}\right)\right]\right\} \quad (6.19)$$

As $t \to \infty$,

$$M_\infty = \frac{4\pi R_p^3 Hc_\infty RT}{3x_{SO_2 \cdot H_2O}} \quad (6.20)$$

and thus

$$\frac{M(t)}{M_\infty} = 1 - \exp\left[\left(-\frac{3D_g x_{SO_2 \cdot H_2O}}{R_p^2 HRT}\right)\left(t + \frac{2R_p\sqrt{t}}{\sqrt{\pi D_g}}\right)\right] \quad (6.21)$$

In the case of irreversible absorption, $x_{SO_2 \cdot H_2O} = 0$, and

$$M(t)_{irr} = 4\pi D_g R_p c_\infty \left(t + \frac{2R_p\sqrt{t}}{\sqrt{\pi D_g}}\right) \quad (6.22)$$

We can form the ratio $M(t)_{irr}/M_\infty$,

$$\frac{M(t)_{irr}}{M_\infty} = \frac{3D_g x_{SO_2 \cdot H_2O}}{R_p^2 HRT}\left(t + \frac{2R_p\sqrt{t}}{\sqrt{\pi D_g}}\right) \quad (6.23)$$

Figure 6.1 shows both $M(t)/M_\infty$ and $M(t)_{irr}/M_\infty$ as a function of time for a droplet of radius 10 μm for pH values of 3, 4, 5, and 6. The solid curves represent $M(t)_{irr}/M_\infty$, and the dashed curves $M(t)/M_\infty$. We see that with irreversible absorption the total sulfur loading is reached in less than a second for all the pH values. When the effect of dissolved SO_2 accumulation is

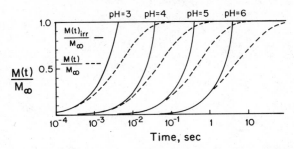

Figure 6.1. Total loading of dissolved sulfur species $M(t)$, assuming reversible and irreversible absorption relative to the total loading at equilibrium, M_∞, for a droplet of radius 10 μm (Beilke and Gravenhorst, 1978).

accounted for, the approach to the total loading is slowed, and at the high pH values may be as long as 10 seconds.

It is important to note that these times are associated with the time needed for a drop to "fill up" with SO_2 and not with the characteristic time for gas-phase diffusion to the drop. Even though we formulated this problem using the transient gas-phase diffusion equation, we expect from the results of the previous section that, because τ_{dg} is so small, the gas-phase concentration profile of SO_2 will be close to or equal to its steady state value during the filling of the drop except perhaps at the lowest pH values for larger drops. That steady state profile of course adjusts as the gas-phase concentration of SO_2 just above the droplet surface changes as dissolved SO_2 accumulates in the drop.

6.2. CHARACTERISTIC TIME TO ACHIEVE INTERFACIAL PHASE EQUILIBRIUM

We next want to obtain an expression for the characteristic time associated with establishing phase equilibrium at a gas-liquid interface. Suppose at $t = 0$, a droplet of pure water is immersed in air containing species A at concentration c_∞. As A is absorbed into the liquid, the concentration in the liquid will eventually reach that in equilibrium with the bulk gas phase C^*. If the partial pressure corresponding to c_∞ is p_∞, then that equilibrium can be expressed by Henry's law, $C^* = Hp_\infty$. Our interest here is in determining the characteristic time for equilibrium at the gas-liquid interface to be established.

To describe the process leading to equilibrium, we first note that to a gas molecule the particle is not distinguishable from a flat surface, so within the liquid phase diffusion of A can be described by

$$\frac{\partial C}{\partial t} = D_1 \frac{\partial^2 C}{\partial x^2} \tag{6.24}$$

where x is the distance into the liquid from the interface and D_1 is the aqueous-phase diffusion coefficient of A. At the gas-liquid interface molecules of A are arriving at the liquid from the gas, those molecules not absorbed are returning from the liquid surface to the gas, and other molecules are diffusing into the liquid phase.

Our object is to solve Eq. (6.24) subject to appropriate initial and boundary conditions. At $t = 0$ there is no A in the liquid phase. Then A starts to dissolve in the liquid and diffuse away from the interface into the bulk liquid. Far from the interface in the liquid the concentration of dissolved A will be zero, although right at the interface equilibrium, described by Henry's law, will be established after a certain characteristic time. By solving Eq. (6.24) we want to determine an expression for that characteristic time. We should note that in Section 6.1 we assumed a gas-phase concentration C_s just above the interface, which presumably is in equilibrium with the liquid-phase composition. More-over, in the example on transient absorption of SO_2 by a droplet, we implicitly assumed Henry's law equilibrium at the gas-liquid interface. Thus, in effect, we were assuming that the characteristic time to achieve interfacial phase equi-librium is short compared with the time scale for changes in the concentration of dissolved SO_2 in the drop. We will now see if such an assumption is justified.

For molecules in three-dimensional random motion the number of mole-cules striking unit area in unit time is $\frac{1}{4}N\bar{c}$, where N is the molecular number density and $\bar{c}$ is the mean speed (Moore, 1962, pp. 217–219),

$$\bar{c} = \left(\frac{8kT}{\pi m} \right)^{1/2} = \left(\frac{8RT}{\pi M} \right)^{1/2} \tag{6.25}$$

and where $m =$ the mass of a molecule and $M =$ molecular weight. Since the partial pressure of the vapor is related to N by $p = NkT$, the number of molecules striking unit area per unit time is, in molar units,

$$\frac{1}{4}\left(\frac{8RT}{\pi M} \right)^{1/2}\left(\frac{p}{RT} \right) = \frac{p}{(2\pi MRT)^{1/2}} \tag{6.26}$$

At the liquid surface molecules are arriving from the gas, molecules are leaving the surface back to the gas, and molecules are diffusing into the liquid phase. Let us call these fluxes R_{-g}, R_{+g}, and R_{+l}, respectively. Since the surface is presumed to have no thickness, these three fluxes must just balance each other. The flux of molecules to the interface from the gas is, as we have just seen, $p/(2\pi MRT)^{1/2}$. If the fraction of the incoming molecules that is incorporated into the liquid is α, the so-called accommodation coefficient, then the net flux from the gas to the interface is

$$R_{-g} = \frac{\alpha p}{(2\pi MRT)^{1/2}} \tag{6.27}$$

The rate of evaporation, R_{+g}, of A from the liquid depends on the surface concentration of A. Suppose the surface concentration is $C_s(t) = C(0, t)$. The evaporation process does not "know" whether equilibrium has been reached; it simply expels molecules at a rate dependent on $C_s(t)$. If the gas phase were at equilibrium with $C_s(t)$, then the flux into the liquid phase would be zero, and

$$R_{-g} = R_{+g} = \frac{\alpha p_s}{(2\pi MRT)^{1/2}} \tag{6.28}$$

where p_s is the partial pressure of A in equilibrium with C_s. Thus, the evaporative flux at any time is

$$R_{+g} = \frac{\alpha p_s(t)}{(2\pi MRT)^{1/2}} \tag{6.29}$$

The flux of A into the liquid is given by $R_{+1} = R_{-g} - R_{+g}$ or

$$R_{+1} = \frac{(p_\infty - p_s(t))\alpha}{(2\pi MRT)^{1/2}} \tag{6.30}$$

At equilibrium, Henry's law holds, so $C^* = Hp_\infty$ and $C_s(t) = Hp_s(t)$, where C^* is the surface concentration in equilibrium with p_∞.

The flux R_{+1} is then equated to the diffusive flux to give

$$-D_1\left(\frac{\partial C}{\partial x}\right)_{x=0} = \frac{\alpha}{H(2\pi MRT)^{1/2}}(C^* - C) \tag{6.31}$$

Thus, the transient mass transfer process leading to phase equilibrium is described by

$$\frac{\partial C}{\partial t} = D_1\frac{\partial^2 C}{\partial x^2} \tag{6.32}$$

subject to

$$C(x,0) = 0 \tag{6.33}$$

$$C(x,t) = 0 \qquad x \to \infty \tag{6.34}$$

$$D_1\frac{\partial C}{\partial x} = \frac{\alpha}{H(2\pi MRT)^{1/2}}(C - C^*) \qquad x = 0 \tag{6.35}$$

The solution of Eqs. (6.32) to (6.35) is (see Appendix 6.A.2)

$$C(x,t) = C^*\mathrm{erfc}\left[\frac{x}{2\sqrt{D_1 t}}\right] - C^*\exp\left(\frac{\kappa x}{D_1}\right)\exp\left(\frac{t}{\tau_p}\right)$$

$$\times \mathrm{erfc}\left[\left(\frac{t}{\tau_p}\right)^{1/2} + \frac{x}{2\sqrt{D_1 t}}\right] \tag{6.36}$$

where $\tau_p = D_1/\kappa^2$ and $\kappa = \alpha H^{-1}(2\pi MRT)^{-1/2}$. At long times

$$C(x,t) = C^*\left\{1 - \exp\left(\frac{\kappa x}{D_1}\right)\exp\left(\frac{t}{\tau_p}\right)\mathrm{erfc}\left[\left(\frac{t}{\tau_p}\right)^{1/2}\right]\right\} \tag{6.37}$$

and as $t \to \infty$, $C(x, t) = C^*$.

The characteristic time of the process is τ_p, given by

$$\tau_p = \frac{2\pi M R T D_1 H^2}{\alpha^2} \tag{6.38}$$

Now, from kinetic theory of gases the average speed of gas molecules is $\bar{c} = (8RT/\pi M)^{1/2}$ so that we can express τ_p as

$$\tau_p = D_1 \left(\frac{4RTH}{\alpha \bar{c}} \right)^2 \tag{6.39}$$

We note that as the Henry's law coefficient H increases, τ_p increases. Physically, a larger H implies a more soluble gas, so we expect that a longer time will be required to establish phase equilibrium since more of the gas must cross the interface before equilibrium is achieved. The accommodation coefficient α is interpreted as the fraction of impinging gas molecules that enter the liquid phase. In the absence of other information, α is usually taken to be unity. We see, however, that as α decreases from 1.0, the charateristic time to achieve interfacial phase equilibrium increases, since fewer of the incoming molecules enter the liquid phase.

Let us evaluate the value of τ_p for some gases of atmospheric interest. In estimating τ_p it is sufficient to take the liquid-phase diffusion coefficient D_1 as 10^{-5} cm^2 sec^{-1}, a value characteristic of many dissolved gases. In addition, we take $T = 298$ K. Under these conditions, Eq. (6.38) becomes $\tau_p = 1.51 \times 10^{-12}$ MH^2/α^2 sec. Evaluating this expression for O_3 and H_2O_2, and using the Henry's law coefficient values from Table 5.2, gives, for $\alpha = 1.0$,

	M	H (Table 5.2)	τ_p, sec
O_3	48	9.4×10^{-3}	6.4×10^{-15}
H_2O_2	34	7.1×10^4	0.26

We see that τ_p can vary enormously depending on the value of the particular Henry's law coefficient. If the accommodation coefficient α is less than 1.0, values of τ_p will increase in accordance with α^{-2}. The validity of assuming instantaneous phase equilibrium will therefore depend on the gas involved, its Henry's law coefficient, and the time scales of the other processes occurring.

6.3. CHARACTERISTIC TIME OF AQUEOUS DISSOCIATION REACTIONS

The next process in the chain is ionization. For SO_2, for example, we know that subsequent to absorption, we have

$$SO_2 \cdot H_2O \rightleftharpoons H^+ + HSO_3^-$$

We are interested in determining the characteristic time to establish this equilibrium. To do so, we wish to derive an expression for the characteristic time to reach equilibrium of the reversible reaction,

$$A \underset{k_r}{\overset{k_f}{\rightleftarrows}} B + C$$

At equilibrium $k_f[A]_e = k_r[B]_e[C]_e$. Let us define the extent of reaction ξ by $[A] = [A]_0 - \xi$, $[B] = [B]_0 + \xi$, and $[C] = [C]_0 + \xi$, and the equilibrium extent ξ_e by $[A]_e = [A]_0 - \xi_e$, $[B]_e = [B]_0 + \xi_e$, and $[C]_e + [C]_0 + \xi_e$. Then we can let

$$[A] = [A]_e - \Delta\xi$$

$$[B] = [B]_e + \Delta\xi$$

$$[C] = [C]_e + \Delta\xi \tag{6.40}$$

where $\Delta\xi = \xi - \xi_e$.

The rate of disappearance of A is given by

$$\frac{d[A]}{dt} = -k_f[A] + k_r[B][C] \tag{6.41}$$

Using Eq. (6.40) together with the equilibrium relation, we obtain from Eq. (6.41),

$$\frac{d\Delta\xi}{dt} = -\alpha\Delta\xi - \beta\Delta\xi^2 \tag{6.42}$$

where $\alpha = [k_f + k_r[B]_e + k_r[C]_e]$ and $\beta = k_r$. Integrating this equation from $\Delta\xi = \Delta\xi_0$ at $t = 0$, we obtain

$$\frac{\Delta\xi}{\Delta\xi_0} \frac{(\alpha + \beta\Delta\xi_0)}{(\alpha + \beta\Delta\xi)} = e^{-\alpha t}$$

Applying this result to A gives

$$\frac{[A] - [A]_e}{[A]_0 - [A]_e} \left[\frac{1 + \beta/\alpha([A]_e - [A]_0)}{1 + \beta/\alpha([A]_e - [A])} \right] = e^{-\alpha t} \tag{6.43}$$

where

$$\beta/\alpha = \frac{1}{\dfrac{k_f}{k_r} + [B]_e + [C]_e} \tag{6.44}$$

and where k_f/k_r is the equilibrium constant K.

Let us apply the foregoing analysis to the case of

$$SO_2 \cdot H_2O \rightleftarrows H^+ + HSO_3^-$$

We note from Eq. (6.43) that if

$$\frac{[SO_2 \cdot H_2O]_e}{K_{s1} + [H^+]_e + [HSO_3^-]_e} \ll 1 \qquad (6.45)$$

then the expression for the approach to equilibrium simplifies to

$$\frac{[SO_2 \cdot H_2O] - [SO_2 \cdot H_2O]_e}{[SO_2 \cdot H_2O]_0 - [SO_2 \cdot H_2O]_e} = e^{-\alpha t} \qquad (6.46)$$

and the characteristic time we are seeking is just α^{-1}. The condition of Eq. (6.45) can be evaluated at pH = 4 and $p_{SO_2} = 10^{-9}$ atm (1 ppb) in which case we find that from Figure 5.2,

$$\frac{[SO_2 \cdot H_2O]_e}{K_{s1} + [H^+]_e + [HSO_3^-]_e} \cong 10^{-2}$$

and the approximation is justified. Thus, the characteristic time to achieve equilibrium is

$$\tau_i = \left[k_f + k_r([H^+]_e + [HSO_3^-]_e) \right]^{-1}$$

For pH = 4, and $k_f = 3.4 \times 10^6$ sec^{-1} and $k_r = 2 \times 10^8$ M sec^{-1}, we find

$$\tau_i \cong 2 \times 10^{-7} \text{ sec}$$

Thus, in the case of the sulfur equilibria it can be assumed that ionization equilibrium is achieved virtually instantaneously upon absorption of SO_2.

6.4. CHARACTERISTIC TIME OF AQUEOUS-PHASE DIFFUSION IN A DROPLET

Consider unsteady state diffusion of a dissolved species in a droplet, initially free of solute, when the surface concentration is raised to C_s at $t = 0$,

$$\frac{\partial C}{\partial t} = D_1 \left(\frac{\partial^2 C}{\partial r^2} + \frac{2}{r} \frac{\partial C}{\partial r} \right) \qquad (6.47)$$

$$C(r, 0) = 0 \qquad 0 \le r \le R_p \qquad (6.48)$$

$$\frac{\partial C}{\partial r} = 0 \qquad r = 0, t > 0 \qquad (6.49)$$

$$C(r, t) = C_s \qquad r = R_p, t > 0 \qquad (6.50)$$

A standard separation of variables solution of Eqs. (6.20) to (6.23) gives

$$\frac{C(r, t)}{C_s} = 1 + \frac{R_p}{r} \sum_{n=1}^{\infty} (-1)^n \frac{2}{n\pi} \sin\left(\frac{n\pi r}{R_p} \right) \exp\left(-\frac{n^2 \pi^2 D_1 t}{R_p^2} \right) \qquad (6.51)$$

The characteristic time for aqueous-phase diffusion, τ_{da}, is obtained from the first term in the exponential in the solution and is

$$\tau_{da} = \frac{R_p^2}{\pi^2 D_1} \tag{6.52}$$

A typical value of D_1 is 10^{-5} cm^2 sec^{-1}, so we can evaluate τ_{da} as a function of R_p as:

R_p, cm	0.1	0.01	0.001
τ_{da}, sec	10^2	1	10^{-2}

The total flow of species into the sphere as a function of time is

$$4\pi R^2 D_1 \left(\frac{\partial C}{\partial r}\right)_{R_p} = 8\pi R_p D_1 C_s \sum_{n=1}^{\infty} \exp\left(-\frac{n^2\pi^2 D_1 t}{R_p^2}\right) \tag{6.53}$$

so that the total amount of A entering the particle from $t = 0$ to $t = t$ is

$$M(t) = 8\pi R_p D_1 C_s \int_0^t \sum_{n=1}^{\infty} \exp\left(-\frac{n^2\pi^2 D_1 t'}{R_p^2}\right) dt' \tag{6.54}$$

and the amount as $t \to \infty$ is $M_\infty = 4\pi R_p^3 C_s/3$. Therefore

$$\frac{M(t)}{M_\infty} = 1 - \frac{6}{\pi^2} \sum_{n=1}^{\infty} \frac{1}{n^2} \exp\left(-\frac{n^2\pi^2 D_1 t}{R_p^2}\right) \tag{6.55}$$

6.5. CHARACTERISTIC TIME FOR AQUEOUS-PHASE CHEMICAL REACTION

To develop an expression for the characteristic time for aqueous-phase chemical reaction, let us consider as an example the oxidation of S(IV). The characteristic time for the chemical reaction is defined as

$$\tau_{ra}^{-1} = -\frac{1}{[S(IV)]} \frac{d[S(IV)]}{dt} \tag{6.56}$$

Thus, one takes the rate expression for $d[S(IV)]/dt$ and divides it by $[S(IV)]$ to obtain τ_{ra}^{-1}. It is also possible to define a characteristic time for chemical reaction relative to the gas-phase concentration,

$$\tau_{rg}^{-1} = -\frac{1}{[SO_2(g)]} \frac{d[S(IV)]}{dt} \tag{6.57}$$

For a uniform aqueous-phase concentration, $[S(IV)] = H_{S(IV)}^* RT[SO_2(g)]$, so that

$$\tau_{rg} = \tau_{ra}/H^*_{S(IV)}RT \qquad (6.58)$$

6.6. COMPARISON OF CHARACTERISTIC TIMES FOR AQUEOUS-PHASE S(IV) OXIDATION

We have developed the following expressions for the characteristic times associated with aqueous-phase chemical reaction in droplets:

1. Characteristic time for gas-phase diffusion

$$\tau_{dg} = \frac{R_p^2}{4D_g}$$

2. Characteristic time to achieve interfacial phase equilibrium

$$\tau_p = \frac{2\pi MRTD_1 H^2}{\alpha^2}$$

3. Characteristic time of aqueous dissociation reactions

$$A \underset{k_r}{\overset{k_f}{\rightleftharpoons}} B + C$$

$$\tau_i = \left[k_f + k_r([B]_e + [C]_e) \right]^{-1}$$

4. Characteristic time for aqueous-phase diffusion

$$\tau_{da} = \frac{R_p^2}{\pi^2 D_1}$$

5. Characteristic time for aqueous-phase chemical reaction

$$\tau_{ra} = -\frac{[S(IV)]}{d[S(IV)]/dt}$$

$$\tau_{rg} = -\frac{[SO_2(g)]}{d[S(IV)]/dt}$$

First, we note that the characteristic times of the aqueous dissociation reactions are very short when compared with the others. Thus, the aqueous ionic equilibria can be assumed to hold at all points in the droplet, and these characteristic times need no longer be considered.

Our main interest is in comparing τ_{dg}, τ_p and τ_{da} to those for chemical reaction, either τ_{ra} or τ_{rg}. Let us start the discussion by comparing τ_{ra} and τ_{da}. If $\tau_{da} \ll \tau_{ra}$, that is, either small droplets or slow rate of reaction, the rate of conversion in the drop is controlled by the rate of reaction. The concentration profile in the drop is uniform since diffusion is fast enough to replenish S(IV) as fast as it is reacted. On the other hand, if $\tau_{da} \gg \tau_{ra}$, that is, large droplet or

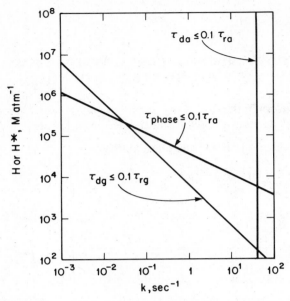

Figure 6.2. Bounds for mass transport limitation as a function of Henry's law constant H or H^* and first-order rate constant for solution-phase reaction, k. Regions to the left and/or below each line represent combinations where mass transport is not limiting (Schwartz, 1984).

fast reactions, the reaction can only proceed as fast as reagent is supplied to the interior of the drop from its surface. The steady-state concentration profile will be nonuniform throughout the drop, decreasing from the surface to the center. If $\tau_{dg} \ll \tau_{rg}$, the gas-phase concentration profile has adequate time to relax to its steady-state value as the reaction proceeds. Finally, if $\tau_p \ll \tau_{ra}$, Henry's law equilibrium can be assumed to hold at the interface.

The criteria that the droplet be saturated at steady state with the reagent gas can be stated as (Schwartz, 1984):

$$\tau_p < 0.1\tau_{ra}$$

$$\tau_{da} < 0.1\tau_{ra}$$

$$\tau_{dg} < 0.1\tau_{rg}$$

The criteria are shown in Figure 6.2 for chemical reaction in a spherical drop of 10 μm diameter as a function of the Henry's law constant and a first-order rate constant k for the chemical reaction. The criteria are satisfied for situations for which the point lies below and to the left of the indicated bounds. The values of D_g and D_1 used are 0.1 and 10^{-5} cm^2 sec^{-1}, respectively, and the sticking coefficient is taken to be $\alpha = 1$.

The line labelled $\tau_{da} < 0.1\tau_{ra}$ is obtained as follows,

$$k \leq \frac{0.1\pi^2 D_1}{R_p^2}$$

Using $D_1 = 10^{-5}$ cm^2 sec^{-1} and $2R_p = 10^{-3}$ cm, we obtain the bound as

$$k \leq 39.5 \text{ sec}^{-1}$$

which is independent of the value of H. The line corresponding to $\tau_{dg} < 0.1\tau_{rg}$ is obtained from the condition

$$\frac{R_p^2}{4D_g} \leq 0.1\left(\frac{1}{HkRT}\right)$$

$$H \leq \left(\frac{0.4D_g}{RTR_p^2}\right)\frac{1}{k}$$

which becomes, for the values used,

$$H \leq 6.55 \times 10^3 k^{-1}$$

Finally, the $\tau_p < 0.1\tau_{ra}$ line is obtained from

$$\frac{2\pi MRTD_1 H^2}{\alpha^2} \leq 0.1\left(\frac{1}{k}\right)$$

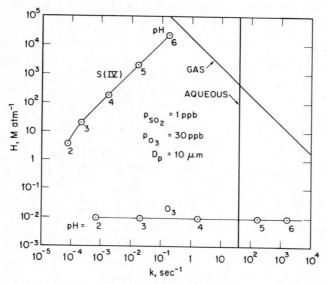

Figure 6.3. Mass transport limitations in the aqueous-phase S(IV)–O$_3$ reaction. Gas and aqueous-phase bounds derived from Figure 6.2. The S(IV) curve is evaluated for $p_{O_3} = 30$ ppb; the O$_3$ curve is evaluated for $p_{SO_2} = 1$ ppb. The values of pH along each curve are indicated by the points. Values of k scale linearly with the partial pressure of the other reagent. Mass transport limitation is absent for points below and/or to the left of the lines (Schwartz, 1984).

which becomes

$$H \leq 2.57 \times 10^5 k^{-1/2} M^{-1/2}$$

where the species has been taken as ozone ($M = 48$).

Figure 6.3 shows an evaluation of the regimes of mass transport limitation in the S(IV)–O_3(aq) reaction represented in terms of a first-order rate constant as in Figure 6.2. The pseudo-first order rate constant is defined by $-d[S(IV)]/dt/[S(IV)]$. The S(IV) curve is evaluated as a function of pH for $p_{O_3} = 30 \times 10^{-9}$ atm (30 ppb). The values at different pH's arise because of the dependence of $H^*_{S(IV)}$ on $[H^+]$. The O_3 curve, on the other hand, is a horizontal line since H_{O_3} is not a function of pH. This line is evaluated assuming $p_{SO_2} = 10^{-9}$ atm (1 ppb). Mass transfer limitations are absent for points (k, H) below and to the left of the indicated bounds. We see that in the O_3(aq) oxidation of S(IV), mass transfer limitations become important at high pH, and the mass transfer process that becomes limiting is aqueous-phase diffusion.

Figure 6.4 shows the regimes of mass transfer limitation for the H_2O_2(aq)–S(IV) reaction. The points labelled H_2O_2 indicate a virtually constant rate between pH 2 and 6. The S(IV) line reflects the dependence of $H^*_{S(IV)}$ on pH. In the H_2O_2 oxidation of S(IV), for pH < 2 aqueous-phase mass transfer for both SO_2 and H_2O_2 becomes important. Note that gas-phase diffusion resistances do not assume any significance for the cases studied.

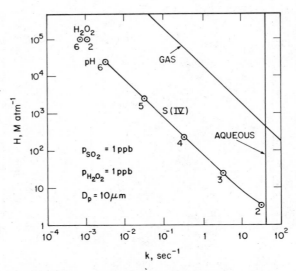

Figure 6.4. Mass transport limitations in the aqueous-phase S(IV)–H_2O_2 reaction. Gas and aqueous-phase bounds derived from Figure 6.2. The S(IV) curve is evaluated for $p_{H_2O_2} = 1$ ppb; the H_2O_2 points are evaluated for $p_{SO_2} = 1$ ppb. The values of pH are indicated by the points. Values of k scale linearly with the partial pressure of the other reagent. Mass transport limitation is absent for points below and/or to the left of the lines (Schwartz, 1984).

6.7.   MASS TRANSFER TO FALLING DROPS

For a stationary drop of radius R_p that retains all gas molecules impinging on it we have seen that at steady state

$$c(r) = c_\infty \left(1 - \frac{R_p}{r}\right) \tag{6.59}$$

We have also seen that the characteristic time for gas-phase diffusion is short compared to those for aqueous-phase reactions and diffusion and consequently that the concentration profile around a droplet may always be taken to be the steady state value. From this solution the magnitude of the flux to the drop is

$$D_g \left(\frac{dc}{dr}\right)_{r=R_p} = \frac{D_g c_\infty}{R_p} \tag{6.60}$$

The dimensionless flux, the Sherwood number, (or the Nusselt number for mass transfer, Nu_{AB}) is defined in terms of a mass transfer coefficient k_c,

$$Sh = \frac{k_c D_p}{D_g} \tag{6.61}$$

For diffusion to a stationary drop, as above, we have an exact solution for $c(r)$, and the mass transfer coefficient k_c defined on the basis of the flux equal to $k_c(c_\infty - c_s)$ is exactly equal to D_g/R_p. Thus, in this case $Sh = 2$.

When the drop is in motion, calculation of the flux of gas molecules is considerably more involved. One usually resorts to empirical correlations for Sh as a function of the other dimensionless groups of the problem, for example, (Bird et al., 1960),

$$Sh = 2 + 0.6 Re^{1/2} Sc^{1/3} \tag{6.62}$$

where the Reynolds number, $Re = v_t D_p/\nu_{air}$, and the Schmidt number, $Sc = \nu_{air}/D_g$, v_t being the terminal velocity of the droplet and ν_{air} the kinetic viscosity of the air.

If the drop is not well mixed internally, it is necessary to compare the characteristic time for aqueous-phase diffusion, τ_{da}, to that for the external transfer to the drop. We have seen that for a 0.1 cm drop, τ_{da} is of the order of 100 sec. Thus, if the only mechanism for mixing is molecular diffusion, for larger drops, aqueous-phase diffusion may be the limiting process. For drops of radii $R_p > 0.1$ mm internal circulations develop (Pruppacher and Klett, 1978), the time scale for which is of order $R_p \mu_1/v_t \mu_{air}$. For a 1 mm radius drop, this time scale is the order of 10^{-2} sec, very short compared with that taken by the drop falling to the ground. Therefore, it can be assumed that for drops of radii larger than about 0.1 mm internal circulations will produce a well-mixed interior.

APPENDIX

6.A.1.   Solution of the Transient Gas-Phase Diffusion Problem Eqs. (6.1) to (6.4)

To solve Eqs. (6.1) to (6.4), let

$$u(r,t) = \frac{r}{R_p}\left(\frac{c_\infty - c(r,t)}{c_\infty}\right)$$

Therefore

$$\frac{c(r,t)}{c_\infty} = 1 - u(r,t)\frac{R_p}{r}$$

and the problem is transformed to

$$\frac{\partial u}{\partial t} = D_g \frac{\partial^2 u}{\partial r^2}$$

$$u(r,0) = 0 \qquad r > R_p,\ t = 0$$

$$u(r,t) = 0 \qquad r \to \infty,\ t > 0$$

$$u(R_p,t) = 1 \qquad r = R_p,\ t > 0$$

We can solve this problem by Laplace or similarity transforms. Let us use the latter. Let $u(\eta) = u(r,t)$ and

$$\eta = \frac{r - R_p}{2\sqrt{D_g t}}$$

Then the equation reduces to

$$\frac{d^2 u}{d\eta^2} - 2\eta u = 0$$

the solution of which is

$$u(\eta) = A + B \int_0^\eta e^{-\xi^2}\,d\xi$$

to be evaluated subject to

$$u(0) = 1 \qquad \eta = 0$$

$$u(\eta) = 0 \qquad \eta \to \infty$$

Therefore, determining A and B, we have

$$u(\eta) = 1 - \frac{2}{\sqrt{\pi}} \int_0^\eta e^{-\xi^2} d\xi$$

The molar flow of species A into the droplet at any time t is

$$4\pi R_p^2 D_g \left(\frac{\partial c}{\partial r} \right)_{R_p} = 4\pi R_p^2 c_\infty D_g \left\{ \frac{R_p}{r^2} - \frac{2R_p}{r^2\sqrt{\pi}} \int_0^{(r-R_p)/2\sqrt{D_g t}} e^{-\xi^2} d\xi \right.$$

$$\left. + \frac{2R_p}{r\sqrt{\pi}} \frac{1}{2\sqrt{D_g t}} e^{-((r-R_p)/2\sqrt{D_g t})^2} \right\}_{r=R_p}$$

$$= 4\pi R_p^2 c_\infty D_g \left(\frac{1}{R_p} + \frac{1}{\sqrt{\pi D_g t}} \right)$$

Then the total quantity of A that has been transferred into the particle from $t = 0$ to $t = t$ is

$$M(t) = \int_0^t 4\pi R_p^2 c_\infty D_g \left(\frac{1}{R_p} + \frac{1}{\sqrt{\pi D_g t'}} \right) dt'$$

$$= 4\pi R_p D_g c_\infty \left(t + \frac{2R_p \sqrt{t}}{\sqrt{\pi D_g}} \right)$$

6.A.2.   Solution of Eqs. (6.32) to (6.35)

We solve Eqs. (6.32) to (6.35) by Laplace transform. Taking the Laplace transform of Eq. (6.32), and using Eq. (6.33), we have

$$D_1 \frac{d^2 \overline{C}}{dx^2} = s\overline{C}$$

subject to

$$\overline{C} = 0 \qquad x \to \infty$$

$$D_1 \frac{d\overline{C}}{dx} = \kappa \overline{C} - \kappa C^*/s \qquad x = 0$$

the solution of which is given in general by

$$\overline{C}(x, s) = A \exp\left((s/D_1)^{1/2} x \right) + B \exp\left(-(s/D_1)^{1/2} x \right)$$

$A = 0$ to satisfy the $x \to \infty$ boundary condition, and from the $x = 0$ boundary condition,

$$B = \frac{C^*/s}{1 + \left(\dfrac{D_1 s}{\kappa^2} \right)^{1/2}}$$

The transform solution is thus

$$\overline{C}(x, s) = \frac{C^*/s}{1 + \left(\dfrac{D_1 s}{\kappa^2} \right)^{1/2}} \exp\left(-(s/D_1)^{1/2} x \right)$$

Inverting (Abramowitz and Segun, 1965, p. 1027),

$$C(x, t) = C^* \mathrm{erfc}\left[\frac{x}{2\sqrt{D_1 t}} \right] - C^* \exp\left(\frac{\kappa x}{D_1} \right) \exp\left(\frac{\kappa^2 t}{D_1} \right) \mathrm{erfc}\left[\frac{\kappa \sqrt{t}}{\sqrt{D_1}} + \frac{\kappa}{2\sqrt{D_1 t}} \right]$$

REFERENCES

Abramowitz, M., and Segun, I. A. *Handbook of Mathematical Functions*, Dover, New York (1965).

Beilke, S., and Gravenhorst, G. "Heterogeneous SO_2 Oxidation in Droplet Phase," *Atmos. Environ.*, **12**, 231–240 (1978).

Bird, R. B., Stewart, W. E., and Lightfoot, E. N. *Transport Phenomena*, Wiley, New York (1960).

Freiberg, J. E., and Schwartz, S. E. "Oxidation of SO_2 in Aqueous Droplets: Mass-Transport Limitation in Laboratory Studies and the Ambient Atmosphere," *Atmos. Environ.*, **15**, 1145–1154 (1981).

Pruppacher, H. R., and Klett, J. D. *Microphysics of Clouds and Precipitation*, D. Reidel, Boston (1978).

Moore, W. J. *Physical Chemistry*, 3rd ed., Prentice-Hall, Englewood Cliffs, NJ (1962).

Schwartz, S. E., and Freiberg, J. E. "Mass-Transport Limitation to the Rate of Reaction of Gases and Liquid Droplets: Application to Oxidation of SO_2 and Aqueous Solution," *Atmos. Environ.*, **15**, 1129–1144 (1981).

Schwartz, S. E. "Gas Aqueous Reactions of Sulfur and Nitrogen Oxides in Liquid Water Clouds," in *SO_2, NO, and NO_2 Oxidation Mechanisms: Atmospheric Considerations*, J. G. Calvert (Ed.), Butterworth, Boston, 173–208 (1984).

PROBLEMS

6.1. Calculate and plot $M(t)/M_\infty$ and $M(t)_{irr}/M_\infty$ as a function of time for a droplet of radius 10 μm for absorption of NH_3 at pH values of 3, 4, 5, and 6 at $T = 298$ K. Compare your results to those given in Figure 6.1 for the SO_2 system.

6.2. Solve Eqs. (6.47) to (6.50) to obtain (6.51), (6.53), (6.54), and (6.55).

6.3. Reconstruct Figure 6.2 for droplets of 0.1 μm and 1.0 μm diameters.

6.4. Reconstruct Figure 6.3 for droplets of 0.1 μm and 1.0 μm diameters.

6.5. Reconstruct Figure 6.4 for droplets of 0.1 μm and 1.0 μm diameters.

6.6. Plot the mass transfer coefficient k_c for spherical drops falling through air as a function of velocity. Assume $T = 298$ K and the diffusing species to be SO_2. For the purposes of this problem, assume that drop size and fall velocity are independent. (We know this is not the case and will develop the theory of terminal velocities of drops in Chapter 8.) Consider drop sizes of $R = 0.1$ mm, 1 mm, 10 mm, and fall velocities of 10^{-2}, 10^{-1}, and 10 m sec^{-1}.

TABLE P6.1. Forward Rate Constants k_f and Parameters A, B, and C in the Equilibrium Constant Expression $\log K = A + B(1000/T) + C(1000/T)^2$ for Aqueous Equilibria

Reaction	k_f, sec^{-1}	A	B	C
$HSO_4^- \rightleftarrows SO_4^{2-} + H^+$	1.8×10^7	-5.95	1.18	0
$SO_2 \cdot H_2O \rightleftarrows HSO_3^- + H^+$	6.1×10^4	-4.84	0.87	0
$HSO_3^- \rightleftarrows SO_3^{2-} + H^+$	5.4×10^0	-8.86	0.49	0
$CO_2 \cdot H_2O \rightleftarrows HCO_3^- + H^+$	2.1×10^4	-14.25	5.19	-0.85
$HCO_3^- \rightleftarrows CO_3^{2-} + H^+$	4.5×10^{-2}	-13.80	2.87	-0.58
$HO_2 \rightleftarrows O_2^- + H^+$	2.3×10^3	-4.9	0	0

6.7. Table P6.1 gives the forward rate constants and parameters A, B, and C in the equilibrium constant expression,

$$\log K = A + B\left(\frac{1000}{T}\right) + C\left(\frac{1000}{T}\right)^2$$

for a number of aqueous phase equilibria. For each of the reactions given in the table evaluate the characteristic time to reach equilibrium at $T = 298$ K and $T = 273$ K. Discuss your results.

PART THREE

Aerosols

SEVEN

Properties of Aerosols

With this chapter we begin the study of aerosols. An aerosol consists, roughly speaking, of a dilute suspension of relatively immobile, relative massive particles in air. Table 7.1 presents a comparison of the relative size, mass, and concentration of gas molecules (e.g., N_2) and aerosols. This chapter is devoted to ways of characterizing aerosol size distributions and to typical atmospheric size distributions. Its object is to gain familiarity with aerosol size distribution data and their manipulation. Subsequent chapters will deal with the mechanics of single aerosol particles, the formation of aerosols by nucleation, and the behavior of aerosol populations.

7.1. THE SIZE DISTRIBUTION FUNCTION

An aerosol can be envisioned as a population of particles each consisting of an integral number of molecules or monomers. The smallest aerosol particle could be defined in principle as that containing two molecules or two monomers. The population can then be characterized by the concentrations of each cluster; that is, N_k = concentration (per cm^3 of air) of particles containing k molecules. While rigorously correct, this "discrete" way of characterizing the distribution quickly becomes unwieldy because of the very large number of molecules that go to make up even the smallest of aerosol particles. For example, a sulfuric acid/water particle at equilibrium at 30 percent relative humidity of 0.01 μm diameter consists of approximately 10^4 molecules of sulfuric acid.

Beyond a relatively small number of molecules, say about 100, an aerosol population can be treated as if its size variation is essentially continuous. In doing so, we replace the discrete size index k by the particle diameter D_p and the discrete number concentration N_k by the size distribution function $n(D_p)$, defined as follows:

$n(D_p)\,dD_p$ = number of particles per cm^3 of air having diameters in
the range D_p to $D_p + dD_p$

TABLE 7.1. Size, Mass, and Concentration of Aerosol
Particles Relative to Gas Molecules

	Diameter	Mass	Concentration
Gas molecules (e.g., N_2)	0.00038 μm ($= 3.8$ Å)	4.6×10^{-23} g	$\approx 10^{19}$ cm^{-3}
Aerosols	0.01 to 10 μm	10^{-18} g to 10^{-9} g	$< 10^8$ cm^{-3}

The total number of particles per cm^3 of air of all sizes is then just

$$N = \int_0^\infty n(D_p)\, dD_p \tag{7.1}$$

From the viewpoint of probability theory, $n(D_p)$ is the probability density function for particle size. Thus, a more precise term for $n(D_p)$ is a size distribution density function, although the word "density" is usually omitted in describing $n(D_p)$. The units of $n(D_p)$ are μm^{-1} cm^{-3}, and those of N are cm^{-3}. If the aerosol population is changing with time then we may write $n(D_p,t)$ and $N(t)$. Similarly, if there is a spatial variation, n can be expressed as $n(D_p; x, y, z, t)$ and N as $N(x, y, z, t)$.

We can define a normalized size distribution function $\tilde{n}(D_p)$ by $\tilde{n}(D_p) = n(D_p)/N$, such that $\tilde{n}(D_p)\, dD_p =$ the fraction of the total number of particles per cm^3 of air having diameters in the range D_p to $D_p + dD_p$. The units of $\tilde{n}(D_p)$ are μm^{-1}.

It is often of interest to know the distributions of both particle surface area and volume with respect to particle size. Considering all particles as spheres, we define the surface area distribution function as

$$n_s(D_p) = \pi D_p^2 n(D_p) \ \left(\mu\text{m}^2\, \mu\text{m}^{-1}\text{cm}^{-3}\right) \tag{7.2}$$

and the volume distribution function as

$$n_v(D_p) = \frac{\pi}{6} D_p^3 n(D_p) \ \left(\mu\text{m}^3\, \mu\text{m}^{-1}\text{cm}^{-3}\right) \tag{7.3}$$

The total particle surface area and volume per cm^3 of air are

$$S = \pi \int_0^\infty D_p^2 n(D_p)\, dD_p = \int_0^\infty n_s(D_p)\, dD_p \ \left(\mu\text{m}^2\,\text{cm}^{-3}\right) \tag{7.4}$$

$$V = \frac{\pi}{6} \int_0^\infty D_p^3 n(D_p)\, dD_p = \int_0^\infty n_v(D_p)\, dD_p \ \left(\mu\text{m}^3\,\text{cm}^{-3}\right) \tag{7.5}$$

Normalized surface area and volume distributions can then be defined by
$\tilde{n}_s(D_p) = n_s(D_p)/S$ (μm^{-1}) and $\tilde{n}_v(D_p) = n_v(D_p)/V$ (μm^{-1}).

If the particles all have density ρ_p (g cm^{-3}) then the distribution of particle mass with respect to particle size is

$$n_m(D_p) = \left(\frac{\rho_p}{10^6}\right)\left(\frac{\pi}{6}\right)D_p^3 n(D_p) = \frac{\rho_p}{10^6} n_v(D_p) \; (\mu\text{g }\mu\text{m}^{-1}\text{cm}^{-3}) \quad (7.6)$$

where the factor of 10^6 is needed to convert ρ_p from g cm^{-3} to μg μm^{-3}, to maintain the units of $n_m(D_p)$ as μg μm^{-1} cm^{-3}.

Because particle diameters in an aerosol population typically vary over several orders of magnitude, it is often convenient to express the size distribution in terms of the logarithm of the diameter, either $\ln D_p$ or $\log D_p$.

7.1.1. Distributions Based on $\log D_p$

Let us define $n(\log D_p)\, d\log D_p$ = number of particles per cm^3 of air in the size range $\log D_p$ to $\log D_p + d\log D_p$. Note that $n(\log D_p)$ is *not* the same function as $n(D_p)$. Rather than introduce new notation for $n(\log D_p)$ to differentiate it from $n(D_p)$, we will always indicate the independent variable, either D_p or $\log D_p$. Formally we cannot take the logarithm of a dimensional quantity. Thus, when we write $\log D_p$ we must think of it as $\log(D_p/1)$, where the "reference" particle diameter is 1 μm and is thus not explicitly indicated. The units of $n(\log D_p)$ are cm^{-3} since $\log D_p$ is dimensionless. The total number concentration of particles is

$$N = \int_{-\infty}^{\infty} n(\log D_p)\, d\log D_p \;(\text{cm}^{-3}) \quad (7.7)$$

and the normalized size distribution function with respect to $\log D_p$ is $\tilde{n}(\log D_p) = n(\log D_p)/N$, which is dimensionless. Note that the limits of integration in Eq. (7.7) are now $-\infty$ to ∞.

Just as we defined surface area and volume distributions with respect to D_p we can do so with respect to $\log D_p$,

$$n_s(\log D_p) = \pi D_p^2 n(\log D_p) \; (\mu\text{m}^2\,\text{cm}^{-3}) \quad (7.8)$$

$$n_v(\log D_p) = \frac{\pi}{6} D_p^3 n(\log D_p) \; (\mu\text{m}^3\,\text{cm}^{-3}) \quad (7.9)$$

with

$$S = \int_{-\infty}^{\infty} \pi D_p^2 n(\log D_p)\, d\log D_p = \int_{-\infty}^{\infty} n_s(\log D_p)\, d\log D_p \qquad (7.10)$$

$$V = \int_{-\infty}^{\infty} \frac{\pi}{6} D_p^3 n(\log D_p)\, d\log D_p = \int_{-\infty}^{\infty} n_v(\log D_p)\, d\log D_p \qquad (7.11)$$

Since $n(D_p)\, dD_p$ = the differential number of particles in the size range D_p to $D_p + dD_p$, this quantity is sometimes expressed as dN, with similar notation for the other distributions. Thus, using this notation we have:

$$dN = n(D_p)\, dD_p = n(\log D_p)\, d\log D_p \qquad (7.12)$$

$$dS = n_s(D_p)\, dD_p = n_s(\log D_p)\, d\log D_p \qquad (7.13)$$

$$dV = n_v(D_p)\, dD_p = n_v(\log D_p)\, d\log D_p \qquad (7.14)$$

Based on this notation, the various size distribution functions are often written as

$$n(D_p) = \frac{dN}{dD_p} \qquad\qquad \tilde{n}(D_p) = \frac{dN}{N\, dD_p}$$

$$n(\log D_p) = \frac{dN}{d\log D_p} \qquad\qquad \tilde{n}(\log D_p) = \frac{dN}{N\, d\log D_p}$$

$$n_s(D_p) = \frac{dS}{dD_p} \qquad\qquad \tilde{n}_s(D_p) = \frac{dS}{S\, dD_p}$$

$$n_s(\log D_p) = \frac{dS}{d\log D_p} \qquad\qquad \tilde{n}_s(\log D_p) = \frac{dS}{S\, d\log D_p}$$

$$n_v(D_p) = \frac{dV}{dD_p} \qquad\qquad \tilde{n}_v(D_p) = \frac{dV}{V\, dD_p}$$

$$n_v(\log D_p) = \frac{dV}{d\log D_p} \qquad\qquad \tilde{n}_v(\log D_p) = \frac{dV}{V\, d\log D_p}$$

To conform with the common notation we will often express the distributions in this manner.

7.1.2. Relating Size Distributions Based on Different Independent Variables

It is important for us to be able to relate a size distribution based on one independent variable, say D_p, to one based on another independent variable, say $\log D_p$. The basis for such relationship is Eq. (7.12). In a particular incremental particle size range D_p to $D_p + dD_p$ the number of particles dN is a certain quantity, and that quantity is the same regardless of how the size distribution function is expressed. Thus, in the particular case of $n(D_p)$ and $n(\log D_p)$ we have that

$$n(D_p) \, dD_p = n(\log D_p) \, d \log D_p \tag{7.15}$$

Say we have $n(D_p)$ and wish to calculate $n(\log D_p)$ from it. Thus,

$$n(\log D_p) = n(D_p) \frac{dD_p}{d \log D_p} \tag{7.16}$$

Now, since $d \log D_p = d \ln D_p / 2.303 = dD_p / 2.303 D_p$, Eq. (7.16) becomes

$$n(\log D_p) = 2.303 D_p n(D_p) \tag{7.17}$$

which is the desired relationship between $n(D_p)$ and $n(\log D_p)$.

This procedure can be generalized to relate any two size distribution functions $n(u)$ and $n(v)$ where u and v are both related to diameter D_p. The generalization of Eq. (7.15) is

$$n(u) \, du = n(v) \, dv \tag{7.18}$$

and if we seek to calculate $n(u)$ in terms of $n(v)$, we write

$$n(u) = n(v) \frac{dv/dD_p}{du/dD_p} \tag{7.19}$$

7.2. PROPERTIES OF SIZE DISTRIBUTIONS

Given an aerosol size distribution, represented either in discrete form as N_k, or in continuous form as $n(D_p)$, it is of interest to be able to compute certain properties of the distribution. Those properties of interest are the so-called *moments* of the distribution, and the two moments of most interest are the mean and the variance.

To define these moments in terms of size distributions, let us assume first that we have a discrete distribution given as N_k, $k = 1, 2, \ldots, M$. We recall that N_k is the number concentration (cm^{-3}) of particles containing k molecules. The mean number of molecules in the population $\bar{k}$ is given by

$$\bar{k} = \sum_{k=1}^{M} kN_k \bigg/ \sum_{k=1}^{M} N_k \tag{7.20}$$

and the variance, a measure of the spread of the distribution around the mean size $\bar{k}$, is given by

$$\sigma^2 = \sum_{k=1}^{M} (k - \bar{k})^2 N_k \bigg/ \sum_{k=1}^{M} N_k \tag{7.21}$$

A value of σ^2 equal to zero would mean that every one of the particles in the distribution is precisely of size $\bar{k}$. An increasing σ^2 indicates that the spread of the distribution about $\bar{k}$ is increasing.

We will deal most frequently with aerosol size distributions expressed in continuous form. Given the size distribution $n(D_p)$, the mean particle diameter of the distribution is defined by

$$\bar{D}_p = \frac{\int_0^\infty D_p n(D_p)\, dD_p}{\int_0^\infty n(D_p)\, dD_p}$$

$$= \frac{1}{N} \int_0^\infty D_p n(D_p)\, dD_p \tag{7.22}$$

The variance of the distribution is

$$\sigma^2 = \frac{\int_0^\infty (D_p - \bar{D}_p)^2 n(D_p)\, dD_p}{\int_0^\infty n(D_p)\, dD_p}$$

$$= \frac{1}{N} \int_0^\infty (D_p - \bar{D}_p)^2 n(D_p)\, dD_p \tag{7.23}$$

Some other properties of a distribution that might be of interest are the mean surface area and mean volume,

$$\bar{S} = \frac{1}{N} \int_0^\infty \pi D_p^2 n(D_p)\, dD_p = \frac{1}{N} \int_0^\infty n_s(D_p)\, dD_p \tag{7.24}$$

$$\bar{V} = \frac{1}{N} \int_0^\infty \frac{\pi}{6} D_p^3 n(D_p)\, dD_p = \frac{1}{N} \int_0^\infty n_v(D_p)\, dD_p \tag{7.25}$$

Table 7.2 presents a number of other mean values of importance in characterizing an aerosol size distribution.

TABLE 7.2.   Mean Values of Importance in Characterizing an Aerosol Size Distribution

Property	Defining Relation	Description
Number mean diameter	$\overline{D}_p = \dfrac{1}{N} \displaystyle\int_0^\infty D_p\, n(D_p)\, dD_p$	Average diameter of the population
Median diameter	$F(D_p,\text{median}) = \dfrac{N}{2}$	Diameter below which one-half the particles lie and above which one-half the particles lie
Mode	$\left[\dfrac{dn(D_p)}{dD_p}\right]_{D_p,\text{mode}} = 0$	The diameter at which the largest number of particles lie, i.e. the most frequently occurring diameter
Surface area mean diameter	$\pi D^2_{p,\text{avg. surface area}}$ $= \dfrac{1}{N}\displaystyle\int_0^\infty n_s(D_p)\, dD_p$	Diameter of that particle whose surface area equals the mean surface area of the population
Volume mean diameter	$\dfrac{\pi}{6} D^3_{p,\text{avg. volume}}$ $= \dfrac{1}{N}\displaystyle\int_0^\infty n_v(D_p)\, dD_p$	Diameter of that particle whose volume equals the mean volume of the population
Surface area median diameter	$\displaystyle\int_0^{D_{p,\text{surf. area median}}} n_s(D_p)\, dD_p$ $= \dfrac{1}{2}\displaystyle\int_0^\infty n_s(D_p)\, dD_p$	The diameter below which one-half the particle surface area lies and above which one-half the particle surface area lies
Volume median diameter	$\displaystyle\int_0^{D_{p,\text{vol. median}}} n_v(D_p)\, dD_p$ $= \dfrac{1}{2}\displaystyle\int_0^\infty n_v(D_p)\, dD_p$	The diameter below which one-half the particle volume lies and above which one-half the particle volume lies

7.3.   THE LOG–NORMAL DISTRIBUTION

The next question that arises in our study of aerosol size distributions is: what functions are commonly used to represent aerosol size distributions? To represent particle size distributions $n(D_p)$ we need a function that is defined only for $D_p \geq 0$ and which is zero for $D_p = 0$ (clearly no particles can exist of size zero) and approaches zero as $D_p \to \infty$ (no particles can exist with infinite size). While many distributions with such properties exist, several of which will be given in Chapter 17, a popular one for representing aerosol size distributions, and one with a host of desirable properties is the *log–normal distribution*.

If a quantity u is normally distributed, the probability density function for u obeys the Gaussian distribution,

$$n(u) = \frac{N}{(2\pi)^{1/2}\sigma_u} \exp\left[-\frac{(u-\bar{u})^2}{2\sigma_u^2}\right] \qquad (7.26)$$

where $n(u)$ is defined for $-\infty < u < \infty$, $\bar{u}$ is the mean of the distribution, σ_u^2 is its variance, and

$$N = \int_{-\infty}^{\infty} n(u)\,du \qquad (7.27)$$

A quantity that is log–normally distributed has its logarithm governed by a normal distribution. If the quantity of interest is particle diameter D_p, then saying that an aerosol population is log–normally distributed means that $u = \ln D_p$ satisfies Eq. (7.26). For now we will use the natural logarithm $\ln D_p$; later we will also express our result in terms of $\log D_p$.

Letting $u = \ln D_p$, we express Eq. (7.26) as

$$n(\ln D_p) = \frac{N}{(2\pi)^{1/2}\ln\sigma_g} \exp\left[-\frac{(\ln D_p - \ln \overline{D}_{pg})^2}{2\ln^2\sigma_g}\right] \qquad (7.28)$$

where we have let $\bar{u} = \ln \overline{D}_{pg}$ and $\sigma_u = \ln\sigma_g$. For the moment we will consider $\overline{D}_{pg}$ and σ_g to be merely the two parameters of the distribution. Shortly we will discuss the physical significance of these parameters. It is more convenient to have the size distribution function expressed in terms of D_p rather than $\ln D_p$. The form of Eq. (7.17) appropriate to this transformation is $n(\ln D_p) = D_p n(D_p)$, so that Eq. (7.28) becomes

$$n(D_p) = \frac{N}{(2\pi)^{1/2}D_p\ln\sigma_g} \exp\left[-\frac{(\ln D_p - \ln \overline{D}_{pg})^2}{2\ln^2\sigma_g}\right] \qquad (7.29)$$

This is the conventional form of the log–normal distribution used in describing aerosol size distributions.

We now wish to examine the physical significance of the two parameters $\overline{D}_{pg}$ and σ_g. To do so let us examine for the moment some properties of the normal distribution Eq. (7.26). The cumulative distribution function $F(u)$ is the probability that u will lie in the range $-\infty$ to u,

$$F(u) = \int_{-\infty}^{u} n(u')\,du' \qquad (7.30)$$

so that for a normally distributed quantity,

$$F(u) = \frac{N}{(2\pi)^{1/2}\sigma_u} \int_{-\infty}^{u} \exp\left[-\frac{(u' - \bar{u})^2}{2\sigma_u^2} \right] du' \tag{7.31}$$

To evaluate this integral we let $\eta = (u' - \bar{u})/\sqrt{2}\,\sigma_u$, and we obtain

$$F(u) = \frac{N}{\sqrt{\pi}} \int_{-\infty}^{(u-\bar{u})/(\sqrt{2}\,\sigma_u)} e^{-\eta^2}\,d\eta \tag{7.32}$$

The *error function* erf z is defined as

$$\text{erf}\,z = \frac{2}{\sqrt{\pi}} \int_0^z e^{-\eta^2}\,d\eta \tag{7.33}$$

where erf $\infty = 1$. If we divide the integral in Eq. (7.32) into one from $-\infty$ to 0 and the second from 0 to $(u - \bar{u})/\sqrt{2}\,\sigma_u$, then the first integral is seen to be equal to $\sqrt{\pi}/2$ and the second to $(\sqrt{\pi}/2)\text{erf}((u - \bar{u})/\sqrt{2}\,\sigma_u)$. Thus, for the normal distribution

$$F(u) = \frac{N}{2} + \frac{N}{2}\text{erf}\left(\frac{u - \bar{u}}{\sqrt{2}\,\sigma_u} \right) \tag{7.34}$$

Now, in the case of the log–normal distribution $u = \ln D_p$, so Eq. (7.34) can be expressed as

$$F(D_p) = \frac{N}{2} + \frac{N}{2}\text{erf}\left(\frac{\ln D_p/\bar{D}_{pg}}{\sqrt{2}\,\ln\sigma_g} \right) \tag{7.35}$$

$F(D_p)/N$ is the fraction of the total number of particles with diameters up to D_p. For $D_p = \bar{D}_{pg}$, since erf(0) = 0, $F(\bar{D}_{pg})/N = 1/2$. Thus, we see that $\bar{D}_{pg}$ is the *median diameter*, that is that diameter for which exactly one-half the particles are smaller and one-half are larger. To understand the role of σ_g, let us consider that diameter D_{po} for which $\sigma_g = D_{po}/\bar{D}_{pg}$. At that diameter

$$\frac{F(D_p)}{N} = \frac{1}{2} + \frac{1}{2}\text{erf}\left(\frac{1}{\sqrt{2}} \right) = 0.841 \tag{7.36}$$

Thus, σ_g is the ratio of the diameter below which 84.1 percent of the particles lie to the median diameter. D_{po} can be located at the point where $F(D_p)/N = 0.841$. σ_g is termed the *geometric standard deviation*.

A monodisperse aerosol has the property that $\sigma_g = 1$. In addition, 67 percent of all particles lie in the range from $\bar{D}_{pg}/\sigma_g$ to $\bar{D}_{pg}\sigma_g$, and 95 percent of all particles lie in the range from $\bar{D}_{pg}/2\sigma_g$ to $2\bar{D}_{pg}\sigma_g$.

Let us calculate the mean diameter $\overline{D}_p$ of a log–normally distributed aerosol. By definition, the mean diameter is found from

$$\overline{D}_p = \frac{1}{N} \int_0^\infty D_p n(D_p) \, dD_p \tag{7.37}$$

which we wish to evaluate in the case of $n(D_p)$ given by Eq. (7.29). In evaluating the integral it is useful to let $u = \ln D_p$, in which case Eq. (7.37) becomes

$$\overline{D}_p = \frac{1}{\sqrt{2\pi}\,\sigma_u} \int_{-\infty}^\infty \exp(u) \exp\left[-\frac{(u - \overline{u})^2}{2\sigma_u^2}\right] du \tag{7.38}$$

By expanding the exponent in the integral and completing the square, we obtain

$$\overline{D}_p = \frac{1}{\sqrt{2\pi}} e^{\overline{u}} e^{\sigma_u^2/2} \int_{-\infty}^\infty \exp\left[-\frac{\left(u - (\overline{u} + \sigma_u^2)\right)^2}{2\sigma_u^2}\right] \frac{du}{\sigma_u} \tag{7.39}$$

To evaluate the integral we let $t = (u - (\overline{u} + \sigma_u^2))/\sqrt{2}\,\sigma_u$ and we get

$$\overline{D}_p = \frac{1}{\sqrt{\pi}} e^{\overline{u}} e^{\sigma_u^2/2} \int_{-\infty}^\infty e^{-t^2} \, dt \tag{7.40}$$

and since the integral equals $\sqrt{\pi}$, the final result is

$$\overline{D}_p = e^{\overline{u}} e^{\sigma_u^2/2}$$

$$= \overline{D}_{pg} \exp\left(\ln^2 \sigma_g / 2\right) \tag{7.41}$$

We see that the mean diameter of a log–normal distribution depends on both $\overline{D}_{pg}$ and σ_g.

7.3.1. Plotting the Log–Normal Distribution

The log–normal distribution has the useful property that when the cumulative distribution function is plotted against the logarithm of particle diameter on special graph paper with one axis scaled according to the error function of Eq. (7.35), so-called log–probability paper, a straight line results. The point at which $F(D_p) = 0.5$ occurs when $\ln D_p = \ln \overline{D}_{pg}$. The point at $F(D_p) = 0.84$ occurs for $\ln D_p = \ln \overline{D}_{pg} + \ln \sigma_g$ or $D_p = \overline{D}_{pg}\sigma_g$. The geometric mean or median is the value of D_p where the straight line plot of F crosses the 50th percentile. The slope of the line is related to the geometric standard deviation σ_g which

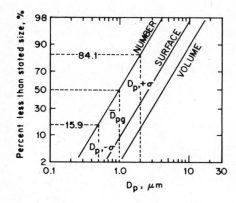

Figure 7.1. Cumulative number, surface area, and volume distributions of a log–normal aerosol size distribution on log–probability paper.

can be calculated from the plot by dividing the 84th percentile diameter (which is one standard deviation from the mean) by the 50th percentile diameter. This property can be expressed as

$$\sigma_g = \frac{\overline{D}_{pg}}{D_{p,-\sigma}} = \frac{D_{p,+\sigma}}{\overline{D}_{pg}} = \left(\frac{D_{p,+\sigma}}{D_{p,-\sigma}}\right)^{1/2} \tag{7.42}$$

where $-\sigma$ and $+\sigma$ are minus and plus one standard deviation from the geometric mean.

Figure 7.1 shows the cumulative log–normal number distribution plotted on log–probability graph paper. $D_{p,-\sigma}$ and $D_{p,+\sigma}$ correspond to the 15.9% and 84.1% points, respectively, on the probability scale. We will discuss the surface area and volume distributions also shown in Figure 7.1 shortly.

7.3.2. Properties of the Log–Normal Distribution

We have developed the log–normal distribution for the number concentration. As we know, in addition to the number distribution, the surface area and volume distributions are of interest. Thus, we wish to examine the surface area and volume distributions of an aerosol whose number distribution is log–normal and given by Eq. (7.29). Since $n_s(D_p) = \pi D_p^2 n(D_p)$ and $n_v(D_p) = (\pi/6)D_p^3 n(D_p)$, let us determine the forms of $n_s(D_p)$ and $n_v(D_p)$ when $n(D_p)$ is log–normal. From Eq. (7.29) we see that these two distributions fall within the general form of $n_\gamma(D_p) = a_\gamma D_p^\gamma n(D_p)$, where $\gamma = 2$ and 3 for the surface area and volume distributions, respectively, and a_γ is the appropriate coefficient, either π or $(\pi/6)$.

Thus, we have

$$n_\gamma(D_p) = \frac{a_\gamma N D_p^\gamma}{(2\pi)^{1/2} D_p \ln \sigma_g} \exp\left[-\frac{(\ln D_p - \ln \overline{D}_{pg})^2}{2\ln^2\sigma_g}\right] \tag{7.43}$$

By letting $D_p^\gamma = \exp(\gamma \ln D_p)$, expanding the exponential and completing the square in the exponent, Eq. (7.43) becomes

$$n_\gamma(D_p) = \frac{N}{(2\pi)^{1/2} D_p \ln \sigma_g} \exp\left[\gamma \ln \overline{D}_{pg} + \frac{\gamma^2}{2} \ln^2 \sigma_g\right]$$

$$\times \exp\left[-\frac{\left(\ln D_p - \left(\ln \overline{D}_{pg} + \gamma \ln^2 \sigma_g\right)\right)^2}{2 \ln^2 \sigma_g}\right] \qquad (7.44)$$

Thus, we see that if $n(D_p)$ is log–normal, $n_\gamma(D_p) = D_p^\gamma n(D_p)$ is also log–normal with the same geometric standard deviation of σ_g as the parent distribution and with the logarithm of the medium diameter given by

$$\ln \overline{D}_{pg\gamma} = \ln \overline{D}_{pg} + \gamma \ln^2 \sigma_g \qquad (7.45)$$

Now if we return to Figure 7.1, we note that the surface area and volume distributions are also log–normal (i.e., represented as straight lines), with the same slope (i.e., the same σ_g) but with median values that are shifted to larger particle sizes in accordance with Eq. (7.45). For the particular distribution shown in Figure 7.1, $\overline{D}_{pg} = 1.0$ μm and $\sigma_g = 2.0$, the resulting surface area and volume median diameters are approximately 2.6 μm and 4.2 μm, respectively.

7.4. ATMOSPHERIC AEROSOLS

Table 7.3 summarizes some properties of atmospheric aerosols. The first column is a measure of particle number concentration, expressed as the so-called Aitkin nuclei concentration. Aitken nuclei are those particles and ions

TABLE 7.3. Properties of Atmospheric Aerosols[a]

Category	Aitken Nuclei, cm^{-3}	V ($D_p < 1$ μm), μm^3 cm^{-3}	V, μm^3 cm^{-3}
Background			
Oceanic	100–400	1–4	
Remote continental	50–1000	0.5–2.5	2–10
Average continental	2000–5000	2.5–8	10–40
Urban influenced	5000–15000	8–30	20–60
Urban Polluted	10^5–4×10^6	30–150	100–300

[a] Willeke and Whitby (1975).

measured by means of an instrument in which water vapor is made to condense on particles by supersaturating the vapor. (To eliminate condensation on light ions, supersaturations in such an instrument should not exceed 270 percent.) Also given in Table 7.3 is the aerosol volume concentration of particles below 1 μm diameter as well as the total aerosol volume concentration.

Atmospheric aerosol size distributions are usually presented graphically in terms of the number distributions,

$$\frac{dN}{d \log D_p} \left(= n(\log D_p) \right) \quad \text{or} \quad \frac{dN}{Nd \log D_p} \left(= \tilde{n}(\log D_p) \right)$$

the surface area distributions,

$$\frac{dS}{d \log D_p} \left(= n_s(\log D_p) \right) \quad \text{or} \quad \frac{dS}{Sd \log D_p} \left(= \tilde{n}_s(\log D_p) \right)$$

or the volume (or mass) distributions,

$$\frac{dV}{d \log D_p} \left(= n_v(\log D_p) \right) \quad \text{or} \quad \frac{dV}{Vd \log D_p} \left(= \tilde{n}_v(\log D_p) \right)$$

Figure 7.2 shows $dN/d \log D_p$ for aerosol samples at Denver's City Maintenance Yard from Oct. 26–30, 1971 as reported by Willeke and Whitby (1975).

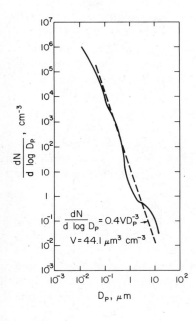

Figure 7.2. The grand average of the aerosol number distribution from October 1971 measurements at Denver's City Maintenance Yard compared with a distribution of the form

$$\frac{dN}{d \log D_p} = KD_p^{-k}$$

with $K = 0.4$ and $k = 3$. (Willeke and Whitby, 1975). Reprinted with permission from Journal of the Air Pollution Control Association.

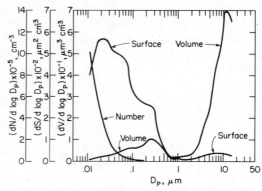

Figure 7.3. Normalized aerosol number, surface area, and volume distributions for the grand average October 1971 measurements at Denver's City Maintenance Yard. (Willeke and Whitby, 1975). Reprinted with permission from Journal of the Air Pollution Control Association.

Figure 7.2 also shows an empirical form, $dN/d \log D_p = K D_p^{-k}$, fit to the distribution. Because of the steep fall-off of the number of particles for diameters larger than 0.1 μm, plots such as Figure 7.2 are not able to show much detail in the distribution. Number distributions, while showing clearly changes in particle number for the smaller sizes, do not show the substantial changes in volume concentration associated with small changes in the number concentration for particles of D_p greater than 1 μm. If one is interested in seeing the relationship of the various size ranges of the distribution to properties such as the surface area or volume, a better plot is one in which $dS/d \log D_p$ or $dV/d \log D_p$ is plotted on a linear ordinate versus $\log D_p$ on the abscissa. Figure 7.3 shows the same data as Figure 7.2 plotted in this manner. From this type of plot it is much easier to discern modes in the distribution and to see the relative number, surface area, or mass in the different size ranges of the distribution.

From Figure 7.3 we see clearly the multimodal nature of atmospheric aerosol surface area and volume distributions that was mentioned in Chapter 1. Thus, plots of $dS/d \log D_p$ or $dV/d \log D_p$ are to be preferred whenever modal detail is desired or the correct relationship of integral areas under the curve is important. The $dN/d \log D_p$ versus $\log D_p$ plot is preferred whenever it is important to display the extreme range of data.

Figure 7.4 shows the volume distributions of aerosol at four sites in California. The first observation we can make is that man's activities, including combustion processes, contribute primarily to the submicron size range, while much of the aerosol from primary natural sources, such as sea salt and soil dust, is concentrated in the size range beyond 1 μm diameter. Second, one notes the multimodal nature of the volume distributions at the three sites reflecting land-based aerosol. As we will see later, the mode in the volume

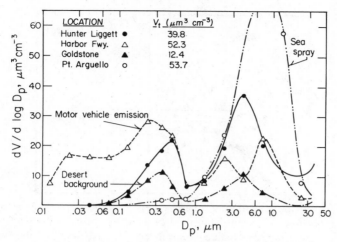

Figure 7.4. Comparison of aerosol volume distributions at four locations in the Southern California area: (1) Hunter Liggett—a non-urban background site; (2) Harbor Freeway—motor vehicle source enriched site; (3) Goldstone—a remote desert site; (4) Pt. Arguello—a site dominated by marine aerosol. V_t is the total volume concentration of aerosol ($\mu m^3\ cm^{-3}$) as estimated from the particle measurements. (Hidy, 1975). Reprinted with permission from Journal of the Air Pollution Control Association.

distribution that occurs in the 0.1 to 1.0 μm diameter range results from the growth of particles by gas-phase chemical reactions that lead to condensable products, so-called gas-to-particle conversion.

7.5. VISIBILITY DEGRADATION

Visibility degradation is the most readily perceived impact of air pollution. Several factors determine how far one can see through the atmosphere, including optical properties of the atmosphere, amount and distribution of light, characteristics of the objects observed, and properties of the human eye. The human ability to see through the atmosphere is dependent on the concentration of suspended particles and gases, which have the ability to scatter and absorb light, causing the appearance of haze, a decrease in contrast, and a change in the perceived color of distant objects.

As we noted in Chapter 2, the *prevailing visibility* is defined as the greatest distance in a given direction at which it is just possible to see and identify (1) a prominent dark object in the daytime, and (2) an unfocused, moderately intense light source at night, and which is attained or surpassed around at least half the horizon circle but not necessarily in continuous sectors. Visibility is reduced by two effects which gas molecules and particles have on visible

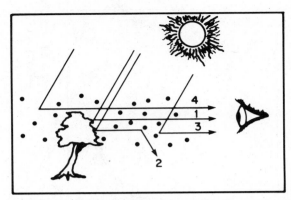

Figure 7.5. Contributions to atmospheric visibility: (1) Residual light from the target reaching the observer. (2) Light from the target scattered out of the observer's line of sight. (3) Airlight from intervening atmosphere scattered into the observer's line of sight. (4) Airlight constituting the horizon sky.

radiation: absorption and scattering of light. Absorption of certain wavelengths of light by gas molecules and particles is sometimes responsible for atmospheric colorations. However, light scattering is the more important phenomenon responsible for impairment of visibility.

Light scattering refers to the deflection of the direction of travel of light by airborne material. Visibility is reduced when there is significant scattering because particles in the atmosphere between the observer and the object scatter light from the sun and other parts of the sky through the line of sight of the observer. This light decreases the contrast between the object and the background sky, thereby reducing visibility. These effects are depicted in Figure 7.5.

Let us examine the effect of atmospheric constituents on visibility reduction. To do so we consider the case in which a black object is being viewed against a white background. We first define the contrast at a distance x from the object, $C(x)$, as the relative difference between the light intensity of the target and the background,

$$C(x) = \frac{I_B(x) - I_0(x)}{I_B(x)} \tag{7.46}$$

where $I_B(x)$ and $I_0(x)$ are the intensities (measured in joules cm^{-2} sec^{-1}) of the background and the object, respectively. At the object ($x = 0$), $I_0(0) = 0$, since the object is assumed to be black and therefore absorbs all light incident on it. Thus $C(0) = 1$. Over the distance x between the object and the observer, $I_0(x)$ will be affected by two phenomena: (1) absorption of light by gases and particles, and (2) addition of light which is scattered into the line of sight. Over a distance dx the intensity change dI_0 is a result of these two effects. The fraction of I_0 diminished is assumed to be proportional to dx, since dx is a measure of the amount of suspended gases and particles present. The fractional reduction in I_0 is written $dI_0 = -(b_{abs} + b_{scat})I_0\,dx$, where $b_{abs}\,dx$ is the fraction of I_0 lost by absorption and $b_{scat}\,dx$ is the fraction of I_0 lost by scattering out of the line of sight. It is common to assume that b_{abs} and b_{scat} are constants (independent of x) which depend on the concentration of particles present. In addition, the intensity I_0 can be increased over the distance dx by scattering of light from the background into the line of sight. The increase can be expressed as $b'I_B(x)\,dx$, where b' is a constant. The net change in intensity is given by

$$dI_0(x) = \left[b'I_B(x) - (b_{abs} + b_{scat})I_0(x)\right] dx \qquad (7.47)$$

By its definition as background intensity, I_B must be independent of x. Thus, along any other line of sight

$$dI_B(x) = 0 = \left[b'I_B - (b_{abs} + b_{scat})I_B\right] dx \qquad (7.48)$$

We see that $b' = b_{abs} + b_{scat}$. Thus, we find that the contrast $C(x)$ varies according to

$$dC(x) = -(b_{abs} + b_{scat})C(x)\,dx \qquad (7.49)$$

and therefore that the contrast decreases exponentially with distance from the object,

$$C(x) = e^{-(b_{abs} + b_{scat})x} \qquad (7.50)$$

The coefficient b_{abs} accounts for absorption of light by both gas molecules and particles, and b_{scat} accounts for scattering of light by both gas molecules and particles. We can decompose b_{abs} and b_{scat} into the gas and particulate components as follows:

$$b_{abs} = b_{ag} + b_{ap}$$

$$b_{scat} = b_{sg} + b_{sp}$$

where

b_{sg} = scattering coefficient of light due to gases (the Rayleigh scattering coefficient)

b_{sp} = scattering coefficient of light due to particles

b_{ag} = absorption coefficient of light due to gases

b_{ap} = absorption coefficient of light due to particles

A ratio b_{scat}/b_{sg} of unity indicates the cleanest possible air ($b_{sp} = 0$). Thus, the higher this ratio, the greater is the contribution of particulate scattering to total light scattering.

Scattering by particulate matter of sizes comparable to the wavelength of visible light (called *Mie scattering*) is mostly responsible for visibility reduction in the atmosphere. The average wavelength of light is about 0.52 μm. Thus, particles in the range 0.1 to 1 μm in radius are the most effective, per unit mass, in reducing visibility. The scattering coefficient b_{scat} has been found to be more or less directly dependent on the atmospheric aerosol concentration in this size range, as long as the relative humidity is sufficiently low that fog formation does not take place (below about 70 percent relative humidity).

The sum of the scattering coefficient (b_{scat}) and the absorption coefficient (b_{abs}) is called the *extinction coefficient*, b_{ext}. The extinction coefficient is commonly expressed in a reciprocal length unit such as inverse meters (m^{-1}).

The lowest visually perceptible brightness contrast is called the liminal contrast or threshold contrast. The threshold contrast has been the object of considerable interest since it determines the maximum distances at which various components of a scene can be discerned. Laboratory experiments indicate that for most daylight viewing conditions, contrast ratios as low as 0.018 to 0.03 are perceptible. Typical observers can detect an 0.02 or greater contrast between large, dark objects and the horizon sky. A threshold contrast value of 2 percent ($C = 0.02$) is usually employed for visual range calculations.

Equation (7.50) can be evaluated at the distance at which a black object has a standard 0.02 contrast ratio against a white background. When the contrast in Eq. (7.50) becomes the threshold contrast, the distance becomes the visual range. If $C = 0.02$ then

$$x = \frac{3.912}{b_{ext}} \qquad (7.51)$$

with x and b_{ext} in similar units (i.e., x in meters and b_{ext} in inverse meters). This is called the Koschmeider equation.

Thus, the visual range can be expressed in terms of an extinction coefficient (b_{ext}) or a distance (x). If the extinction coefficient is measured along a sight path, then x is the visual range. If the extinction coefficient is measured at a point, then x is taken to be the local visual range. The two values of x are equal in a homogeneous atmosphere.

The derivation of Eqs. (7.50) and (7.51) is based on certain assumptions about atmospheric conditions and human perception. The fundamental assumptions are (Cohen, 1975):

1. A perfectly black object (one that reflects no light) is perceived against an ideal white background.

2. An observer can detect a contrast ratio of 0.02 (the threshold contrast).

3. The atmosphere is homogeneous such that scattering and absorption of radiation are the same everywhere.

4. Sky brightness is the same at the object, the background, and the observer (cloudless sky).

5. The viewing distance is horizontal and the earth's curvature is ignored.

It should be noted that the visual range for nonblack targets strongly depends upon the initial contrast ratio, which in turn depends on color, angle, and intensity of illumination. To maximize object visibility the object should be of such a color as to have maximum contrast relative to the background, and the observation should be made at wavelengths that maximize transmission between observer and object.

7.5.1. Components of the Extinction Coefficient

Scattering of Light.

Rayleigh Scattering (b_{sg}). Lord Rayleigh, in seeking an explanation of the blue sky, observed that the sky is bluest when air is purest and correctly referred the color to its actual cause, scattering of sunlight by the molecules of the permanent gases of air. Rayleigh demonstrated that an atmosphere containing only the primary gases scatters light in proportion to the inverse fourth power of the wavelength. This ideal atmosphere is frequently referred to as the Rayleigh atmosphere. At sea level the Rayleigh atmosphere has an extinction coefficient of approximately 13.2×10^{-6} m^{-1} at 0.52 μm wavelength, limiting visibility to about 296 kilometers.

Rayleigh scattering decreases with altitude and is proportional to air density. At 0.52 μm wavelength:

Altitude Above Sea Level, km	b_{sg} at 0.52 μm $\times 10^6$ m^{-1}
0	13.2
1.0	11.4
2.0	10.6
3.0	9.7
4.0	8.8

Rayleigh scattering thus represents a simple, definable, and measurable background level of extinction against which other extinction components (e.g., man-made pollutants) can be compared.

Particle Scattering (b_{sp}). An important parameter that characterizes the pattern of light scattering by a particle is the ratio of the particle diameter to the wavelength of visible light. Visible light that affects the retina of the human eye has a bandwidth of approximately 0.4 to 0.7 μm.

Large particles (of size greater than a few micrometers) scatter light by three processes: (1) reflection from the particle surface, (2) diffraction around the edges of the particle, and (3) refraction upon passing through the interior of the particle. Most of the light scattered by large particles is not significantly altered in direction from its original path (the forward direction). Particles most effective in scattering light are those with sizes comparable to the wavelength of visible light (0.4 to 0.7 μm). A much greater fraction of the incident light is scattered away from the forward direction by particles in this size range than by large particles. Most of the scattered light is deflected by more than 1 degree but less than 45 degrees from the forward direction. Particles of very small size (less than 0.1 μm) scatter light equally in the forward and backward directions. In addition, small particles scatter light of short wavelengths more effectively than light of long wavelengths. This effect is, in fact, responsible for the reddish hue of sunsets, since the shorter-wavelength blue component of sunlight is scattered out of the line of sight, leaving the red components to reach the observer.

When a scattered light beam strikes another particle, it is scattered (secondary scattering), and scattered again, and so on (multiple scattering). In the case of sunlight passing through the atmosphere, all the particles in the atmosphere will send scattered light in all directions so that the atmosphere itself appears luminous. This phenomenon is called airlight.

The addition of small amounts of submicron particles throughout the viewing distance tends to whiten the horizon sky, making distant dark objects and intervening airlight appear more grey. Particles generally scatter more light in the forward direction than in other directions; thus, haze appears bright in the forward-scatter mode and dark in the back-scatter mode (see Figure 7.5).

Absorption of Light.

Gas Absorption (b_{ag}). Nitrogen dioxide (NO_2) is the only light-absorbing atmospheric gas present in optically significant quantities. NO_2 absorbs light selectively and is strongly blue-absorbing; it will color plumes red, brown, or yellow. In spite of the coloration properties of NO_2, the brown haze characteristic of smoggy atmospheres is due largely to particles rather than to NO_2 (Charlson and Ahlquist, 1969).

Particle Absorption (b_{ap}). The amount of particle absorption depends on the composition and size distribution of the particles. The most important contributor to absorption appears to be graphitic carbon (in the form of soot). The source of this highly absorbing submicron-size soot is the combustion of liquid fuels, particularly in diesel engines. The effects of particle absorption in the extinction coefficient vary. In "clean" areas b_{ap} can be 10 percent or less of b_{sp}. In urban areas b_{ap} can reach 50 percent of b_{sp} or greater.

TABLE 7.4. Contribution of Chemical Species to the Extinction Coefficient, b_{ext}

Denver Wintertime Aerosol[a]		
Fine Particle Species		Mean Percent Contribution
$(NH_4)_2SO_4$		20.2
NH_4NO_3		17.2
Organic C		12.5
Elemental C (scattering)	6.5	
Elemental C (absorption)	31.2	
Elemental C (subtotal)		37.7
Other		6.6
NO_2		5.7
	Total	100

[a]Groblicki et al. (1981).

The chemical species responsible for visibility impairment are those found in the fine particle mode. Results from the ACHEX experiment (Hidy, 1975) in the South Coast Air Basin of California showed that sulfates, nitrates, and organics were the main contributors to the light-scattering coefficient (White and Roberts, 1977). The recent Denver winter haze study produced results listed in Table 7.4.

Recently, Trijonis et al. (1982) completed an investigation into visibility and aerosol relationships for California. The results of that study showed that Rayleigh scattering caused only about 5 percent of total extinction in the most polluted areas. Light absorption by NO_2 contributed 7 to 11 percent of total extinction throughout the state. Sulfate accounted for 40 to 70 percent of total extinction in Los Angeles and San Diego and 15 to 35 percent in the remainder of California. Nitrates apparently contributed 10 to 40 percent of total extinction in northern California. However, black (graphitic) carbon, the most significant remaining component, was not accounted for in this study as a single species contributing to visibility reduction in the state. From Table 7.4 we note that in Denver during winter, elemental carbon is responsible for about 40 percent of visibility reduction.

The role of fine carbonaceous particles in visibility degradation has been an area of recent and intense study (Conklin et al., 1981; Cass et al., 1982, 1984; Gray et al., 1985). It has been estimated that light absorption by black (graphitic) carbon particles is currently responsible for as much as 17 percent of the total extinction coefficient in the wintertime in downtown Los Angeles (Conklin et al., 1981). The disproportionately large influence of black carbon upon light extinction, also reflected in findings from the Denver winter haze study, arises in part, as we will see, because black carbon is more effective than nonabsorbing aerosol particles (such as sulfates and nitrates) in attenuating light (Faxvog and Roessler, 1978).

Larson et al. (1984) have analyzed atmospheric composition and visibility in Los Angeles on two days in 1983: one day, April 7, representing relatively unpolluted conditions, and the second, August 25, characterized by heavy smog. Table 7.5 gives the ambient measured concentrations of the species sampled on the two days. In preparing Table 7.5 Larson et al. (1984) used the procedure of Stelson and Seinfeld (1981) for developing a material balance on the chemical composition of the aerosol samples. Stelson and Seinfeld (1981) showed that urban aerosol mass can be accounted for from measurements of SO_4^{2-}, Cl^-, Br^-, NO_3^-, NH_4^+, Na^+, K^+, Ca^{2+}, Fe, Mg, Al, Si, Pb, carbonaceous material, and aerosol water. Their method assumes that trace metals are present in the form of common oxides:

Element	Oxide Form
Al	Al_2O_3
Ca	CaO
Fe	Fe_2O_3
Si	SiO_2
Mg	MgO
Pb	PbO
Na	Na_2O
K	K_2O

In Table 7.5 this procedure was followed with the exception of Na, which was assumed to be in the form of an ionic solid. Mg was present at negligible levels, and thus its chemical form was unimportant to the aerosol mass balance. To account for hydrogen and oxygen present in the hydrocarbons, the mass of organic carbonaceous material was taken to be 1.2 times the organic carbon mass measured (Countess et al., 1980). The ionic material was assumed to be distributed as follows:

Na^+ was associated with Cl^-.

NH_4^+ was associated with SO_4^{2-}.

NH_4^+ remaining, if any, was associated with NO_3^-.

Na^+ remaining, if any, was associated with remaining NO_3^-, if any.

Na^+ remaining, if any, was associated with remaining SO_4^{2-}, if any.

Figure 7.6 shows the aerosol volume distributions and gives the total extinction coefficients on the two days at $\lambda = 0.55$ μm. The estimated contributions to b_{ext} on the two days were:

TABLE 7.5. **Atmospheric Concentrations Measured on Two Days in Los Angeles**[a]

Component (concentration)	Clear day April 7, 1983	Heavy Smog August 25, 1983
$(NH_4)_2SO_4$ (μg m^{-3})	3.54	14.90
NH_4NO_3 (μg m^{-3})	1.23	1.79
$NaNO_3$ (μg m^{-3})	—	12.80
Na_2SO_4 (μg m^{-3})	—	—
elemental carbon (μg m^{-3})	0.99	6.37
organic carbon (μg m^{-3})	6.78	32.74
Al_2O_3 (μg m^{-3})	2.82	9.34
SiO_2 (μg m^{-3})	4.53	15.54
K_2O (μg m^{-3})	0.36	1.45
CaO (μg m^{-3})	0.45	1.83
Fe_2O_3 (μg m^{-3})	0.91	4.58
PbO (μg m^{-3})	0.06	0.72
NO_2 (ppm)	0.04	0.10
O_3 (ppm)	0.05	0.21
CO (ppm)	1.6	3.39
temperature (°C)	22.0	29.8
relative humidity (%)	23.6	50.5

[a] Larson et al. (1984).

	4/7/83	8/25/83
b_{sp}, m^{-1}	0.259×10^{-4}	4.08×10^{-4}
b_{sg}, m^{-1} (Rayleigh)	0.111×10^{-4}	0.107×10^{-4}
b_{ag}, m^{-1} (NO_2)	0.012×10^{-4}	0.030×10^{-4}
b_{ap}, m^{-1} (carbon)	0.093×10^{-4}	0.787×10^{-4}
Calculated b_{ext}, m^{-1}	0.475×10^{-4}	5.00×10^{-4}

Note that the total calculated b_{ext} on the polluted day was somewhat smaller than that measured since not all atmospheric constituents were included in the calculation.

Our current knowledge of the relationship of pollutants to visibility can be summarized as follows (Cass, 1979; Tang et al., 1981; Waggoner et al., 1981):

1. Scattering by particles causes 60 to 95 percent of visibility reduction.
2. SO_4^{2-} is almost always the most important scattering material, followed by organic carbon. NO_3^- may be important in some locations.

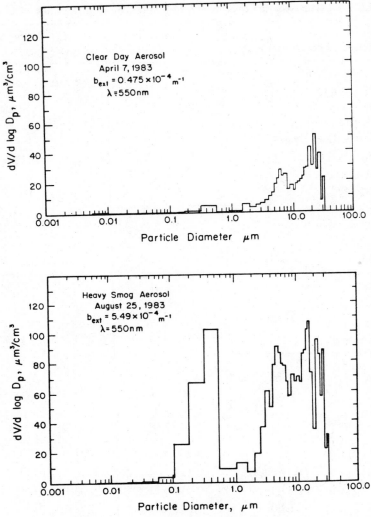

Figure 7.6. Aerosol volume distributions measured on two days in Los Angeles (Larson et al., 1984).

3. Absorption by soot particles causes 5 to 40 percent of visibility reduction.

4. NO_2 appears to cause little visibility reduction except in causing the appearance of plumes from electric power generating facilities.

5. Soot is about three times as efficient as SO_4^{2-}, NO_3^-, or organics in terms of visibility reduction per unit mass of airborne particles.

7.5.2. Light Extinction Due to Single-Component Spherical Aerosols

The aerosol scattering and absorption coefficients can be determined from the single particle light extinction efficiencies, $K_s(m, p)$ and $K_a(m, p)$, where m in the complex refractive index of each particle and $p = \pi D_p/\lambda$, the dimensionless parameter relating the particle diameter to the wavelength λ of the incident light, and the aerosol size distribution function by

$$b_{sp} = \int_0^\infty \frac{\pi}{4} D_p^2 K_s(m, p) n(D_p) \, dD_p \tag{7.52}$$

$$b_{ap} = \int_0^\infty \frac{\pi}{4} D_p^2 K_a(m, p) n(D_p) \, dD_p \tag{7.53}$$

The single particle light extinction efficiencies K_s and K_a can be derived theoretically by Mie's solution to Maxwell's equation (van de Hulst, 1957; Kerker, 1969). The total extinction coefficient b_{ext} is found by summing Eqs. (7.52) and (7.53), where we can define the single particle light extinction efficiency $K_e = K_s + K_a$.

The particle extinction coefficient can also be expressed in terms of the aerosol volume distribution, $dV/d \log D_p$,

$$b_{ext} = \int_{-\infty}^\infty G_e(m, D_p, \lambda) \frac{dV}{d \log D_p} d \log D_p \tag{7.54}$$

where the particle volume extinction efficiency, G_e, is related to $K_e(m, p)$ by

$$G_e(m, D_p, \lambda) = \frac{3}{2D_p} K_e(m, p) \tag{7.55}$$

The volume scattering and absorption efficiencies, G_s and G_a, respectively, can be used to determine analogous relationships for b_{ap} and b_{sp}.

Similarly, b_{ext} can be expressed as a convolution of the mass extinction efficiency, E_e, and the particle mass distribution, $f(x)$:

$$b_{ext} = \int_0^\infty E_e(m, x, \lambda) f(x) \, dx \tag{7.56}$$

where $x = \log(D_p/D_{p0})$, $f(x) = dM/dx$, and

$$E_e(m, x, \lambda) = \frac{3}{2D_p \rho_p} K_e(m, p) \tag{7.57}$$

The logarithmic transformation from particle size D_p to x is used to accommodate the wide variation in particle size. The mass scattering and absorption

**TABLE 7.6.   Refractive Indices and Bulk Densities for
Selected Aerosol Chemical Species**

Chemical Species	Refractive Index at $\lambda = 0.5\,\mu m$	ρ_p, g cm^{-3}
Water	1.33–0i	1.00
Ammonium Sulfate	1.53–0i	1.76
Soot	1.96–0.66i	2.0
Silica	1.55–0i	2.66
Model Aerosol	1.54–0.015i	1.7

efficiencies, E_s and E_a, respectively, are then defined as:

$$E_s(m, x, \lambda) = \frac{3}{2 D_p \rho_p} K_s(m, p) \tag{7.58}$$

$$E_a(m, x, \lambda) = \frac{3}{2 D_p \rho_p} K_a(m, p) \tag{7.59}$$

The mass scattering and absorption efficiencies are strongly dependent upon particle size and chemical composition through the dependences of K_s and K_a on these quantities. Refractive indices and bulk densities for some aerosol species are given in Table 7.6.

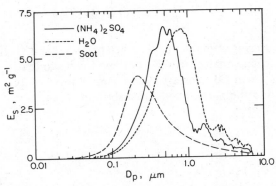

Figure 7.7.   Mass scattering efficiencies for homogeneous spheres. $(NH_4)_2SO_4$ given by the solid curve ($\rho_p = 1.76$ g cm^{-3}, $m = 1.53$–0i); water given by the short-dash curve ($\rho_p = 1.0$ g cm^{-3}, $m = 1.33$–0i); graphitic carbon (soot) given by the long-dash curve ($\rho_p = 2.0$ g cm^{-3}, $m = 1.96$–0.66i). Wavelength of radiation $\lambda = 0.53\,\mu$m. (Ouimette and Flagan, 1982). Reprinted with permission from Atmospheric Environment, Copyright (1982), Pergamon Press, Ltd.

The mass scattering efficiencies of homogeneous spheres composed of water, ammonium sulfate, and soot are shown as a function of particle size in Figure 7.7 at a wavelength of $\lambda = 0.53$ μm. We see that particles between 0.2 and 0.9 μm scatter light quite efficiently.

For particles for which $D_p \ll \lambda$, the scattering cross section is proportional to D_p^6, and thus the scattering per unit mass is proportional to D_p^3. For large particles, $D_p \gg \lambda$, the cross section is proportional to D_p^2, and hence the scattering per unit mass is proportional to D_p^{-1}. These dependencies are evident from the carbon curve in Figure 7.7. The larger absorption indices of opaque materials results in the maximum light scattering occurring for smaller particle sizes (about 0.2 μm for carbon) than those for transparent materials (0.85 μm for water). Calculations for a wide variety of transparent materials show that the maximum scattering cross section per unit mass generally occurs in the 0.7 $\lambda < D_p < 2.2$ λ particle size range. For absorbing materials the corresponding scattering maximum occurs in the 0.15 $\lambda < D_p < 0.5$ λ range (Faxvog and Roessler, 1978).

The single-particle absorption efficiency, K_a, has nonzero values only for a nonzero imaginary part of the refractive index. The variation in E_a with particle size for pure carbon spheres at $\lambda = 0.53$ μm is shown in Figure 7.8. Similarly to the scattering efficiency, the soot absorption efficiency has a maximum at 0.2 μm. The absorption cross section is proportional to D_p^2 for particles of $D_p \gg \lambda$ and to D_p^3 for particles of $D_p \ll \lambda$. On a unit mass basis, therefore, the absorption cross section should behave as D_p^{-1} for large particles and become independent of particle diameter in the small particle range. Figure 7.8, which shows the mass absorption coefficient for two different soot particles, shows this behavior. The maximum absorption occurs for particle diameters near 0.2 μm. However, the absorption efficiency approaches a

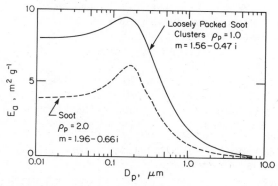

Figure 7.8. Mass absorption efficiencies for homogeneous spheres. Graphitic carbon (soot) given by the dashed curve. The solid curve represents loosely packed soot clusters which are still spherical (Ouimette and Flagan, 1982). Reprinted with permission from Atmospheric Environment, Copyright (1982), Pergamon Press, Ltd.

constant nonzero value for very small particles. Thus, very small particles may contribute substantially to light absorption but not scattering.

REFERENCES

Cass, G. R., "On the Relationship Between Sulfate Air Quality and Visibility with Examples in Los Angeles," *Atmos. Environ.*, **13**, 1069–1084 (1979).

Cass, G. R., Boone, P. M., and Macias, E. S. "Emissions and Air Quality Relationships for Atmospheric Carbon Particles in Los Angeles," in *Particulate Carbon: Atmospheric Life Cycles*, G. T. Wolff and R. L. Klimisch (Eds.), Plenum, New York, (1982).

Cass, G. R., Conklin, M. H., Shah, J. J., Huntzicker, J. J., and Macias, E. S. "Elemental Carbon Concentrations: Estimation of an Historical Data Base," *Atmos. Environ.*, **18**, 153–162 (1984).

Charlson, R. J., and Ahlquist, N. C., "Brown Haze: NO_2 or Aerosol?" *Atmos. Environ.*, **3**, 653–656 (1969).

Cohen, A. "Horizontal Visibility and the Measurement of Atmospheric Optical Depth of Lidar." *Appl. Optics*, **14**, 2878–2882 (1975).

Conklin, M. H., Cass, G. R., Chu, L. C., and Macias, E. S. "Winter Time Carbonaceous Aerosols in Los Angeles," in *Atmospheric Aerosol-Source/Air Quality Relationships*, E. S. Macias and P. K. Hopke (Eds.), ACS Symposium Series 167, Washington, D.C. (1981).

Countess, R. J., Wolff, G. T., and Cadle, S. H. "The Denver Winter Aerosol: A Comprehensive Chemical Characterization," *J. Air Pollution Control Assoc.*, **30**, 1194–1200 (1980).

Davison, R. L., Natusch, D. F. S., Wallace, J. R., and Evans, C. A., Jr. "Trace Elements in Fly Ash-Dependence of Concentration on Particle Size," *Environ. Sci. Technol.*, **8**, 1107–1113 (1974).

Faxvog, F. R., and Roessler, D. M., "Carbon Aerosol Visibility versus Particle Size Distribution," *Appl. Optics*, **17**, 2612–2616 (1978).

Gray, H. A., Cass, G. R., Huntzicker, J. J., Heyerdahl, B. K., and Rau, J. A. "Characteristics of Atmospheric Organic and Elemental Carbon Particle Concentrations in Los Angeles," *Environ. Sci. Technol.*, **19**, in press (1985).

Groblicki, P. J., Wolff, G. T., and Countess, R. J. "Visibility-Reducing Species in the Denver 'Brown Cloud'—I. Relationships Between Extinction and Chemical Composition," *Atmos. Environ.*, **15**, 2473–2484 (1981).

Hidy, G. M. "Summary of the California Aerosol Characterization Experiment," *J. Air Pollution Control Assoc.*, **25**, 1106–1114 (1975).

Kerker, M. *The Scattering of Light and Other Electromagnetic Radiation*, Academic Press, New York (1969).

Larson, S., Cass, G., Hussey, K., and Luce, F. "Visibility Model Verification by Image Processing Techniques," Final Report to State of California Air Resources Board under Agreement A2-077-32 (1984).

Ouimette, J. R., and Flagan, R. C., "The Extinction Coefficient of Multicomponent Aerosols," *Atmos. Environ.*, **16**, 2405–2419 (1982).

Stelson, A. W., and Seinfeld, J. H. "Chemical Mass Accounting of Urban Aerosol," *Environ. Sci. Technol.*, **15**, 671–679 (1981).

Tang, I. N., Wong, W. T., and Munkelwitz, H. R. "The Relative Importance of Atmospheric Sulfates and Nitrates in Visibility Reduction," *Atmos. Environ.*, **15**, 2463–2471 (1981). See also *Atmos. Environ.*, **16**, 2753 (1982).

Trijonis, J., Cass, G. R., McRae, G., Horie, Y., Lim, W., Chang, N., and Cahill, T. "Analysis of Visibility/Aerosol Relationships and Visibility Modeling/Monitoring Alternatives for California," Final Report to California Air Resources Board, Sacramento (1982).

van de Hulst, H. C., *Light Scattering by Small Particles*, Wiley, New York (1957).

Waggoner, A. P., Weiss, R. E., Ahlquist, N. C., Covert, D. S., Will, S., and Charlson, R. J. "Optical Characteristics of Atmospheric Aerosols," *Atmos. Environ.*, **15**, 1891–1909 (1981).

White, W. H., and Roberts, P. T. "On the Origins of Visibility Reducing Aerosols in the Los Angeles Air Basin," *Atmos. Environ.*, **11**, 803–812 (1977).

Willeke, K., and Whitby, K. T. "Atmospheric Aerosols: Size Distribution Interpretation," *J. Air Pollution Control Assoc.*, **25**, 529–534 (1975).

PROBLEMS

7.1. Given the following data on the number of aerosol particles in the size ranges listed, tabulate and plot the normalized size distributions $\tilde{n}(D_p) = n(D_p)/N$ and $\tilde{n}(\log D_p) = n(\log D_p)/N$ as discrete histograms.

Size Interval μm	Mean of Size Interval μm	Number of Particles in Interval
0–0.2	0.1	10
0.2–0.4	0.3	80
0.4–0.6	0.5	132
0.6–0.8	0.7	142
0.8–1.0	0.9	138
1.0–1.2	1.1	112
1.2–1.4	1.3	75
1.4–1.6	1.5	65
1.6–1.8	1.7	52
1.8–2.1	1.95	65
2.1–2.7	2.4	62
2.7–3.6	3.15	32
3.6–5.1	4.35	35

7.2. For the data given in Problem 7.1, plot the surface area and volume distributions $n_s(D_p)$, $n_s(\log D_p)$, $n_v(D_p)$, and $n_v(\log D_p)$ in both non-normalized and normalized form as discrete histograms.

7.3. You are given an aerosol size distribution function $n_m(m)$ such that $n_m(m)\,dm$ = aerosol mass per cm^3 of air contained in particles having masses in the range m to $m + dm$. It is desired to convert that distribution function to a mass distribution based on $\log D_p$. Show that

$$n_m(\log D_p) = 6.9 \, m^2 \, n_m(m)$$

7.4. Show that the variance of the size distribution of a log–normally distributed aerosol is

$$\overline{D}_p^2 \left[\exp\left(\ln^2 \sigma_g \right) - 1 \right]$$

7.5. Starting with semi-logarithmic graph paper, construct a log–probability coordinate axis and show that a log–normal distribution plots as a straight line on these coordinates.

7.6. The data given below were obtained for a log–normally distributed aerosol size distribution:

Size Interval μm	Geometric Mean of Size Interval, μm	Number of Particles in Interval[a]
0.1–0.2	0.1414	50
0.2–0.4	0.2828	460
0.4–0.7	0.5292	1055
0.7–1.0	0.8367	980
1.0–2.0	1.414	1705
2.0–4.0	2.828	680
4.0–7.0	5.292	102
7.0–10	8.367	10
10–20	14.14	2

[a]Assume that the particles are spheres with density $\rho_p = 1.5$ g cm^{-3}.

(a) Complete the above table by computing the following quantities: $\Delta N_i / \Delta D_{pi}$, $\Delta N_i / N \Delta D_{pi}$, $\Delta S_i / \Delta D_{pi}$, $\Delta S_i / S \Delta D_{pi}$, $\Delta M_i / \Delta D_{pi}$, $\Delta M_i / M \Delta D_{pi}$, $\Delta N_i / \Delta \log D_{pi}$, $\Delta N_i / N \Delta \log D_{pi}$, $\Delta S_i / \Delta \log D_{pi}$, $\Delta S_i / S \Delta \log D_{pi}$, $\Delta M_i / \Delta \log D_{pi}$, and $\Delta M_i / M \Delta \log D_{pi}$, where $M =$ particle mass.

(b) Plot $\Delta N_i / \Delta \log D_{pi}$, $\Delta S_i / \Delta \log D_{pi}$, and $\Delta M_i / \Delta \log D_{pi}$ as histograms.

(c) Determine the geometric mean diameter and geometric standard deviation of the log–normal distribution to which these data adhere and plot the continuous distributions on the three plots from part (b).

7.7. For a log–normally distributed aerosol different mean diameters can be defined by

$$\overline{D}_{pv} = \overline{D}_{pg} \exp\left(v \ln^2 \sigma_g \right)$$

where v is a parameter that defines the particular mean diameter of interest. Show that

Diameter	ν
Mode (most frequent value)	-1
Geometric mean or median	0
Number (arithmetic) mean	0.5
Surface area mean	1
Mass mean	1.5
Surface area median	2
Volume median	3

Plot a normalized log–normal particle size distribution over a range of D_p from 0 to 7 μm with $\overline{D}_{pg} = 1.0$ μm and $\sigma_g = 2.0$ and identify each of the above diameters on the plot. Hint: You may find this integral of use

$$\int_{L_1}^{L_2} e^{ru} \exp\left(-\frac{(u - \bar{u})^2}{2\sigma_u^2}\right) du = (\pi/2)^{1/2} \sigma_u e^{r\bar{u}} e^{r^2\sigma_u^2/2}$$

$$\times \left[\text{erf}\left(\frac{L_2 - (\bar{u} + r\sigma_u^2)}{\sqrt{2}\,\sigma_u}\right) - \text{erf}\left(\frac{L_1 - (\bar{u} + r\sigma_u^2)}{\sqrt{2}\,\sigma_u}\right) \right]$$

7.8. Assume that an aerosol has a log–normal distribution with $\overline{D}_{pg} = 5.5$ μm and $\sigma_g = 1.36$.

(a) Plot the number and volume distributions of this aerosol on log–probability paper.

(b) It is desired to represent this aerosol by a distribution of the form

$$F_v(D_p) = 1 - \exp\left(-cD_p^b\right)$$

where $F_v(D_p)$ is the fraction of the total aerosol volume in particles of diameter less than D_p. Determine the values of the constants c and b needed to match this distribution to the given aerosol.

7.9. Given the following size frequency for a dust:

Size Interval, μm	% by Number
7–17.5	10
17.5–21	10
21–25	10
25–28	10
28–30	10
30–33	10
33–36	10
36–41	10
41–49	10
49–70	10

(a) Plot the cumulative frequency distributions (in %) of the number, surface area, and mass on linear graph paper assuming all particles are spheres with $\rho_p = 1.6$ g cm^{-3}.

(b) Is this a log-normally distributed dust?

7.10. The following particle size distribution data are available for an aerosol:

D_p	% by Volume Less Than
9.8	3.2
13.8	10.0
19.6	26.7
27.7	46.8
39.1	72.0
55.3	87.5

(a) What is the volume median diameter and geometric standard deviation of the volume distribution of this aerosol?

(b) What is the surface area median diameter?

7.11. Calculate the scattering and absorption coefficients, b_{sp} and b_{ap}, for a log-normally distributed carbon aerosol of mass concentration 20 μg m^{-3}, with $\overline{D}_{pg} = 0.02$ μm and $\sigma_g = 0.3$, at a wavelength of radiation $\lambda = 0.53$ μm. What is the visibility under these conditions?

7.12. Plot the visibility (in km) at $\lambda = 0.53$ μm as a function of mass concentration (in μg m^{-3}) for a carbon aerosol of $\overline{D}_{pg} = 0.02$ μm and $\sigma_g = 0.3$. Consider mass concentrations ranging from 1 to 1000 μg m^{-3}.

7.13. Assuming the aerosol to be an external mixture of 50 percent soot and 50 percent ammonium sulfate, calculate the visibility at the Harbor Freeway in Los Angeles on the day that the data in Figure 7.8 were obtained.

EIGHT

Dynamics of Single Aerosol
Particles

In this chapter we consider the processes that involve a single aerosol particle in a suspending fluid and the interaction of that particle with the suspending fluid itself or with other molecules contained in the suspending fluid. Thus, we treat the drag force exerted by the fluid on the particle, the motion of a particle through a fluid due to an imposed external force and due to the bombardment of the particle by the molecules of the fluid, and mass and heat transfer to the particle. We begin by considering how we characterize the size of the particle in an appropriate way in order to describe transport processes involving momentum, mass, and energy.

8.1. THE KNUDSEN NUMBER

As we begin our study of the dynamics of aerosol particles in a fluid (e.g., air), we would like to have a way of determining, from the point of view of transport processes, how the fluid " views" the particle. As usual, in transport phenomena, one seeks an appropriate dimensionless group that reflects this comparison. The key dimensionless group that defines the nature of the suspending fluid relative to the particle is the *Knudsen number* $\mathrm{Kn} = 2\lambda/D_p$, where λ is the mean free path of the fluid. Thus, the Knudsen number is the ratio of two length scales, a length scale characterizing the "graininess" of the fluid with respect to the transport of momentum, mass, or heat and a length scale characterizing the particle, its radius.

8.1.1. The Mean Free Path

Before we discuss the physical interpretation of the Knudsen number, we must be quite precise with respect to the definition of the mean free path. The mean free path of a gas molecule can be defined as the average distance travelled between collisions with other gas molecules. If the gas consists entirely of molecules of a single type, call them B, then the mean free path can be denoted as λ_{BB}. Even though air consists of molecules of N_2 and O_2, it is customary to talk about the mean free path of air as if air were a single chemical species. We will denote air by B in what follows. If the gas consists of molecules of two types, A and B, then several mean free paths can be defined.

λ_{AB} is the average distance travelled by a molecule of A before it encounters a molecule of B, with the likewise interpretation for λ_{BA}. Although the idea of a mean free path can be extended to aerosol particles, it is considerably more difficult to define the mean free path of an aerosol particle than for a gas molecule. Aerosol particles collide only very infrequently with other particles, and, when they do, it is usually assumed that the two particles adhere. Thus, aerosol-aerosol collisions are not an appropriate basis on which to define a particle mean free path. On the other hand, because of their large size and mass relative to that of gas molecules, an aerosol particle experiences a large number of collisions per unit time with the surrounding gas molecules and is not influenced significantly by any one single collision. Consequently, the motion of an aerosol particle can be viewed as more or less continuous in nature, a view that, however, does not provide a convenient length to be identified as a mean free path. Fortunately, it will not be necessary for us to compute a particle mean free path in order to calculate the transport properties of aerosols.

If we are interested in characterizing the nature of the suspending air relative to a particle, the mean free path that appears in the definition of the Knudsen number is λ_{air}.* If the particle radius greatly exceeds λ_{air}, then the air appears to the particle as a continuum. Thus, when $Kn \ll 1$, we say that the particle is in the *continuum regime*, and the usual equations of continuum mechanics apply. When the mean free path of air molecules substantially exceeds the particle radius, the particle exists in a more or less rarified medium, and its transport properties must be obtained from kinetic theory of gases. This $Kn \gg 1$ limit is called the *free molecule* or *kinetic regime*. The particle size range intermediate between these two extremes is called the *transition regime*.

If we are interested in the diffusion of a vapor molecule A toward a particle, both of which are contained in a background gas B (e.g., air) then the description of that diffusion process depends on the value of the Knudsen number defined on the basis of λ_{AB}, $Kn = 2\lambda_{AB}/D_p$. The same definitions of regimes of behavior, continuum, free molecule, and transition can be made in that case as when determining how the particle interacts with air molecules.

The mean free path λ of a gas molecule is defined as the average distance travelled between collisions. If in one second a molecule travels ($\bar{c} \times 1$ sec) cm and makes Z collisions, $\lambda = \bar{c}/Z$. The mean speed of gas molecules is

*Ordinarily air will be the predominant vapor species in situations of interest to us. Only if other vapor species reach appreciable concentrations would the mean free path needed to characterize the suspending gas be different from λ_{air}.

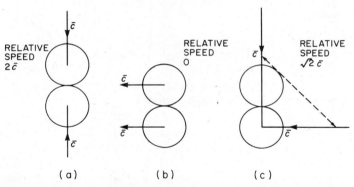

Figure 8.1. Relative speeds. (a) Head-on collision. (b) Grazing collision. (c) Right-angle collision. For molecules moving in the same direction with the same velocity, the relative velocity of approach is zero. If they approach head-on, the relative velocity of approach is $2\bar{c}$. If they approach at $90°$, the relative velocity of approach is the sum of the velocity components along the line joining the centers, that is, $\frac{1}{2}\sqrt{2}\,\bar{c} + \frac{1}{2}\sqrt{2}\,\bar{c} = \sqrt{2}\,\bar{c}$. The third situation is taken to represent the average situation so we write $Z = \sqrt{2}\,\pi\sigma^2\bar{c}N$.

$\bar{c} = (8kT/\pi m)^{1/2} = (8RT/\pi M)^{1/2}$, where m is the mass of the molecule and M is its molecular weight (Moore, 1962, p. 238). Thus, to calculate λ we need to calculate Z. Let σ be the diameter of the molecule. In one second a molecule travels a distance $\bar{c}$ and collides with all molecules whose centers are in the cylinder of radius σ and height $\bar{c}$. If N is the number of molecules per unit volume, then the number of molecules in the cylinder is $\pi\sigma^2\bar{c}N$, and the number of collisions made by one molecule in one second is just equal to the number of molecules in the cylinder, $Z = \pi\sigma^2\bar{c}N$. Actually to account for the fact that the molecules may be travelling in any direction, we introduce a factor of $\sqrt{2}$ as shown in Figure 8.1, to give $Z = \sqrt{2}\,\pi\sigma^2\bar{c}N$. Consequently, the mean free path λ is given by

$$\lambda = \frac{1}{\sqrt{2}\,\pi\sigma^2 N} \tag{8.1}$$

If there are N molecules per cm^3 and each experiences Z collisions per sec, the total number of collisions occurring per cm^3 per second equals $\frac{1}{2}ZN$, where the one-half is needed so we do not count each collision twice. Thus, the total number of collisions $= \frac{1}{2}\sqrt{2}\,\pi\sigma^2\bar{c}N^2$. This expression is generalized for unlike molecules to

$$Z_{AB} = \pi\sigma_{AB}^2\left(\frac{8kT}{\pi m_{AB}}\right)^{1/2} N_A N_B \tag{8.2}$$

where σ_{AB} is the average diameter, $\sigma_{AB} = (\sigma_{AA} + \sigma_{BB})/2$, and m_{AB} is the reduced mass,

$$\frac{1}{m_{AB}} = \frac{1}{m_A} + \frac{1}{m_B} \tag{8.3}$$

Jeans showed that the effective mean free path of molecules of A, λ_{AB}, in a binary mixture of A and B is (Davis, 1983)

$$\lambda_{AB} = \frac{1}{\sqrt{2}\,\pi N_A \sigma_{AA}^2 + \pi(1 + z)^{1/2} N_B \sigma_{AB}^2} \tag{8.4}$$

where N_A and N_B are the molecular number concentrations of A and B, σ_{AA} and σ_{AB} are the collision diameters for binary collisions between molecules of A and molecules of A and B, respectively, and $z = m_A/m_B$, the ratio of molecular masses. (Note that $z = m_A/m_B = M_A/M_B$, the ratio of molecular weights.) If species A is in dilute concentration, $N_A \ll N_B$, and we obtain

$$\lambda_{AB} = \frac{1}{\pi(1 + z)^{1/2} N_B \sigma_{AB}^2} \tag{8.5}$$

$$\lambda_{BA} = \frac{1}{\sqrt{2}\,\pi N_B \sigma_{BB}^2} \tag{8.6}$$

In this case $N_B = p/kT$, where p is the pressure of the system. From Eqs. (8.5) and (8.6) we compute the ratio of the mean free paths of B and A as

$$\frac{\lambda_{BA}}{\lambda_{AB}} = \left(\frac{\sigma_{AB}}{\sigma_{BB}}\right)^2 \left(\frac{1 + z}{2}\right)^{1/2} \tag{8.7}$$

We will see shortly that it will be important for us to have a relationship between the mean free path λ_{AB} and the binary diffusivity D_{AB}. In fact, the mean free path cannot be measured directly; rather, its value is inferred from that of a measurable macroscopic property, such as viscosity, thermal conductivity, or molecular diffusivity, that can be related to the mean free path theoretically.

From the Chapman–Enskog theory for the binary diffusivity (Chapman and Cowling, 1970)

$$D_{AB} = \frac{3}{8\pi} \frac{\left(\pi k^3 T^3 (1 + z)/2m_A\right)^{1/2}}{p\sigma_{AB}^2 \Omega_{AB}^{(1,1)}} \tag{8.8}$$

where $\Omega_{AB}^{(1,1)}$ is the collision integral, which has been tabulated by Hirschfelder et al. (1954) as a function of the reduced temperature $T^* = kT/\varepsilon_{AB}$, where ε_{AB} is the Lennard–Jones molecular interaction parameter. For hard spheres

$\Omega_{AB}^{(1,1)} = 1$, and Eq. (8.8) reduces to the Chapman–Enskog first approximation $D_{AB}^{(0)}$. Using $\bar{c}_A = (8kT/\pi m_A)^{1/2}$ and Eqs. (8.5) and (8.8), and making the hard-sphere approximation, we obtain the following relationship between the mean free path λ_{AB} and the binary diffusivity D_{AB},

$$\frac{D_{AB}}{\lambda_{AB}\bar{c}_A} = \frac{3\pi}{32}(1 + z) \tag{8.9}$$

from which we can identify certain limiting cases,

$$\frac{D_{AB}}{\lambda_{AB}\bar{c}_A} = \begin{cases} 0.2945 & z \ll 1 \\ 0.5890 & z = 1 \\ 3\pi z/32 & z \gg 1 \end{cases} \tag{8.10}$$

Most cases of interest to us will involve z of order unity. Nevertheless, most studies of gas-aerosol transport phenomena are based on the assumption of $z \ll 1$, either explicitly or implicitly.

8.1.2. Transport Properties of Gases as Mean Free Path Phenomena

In the elementary kinetic theory of gases transport properties such as viscosity, thermal conductivity, and molecular diffusivity are related to the mean free path by a simple argument involving the flux of gas molecules across planes separated by a distance l_D. Consider, for a moment, the process of molecular diffusion. If the concentration in a mixture of two gases is not uniform, the gases diffuse into one another until the composition is uniform. The molecular diffusion coefficient D_{AB} can be related to the individual mean speeds and mean free paths. To illustrate the simplest case, consider only a single gas, some of the molecules of which are painted red, which has a concentration gradient in the y-direction. The number N' of red molecules is greater in one direction along the y-axis than the other, and consequently, if the total pressure is uniform throughout the gas, the number N'' of unpainted molecules must also vary along the y-direction. Let us say that the "mean free path" for this diffusion phenomenon is l_D, so that l_D is the distance both above and below the plane at y where the painted and unpainted molecules experienced their last collisions. We are purposely not defining l_D precisely at this point. Figure 8.2 depicts planes at $y + l_D$, y, and $y - l_D$. For molecules in three-dimensional random motion the number of molecules striking unit area in unit time is $\frac{1}{4}N\bar{c}$ (Moore, 1962, pp. 217–219). If l_D is the average distance from the control surface at which the molecules originated that cross the surface at y, then the upward flux of painted molecules is $\frac{1}{4}\bar{c}N(y - l_D)$ and the downward flux of painted molecules is $\frac{1}{4}\bar{c}N(y + l_D)$.

The net upward flux of painted molecules through the plane at $y = 0$ is (molecules cm^{-2} sec^{-1})

$$j = \tfrac{1}{4}\bar{c}\left[N'(y - l_D) - N'(y + l_D)\right] \tag{8.11}$$

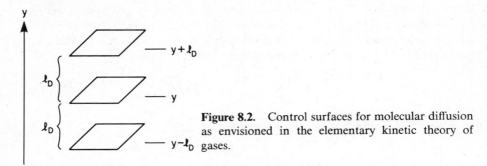

Figure 8.2. Control surfaces for molecular diffusion as envisioned in the elementary kinetic theory of gases.

Expanding both $N'(y - l_D)$ and $N'(y + l_D)$ in Taylor series about y, we obtain

$$j = -\tfrac{1}{2}\bar{c}l_D\left(\frac{\partial N'}{\partial y}\right)_y \qquad (8.12)$$

Comparing Eq. (8.12) with the continuum expression

$$j = -D\left(\frac{\partial N'}{\partial y}\right) \qquad (8.13)$$

gives $l_D = 2D/\bar{c}$. Since the red molecules differ from the others only by a coat of paint, l_D and D apply to all molecules of the gas. Thus, the diffusional mean free path l_D is defined in terms of the molecular diffusivity of the vapor, and its mean speed, specifically that given by $2D_{AB}/\bar{c}_A$. The length l_D is not defined independently.

8.2.　THE DRAG ON A SINGLE PARTICLE–STOKES LAW

To begin to understand the dynamical behavior of aerosol particles we consider the drag force exerted on an aerosol particle as it moves in a fluid. To calculate the drag force exerted by a fluid on a particle moving in that fluid we must solve the equations of fluid motion to determine the velocity and pressure fields around the particle.

The velocity $\mathbf{u} = [u_1, u_2, u_3]$ and pressure p in an incompressible Newtonian fluid are governed by the equation of continuity,

$$\frac{\partial u_k}{\partial x_k} = 0 \qquad (8.14)$$

and the Navier–Stokes equations (Bird et al., 1960),

$$\rho\left[\frac{\partial u_j}{\partial t} + u_k\frac{\partial u_j}{\partial x_k}\right] = \frac{\partial p}{\partial x_j} + \mu\frac{\partial^2 u_j}{\partial x_k \partial x_k} + \rho g_j \qquad j = 1, 2, 3 \quad (8.15)$$

where we use the so-called *summation convention.** g_j is the component of the gravity force in the jth direction. In what follows we will neglect the gravity term.

By introducing a characteristic velocity u_0 and length l, the continuity and Navier-Stokes equations can be made dimensionless,

$$\frac{\partial u_k^*}{\partial x_k^*} = 0 \tag{8.16}$$

$$\frac{\partial u_j^*}{\partial t} + u_k^* \frac{\partial u_j^*}{\partial x_k^*} = -\frac{\partial p^*}{\partial x_j^*} + \frac{1}{Re} \frac{\partial^2 u_j^*}{\partial x_k^* \partial x_k^*} \tag{8.17}$$

where the asterisk indicates a dimensionless variable. The *Reynolds number* $Re = u_0 l \rho/\mu$, the ratio of inertial to viscous forces in the flow. For flow around a submerged body, l can be chosen as a characteristic dimension of the body, say its diameter, and u_0 can be chosen as the speed of the undisturbed fluid upstream of the body.[†] We will be interested in steady state situations.

When viscous forces dominate inertial forces, $Re \ll 1$, the type of flow that results is called a *creeping flow* or low-Reynolds number flow, in which case the

---

*When dealing with conservation equations in this book we will use either conventional (x, y, z) coordinate notation or, if more concise, (x_1, x_2, x_3) coordinate notation. Correspondingly, fluid velocity components in the (x, y, z) system will be denoted by (u, v, w), whereas in the (x_1, x_2, x_3) system they will be denoted by (u_1, u_2, u_3).

The equation of continuity for an incompressible fluid in (x, y, z), (u, v, w) notation is

$$\frac{\partial u}{\partial x} + \frac{\partial v}{\partial y} + \frac{\partial w}{\partial z} = 0$$

and in (x_1, x_2, x_3), (u_1, u_2, u_3) notation is

$$\frac{\partial u_1}{\partial x_1} + \frac{\partial u_2}{\partial x_2} + \frac{\partial u_3}{\partial x_3} = 0$$

The so-called summation convention can be used to represent an equation such as that above in a concise manner. In the summation convention a repeated subscript in a term indicates summation over the three components of that term. Thus,

$$\frac{\partial u_k}{\partial x_k} = \frac{\partial u_1}{\partial x_1} + \frac{\partial u_2}{\partial x_2} + \frac{\partial u_3}{\partial x_3}$$

$$u_k \frac{\partial c}{\partial x_k} = u_1 \frac{\partial c}{\partial x_1} + u_2 \frac{\partial c}{\partial x_2} + u_3 \frac{\partial c}{\partial x_3}$$

[†]For flow past a sphere the Reynolds number can be defined based on the sphere's radius or its diameter. In the first case, the Reynolds number is conventionally given the symbol $R = u_0 R_p/\nu$, whereas in the second it is called $Re = u_0 D_p/\nu$. Clearly $Re = 2R$. In this book we will use the Reynolds number Re defined on the basis of the sphere diameter.

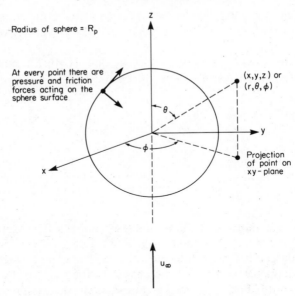

Figure 8.3. Coordinate system used in describing the flow of a fluid about a rigid sphere.

continuity and Navier–Stokes equations become

$$\frac{\partial u_k^*}{\partial x_k^*} = 0 \tag{8.18}$$

$$\frac{1}{Re}\frac{\partial^2 u_j^*}{\partial x_k^* \, \partial x_k^*} = \frac{\partial p^*}{\partial x_j^*} \tag{8.19}$$

The solution of these equations for the velocity and pressure distribution around a sphere in creeping flow was first obtained by Stokes. The assumptions invoked to obtain that solution are (1) an infinite medium, (2) a rigid sphere, and (3) no slip at the surface of the sphere. Using the spherical coordinate system defined in Figure 8.3, the two non-zero velocity components and the pressure are given by (Bird et al., 1960, p. 132),

$$u_r = u_\infty\left[1 - \tfrac{3}{2}(R_p/r) + \tfrac{1}{2}(R_p/r)^3\right]\cos\theta \tag{8.20}$$

$$u_\theta = -u_\infty\left[1 - \tfrac{3}{4}(R_p/r) - \tfrac{1}{4}(R_p/r)^3\right]\sin\theta \tag{8.21}$$

$$p = p_0 - \tfrac{3}{2}(\mu u_\infty/R_p)(R_p/r)^2\cos\theta \tag{8.22}$$

where R_p is the sphere radius, p_0 is the pressure in the plane $z = 0$ far from

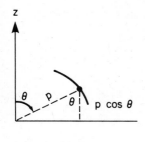

(A)

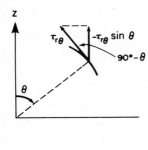

(B)

Figure 8.4. (A) Coordinate system for normal force acting on the surface of a sphere in flow around the sphere. (B) Coordinate system for tangential force acting on the surface of a sphere for flow around the sphere.

the sphere, u_∞ is the approach velocity far from the sphere, and gravity has been neglected.

Our object is to calculate the net force exerted by the fluid on the sphere in the direction of flow. The force consists of two contributions. At each point on the surface of the sphere there is a pressure on the solid acting perpendicularly to the surface. This is the *normal force*. At each point there is also a *tangential force* exerted by the fluid due to the shear stress caused by the velocity gradients in the vicinity of the surface.

To obtain the normal force on the sphere we integrate the component of the pressure acting perpendicularly to the surface. (See Figure 8.4.A.)

The z-component of the pressure at a point on the surface at the azimuthal angle θ is $-p \cos \theta$, where the negative sign is needed since the pressure acts in the $-z$ direction if $-90° < \theta < 90°$. Then the normal force over the entire surface is

$$F_n = \int_0^{2\pi} \int_0^{\pi} \left(-p|_{r=R_p} \cos \theta \right) R_p^2 \sin \theta \, d\theta \, d\phi \tag{8.23}$$

Since $p|_{r=R_p} = p_0 - \frac{3}{2}(\mu u_\infty / R_p) \cos \theta$,

$$F_n = 2\pi \mu R_p u_\infty \tag{8.24}$$

The tangential force acting in the θ-direction due to shear is $-\tau_{r\theta}$, where

$$\tau_{r\theta} = -\mu\left[r\frac{\partial}{\partial r}\left(\frac{u_\theta}{r}\right) + \frac{1}{r}\frac{\partial u_r}{\partial \theta}\right] \qquad (8.25)$$

Since $\tau_{r\theta}$ is defined as the force acting in the $+\theta$-direction for the geometry shown in Figure 8.4.B, the force is $-\tau_{r\theta}$. Evaluating $\tau_{r\theta}$ from the solution gives

$$\tau_{r\theta} = \tfrac{3}{2}(\mu u_\infty R_p)(R_p/r)^4\sin\theta \qquad (8.26)$$

and

$$\tau_{r\theta}|_{r=R_p} = \tfrac{3}{2}(\mu u_\infty/R_p)\sin\theta \qquad (8.27)$$

The z-component of the tangential force is $(-\tau_{r\theta})\sin\theta$, as shown in Figure 8.4.B. Thus, the tangential force over the entire surface is

$$F_t = \int_0^{2\pi}\int_0^{\pi}\left(\tau_{r\theta}|_{r=R_p}\sin\theta\right)R_p^2\sin\theta\,d\theta\,d\phi$$

$$= 4\pi\mu R_p u_\infty \qquad (8.28)$$

The total drag force exerted by the fluid on the sphere is

$$F_{\mathrm{drag}} = F_n + F_t = 6\pi\mu R_p u_\infty \qquad (8.29)$$

which is called *Stokes law*. If we include gravity, then the total force on the sphere is the sum of the drag force and the buoyant force. When the direction of flow and the direction of gravity coincide, the buoyant force to be added to the drag force is

$$F_{\mathrm{buoyant}} = \tfrac{4}{3}\pi R_p^3\rho g \qquad (8.30)$$

At Re $= 1$, the drag force predicted by Stokes law is 13 percent low due to the neglect of the inertial terms in the equation of motion. The correction to account for higher Reynolds numbers is (Re ≤ 2)*

$$F_{\mathrm{drag}} = 6\pi\mu R_p u_\infty\left[1 + \tfrac{3}{16}\mathrm{Re} + \tfrac{9}{160}\mathrm{Re}^2\ln 2\,\mathrm{Re}\right] \qquad (8.31)$$

*To gain a feeling for the order of magnitude of Re for typical aerosol particles at $T = 20°C$, $p = 1$ atm in air falling at their terminal velocities:

D_p, μm	20	60	100	300
Re	0.02	0.4	2	20

To account for the drag force over entire range of Reynolds number, we can express the drag force in terms of an empirical *drag coefficient* C_D as

$$F_{\text{drag}} = C_D A_p \rho \left(u_\infty^2 / 2 \right) \qquad (8.32)$$

where A_p is the projected area of the body normal to the flow. Thus, for a spherical particle of diameter D_p,

$$F_{\text{drag}} = \tfrac{1}{8} \pi C_D \rho D_p^2 u_\infty^2 \qquad (8.33)$$

where

$$
C_D = \begin{cases}
24/\text{Re} & \text{Re} < 0.1 \text{ (Stokes law)} \\
(24/\text{Re})\left[1 + \tfrac{3}{16}\,\text{Re} + \tfrac{9}{160}\,\text{Re}^2 \ln\left(2\,\text{Re} \right) \right] & 0.1 < \text{Re} < 2 \\
(24/\text{Re})\left[1 + 0.15\,\text{Re}^{0.687} \right] & 2 < \text{Re} < 500 \\
0.44 & 500 < \text{Re} < 2 \times 10^5
\end{cases}
$$

$$(8.34)$$

For the particles of interest to us in air pollution applications Re is generally less than 0.1.

8.3. NON-CONTINUUM EFFECTS—CUNNINGHAM CORRECTION FACTOR

Stokes law is based on continuum fluid mechanics. When the particle diameter D_p approaches the same order as the mean free path λ of the suspending fluid (e.g., air), the resisting force offered by the fluid is smaller than that predicted by Stokes law. To account for non-continuum effects that become important as D_p becomes smaller and smaller, the Cunningham correction factor, C_c, is introduced into Stokes law, written now in terms of particle diameter D_p,

$$F_{\text{drag}} = \frac{3\pi\mu u_\infty D_p}{C_c} \qquad (8.35)$$

where

$$C_c = 1 + \frac{2\lambda}{D_p}\left[1.257 + 0.4\exp\left(-1.1 D_p/2\lambda \right) \right] \qquad (8.36)$$

Values of C_c as a function of D_p in air at 25°C ($\lambda = 0.065\ \mu\text{m}$) are given in Table 8.1. The limiting behavior of C_c for large and small particle diameter is

$$
C_c = \begin{cases}
1 + (1.257)2\lambda/D_p & D_p \gg \lambda \\
1 + (1.657)2\lambda/D_p & D_p \ll \lambda
\end{cases}
\qquad (8.37)
$$

**TABLE 8.1. Cunningham Correction Factor C_c
for Spherical Particles in Air at 20°C, 1 atm**

$D_p(\mu m)$	C_c
0.001	216.
0.002	108.
0.005	43.6
0.01	22.2
0.02	11.4
0.05	4.95
0.1	2.85
0.2	1.865
0.5	1.326
1.0	1.164
2.0	1.082
5.0	1.032
10.0	1.016
20.0	1.008
50.0	1.003
100.0	1.0016

It is sometimes convenient to express the drag force on a particle in terms of
a *friction coefficient* f by $F_{drag} = fu_\infty$. In the Stokes law regime, then $f = 3\pi\mu D_p$,
and in general $f = 3\pi\mu D_p/C_c$.

8.4. MOTION OF AN AEROSOL PARTICLE IN AN EXTERNAL FORCE FIELD

Up to this point we have considered the flow of fluid around a particle moving
at a steady velocity u_∞ through a quiescent fluid and determined the drag
force acting on that particle. The motion of a particle arises in the first place
due to the action of some external force on the particle, such as gravity or
electrical forces. The drag force arises as soon as there is a difference between
the velocity of the particle and that of the fluid. The basis of the description of
the behavior of a particle in a fluid is an equation of motion for the particle.
To derive an equation of motion for a particle let us begin with a force balance
on a moving particle of mass m_p written in vector form,

$$m_p \frac{d\mathbf{v}}{dt} = \sum_i \mathbf{F}_i \qquad (8.38)$$

where **v** is the velocity of the particle and $\mathbf{F}_i$ is the force acting on the particle by mechanism i. Typical mechanisms include gravity, drag force, or electrical force. The drag force will always be present as long as the particle is not moving in a vacuum.

Our interest is in the motion of a particle in a fluid with velocity **v** only in the presence of gravity and drag forces,

$$m_p \frac{d\mathbf{v}}{dt} = m_p \mathbf{g} + \frac{3\pi\mu D_p}{C_c}(\mathbf{u} - \mathbf{v}) \tag{8.39}$$

where we assume that even though the particle motion is unsteady, this acceleration is slow enough so that at any instant Stokes law still applies for the drag force on the particle. If we divide this equation by $3\pi\mu D_p/C_c$, we obtain

$$\tau \frac{d\mathbf{v}}{dt} + \mathbf{v} = \mathbf{u} - \tau\mathbf{g} \tag{8.40}$$

where $\tau = m_p C_c/3\pi\mu D_p$, the characteristic relaxation time of the particle. For a spherical particle of density ρ_p in a fluid of density ρ, $m_p = (\pi/6)D_p^3(\rho_p - \rho)$, where the factor $(\rho_p - \rho)$ is needed because $(\pi/6)D_p^3\rho g$ is the buoyancy force on the particle. (Recall Eq. (8.30).) However, since $\rho_p \gg \rho$, $m_p \simeq (\pi/6)D_p^3\rho_p$, and $\tau = D_p^2\rho_p C_c/18\mu$.

For $t \gg \tau$, the particle attains a constant velocity, its terminal settling velocity v_t,

$$v_t = \tau g = \frac{1}{18}\frac{D_p^2\rho_p g C_c}{\mu} \tag{8.41}$$

The time scale of the approach to steady motion is governed by the magnitude of τ. Values of τ for unit density spheres at 20°C in air are:

D_p, μm	0.05	0.1	0.5	1.0
τ, sec	4×10^{-8}	9.2×10^{-8}	1×10^{-6}	3.6×10^{-6}

D_p μm	5.0	10.0	50.0
τ, sec	7.9×10^{-5}	3.1×10^{-4}	7.7×10^{-3}

Thus, the characteristic time for most particles of interest to achieve steady motion in air is extremely short. Likewise, if a particle enters a moving air stream, it adopts the velocity of the stream after the time τ.

8.5. BROWNIAN MOTION OF AEROSOL PARTICLES

Particles suspended in a fluid undergo irregular random motion due to bombardment by surrounding fluid molecules. Brownian motion is the name given to such motion. To describe the Brownian motion process we need not consider the details of the particle-fluid interaction, but only assume that the particle motion consists of statistically independent successive displacements.

Consider an aerosol particle that is settling in air due to the action of gravity. As we have seen, the particle eventually reaches a terminal velocity that depends on the size of the particle and the viscosity of the air. A drag force is generated, proportional to the velocity of the particle, that acts in a direction opposite to the direction of motion of the particle. Imagine now that the diameter of the particle is continually reduced. A particle of sufficiently large size, say larger than 100 μm, would experience only the drag force and its motion would be more or less unaffected by molecular bombardment. As the particle decreases in size the fluctuations in its motion due to molecular bombardment become increasingly noticeable until at last the particle acts as if its Brownian motion is the chief motion of the particle.

Previously we wrote an equation of motion for the particle in which the acceleration experienced by the particle is equated to the sum of the forces acting on the particle. The forces we have considered up to this point, namely gravity and the drag force, are essentially "deterministic." As the particle gets smaller we want to include the force imparted to the particle by molecular bombardment as a contribution to its acceleration. We can continue to use the idea of an equation of motion but now adding the force associated with Brownian motion. The equation of motion written to include the Brownian force has its roots in two worlds: the macroscopic world represented by the drag force and the microscopic world represented by the Brownian force. This equation was first formulated by the French physicist Paul Langevin in 1908 and it now bears his name.

The basis for analyzing Brownian motion is the equation of motion of a single particle, Eq. (8.39). Assuming that the only forces acting on a particle are the random acceleration $\mathbf{a}(t)$ caused by the bombardment by the bath molecules and Stokes drag, we write the equation of motion as

$$m_p \frac{d\mathbf{v}}{dt} = \frac{-3\pi\mu D_p}{C_c}\mathbf{v} + m_p\mathbf{a}(t) \qquad (8.42)$$

Dividing through by m_p, we write Eq. (8.42) as

$$\frac{d\mathbf{v}}{dt} = -b\mathbf{v} + \mathbf{a}(t) \qquad (8.43)$$

where $b = 3\pi\mu D_p/C_c m_p = \tau^{-1}$, the inverse of the relaxation time of the particle. The random acceleration $\mathbf{a}(t)$ is a discontinuous term, since it is intended to represent the force exerted by the suspending fluid molecules that imparts an irregular, jerky motion to the particle. That the equation of motion can be decomposed into continuous and discontinuous pieces is an ad hoc assumption that is intuitively appealing and, moreover, leads to successful predictions of observed behavior. Equation (8.44) is referred to as a *Langevin equation*.

Since the motion, and therefore the trajectory, of any one particle is a random process due to $\mathbf{a}(t)$, in order to study the Brownian motion phenomenon, it is necessary to consider the behavior of an entire population, or *ensemble*, of particles. Consider the trajectory of one particle along the y-direction released at the origin at $t = 0$. The displacement from $y = 0$ at time t for this particle can be called $y(t)$. If a large number of particles are released from the origin and we average all their y-displacements at time t, we expect that average, denoted by $\langle y(t) \rangle$, to be zero since there is no preferred direction inherent in $\mathbf{a}(t)$. On the other hand, $\langle y^2(t) \rangle$, the mean square displacement of all the particles, is nonzero, and is, in fact, a measure of the intensity of the Brownian motion. Since the mean square displacement is an important descriptor of the Brownian motion process, let us see what we can learn about this quantity.

Let the position vector $\mathbf{r} = (x, y, z)$. Thus we seek to obtain an expression for the mean square displacement $\langle r^2 \rangle$. We begin by taking the dot product of $\mathbf{r}$ and Eq. (8.43).

$$\mathbf{r} \cdot \frac{d\mathbf{v}}{dt} = -b\mathbf{r} \cdot \mathbf{v} + \mathbf{r} \cdot \mathbf{a} \tag{8.44}$$

Then ensemble averaging this equation gives

$$\langle \mathbf{r} \cdot \frac{d\mathbf{v}}{dt} \rangle = -b\langle \mathbf{r} \cdot \mathbf{v} \rangle + \langle \mathbf{r} \cdot \mathbf{a} \rangle \tag{8.45}$$

Since we assume that there is no preferred direction inherent in $\mathbf{a}$, $\langle \mathbf{r} \cdot \mathbf{a} \rangle$ will be equal to zero, giving

$$\langle \mathbf{r} \cdot \frac{d\mathbf{v}}{dt} \rangle = -b\langle \mathbf{r} \cdot \mathbf{v} \rangle \tag{8.46}$$

Now since

$$\langle \mathbf{r} \cdot \frac{d\mathbf{v}}{dt} \rangle = \frac{d}{dt}\langle \mathbf{r} \cdot \mathbf{v} \rangle - \langle v^2 \rangle \tag{8.47}$$

Eq. (8.46) becomes

$$\frac{d}{dt}\langle \mathbf{r} \cdot \mathbf{v} \rangle = -b\langle \mathbf{r} \cdot \mathbf{v} \rangle + \langle v^2 \rangle \tag{8.48}$$

The temperature of a Brownian particle suspended in a fluid is the same as that of the fluid, but the kinetic energy of its ceaseless motion must be determined from the kinetic energy of the molecules of the fluid. Because temperature is just a way of expressing the translational kinetic energy of the fluid molecules, the brief transfer of kinetic energy to the Brownian particle must be accompanied by a local cooling of the fluid. Thus, even at thermodynamic equilibrium, small but persistent random fluctuations in temperature about the equilibrium temperature always exist. We now assume that the total kinetic energy of the system $m_p \langle v^2 \rangle = 3kT$ from equipartition of energy, so that $\langle v^2 \rangle = 3kT/m_p$. Thus, Eq. (8.46) is

$$\frac{d}{dt} \langle \mathbf{r} \cdot \mathbf{v} \rangle = -b \langle \mathbf{r} \cdot \mathbf{v} \rangle + \frac{3kT}{m_p} \tag{8.49}$$

Integrating,

$$\langle \mathbf{r} \cdot \mathbf{v} \rangle = \frac{3kT}{bm_p} + c \exp(-bt) \tag{8.50}$$

Now, we note that

$$\langle \mathbf{r} \cdot \mathbf{v} \rangle = \left\langle \mathbf{r} \cdot \frac{d\mathbf{r}}{dt} \right\rangle = \frac{1}{2} \frac{d}{dt} \langle r^2 \rangle \tag{8.51}$$

so that Eq. (8.50) becomes

$$\frac{1}{2} \frac{d}{dt} \langle r^2 \rangle = \frac{3kT}{bm_p} + c \exp(-bt) \tag{8.52}$$

We saw in Section 8.4 that for $t \gg \tau \, (= b^{-1})$, any initial disturbance of the particle's velocity decays sufficiently so that the particle motion obeys a pseudo-steady state. We will assume that to be the case here, namely that the Brownian motion of the particle is sufficiently slow that the particle has time to "relax" after each fluctuating impulse. Consequently, we drop the exponential in Eq. (8.52) to obtain

$$\frac{1}{2} \frac{d}{dt} \langle r^2 \rangle = \frac{3kT}{bm_p} \tag{8.53}$$

which, upon integration, becomes

$$\langle r^2 \rangle = \frac{6kT}{bm_p} t = \frac{2kTC_c t}{\pi \mu D_p} \tag{8.54}$$

The Brownian motion is assumed to be isotropic so $\langle x^2 \rangle = \langle y^2 \rangle = \langle z^2 \rangle$

$= \frac{1}{3}\langle r^2 \rangle$. Thus,

$$\langle x^2 \rangle = \langle y^2 \rangle = \langle z^2 \rangle = \frac{2kTC_c t}{3\pi\mu D_p} \tag{8.55}$$

This result, first derived by Einstein in 1905 by a different route, has been confirmed experimentally in numerous ways and, because of its extreme accuracy, has even been used to determine the Boltzmann constant k and Avogadro's number, $N_A = R/k$.

We should note that we have obtained the foregoing results in a more or less formal manner without attempting to justify from a rigorous mathematical point of view the validity of the Langevin equation as the basic description of particle motion. The theoretical results we have presented can be rigorously justified. The subject of Brownian motion is, in fact, one of significant mathematical subtlety. A good starting point for the reader wishing to go more deeply into its theory is the classic article by Chandrasekhar (1943), which is reprinted in Wax (1954).

The movement of particles due to Brownian motion can be described as a diffusion process. The number concentration N of particles undergoing Brownian motion can be assumed to be governed by the diffusion equation

$$\frac{\partial N}{\partial t} = D\nabla^2 N \tag{8.56}$$

where D is the Brownian diffusivity. To obtain an expression for D, we want to relate the properties of the diffusion equation to Eq. (8.55). To do so, let us calculate the mean-square displacement of N_0 particles all of which start from the origin at $t = 0$, which is conceptually the same as many simultaneous realizations of a single particle random walk from the origin. Multiply Eq. (8.56) by x^2 and integrate the resulting equation over x from $-\infty$ to ∞. The result for the left-hand side is

$$\int_{-\infty}^{\infty} x^2 \frac{\partial N}{\partial t}\, dx = N_0 \frac{\partial \langle x^2 \rangle}{\partial t} \tag{8.57}$$

and for the right-hand side is

$$\int_{-\infty}^{\infty} x^2 D \frac{\partial^2 N}{\partial x^2}\, dx = 2DN_0 \tag{8.58}$$

Equating Eq. (8.57) and (8.58) gives

$$\frac{\partial \langle x^2 \rangle}{\partial t} = 2D \tag{8.59}$$

and

$$\langle x^2 \rangle = 2Dt \qquad (8.60)$$

We now equate this result for $\langle x^2 \rangle$ with that from Eq. (8.55) to obtain an explicit relation for D,

$$D = \frac{kTC_c}{3\pi\mu D_p} \qquad (8.61)$$

which, without the factor C_c, is known as the Stokes-Einstein relation. When $D_p \gg \lambda$, $C_c \simeq 1$, and D varies as D_p^{-1}. When $D_p \ll \lambda$, $C_c \simeq 1 + (2\lambda/D_p)(1.657)$, and D can be approximated by $2(1.657)\lambda kT/3\pi\mu D_p^2$, so that in the free molecule regime D varies as D_p^{-2}.

Diffusion coefficients for particles ranging from 0.001 to 1.0 μm diameter are shown, together with the Cunningham correction factor C_c, in air at 20°C and 1 atm, in Figure 8.5. The change from the D_p^{-2} dependence to the D_p^{-1} dependence is evident in the change of slope of the line of D versus D_p. Values of D, the Schmidt number Sc $= \nu/D$, and the terminal settling velocity are given in Table 8.2

The importance of Brownian diffusion as compared to gravitational settling can be judged by comparing the distances that a particle travels in both cases (Twomey, 1977). Over a time of 1 second a 1 μm radius particle diffuses a distance of the order of 4 μm, while it falls about 200 μm under gravity. A 0.1 μm radius particle, on the other hand, diffuses a distance of about 20 μm in 1 second compared to a fall distance of 4 μm. Even though the 1 μm particle's

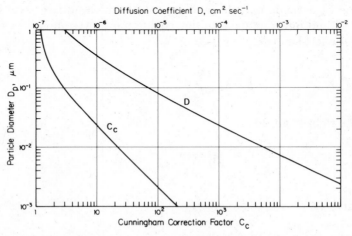

Figure 8.5. Diffusion coefficient and Cunningham correction factor as a function of particle size.

TABLE 8.2. Diffusion Coefficient, Schmidt Number, and Settling Velocity for Spherical Particles in Air at 293 K

$D_p(\mu m)$	$D(\text{cm}^2 \text{ sec}^{-1})$	Schmidt Number ν/D	v_t (cm sec^{-1}) $(\rho_p = 1 \text{ g cm}^{-3})$
0.001	5.14×10^{-2}	2.92	
0.002	1.29×10^{-2}	1.16×10^1	
0.005	2.07×10^{-3}	7.25×10^1	
0.01	5.25×10^{-4}	2.87×10^2	
0.02	1.34×10^{-4}	1.12×10^3	
0.05	2.35×10^{-5}	6.39×10^3	
0.1	6.75×10^{-6}	2.22×10^4	8.62×10^{-5}
0.2	2.22×10^{-6}	6.76×10^4	2.26×10^{-4}
0.5	6.32×10^{-7}	2.32×10^5	1.00×10^{-3}
1.0	2.77×10^{-7}	5.42×10^5	3.52×10^{-3}
2.0			1.31×10^{-2}
5.0			7.80×10^{-2}
10.0			3.07×10^{-1}
20.0			1.22
50.0			7.58
100.0			30.3

motion is dominated by inertia and gravity, it still diffuses several times its own radius in 1 second. The motion of the 0.1 μm particle is dominated by Brownian diffusion, although over time scales of the order of hours its total displacement is still governed by gravity. For a 0.01 μm radius particle, Brownian diffusion further outweighs gravity; its diffusive displacement in 1 second is almost 1000 times its displacement due to gravity, and several weeks would be required for the small orderly gravity effect to equal that of the random Brownian motion.

8.5.1. Mobility and Drift Velocity

In the development of Brownian motion up to this point we have assumed that the only external force acting on the particle is the fluctuating acceleration $\mathbf{a}(t)$. If we generalize Eq. (8.42) to include an external force $\mathbf{F}_{\text{ext}}$, we get

$$m_p \frac{d\mathbf{v}}{dt} = \mathbf{F}_{\text{ext}} - bm_p\mathbf{v} + m_p\mathbf{a} \qquad (8.62)$$

As before, assuming that we are interested in times for which $t \gg b^{-1}$, then the approximate force balance is

$$0 = \mathbf{F}_{\text{ext}} - bm_p\langle\mathbf{v}\rangle \qquad (8.63)$$

where the ensemble mean velocity $\langle \mathbf{v} \rangle = \mathbf{F}_{ext}/bm_p$, is identified as the *drift velocity* $\mathbf{v}_d$. The drift velocity is that which the particle population experiences due to the presence of the external force. For example, in the case where the external force is simply gravity the drift velocity is just the terminal settling velocity v_t.

The particle *mobility* B is then defined by

$$\mathbf{v}_d = B\mathbf{F}_{ext} \tag{8.64}$$

The mobility is seen to be just the drift velocity that would be attained under unit external force. Finally, the Brownian diffusivity can be written in terms of the mobility by

$$D = BkT \tag{8.65}$$

a result known as the Einstein relation.

8.5.2. Mean Free Path of an Aerosol Particle

The concept of mean free path is an obvious one for gas molecules. In the motion of an aerosol particle undergoing Brownian motion there is not an obvious length that can be identified as a mean free path. Nonetheless, the particle random motion can be likened to that of gas molecules and can be characterized by a mean thermal speed $\bar{c}_p = (8kT/\pi m_p)^{1/2}$.

As we have seen in Section 8.1, the mean free path of a gas molecule is usually evaluated by combining a measured macroscopic transport property of the gas, such as its viscosity or binary diffusivity, with a kinetic theory expression for the property and solving for the mean free path. A similar procedure can be used to obtain a particle mean free path λ_p from the Brownian diffusion coefficient and an appropriate kinetic theory expression for the diffusion flux. Following an argument identical to that in Section 8.1, diffusion of aerosol particles can be viewed as a mean free path phenomenon so that $D = \frac{1}{2}\bar{c}_p\lambda_p$ and

$$\lambda_p = \frac{2kT}{3\pi\mu D_p\bar{c}_p} \tag{8.66}$$

The particle diffusion Knudsen number is then defined by

$$\mathrm{Kn}_p = \frac{2\lambda_p}{D_p} = \frac{4kTC_c}{3\pi\mu\bar{c}_p D_p^2} \tag{8.67}$$

Approximate values of Kn_p as a function of particle radius are:

$D_p/2$, μm	0.001	0.01	0.1	1.0	10.0
Kn_p	100	5	0.1	0.005	0.01

8.5.3. Phoretic Effects

Phoretic effects produce a directional preference in the Brownian diffusion of aerosol particles due to a difference in momentum imparted to a particle by molecules coming from different directions. One phoretic effect is *thermophoresis*, which is particle motion caused by higher energy molecules on one side of the particle. A gradient in molecular energies will be associated with a macroscopic temperature gradient, so the result of thermophoresis is that aerosol particles will tend to diffuse away from warmer regions toward cooler regions. *Photophoresis* results when incident radiation heats one side of a particle more than the other, leading to differences in the energies of gas molecules adjacent to the surface of the particle.

Diffusiophoresis occurs in the presence of a gradient of vapor molecules that are either lighter or heavier than air molecules. For example, consider an evaporating surface above which a gradient of water vapor concentration exists. Water molecules are less massive than air molecules so a decrease in water vapor concentration with distance above the evaporating surface will lead to a net downward force on aerosol particles that is the result of the downward flux of air molecules needed to balance the upward flux of water molecules.

Thus, phoretic effects depend on local gradients of molecular momentum caused by differences in energy, or velocity, or by differences in mass. These effects depend on particle size and shape. The theories of thermophoresis and diffusiophoresis are developed by Derjaguin and Yalamov (1972) and will not be considered here.

8.6. MASS AND HEAT TRANSFER TO SINGLE AEROSOL PARTICLES

Mass and energy transport to or from aerosol particles accompanies their growth or evaporation. Let us consider a particle of pure species A in a background gas species B (e.g., air) that also contains vapor molecules of A. Particle growth or evaporation depends on the direction of the net flux of vapor molecules relative to the particle. Expressions for the vapor concentration and temperature profiles around a growing or evaporating particle can be obtained by solution of the appropriate mass and energy conservation equations.

Before writing the conservation equations it is useful to compare the relative rates of the processes occurring. Relations for the characteristic times associated with vapor diffusion in air and diffusion in the particle were developed in Chapter 6. We saw that the characteristic time for vapor diffusion is indeed short when compared with those for other processes that occur in conjunction with particle phenomena. Two characteristic times that enter the current problem, not explicitly treated in Chapter 6 but completely analogous to that for mass transfer, are those for heat conduction around and in the particle. The

TABLE 8.3.   Characteristic Times for Processes Associated with Growth or Evaporation of Particles

Heat conduction in air	R_p^2/α
Heat conduction in particle	R_p^2/α_p
Vapor diffusion	R_p^2/D
Particle growth or evaporation	$c_p R_p^2 / D x_{A_\infty} c$

	Heat Conduction in Air	Heat Conduction in Particle	Vapor Diffusion	Particle Growth
$\dfrac{\tau}{\tau_{\text{cond}}}$	1	α/α_p	$\alpha/D = \text{Le}^a$	$c_p \alpha / c D x_{A_\infty}$
Dibutylphthalate	1	310	4.2	$380/x_{A_\infty}$
Organics	1	200	2–4	$(10\text{--}100)/x_{A_\infty}$
Water	1	90	0.86	$20/x_{A_\infty}$
Metals	1	~ 5	1.5	$5000/x_{A_\infty}$

^{a}Le = Lewis Number.

characteristic time for heat conduction in air around a particle of radius R_p is proportional to R_p^2/α, where $\alpha = k/\rho C_p$ is the thermal diffusivity of air. The characteristic time for heat conduction in a particle is proportional to R_p^2/α_p, where $\alpha_p = k_p/\rho_p C_{p_p}$ is the thermal diffusivity of the particle. The characteristic time for vapor diffusion is proportional to R_p^2/D, where D is the molecular diffusivity of A in air (B).

For a particle that is growing or evaporating we will wish to estimate a characteristic time for the size change. We will do so subsequently. The expression we will obtain is given in Table 8.3 together with those of the other processes we have been discussing. Table 8.3 presents a comparison of the characteristic times for the four processes taken relative to that for heat conduction in air for four substances.

The time scales for the diffusion processes in the gas phase are much shorter than that for particle growth. The time scale for heat conduction in aqueous or organic particles is less than that for particle growth, but still greater than that for heat conduction in air.

In light of these differing time scales, a physical picture of the formation and subsequent growth processes emerges. The entire process is initiated by the formation of a new particle by homogeneous nucleation, a process that we will consider in detail in the next chapter.

As growth begins, vapor diffusion proceeds on a much faster time scale than growth. Even before significant growth occurs, vapor diffusion evolves through hundreds of time constants. Consequently, the vapor concentration profile within tens of radii from the particle is at steady state, whereas the more distant part of the profile is still changing.

The growth rate is determined by the diffusional flux of vapor. Since the vapor concentration profile near the particle approaches steady state before appreciable growth occurs, the steady state diffusional flux may be used to calculate the particle growth rate. As growth proceeds hundreds of times more slowly than diffusion, the profile near the particle remains close to its steady-state value at all times, whereas the region of transience propagates farther from the particle.

An energy balance describes the effects of latent heat release by condensation at the particle surface. Heat conduction occurs both in the particle interior and in the exterior gas phase. The ratio of the characteristic time for conduction in a particle to that for outward conduction in the vapor is of the order of 100 for most nonmetals in air and the order of 10 for metals. The high value of this ratio suggests that the latent heat is primarily conducted outward. As vapor condensation begins, the particle surface temperature rises until the rate of outward heat conduction balances the rate of latent heat generation. The formation of the external temperature and the vapor concentration profiles occurs on approximately the same time scale. Consequently, the steady-state fluxes of heat and vapor may be related by a steady-state energy balance to determine the steady-state surface temperature at all times during the particle growth.

For most aerosol systems the surface temperature is elevated by only a few degrees Kelvin, and as a result, the total molar density of the gas c may be assumed constant. The saturation pressure at the particle surface is elevated to the thermodynamic value at the surface temperature, providing the surface boundary condition for the vapor diffusion process.

An additional consequence of the diffusion of vapor to the particle is Stefan flow, a net flow of gas toward the particle. The particle growth rate and the Stefan flow velocity at the surface are related by a mass balance. The Stefan flow is several orders of magnitude faster than the particle growth rate. Therefore, the velocity induced by the outward motion of the growing particle surface is negligible.

It is evident that all processes except particle growth reach steady state in the vicinity of the particle well before the onset of significant growth. This physical picture suggests that we seek steady-state solutions to the conservation equations for a particle of fixed radius, from which to calculate expressions for the velocity profile and the particle growth rate. These expressions can then be used in the full conservation equations applying to a growing particle, describing the monomer vapor concentration and temperature profiles on a time scale relating to particle growth.

We will now develop the theory governing mass and heat transfer to single aerosol particles when the particle is large compared to the mean free path of the diffusing substance. This is the so-called continuum regime. Based on the above discussion we will determine the steady state profiles of vapor concentration and temperature around a particle of radius R_p. Recall that when we solved Eq. (6.1) to determine the transient concentration profile around a particle we neglected the convective contribution to the mass flux, the so-called Stefan flow term, on the assumption that the diffusing species was dilute relative to the background gas. At that point, since our primary object was to obtain a characteristic time for the diffusion process, there was no need to include the Stefan flow contribution. Now we wish to develop the full equations.

In a binary system the total molar flux at any radial position r is $N_{A_r} + N_{B_r} = cv_r^*$, where v_r^* is the molar average velocity in the r-direction and c is the total molar concentration. Since species B (air) is assumed not to be transferring to or from the particle, $N_{B_r} = 0$ at all r. Thus, the molar flux of A at any radial position $N_{A_r} = cv_r^*$.

A mass balance on a spherical shell gives

$$\frac{d}{dr}\left(r^2 N_{A_r}\right) = 0 \tag{8.68}$$

The molar flux of species A through stagnant B is given by Fick's law (Bird et al., 1960)

$$N_{A_r} = x_A\left(N_{A_r} + N_{B_r}\right) - cD\frac{dx_A}{dr}$$

$$= x_A N_{A_r} - cD\frac{dx_A}{dr} \tag{8.69}$$

Substituting the expression for N_{A_r} from Eq. (8.69) into Eq. (8.68) and solving subject to the boundary conditions

$$\begin{aligned} x_A = x_{A_s} \quad & r = R_p \\ x_A = x_{A_\infty} \quad & r \to \infty \end{aligned} \tag{8.70}$$

gives the mole fraction profile of A around the particle,

$$\frac{1 - x_A}{1 - x_{A_\infty}} = \left(\frac{1 - x_{A_s}}{1 - x_{A_\infty}}\right)^{R_p/r} \tag{8.71}$$

The flux of species A at any radial position r is

$$N_{A_r} = -\left(\frac{R_p}{r}\right)^2 \frac{cD}{R_p} \ln\left[\frac{1 - x_{A_s}}{1 - x_{A_\infty}}\right] \tag{8.72}$$

If $x_{A_s} < x_{A_\infty}$, the flow of molecules of A is toward the particle (in the negative

r-direction) and vice versa. The flux of A at the particle surface is

$$N_{A_{R_p}} = -\frac{cD}{R_p}\ln\left[\frac{1-x_{A_s}}{1-x_{A_\infty}}\right] \tag{8.73}$$

A mass balance on the growing or evaporating particle is

$$c_p\frac{d}{dt}\left(\frac{4}{3}\pi R_p^3\right) = 4\pi R_p^2 N_{A_{R_p}} \tag{8.74}$$

where c_p is the molar density of the particle, ρ_p/M_A. Using Eq. (8.73) with Eq. (8.74) gives

$$R_p\frac{dR_p}{dt} = \frac{cD}{c_p}\ln\left[\frac{1-x_{A_s}}{1-x_{A_\infty}}\right] \tag{8.75}$$

The mole fraction of A in the gas phase just above the particle surface, x_{A_s}, depends on the temperature T_s of the particle. That mole fraction is, by the ideal gas law, p_{A_s}/p, where p_{A_s} is the vapor pressure of A at T_s. The steady state temperature distribution around the particle is governed by

$$u_r\frac{dT}{dr} = \alpha\frac{1}{r^2}\frac{d}{dr}\left(r^2\frac{dT}{dr}\right) \tag{8.76}$$

to be solved subject to

$$\begin{aligned} T &= T_s & r &= R_p \\ T &= T_\infty & r &\to \infty \end{aligned} \tag{8.77}$$

The velocity u_r is the mass average velocity at radial position r. To solve Eq. (8.76) we need to determine u_r in terms of known quantities. The molar and mass average velocities in a binary system are defined in terms of the individual species velocities by (Bird et al., 1960)

$$\begin{aligned} u^* &= x_A u_A + x_B u_B \\ u &= \omega_A u_A + \omega_B u_B \end{aligned} \tag{8.78}$$

where ω is the mass fraction. If A is in dilute amounts, Eq. (8.78) can be approximated by $u^* = x_A(u_A - u_B)$ and $u = \omega_A(u_A - u_B)$. Equating these two expressions gives $u = \omega_A u^*/x_A$. Then ω_A/x_A is given by M_A/M, where M is the mean molecular weight, $M = x_A M_A + x_B M_B$. If we now approximate M by M_B, we have a relationship between the mass and molar average velocities in a binary system of dilute A,

$$u_r \cong u_r^*\frac{M_A}{M_B} \tag{8.79}$$

This relation may be used with the expression for the molar average velocity,

$$u_r^* = -\left(\frac{R_p}{r}\right)^2 \frac{D}{R_p} \ln\left[\frac{1 - x_{A_s}}{1 - x_{A_\infty}}\right] \tag{8.80}$$

in Eq. (8.76). Solving Eq. (8.76) subject to Eq. (8.77) gives (Pesthy et al., 1981)

$$\frac{T - T_\infty}{T_s - T_\infty} = \frac{\left(\dfrac{1 - x_{A_s}}{1 - x_{A_\infty}}\right)^{\mathrm{Le}^{-1}(M_A/M_B)(R_p/r)} - 1}{\left(\dfrac{1 - x_{A_s}}{1 - x_{A_\infty}}\right)^{\mathrm{Le}^{-1}(M_A/M_B)} - 1} \tag{8.81}$$

where the Lewis number, Le $= \alpha/D$.

It can be shown that if

$$\mathrm{Le}^{-1}(M_A/M_B)\ln\left(\frac{1 - x_{A_s}}{1 - x_{A_\infty}}\right) \ll 1 \tag{8.82}$$

the temperature profile simplifies to the well-known result for pure conduction,

$$\frac{T - T_\infty}{T_s - T_\infty} = \frac{R_p}{r} \tag{8.83}$$

which is the solution of

$$\frac{d^2T}{dr^2} + \frac{2}{r}\frac{dT}{dr} = 0 \tag{8.84}$$

subject to Eq. (8.77). Thus, the condition Eq. (8.82) provides a criterion for neglecting the convective term in Eq. (8.76). This criterion depends essentially on the concentration of A being dilute. The comparable "dilute" limit for the mole fraction profile is

$$\frac{x_A - x_{A_\infty}}{x_{A_s} - x_{A_\infty}} = \frac{R_p}{r} \tag{8.85}$$

which is the solution of

$$\frac{d^2x_A}{dr^2} + \frac{2}{r}\frac{dx_A}{dr} = 0 \tag{8.86}$$

Henceforth we will assume that A is sufficiently dilute that the mole fraction and temperature profiles are given by Eqs. (8.85) and (8.83). Thus, Eq. (8.82) provides a criterion for when the convective or Stefan flow contribution may be neglected. In most applications involving mass and heat transfer to aerosol particles it is generally neglected. (See, for example, Davis (1983).)

Up to this point we have been treating x_{A_s} and T_s as if they were known. Actually the value of x_{A_s} depends on T_s as we have noted. To determine T_s we write an energy balance on the particle assuming outward conduction only,

$$N_{A_{R_p}} \Delta H_v \left(4\pi R_p^2 \right) = k \left(\frac{dT}{dr} \right)_{r=R_p} \left(4\pi R_p^2 \right) \tag{8.87}$$

The left-hand side is the molar flow rate of vapor contributing to the latent heat energy of the particle, and the right-hand side is the rate of heat conduction from the particle. Using the dilute vapor approximations, Eqs. (8.83) and (8.85) with Eq. (8.87), we obtain

$$k(T_s - T_\infty) = c\Delta H_v D[x_{A_\infty} - x_{A_s}] \tag{8.88}$$

where x_{A_s} is a function of T_s. For convenience Eq. (8.88) can be expressed in terms of $\Delta_T = (T_s - T_\infty)/T_\infty$ as

$$\Delta_T = \left(\frac{\Delta H_v}{RT_\infty} \right) \left(\frac{R}{M_B C_p} \right) \text{Le}^{-1} [x_{A_\infty} - x_{A_s}] \tag{8.89}$$

The saturation mole fraction may be replaced by the integrated Clausius-Clapeyron equation which yields the implicit equation for Δ_T,

$$\Delta_T = \left(\frac{\Delta H_v}{RT_\infty} \right) \left(\frac{R}{M_B C_p} \right) \text{Le}^{-1} \left\{ x_{A_\infty} - x_{A_s}(T_\infty) \exp \left[\frac{\Delta H_v}{RT_\infty} \left(\frac{\Delta_T}{1 + \Delta_T} \right) \right] \right\} \tag{8.90}$$

Under conditions typical for many vapors, $x_{A_\infty} \gg x_{A_s}(T_\infty)$, and Eq. (8.90) becomes explicit for Δ_T,

$$\Delta_T \cong \left(\frac{\Delta H_v}{RT_\infty} \right) \left(\frac{R}{M_B C_p} \right) \text{Le}^{-1} x_{A_\infty} \tag{8.91}$$

Equation (8.85) can be expressed in terms of molar concentrations as

$$\frac{c_{A_\infty} - c_A}{c_{A_\infty} - c_{A_s}} = \frac{R_p}{r} \tag{8.92}$$

If there is no back vapor pressure $c_{A_s} = 0$. The total flow of vapor A toward the particle is denoted by J_c, the subscript c referring to the continuum regime,

$$J_c = 4\pi R_p D(c_{A_\infty} - c_{A_s}) \tag{8.93}$$

This result was first obtained by Maxwell (1877) and the expression Eq. (8.103) is often called the Maxwellian flux.

Under the dilute conditions we have been considering, the particle growth equation Eq. (8.75) becomes, in terms of diameter,

$$R_p \frac{dR_p}{dt} = \frac{D}{c_p}(c_{A_\infty} - c_{A_s}) \tag{8.94}$$

When $c_{A_s} = 0$ and c_{A_∞} is constant, Eq. (8.94) can be integrated to give

$$R_p^2 = R_{p0}^2 + \frac{2Dc_{A_\infty}}{c_p}t \tag{8.95}$$

We can now refer back to the characteristic time for particle growth given in Table 8.3. If we consider a small change in R_p so that Eq. (8.95) may be linearized, we can derive an expression for the characteristic time for changes in R_p. To do so, let $R_p = R_{p0} + \varepsilon$, and derive a first-order equation for $d\varepsilon/dt$. The decay coefficient of ε is the inverse of the characteristic time and is found to be $R_p^2 c_p/Dx_{A_\infty}c$. The ratio of this characteristic time to that for heat conduction in air is given in Table 8.3 for each of the four substances and is seen to depend on the value of x_{A_∞}. Regardless of the specific value of x_{A_∞} we see that this ratio exceeds 10^2 to 10^3, indicating, as assumed at the outset, that the characteristic time for particle growth or evaporation is considerably longer than those for the diffusion and conduction processes.

8.7. THE TRANSITION REGIME

The steady state flow of vapor molecules to a sphere of diameter D_p, when the particle is sufficiently large compared to the mean free path of the diffusing vapor molecules, is given by Maxwell's equation Eq. (8.93). Since Eq. (8.93) is based on solution of the continuum transport equation, it is no longer valid when the mean free path of the diffusing vapor molecules is of the same order as the particle diameter. When this occurs, the phenomena are said to lie in the transition regime.

In the transition regime the concentration distribution of the diffusing species and background gas are governed rigorously by the Boltzmann equation. There does not exist a general solution to the Boltzmann equation valid over the full range of Knudsen numbers for arbitrary masses of the diffusing species and the background gas. Consequently, most investigations of mass and heat transfer in the transition regime have avoided solution of the Boltzmann equation and instead have been based on a conceptual picture of the transition regime transport process in which non-continuum effects are limited to a region $D_p/2 \leq r \leq l_D$ beyond the particle surface. It is assumed that vapor molecules within the distance l_D of the sphere surface behave as if in a vacuum, and l_D is, in fact, a "diffusional mean free path." Beyond l_D the diffusing vapor molecules are assumed to obey continuum behavior. Even though continuum diffusion theory is not valid within l_D of the surface, it is desirable to be able to use continuum diffusion theory over the entire field of interest. The idea is to match the flux predicted by continuum diffusion theory with that predicted by free molecule theory within the region l_D to obtain a boundary condition on the continuum diffusion equation. If the correct boundary condition is imposed so as to require the correct flux at the surface, the concentration field obtained from solution of the continuum diffusion equation will approach its proper value at the surface to account for the free molecule flux. The idea of matching continuum and free molecule flux expressions was first conceived by Fuchs and is called *flux matching*. There are several approaches to developing transition regime diffusion formulas. We will first show that of Dahneke (1983).

The flux of vapor molecules to a surface within a distance l_D of the surface is given (dropping the subscript A for convenience) by Eq. (8.11),

$$j = \tfrac{1}{4}\bar{c}\big[c(l_D) - c_s\big] \tag{8.96}$$

where surface curvature is neglected. Now, utilizing the concept of flux matching, if the concentration distribution beyond l_D is governed by the continuum diffusion equation, we impose the following boundary condition on it at $y = 0$,

$$\tfrac{1}{4}\bar{c}\big[c(l_D) - c_s\big] = D\left(\frac{\partial c}{\partial y}\right)_{y=0} \tag{8.97}$$

This boundary condition can be placed in dimensionless form by defining a dimensionless length $x = y/L'$, L' being a characteristic length scale of the problem, and the Knudsen number, $\mathrm{Kn}_D = l_D/L' = 2D/\bar{c}L'$, (Recall Eq. (8.13).)

$$c(\mathrm{Kn}_D) - c_s = 2\mathrm{Kn}_D\left(\frac{\partial c}{\partial x}\right)_{x=0} \tag{8.98}$$

Now let us apply these ideas to the diffusion of vapor molecules to a sphere. Thus, we need to solve Eq. (8.86) subject to

$$c = c_\infty \quad r \to \infty \tag{8.99}$$

$$c\left[\frac{D_p}{2}(1 + \mathrm{Kn}_D)\right] - c_s = 2(D_p/2)\mathrm{Kn}_D\left(\frac{\partial c}{\partial r}\right)_{r=D_p/2} \tag{8.100}$$

where $\text{Kn}_D = 2l_D/D_p$. Solving Eq. (8.86) subject to Eqs. (8.99) and (8.100) gives

$$\frac{c_\infty - c(r)}{c_\infty - c_s} = \left(\frac{D_p}{2r}\right)\beta \qquad (8.101)$$

where β is a correction factor to the continuum profile given by

$$\beta = \frac{1 + \text{Kn}_D}{1 + 2\text{Kn}_D(1 + \text{Kn}_D)} \qquad (8.102)$$

The resulting flow of vapor molecules to the sphere is

$$J = 2\pi D_p D(c_\infty - c_s)\beta = \beta J_c \qquad (8.103)$$

We see that $\beta = 1$ as $\text{Kn}_D \to 0$, and Eq. (8.103) reduces to J_c. On the other hand,

$$\lim_{\text{Kn}_D \to \infty} \beta = \frac{1}{2\text{Kn}_D} = \frac{1}{2(4D/D_p\bar{c})} \qquad (8.104)$$

and

$$\lim_{\text{Kn}_D \to \infty} J = \tfrac{1}{4}\pi D_p^2\bar{c}(c_\infty - c_s) = J_{fm} \qquad (8.105)$$

8.7.1. Fuchs Theory of the Transition Regime

The original flux matching idea was, as noted above, due to Fuchs. (See Fuchs (1964).) He suggested that a distance Δ from the sphere surface be the point at which the free molecule and continuum fluxes are matched. In particular, one equates the continuum flux at $r = D_p/2 + \Delta$ to the net molecular flux to the sphere surface,

$$\pi D_p^2(\tfrac{1}{4}\bar{c})\left[c\left(\frac{D_p}{2} + \Delta\right) - c_s\right] = D\left(\frac{\partial c}{\partial r}\right)_{r=D_p/2+\Delta} 4\pi\left(\frac{D_p}{2} + \Delta\right)^2 \qquad (8.106)$$

Then solving Eq. (8.86) subject to Eqs. (8.99) and (8.106) gives

$$\frac{c_\infty - c(r)}{c_\infty - c_s} = \left(\frac{D_p}{2r}\right)\beta_F \qquad (8.107)$$

where the correction factor is given by

$$\beta_F = \frac{1 + 2\Delta/D_p}{1 + \dfrac{4D(1 + 2\Delta/D_p)}{\bar{c}(D_p/2)}} \qquad (8.108)$$

The value of Δ was not specified in the original theory and must be assumed, adjusted empirically or estimated by independent theory. By relating the binary diffusivity and the mean free path by $D_{AB}/\lambda_{AB}\bar{c}_A = 1/3$ and letting $\mathrm{Kn} = 2\lambda_{AB}/D_p$, the Fuchs flux relation can be written as

$$\frac{J}{J_{fm}} = \frac{1 + \mathrm{Kn}\,\Delta/\lambda_{AB}}{1 + \mathrm{Kn}\,\Delta/\lambda_{AB} + 3/4\mathrm{Kn}^{-1}} \tag{8.109}$$

or as

$$\frac{J}{J_c} = \frac{3}{4}\,\frac{1 + \mathrm{Kn}\,\Delta/\lambda_{AB}}{\frac{3}{4} + \mathrm{Kn} + (\Delta/\lambda_{AB})\mathrm{Kn}^2} \tag{8.110}$$

where $J_{fm}/J_c = 3/4\mathrm{Kn}$.

In subsequent efforts to produce an improved transition regime interpolation formula Fuchs and Sutugin (1971) fitted Sahni's (1966) solution to the Boltzmann equations for $z \ll 1$ by means of

$$\frac{J}{J_c} = \frac{1 + \mathrm{Kn}}{1 + 1.71\mathrm{Kn} + 1.333\mathrm{Kn}^2} \tag{8.111}$$

Since Eq. (8.111) is based on results for $z \ll 1$ it is strictly limited to light molecules in a heavier background gas.

For $\mathrm{Kn} \to 0$, Eqs. (8.110) and (8.111) reduce to $J/J_c = 1$ and for $\mathrm{Kn} \to \infty$, Eq. (8.110) reduces to $J/J_c = 3/4\mathrm{Kn}$, whereas Eq. (8.111) yields $J/J_c = 3/4\mathrm{Kn}$. Thus the two interpolation formulas have the same asymptotic limits.

8.7.2. Comparison of Transition Regime Formulas

Table 8.4 summarizes the transition regime expressions we have developed in this section.

As a closing point it is worthwhile to comment on the definitions of the mean free path in these formulas. We recall the expression Eq. (8.9) for $D_{AB}/\lambda_{AB}\bar{c}_A$ when A is in dilute concentration and for hard sphere molecules. Thus, we see that $D_{AB}/\lambda_{AB}\bar{c}_A = \frac{1}{3}$ generally does not conform with the kinetic theory prediction. Nevertheless, the definitions in Table 8.4 are needed for the transition regime interpolation formulas to approach the proper limits as $\mathrm{Kn} \to 0$ and $\mathrm{Kn} \to \infty$.

8.7.3. The Accommodation Coefficient

Up to this point we have assumed that once a vapor molecule encounters the surface of a particle its probability of sticking is unity. This assumption can be generalized by introducing a particle sticking probability or accommodation coefficient δ.* In so doing, the flux of vapor molecules to a surface within a

---

*In Chapter 6 we denoted the accommodation coefficient by α. Here we use δ to avoid any confusion with the thermal diffusivity.

TABLE 8.4. Transition Regime Formulas for Diffusion of Species A in a Background Gas B to an Aerosol

Author	J/J_c	Mean Free Path Definition
Fuchs (1934) (see Fuchs (1964))	$\dfrac{3}{4}\dfrac{1 + \mathrm{Kn}\,\Delta/\lambda_{AB}}{3/4 + \mathrm{Kn} + (\Delta/\lambda_{AB})\mathrm{Kn}^2}$	$\dfrac{D_{AB}}{\lambda_{AB}\bar{c}_A} = \dfrac{1}{3}$
Fuchs and Sutugin (1971)	$\dfrac{1 + \mathrm{Kn}}{1 + 1.71\mathrm{Kn} + 1.333\mathrm{Kn}^2}$	$\dfrac{D_{AB}}{\lambda_{AB}\bar{c}_A} = \dfrac{1}{3}$
Dahneke (1983)	$\dfrac{1 + \mathrm{Kn}_D}{1 + 2\mathrm{Kn}_D(1 + \mathrm{Kn}_D)}$	$\mathrm{Kn}_D = \dfrac{2l_D}{D_p}$
		$l_D = \dfrac{2D_{AB}}{\bar{c}_A}$

distance of l_D of the surface is given by Eq. (8.96) modified to include the sticking probability,

$$j = \tfrac{1}{4}\delta\bar{c}\big[c(l_D) - c_s\big] \tag{8.112}$$

We can retrace the development of this section including the sticking probability δ and we find

$$\beta = \frac{1 + \mathrm{Kn}_D}{1 + 2\mathrm{Kn}_D(1 + \mathrm{Kn}_D)/\delta} \tag{8.113}$$

and

$$\beta_F = \frac{1 + 2\Delta/D_p}{1 + \dfrac{4D(1 + 2\,\Delta/D_p)}{\bar{c}\delta(D_p/2)}} \tag{8.114}$$

The Fuchs relation including the sticking probability is

$$\frac{J}{J_{fm}} = \frac{1 + \mathrm{Kn}\,\Delta/\lambda_{AB}}{1 + \mathrm{Kn}\,\Delta/\lambda_{AB} + \tfrac{3}{4}\delta\mathrm{Kn}^{-1}} \tag{8.115}$$

or

$$\frac{J_{fm}}{J_c} = \frac{3\delta}{4\mathrm{Kn}} \tag{8.116}$$

The importance of the value of the accommodation coefficient on β can be seen from Eq. (8.113). For example, if $\mathrm{Kn}_D = 0.01$ and δ takes the values 1.0, 0.01, and 0.001, then β is 0.99, 0.33, and 0.048. Since sticking probabilities may be even smaller than 0.001, the correction factor β may be quite important in systems where $Kn_D \ll 1$. The measurement of accommodation coefficients has been an active area in gas-aerosol research (Wagner, 1982; Rubel and Gentry, 1984).

REFERENCES

Bird, R. B., Stewart, W. E., and Lightfoot, E. N. *Transport Phenomena*, Wiley, New York (1960).

Chandrasekhar, S. "Stochastic Problems in Physics and Astronomy," *Rev. Modern Phys.*, **15**, 1–89 (1943).

Chapman, S., and Cowling, T. G. *The Mathematical Theory of Non-Uniform Gases*, Cambridge Univ. Press, Cambridge (1970).

Dahneke, B. "Simple Kinetic Theory of Brownian Diffusion in Vapors and Aerosols," in *Theory of Dispersed Multiphase Flow*, R. E. Meyer (Ed.), Academic Press, New York, 97–133 (1983).

Davis, E. J. "Transport Phenomena with Single Aerosol Particles," *Aerosol Sci. Technol.*, **2**, 121–144 (1983).

Derjaguin, B. V., and Yalamov, Y. I. "The Theory of Thermophoresis and Diffusiophoresis of Aerosol Particles and Their Experimental Testing," in *Topics in Current Aerosol Research* (*Part 2*), G. M. Hidy and J. R. Brock (Eds.), Pergamon, New York, 1–200 (1972).

Fuchs, N. A. *The Mechanics of Aerosols*, Pergamon, New York (1964).

Fuchs, N. A., and Sutugin, A. G. "High-Dispersed Aerosols," in *Topics in Current Aerosol Research*, G. M. Hidy and J. R. Brock (Eds.), Pergamon, New York, 1–60 (1971).

Hirschfelder, J. O., Curtiss, C. O., and Bird, R. B. *Molecular Theory of Gases and Liquids*, Wiley, New York (1954).

Maxwell, J. C. in *Encyclopedia Brittanica*, Vol. 2, p. 82 (1877).

Moore, W. J. *Physical Chemistry*, 3rd ed., Prentice-Hall, Englewood Cliffs, NJ (1962).

Pesthy, A. J., Flagan, R. C., and Seinfeld, J. H. "The Effect of a Growing Aerosol on the Rate of Homogeneous Nucleation of a Vapor," *J. Colloid Interface Sci.*, **82**, 465–479 (1981).

Pruppacher, H. R., and Klett, J. O. *Microphysics of Clouds and Precipitation*, D. Reidel, Boston (1978).

Rubel, G. O., and Gentry, J. W. "Measurement of the Kinetics of Solution Droplets in the Presence of Adsorbed Monolayers: Determination of Water Accommodation Coefficients," *J. Phys. Chem.*, **88**, 3142–3148 (1984).

Sahni, D. C. "The Effect of a Black Sphere on the Flux Distribution in an Infinite Moderator," *J. Nuclear Energy*, **20**, 915–920 (1966).

Twomey, S. *Atmospheric Aerosols*, Elsevier, New York (1977).

Wagner, P. E. "Aerosol Growth by Condensation," in *Aerosol Microphysics II—Chemical Physics of Microparticles*, W. H. Marlow (Ed.), Springer-Verlag, Berlin, 129–178 (1982).

Wax, N. (Ed.), *Selected Papers on Noise and Stochastic Processes*, Dover, New York, (1954).

PROBLEMS

8.1. (a) Knowing a particle's density ρ_p and its settling velocity v_t, show how to determine its diameter. Consider both the non-Stokes and the Stokes law regions.

   (b) Determine the size of a water droplet that has $v_t = 1$ cm sec^{-1} at $T = 20°C$, 1 atm.

8.2. (a) A unit density sphere of a diameter 100 μm moves through air with a velocity of 25 cm sec^{-1}. Compute the drag force offered by the air, in dynes.

(b) A unit density sphere of diameter 1 μm moves through air with a velocity of 25 cm sec^{-1}. Compute the drag force offered by the air, in dynes.

8.3. Calculate the terminal settling velocities of silica particles ($\rho_p = 2.65$ g cm^{-3}) of 0.05 μm, 0.1 μm, 0.5 μm and 1.0 μm diameters.

8.4. Develop a table of terminal settling velocities of water drops in still air at $T = 20°$C, 1 atm. Consider drop diameters ranging from 1.0 μm to 1000 μm. (Note that for drop diameters exceeding about 1000 μm (1 mm) the drops can no longer be considered spherical as they fall. In this case one must resort to empirical correlations. Use the Beard correlation on p. 323 of Pruppacher and Klett (1978).)

8.5. Consider the growth of a particle of dibutylphthalate (DBP) in air at 298 K containing DBP at a background mole fraction of 0.10. The vapor pressure of DBP is sufficiently low that it may be assumed to be negligible.

(a) Compute the steady state mole fraction and temperature profiles around a DBP particle of 1 μm diameter. Assume continuum regime conditions to hold.

(b) Compute the flux of DBP (moles cm^{-2} sec^{-1}) at the particle surface.

(c) Evaluate the differences between the mole fraction and temperature profiles when the convective (Stefan flow) terms are retained and ignored. Discuss.

(d) Evaluate the dimensionless temperature rise Δ_T resulting from the condensation of the vapor on the particle.

(e) Plot the particle radius as a function of time starting at 0.5 μm assuming that the background mole fraction of DBP remains constant at 0.10.

The following parameters may be used in the calculation:

$$c/c_p = 0.011 \qquad\qquad \Delta H_v/R = 8930 \text{ K}$$
$$D = 0.0282 \text{ cm}^2 \text{ sec}^{-1} \qquad R/M_B C_p = 0.274$$
$$M_A/M_B = 9.61$$
$$\delta \text{ (accommodation coefficient)} = 1$$

8.6. In Problem 8.5 for the purpose of computing the mass and energy transport rates to the particle it was assumed that continuum conditions held.

(a) Evaluate the validity of using continuum transport theory for the conditions of Problem 8.5.

(b) Plot the particle radius as a function of time under the conditions of Problem 8.5 for a DBP particle initially of 0.5 μm radius if the accommodation coefficient is $\delta = 0.1, 0.01$, and 0.001.

(c) Plot the particle radius as a function of time under the conditions of Problem 8.5 for a DBP particle initially of 0.01 μm radius if the accommodation coefficient is $\delta = 1, 0.1, 0.01$, and 0.001.

NINE

Thermodynamics of Aerosols and Nucleation Theory

In this chaper we will deal with two important questions concerning aerosols. The first is: What are the thermodynamic equilibrium properties of small particles in the atmosphere? The second is: How and at what rate do new particles form from the vapor phase? Since the most important "solvent" for constituents of atmospheric particles and drops is water, we will pay particular attention to the thermodynamic properties of aqueous solution droplets.

The formation of new particles from a continuous phase is referred to as nucleation, of which we can distinguish two essential types. *Heterogeneous nucleation* is the nucleation on a foreign substance or surface, such as an ion or a solid salt particle. *Homogeneous nucleation* is the nucleation of vapor on embryos comprised of vapor molecules in the absence of foreign substances. Moreover, nucleation processes can be characterized as *homomolecular* (involving a single gaseous species) or *heteromolecular* (in which a solution droplet is formed from two or more vapor species). Consequently, we can identify four types of nucleation processes:

1. Homogeneous–homomolecular: self-nucleation of a single vapor species. No foreign nuclei or surfaces involved.
2. Homogeneous–heteromolecular: self-nucleation of two or more vapor species. No foreign nuclei or surfaces involved.
3. Heterogeneous–homomolecular: nucleation of a single vapor species on a foreign substance.
4. Heterogeneous–heteromolecular: nucleation of two or more vapor species on a foreign substance.

9.1. EQUILIBRIUM VAPOR PRESSURE OVER A CURVED SURFACE—THE KELVIN EFFECT

The key aspect that characterizes the thermodynamics of atmospheric particles and drops is their curved interface. In this section we want to derive an equation that relates the vapor pressure of a pure species A over the surface of

343

a drop to that over a flat surface. To do so we begin by considering the change in Gibbs free energy accompanying the formation of a single drop of pure material A of radius R_p containing g molecules of the substance,

$$\Delta G = G_{\text{embryo system}} - G_{\text{pure vapor}}$$

Let us say that the total number of molecules in the starting condition of pure vapor is N_T; after the embryo forms, the number of vapor molecules remaining is $N_1 = N_T - g$. Then, if g_v and g_l are the Gibbs free energies of a molecule in the vapor and liquid phases, respectively,

$$\Delta G = N_1 g_v + g g_l + 4\pi R_p^2 \sigma - N_T g_v \tag{9.1}$$

where $4\pi R_p^2 \sigma$ is the free energy associated with an interface with radius of curvature R_p and surface tension σ. This equation can be written as

$$\Delta G = g(g_l - g_v) + 4\pi R_p^2 \sigma \tag{9.2}$$

Note that the number of molecules in the drop, g, and its radius R_p are related by $g = \frac{4}{3}\pi R_p^3 / v_l$, where v_l is the volume occupied by a molecule in the liquid phase. Thus,

$$\Delta G = \left(\frac{\frac{4}{3}\pi R_p^3}{v_l} \right)(g_l - g_v) + 4\pi R_p^2 \sigma \tag{9.3}$$

We now need to evaluate $g_l - g_v$, the difference in the Gibbs free energy per molecule of molecules in the liquid and vapor states. To do so we note that at constant temperature $dg = v\,dp$. Thus, $dg = (v_l - v_v)\,dp$. Since $v_v \gg v_l$ for all conditions of interest to us, we can neglect v_l relative to v_v in this equation, giving $dg = -v_v\,dp$. The vapor phase is assumed to be ideal so $v_v = kT/p$. Thus,

$$g_l - g_v = -kT \int_{p_A^0}^{p_A} \frac{dp}{p} \tag{9.4}$$

where p_A^0 is the vapor pressure of pure A over a flat surface, and p_A is the actual equilibrium partial pressure over the liquid. Then

$$g_l - g_v = -kT \ln \frac{p_A}{p_A^0} \tag{9.5}$$

We can define the ratio p_A/p_A^0 as the *saturation ratio S*.

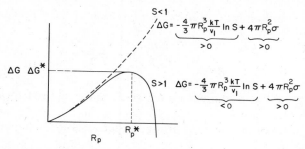

Figure 9.1. Gibbs free energy change for formation of a droplet of radius R_p from a vapor with saturation ratio S.

Substituting Eq. (9.5) into Eq. (9.3) we obtain the expression for the Gibbs free energy change,

$$\Delta G = -\tfrac{4}{3}\pi R_p^3 \frac{kT}{v_l} \ln S + 4\pi R_p^2 \sigma \tag{9.6}$$

Figure 9.1 shows a sketch of the behavior of ΔG as a function of R_p. We see that if $S < 1$, ΔG increases monotonically with R_p. On the other hand, if $S > 1$, ΔG consists of positive and negative contributions. At small values of R_p the surface tension term dominates and the behavior of ΔG as a function of R_p is close to that in the case of $S < 1$. As R_p increases, the first term becomes more important, so that ΔG achieves a maximum at $R_p = R_p^*$, found from setting $(\partial \Delta G / \partial R_p)_{T,p} = 0$,

$$R_p^* = \frac{2\sigma v_l}{kT \ln S} \tag{9.7}$$

The corresponding value of the number of molecules at the critical size is

$$g^* = \frac{32\pi \sigma^3 v_l^2}{3(kT \ln S)^3} \tag{9.8}$$

The value of ΔG at $R_p = R_p^*$ is

$$\Delta G^* = \tfrac{4}{3}\pi R_p^{*2} \sigma = \tfrac{4}{3}\pi \sigma \left(\frac{2\sigma v_l}{kT \ln S} \right)^2 \tag{9.9}$$

Since ΔG is a maximum at $R_p = R_p^*$, the equilibrium at that point is a metastable one.

Equation (9.7) relates the equilibrium radius of a droplet of pure substance to the physical properties of the substance, σ and v_l, and to the saturation ratio S of its environment. Equation (9.7) can be rearranged so that the equilibrium saturation ratio is given as a function of the radius of the drop,

$$\ln S = \frac{2\sigma v_l}{kTR_p} = \frac{4\sigma v_l}{kTD_p} \qquad (9.10)$$

Expressed in this form, the equation is frequently referred to as the Kelvin equation.

The Kelvin equation can be expressed in terms of molar units as

$$\ln S = \frac{2\sigma M}{RT\rho_l R_p} = \frac{2\sigma \bar{v}_l}{RTR_p} = \frac{4\sigma \bar{v}_l}{RTD_p} \qquad (9.11)$$

where M is the molecular weight of the substance and ρ_l is the liquid phase density. As indicated, M/ρ_l can simply be expressed as $\bar{v}_l$, the molar volume of the liquid phase.

The Kelvin equation tells us that the vapor pressure over a curved interface always exceeds that of the same substance over a flat surface. A rough physical interpretation of this so-called Kelvin effect is as follows. The vapor pressure of a liquid is determined by the energy necessary to separate a molecule from the attractive force exerted by its neighbors and bring it into the gas phase. When a curved interface exists, as in a small droplet, there are fewer molecules immediately adjacent to a molecule on the surface than when the surface is flat. Consequently, it is easier for the molecules on the surface of a small drop to escape into the vapor phase and the vapor pressure over a curved interface is greater than that over a plane surface.

Table 9.1 gives g^* and R_p^* for water at $T = 273$ K and 298 K as a function of S. As expected, we see that as S increases both g^* and R_p^* decrease. Table 9.2 contains surface tension and density data for five organic molecules, and values of g^* and R_p^* for these five substances at $T = 298$ K are given in Table

TABLE 9.1.   Critical Number and Radius for Water Droplets

S	$T = 273$ K[a]		$T = 298$ K[b]	
	$R_p^*,$ Å	g^*	$R_p^*,$ Å	g^*
1	∞	∞	∞	∞
2	17.3	726	15.1	482
3	10.9	182	9.5	121
4	8.7	91	7.6	60
5	7.5	58	6.5	39

[a] $\sigma = 75.6$ dynes cm^{-1}; $v_l = 2.99 \times 10^{-23}$ cm^3 molecule^{-1}.
[b] $\sigma = 72$ dynes cm^{-1}; $v_l = 2.99 \times 10^{-23}$ cm^3 molecule^{-1}.

TABLE 9.2. Surface Tensions and Densities of Five Organic Species at 298 K

Species	M	ρ_l, g cm$^{-3\,b}$	v_l, cm^3 $\times 10^{23}$ molecule^{-1}	σ, dynes cm^{-1}
acetone (C_3H_6O)	58.08	0.787	12.25	23.04
benzene (C_6H_6)	78.11	0.879	14.75	28.21
carbon tetrachloride (CCl_4)	153.82	1.594	16.02	26.34
ethanol (C_2H_6O)	46.07	0.789	9.694	22.14
styrene (C_8H_8)	104.2	0.906	19.10	31.49

[a]*Handbook of Chemistry and Physics*, 56th Ed.
[b]All densities are at $T = 293$ K except that for acetone, at 298 K.

TABLE 9.3. Critical Number and Radius for Five Organic Species at 298 K

Species				S		
		1	2	3	4	5
acetone	g^*	∞	265	67	33	21
	R_p^*, Å	∞	19.8	12.5	9.9	8.5
benzene	g^*	∞	706	177	88	56
	R_p^*, Å	∞	29.2	18.4	14.6	12.6
carbon tetrachloride	g^*	∞	678	170	85	54
	R_p^*, Å	∞	29.6	18.7	14.8	12.7
ethanol	g^*	∞	147	37	18	12
	R_p^*, Å	∞	15.1	9.5	7.5	6.5
styrene	g^*	∞	1646	413	206	132
	R_p^*, Å	∞	42.2	26.6	21.1	18.2

9.3. The critical radius R_p^* depends on the product of σv_l. For the five organic liquids $\sigma < \sigma_{water}$ but $v_l > v_{l,water}$. The organic surface tensions are about $\frac{1}{3}$ that of water and their molecular volumes range from 3 to 6 times that of water. The product σv_l for ethanol is approximately the same as that of water, and consequently we see that the R_p^* values for the two species are virtually identical. Since g^* involves an additional factor of v_l, even though the R_p^* values coincide for ethanol and water, the critical numbers g^* differ appreciably because of the large size of the ethanol molecule.

TABLE 9.4. Equilibrium Vapor Pressure Increase Over a Pure Water Droplet as a Function of Droplet Diameter at $T = 298$ K

D_p, μm	1.0	0.5	0.1	0.05	0.01	0.005
$\dfrac{p_{H_2O} - p^0_{H_2O}}{p^0_{H_2O}}$	0.0021	0.0042	0.021	0.043	0.23	0.52

Table 9.4 gives the vapor pressure difference $(p_{H_2O} - p^0_{H_2O})/p^0_{H_2O}$ for a pure water droplet as a function of diameter at 298 K. We see that the vapor pressure is increased by 2.1 percent for a 0.1 μm and 23 percent for a 0.01 μm drop over that for a flat surface. Roughly we may consider 0.05 μm diameter as the point at which the Kelvin effect begins to become important.

9.2. EQUILIBRIUM OF AN AQUEOUS SOLUTION DROPLET

In the previous section we developed the equilibrium vapor pressure of a droplet of pure substance. Atmospheric droplets virtually always contain dissolved solutes, and so we wish to extend the analysis to include this situation. Let us now consider a solution droplet consisting of a solute B in a solvent A. For most cases of interest to us, the solvent A will be water.

Consider a droplet of diameter D_p containing n_A moles of solvent (e.g., water), and n_B moles of solute (e.g., a nonvolatile salt). The mole fraction of solvent $x_A = n_A/(n_A + n_B)$, and if $\bar{v}_A$ and $\bar{v}_B$ are the partial molar volumes of the two components in solution, the total volume of the drop $(\pi/6)D_p^3 = n_A\bar{v}_A + n_B\bar{v}_B$. Since the solute is nonvolatile, n_B is fixed regardless of the value of D_p.

The vapor pressure of solvent over such a solution with a flat surface is, by extension of Raoult's law, $p^0_{A_{sol}} = \gamma_A x_A p^0_A$, where p^0_A is the vapor pressure of pure solvent A over a flat surface, and γ_A is its activity coefficient in the solution. Substituting this expression into the Kelvin equation we have

$$\ln \frac{p_A}{p^0_A \gamma_A x_A} = \frac{4\sigma\bar{v}_A}{RTD_p} \tag{9.12}$$

or

$$\ln \frac{p_A}{p^0_A} = \frac{4\sigma\bar{v}_A}{RTD_p} + \ln\gamma_A + \ln x_A \tag{9.13}$$

Noting that

$$\frac{1}{x_A} = 1 + \frac{n_B}{n_A} = 1 + \frac{n_B\bar{v}_A}{(\pi/6)D_p^3 - n_B\bar{v}_B} \tag{9.14}$$

we have

$$\ln \frac{p_A}{p_A^0} = \frac{4\sigma\bar{v}_A}{RTD_p} + \ln\gamma_A - \ln\left[1 + \frac{n_B\bar{v}_A}{(\pi/6)D_p^3 - n_B\bar{v}_B}\right] \quad (9.15)$$

This is the relation between the vapor pressure over a solution droplet to that of the pure solvent over a flat surface at the same temperature as a function of the drop diameter D_p. If the solution is dilute, the volume occupied by the solute can be neglected relative to the total volume—that is, $n_B\bar{v}_B \ll (\pi/6)D_p^3$. Also, under dilute conditions the activity coefficient γ_A can be assumed to be close to its infinite dilution limit, $\gamma_A = 1$. In that case, Eq. (9.15) becomes

$$\ln \frac{p_A}{p_A^0} = \frac{4\sigma\bar{v}_w}{RTD_p} - \frac{6n_B\bar{v}_w}{\pi D_p^3} \quad (9.16)$$

where $\bar{v}_A$ is now interpreted as the molar volume of pure water $\bar{v}_w$. It is customary to express Eq. (9.16) as

$$\ln \frac{p_A}{p_A^0} = \frac{A}{D_p} - \frac{B}{D_p^3} \quad (9.17)$$

where $A = 4\sigma\bar{v}_w/RT$ and $B = 6n_B\bar{v}_w/\pi$.

We saw that for a pure water drop the vapor pressure over a curved interface always exceeds that over a flat interface. By contrast, the vapor pressure p_A over an aqueous solution droplet may be larger or smaller than the vapor pressure of pure water over a flat surface p_A^0 depending on the magnitude of the solute-effect term, B/D_p^3, relative to the curvature term, A/D_p. If $D_p^2 A < B$, then $p_A < p_A^0$ and an aqueous solution droplet is in equilibrium with a subsaturated environment.

Figure 9.2 shows a sketch of $\ln p_A/p_A^0$ versus D_p. The value of D_p at which $p_A = p_A^0$ is denoted D_{pp}, called the *potential diameter*, and is given by $(B/A)^{1/2}$. The curve of $\ln p_A/p_A^0$ reaches a maximum at D_{pc}, the so-called *critical diameter*, equal to $(3B/A)^{1/2}$. We see that $D_{pc} = \sqrt{3} D_{pp}$ regardless of the solute or its properties. The maximum value of p_A/p_A^0 occurs at the critical diameter and is given by

$$\frac{p_A}{p_A^0} = 1 + \left(\frac{4A^3}{27B}\right)^{1/2} \quad (9.18)$$

The general class of curves shown in Figure 9.2 is called the Köhler curve.

The steeply rising portion of the Köhler curve represents a region where solute effects dominate, and the $-B/D_p^3$ term leads to a rapid increase in p/p_A^0 to unity as D_p increases. When $p = p_A^0$, both terms are equal. Beyond

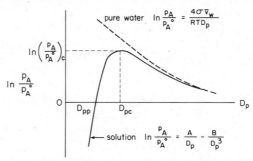

Figure 9.2. The ratio of the vapor pressure p_A of a solvent A over a solution droplet to its pure component vapor pressure over a flat surface p_A^0, as a function of the diameter of the droplet. Curves of this type are called Köhler curves.

D_{pp}, S becomes greater than 1 and the Kelvin effect begins to predominate. At the point of maximum, or critical, saturation the Kelvin effect contribution is three times as large as the solute effect term. Thereafter the curve approaches closely the Kelvin equation, which represents the envelope of all Köhler curves.

Let us examine the general character of the Köhler curves. Any point on the curve gives the equilibrium saturation ratio of water (i.e., relative humidity) at which a solution droplet of a given solute amount and diameter exists. Ordinarily, we would describe the process in reverse, namely that, given an ambient saturation ratio, or relative humidity, and given the amount of dissolved solute, the curve tells us the equilibrium particle size. We note however that for $S > 1$, there are two equilibrium diameters predicted for any saturation ratio. Does this mean that particles of two different sizes containing identical quantities of solute can exist in equilibrium simultaneously? To answer this question let us consider the behavior of a droplet at a fixed ambient saturation ratio S. Consider first a particle lying on the portion of the curve for which $D_p < D_{pc}$. A drop will constantly experience small perturbations caused by the gain or loss of a few molecules of water. Say the drop at equilibrium grows slightly due to the addition of a few molecules of water. At its momentary larger size the equilibrium vapor pressure for the drop is larger than the fixed ambient value and the drop evaporates water to return to its prior equilibrium. This equilibrium is therefore stable. Now consider a drop on the portion of the curve for which $D_p > D_{pc}$ that experiences a slight perturbation that causes the drop to grow by a few molecules of water. At the larger size the equilibrium vapor pressure is lower than the ambient. Thus, water molecules will continue to flow to the drop and it will grow even larger. Conversely, a slight shrinkage leads to a drop that has a higher equilibrium vapor pressure than the ambient so the drop continues to evaporate. If it is a drop of pure water, it will evaporate completely. If it contains a solute, it will diminish in size until it intersects the equilibrium size on the ascending branch of the Köhler curve.

If the ambient saturation ratio happens to exceed the critical saturation ratio S_c, whatever the size of the drop, its equilibrium vapor pressure is less than that with which it is in contact and growth continues indefinitely. In such a way, a droplet can grow to a size much larger than the initial size of the nucleus. It is, in fact, through this process that cloud or fog droplets of 10 μm or more in diameter grow from nuclei of perhaps only 0.01 μm diameter. Moreover, in cloud physics a droplet is not considered to be a cloud droplet unless its diameter exceeds its critical diameter. The critical saturation ratio of a particle is as important, or more important, than its initial size in determining whether or not the particle will become activated for growth. When a fixed ambient saturation ratio exists, all particles whose S_c are below the ambient S grow indefinitely as long as $S > S_c$. Particles whose S_c are above the ambient S come to a stable equilibrium size at the appropriate point on the Köhler curve. Under natural cloud conditions the saturation ratio of water varies with time. If the maximum value it achieves is S_{max}, then only those particles with $S_c < S_{max}$ will grow to become cloud droplets. In subsaturated air, $S < 1$, no particles can grow to become cloud or fog droplets since the critical saturation ratio for a particle must exceed 1.

The expression for the vapor pressure over the solution involves n_B, the number of moles of solute. When the solute is a salt, it may be highly dissociated in solution. The dissociation is not complete except at infinite

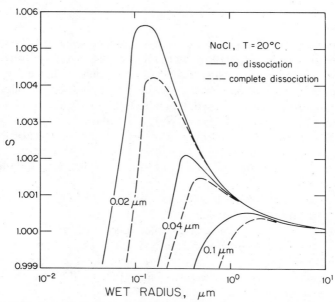

Figure 9.3. Köhler curves for aqueous NaCl droplets at 20°C assuming no dissociation and complete dissociation of the salt in solution for dry radii of 0.02 μm, 0.04 μm, and 0.1 μm.

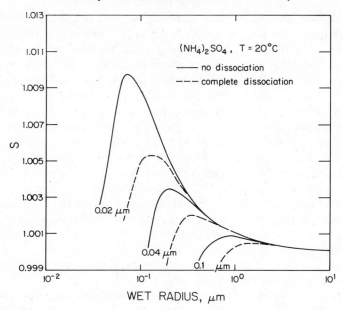

Figure 9.4. Köhler curves for aqueous $(NH_4)_2SO_4$ droplets at 20°C assuming no dissociation and complete dissociation of the salt in solution for dry radii of 0.02 μm, 0.04 μm, and 0.1 μm.

dilution, and at finite dilutions some undissociated salt is present together with its component ions. In calculating the number of moles, a dissociated molecule that has dissociated into i ions is treated as i molecules, whereas an undissociated molecule is counted only once. For the actual solution, an effective i, the so-called van't Hoff factor, is used, which reflects the degree of dissociation of the particular salt. For example, for $(NH_4)_2SO_4$ the maximum value of i is 3. Although the value of i is a function of concentration, it is generally taken to be constant so that i does not become a function of D_p. Given the initial mass of solute, m_B, the number of moles resulting in solution from this mass of solute is $n_B = im_B/M_B$.

Figures 9.3 and 9.4 show the Köhler curves for NaCl and $(NH_4)_2SO_4$ at $T = 20°C$ for initial dry nuclei of 0.02 μm, 0.04 μm, and 0.1 μm radii assuming both no dissociation and complete dissociation. For both NaCl and $(NH_4)_2SO_4$, complete dissociation results in lower saturation values. In other words, at $S = S'$, beginning with a dry particle, if complete dissociation occurs, the equilibrium wet diameter is larger than in the case of no dissociation. As the diameter of the wet particle increases, the curves for no and complete dissociation converge to the same limit for both salts. This behavior occurs because as diameter increases, the first term in Eq. (9.17) dominates, and that term is not a function of composition.

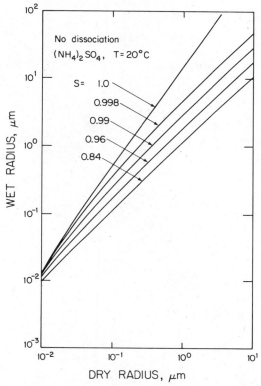

Figure 9.5. Wet radius as a function of dry radius for aqueous $(NH_4)_2SO_4$ solution droplets at $T = 20°C$ at saturation ratios (relative humidities) of 100%, 99.8%, 99%, 96%, and 84%. No dissociation assumed.

Figures 9.5 and 9.6 show the wet radius versus dry radius for $(NH_4)_2SO_4$ at saturation ratios (relative humidities) of 100%, 99.8%, 99%, 96%, and 84%, assuming no dissociation and complete dissociation, respectively. Again we see that for a given value of S and dry radius, complete dissociation (effectively more "solute") results in a larger wet particle.

The above development can be extended to include solution nonideality. The water activity a_A in a binary solution of a solute B at molality m is given by

$$a_A = \gamma_A x_A = \exp\left(\frac{-\nu m M_A \Phi_T}{1000} \right) \tag{9.19}$$

where ν is the number of moles of ions formed from complete ionization of one mole of solute and Φ_T is the practical osmotic coefficient, which will be discussed in Section 9.7.

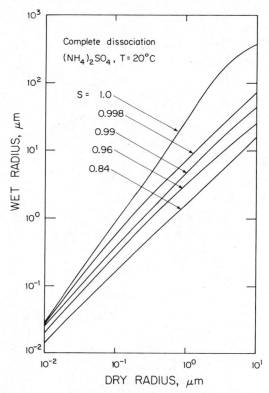

Figure 9.6. Wet radius as a function of dry radius for aqueous $(NH_4)_2SO_4$ solution droplets at $T = 20°C$ at saturation ratios (relative humidities) of 100%, 99.8%, 99%, 96%, and 84%. Complete dissociation assumed.

9.3. HOMOGENEOUS NUCLEATION THEORY

In this section we develop the theory of homogeneous nucleation in the format of so-called classical nucleation theory. Classical nucleation theory, as it is commonly presented (see, for example, McDonald (1962, 1963)), follows the material in Frenkel (1955), which is originally due to Becker and Döring (1935), as an improvement on a thermodynamic approach of Volmer and Weber (1926). The classical theory involves many approximations which have been investigated rather thoroughly in studies subsequent to those cited above. Although it is beyond the scope of this book to attempt to discuss some of the more recent improvements to classical nucleation theory, we refer the reader to Springer (1978) as a good starting point for a more in-depth study of homogeneous nucleation.

9.3.1.   Equilibrium Cluster Distribution

In a dilute mixture of a vapor A in air, an instantaneous snapshot would show that nearly all molecules of A exist independently or in small clusters containing two, three, or possibly four molecules; larger clusters of solute molecules would be extremely rare (Katz and Donohue, 1979). Moreover, the concentration of independent molecules, or monomers, will generally be very much larger than the concentration of all other clusters combined. As a result, when a cluster grows it does so almost exclusively by the addition of single molecules.

At equilibrium the concentrations of all clusters are constant, such that every forward process (i.e., the addition of single molecules) is matched by its corresponding reverse process (i.e., the loss of single molecules from a cluster). In a sufficiently dilute situation, the rate at which single molecules evaporate from a cluster depends only on the properties of the cluster, its size and temperature.

Let the equilibrium concentration of clusters containing g molecules be denoted as N_g^e, $g = 2, 3, \ldots$. Equation (9.6) gives the Gibbs free energy change for a system of pure vapor to one containing vapor plus a drop containing g molecules. This expression can be written in terms of g as

$$\Delta G = bg^{2/3} - gkT \ln S \qquad (9.20)$$

where $b = 3\sigma v_l (4\pi / 3v_l)^{1/3}$. For a fluid at equilibrium, in this case in both phase and thermal equilibrium, it is generally accepted that the concentration of clusters obeys a Boltzmann distribution,

$$N_g^e = N_1 \exp(-\Delta G / kT) \qquad (9.21)$$

where N_1 is the total number of molecules of solute A in the system. (Since in a dilute system the number of molecules of A tied up in clusters will be negligibly small compared with the total number of molecules of A, N_1 can be simply taken as the total number of molecules of A.) Using Eq. (9.20) in Eq. (9.21) gives

$$N_g^e = N_1 \exp\left(g \ln S - \frac{bg^{2/3}}{kT} \right)$$

$$= N_1 S^g \exp(-bg^{2/3} / kT) \qquad (9.22)$$

Because of the approximate nature of the expression for ΔG that we are using, for small g and very large g, Eq. (9.22) departs from reality. For example, when $g = 1$, N_g^e should be identical with N_1, but Eq. (9.22) does not produce this identity. N_g^e cannot exceed N_1, but Eq. (9.22) predicts that at

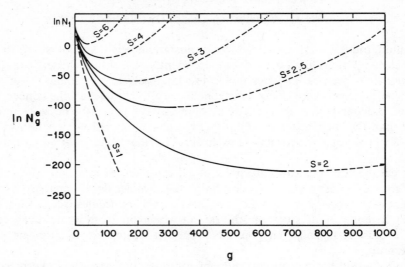

Figure 9.7. Equilibrium cluster distribution for various values of the saturation ratio S.

sufficiently large g, N_g^e can be greater than N_1. N_g^e is sketched as a function of g and S in Figure 9.7. Clearly, the relation Eq. (9.22) is no longer valid when the accumulated value of the product gN_g^e begins to approach N_1 in magnitude. By differentiating Eq. (9.22) at constant T, N_1, and $S(S > 1)$, we see that N_g^e is a minimum at $g = g^*$ where

$$kT \ln S = \tfrac{2}{3} b g^{* -1/3} \tag{9.23}$$

Recalling that $4\pi R_p^2 \sigma = b g^{2/3}$, this becomes

$$kT \ln S = \frac{8\pi\sigma R_p^2}{3g^*} \tag{9.24}$$

or, equivalently,

$$\ln S = \frac{2\sigma v_l}{kTR_p^*} = \frac{2\sigma M_A}{RT\rho_l R_p^*} \tag{9.25}$$

Thus, the minimum in N_g^e as a function of g occurs at the g^* (or R_p^*) as given by the Kelvin equation. The larger the value of S, the smaller g^* is and the larger is the value of N_g^e at the minimum,

$$N_{g*}^e = N_1 S^{g^*} \exp\left(-bg^{*2/3}/kT\right) \tag{9.26}$$

Since g^* is at the maximum of ΔG, the N_g^e distribution should be a minimum at g^*. Physically, we do not expect that for $g > g^*$, the cluster concentrations should increase with increasing g. Thus, the equilibrium distribution N_g^e given by Eq. (9.22) is taken to be valid only up to g^*, where

$$g^* = \left(\frac{\frac{2}{3}b}{kT \ln S} \right)^3 = \frac{32\pi\sigma^3 v_l^2}{3(kT \ln S)^3} \tag{9.27}$$

or equivalently where $R_p^* = 2\sigma v_l / kT \ln S$. Using Eq. (9.27) we obtain

$$N_{g*}^e = N_1 \exp\left[-\frac{16\pi\sigma^3 v_l^2}{3(kT)^3 (\ln S)^2} \right] \tag{9.28}$$

Even though N_g^e as predicted by Eq. (9.22) is not accurate for g approaching 1 and for very large g, it can be taken as appropriate in the region around g^*. Fortunately, it is precisely this region in which we will be interested in considering nucleation.

The equilibrium distribution of clusters N_g^e can be interpreted in a kinetic sense as follows. At equilibrium the rate of formation of the g-mer by monomer addition to the $(g - 1)$-mer is equal to the rate of loss of g-mers by evaporation of single molecules from a g-mer. Thus,

$$\beta a_{g-1} N_{g-1}^e = e'_g a_g N_g^e \tag{9.29}$$

where β is the flux of monomer molecules to a unit area of surface, a_{g-1} and a_g are the surface areas of a $(g - 1)$-mer and a g-mer, respectively, and e'_g is the flux of monomers per unit area leaving a g-mer. To obtain an expression for β we recall that the number of molecules striking unit area per unit time in a gas is $N\bar{c}/4$, where $\bar{c} = (8kT/\pi m)^{1/2}$. Since the partial pressure of monomer, $p_1 = N_1 kT$,

$$\beta = \frac{1}{4}\left(\frac{8kT}{\pi m_1} \right)^{1/2} \frac{p_1}{kT} = \frac{p_1}{(2\pi m_1 kT)^{1/2}} \tag{9.30}$$

For sufficiently large g, a_{g-1} is approximately equal to a_g and Eq. (9.29) simplifies to

$$\beta N_{g-1}^e = e'_g N_g^e \tag{9.31}$$

Even though at dilute solute concentrations the evaporation rate e'_g can be assumed to depend only on the size of the cluster and its temperature, it is actually a complicated and generally unknown function of g and T. Fortunately, as long as we already have postulated the form of N_g^e as Eq. (9.22) it is not necessary to know e'_g explicitly.

9.3.2.   Kinetics of Homogeneous Nucleation

In general, the net rate at which clusters containing $g - 1$ molecules become clusters containing g molecules is

$$J_g = \beta a_{g-1} N_{g-1} - e'_g a_g N_g \qquad (9.32)$$

where N_{g-1} and N_g are the *non-equilibrium* concentrations of $(g - 1)$-mers and g-mers, respectively. Of course, at equilibrium $J_g = 0$, $N_{g-1} = N^e_{g-1}$, $N_g = N^e_g$ and Eq. (9.29) is obtained. Given β, e'_g, and the concentrations of clusters, the net formation rate of any g-mer can, in principle, be calculated from Eq. (9.32). However, the only term in Eq. (9.32) that is really known is β (and the surface areas a_{g-1} and a_g). The evaporation rate e'_g, according to our assumption of a dilute mixture, does not depend on the monomer concentration but only on the size of the cluster and temperature. It is useful to invoke Eq. (9.29) and write Eq. (9.32) as

$$J_g = \beta a_{g-1} N^e_{g-1} \left[\frac{N_{g-1}}{N^e_{g-1}} - \frac{N_g}{N^e_g} \right] \qquad (9.33)$$

A number balance on N_g gives

$$\frac{dN_g}{dt} = J_g - J_{g+1} \qquad (9.34)$$

that is, the rate of accumulation of g-mers is the difference between the net rate at which g-mers are formed from $(g - 1)$-mers and the net rate at which $(g + 1)$-mers are formed from g-mers.

It is at this point that we invoke the key assumption of homogeneous nucleation theory, that is that a pseudo-steady state is quickly achieved so that at any instant the rate of formation of g-mers is equal to the net rate of formation of $(g + 1)$-mers, and so on, so that J becomes a constant independent of g. (Note that this assumption is *not* equivalent to equilibrium. At equilibrium, $J_g = 0$, whereas at the pseudo-steady state, $J_g = J_{g+1} = \cdots = J$. Thus, the pseudo-steady state approximation leads to a constant flux of particles moving through the cluster distribution rather than the zero flux that exists at equilibrium.) Thus, Eq. (9.33) becomes

$$J = \beta a_{g-1} N^e_{g-1} \left[\frac{N_{g-1}}{N^e_{g-1}} - \frac{N_g}{N^e_g} \right] \qquad (9.35)$$

Note that the terms on the right-hand side of Eq. (9.35) differ only in the value of the index g. Summing Eq. (9.33) from $g = 2$ to some sufficiently large

$g = G - 1$, successive terms cancel and we obtain,

$$\sum_{g=1}^{G-1} \frac{J}{\beta a_g N_g^e} = \frac{N_1}{N_1^e} - \frac{N_G}{N_G^e} \tag{9.36}$$

We specify that the non-equilibrium and equilibrium monomer concentrations are equivalent, so $N_1/N_1^e = 1$, and that $N_G/N_G^e = 0$. This latter assumption can be understood as follows. Physically we expect N_G to be a slowly decreasing function of G, whereas N_G^e for $G > g^*$ is an increasing function (even though it is physically unrealistic). Thus, for sufficiently large G, N_G/N_G^e becomes negligibly small and can be set equal to zero. Factoring J out of the summation and rearranging gives

$$J = \frac{1}{\sum_{g=1}^{G-1} \frac{1}{\beta a_g N_g^e}} \tag{9.37}$$

By now making two very accurate mathematical approximations (Cohen, 1970), the summation can be evaluated analytically. The first approximation is the conversion of the summation to an integral,

$$J = \frac{1}{\int_1^{G-1} \frac{dg}{\beta a(g) N^e(g)}} \tag{9.38}$$

Since $N^e(g)$ goes through a sharp minimum at $g = g^*$, $1/N^e(g)$ goes through a sharp maximum. Thus, the second approximation is to consider only the contribution of the integrand in the region around $g = g^*$. To do so, we expand $N^e(g)$ in a Taylor series about $g = g^*$,

$$N^e(g) = N_1 \exp\left[-\frac{\Delta G^*}{kT} - \frac{1}{kT}\left(\frac{d\Delta G}{dg}\right)_{g^*}(g - g^*) \right.$$

$$\left. - \frac{1}{2kT}\left(\frac{d^2\Delta G}{dg^2}\right)_{g^*}(g - g^*)^2 \right]$$

$$= N_1 \exp\left[-\frac{\Delta G^*}{kT} - \frac{1}{2kT}\left(\frac{d^2\Delta G}{dg^2}\right)_{g^*}(g - g^*)^2 \right] \tag{9.39}$$

where, by definition, $(d\Delta G/dg)_{g^*} = 0$. Now from Eq. (9.20),

$$\frac{\Delta G}{kT} = \frac{bg^{2/3}}{kT} - g \ln S \tag{9.40}$$

and

$$\frac{d^2 \Delta G}{dg^2} = -\frac{2}{9} \frac{b}{kT} g^{-4/3}$$

(9.41)

so that

$$N^e(g) = N_1 \exp\left[-\frac{\Delta G^*}{kT} + \frac{1}{2}\left(\frac{2b}{kT}\right) g^{*-4/3}(g - g^*)^2\right]$$

(9.42)

Substituting Eq. (9.42) into the integral in Eq. (9.38) gives

$$\int_1^{G-1} \frac{dg}{\beta a(g) N^e(g)} = \frac{1}{\beta a(g^*) N^e(g^*)} \int_0^\infty \exp\left[-\frac{\gamma}{2}(g - g^*)^2\right] dg$$

(9.43)

where $\gamma = 2bg^{*-4/3}/9kT$. Note that as long as $g^* \gg 1$, we can change the lower limit on the integral to zero. Recognizing the integral in Eq (9.43) as an error function, we obtain from Eq. (9.38),

$$J = \beta a(g^*) N^e(g^*)\left(\frac{\gamma}{2\pi}\right)^{1/2}$$

(9.44)

Using $\beta = p_1/(2\pi m_1 kT)^{1/2}$, $a(g^*) = 4\pi R_p^{*2}$, $N^e(g^*) = N_1 \exp[-16\pi\sigma^3 v_l^2/3(kT)^3(\ln S)^2]$, and $(\gamma/2\pi)^{1/2} = (bg^{*-4/3}/9\pi kT)^{1/2}$, Eq. (9.44) becomes

$$J = \left[\frac{p_1}{(2\pi m_1 kT)^{1/2}}\right]\left[\frac{2\sigma^{1/2}v_l}{(kT)^{1/2}}\right] N_1 \exp\left[-\frac{16\pi\sigma^3 v_l^2}{3(kT)^3(\ln S)^2}\right]$$

(9.45)

The first term in brackets is recognized as β, the monomer flux to a unit area and the third term is just $N^e(g^*)$, the *equilibrium* concentration of clusters of the critical size g^*. Since we know that the *pseudo-steady state* cluster concentration differs from the *equilibrium* cluster concentration, the middle term in brackets represents a correction factor for that difference. Equation (9.45) is sometimes written as

$$J = C^* Z N^e(g^*)$$

(9.46)

where

$$C^* = \frac{4\pi R_p^{*2} p_1}{(2\pi m_1 kT)^{1/2}}$$

(9.47)

the rate of arrival of monomer molecules at the critical cluster (molecules sec^{-1}) and

$$Z = \frac{\sigma^{1/2}v_l}{2\pi R_p^{*2}(kT)^{1/2}} \tag{9.48}$$

the so-called Zeldovich non-equilibrium factor.

Let us summarize what we have obtained in our development of homogeneous nucleation theory. In order for homogeneous nucleation to occur, it is necessary that the free energy barrier, the peak of which is at $g = g^*$, be surmounted. The lower the saturation ratio S, the larger the critical cluster size g^*. At equilibrium the cluster concentrations are given by a Boltzmann distribution which predicts that clusters containing more than a very few molecules are exceedingly rare. In order to obtain nucleation, the equilibrium cluster distribution N_g^e has to be perturbed to produce a non-equilibrium distribution N_g and "current" J. This current results when the saturation ratio can be maintained at a sufficiently large value to provide a chain of bombardments of vapor molecules on clusters that produces a net flow through the cluster distribution. Even when such a net flow exists, the characteristic time for response of the cluster concentrations to changes in S is assumed to be short compared with the characteristic time for changes in S. As a result, the non-equilibrium cluster concentrations N_g can be assumed to be in a pseudo-steady state in the same manner as free radical concentrations can often be assumed to be in a pseudo-steady state in chemical reactions. The pseudo-steady state approximation applied to the non-equilibrium cluster concentrations leads, in fact, to a flux or current J that is a constant throughout the hierarchy of clusters. To maintain the nucleation rate at a constant value J it is necessary that the saturation ratio of vapor be maintained at its constant value. Clearly, without outside reinforcement of the vapor concentration, the saturation ratio will eventually fall due to the depletion of vapor molecules to form stable nuclei. The case in which the vapor concentration is augmented by a source of fresh vapor is referred to as nucleation with a continuously reinforced vapor.

9.3.3. Evaluation of the Homogeneous Nucleation Rate for Water

Let us evaluate the nucleation rate J for water as a function of the saturation ratio S. To do so, we use Eq. (9.45) together with the parameters given in Table 9.5 to evaluate both J and g^* for values of S ranging from 1.5 to 10.0. We see that the nucleation rate varies *over 70 orders of magnitude* from $S = 2$ to $S = 10$. As S increases, the critical cluster size g^* decreases from 525 at $S = 2$ to 14 at $S = 10$. Clearly, the more saturated the air the smaller the cluster needed to surmount the free energy barrier. Figure 9.8 shows the critical number g^* and the droplet current J as a function of S for water at 20°C.

It is of interest to compare the equilibrium and pseudo-steady state cluster distributions under a particular set of conditions. The equilibrium cluster

TABLE 9.5. Nucleation Rate and Critical Cluster Size for Water at $T = 293$ K

$$J = \frac{p_1}{(2\pi m_1 kT)^{1/2}}\left(\frac{2\sigma^{1/2}v_l}{(kT)^{1/2}}\right)N_1\exp\left[-\frac{16\pi\sigma^3 v_l^2}{3(kT)^3(\ln S)^2}\right]$$

$$g^* = \frac{32\pi\sigma^3 v_l^2}{3(kT\ln S)^3}$$

$\sigma = 72.75$ dyne cm^{-1}

$v_l = 2.99 \times 10^{-23}$ cm^3 molecule^{-1}

$N_1 = p_{H_2O}^0 S/kT$

$k = 1.380 \times 10^{-16}$ dyne cm K^{-1} molecule^{-1}

$m_1 = 2.99 \times 10^{-23}$ g molecule^{-1}

$p_{H_2O}^0 = 17.525$ torr

S	J, cm^{-3} sec^{-1}	g^*
2	4.04×10^{-54}	525
2.5	4.28×10^{-20}	227
3	3.68×10^{-6}	132
3.5	94	89
4	3.36×10^6	66
4.5	4.02×10^9	51
5	6.66×10^{11}	42
5.5	3.17×10^{13}	35
6	6.53×10^{14}	30
6.5	7.51×10^{16}	27
7	5.63×10^{16}	24
7.5	3.06×10^{17}	21
8	1.30×10^{18}	19
8.5	4.54×10^{18}	18
9	1.36×10^{19}	16
9.5	3.57×10^{19}	15
10	8.47×10^{19}	14

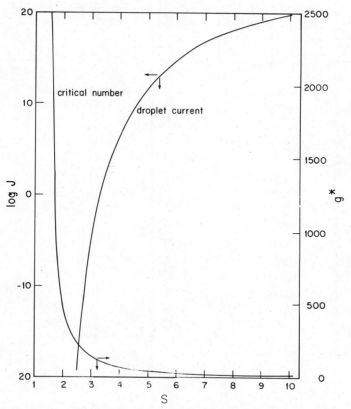

Figure 9.8. Critical cluster size g^* and droplet current J for homogeneous nucleation of water at 293 K.

distribution N_g^e can be used as the starting point to calculate the pseudo-steady state distribution N_g. Since

$$J = \beta a_g N_g - e_{g+1} a_{g+1} N_{g+1} \tag{9.49}$$

we can let $U_g = N_g / N_g^e$ and Eq. (9.33) is just

$$J = \beta a_g (U_g - U_{g+1}) \tag{9.50}$$

Assume that for some $G \gg g^*$, $N_G \ll N_G^e$ which gives us the condition $U_G = 0$. From Eq. (9.37)

$$J = \frac{1}{\sum_{g=1}^{G-1} \dfrac{1}{\beta a_g N_g^e}} \tag{9.51}$$

TABLE 9.6. Equilibrium (N_g^e) and Pseudo-Steady State (N_g)
Cluster Concentrations for Water at $T = 293$ K and $S = 3.5$

g	$U_g = N_g/N_g^e$	N_g^e	N_g
1	1.0	2.022576×10^{18}	2.022576×10^{18}
10	1.0	6.8197×10^6	6.8197×10^6
20	1.0	218.696	218.696
30	1.0	0.280456	0.280456
40	0.99996	2.8248×10^{-3}	2.82447×10^{-3}
50	0.99868	1.1374×10^{-4}	1.1359×10^{-4}
60	0.9845	1.2738×10^{-5}	1.2541×10^{-5}
70	0.9146	3.1732×10^{-6}	2.9022×10^{-6}
80	0.7354	1.5138×10^{-6}	1.1134×10^{-6}
89[a]	0.4991	1.2402×10^{-6}	6.1908×10^{-7}
100	0.2307	1.6231×10^{-6}	3.7440×10^{-7}
110	0.0848	3.170×10^{-6}	2.688×10^{-7}
120	0.0236	8.827×10^{-6}	2.080×10^{-7}
130	5.08×10^{-3}	3.370×10^{-5}	1.693×10^{-7}
150	1.09×10^{-4}	1.119×10^{-3}	1.224×10^{-7}
169	2.95×10^{-7}	7.472×10^{-2}	2.205×10^{-8}

[a] Critical cluster size.

Once J has been calculated U_g can be determined from

$$U_g = J \sum_{g'=g}^{G-1} \frac{1}{\beta a_{g'} N_{g'}^e} \qquad (9.52)$$

We choose a value for G and evaluate the summation for $g = 1$. If $U_1 \neq 1$, then the value of G chosen is too small. Table 9.6 gives the equilibrium and pseudo-steady state cluster concentrations for water for the same conditions as in Table 9.5 for $S = 3.5$. We note that, as expected, N_g^e begins to increase when g exceeds g^*, whereas N_g continues to decay. By trial and error it was determined that a choice of $G = 170$ was sufficient to satisfy the condition $U_1 = 1$ under these conditions.

It is interesting to contrast the nucleation of pure water with the situation considered in Section 9.2 in which a nonvolatile solute is present. In that case spontaneous growth can take place without the need for the establishment of a cluster distribution. When the ambient saturation ratio exceeds the critical saturation shown in Figure 9.2, the solution droplet will gain water at an accelerating rate, since the addition of water to the droplet cannot alleviate the difference between the vapor pressure of water over the droplet and the partial pressure of water vapor in the ambient air. In this way a droplet can grow to cloud droplet size ($\approx 10\ \mu$m) in seconds. In clouds the droplets eventually stop growing because the saturation ratio of water is continually lowered due to the transfer of water vapor to growing droplets.

9.4. HOMOGENEOUS–HETEROMOLECULAR NUCLEATION

We have seen that in homogeneous–homomolecular nucleation, nucleation does not occur unless the vapor phase is supersaturated with respect to the species. When two or more vapor species are present, neither of which is supersaturated, nucleation can still take place as long as the participating vapor species are supersaturated with respect to a liquid solution droplet. Thus, heteromolecular nucleation can occur when a mixture of vapors is subsaturated with respect to the pure substances as long as there is supersaturation with respect to a solution of these substances. The theory of homogeneous–heteromolecular nucleation parallels that of homogeneous–homomolecular nucleation extended to include two or more nucleating vapor species. We consider here only two such species, thus binary homogeneous nucleation, the extension to more than two species being straightforward in principle if not in fact.

Let us consider a mixture of two vapor species, A and B, in air. The free energy of formation of a cluster of radius R_p containing n_A molecules of A and n_B molecules of B from a mixture of ideal gases with partial pressures p_A and p_B is

$$\Delta G = -n_A kT \ln \frac{p_A}{p_{A_{\text{sol}}}^0} - n_B kT \ln \frac{p_B}{p_{B_{\text{sol}}}^0} + 4\pi R_p^2 \sigma \qquad (9.53)$$

where $p_{A_{\text{sol}}}^0$ and $p_{B_{\text{sol}}}^0$ are the vapor pressures of A and B over a *flat solution* of the same composition as the droplet. Whereas (at constant temperature) in the case of a single vapor species, ΔG is a function of the number of molecules g, here ΔG depends on both n_A and n_B. For very small values of R_p, ΔG is dominated by the surface energy term, and for small values of n_A and n_B, ΔG increases with size. Instead of considering ΔG as a function of g, it is now necessary to view ΔG as a surface in the $n_A - n_B$ plane. Reiss (1950) showed that the three-dimensional surface $\Delta G(n_A, n_B)$ has a saddle point that represents the minimum height of the free energy barrier. As usual, we will denote this height by ΔG^* and the values of n_A and n_B at this point by n_A^* and n_B^*. The following conditions hold at the saddle point:

$$\left(\frac{\partial \Delta G}{\partial n_A} \right)_{n_B} = \left(\frac{\partial \Delta G}{\partial n_B} \right)_{n_A} = 0 \qquad (9.54)$$

Differentiating Eq. (9.53) and expressing n_A and n_B in terms of partial molar volumes $\bar{v}_A$ and $\bar{v}_B$, we obtain (Mirabel and Katz, 1974)

$$RT \ln \frac{p_A}{p_{A_{sol}}^0} = \frac{2\sigma \bar{v}_A}{R_p} - \frac{3x_B \bar{v}}{R_p} \frac{d\sigma}{dx_B} \tag{9.55}$$

$$RT \ln \frac{p_B}{p_{B_{sol}}^0} = \frac{2\sigma \bar{v}_B}{R_p} - \frac{3(1 - x_B)\bar{v}}{R_p} \frac{d\sigma}{dx_B} \tag{9.56}$$

where $x_B = n_B/(n_A + n_B)$ and the molar volume of solution $\bar{v} = (1 - x_B)\bar{v}_A + x_B \bar{v}_B$. (Note that this definition of $\bar{v}$ is an approximation since in mixing two species in general 1 cm^3 of A mixed with 1 cm^3 of B does not produce precisely 2 cm^3 of solution.) Equations (9.55) and (9.56) can be called the generalized Kelvin equations.

When solving Eqs. (9.55) and (9.56) to determine radius R_p and mole fraction x_B, it is important to note that $p_{A_{sol}}^0$, $p_{B_{sol}}^0$, σ, $\bar{v}_A$, and $\bar{v}_B$ are all implicit functions of x_B. Yue (1979) has reviewed various methods of solving these equations. One way of determining the location of the saddle point is to construct a table of ΔG as a function of n_A and n_B and then find the "pass" in the ΔG surface by visual inspection. For example, Table 9.7 shows the values

TABLE 9.7. Values of $\Delta G (\times 10^{12}$ erg) for Different n_A and n_B ($A = H_2O$; $B = H_2SO_4$).
Pressures used are $p_A = 2 \times 10^4$ and $p_B = 1.15 \times 10^{-11}$ mm Hg[a]

n_A/n_B	75	76	77	78	79	80	81	82
128	5.64	5.82	5.94	6.00	6.02	5.99	5.94	5.86
129	5.51[b]	5.73	5.88	5.97	6.01	6.02	5.98	5.91
130	5.63	5.61	5.80	5.93	6.00	6.02	6.01	5.96
131	5.73	5.54	5.70	5.86	5.96	6.01	6.02	6.00
132	5.91	5.65	5.56	5.77	5.91	5.99	6.02	6.02
133	5.89	5.75	5.57	5.66	5.84	5.95	6.01	6.08
134	5.95	5.83	5.68	5.51	5.74	5.89	5.98	6.02
135	6.00	5.91	5.77	5.60	5.62	5.81	5.93	6.00
136	6.04	5.97	5.85	5.70	5.51	5.71	5.87	5.97
137	6.06	6.01	5.92	5.79	5.63	5.57	5.78	5.91
138	6.08	6.05	5.98	5.87	5.72	5.54	5.67	5.84
139	6.07	6.07	6.02	5.94	5.81	5.64	5.52	5.74

[a] Hamill et al. (1977).
[b] Single underline represents the path of minimum free energy; double underlined value is the saddle point free energy.

of ΔG at 218 K for n_A and n_B ($A = H_2O$; $B = H_2SO_4$) at $p_A = 2 \times 10^{-4}$ mm Hg and $p_B = 1.15 \times 10^{-11}$ mm Hg. The single underlined numbers represent the path of minimum free energy and the double underlined value is the saddle point, n_A^* and n_B^*. (Due to the extrapolation to 218 K and the linear interpolation there is an uncertainty in $p_{A_{sol}}^0$ and $p_{B_{sol}}^0$ that is reflected by the values of ΔG in a particular column not having a single minimum. This effect is spurious.)

For systems of interest to us one species will generally be in much higher concentration, for example, $N_A \gg N_B$, where N_A and N_B are the vapor phase concentrations. The number concentration of clusters at the critical point is $(N_A + N_B)\exp(-\Delta G^*/kT)$, which can be approximated by $N_A \exp(-\Delta G^*/kT)$. The rate at which new molecules are incorporated into the critical sized cluster is controlled by the rate of arrival of B molecules. The rate at which molecules of B are incorporated into the critical sized cluster is

$$\left(4\pi R_p^{*2}\right)\frac{p_B}{\left(2\pi m_B kT\right)^{1/2}}$$

and the nucleation rate is then expressed simply as this rate multiplied by the equilibrium critical cluster concentration,

$$J = 4\pi R_p^{*2}\frac{N_B kT}{\left(2\pi m_B kT\right)^{1/2}}N_A \exp(-\Delta G^*/kT) \tag{9.57}$$

Note that in its simplest form the nucleation rate expression does not involve a Zeldovich non-equilibrium correction factor as in the case of homogeneous–homomolecular nucleation.

In general when $N_A \gg N_B$, particle growth is determined by the rate of impingement of B molecules. After one B molecule strikes a cluster, many A molecules impinge and evaporate to achieve an equilibrium until another B molecule arrives and the process is repeated all over again.

Heteromolecular nucleation was first investigated by Flood (1934). Reiss (1950) provided a detailed account of the contributions to ΔG from which he was able to show that the size and composition of the critical cluster actually corresponds to a saddle point on the $\Delta G(n_A, n_B)$ surface. The nucleation rate is then physically equivalent to the total flux of clusters migrating across the boundary corresponding to the critical size, that is, the total current of clusters going through the "pass" at the saddle point in the $\Delta G(n_A, n_B)$ surface. Doyle (1961) was the first to apply Reiss's theory of binary homogeneous nucleation to mixtures of H_2O and H_2SO_4 vapors. At 298 K and 50 percent relative humidity, Doyle found that rapid nucleation would take place if the partial pressure of H_2SO_4 exceeded about 10^{-9} Torr. This extremely low partial pressure of H_2SO_4 corresponds to roughly 10^{-6} ppm, and the prediction that such minute amounts of H_2SO_4 may trigger nucleation in an atmosphere that has only a 50 percent relative humidity suggests an important air pollution impact, since we know H_2SO_4 is a product of the gas-phase oxidation of SO_2. Consequently, we will focus shortly on the $H_2O-H_2SO_4$ system in our application of binary homogeneous nucleation theory.

Shugard et al. (1974) and Wilemski (1975) recognized that Reiss's (1950) binary homogeneous nucleation rate expression, Eq. (9.57), does not produce the proper limiting behavior to the homomolecular nucleation rate if the mole fraction of one of the constituent vapors of the binary mixture approaches zero. Stauffer (1976) proposed a correct treatment that rectified the improper limit behavior in the earlier formula. He pointed out that the assumption that the nucleation current is always parallel to the bottom of the valley in the ΔG surface at the saddle point is incorrect. Stauffer showed that the nucleation current is parallel to the valley floor only when the impingement rates of A and B are identical, and obtained a generalized steady state binary nucleation rate expression that is valid in the limit when either species is present only in minute amounts.

9.5.   BINARY NUCLEATION IN THE $H_2O-H_2SO_4$ SYSTEM

The importance of sulfuric acid in aerosol formation in a humid atmosphere has been emphasized in a number of studies (Kiang et al., 1973; Mirabel and Katz, 1974; Shugard et al., 1974; Reiss et al., 1976). In addition, it is generally accepted that the stratospheric aerosol consists primarily of $H_2O-H_2SO_4$ solution droplets (Hamill et al., 1977). Thus, we consider this system not only as an application of binary homogeneous nucleation theory but also because of its atmospheric relevance.

9.5.1.   Properties of Sulfuric Acid Solution Droplets

The generalized Kelvin equations Eq. (9.55) and (9.56) give the saddle point values of particle size and water and sulfuric acid mole fractions, from which all other properties of interest, such as solution density and surface tension, may be calculated (Yue, 1979). The variation of the vapor pressure of H_2SO_4 in a mixture with water over a flat surface as a function of composition at ambient temperatures is shown in Figure 9.9. Figure 9.10 shows the equilibrium concentration of H_2SO_4 in a spherical droplet of $H_2O-H_2SO_4$ as a function of the relative humidity and the particle diameter. We see that the H_2SO_4 mole fraction in the droplet is highly dependent on the particle size and the relative humidity. Also notice that for a fixed droplet size, the water concentration increases as the relative humidity increases. Thus, Figure 9.11 shows that due to the additional water molecules, the particle size increases for a fixed number of H_2SO_4 molecules in the particle, as the relative humidity increases.

In Figure 9.12, sulfuric acid aqueous solution properties are shown as a function of the mass fraction of H_2SO_4. Included in Figure 9.12 are the

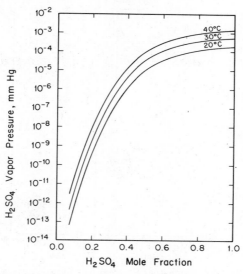

Figure 9.9. Equilibrium vapor pressure of H$_2$SO$_4$ in a mixture with water over a flat surface as a function of composition and temperature (Gelbard, 1978).

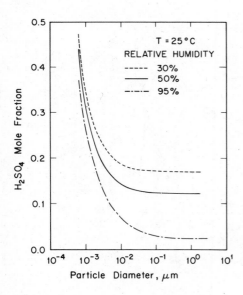

Figure 9.10. Equilibrium concentration of H$_2$SO$_4$ in a spherical droplet of H$_2$SO$_4$ and H$_2$O, as a function of the relative humidity and particle diameter (Gelbard, 1978).

equilibrium relative humidity over a flat solution surface, the solution density ρ, the boiling point, and the surface tension. In addition, the solution normality, the mass concentration $x\rho$, the particle growth factor D_p/D_{p0}, the ratio of the actual diameter of the droplet to that if the water associated with it were completely removed, and the Kelvin effect parameter $D_{p0} \ln p/p^0$ are shown in Figure 9.12.

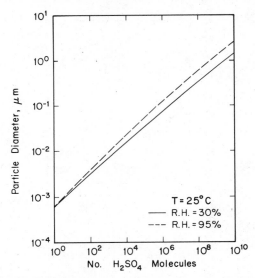

Figure 9.11. Equilibrium particle size as a function of the relative humidity and the number of H_2SO_4 molecules in an aqueous sulfuric acid droplet (Gelbard, 1978).

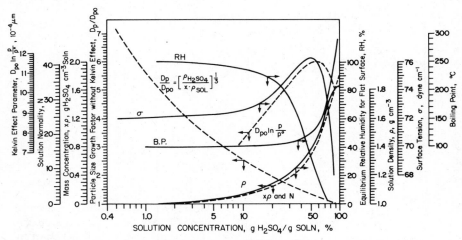

Figure 9.12. Properties of sulfuric acid droplets (Liu and Levi, 1980).

To illustrate how to use Figure 9.12, Liu and Levi (1980) present the following illustration. Consider a 1 μm diameter solution droplet in equilibrium at 50 percent relative humidity. Using the curve labelled RH we find that the solution concentration, x, is 0.425 g H_2SO_4 per g of solution. At this concentration the solution has a density, ρ, of 1.32 g cm^{-3}, a boiling point of 115°C, a surface tension, σ, of 76 dyne cm^{-1}, a normality of 11N, and a mass

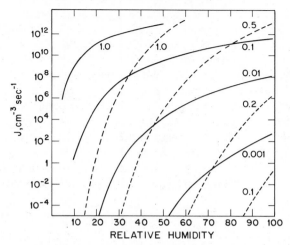

Figure 9.13. Calculated heteromolecular nucleation rates for binary mixtures of H_2SO_4–H_2O (solid lines) and HNO_3–H_2O (dashed lines) as a function of relative humidity and various activities ranging from 0.001 to 1.0 (Kiang et al., 1973).

concentration, $x\rho$, of 0.55 g H_2SO_4 cm^{-3} of solution. The particle size growth factor, D_p/D_{p0}, is 1.48, and the Kelvin effect parameter, $D_{p0}\ln(p/p^0)$, is 11.3×10^{-4} μm. Thus, the H_2O–H_2SO_4 solution droplet would become a droplet of pure H_2SO_4 of $1/1.48 = 0.68$ μm if all the water were removed. Say the ambient relative humidity is increased to 90 percent. The particle size growth factor at this humidity is 2.12. Thus, the 1 μm diameter drop at 50 percent R.H. will grow to become a drop of $(2.12/1.48)(1) = 1.43$ μm diameter at 90 percent R.H. Finally, a Kelvin effect parameter of 11.3×10^{-4} μm indicates that $\ln(p/p^0) = 11.3 \times 10^{-4}/0.68 = 16.62 \times 10^{-4}$. Thus, $p/p^0 = 1.00166$, and in this case the Kelvin effect is negligible; the increase in water vapor pressure due to the droplet curvature is only 0.166 percent above that for a flat surface.

9.5.2. Nucleation of H_2O–H_2SO_4 Droplets

Figure 9.13 shows nucleation rates for H_2SO_4–H_2O and HNO_3–H_2O solution droplets as a function of relative humidity and various activities a, defined as the ratio of the partial pressure of the vapor to its equilibrium vapor pressure over the pure liquid. Roughly a nine orders of magnitude higher concentration of HNO_3 is required to produce the same nucleation rate as with H_2SO_4. Figure 9.13 illustrates the point made at the beginning of Section 9.4 that heteromolecular nucleation can occur when either species is subsaturated with respect to its pure component vapor pressure. Whereas homogeneous homomolecular nucleation does not occur unless $S > 1$, we see that even at H_2SO_4 activities as low as 0.001 appreciable nucleation can be achieved.

As SO_2 is oxidized to H_2SO_4, the H_2SO_4 formed may undergo heteromolecular nucleation with H_2O to form new H_2SO_4/H_2O particles or may, in the presence of foreign particles, deposit onto the pre-existing particles. To estimate which of these two competitive processes is dominant under a particular set of conditions, Middleton and Kiang (1978) have compared the characteristic times required for nucleation of H_2SO_4/H_2O aerosols and for condensation of H_2SO_4 vapor molecules on foreign particles. Call these two times τ_N and τ_P. If R_g represents the rate of production of H_2SO_4 by gas-phase oxidation of SO_2, and A_p is the total surface area of pre-existing particles, then a balance on the number concentration of H_2SO_4 molecules can be written as

$$\frac{dN_{H_2SO_4}}{dt} = R_g - \beta' A_p N_{H_2SO_4} \tag{9.58}$$

where $\beta' N_{H_2SO_4}$ is the rate of impingement of H_2SO_4 molecules per unit area and $\beta' = (kT/2\pi m_1)^{1/2}$. From Eq. (9.58), we find that the characteristic time for removal of H_2SO_4 molecules by condensation on existing particles is

$$\tau_P = \frac{1}{\beta' A_p} = \left(\frac{2\pi m_{H_2SO_4}}{kT} \right)^{1/2} \frac{1}{A_p} \tag{9.59}$$

The characteristic time τ_N to achieve a certain nucleation rate is calculated as follows. We assume that the production rate R_g of H_2SO_4 vapor is constant. At $t = 0$, $N_{H_2SO_4} = 0$ and the nucleation rate is zero. $N_{H_2SO_4}$ increases linearly with time due to R_g until, after a build-up time τ_N, the concentration of H_2SO_4 vapor reaches the point at which appreciable nucleation takes place. At this point, $N_{H_2SO_4}$ decreases due to the resulting gas-to-particle conversion. The heteromolecular nucleation rate J is in general a function of both a and relative humidity RH. Define τ_N as $N_{H_2SO_4}/R_g$, where $N_{H_2SO_4}$ is evaluated at its maximum. The number concentration of H_2SO_4 can be related to its activity at a particular temperature. At $T = 298$ K, for example, the vapor pressure of H_2SO_4 is 10^{-6} torr and $N_{H_2SO_4} = a10^{10.5}$. Now, the nucleation rate J can be determined by a pseudo-steady state approximation on sulfuric acid vapor. Stauffer et al. (1973) show the details of the calculation. We note only that to evaluate τ_N at a particular relative humidity it is necessary to estimate J as a function of R_g and activity a that is consistent with the value of $N_{H_2SO_4}$.

Figure 9.14 shows the two characteristic times as a function of relative humidity for the two H_2SO_4 production rates of $10^{4.8}$ and $10^{7.3}$ cm^{-3} sec^{-1}, corresponding to 0.1 ppm SO_2 converted to H_2SO_4 at rates of 0.1 and 3 percent hr^{-1}, respectively, and aerosol surface areas of 10^2 and 10^3 μm^2 cm^{-3}, corresponding to rural and urban conditions, respectively. We see that at the lower SO_2 conversion rate, the characteristic time for nucleation to occur greatly exceeds that for condensation so the latter can be expected to pre-

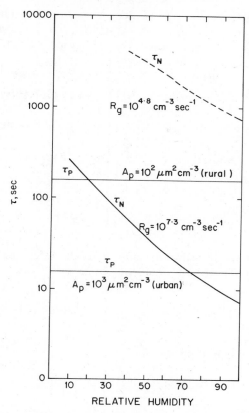

Figure 9.14. Estimates for the characteristic time required for the condensation of sulfuric acid vapor on preexisting particles (τ_P) and the characteristic time required for nucleation of $H_2SO_4-H_2O$ aerosols (τ_N) as a function of relative humidity. Two H_2SO_4 production rates $R_g = 10^{4.8}$ and $10^{7.3}$ cm^3 sec^{-1} are considered, and two total particle surfaces areas, $A_p = 10^2$ μm^2 cm^{-3}, representing rural levels, and $A_p = 10^3$ μm^2 cm^{-3}, representing urban levels, are considered (Middleton and Kiang, 1978).

dominate as the mechanism for gas-to-particle conversion. At the higher production rate at high humidities, the nucleation time can actually become shorter than the condensation time, indicating that heteromolecular nucleation can be expected to become important under these conditions.

9.6. NUCLEATION FROM CHEMICAL REACTION

Particle formation can occur when two volatile and noncondensable vapor species react to form a product with an exceptionally low vapor pressure. Notable examples of atmospheric importance are the reactions of NH_3 and

HCl to produce NH_4Cl. The rate of nucleation of the product, say NH_4Cl, depends on the concentrations of the reactants. To develop the nucleation theory in this case let us consider the NH_3–HCl system. The NH_3–HCl system can be represented as an equilibrium as

$$NH_3(g) + HCl(g) \rightleftarrows NH_4Cl(g) \rightleftarrows NH_4Cl(s)$$

At equilibrium the following relationship exists among the chemical potentials,

$$\mu_{NH_3(g)} + \mu_{HCl(g)} = \mu_{NH_4Cl(g)} = \mu_{NH_4Cl(s)} \tag{9.60}$$

The chemical potential of an ideal gas is

$$\mu_i = \mu_i^0 + RT \ln(p_i/p_0) \tag{9.61}$$

where p_i is the partial pressure of i and p_0 is the reference pressure, 1 atm. Substituting Eq. (9.61) into Eq. (9.60) we obtain

$$\mu_{NH_3}^0(T) + \mu_{HCl}^0(T) - \mu_{NH_4Cl(g)}^0(T) = -RT \ln \frac{p_{NH_3} p_{HCl}}{p_0 p_{NH_4Cl(g)}} \tag{9.62}$$

If we consider the equilibrium

$$NH_3(g) + HCl(g) \rightleftarrows NH_4Cl(s)$$

we have

$$\mu_{NH_4Cl(s)} = \mu_{NH_3}^0(T) + \mu_{HCl}^0(T) + RT \ln K_p \tag{9.63}$$

where $K_p = p_{NH_3} p_{HCl}/p_0^2$. For a solid the chemical potential at any pressure is approximately equal to that at 1 atm since $(\partial \mu_i/\partial p)_T = v_i$, where v_i is the molar volume of the solid. Thus for NH_4Cl, $\mu_{NH_4Cl(s)} = \mu_{NH_4Cl(s)}^0(T)$, and Eq. (9.63) becomes

$$\mu_{NH_4Cl(s)}^0(T) - \mu_{NH_3}^0(T) - \mu_{HCl}^0(T) = RT \ln K_p \tag{9.64}$$

To develop a formula to predict K_p as a function of T, we differentiate Eq. (9.64) with respect to T,

$$\frac{d \ln K_p}{dT} = \frac{1}{R} \frac{d}{dT} \left[\frac{\mu_{NH_4Cl(s)}^0(T) - \mu_{NH_3}^0(T) - \mu_{HCl}^0(T)}{T} \right] \tag{9.65}$$

Since for an ideal gas mixture

$$\frac{d}{dT}\left(\frac{\mu_i^0(T)}{T}\right) = -\frac{h_i}{T^2} \tag{9.66}$$

where h_i is the enthalpy of pure i at temperature T, Eq. (9.65) becomes

$$\frac{d \ln K_p}{dT} = \frac{-h_{NH_4Cl(s)} + h_{NH_3} + h_{HCl}}{RT^2}$$

$$= \frac{\Delta H_0}{RT^2} + \frac{1}{RT^2}\int_{298}^{T}\left(C_{p_{NH_3}} + C_{p_{HCl}} - C_{p_{NH_4Cl}}\right)dT' \tag{9.67}$$

where $\Delta H_0 =$ the heat of reaction at 298 K. Integrating Eq. (9.67) leads to

$$\ln K_p = C - \frac{\Delta H_0}{RT} + \int_{298}^{T}\frac{1}{RT''^2}\int_{298}^{T''}\left(C_{p_{NH_3}} + C_{p_{HCl}} - C_{p_{NH_4Cl}}\right)dT'\,dT''$$

$$\tag{9.68}$$

Let us now derive an applicable Kelvin equation for this system. If the mechanism for nucleation is assumed to be

$$NH_4Cl(g) \rightleftarrows NH_4Cl(s)$$

then the Gibbs free energy change for the nucleation step is

$$\Delta G = \left(\mu_{NH_4Cl(s)} - \mu_{NH_4Cl(g)}\right)n_{NH_4Cl} + 4\pi R_p^2\sigma \tag{9.69}$$

where n_{NH_4Cl} is the number of moles of NH_4Cl that transfer from the vapor to the solid phase. Minimizing ΔG with respect to n_{NH_4Cl},

$$\frac{d\,\Delta G}{dn_{NH_4Cl}} = 0 = \mu_{NH_4Cl(s)} - \mu_{NH_4Cl(g)} + 8\pi R_p\sigma\frac{dR_p}{dn_{NH_4Cl}} \tag{9.70}$$

Since $\frac{4}{3}\pi R_p^3\rho = n_{NH_4Cl}M_{NH_4Cl}$,

$$R_p = \left[\frac{3n_{NH_4Cl}M_{NH_4Cl}}{4\pi\rho}\right]^{1/3} \tag{9.71}$$

Eq. (9.70) becomes

$$\mu_{NH_4Cl(g)} - \mu_{NH_4Cl(s)} = \frac{2M_{NH_4Cl}\sigma}{R_p\rho} \tag{9.72}$$

Now using $\mu_{NH_4Cl(g)} = \mu_{NH_3} + \mu_{HCl}$ and $\mu_{NH_4Cl(s)} = \mu^0_{NH_4Cl}$, together with Eq. (9.61), Eq (9.72) becomes

$$\mu^0_{NH_4Cl(s)}(T) - \mu^0_{NH_3}(T) - \mu^0_{HCl}(T) - RT \ln \frac{p_{NH_3} p_{HCl}}{p_0^2} = -\frac{2 M_{NH_4Cl}\sigma}{R_p \rho}$$

(9.73)

Using Eq. (9.64), Eq. (9.73) becomes

$$\ln \frac{p_{NH_3} p_{HCl}}{p_0^2 K_p} = \frac{2 M_{NH_4Cl}\sigma}{RT\rho R_p}$$

(9.74)

We find that the Kelvin equation for the critical cluster size depends on the ratio of the product of the partial pressures of NH_3 and HCl to the equilibrium constant K_p. The product $p_{NH_3} p_{HCl}$ must exceed K_p for a critical cluster to exist. Physically this condition merely means that the product of the gas phase partial pressures must exceed the equilibrium partial pressure product at that temperature for a solid phase to exist. It is equivalent to the condition that $S > 1$ for a critical cluster to exist for homogeneous–homomolecular nucleation.

Let us compute the critical cluster size and the number of NH_4Cl molecules in a specific case. Countess and Heicklen (1973) studied the growth of NH_4Cl particles from the reaction of NH_3 and HCl in a flow reactor. The experimental procedure involved mixing 60 ppm of NH_3 and 60 ppm of HCl in 1 atm of nitrogen at 293 K. The critical cluster size can be computed from Eq. (9.74). First, we need to know K_p at 293 K. We may use

$$\ln K_p = 34.266 - \frac{21,196}{T}$$

(9.75)

Parameters needed for the NH_4Cl system are $\sigma = 150$ dynes cm^{-1}, $\rho = 1.527$ g cm^{-3}, and $M_{NH_4Cl} = 53.49$ g $mole^{-1}$. Using Eq. (9.74) we obtain the radius of the critical cluster of NH_4Cl as 2.316×10^{-8} cm. Since the molecular volume of NH_4Cl is $53.49/(1.527)(6.023 \times 10^{23}) = 5.816 \times 10^{-23}$ cm³, and the volume of the critical cluster is 5.208×10^{-23} cm³, we find that 0.895, or approximately one, molecule comprises the critical cluster at the conditions of the experiment. The reason for the very small predicted size of the critical cluster is that the concentrations of 60 ppm each of NH_3 and HCl so exceed the equilibrium constant K_p at 293 K that the effective saturation ratio is $(3.6 \times 10^3/2.911 \times 10^{-5}) = 1.24 \times 10^8$. At such a large value, the critical cluster size is predicted to be a single molecule.

9.7. AMMONIA IN THE ATMOSPHERE

The principal role played by ammonia (NH_3) gas in the urban atmosphere is in neutralizing acidic substances such as sulfuric acid (H_2SO_4) and nitric acid (HNO_3) which are products of the gas-phase oxidations of SO_2 and NO_x, respectively. Ammonia is not known to participate in the gas-phase reactions of photochemical smog nor, at the levels typical of the urban atmosphere, has it been cited as leading to effects on human health. In spite of the role of NH_3 solely as a neutralizer of acidic species, its chemistry in the atmosphere is somewhat complex. The complexity arises because the products formed upon reaction of NH_3, two of the most important of which being ammonium sulfate ($(NH_4)_2SO_4$, and ammonium nitrate, NH_4NO_3, exist in the atmosphere in condensed or particulate form, and whether these two substances will exist at all depends on the quantities of NH_3 and the acid precursor present. Thus, a study of the chemistry of NH_3 in the urban atmosphere often reduces to an analysis of the chemistry of the system of NH_3, H_2SO_4, HNO_3, and water. The key question to be answered about this chemistry is: Given certain concentrations of NH_3, H_2SO_4, and water (i.e., relative humidity), what are the chemical forms of the products that result and will they exist in the gaseous or aerosol phases?

On the basis of a reasonable quantity of ambient data and extensive thermodynamic predictions, the hypothesis that equilibrium generally exists between gaseous and aerosol phases appears to be largely substantiated (Stelson et al., 1979; Stelson and Seinfeld, 1982a; Tanner 1983; Hildemann et al., 1984). It may be anticipated that the ambient gas-aerosol system will be at equilibrium if the rates of change of the concentrations of gaseous species such as HNO_3, H_2SO_4, NH_3, and H_2O are slow compared with the characteristic times for diffusion of these species to the particles and for equilibrium within the particle. In most ambient situations it is expected that the assumptions required for equilibrium to hold are valid since the characteristic time for mass transfer to and from an aerosol particle is of the order of a fraction of a second (see Chapter 6).

Because of the frequent predominance of sulfate, nitrate, ammonium, and water by total aerosol mass, ambient atmospheric aerosol can often be characterized as consisting of a concentrated aqueous solution of ammonium nitrate, ammonium bisulfate, and sulfate, nitric, and sulfuric acids and two mixed salts of ammonium sulfate and nitrate. (Which of these species predominates depends on ambient conditions.) To predict the quantity and composition of such an aerosol, a prediction of the rate of formation of nitric acid and sulfuric acid from SO_2 and NO_x precursors must be coupled to an equilibrium description of the aerosol. Knowledge of temperature, relative humidity and gaseous ammonia concentration is assumed in such a calculation.

9.7.1. Qualitative Observations on the
Ammonium / Sulfate / Nitrate   System

The system of interest consists of the following possible components: liquid phase: NH_4^+, H^+, HSO_4^-, SO_4^{2-}, NO_3^-, H_2O; solid phase: NH_4HSO_4, $(NH_4)_2SO_4$, NH_4NO_3, $(NH_4)_2SO_4 \cdot 2NH_4NO_3$, $(NH_4)_2SO_4 \cdot 3NH_4NO_3$, $(NH_4)_3(SO_4)_2$; gas phase: NH_3, HNO_3, H_2SO_4, H_2O.

Two observations are useful in determining a priori the composition of the aerosol that exists in such a system: (i) sulfuric acid possesses an extremely low vapor pressure and (ii) $(NH_4)_2SO_4$(s or aq) is the preferred form of sulfate. The second observation means that, if possible, each mole of sulfate will remove two moles of ammonia from the gas phase, and the first observation implies that the amount of sulfuric acid in the gas phase will be negligible. Based on these observations we can delineate two regimes of interest. If we let $[NH_3]$, $[SO_4^{2-}]$, and $[NO_3^-]$ denote the total (gas + aqueous + solid) concentrations of ammonia, sulfate, and nitrate, respectively, then the two cases are:

> **I.** $[NH_3] < 2[SO_4^{2-}]$
> **II.** $[NH_3] > 2[SO_4^{2-}]$

Case I. $[NH_3] < 2[SO_4^{2-}]$. In this case there is insufficient NH_3 to neutralize the sulfate. Thus the liquid phase will be acidic. The vapor pressures of both NH_3 and H_2SO_4 will be low, and the sulfate will tend to drive the nitrate from the liquid phase. Since the NH_3 partial pressure will be low, ammonium nitrate levels will be low.

Case II. $[NH_3] > 2[SO_4^{2-}]$. In this case there is excess NH_3, so that the liquid phase can be assumed to be fully neutralized. As a result, species containing H^+ and HSO_4^-, since the latter is proportional to that of H^+, will be in negligible concentrations.

From the above discussion we can summarize our qualitative understanding of the ammonium/sulfate/nitrate system as follows. Available NH_3 will be first taken up by available H_2SO_4. Any NH_3 remaining is then available to react with HNO_3 to produce ammonium nitrate.

9.7.2. The Ammonium Nitrate System—Theoretical Predictions

Ammonium nitrate is a secondary pollutant formed from reaction between NH_3 and HNO_3 vapor. From thermodynamic considerations Stelson et al. (1979) and Stelson and Seinfeld (1982a, b) have shown that atmospheric NH_4NO_3 should be in equilibrium with precursor HNO_3 and NH_3 concentrations. The validity of this assumption has been tested in field experiments by Doyle et al. (1979) and Hildemann et al. (1984), where it was found that the

NH_4NO_3 equilibrium constant derived from published thermochemical data is generally consistent with atmospheric observations.

Equilibrium concentrations of gaseous NH_3 and HNO_3, and the resulting concentration of solid or aqueous NH_4NO_3, can be calculated from fundamental thermodynamic principles using the method presented by Stelson and Seinfeld (1982a). The procedure is composed of several steps, requiring as input the ambient temperature and relative humidity (RH). First, the equilibrium state of NH_4NO_3 is defined. If the ambient relative humidity is less than the relative humidity of deliquescence (RHD), given by

$$\ln(\text{RHD}) = \frac{723.7}{T} + 1.7037,$$

then the equilibrium state of NH_4NO_3 is modeled as a solid. Supersaturated solutions also are possible. Formation of solid NH_4NO_3, from the gas phase precursors, is described by the equilibrium

$$NH_3(g) + HNO_3(g) \rightleftarrows NH_4NO_3(s)$$

The dissociation constant is given by $K_p = p_{NH_3} p_{HNO_3}$, where p_{NH_3} and p_{HNO_3} are the partial pressures of NH_3 and HNO_3, respectively. K_p can be estimated by integrating the van't Hoff equation. The resulting equation for K_p, in units of ppb^2 (assuming 1 atm of total pressure) is

$$\ln K_p = 84.6 - \frac{24220}{T} - 6.1 \ln\left(\frac{T}{298}\right). \tag{9.76}$$

At relative humidities above that of deliquescence, NH_4NO_3 will be found in the aqueous state. A dissociation constant for the comparable reaction involving aqueous NH_4NO_3 can be found and is a function of both temperature and relative humidity. Temperature dependent equilibrium relative humidities above ionic solutions can be calculated from Eq. (9.19),

$$\text{RH} = 100 \exp\left[\frac{-\nu m M_w \Phi_T}{1000}\right] \tag{9.77}$$

where ν is the number of moles of ions formed by ionization of one mole of solute, M_w the molecular weight of water, m the molality of the solution, and Φ_T is the osmotic coefficient given by (Robinson and Stokes, 1965)

$$\Phi_T = 1 + \frac{1}{m} \int_0^m m \, d(\ln \gamma_\pm) \tag{9.78}$$

where $\gamma_\pm$ is the mean molal activity of NH_4NO_3 in the solution at temperature T. The activity coefficient depends on temperature and molality.

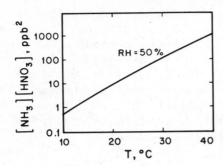

Figure 9.15. NH_4NO_3 equilibrium dissociation constant as a function of temperature. RH = 50%.

Stelson and Seinfeld (1981) have shown that solution concentrations of 8–26 M can be expected in wetted aerosol particles. At such concentrations the solutions are strongly nonideal, and appropriate thermodynamic activity coefficient correlations have only recently been developed. In particular, Tang (1980), Stelson and Seinfeld (1982a, b, c) and Stelson et al. (1984) have developed activity coefficient expressions for aqueous systems of nitrate, sulfate, ammonium and nitric and sulfuric acids at concentrations exceeding 1 M.

An iterative scheme is used to match the relative humidity calculated from (9.77) to the ambient relative humidity. This calculation gives the equilibrium solution molality and activity that are needed to evaluate K_p, the equilibrium dissociation constant, from the expression

$$\ln\left(K_p/(\gamma_\pm m)^2\right) = 54.18 - \frac{15860}{T} + 11.206\ln\left(\frac{T}{298}\right). \qquad (9.79)$$

If the ambient relative humidity is between that of deliquescence and the value given by (9.77) for a saturated solution at $m = 25.954$, linear interpolation is used between the corresponding dissociation constants. For typical atmospheric conditions, the equilibrium dissociation constant varies from about 0.8 ppb^2 at 283 K to about 10^3 ppb^2 at 313 K at 50 percent relative humidity (Figure 9.15).

First, the equilibrium dissociation constant K_p, for pure ammonium nitrate is calculated from the ambient temperature and relative humidity (Stelson and Seinfeld, 1982a). Then the total nitrate, [TN], and total ammonia, [TA], available to form ammonium nitrate is calculated as

$$[TN] = \left[HNO_3(g)\right]_m + \left[NO_3^-\right]_m \qquad (9.80)$$

$$[TA] = \left[NH_3(g)\right]_m + \left[NH_4^+\right]_m, \qquad (9.81)$$

where $[HNO_3(g)]_m$ is the measured gaseous nitric acid concentration, $[NH_3(g)]_m$ is the measured gaseous ammonia concentration, and $[NO_3^-]_m$ and $[NH_4^+]_m$ are the measured aerosol nitrate and ammonium concentrations, respectively, available or free to form NH_4NO_3. Then the equilibrium constraint

$$[NH_3(g)][HNO_3(g)] \leqq K_p$$

is imposed. If $[TN][TA] \leq K_p$, no ammonium nitrate is predicted to be present because there is not enough total nitrate and total ammonia to support aerosol NH_4NO_3 formation. If $[TN][TA] > K_p$ then aerosol ammonium nitrate is predicted to form from the gas-phase precursors such that the product $[NH_3(g)]_c[HNO_3(g)]_c = K_p$. The subscript c indicates a theoretically computed pollutant concentration that may differ from measured values. Conservation of TA and TN gives the final expression for the ammonium nitrate formed as

$$[NH_4NO_3]_c = \tfrac{1}{2}\Big\{[TA] + [TN]$$

$$- \big[([TA] + [TN])^2 - 4([TA][TN] - K_p)\big]^{1/2}\Big\} \quad (9.82)$$

and the gas-phase concentrations

$$[NH_3(g)]_c = [TA] - [NH_4NO_3]_c \quad (9.83)$$

and

$$[HNO_3(g)]_c = [TN] - [NH_4NO_3]_c. \quad (9.84)$$

Thus the inputs to the calculation are TA, TN, T, and RH, and the outputs are the calculated aerosol and gas-phase concentrations, and the dissociation constant, K_p. K_p and the calculated concentrations are very sensitive to T, and also to RH if the RH is high (Fig. 9.16).

Addition of ammonium sulfate to solutions containing aqueous ammonium nitrate would lower the vapor-pressure product $[NH_3][HNO_3]$ in equilibrium with the aerosol phase (Fig. 9.16). In Fig. 9.16, Y is the ionic-strength fraction of ammonium nitrate and is calculated as

$$Y = \frac{[NH_4NO_3]}{[NH_4NO_3] + 3[(NH_4)_2SO_4]} \quad (9.85)$$

Note that the concentration product of nitric acid and ammonia in equilibrium with a mixed sulfate/nitrate solution having a value of $Y = 0.5$ is about half as high as that in equilibrium with a pure ammonium nitrate solution. The temperature dependence of the partial-pressure product for the aqueous mixed salt case should be similar to that of the pure salt.

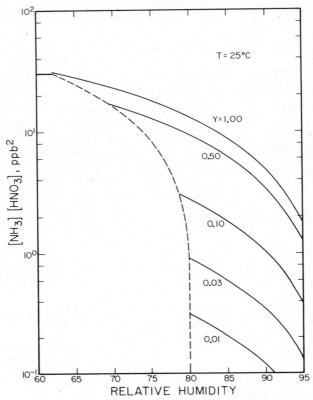

Figure 9.16. NH_4NO_3 equilibrium dissociation constant for an ammonium/sulfate/nitrate solution as a function of relative humidity and ammonium nitrate ionic strength fraction

$$Y = \frac{[NH_4NO_3]}{[NH_4NO_3] + 3[(NH_4)_2SO_4]}$$

at 298 K (Stelson and Seinfeld, 1982c).

REFERENCES

Arnold, S., Murphy, E. K., and Sageev, G. "Aerosol Particle Molecular Spectroscopy," *Appl. Optics*, **24**, 1048–1053 (1985).

Becker, R., and Döring, W. "Kinetische Behandlung der Keimbildung in Übersättigten Dampfen," *Ann. Phys. (Leipzig)*, **24**, 719–752 (1935).

Cohen, E. R. "The Accuracy of the Approximations in Classical Nucleation Theory," *J. Statistical Phys.*, **2**, 147–152 (1970).

Countess, R., and Heicklen, J. "Kinetics of Particle Growth. II. Kinetics of the Reaction of Ammonia with Hydrogen Chloride and the Growth of Particulate Ammonium Chloride," *J. Phys. Chem.*, **77**, 444–447 (1973).

Doyle, G. J. "Self-Nucleation in the Sulfuric Acid-Water System," *J. Chem. Phys.*, **35**, 795–799 (1961).

Doyle, G. J., Tuazon, E. C., Graham, R. A., Mischke, T. M., Winer, A. M. and Pitts, J. N., Jr. "Simultaneous Concentrations of Ammonia and Nitric Acid in a Polluted Atmosphere and Their Equilibrium Relationship to Particulate Ammonium Nitrate," *Environ. Sci. Technol.*, **13**, 1416–1419 (1979).

Flood, H. "Tröpfenbildung in Übersättigten Äthylalkohol-Wasserdampfgemischen," *Z. Phys. Chem.*, **A170**, 286–294 (1934).

Frenkel, J. *Kinetic Theory of Liquids*, Dover, New York (1955).

Gelbard, F. *The General Dynamic Equation for Aerosols*, Ph.D. thesis, California Institute of Technology, Pasadena, CA (1978).

Hamill, P., Kiang, C. S., and Cadle, R. D. "The Nucleation of H_2SO_4–H_2O Solution Aerosol Particles in the Stratosphere," *J. Atmos. Sci.*, **34**, 150–162 (1977).

Hildemann, L. M., Russell, A. G., and Cass, G. R. "Ammonia and Nitric Acid Concentrations in Equilibrium with Atmospheric Aerosols: Experiment vs Theory," *Atmos. Environ.*, **18**, 1737–1750 (1984).

Katz, J. L., and Donohue, M. D. "A Kinetic Approach to Homogeneous Nucleation Theory," in *Advances in Chemical Physics*, Vol. 40, Wiley, New York, 137–155 (1979).

Kiang, C. S., Stauffer, D., Mohnen, V. A., Bricard, J., and Vigla, D. "Heteromolecular Nucleation Theory Applied to Gas-to-Particle Conversion," *Atmos. Environ.*, **7**, 1279–1283 (1973).

Liu, B. Y. H., and Levi, J. "Generation of Submicron Sulfuric Acid Aerosol by Vaporization and Condensation," in *Generation of Aerosols and Facilities for Exposure Experiments*, K. Willeke (Ed.), Ann Arbor Science, Ann Arbor, Michigan, 317–336 (1980).

McDonald, J. E. "Homogeneous Nucleation of Vapor Condensation I. Thermodynamic Aspects," *Am. J. Phys.*, **30**, 870–877 (1962).

McDonald, J. E. "Homogeneous Nucleation of Vapor Condensation II. Kinetic Aspects," *Am. J. Phys.*, **31**, 31–41 (1963).

Middleton, P., and Kiang, C. S. "A Kinetic Aerosol Model for the Formation and Growth of Secondary Sulfuric Acid Particles," *J. Aerosol Sci.*, **9**, 359–385 (1978).

Mirabel, P., and Katz, J. L. "Binary Homogeneous Nucleation as a Mechanism for the Formation of Aerosols," *J. Chem. Phys.*, **60**, 1138–1144 (1974).

Peterson, T. W., and Seinfeld, J. H. "Heterogeneous Condensation and Chemical Reaction in Droplets—Application to the Heterogeneous Atmospheric Oxidation of SO_2," in *Adv. Environ. Sci. Technol.*, **10**, J. N. Pitts, Jr. and R. Metcalf (Eds.), Wiley, New York, 125–180 (1980).

Reiss, H. "The Kinetics of Phase Transition in Binary Systems," *J. Chem. Phys.*, **18**, 840–848 (1950).

Reiss, H., Margolese, D. I., and Schelling, F. J. "Experimental Study of Nucleation in Vapor Mixtures of Sulfuric Acid and Water," *J. Colloid Interface Sci.*, **56**, 511–526 (1976).

Robinson, R. A., and Stokes, R. H., *Electrolyte Solutions*, Butterworth, London (1965).

Shugard, W. J., Heist, R. H., and Reiss, H. "Theory of Vapor Phase Nucleation in Binary Mixtures of Water and Sulfuric Acid," *J. Chem. Phys.*, **61**, 5298–5305 (1974).

Springer, G. S. "Homogeneous Nucleation," in *Advances in Heat Transfer*, Vol. 14, Academic Press, New York, 281–346 (1978).

Stauffer, D. "Kinetic Theory of Two-Component (Heteromolecular) Nucleation and Condensation," *J. Aerosol Sci.*, **7**, 319–333 (1976).

Stauffer, D., Mohnen, V. A., and Kiang, C. S. "Heteromolecular Condensation Theory Applied to Particle Growth," *J. Aerosol Sci.*, **4**, 461–471 (1973).

Stelson, A. W., and Seinfeld, J. H. "Chemical Mass Accounting of Urban Aerosol," *Environ. Sci. Technol.*, **15**, 671–679 (1981).

Stelson, A. W., and Seinfeld, J. H. "Relative Humidity and Temperature Dependence of the Ammonium Nitrate Dissociation Constant," *Atmos. Environ.* **16**, 983–993 (1982a).

Stelson, A. W., and Seinfeld, J. H. "Relative Humidity and pH Dependence of the Vapor Pressure of Ammonium Nitrate-Nitric Acid Solutions at 25°C," *Atmos. Environ.*, **16**, 993–1000 (1982b).

Stelson, A. W., and Seinfeld, J. H. "Thermodynamic Prediction of the Water Activity, NH_4NO_3 Dissociation Constant, Density and Refractive Index for the NH_4NO_3–$(NH_4)_2SO_4$–H_2O System at 25°C," *Atmos. Environ.*, **16**, 2507–2514 (1982c).

Stelson, A. W., Friedlander, S. K., and Seinfeld, J. H. "A Note on the Equilibrium Relationship Between Ammonia and Nitric Acid and Particulate Ammonium Nitrate," *Atmos. Environ.* **13**, 369–371 (1979).

Stelson, A. W., Bassett, M. E., and Seinfeld, J. H. "Thermodynamic Equilibrium Properties of Aqueous Solutions of Nitrate, Sulfate and Ammonium," in *Chemistry of Particles, Fogs and Rain*, J. L. Durham (Ed.), Butterworth, Boston, 1–52 (1984).

Tang, I. N. "On the Equilibrium Partial Pressures of Nitric Acid and Ammonia in the Atmosphere," *Atmos. Environ.* **14**, 819–828 (1980).

Tanner, R. L. "An Ambient Experimental Study of Phase Equilibrium in the Atmos. System: Aerosol H^+, NH_4^+, SO_4^{2-}, NO_3^-–NH_3(g), HNO_3(g)," *Atmos. Environ.* **16**, 2935–2942 (1983).

Volmer, M., and Weber, A. "Keimbildung in Übersättigten Gebilden," *Zeitschrift Phys. Chem.*, **119**, 277–301 (1926).

Wilemski, G. "Binary Nucleation. I. Theory Applied to Water-Ethanol Vapors," *J. Chem. Phys.*, **62**, 3763–3771 (1975).

Yue, G. K. "A Quick Method for Estimating the Equilibrium Size and Composition of Aqueous Sulfuric Acid Droplets," *J. Aerosol Sci.*, **10**, 75–86 (1979).

PROBLEMS

9.1. Construct Köhler curves for NH_4NO_3 at $T = 20°C$ for initial dry nuclei of 0.02 μm, 0.04 μm, and 0.1 μm radius assuming both no dissociation and complete dissociation. Compare your curves to Figures 9.3 and 9.4. Discuss your results.

9.2. Classical homogeneous nucleation theory leads to the nucleation rate expressed by Eq. (9.46) as $J = C^*ZN^e(g^*)$, where Z is the Zeldovich non-equilibrium correction factor. Show that Z may be expressed as

$$Z = \frac{N(g^*)}{N^e(g^*)} - \frac{N(g^*+1)}{N^e(g^*+1)}$$

9.3. For the homogeneous nucleation of water at 20°C at a saturation ratio $S = 3.5$, calculate the sensitivity of the nucleation rate to small changes in saturation ratio and surface tension; that is, find x and y in

$$\frac{\Delta J}{J} = \left(\frac{\Delta S}{S}\right)^x \left(\frac{\Delta \sigma}{\sigma}\right)^y$$

9.4. Consider a 0.01 μm diameter sulfuric acid–water droplet at 50 percent RH. What is the increase in the equilibrium vapor pressure over the curved droplet surface over that for the corresponding flat surface?

9.5. Most hygroscopic aerosols are deliquescent, that is, they do not become wet until a certain relative humidity called the deliquescent point. For example, initially dry ammonium sulfate particles will remain dry as the relative humidity is increased until a humidity of 81 percent, at which they deliquesce to form liquid droplets. (When the RH is reduced from above the deliquescent point, the transition back to a dry particle does not occur at 81 percent but at a lower value, actually between 36 and 40 percent. The existence of wet $(NH_4)_2SO_4$ particles at humidities below 81 percent is a metastable one, and the ultimate crystallization humidity can be found only experimentally.) Describe how the deliquescent point for a particular salt may be calculated theoretically.

9.6. Arnold et al. (1985) have considered the response of an aqueous solution droplet when heated by a short pulse of laser light. When infrared radiation is absorbed by a solution droplet in equilibrium with water vapor, the temperature of the drop increases, leading to an increase in the vapor pressure of water over the droplet's surface and evaporation of some water from the drop. The vapor pressure of water at the surface of the solution drop is the product of the vapor pressure of pure water, p_w^0, and the mole fraction of water in the solution, x_w. When the drop is heated, the vapor pressure increases and some water evaporates, causing a decrease in the size of the drop and a decrease in the mole fraction of water in the drop. As long as the radiation is applied, eventually the product of the elevated vapor pressure and the depressed mole fraction equals the ambient partial pressure of water and a new equilibrium size is reached. Once the radiative heating ceases, the drop returns to its original temperature and size. The object of this problem is to calculate that rate of return. Our analysis will focus on small changes in temperature, mole fraction, and size as might result from a brief pulse from a low power laser.

(a) We saw in Chapter 6 that the characteristic time for establishing a steady state concentration profile around a droplet is of order R_p^2/D_g. Show that the characteristic time for establishing a steady state temperature profile around a droplet is proportional to $\rho C_p R_p^2/k$, where ρ, C_p, and k are the density, heat capacity, and thermal conductivity of air. Show that for a particle of radius 2.5 μm in air at atmospheric pressure and room temperature the characteristic time to establish steady state concentration and temperature profiles is the order of 10^{-7} s. Thus, we conclude that as long as the characteristic times of the heating and cooling problems are long compared with 10^{-7} s, we may assume that the water vapor concentration and temperature profiles around the drop are the steady state profiles,

$$\frac{c(r) - c_\infty}{c_s - c_\infty} = \frac{R_p}{r}$$

$$\frac{T(r) - T_\infty}{T_s - T_\infty} = \frac{R_p}{r}$$

where c_s and c_∞ are the water vapor concentrations just above the drop's surface and in the ambient air, respectively, and T_s and T_∞ are the temperatures of the droplet surface and the ambient. We will assume that the drop is large enough so that continuum transport theory applies.

(b)   We assume that the drop consists of an electrolyte solution which can be characterized by a van't Hoff factor i. Then the vapor pressure of water over the solution p_s is related to the vapor pressure of pure water p_w^0 by $p_s = [1 - i(1 - x_w)] p_w^0$. (Curvature effects will be neglected.) Written in terms of concentrations, $c_s = [1 - i(1 - x_w)] c_w^0$, where c_w^0 is the water vapor concentration above pure water, $c_w^0 = p_w^0 / RT$.

   If the changes in temperature and radius due to heating are small, show that the change in c_s due to changes in both x_w and c_w^0 can be expressed as

$$\delta c_s = i c_w^0 \delta x_w + [1 - i(1 - x_w)]\, \delta c_w^0$$

(c)   Show that the change in c_w^0, $\delta c_w^0 = c_w^0(T_s) - c_w^0(T_\infty)$, resulting from a small change in temperature, $\delta T = T_s - T_\infty$, can be expressed as

$$\delta c_w^0 = c_w^0(T_\infty)\left(\frac{\Delta H_v}{RT_\infty} - 1 \right) \frac{\delta T}{T_\infty}$$

(d)   Show that, if the density of the droplet is constant, the change in mole fraction of water that results from a small change in the radius of the drop, δR_p, is

$$\delta x_w = \frac{3 x_w (1 - x_w)}{f_w} \frac{\delta R_p}{R_p}$$

where f_w is the mass fraction of water in the drop.

   The results of parts (c) and (d) can be combined with that of part (b) to obtain the expression for the perturbation in the water vapor concentration above the drop surface as related to perturbations in the radius and temperature of the drop,

$$\delta c_s = c_w^0(T_\infty) \left\{ \frac{3i x_w (1 - x_w)}{f_w} \frac{\delta R_p}{R_p} \right.$$

$$\left. + [1 - i(1 - x_w)] \left(\frac{\Delta H_v}{RT_\infty} - 1 \right) \frac{\delta T}{T_\infty} \right\}$$

(e) Show that the change of drop radius with time is related to δc_s by

$$\rho_p R_p \frac{dR_p}{dt} = -M_w D_g \delta c_s$$

where D_g is the molecular diffusivity of water vapor in air and M_w is the molecular weight of water.

Since we are interested in small changes in radius, we will now let $R_p(t) = R_{p0} + \varepsilon(t)$. Thus, the differential equation for R_p can be expressed in terms of ε as, where $R_{p0} \gg \varepsilon(t)$,

$$\frac{d\varepsilon}{dt} = -\frac{M_w D_g c_w^0(T_\infty)}{\rho_p R_{p0}} \left\{ \frac{3i x_w (1 - x_w)}{f_w} \frac{\varepsilon}{R_{p0}} \right.$$

$$\left. + [1 - i(1 - x_w)] \left(\frac{\Delta H_v}{RT_\infty} - 1 \right) \frac{\delta T}{T_\infty} \right\}$$

This differential equation describes the response of the perturbation in the radius of the drop caused by a temperature perturbation δT.

(f) To obtain the differential equation for $\varepsilon(t)$ in terms of measurable quantities, we need finally to relate the temperature perturbation δT to the radiative power absorbed by the droplet. The power absorbed by a sphere is given by the product of an absorption efficiency Q_a and the power incident on the drop's cross-sectional area, $\pi R_p^2 I$. If we assume that the power absorbed is dissipated through both thermal conduction to the air and evaporation, show that the temperature change resulting from absorption of the radiation is related to the incident intensity and the change in concentration by

$$\delta T = \frac{1}{k} \left(\frac{Q_a I R_p}{4} - \Delta H_v D_g \delta c_s \right)$$

(g) By combining the results of parts (d), (e), and (f), show that the differential equation for the transient perturbation in the drop radius can be written as

$$\frac{d\varepsilon}{dt} = -\gamma\varepsilon - \alpha I$$

where

$$\gamma = \frac{3D_g c_w^0(T_\infty) i x_w(1 - x_w) M_w}{\rho_p R_{p0}^2 f_w(1 + \Delta H_v Z)} + \frac{Q_a I M_w Z}{4\rho_p R_{p0}(1 + \Delta H_v Z)}$$

$$\alpha = \left(\frac{M_w Z}{1 + \Delta H_v Z}\right)\frac{Q_a}{4\rho_p}$$

$$Z = D_g[1 - i(1 - x_w)]c_w^0(T_\infty)\left(\frac{\Delta H_v}{RT_\infty} - 1\right)\bigg/kT_\infty$$

The characteristic relaxation time of the particle radius resulting from laser heating is thus γ^{-1}. Calculate this relaxation time for a droplet of initial radius 2.5 μm with $x_w = 0.95$, $\rho_p = 1$ g cm^{-3}, in air at standard temperature and pressure. You may neglect the second term in the expression for γ.

9.7. Atmospheric aerosols may grow through gas-to-particle conversion. As a specific example, we consider here the iron-catalyzed oxidation of SO_2 in an aqueous aerosol particle. The problem is conceptually similar to that considered in Section 5.6; only certain details differ. In Chapter 5 we neglected size changes of the droplet associated with aqueous-phase oxidation; here, if we are dealing with an aerosol particle of submicron size, size changes may be important. In addition, when dealing with cloud-sized drops, the solution was sufficiently dilute so that it could be treated as ideal; because the solution associated with a micron-sized particle is relatively concentrated, it is necessary to account for nonideality.

We consider an aerosol particle that has pH = 5 at time zero and is in equilibrium with air containing SO_2 at a concentration of 1 ppm and NH_3 with a concentration of 10 ppb. The initial pH is established with an amount of Mg^{2+}. The particle also contains Fe^{3+}. The initial counter-ion for both Mg^{2+} and Fe^{3+} is SO_4^{2-}. Vapor–liquid equilibrium for SO_2, NH_3, and H_2O is assumed to hold at all times, together with chemical equilibrium in the aqueous phase and with electroneutrality. Because of the high concentrations, the equilibrium expressions used in Chapter 5 must be modified to include activity coefficients. For example, for

$$HSO_3^- \rightleftarrows H^+ + SO_3^{2-}$$

we have

$$K_{s2} = \frac{[\text{H}^+][\text{SO}_3^{2-}]\gamma_{+}\gamma_{2-}}{[\text{HSO}_3^-]\gamma_-}$$

For ionic strength $I < 0.5$, we can use the expression from Section 5.7,

$$\log \gamma_z = -0.5085 z^2 \left(\frac{I^{1/2}}{1 + I^{1/2}} - 0.2I \right)$$

where z is the ionic charge.

The condition for water equilibrium between the gas and aqueous phases for an ideal solution is that the vapor pressure of water over the solution equals its partial pressure in the gas. This condition can be expressed more generally as equality of the water activity in the solution, a_w, and the relative humidity RH as a fraction. Many approaches exist for estimating the water activity in electrolyte solutions (Robinson and Stokes, 1965). We will use one of the simplest formulations here, the ZSR approach, which states that

$$\sum_i \frac{m_i}{m_{bi}(a_w)} = 1$$

where m_i = molality of species i in the multicomponent solution (moles i/kg H_2O) and $m_{bi}(a_w)$ = molality of species i in a binary solution with water at activity a_w. The summation is taken over all species in the solution. The equation is satisfied only for one value of a_w, so that given data or a correlation for m_{bi} as a function of a_w, the value of a_w for which the equation is satisfied can be determined by iteration.

In a binary solution of electrolyte and water, if the molality of the solute is m, the mole fraction of water is given by

$$x_w = \frac{55.51}{\nu m + 55.51}$$

where ν is the order of the electrolyte, equal to $\nu_+ + \nu_-$, where one mole of the electrolyte is assumed to exist in solution as ν_+ moles of cations and ν_- moles of anions. The general relation between the molar concentration of species i, c_i, and its molality, m_i, is

$$m_i = \frac{c_i}{\rho - \Sigma_i M_i c_i}$$

In the case we will consider we will assume that the solution density is influenced only by sulfate and is given by $\rho = 0.9989 + 0.05715 m_{\text{SO}_4}$.

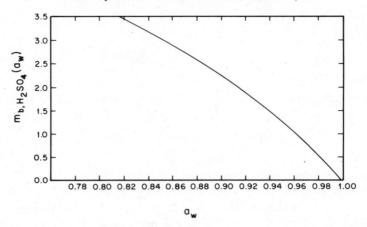

Figure P9.1. Molality of sulfuric acid in a binary solution with water as a function of water activity.

We wish to calculate the change in pH, size, ionic strength, and composition of an aqueous aerosol particle exposed at $t = 0$ to the conditions above. We will consider ambient relative humidities of 95 percent and 99 percent, and $T = 298$ K. The Kelvin effect will be neglected. For the purposes of calculating water activity, we assume that only H_2SO_4 and NH_4OH affect a_w, namely that

$$\frac{m_{H_2SO_4}}{m_{b,H_2SO_4}(a_w)} + \frac{m_{NH_4OH}}{m_{b,NH_4OH}(a_w)} = 1$$

The relation between m_{b,H_2SO_4} and a_w is given in Figure P9.1, and for the binary $NH_4OH–H_2O$ solution it may be assumed that $a_w = x_w^2$ (Peterson and Seinfeld, 1980). The dissolved S(IV) is catalytically oxidized to S(VI) by Fe^{3+} according to the rate expression given in Section 5.4.4,

$$\frac{d\,[S(VI)]}{dt} = 1.2 \times 10^6 [Fe^{3+}][S(IV)]\,\alpha_2$$

Assuming $[Fe^{3+}]_0 = 10^{-2}$ M and 10^{-16} g of S(VI) present at $t = 0$, calculate, over a duration of 60 minutes, the variation in pH, diameter, ionic strength, and concentrations of S(IV), S(VI), $[Fe^{3+}]$, and NH_4^+. Assume RH values of 95 and 99 percent. Recall that the initial pH of the drop is to be 5, a condition used to fix the quantity of Mg^{2+} in the drop.

TEN

Dynamics of Aerosol Populations

Up to this point we have considered the physics and chemistry of atmospheric aerosols from the point of view of the behavior of a single particle. In this chapter we now allow the particles in an aerosol population to interact by specifically treating the changes that occur in the population when particles collide and adhere, that is, when they coagulate. We begin by calculating the rate at which two spherical particles in Brownian motion will collide and then consider coagulation induced by velocity gradients in the fluid and by differential settling velocities of particles. Next we compute the enhancement or retardation to the coagulation rate due to interparticle forces. The remainder of the chapter is devoted to solution of the equations governing the size distribution of an aerosol and examination of the physical regimes of behavior of an aerosol population.

10.1. RATE OF COAGULATION OF TWO PARTICLES BY BROWNIAN MOTION

Aerosol particles suspended in a fluid may come into contact because of their Brownian motion. Assume that a fluid contains a population of equal-sized particles of radius R_p at concentration N_0. Imagine one of the particles to be stationary with its center at the origin of the coordinate system. We wish to calculate the rate at which particles collide with this stationary particle as a result of Brownian motion. We disregard the fact that as particles collide with the test particle the size and shape of the particle will change. This assumption does not lead to appreciable error in the early stages of coagulation. Moreover, since spherical particles come into contact when the distance between their centers is equal to the sum of their radii, from a mathematical point of view the stationary particle can be replaced by an "absorbing" sphere of radius $2R_p$ and the other particles by point masses. Assuming that the distribution of particles around the fixed text particle is described by the continuum diffusion equation, then that distribution satisfies

$$\frac{\partial N}{\partial t} = D\left(\frac{\partial^2 N}{\partial r^2} + \frac{2}{r}\frac{\partial N}{\partial r}\right) \tag{10.1}$$

where D is the Brownian diffusion coefficient for the particles. The initial and boundary conditions for Eq. (10.1) are

$$N(r,0) = N_0 \tag{10.2}$$

$$N(r,t) = N_0 \qquad r \to \infty \tag{10.3}$$

$$N(2R_p,t) = 0 \tag{10.4}$$

The boundary condition at $r = 2R_p$ expresses the assumption that the fixed particle is a perfect absorber, that is, that particles adhere at every collision. Although little is known quantitatively about the sticking coefficient of aerosol particles, their low kinetic energies make bounce-off unlikely. We shall therefore assume here a sticking coefficient of unity.

The solution of Eqs. (10.1) to (10.4) is

$$N(r,t) = N_0\left[1 - \frac{2R_p}{r} + \frac{4R_p}{r\sqrt{\pi}}\int_0^{\frac{r-2R_p}{2\sqrt{Dt}}} e^{-\eta^2}\,d\eta\right]$$

$$= N_0\left[1 - \frac{2R_p}{r}\,\mathrm{erfc}\left(\frac{r-2R_p}{2\sqrt{Dt}}\right)\right] \tag{10.5}$$

and the rate (sec^{-1}) at which particles arrive at the surface $r = 2R_p$ is

$$J = 16\pi R_p^2 D\left(\frac{\partial N}{\partial r}\right)_{r=2R_p} = 8\pi R_p DN_0\left(1 + \frac{2R_p}{\sqrt{\pi Dt}}\right) \tag{10.6}$$

We see that the collision rate is initially rapid, but as $2R_p/(\pi Dt)^{1/2} \ll 1$, the collision rate approaches the steady state value $8\pi R_p DN_0$. Physically, at $t = 0$ other particles may happen to be in the vicinity of the absorbing one, and the first collisions occur very quickly. After the particles nearby have coagulated or diffused away, the rate of coagulation relaxes to its steady state value.

Suppose now that the particle we have assumed to be stationary is also undergoing Brownian motion. Also, let us relax the assumption that the two particles are of equal size. Let the formerly stationary particle have radius R_{p1} and the others in the fluid have radii R_{p2}. To formulate the coagulation process in the framework of the diffusion equation, Eq. (10.1), we first need to find the diffusion coefficient D_{12} that characterizes the diffusion of particles of radius R_{p2} relative to those of radius R_{p1}. As both particles are undergoing

Brownian motion, suppose that in time interval dt they experience displacements $d\mathbf{r}_1$ and $d\mathbf{r}_2$. Then, their mean square relative displacement is

$$\langle |d\mathbf{r}_1 - d\mathbf{r}_2|^2 \rangle = \langle dr_1^2 \rangle + \langle dr_2^2 \rangle - 2\langle d\mathbf{r}_1 \cdot d\mathbf{r}_2 \rangle \qquad (10.7)$$

Since the motions of the two particles are assumed to be independent, $\langle d\mathbf{r}_1 \cdot d\mathbf{r}_2 \rangle = 0$. Thus,

$$\langle |d\mathbf{r}_1 - d\mathbf{r}_2|^2 \rangle = \langle dr_1^2 \rangle + \langle dr_2^2 \rangle \qquad (10.8)$$

Referring back to our discussion of Brownian motion, we can identify the diffusion coefficient D_{12} by Eq. (8.54),

$$\langle |d\mathbf{r}_1 - d\mathbf{r}_2|^2 \rangle = 6D_{12}\, dt \qquad (10.9)$$

On the other hand, the two individual Brownian diffusion coefficients are defined by $\langle dr_1^2 \rangle = 6D_1\, dt$ and $\langle dr_2^2 \rangle = 6D_2\, dt$. Consequently, we find that

$$D_{12} = D_1 + D_2 \qquad (10.10)$$

On the basis of this result we may again regard the particle with radius R_{p1} as stationary and those with radius R_{p2} as diffusing toward it. The diffusion equation, Eq. (10.1), then governs $N_2(r, t)$, the concentration of particles with radius R_{p2}, with the diffusion coefficient D_{12}. The boundary condition at $r = 2R_p$ now applies at $r = R_{p1} + R_{p2}$. The solution is the rather obvious extension of Eq. (10.5),

$$N_2(r, t) = N_{20}\left[1 - \frac{R_{p1} + R_{p2}}{r}\, \mathrm{erfc}\left(\frac{r - (R_{p1} + R_{p2})}{2\sqrt{D_{12}t}} \right) \right] \qquad (10.11)$$

and the rate (sec^{-1}) at which #2 particles arrive at the surface $r = R_{p1} + R_{p2}$ is

$$J = 4\pi (R_{p1} + R_{p2}) D_{12} N_{20}\left(1 + \frac{R_{p1} + R_{p2}}{\sqrt{\pi D_{12}t}} \right) \qquad (10.12)$$

The steady state rate of collision is

$$J = 4\pi (R_{p1} + R_{p2}) D_{12} N_{20} \qquad (10.13)$$

The collision rate we have derived is the rate, expressed as the number of #2 particles per second, that collide with a single #1 particle. When there is more than one #1 particle, the total collision rate between #1 and #2 particles per unit volume of fluid is the above derived collision rate multiplied by the concentration of #1 particles, call it N_{10}. Thus, the steady state coagulation rate (cm^{-3} sec^{-1}) between #1 and #2 particles is

$$J_{12} = 4\pi(R_{p1} + R_{p2})D_{12}N_{10}N_{20} \qquad (10.14)$$

At this point there is no need to retain the subscript 0 on the concentrations of #1 and #2 particles so the rate can be expressed as $J_{12} = K_{12}N_1N_2$, where

$$K_{12} = 4\pi(R_{p1} + R_{p2})(D_1 + D_2) \qquad (10.15)$$

is the Brownian coagulation coefficient for particles of radii R_{p1} and R_{p2}, with D_{12} replaced by $D_1 + D_2$.

Expressed in terms of particle diameter, Eq. (10.15) is

$$K_{12} = 2\pi(D_{p1} + D_{p2})(D_1 + D_2) \qquad (10.16)$$

In the continuum regime the Brownian diffusivities are given by the Stokes–Einstein formula $D_i = kT/3\pi\mu D_{pi}$. Using the Stokes–Einstein expressions for D_1 and D_2, Eq. (10.16) becomes

$$K_{12} = \frac{2kT}{3\mu}(D_{p1} + D_{p2})\left(\frac{1}{D_{p1}} + \frac{1}{D_{p2}}\right) \qquad (10.17)$$

The coagulation coefficient K_{12} can be expressed in terms of particle volume as

$$K_{12} = \frac{2kT}{3\mu}(v_1^{1/3} + v_2^{1/3})\left(\frac{1}{v_1^{1/3}} + \frac{1}{v_2^{1/3}}\right) \qquad (10.18)$$

The above development is based on the assumption that continuum diffusion theory is a valid description of the concentration distribution of particles surrounding a central absorbing particle. As in the case of molecular diffusion of vapor molecules to an absorbing sphere, considered in Section 8.6, we must be cautious in applying continuum diffusion theory for particles right up to the absorbing particle's surface. When the apparent mean free path of the diffusing aerosol particle is comparable with the radius of the absorbing particle, the boundary condition at the absorbing particle surface must be corrected to account for the nature of the diffusion process in the vicinity of the surface. The continuum diffusion equation can be applied to the Brownian motion of particles only for diffusion times that are large compared with the relaxation time τ of the particle or for distances that are large compared with a characteristic mean free path of the particle. The diffusion equation cannot describe the motion of a particle inside a layer of thickness l_D adjacent to an absorbing surface.

In developing a correction to the collision rate to account for the case in which the particle mean free path l_D is appreciable compared to particle radius, we can follow virtually the same approach as we did for vapor molecules in Section 8.7. At the outset we need only identify a particle mean free path l_D; its actual definition will emerge from the analysis that follows.

Suppose as before that particles with radii R_{p2} are diffusing toward a central particle of radius R_{p1}. The concentration $N_2(r, t)$ is presumed to obey the continuum diffusion equation, Eq. (10.1), with initial condition Eq. (10.2) and boundary condition as $r \to \infty$ of Eq. (10.3). To account for a finite particle mean free path we replace the boundary condition Eq. (10.4) at $r = R_p = R_{p1} + R_{p2}$ with

$$N_2(R_p + l_D, t) = D_{12}\left(\frac{\partial N_2}{\partial r}\right)_{r = R_{p1} + R_{p2}} \qquad (10.19)$$

We define the Knudsen number for this process as

$$\mathrm{Kn}_D = \frac{2D_{12}}{\bar{c}_{12} R_p} \qquad (10.20)$$

where $\bar{c}_{12} = (\bar{c}_1^2 + \bar{c}_2^2)^{1/2}$, then Eq. (10.19) can be nondimensionalized as

$$N_2(R_p(1 + \mathrm{Kn}_D), t) = 2R_p \mathrm{Kn}_D\left(\frac{\partial N_2}{\partial r}\right)_{r = R_p} \qquad (10.21)$$

The boundary value problem, Eqs. (10.1) to (10.3) and Eq. (10.19) can be solved by the method of Laplace transforms to give the following steady state coagulation rate (Dahneke, 1983),

$$J = 4\pi(R_{p1} + R_{p2})(D_1 + D_2)\beta N_{20} \qquad (10.22)$$

where the correction factor to the continuum rate is Eq. (8.102)

$$\beta = \frac{1 + \mathrm{Kn}_D}{1 + 2\mathrm{Kn}_D(1 + \mathrm{Kn}_D)} \qquad (10.23)$$

We see that β has the same functional form as in the vapor molecule case, only the definition of the Knudsen number varies in the particle coagulation case.

Let us examine the two asymptotic limits of this coagulation rate. In the continuum limit, $\mathrm{Kn}_D \to 0$, $\beta = 1$, and the collision rate reduces to Eq. (10.13). In the free molecule limit,

$$\lim_{\mathrm{Kn}_D \to \infty} J = 4\pi(R_{p1} + R_{p2})(D_1 + D_2)N_{20}\left(\frac{1}{2\,\mathrm{Kn}_D}\right) \qquad (10.24)$$

Using Eq. (10.20), we find

$$\lim_{Kn_D \to \infty} J = \pi(R_{p1} + R_{p2})^2 \bar{c}_{12} N_{20} \tag{10.25}$$

This collision rate is, of course, that one would obtain on the basis of molecular effusion theory, that is $(1/4N\bar{c})(4\pi R_p^2)$.

Thus, the generalized expression for the coagulation rate per unit volume of fluid valid over the entire range of Knudsen number is (again dropping the subscript 0 on N_1 and N_2)

$$J_{12} = 4\pi(R_{p1} + R_{p2})(D_1 + D_2)\beta N_1 N_2 \tag{10.26}$$

where the generalized coagulation coefficient is

$$K_{12} = 4\pi(R_{p1} + R_{p2})(D_1 + D_2)\beta \tag{10.27}$$

Also, as in the vapor diffusion case a slightly different form of β was derived by Fuchs (1964). The difference between β given by Eq. (10.23) and that derived by Fuchs is less than 4 percent (Dahneke, 1983). In fact, for numerical evaluation of K_{12} we will employ the Fuchs correction factor due to its popularity (see, for example, Wagner and Kerker, 1977).

The free molecule coagulation coefficient

$$K_{12} = \pi(R_{p1} + R_{p2})^2 \bar{c}_{12}$$

$$= \frac{\pi}{4}(D_{p1} + D_{p2})^2 \bar{c}_{12} \tag{10.28}$$

can be expressed strictly in terms of particle diameter by noting that

$$\bar{c}_{12} = \frac{4(3kT)^{1/2}}{\pi \rho_p^{1/2}}\left(\frac{1}{D_{p1}^3} + \frac{1}{D_{p2}^3}\right)^{1/2} \tag{10.29}$$

where particle density ρ_p is assumed to be independent of size. Combining Eqs. (10.28) and (10.29) gives

$$K_{12} = \left(\frac{3kT}{\rho_p}\right)^{1/2}(D_{p1} + D_{p2})^2\left(\frac{1}{D_{p1}^3} + \frac{1}{D_{p2}^3}\right)^{1/2} \tag{10.30}$$

or, in terms of particle volumes,

$$K_{12} = \left(\frac{3}{4\pi}\right)^{1/6}\left(\frac{6kT}{\rho_p}\right)^{1/2}(v_1^{1/3} + v_2^{1/3})^2\left(\frac{1}{v_1} + \frac{1}{v_2}\right)^{1/2} \tag{10.31}$$

Figure 10.1 shows K_{12} as a function of the two particle diameters D_{p1} and D_{p2} over the range of diameters 0.001 μm to 10 μm. In carrying out the calculations to generate Figure 10.1 we have included the Cunningham slip

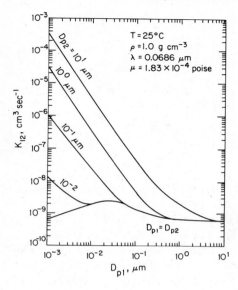

Figure 10.1. Brownian coagulation coefficient K_{12} for coagulation in air at $T = 25°C$ of particles with diameters D_{p_1} and D_{p_2}. The curves were calculated using the correlation of Fuchs in Table 10.1.

correction in the diffusion coefficients in a form due to Phillips (1975) and have used the noncontinuum correction factor due to Fuchs. The complete form of K_{12} is given in Table 10.1. In using Figure 10.1 we find the smaller of the two particles as the abscissa and then locate the line corresponding to the larger particle.

The smallest value of the coagulation coefficient occurs when both particles are of the same size. When the continuum regime formula holds, that is, $Kn_D \ll 1$, the coagulation coefficient for two equal-sized particles is indepen-

---

TABLE 10.1.   Fuchs Form of the Brownian Coagulation Coefficient K_{12}

$$K_{12} = 2\pi(D_1 + D_2)(D_{p1} + D_{p2})\left[\frac{D_{p1} + D_{p2}}{D_{p1} + D_{p2} + 2g_{12}} + \frac{8(D_1 + D_2)}{\bar{c}_{12}(D_{p1} + D_{p2})}\right]^{-1}$$

$$D_i = \frac{kT}{3\pi\mu D_{pi}}\left[\frac{5 + 4Kn_i + 6Kn_i^2 + 18Kn_i^3}{5 - Kn_i + (8 + \pi)Kn_i^2}\right] \quad \text{Phillips (1975)}$$

$$g_{12} = (g_1^2 + g_2^2)^{1/2}$$
$$g_i = (1/(3D_{pi}l_i))[(D_{pi} + l_i)^3 - (D_{pi}^2 + l_i^2)^{3/2}] - D_{pi}$$
$$l_i = 8D_i/\pi\bar{c}_i$$
$$\bar{c}_i = (8kT/\pi m_i)^{1/2}$$
$$Kn_i = 2\lambda_{air}/D_{pi}$$
$$\bar{c}_{12} = (\bar{c}_1^2 + \bar{c}_2^2)^{1/2}$$

dent of particle size and is given by

$$K_{12} = \frac{8kT}{3\mu} \tag{10.32}$$

On the other hand, in free molecule regime coagulation with $D_{p1} = D_{p2}$, the coagulation coefficient becomes

$$K_{12} = 4\left(\frac{6kT}{\rho_p}\right)^{1/2} D_{p1}^{1/2} \tag{10.33}$$

We see from Figure 10.1 that for coagulation of equal-sized particles when both particle diameters exceed about 1 μm, K_{12} is a constant, $8kT/3\mu$. On the other hand, when both particles are smaller than 0.01 μm, we see that as D_p increases, K_{12} increases according to Eq. (10.33). A maximum coagulation coefficient for coagulation of equal-sized particles is reached at about 0.02 μm diameter. Physically, the maximum in the coagulation coefficient for equal-sized particles can be explained as follows. We expect the coagulation coefficient for large particles to be low because of their sluggishness, that is the Brownian diffusivity decreases with particle size. On the other hand, whereas very small particles have relatively high particle velocities, their cross-sectional area for collision is small and they tend to miss each other. The maximum in the coagulation coefficient for equal-sized particles reflects a balance between particle mobility and cross-sectional area for collision, and a maximum in the coagulation coefficient is achieved for particle diameters of about 0.02 μm.

Consider now the coagulation of unequal-sized particles. First, we note that the coagulation coefficient for unequal-sized particles is always larger than that for either of the two particles coagulating with a particle of its same size. Say we have two equal-sized particles with their coagulation rate. Then say we increase the size of one of the particles. The coagulation coefficient increases because the increase in target area goes as D_p^2 whereas the Brownian diffusion coefficient decreases only as D_p. This effect is seen clearly in Figure 10.1 if we choose the smaller particle size on the abscissa and move vertically up a line intersecting larger and larger sizes for the second particle. In the continuum regime if $D_{p2} \gg D_{p1}$, the coagulation coefficient approaches the limiting value

$$\lim_{D_{p2} \gg D_{p1}} K_{12} = \frac{2kT}{3\mu} \frac{D_{p2}}{D_{p1}} \tag{10.34}$$

In the free molecule regime if $D_{p2} \gg D_{p1}$, the coagulation coefficient has the asymptotic behavior,

$$\lim_{D_{p2} \gg D_{p1}} K_{12} = \left(\frac{3kT}{\rho_p}\right)^{1/2} \frac{D_{p2}^2}{D_{p1}^{3/2}} \tag{10.35}$$

By comparing Eqs. (10.34) and (10.35) we see that with D_{p1} fixed, K_{12} increases more rapidly with D_{p2} for free molecule regime than for continuum regime coagulation.

There have been a number of studies over the years aimed at evaluating experimentally the predicted coagulation coefficients. Experiments conducted with continuum regime aerosols confirm the theoretical coefficients. Because of their small size, free molecule regime aerosols have presented a more challenging experimental problem. Two recent studies on the coagulation of free molecule regime aerosols are those of Kim and Liu (1984) and Okuyama et al. (1984).

Our development has assumed that all particles behave as spheres. It has been found that, when coagulating, certain particles form chain-like aggregates whose behavior can no longer be predicted on the basis of ideal, spherical particles. A recent study of the coagulation of such particles is that of Lee and Shaw (1984).

10.2.   COAGULATION IN LAMINAR SHEAR FLOW, TURBULENCE, AND BY GRAVITATIONAL SETTLING

10.2.1.   Coagulation in Laminar Shear Flow

Particles in a fluid in which a velocity gradient exists have a relative motion that may bring them into contact and cause coagulation. The simplest model for this process was developed by Smoluchowski in 1916. The model is based on the assumptions of a uniform shear field, no fluid dynamic interactions between the particles, and no Brownian motion. If the shear rate in the fluid is Γ, the coagulation coefficient is given by

$$K_{12}^{LS} = \frac{\Gamma}{6}\left(D_{p1} + D_{p2}\right)^3 \qquad (10.36)$$

The relative magnitudes of the laminar shear and Brownian coagulation coefficients for equal-sized particles in the continuum regime is given by the ratio

$$\frac{K_{12}^{LS}}{K_{12}} = \frac{\Gamma\mu}{2kT}D_p^3 \qquad (10.37)$$

From this ratio we find the shear rates required for the two processes to be comparable are quite high for D_p the order of 1 μm. For example, for $D_p = 2$ μm, $\Gamma \cong 60$ sec^{-1} to achieve a ratio of order unity. Since the atmosphere is always in a turbulent state, we must turn to a consideration of coagulation in turbulent flow in order to assess the importance of shear-induced aerosol coagulation.

10.2.2. Coagulation in Turbulent Flow

Velocity gradients in a turbulent fluid will cause relative particle motion and induce coagulation just as in a laminar shear flow. The difficulty in analyzing the process rests with identifying an appropriate velocity gradient in the turbulence. In fact, a characteristic turbulent shear rate at the small length scales applicable to aerosols is $(\varepsilon_k/\nu)^{1/2}$, where ε_k is the rate of dissipation of kinetic energy per unit mass and ν is the kinematic viscosity of the fluid (Tennekes and Lumley, 1972). The analysis of Saffman and Turner (1956) gives the coagulation coefficient for turbulent shear as*

$$K_{12}^{TS} = \left(\frac{\pi^2 \varepsilon_k}{120\nu} \right)^{1/2} \left(D_{p1} + D_{p2} \right)^3 \qquad (10.38)$$

The relative magnitudes of the turbulent shear and Brownian coagulation coefficients for equal-sized particles in the continuum regime is given by the ratio

$$\frac{K_{12}^{TS}}{K_{12}} = \frac{3\mu \left(2\pi \varepsilon_k/120\nu \right)^{1/2} D_p^3}{kT} \qquad (10.39)$$

Measured values of ε_k are of order of 10 sec^{-1}, so Brownian and turbulent shear coagulation are expected to become equal for particles of about 5 μm diameter.

10.2.3. Coagulation Due to Gravitational Settling

Coagulation can result when a population of particles is settling because heavier particles catch up to lighter particles and collide with them. We will actually consider this process in Chapter 16 where we will be interested in the scavenging of particles by falling raindrops. Suffice it to say at this point that if $D_{p1} \gg D_{p2}$, the target area is that of the larger particle, $\pi D_{p1}^2/4$, and the coagulation coefficient is just the product of the target area and the relative distance swept out by the larger particle per unit time,

$$K_{12}^{GS} = \frac{\pi D_{p1}^2}{4} \left(v_{t_1} - v_{t_2} \right) \qquad (10.40)$$

where v_{t_1} and v_{t_2} are the two terminal settling velocities.

---

*There is a numerical error in the coefficient in the original Saffman and Turner (1956) paper which has been corrected in Eq. (10.38).

10.3.   EFFECT OF PARTICLE FORCE FIELDS ON BROWNIAN COAGULATION

In our development of Brownian motion we did not include the effect of external force fields on the particle motion. To do so is straightforward and we now extend our treatment of coagulation to include interparticle forces. The flux of particles resulting from simultaneous Brownian diffusion and migration in an external force field is given by

$$\mathbf{j} = -D\nabla N + \mathbf{v}N \tag{10.41}$$

where $\mathbf{v}$ is the migration velocity. If we consider the flux of #2 particles to a #1 particle due to Brownian diffusion and an interparticle force $\mathbf{F}_{12}$, then, since, as we saw in Eq. (8.64), the migration velocity can be written as the product of the particle mobility B and the force, Eq. (10.41) can be expressed as

$$\mathbf{j}_{12} = -D_2\nabla N_2 + B_2\mathbf{F}_{12}N_2 \tag{10.42}$$

Further, using Eq. (8.65), $D = BkT$, and representing the force as the negative of the gradient of a potential,

$$\mathbf{F}_{12} = -\nabla\Phi \tag{10.43}$$

then the flux can be written as

$$\mathbf{j}_{12} = -D_2\exp(-\Phi/kT)\{\nabla(N_2\exp(\Phi/kT))\} \tag{10.44}$$

Now let us assume that $\Phi = \Phi(r)$, where r is the distance between the particle centers. Also we assume steady state conditions and integrate the flux over a spherical surface surrounding particle #1,

$$J_{12} = 4\pi r^2 D_2\exp(-\Phi(r)/kT)\frac{d}{dr}(N_2\exp(\Phi(r)/kT)) \tag{10.45}$$

where the direction of the flux is in the negative r direction. Integrating the flux from $r = \infty$ to $r = r$ subject to $N_2 = N_{20}$ and $\Phi(r) = 0$ at $r = \infty$ yields

$$N_2(r) = N_{20}\exp(-\Phi(r)/kT) + \frac{J_{12}\exp(-\Phi(r)/kT)}{4\pi D_2}\int_{\infty}^{r}\frac{\exp(\Phi(x)/kT)}{x^2}\,dx \tag{10.46}$$

If we now invoke the coagulation boundary condition $N_2(r) = 0$ at $r = R_{p1} + R_{p2}$, and replace D_2 by D_{12} as discussed in Section 10.1, we obtain the steady state collision flux as

$$J_{12} = \frac{4\pi D_{12}(R_{p1} + R_{p2})N_{20}}{(R_{p1} + R_{p2})\displaystyle\int_{R_{p1}+R_{p2}}^{\infty} \frac{\exp(\Phi(x)/kT)}{x^2}\, dx} \qquad (10.47)$$

Since the collision rate due to Brownian motion only is the numerator of Eq. (10.47), we see that the presence of an interparticle force, as represented by the potential $\Phi(r)$, leads to a collision rate that is the pure Brownian motion collision rate divided by the factor,

$$W = (R_{p1} + R_{p2})\int_{R_{p1}+R_{p2}}^{\infty} \frac{\exp(\Phi(x)/kT)}{x^2}\, dx \qquad (10.48)$$

Thus, $K_{12} = K_{12}^{\text{Brownian}}/W$.

10.3.1. van der Waals Forces

van der Waals forces result from momentary dipoles in uncharged, nonpolar molecules caused by fluctuations in the electron cloud, which can attract similar dipoles in other molecules. The potential of the attractive force can be expressed as

$$\Phi_v = -4\phi_1\left(\frac{\phi_2}{r}\right)^6 \qquad (10.49)$$

where ϕ_1 and ϕ_2 are constants with units of energy and length, respectively, that depend on the particular species involved, values of which are tabulated in Hirschfelder et al. (1954). Hamaker (1937) calculated the van der Waals potential between two spherical particles of radii R_{p1} and R_{p2} whose centers are separated by a distance r as

$$\Phi_v(r) = -\frac{\pi^2 Q}{6}\left\{ \frac{2R_{p1}R_{p2}}{r^2 - (R_{p1} + R_{p2})^2} + \frac{2R_{p1}R_{p2}}{r^2 - (R_{p1} - R_{p2})^2} \right.$$

$$\left. + \ln\left[\frac{r^2 - (R_{p1} + R_{p2})^2}{r^2 - (R_{p1} - R_{p2})^2}\right]\right\} \qquad (10.50)$$

where $Q = 4\phi_1\phi_2^6/v_m^2$, and where $v_m =$ molecular volume. For equal-sized particles, let $x = 2R_p/r$, and

$$\Phi_v(x) = -\frac{\pi^2 Q}{6}\left[\frac{x^2}{2(1 - x^2)} + \frac{x^2}{2} + \ln(1 - x^2)\right] \qquad (10.51)$$

TABLE 10.2.
TABLE 10.2. Correction Factors for Coagulation Coefficient due to van der Waals Forces at $T = 293$ K

Species	M	ρ, g cm^{-3}	ϕ_1/k	ϕ_2	Q/kT	$1/W_v$
acetone	58.08	0.7899	519.00	4.669	4.7878	1.3811
benzene	78.12	0.8786	335.00	5.628	6.4828	1.4268
cyclohexane	84.16	0.7786	324.00	6.093	6.8310	1.4350
ethanol	46.07	0.7893	391.00	4.455	4.3196	1.3664
ethyl acetate	88.12	0.9003	531.00	5.163	5.0544	1.3890
methanol	32.04	0.7914	507.00	3.585	3.1614	1.3242
n-octane	114.23	0.7025	333.00	7.407	10.0131	1.4987
toluene	92.15	0.8669	377.00	5.392	3.9475	1.3539
water	18.02	1.0000	373.00	2.680	2.0490	1.2715

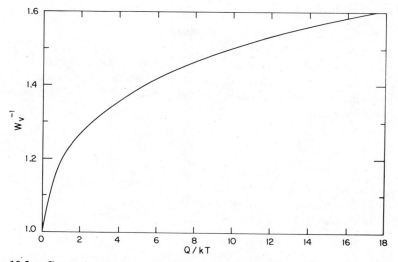

Figure 10.2. Correction factor to the Brownian coagulation coefficient for equal-sized particles in the continuum regime from van der Waals forces.

Using Eq. (10.51), the correction factor W_v for equal-sized particles is

$$W_v = \int_0^1 \exp\left[-\frac{\pi^2 Q}{6kT} \left(\frac{x^2}{2(1-x^2)} + \frac{x^2}{2} + \ln(1-x^2) \right) \right] dx \quad (10.52)$$

Thus we see that the correction factor W_v is independent of particle size for identically sized particles and depends only on the factor Q/kT.

W_v can be evaluated as a function of Q/kT by numerically evaluating the integral in Eq. (10.52). Figure 10.2 shows this dependence. Table 10.2 gives the coagulation correction factors, expressed as $1/W_v$, for equal-sized particles of a number of species. For this range of species the correction factor ranges from 1.25 to 1.50, indicating that increases in rates of coagulation for equal-sized particles resulting from van der Waals forces can be expected not to exceed 50 percent.

The preceding development has been based on a continuum regime treatment. Marlow (1981, 1982) has extended this development to the transition and free molecule regimes, and determined that the effect of van der Waals forces on coagulation rates can be considerably more pronounced in these size ranges than for particles in the continuum regime. Moreover, Okuyama et al. (1984), in measurements on the size distributions of ultrafine coagulating aerosols, have found that observed coagulation rates are consistent with those predicted by Marlow. Due to the complexity of the transition and free molecule regime theories, we do not present them here. The interested reader is referred to Marlow (1981, 1982).

10.3.2. Coulomb Forces

Charged particles may experience either enhanced or retarded coagulation rates depending on their charges. The potential energy of interaction between two particles containing z_1 and z_2 charges (including sign) whose centers are separated by a distance r is

$$\Phi_c = \frac{z_1 z_2 e^2}{\varepsilon r} \quad (10.53)$$

where e is the electronic charge and ε is the dielectric constant of the medium. For air at 293 K and 1 atm, $\varepsilon = 1.000536$. If Eq. (10.53) is substituted into Eq. (10.48) the integral can be evaluated analytically to obtain

$$W_c = \frac{e^\kappa - 1}{\kappa} \quad (10.54)$$

where $\kappa = z_1 z_2 e^2 / \varepsilon (R_{p1} + R_{p2}) kT$. The constant κ can be interpreted as the ratio of the electrostatic potential energy at contact to the thermal energy kT. For $\kappa > 0$ (like charge), $W_c > 1$, and coagulation is retarded from that for pure

TABLE 10.3. Coagulation Correction Factors for Coulomb Forces Between Equal-Sized Particles

κ	W_c^{-1}(like)	W_c^{-1}(unlike)	$1/2[W_c^{-1}$(like)$ + W_c^{-1}$(unlike)$]$
0.1	0.9508	1.0508	1.0008
0.25	0.8802	1.1302	1.0052
0.5	0.7708	1.2708	1.0208
0.75	0.6714	1.4214	1.0464
1.0	0.5820	1.5820	1.0820
5.0	0.0339	5.0339	2.5339
10.0	0.00045	10.00045	5.00045

Brownian motion. Conversely, for $\kappa < 0$ (unlike charges), $W_c < 1$, and the coagulation rate is enhanced. If we consider a situation where there exist equal numbers of positively and negatively charged particles, we can estimate the coagulation correction coefficient W_c^{-1} as the average of the like- and unlike-correction coefficients. This estimate is shown in Table 10.3. We see that an aerosol consisting of an equal number of positively and negatively charged particles will exhibit an overall enhanced rate of coagulation because the enhanced rate of unlike charged particles more than compensates for the retarded rate of like charged particles.

Pruppacher and Klett (1978) show that the average number of charges on a particle, regardless of sign, is given by

$$\bar{z} = \frac{1}{e}\left(\frac{D_p kT}{\pi}\right)^{1/2} \tag{10.55}$$

Equation (10.55) can be evaluated as a function of particle diameter to give

D_p, μm	0.02	0.1	1.0	10	20	50
$\bar{z}$	0.3	0.7	2.1	6.7	9.5	15

For all of these particle diameters, κ is of the order of 10^{-11} or smaller so $W_c^{-1} = 1$. Consequently, it is not expected that Coulomb forces will be important in affecting the coagulation rates of atmospheric particles. Only if an aerosol is charged far in excess of its equilibrium charge will there be any effect on the coagulation coefficient.

There exists a maximum number of charges that a particle can carry. At this point a solid particle will emit an ion or an electron and a liquid droplet will break apart, the break-up occurring when the force due to the charges exceeds the surface tension forces that act to hold the droplet intact. This maximum number of charges is called the *Rayleigh limit*. The Rayleigh limit, z_{RL}, of

elementary charges on a particle as a function of particle diameter, assuming a
surface tension of 21 dynes cm^{-1}, is

D_p, μm	0.1	1.0	10.0
z_{RL}	10^3	2×10^4	8×10^5

Using the values of z_{RL} given above, we can reevaluate the coagulation
correction factor W_c^{-1} as

0.1 μm		1 μm		10 μm	
W_c^{-1} (like)	W_c^{-1} (unlike)	W_c^{-1} (like)	W_c^{-1} (unlike)	W_c^{-1} (like)	W_c^{-1} (unlike)
≈ 1.0	≈ 1.0	0.999	1.001	0.81	1.22

Thus, a collection of supermicron particles, all charged to the Rayleigh limit,
can have an enhanced coagulation rate over the pure Brownian rate.

10.4. THE DISCRETE GENERAL DYNAMIC EQUATION

A spatially homogeneous aerosol of uniform chemical composition can be fully
characterized by the number densities of particles of various sizes as a function
of time. Define $N_k(t)$ as the number density (cm^{-3}) of particles containing k
monomers, where a monomer can be considered as a single molecule of the
species comprising the particle. The basic processes that influence $N_k(t)$ are
coagulation and evaporation (the loss of single molecules from a k-mer). We
specifically neglect processes in which a k-mer spontaneously dissociates into
two particles, of sizes $\tilde{k}$ and $k - \tilde{k}$ if $\tilde{k} > 1$. (Homogeneous nucleation, the
process by which original stable particles are formed, is, for the moment,
included within the definition of coagulation.)

The dynamic equation governing $N_k(t)$, $k \geq 2$, can be developed as follows.
We have seen that the rate of collision between particles of two types (sizes) is
$J_{12} = K_{12}N_1N_2$, expressed in units of number of collisions per cm^3 of fluid per
second. Let us write this rate as $K_{ij}N_iN_j$, in terms of the number concentrations of particles containing i and j monomers. Our object is to derive an
equation governing the concentration $N_k(t)$ due to coagulation and evaporation. Consider first the contribution of coagulation to this equation.

The rate of formation of a k-mer by agglomeration of two smaller particles
whose monomers sum to k is

$$\frac{1}{2} \sum_{j=1}^{k-1} K_{k-j,j} N_{k-j}(t) N_j(t)$$

Let us see where the factor of one-half comes from. We know that $K_{k-j,j} = K_{j,k-j}$ and the summation counts each agglomeration twice so we need a factor of one half. If k is an even integer, the term $K_{k/2,\,k/2}N_{k/2}^2$ occurs only once in the summation, but the factor of one half is still needed due to the indistinguishability of two equal-sized particles.

To see this point about indistinguishability suppose that we have all particles of size $k/2$ (F. Gelbard, personal communication). If one-half of these particles are painted red and one-half painted blue, then the rate of coagulation of red and blue particles is $K_{k/2,\,k/2}(N_{k/2}/2)(N_{k/2}/2) = 1/4K_{k/2,\,k/2}N_{k/2}^2$. However, this rate is not equal to the total rate of coagulation occurring in the population, since we must also account for coagulation of red particles among themselves and blue particles among themselves. Let us now paint one-half the red particles as green and one-half the blue particles as yellow. The rate of coagulation within each of the initial particles categories is

$$K_{k/2,\,k/2}\left[\underbrace{\left(\frac{N_{k/2}}{4}\right)}_{\text{red}}\underbrace{\left(\frac{N_{k/2}}{4}\right)}_{\text{green}}+\underbrace{\left(\frac{N_{k/2}}{4}\right)}_{\text{blue}}\underbrace{\left(\frac{N_{k/2}}{4}\right)}_{\text{yellow}}\right]$$

We can continue this marking process indefinitely (as long as we have new colors) and the result for the total rate of coagulation occurring in the population of equal-sized particles is

$$K_{k/2,\,k/2}N_{k/2}^2\left[\frac{1}{2^2}+\frac{1}{2^3}+\frac{1}{2^4}+\cdots\right]$$

Since $\sum_{n=2}^{\infty}2^{-n}=1/2$, the total coagulation rate is

$$\tfrac{1}{2}K_{k/2,\,k/2}N_{k/2}^2$$

The factor of one-half in the equal-sized case is thus a result of the indistinguishability of the coagulating particles.

The rate of depletion of a k-mer by agglomeration with all other particles is

$$N_k(t)\sum_{j=1}^{\infty}K_{kj}N_j(t)$$

for $j=k$ this rate must be divided by 2 because of indistinguishability, but because each collision removes two k-mers, the rate must be multiplied by 2.

The rate of loss of k-mers due to evaporation is written as $e_kN_k(t)$, $k\geq 2$, where e_k is the rate of escape of monomers from a k-mer.* The rate of formation of k-mers by evaporation is then just $(1+\delta_{1,\,k})e_{k+1}N_{k+1}(t)$, $k\geq 1$,

---

*Recall that in Chapter 9 we defined e_k' as the flux of monomers per unit area leaving a k-mer. Here, e_k is the rate of escape of monomers from a k-mer. Thus, $e_k=e_k'a_k$.

where

$$\delta_{j,k} = \begin{cases} 1 & j = k \\ 0 & j \neq k \end{cases}$$

We see that for $k = 1$, if a dimer dissociates, one obtains two monomer molecules.

Combining the coagulation and evaporation contributions, we obtain the general balance equation for k-mers, $k \geq 2$, the so-called *Discrete General Dynamic Equation*,

$$\frac{dN_k}{dt} = \tfrac{1}{2} \sum_{j=1}^{k-1} K_{j,k-j} N_j N_{k-j} - N_k \sum_{j=1}^{\infty} K_{k,j} N_j - e_k N_k + e_{k+1} N_{k+1}$$

(10.56)

The first two terms on the right-hand side of Eq. (10.56) express the rate of change of N_k as a result of collisional (coagulation) processes, and the last two terms describe the contribution of monomer evaporation. In the absence of evaporation, we have the *Discrete Coagulation Equation*,

$$\frac{dN_k}{dt} = \tfrac{1}{2} \sum_{j=1}^{k-1} K_{j,k-j} N_j N_{k-j} - N_k \sum_{j=1}^{\infty} K_{k,j} N_j \qquad (10.57)$$

Equation (10.56) is a rigorous representation of the kinetics of a system of particles undergoing simultaneous coalescence and evaporation. It proves to be convenient, however, to represent the process of accretion of monomers by other particles in a manner analogous to that of evaporation. Thus, we define $p_k N_k$ as the rate of gain of $(k + 1)$-mers due to collision of a k-mer with a monomer, where $p_k(\sec^{-1})$ is the frequency with which a monomer collides with a k-mer. This is the process we commonly refer to as heterogeneous condensation. With this modification, Eq. (10.56) becomes

$$\frac{dN_k}{dt} = \tfrac{1}{2} \sum_{j=2}^{k-2} K_{j,k-j} N_j N_{k-j} - N_k \sum_{j=1}^{\infty} K_{k,j} N_j$$

$$+ p_{k-1} N_{k-1} - (p_k + e_k) N_k + e_{k+1} N_{k+1} \qquad (10.58)$$

where $p_k = K_{1,k} N_1$.

In this formulation, it is assumed that the smallest particle is one of size $k = 2$. No distinction has yet been made among the processes of coagulation, homogeneous nucleation, and heterogeneous condensation. In reality, there is a minimum number of monomers in a stable nucleus, g^*, and generally $g^* \gg 2$. In the presence of a supersaturated vapor, stable clusters of size g^* will form continuously at a rate given by the classical theory of homogeneous nucleation. Let us denote the rate of formation of stable clusters containing g^* monomers from homogeneous nucleation as $J_0(t)$. Then, coagulation and heterogeneous condensation of vapor on particles of size $k \geq g^*$ become distinct processes in Eq. (10.56). By changing the smallest size stable particle from 2 to g^*, Eq. (10.58) becomes

$$\frac{dN_k}{dt} = \frac{1}{2} \sum_{j=g^*}^{k-g^*} K_{j,k-j} N_j N_{k-j} - N_k \sum_{j=g^*}^{\infty} K_{k,n} N_j$$

$$+ p_{k-1} N_{k-1} - (p_k + e_k) N_k + e_{k+1} N_{k+1} + J_0(t) \delta_{g^*}$$

$$k = g^*, g^* + 1, \ldots \tag{10.59}$$

10.5. THE CONTINUOUS GENERAL DYNAMIC EQUATION

Although Eq. (10.59) is still a rigorous representation of the system, it is impractical to deal with discrete equations because of the enormous range of k. Thus, it is customary to replace the discrete number density $N_k(t)$ (cm^{-3}) by the continuous size distribution density function $n(v, t)$ (μm^{-3} cm^{-3}), where $v = k \Delta v$, Δv being the volume associated with a monomer. Thus, $n(v, t) \, dv$ is defined as the number of particles per cubic centimeter having volumes in the range v to $v + dv$. If we let $v_0 = g^* \Delta v$, then Eq. (10.59) becomes in the limit of a continuous distribution of sizes

$$\frac{\partial n(v, t)}{\partial t} = \frac{1}{2} \int_{v_0}^{v - v_0} K(v - \tilde{v}, \tilde{v}) n(v - \tilde{v}, t) n(\tilde{v}, t) \, d\tilde{v}$$

$$- \int_{v_0}^{\infty} K(\tilde{v}, v) n(v, t) n(\tilde{v}, t) \, d\tilde{v} - \frac{\partial}{\partial v} [I_0(v) n(v, t)]$$

$$+ \frac{\partial^2}{\partial v^2} [I_1(v) n(v, t)] + J_0(v) \delta(v - v_0) \tag{10.60}$$

where

$$I_0(v) = \Delta v (p_k - e_k) \tag{10.61}$$

$$I_1(v) = \frac{\Delta v^2}{2} (p_k + e_k) \tag{10.62}$$

Since $p_k - e_k$ is the frequency with which a k-mer experiences a net gain of one monomer, $I_0(v)$ is the rate of change of the volume of a particle of size

$v = k\,\Delta v$. The sum $p_k + e_k$ is the total frequency with which monomers enter and leave a k-mer. $I_1(v)$ assumes the role of a diffusion coefficient from kinetic theory. Brock (1972), however, has obtained relations for I_0 and I_1 based on a continuous size distribution which provide additional insight into their nature. When we consider only condensational growth, if we let $n'(\tilde{v}, t)$ represent the size distribution function of the small condensing nuclei, then the evolution of $n(v, t)$ is described by

$$\frac{\partial n(v, t)}{\partial t} = \int_0^{\tilde{v}_m} K(v - \tilde{v}, \tilde{v}) n(v - \tilde{v}, t) n'(\tilde{v}, t)\, d\tilde{v}$$

$$- \int_0^{\tilde{v}_m} K(v, \tilde{v}) n(v, t) n'(\tilde{v}, t)\, d\tilde{v} \qquad (10.63)$$

where the condensing species are assumed to have volumes such that $\tilde{v} \ll v$, and where $\tilde{v}_m$ is the largest volume of the condensing species. By taking advantage of the fact that $\tilde{v}/v \ll 1$, the first integrand can be expanded in a Taylor series to yield

$$\frac{\partial n(v, t)}{\partial t} = -\frac{\partial}{\partial v}\left[I_0(v, t) n(v, t)\right] + \frac{\partial^2}{\partial v^2}\left[I_1(v, t) n(v, t)\right] \quad (10.64)$$

where

$$I_0(v, t) = \int_0^{\tilde{v}_m} K(v, \tilde{v})\tilde{v} n'(\tilde{v}, t)\, d\tilde{v} \qquad (10.65)$$

$$I_1(v, t) = \tfrac{1}{2}\int_0^{\tilde{v}_m} K(v, \tilde{v})\tilde{v}^2 n'(\tilde{v}, t)\, d\tilde{v} \qquad (10.66)$$

For $v \gg \tilde{v}$, it is reasonable to assume that $K(v, \tilde{v}) = K(v)$, namely, that the collision rate depends only on the volume of the particle. If, in addition, we assume that all condensing nuclei are of a uniform size $\tilde{v}_1 \le \tilde{v}_m$, then $n'(\tilde{v}, t) = N_{CN}\delta(\tilde{v} - \tilde{v}_1)$, and

$$I_0(v) = K(v)\tilde{v}_1 N_{CN} \qquad (10.67)$$

$$I_1(v) = \tfrac{1}{2}K(v)\tilde{v}_1^2 N_{CN} \qquad (10.68)$$

where N_{CN} is assumed to be constant. Brock (1972) and Ramabhadran et al. (1976) have shown that the term in Eq. (10.64) involving I_1 can ordinarily be neglected. We shall do so and simply write I_0 as I.

In Eq. (10.60), a stable particle has been assumed to have a lower limit of volume of v_0. From the standpoint of the solution of Eq. (10.60), it is advantageous to replace the lower limits v_0 of the coagulation integrals by zero. Ordinarily this does not cause any difficulty, since the initial distribution $n(v, 0) = n_0(v)$ may be specified as zero for $v < v_0$, and no particles of volume $v < v_0$ can be produced for $t > 0$. Homogeneous nucleation provides a steady source of particles of size v_0, according to the rate defined by $J_0(t)$. Then the full equation governing $n(v, t)$ is

$$\frac{\partial n(v, t)}{\partial t} + \frac{\partial}{\partial v}[I(v, t)n(v, t)]$$

$$= \frac{1}{2}\int_0^v K(v - \tilde{v}, \tilde{v})n(v - \tilde{v}, t)n(\tilde{v}, t)\, d\tilde{v}$$

$$-n(v, t)\int_0^\infty K(v, \tilde{v})n(\tilde{v}, t)\, d\tilde{v} + J_0(t)\delta(v - v_0)$$

$$(10.69)$$

This equation is called the *Continuous General Dynamic Equation* for aerosols (Gelbard and Seinfeld, 1979). Its initial and boundary conditions are

$$n(v, 0) = n_0(v) \tag{10.70}$$

$$n(0, t) = 0 \tag{10.71}$$

In the absence of nucleation or sources, $J_0(t) = 0$, and growth, $I(v, t) = 0$, we have the *Continuous Coagulation Equation*,

$$\frac{\partial n(v, t)}{\partial t} = \frac{1}{2}\int_0^v K(v - \tilde{v}, \tilde{v})n(v - \tilde{v}, t)n(\tilde{v}, t)\, d\tilde{v}$$

$$-n(v, t)\int_0^\infty K(v, \tilde{v})n(\tilde{v}, t)\, d\tilde{v} \tag{10.72}$$

The continuous coagulation equation may be transformed into that governing $n(D_p, t)$ using the transformation Eq. (7.19). The result is

$$\frac{\partial n(D_p, t)}{\partial t} = D_p^2 \int_0^{D_p/2^{1/3}} (D_p^3 - \tilde{D}_p^3)^{-2/3} K\left[(D_p^3 - \tilde{D}_p^3)^{1/3}, \tilde{D}_p\right]$$

$$\times n\left((D_p^3 - \tilde{D}_p^3)^{1/3}, t\right)n(\tilde{D}_p, t)\, d\tilde{D}_p$$

$$-n(D_p, t)\int_0^\infty K(D_p, \tilde{D}_p)n(\tilde{D}_p, t)\, d\tilde{D}_p \tag{10.73}$$

If particle concentrations are sufficiently small, coagulation can be neglected, in which case each particle evolves independently of the other particles present.* The dynamic processes included in Eq. (10.69) in addition to

---

*Actually, if a population of particles is growing by condensation of vapor in a closed system, the particles will "compete" for the finite supply of vapor molecules, and thus the growth rate of each particle is dependent on the other particles present. We do not consider that case here.

coagulation are growth (condensation) and formation of fresh particles by nucleation. Actually we can replace the nucleation term, $J_0(t)\delta(v - v_0)$, by a general source rate $S(v, t)$ that includes nucleation as well as any other particle sources, such as emissions, that might be present. The resulting equation can be called the *Condensation Equation* and is

$$\frac{\partial n(v, t)}{\partial t} + \frac{\partial}{\partial v}(I(v, t)n(v, t)) = S(v, t) \tag{10.74}$$

10.6. SOLUTION OF THE COAGULATION EQUATION

In this section we will present solutions of the discrete and continuous forms of the coagulation equation, Eqs. (10.57) and (10.72), respectively. A classic solution of the coagulation equation is that for constant coagulation coefficient K. Such a situation is most relevant for the early stages of coagulation of a monodisperse aerosol in the continuous regime when $K(v, \tilde{v}) = 8kT/3\mu$.

10.6.1. Discrete Coagulation Equation

Assume $K_{k, j} = K$ in Eq. (10.57) and we obtain

$$\frac{dN_k}{dt} = \tfrac{1}{2}K \sum_{j=1}^{k-1} N_{k-j}(t)N_j(t) - KN_k(t) \sum_{j=1}^{\infty} N_j(t) \tag{10.75}$$

Noting that the total number of concentration of particles is

$$N(t) = \sum_{j=1}^{\infty} N_j(t) \tag{10.76}$$

Eq. (10.75) becomes

$$\frac{dN_k}{dt} = \tfrac{1}{2}K \sum_{j=1}^{k-1} N_{k-j}(t)N_j(t) - KN(t)N_k(t) \tag{10.77}$$

In order to solve Eq. (10.77) we need to know $N(t)$. By summing Eq. (10.77) over k from 1 to ∞, we obtain

$$\frac{dN}{dt} = \tfrac{1}{2}K \sum_{k=1}^{\infty} \sum_{j=1}^{k-1} N_{k-j}N_j - KN^2(t) \tag{10.78}$$

The double summation on the right hand side of Eq. (10.78) is seen to be equal to $N^2(t)$, so Eq. (10.78) becomes

$$\frac{dN}{dt} = -\tfrac{1}{2}KN^2(t) \tag{10.79}$$

If $N(0) = N_0$, the solution of Eq. (10.79) is

$$N(t) = \frac{N_0}{1 + t/\tau_c} \tag{10.80}$$

where $\tau_c = 2/KN_0$, a characteristic time for coagulation.

We can readily solve Eq. (10.77) inductively. Consider $k = 1$,

$$\frac{dN_1}{dt} = -KN_1 N \tag{10.81}$$

so using Eq. (10.80) and solving (10.81) gives

$$N_1(t) = \frac{N_1(0)}{(1 + t/\tau_c)^2} \tag{10.82}$$

Similarly, solving

$$\frac{dN_2}{dt} = \tfrac{1}{2}KN_1^2 - KN_2 N \tag{10.83}$$

gives

$$N_2(t) = \frac{N_2(0)(t/\tau_c)}{(1 + t/\tau_c)^3} \tag{10.84}$$

Continuing, we find

$$N_k(t) = \frac{N_k(0)(t/\tau_c)^{k-1}}{(1 + t/\tau_c)^{k+1}} \qquad k = 1, 2, \dots \tag{10.85}$$

Note that when $t/\tau_c \gg 1$, $N(t) \cong N_0/(t/\tau_c) = 2/Kt$, and the total number of particles decreases as t^{-1}, independent of the initial number N_0. In this large time limit, $N_k(t) \cong N_k(0)(t/\tau_c)^{-k}$, so the number concentration of each k-mer decreases as t^{-k}. In the short time limit, $t/\tau_c \ll 1$, $N_k(t) = N_k(0)(t/\tau_c)^{k-1}$, and N_k increases as t^{k-1}.

10.6.2. Continuous Coagulation Equation

We now consider the solution of the continuous coagulation equation, Eq. (10.72), with $K(v, \tilde{v}) = K$,

$$\frac{\partial n(v, t)}{\partial t} = \tfrac{1}{2}K \int_0^v n(v - \tilde{v}, t) n(\tilde{v}, t)\, d\tilde{v} - Kn(v, t)N(t) \tag{10.86}$$

Using Eq. (10.80) for $N(t)$, this equation becomes

$$\frac{\partial n(v,t)}{\partial t} + \frac{KN_0}{1 + t/\tau_c}n(v,t) = \tfrac{1}{2}K\int_0^v n(v - \tilde{v},t)n(\tilde{v},t)\,d\tilde{v} \quad (10.87)$$

To solve this equation we can employ an integrating factor and an assumed form for the solution or attack it directly with the Laplace transformation. We illustrate now the solution using the integrating factor and then subsequently the Laplace transform approach.

Use the integrating factor,

$$\exp\left[\int_0^t \frac{KN_0}{1 + t'/\tau_c}\,dt'\right] = (1 + t/\tau_c)^2 \quad (10.88)$$

and Eq. (10.87) becomes

$$\frac{\partial}{\partial t}\left[(1 + t/\tau_c)^2 n(v,t)\right] = \tfrac{1}{2}K(1 + t/\tau_c)^2\int_0^v n(v - \tilde{v},t)n(\tilde{v},t)\,d\tilde{v}$$

$$(10.89)$$

If we let $y = N_0^{-1}(1 + t/\tau_c)^{-1}$ and $w = (1 + t/\tau_c)^2 n(v,t)$ then Eq. (10.89) can be transformed to

$$\frac{\partial w(v,y)}{\partial y} = -\int_0^v w(v - \tilde{v},y)w(\tilde{v},y)\,d\tilde{v} \quad (10.90)$$

As a solution let us try $w(v,y) = A\exp(-bv)$ where A and b are to be determined, and we find that

$$w(v,y) = A\exp(-Ayv) \quad (10.91)$$

so

$$(1 + t/\tau_c)^2 n(v,t) = A\exp\left[-\frac{Av}{N_0(1 + t/\tau_c)}\right] \quad (10.92)$$

At $t = 0$,

$$n(v,0) = A\exp(-Av/N_0) \quad (10.93)$$

The total initial number and volume are

$$\int_0^\infty n(v,0)\,dv = N_0 \qquad \int_0^v vn(v,0)\,dv = V_0 \quad (10.94)$$

These definitions, together with Eq. (10.93), can be used to fix A as N_0/V_0. Thus, the desired solution is

$$n(v, t) = \frac{N_0/V_0}{(1 + t/\tau_c)^2} \exp\left[-\frac{v/V_0}{(1 + t/\tau_c)} \right] \qquad (10.95)$$

For additional solutions of the discrete and continuous coagulation equations the interested reader may wish to consult Drake (1972), Mulholland and Baum (1980) and Tambour and Seinfeld (1980).

Solution of the Coagulation Equation by the Laplace Transform. Define the Laplace transform of $n(v, t)$ as

$$\bar{n}(s, t) = \int_0^\infty e^{-sv} n(v, t) \, dv \qquad (10.96)$$

and transforming Eq. (10.86) leads to

$$\frac{d\bar{n}(s, t)}{dt} = \frac{1}{2} K \bar{n}(s, t)^2 - KN(t) \bar{n}(s, t) \qquad (10.97)$$

Now let

$$\bar{n}(s, t) = \bar{\psi}(s, t) \exp\left\{ -\int_0^t KN(t') \, dt' \right\} \qquad (10.98)$$

and

$$\frac{d\bar{\psi}(s, t)}{dt} = \tfrac{1}{2} K \bar{\psi}^2(s, t) \exp\left\{ -\int_0^t KN(t') \, dt' \right\} \qquad (10.99)$$

Applying $\bar{n}(s, 0) = \bar{n}_0(s)$, Eq. (10.99) can be solved to yield

$$\bar{n}(s, t) = \frac{\exp\left\{ -\int_0^t KN(t') \, dt' \right\}}{\dfrac{1}{\bar{n}_0(s)} - \dfrac{1}{2} K \int_0^t \exp\left\{ -\int_0^{t'} KN(t'') \, dt'' \right\} dt'} \qquad (10.100)$$

Let us assume at this point that the initial distribution is

$$\bar{n}_0(v) = \frac{N_0}{v_0} \exp(-v/v_0) \qquad (10.101)$$

so $\bar{n}_0(s) = N_0/(1 + sv_0)$. Then

$$n(v,t) = \frac{N_0}{v_0} e^{-v/v_0} \left\{ \exp\left[-\int_0^t \left(KN(t') - \frac{vN_0 K}{2v_0} \exp\left(-\int_0^{t'} KN(t'') \, dt'' \right) \right) dt' \right] \right\}$$

(10.102)

Now using $N(t) = N_0/(1 + t/\tau_c)$, we find

$$n(v,t) = \frac{N_0}{v_0} (1 + t/\tau_c)^{-2} \exp\left[-\frac{v/v_0}{1 + t/\tau_c} \right]$$

$$= \frac{N_0}{v_0} \left(\frac{N(t)}{N_0} \right)^2 \exp\left[-\frac{vN(t)}{v_0 N_0} \right]$$

(10.103)

10.7. SOLUTION OF THE CONDENSATION EQUATION

When coagulation can be neglected, and the only dynamic process influencing individual particles is growth, the size distribution function $n(v, t)$ is governed by the condensation equation, Eq. (10.74). This equation describes how the size distribution evolves as a result of the growth of each particle at a rate $dv/dt = I(v, t)$ and as a result of sources of new particles, $S(v, t)$. In this section we will study the evolution of an aerosol size distribution when growth and particle sources are the main processes of interest. The source term $S(v, t)$ represents the rate of change of the size distribution function due to the input of new particles to the system, that is $S(v, t) \, dv$ is the number of particles introduced into the system per unit time having particle volumes in the range $(v, v + dv)$. If the input of fresh particles is a result of nucleation, then one might want to set $S(v, t) = J_0(t) \delta(v - v_0)$. On the other hand, for an input from a primary emission source, one would need to specify the total emission rate and the size distribution of particles from the source.

Let us begin by considering particle growth in the absence of particle sources. The flow of molecules to the surface of a spherical particle for a particle in the continuum regime is given by the Maxwell equation, $J_c = 2\pi D D_p (N_\infty - N_s)$. Clearly, J_c is also equal to the rate of increase in the number of molecules in the particle, so the rate of growth of the drop volume is

$$\frac{dv}{dt} = I(D_p) = v_m J_c$$

(10.104)

where v_m is the molecular volume of the monomer. The corresponding increase in particle diameter is

$$I_D(D_p) = \frac{dD_p}{dt} = \frac{dD_p}{dv}\frac{dv}{dt} = \left(\frac{2}{\pi}\right)\frac{1}{D_p^2}I(D_p) \qquad (10.105)$$

Thus, the continuum diffusion growth law based on particle diameter is

$$I_D(D_p) = [4Dv_m(N_\infty - N_s)]/D_p \qquad (10.106)$$

which can be written as

$$I_D(D_p) = \frac{A_D}{D_p} \qquad (10.107)$$

where $A_D = 4Dv_m p^0(S - 1)/kT.$*

The condensation equation incorporating the continuum diffusion growth law Eq. (10.107) is

$$\frac{\partial n(D_p,t)}{\partial t} + \frac{\partial\left[(A_D/D_p)n(D_p,t)\right]}{\partial D_p} = 0 \qquad (10.108)$$

By expanding the derivative, Eq. (10.108) can be put into a simplified form of the diffusion-convection equation with a decay term

$$\frac{\partial n(D_p,t)}{\partial t} + \left(\frac{A_D}{D_p}\right)\frac{\partial n(D_p,t)}{\partial D_p} = \left(\frac{A_D}{D_p^2}\right)n(D_p,t) \qquad (10.109)$$

The aerosol growth equation Eq. (10.109) can be put in a simpler form using a change of variable:

$$\frac{\partial F(D_p,t)}{\partial t} = -I_D(D_p)\frac{\partial F(D_p,t)}{\partial D_p} \qquad (10.110)$$

*The saturation ratio plays an important role in determining the rates of aerosol growth. The saturation ratio is governed by a monomer conservation relation, since all molecules leaving the vapor phase are assumed to add to the particles present:

$$\left[\frac{p^0}{kT}\right]\frac{dS(t)}{dt} = -\int_0^\infty n(D_p,t)I_D(D_p,S)\,dD_p$$

At the critical nucleus size, D_p^*, the addition of molecules to the particle size distribution occurs at the rate of nucleation such that

$$\left[\frac{p^0}{kT}\right]\frac{dS(t)}{dt} = -\int_{D_p^*}^\infty n(D_p,t)I_D(D_p,S)\,dD_p - n_D(D_p^*,t)I_D(D_p^*,S)$$

We consider the case here in which the supersaturation is held fixed externally.

where $F(D_p, t) = I_D(D_p) n(D_p, t)$. The characteristic equations for Eq. (10.110) are

$$\frac{dt}{1} = \frac{dD_p}{I_D(D_p)} = \frac{dF(D_p, t)}{0} \tag{10.111}$$

Equation (10.111) implies that F is a constant along the characteristic curves. The boundary conditions for the aerosol growth equation are taken as:

$$n(0, t) = 0 \tag{10.112}$$

$$n(D_p, 0) = n_0(D_p) \tag{10.113}$$

The interpretation of these boundary conditions is that there are no particles of zero diameter, and that the initial particle size distribution is specified. Since the value of F is a constant along the characteristic curves, the value of F along any characteristic intersecting $D_p = 0$ must be zero. Only the solution in the domain of influence of the initial distribution need be calculated. The characteristic curves satisfy

$$\frac{dD_p}{dt} = I_D \tag{10.114}$$

The solution for the characteristic curves using the continuum diffusion growth law Eq. (10.107) is

$$2 A_D t = D_p^2 - D_{p0}^2 \tag{10.115}$$

where D_{p0} = a constant, the initial diameter for a given characteristic. The characteristic curves for a typical set of parameters are shown in Figure 10.3. The characteristics at the larger diameters have a very large slope, indicating that the particle distribution will not shift very much. The smaller diameters will undergo a much greater shift since the characteristics are moving rapidly to larger diameters.

The constant value of F along the characteristic curve is determined by the definition of F evaluated at the diameter through which the curve passes at $t = 0$:

$$F = F(D_{p0}, 0) = I_D(D_{p0}) n_0(D_{p0}) \tag{10.116}$$

Using Eq. (10.115) to eliminate the constant D_{p0} and noting the definition of $F(D_p, t)$ allows us to obtain the solution for $n(D_p, t)$ in terms of the initial distribution function:

$$n(D_p, t) = \frac{D_p}{\left(D_p^2 - 2 A_D t \right)^{1/2}} n_0 \left((D_p - 2 A_D t)^{1/2} \right) \quad D_p > \sqrt{2 A_D t}$$

$$\tag{10.117}$$

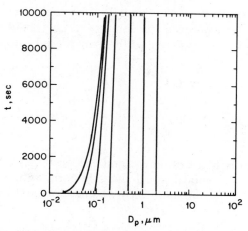

Figure 10.3. Characteristic curves for the aerosol growth equation for the growth law

$$\frac{dD_p}{dt} = \frac{A_D}{D_p}$$

with $A_D = 1.06 \times 10^{-6}\ \mu m^2\ sec^{-1}$.

Aerosol size distribution data are sometimes represented by the log-normal distribution function, Eq. (7.29),

$$n(D_p) = \frac{N_0}{\sqrt{2\pi}\,D_p \ln \sigma_g} \exp\left[-\frac{\ln^2\left(D_p/\overline{D}_{pg}\right)}{2\ln^2\sigma_g} \right] \qquad (10.118)$$

The solution to the aerosol growth equation using the log-normal form for the initial distribution is

$$n(D_p, t) = \frac{D_p}{\left(D_p^2 - 2A_D t\right)} \frac{N_0}{\sqrt{2\pi}\,\ln \sigma_g} \exp\left[-\frac{\ln^2\left(\left(D_p^2 - 2A_D t\right)^{1/2}/\overline{D}_{pg}\right)}{2\ln^2\sigma_g} \right]$$

$$(10.119)$$

For an aerosol distribution undergoing pure growth with no particle sources or losses due to coagulation, the total particle number concentration is preserved. If the solution in Eq. (10.119) is valid, it must satisfy the following integral relation:

$$N_0 = \int_{\sqrt{2A_D t}}^{\infty} n(D_p, t)\, dD_p \qquad (10.120)$$

Note that the lower limit of this integral is determined by the characteristic curve through the origin, since the solution is only valid for $D_p > \sqrt{2A_D t}$. Equation (10.120) is readily simplified by using the substitution

$$u = \left(D_p^2 - 2A_D t \right)^{1/2} \tag{10.121}$$

$$du = \frac{D_p}{\left(D_p^2 - 2A_D t \right)^{1/2}} \, dD_p \tag{10.122}$$

The lower and upper limits of the integral become 0 and ∞, respectively. The resulting integral is identical at all times in form with the integral of the original log-normal distribution, which we know is equal to the total number concentration:

$$N_0 = \int_0^\infty \frac{N_0}{\sqrt{2\pi}\, u \ln \sigma_g} \exp\left[-\frac{\ln^2\left(u/\overline{D}_{pg} \right)}{2 \ln^2 \sigma_g} \right] du \tag{10.123}$$

We see that the growth rates of the smallest particles are orders of magnitude larger than those of the larger particles. The range of diameters having significant values of the distribution function also covers several orders of magnitude. It is sometimes important to rescale the diameter variable in order to expand the region of the smaller diameters in which significant growth is taking place. Another helpful change is the reduction of the infinite domain of the diameter to a finite domain. These factors all suggest the substitution of a logarithmic variable for the particle diameter. Gelbard and Seinfeld (1978) have suggested the following logarithmic variable:

$$w = \frac{\ln\left[D_p/D_{pa} \right]}{\ln\left[D_{pb}/D_{pa} \right]} \tag{10.124}$$

where D_{pa} = the lower limit of the computational domain and D_{pb} = the upper limit of the computational domain. Defining $\zeta = D_{pb}/D_{pa}$, the following relations are used in expressing the aerosol growth equation in terms of the size distribution $n(w, t)$,

$$D_p = D_{pa} \exp[w \ln \zeta]$$

$$I_D = \frac{dD_p}{dt} = \frac{dD_p}{dw} \frac{dw}{dt} = \frac{dD_p}{dw} I_w$$

The form of the aerosol growth equation in terms of $n(w, t)$ is

$$\frac{\partial n(w, t)}{\partial t} + \frac{\partial}{\partial w} \left[I_w n(w, t) \right] = 0 \tag{10.125}$$

where $n(w, t)$ is related to $n(D_p, t)$ by Eq. (7.18),

$$n(w, t) = D_p \ln \zeta \, n(D_p, t) \qquad (10.126)$$

and

$$I_w(w) = \frac{A_D}{D_{pa}^2 \ln \zeta} \exp(-2w \ln \zeta) \qquad (10.127)$$

By dividing Eq. (10.126) by $\ln \zeta$ we produce a dependent variable of physical interest, $D_p n(D_p, t)$:

$$\frac{n(w, t)}{\ln \zeta} = D_p n(D_p, t) \qquad (10.128)$$

The growth law is unchanged in this formulation. The log-normal initial distribution has the following form for the scaled problem:

$$D_p n_0(D_p) = \frac{N_0}{\sqrt{2\pi} \ln \sigma_g} \exp\left\{ \frac{\left[\ln(D_{pa}/\overline{D}_{pg}) + w \ln \zeta \right]^2}{2 \ln^2 \sigma_g} \right\} \qquad (10.129)$$

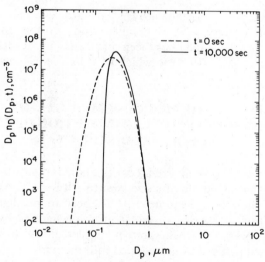

Figure 10.4. Aerosol size distributions at $t = 0$ and $t = 10^4$ sec for an initially log–normal size distribution with $N_0 = 2.26 \times 10^7 \, \text{cm}^{-3}$, $\overline{D}_{pg} = 0.2 \, \mu\text{m}$, and $\sigma_g = 1.4$ and for a growth law

$$\frac{dD_p}{dt} = \frac{A_D}{D_p}$$

with $A_D = 1.06 \times 10^{-6} \, \mu\text{m}^2 \, \text{sec}^{-1}$.

TABLE 10.4.   Properties of Coagulation and Condensation

Process	$\dfrac{N(t)}{N(0)}$	$\dfrac{V(t)}{V(0)}$
Coagulation	< 1	1
Condensation	1	> 1
Coagulation and Condensation	< 1	> 1

Figure 10.4 shows the aerosol size distribution at $t = 0$ and $t = 10^4$ sec for a log-normal initial distribution Eq. (10.118) with $N_0 = 2.26 \times 10^7$, $\overline{D}_{pg} = 0.2 \ \mu m$, and $\sigma_g = 1.4$ and for the growth parameter $A_D = 1.06 \times 10^{-6}$. The difference in growth between the small and large particles, seen from the characteristic curves in Figure 10.3, is even more evident in Figure 10.4.

Table 10.4 compares the properties of coagulation and condensation with respect to the total number of particles and the total particle volume. Coagulation reduces particle number but the total particle volume remains constant. Condensation, since it involves gas-to-particle conversion, increases total particle volume, but the total number of particles remains constant. If both processes are occurring simultaneously, total particle number decreases and total particle volume increases. A detailed study of the interplay between coagulation and condensation has been presented by Ramabhadran et al. (1976) and Peterson et al. (1978) to which we refer the interested reader.

10.8.   EFFECT OF THE MECHANISM OF GAS-TO-PARTICLE CONVERSION ON THE EVOLUTION OF AN AEROSOL SIZE DISTRIBUTION

Atmospheric aerosols evolve in size by coagulation and gas-to-particle conversion. To interpret the evolution of a size spectrum it is necessary to understand the influences of these two phenomena. It has been found that aerosols in the size range 0.01 μm to 1.0 μm diameter grow principally by gas-to-particle conversion, the process by which vapor molecules diffuse to the surface of a particle and subsequently are incorporated into the particle.

The rate-controlling step in gas-to-particle conversion may be a result of one or a combination of three mechanisms: the rate of diffusion of the vapor molecule to the surface of the particle; the rate of a surface reaction involving the adsorbed vapor molecule and the particle surface; and the rate of a reaction involving the dissolved species occurring uniformly throughout the volume of the particle. The particle growth rates that result in the three cases can be referred to as diffusion-controlled, surface reaction-controlled, and volume reaction-controlled growth, respectively. In fact, it has been suggested that information about possible chemical conversion mechanisms can be inferred from data on the evolution of an aerosol size distribution (Seinfeld and Ramabhadran, 1975; Heisler and Friedlander, 1977; Gelbard and Seinfeld, 1979: McMurry and Wilson, 1982). By calculating growth rates for particles of different sizes, the functional dependence of growth rate on particle size can be determined and compared with theoretical expressions relating particle growth to particle size (i.e., growth laws). In this way it is possible to suggest chemical mechanisms that are consistent with the data.

The main object of this section is to theoretically compare aerosol size spectra evolving by the mechanisms of diffusion-, surface reaction-, and volume reaction-controlled growth. The results will provide a basis for the interpretation of atmospheric and laboratory aerosol size spectra with respect to the governing growth mechanisms.

Let us consider Eq. (10.74) written in terms of particle mass m as the size variable, so that $n(m, t)$ is the size distribution function based on particle mass and $I_m(m, t)$ is the rate of change of the mass of a particle of mass m due to condensation. In the absence of particle sources $S(m, t) = 0$, and the condensation equation is

$$\frac{\partial n}{\partial t} + \frac{\partial}{\partial m}\left(I_m(m, t)n\right) = 0 \qquad (10.130)$$

To study the evolution of an aerosol from an initial distribution,

$$n(m, 0) = n_0(m) \qquad (10.131)$$

under different modes of gas-to-particle conversion requires the solution of Eq. (10.130) for the forms of $I_m(m, t)$ corresponding to the modes of conversion.

It is advantageous to place Eq. (10.130) in dimensionless form since we will be comparing several solutions of it that correspond to different physical situations. We define the dimensionless time and particle mass,

$$\tau = \frac{t I_m^r}{\rho_p \lambda^3}, \qquad \mu = \frac{m}{\rho_p \lambda^3}$$

ρ_p is the density of the particle, λ is the mean free path of the vapor, and I_m^r is a reference value of I_m. By then defining the reference size distribution function n^r and the dimensionless growth rate, $I(\mu, \tau) = I_m(m, t)/I_m^r$, we obtain the dimensionless form of Eq. (10.130),

$$\frac{\partial \psi}{\partial \tau} + \frac{\partial}{\partial \mu}\left(I(\mu, \tau)\psi\right) = 0 \qquad (10.132)$$

where $\psi(\mu, \tau) = n(m, t)/n^r$.

The object of this section is to examine solutions of Eq. (10.132) for several forms of the growth law $I(\mu, \tau)$. In particular, three forms of I will be studied corresponding to three different rate-controlling mechanisms for gas-to-particle conversion.

10.8.1. Diffusion-Controlled Growth

The rate of change of the mass of a particle resulting from diffusion of vapor molecules of species A to the particle is expressed by (8.103),

$$I_m = \left(\frac{48\pi^2 m}{\rho_p} \right)^{1/3} \frac{D_A M_A}{RT} (p_A - p_{A_s}) \beta(\text{Kn}) \qquad (10.133)$$

where we will use $\beta(\text{Kn})$ as $\beta_{FS}(\text{Kn})$ given by (8.111).

The vapor pressure of A just above the surface can be related to the particle mass through the Kelvin equation, Eq. (9.11),

$$\frac{p_{A_s}}{p_A^0} = \exp\left[\left(\frac{32\pi}{3} \right)^{1/3} \frac{\sigma\rho_p^{1/3}\bar{v}}{RTm^{1/3}} \right] \qquad (10.134)$$

We define the saturation ratio $S = p_A/p_A^0$ and the reference growth rate,

$$I_m^r = (48\pi^2)^{1/3} \frac{\lambda D_A M_A p_A^0}{RT} \qquad (10.135)$$

Then the dimensionless growth rate corresponding to Eqs. (10.133) and (10.134) is

$$I(\mu, \tau) = \mu^{1/3}\left[S(\tau) - \exp(\omega\mu^{-1/3}) \right] \beta(\text{Kn}) \qquad (10.136)$$

where the dependence on time τ enters through S and where

$$\omega = \left(\frac{32\pi}{3} \right)^{1/3} \frac{\sigma\bar{v}}{RT} \qquad (10.137)$$

and

$$\text{Kn} = \left(\frac{3\mu}{4\pi} \right)^{-1/3} \qquad (10.138)$$

In the case of so-called perfect absorption, $p_{A_s} = 0$, and Eq. (10.136) reduces to

$$I(\mu, \tau) = \mu^{1/3} S \beta(\text{Kn}) \qquad (10.139)$$

The continuum and free molecule limits can be examined with reference to Eq. (10.139). We find

$$I(\mu, \tau) = \begin{cases} S\mu^{1/3} & \text{Kn} \to 0 \\ \left(\dfrac{81}{256\pi}\right)^{1/3} S\mu^{2/3} & \text{Kn} \to \infty \end{cases} \tag{10.140}$$

10.8.2. Surface Reaction-Controlled Growth

The second case we consider is that of surface reaction-controlled growth, namely when the rate of particle growth is controlled by the rate at which adsorbed A on the particle surface is converted to another species B. Thus, we take, as the simplest representation of such a situation, the sequence,

$$A(g) \rightleftarrows A(s) \to B$$

where $A(s)$ denotes an adsorbed vapor molecule A on the surface that subsequently is converted to species B.

If the concentration of adsorbed A on the surface is C_s, and the rate of conversion to B is first order, with rate constant k_s, the rate of gain of particle mass due to the surface reaction is $4\pi R_p^2 M_B k_s C_s$. At steady state this rate must equal the rate of diffusion of molecules of A to the surface, which is given by Eq. (10.133). Thus,

$$4\pi R_p^2 M_B k_s C_s = \left(\frac{48\pi^2 m}{\rho_p}\right)^{1/3} \frac{D_A M_A}{RT}(p_A - p_{A_s})\beta(\text{Kn}) \tag{10.141}$$

Let us assume that adsorption equilibrium can be expressed by a relation of the form,

$$C_s = H_s p_A^0 \tag{10.142}$$

Then C_s can be determined from Eqs. (10.141), (10.142), and (10.134) as

$$C_s = \left[\left(\frac{48\pi^2 m}{\rho_p}\right)^{1/3} \frac{D_A M_A}{RT} p_A \beta(\text{Kn})\right]$$

$$\times \left\{4\pi R_p^2 M_B k_s + \left(\frac{48\pi^2 m}{\rho_p}\right)^{1/3} \frac{D_A M_A}{RTH_s}\right.$$

$$\left.\times \exp\left[\left(\frac{32\pi}{3}\right)^{1/3} \frac{\sigma \rho_p^{1/3}\bar{v}}{RTm^{1/3}}\right]\beta(\text{Kn})\right\}^{-1} \tag{10.143}$$

When the rate-determining step is surface reaction, the second term in the denominator of Eq. (10.143) dominates the first term and Eq. (10.143) reduces to

$$C_s \simeq p_A H_s \exp\left[-\left(\frac{32\pi}{3}\right)^{1/3} \frac{\sigma\rho_p^{1/3}\bar{v}}{RTm^{1/3}}\right] \qquad (10.144)$$

The corresponding rate of particle growth is

$$I_m = 4\pi R_p^2 M_B k_s p_A H_s \exp\left[-\left(\frac{32\pi}{3}\right)^{1/3} \frac{\sigma\rho_p^{1/3}\bar{v}}{RTm^{1/3}}\right] \qquad (10.145)$$

Defining the reference growth rate,

$$I_m^r = (36\pi)^{1/3} M_B k_s p_A^0 H_s \qquad (10.146)$$

we obtain the surface reaction-controlled dimensionless growth rate as

$$I(\mu, \tau) = S\mu^{2/3}\exp(-\omega\mu^{-1/3}) \qquad (10.147)$$

10.8.3. Volume Reaction-Controlled Growth

Finally we consider the case in which the rate of growth is controlled by the conversion of dissolved A to a second species B. The sequence can be depicted as

$$A(g) \rightleftarrows A(1) \rightarrow B$$

If the concentration of dissolved A is C_v and the rate of conversion to B is first order, with rate constant k_v, the rate of gain of particle mass due to volume reaction is $4/3\pi R_p^3 M_B k_v C_v$. At steady state this rate must equal the rate of diffusion of molecules of A to the particle. Thus,

$$\tfrac{4}{3}\pi R_p^3 M_B k_v C_v = \left(\frac{48\pi^2 m}{\rho_p}\right)^{1/3} \frac{D_A M_A}{RT}(p_A - p_{A_s})\beta(\text{Kn}) \qquad (10.148)$$

As before, we assume that the equilibrium can be expressed by C_v

$$C_v = H_v p_A^0 \qquad (10.149)$$

Then C_v can be determined from Eqs. (10.148), (10.149), and (10.134) as

$$C_v = \left[\left(\frac{48\pi^2 m}{\rho_p}\right)^{1/3}\frac{D_A M_A}{RT}p_A\beta(\mathrm{Kn})\right]$$

$$\times\left\{\tfrac{4}{3}\pi R_p^3 M_B k_v + \left(\frac{48\pi^2 m}{\rho_p}\right)^{1/3}\frac{D_A M_A}{RTH_v}\exp\left[\left(\frac{32\pi}{3}\right)^{1/3}\frac{\sigma\rho_p^{1/3}\bar{v}}{RTm^{1/3}}\right]\beta(\mathrm{Kn})\right\}^{-1}$$

$$(10.150)$$

When the rate-determining step is volume reaction, the second term in the denominator of Eq. (10.150) dominates the first term and Eq. (10.150) reduces to

$$C_v \simeq p_A H_v \exp\left[-\left(\frac{32\pi}{3}\right)^{1/3}\frac{\sigma\rho_p^{1/3}\bar{v}}{RTm^{1/3}}\right] \tag{10.151}$$

The corresponding rate of particle growth is

$$I_m = \frac{4}{3}\pi R_p^3 M_B k_v\, p_A H_v \exp\left[-\left(\frac{32\pi}{3}\right)^{1/3}\frac{\sigma\rho_p^{1/3}\bar{v}}{RTm^{1/3}}\right] \tag{10.152}$$

Defining the reference growth rate,

$$I_m^r = \lambda^3 M_B k_v\, p_A^0 H_v \tag{10.153}$$

we obtain the volume reaction-controlled dimensionless growth rate as

$$I(\mu,\tau) = S\mu\exp(-\omega\mu^{-1/3}) \tag{10.154}$$

10.8.4. Dimensionless Size Spectra Evolution

We now consider size spectra $\psi(\mu,\tau)$ corresponding to the three growth cases just developed. The initial distribution $\psi_0(\mu)$ was adapted from one measured in a power plant plume. (See case d in Table 3 of Eltgroth and Hobbs, 1979.) The dimensionless size distributions are presented in terms of the dimensionless mass distribution $M(\log D_p,\tau)$, where $(\rho_p\lambda^3)^2 n' M(\log D_p,\tau)\, d\log D_p$ is the mass of particles having logarithm of diameter in the range $(\log D_p, \log D_p + d\log D_p)$. Thus, M is related to ψ by

$$M(\log D_p,\tau) = 6.9\mu^2\psi(\mu,\tau) \tag{10.155}$$

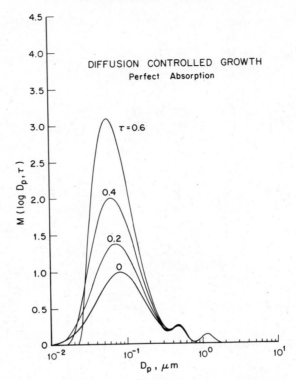

Figure 10.5. Evolution of dimensionless aerosol mass distribution at dimensionless times $\tau = 0$, 0.2, 0.4 and 0.6 for diffusion-controlled growth with perfect absorption (Seinfeld and Bassett, 1982).

For the initial distribution used, the value of n^r was chosen so that the maximum value of $M(\log D_p, 0)$ is 1.0. This value of n^r is 1.645×10^{14} μg^{-1} cm^{-3}.

It is necessary to specify the parameters S and ω. The saturation ratio S will be chosen as 2.878 corresponding to a critical diameter $D_p^* = 4\sigma\bar{v}/RT \ln S$ of 0.01 μm for a sulfuric acid/water aerosol at 25°C. The Kelvin parameter ω is then equal to 0.1282. Since S is taken as independent of time, the growth laws I are functions of μ only.

Figure 10.5 shows the evolution of the dimensionless mass distribution at $\tau = 0$, 0.2, 0.4, and 0.6 for case (1), diffusion-controlled growth with perfect absorption. As expected, we see that the smaller particles grow proportionally faster than the larger ones. The dependence of I on particle diameter gradually shifts from D_p^2 for the smallest particles (free molecule regime) to D_p for the largest particles (continuum regime), as indicated in Eq. (10.140).

In diffusion-controlled growth with a nonzero vapor pressure over the particle surface, addition of a vapor pressure leads to a much slower growth of

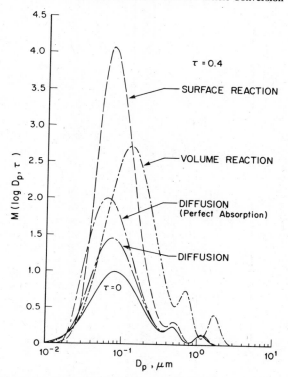

Figure 10.6. Aerosol mass distribution at dimensionless time $\tau = 0.4$ resulting from growth by diffusion, with and without perfect absorption, surface reaction, and volume reaction (Seinfeld and Bassett, 1982).

the smaller particles than the case in Figure 10.5. This, in turn, reduces the tendency of the major mode in the mass distribution to steepen.

In the case of surface reaction-controlled growth, we note that the large particles, for which the Kelvin effect is negligible, grow at a rate proportional to D_p^2. Recall that in diffusion-controlled growth the smallest particles also grow at a rate proportional to D_p^2. The larger particles growing by diffusion grow at a rate proportional to D_p. Thus, we expect that of two continuum regime particles, one growing by diffusion and one by surface reaction, the particle growing by surface reaction does so at a greater rate. When gas-to-particle conversion occurs by volume reaction, large particles grow at a rate proportional to D_p^3. Thus, these particles grow more rapidly than in either diffusion or surface reaction cases.

In Figure 10.6 the distributions from all three mechanisms at $\tau = 0.4$ are shown, providing a summary of the effects just discussed. The location of the main peak provides an indication of the relative importance of the growth of small and large particles. For the volume reaction case, where the ratio of large

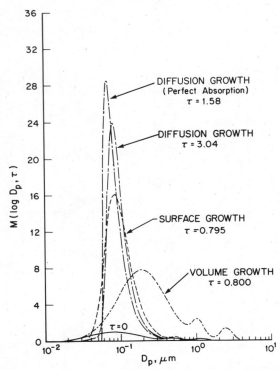

Figure 10.7. Aerosol mass distributions at the time when the mass added by gas-to-particle conversion is seven times the initial mass (Seinfeld and Bassett, 1982).

particle growth to small particle growth is the greatest, the particle diameter at which the peak is located is the greatest. On the other hand, for diffusional growth with no vapor pressure, where the growth of small particles is the most important, the particle diameter at which the peak is located is smaller than for any of the other cases.

These results indicate that the mechanism of growth of an aerosol can be inferred from the evolution of its size spectrum. Figure 10.7 shows three size distributions at times when the total mass added to the particulate phase is the same (seven times the initial aerosol mass). Thus, the different size distributions are solely the result of the manner in which the different mechanisms distribute mass among the different particle sizes.

The distribution for the volume reaction case has significantly more large particles than any other. Thus, it should be fairly easy to distinguish experimentally between a volume reaction and the other mechanisms. On the other hand, it would probably be difficult to distinguish between the surface reaction case and diffusion growth without a vapor pressure. It would probably be impossible to distinguish experimentally between diffusion growth with a vapor pressure and a surface reaction.

10.9. KINETIC APPROACH TO HOMOGENEOUS NUCLEATION THEORY

In Chapter 9 we developed homogeneous nucleation theory essentially from a thermodynamic point of view. Having developed the general dynamic equation it is now possible to return to homogeneous nucleation and treat it as a purely kinetic phenomenon. Consider a situation in which a single condensable species is being produced in a constant volume system at a rate R_g (molecules cm^{-3} sec^{-1}). The balance on monomer molecules is

$$\frac{dN_1}{dt} = R_g - N_1 \sum_{j=1}^{\infty} K_{1j}N_j + \sum_{j=2}^{\infty} (1 - \delta_{2j})e_j N_j \qquad (10.156)$$

and that on particles containing g monomers is Eq. (10.56)

$$\frac{dN_g}{dt} = \frac{1}{2} \sum_{j=1}^{g-1} K_{j,g-1}N_j N_{g-j} - N_g \sum_{j=1}^{\infty} K_{g,j}N_j - e_g N_g + e_{g+1}N_{g+1}$$

$$(10.157)$$

The evaporation coefficient e_g is obtained by equating the rates at which molecules enter and leave a cluster of size g at equilibrium, as was done in Eq. (9.31). The presumption is that molecules will evaporate from a cluster at a rate that depends only on the size and properties of the cluster and the temperature. At equilibrium this rate equals the rate at which monomers collide and stick to particles containing $g - 1$ molecules. From Eq. (9.31) we can estimate e_g as

$$e_g = \beta \frac{N_{g-1}^e}{N_g^e} = K_{g,g-1}N_s \exp\left[\frac{b}{kT}\left(g^{2/3} - (g-1)^{2/3}\right)\right] \qquad (10.158)$$

where N_s is the equilibrium saturation concentration of monomer over a flat surface at temperature T.

Equations (10.156) to (10.158) constitute the basis of the kinetic approach to homogeneous nucleation theory. Since we expect clusters to lie in the free molecule regime, the coagulation coefficient is Eq. (10.31),

$$K_{i,j} = \left(\frac{3v_1}{4\pi}\right)^{1/6}\left(\frac{6kT}{\rho_p}\right)^{1/2}\left(\frac{1}{i} + \frac{1}{j}\right)^{1/2}\left(i^{1/3} + j^{1/3}\right)^2 \qquad (10.159)$$

It is useful to define dimensionless time and number concentrations (McMurry, 1980). The parameter driving the behavior of the system is the monomer generation rate R_g, so we incorporate R_g into these two quantities. We let $\tau = (R_g K_{1,1})^{1/2}t$ and $N_g^* = (K_{1,1}/R_g)^{1/2}N_g$ be the dimensionless time and g-mer concentration, respectively. In addition, we let $E = N_s(K_{1,1}/R_g)^{1/2}$ and $C_{ij} = K_{i,j}/K_{1,1}$. Then the dimensionless monomer and g-mer balance equations become

$$\frac{dN_1^*}{d\tau} = 1 - N_1^* \sum_{j=1}^{\infty} C_{ij} N_j^*$$

$$+ \sum_{j=2}^{\infty} (1 - \delta_{2j}) C_{1,j-1} E \exp\left[\left(\frac{b}{kT}\right)\left(j^{2/3} - (j-1)^{2/3}\right)\right] N_j^*$$

$$\tag{10.160}$$

$$\frac{dN_g^*}{d\tau} = \tfrac{1}{2} \sum_{j=1}^{g-1} C_{j,g-j} N_j^* N_{g-j}^* - N_g^* \sum_{j=1}^{\infty} C_{g,j} N_j^*$$

$$+ N_{g+1}^* C_{1g} E \exp\left[\left(\frac{b}{kT}\right)\left((j+1)^{2/3} - j^{2/3}\right)\right]$$

$$- N_g^* C_{1,g-1} E \exp\left[\left(\frac{b}{kT}\right)\left(j^{2/3} - (j-1)^{2/3}\right)\right] \tag{10.161}$$

Note that the saturation ratio $S = N_1/N_s = N_1^*/E$.

We can note some qualitative features of this system. As $E \to 0$, we expect evaporation to be unimportant. A small E implies either a large rate of monomer generation R_g or a small value of the saturation number concentration of monomer. As surface tension σ increases, b increases, leading to an increase in the importance of evaporation.

REFERENCES

Brock, J. R. "Condensational Growth of Atmospheric Aerosols," *J. Colloid Interface Sci.*, **39**, 32–36 (1972).

Dahneke, B. "Simple Kinetic Theory of Brownian Diffusion in Vapors and Aerosols," in *Theory of Dispersed Multiphase Flow*, R. E. Meyer (Ed.), Academic Press, New York, 97–138 (1983).

Drake, R. L. "A General Mathematical Survey of the Coagulation Equation," in *Topics in Current Aerosol Research* (Part 2) G. M. Hidy and J. R. Brock (Eds.), Pergamon, New York, 201–376 (1972).

Eltgroth, M. W., and Hobbs, P. V. "Evolution of Particles in the Plumes of Coal-Fired Power Plants—II. A Numerical Model and Comparisons with Field Measurements," *Atmos. Environ.*, **13**, 953–976 (1979).

Friedlander, S. K. *Smoke, Dust and Haze: Fundamentals of Aerosol Behavior*, Wiley, New York (1977).

Fuchs, N. A. *Mechanics of Aerosols*, Pergamon, New York (1964).

Gelbard, F., and Seinfeld, J. H. "Numerical Solution of the Dynamic Equation for Particulate Systems," *J. Comput. Phys.*, **28**, 357–375 (1978).

Gelbard, F., and Seinfeld, J. H. "Exact Solution of the General Dynamic Equation for Aerosol Growth by Condensation," *J. Colloid Interface Sci.*, **68**, 173–183 (1979).

Gelbard, F., and Seinfeld, J. H. "The General Dynamic Equation for Aerosols-Theory and Application to Aerosol Formation and Growth," *J. Colloid Interface Sci.*, **68**, 363–382 (1979).

Hamaker, H. C. "The London-van der Waals Attraction Between Spherical Particles," *Physica*, **4**, 1058–1072 (1937).

Heisler, S. L., and Friedlander, S. K. "Gas-to-Particle Conversion in Photochemical Smog; Growth Laws and Mechanisms for Organics," *Atmos. Environ.*, **11**, 158–168 (1977).

Hidy, G. M., Mueller, P. K., Grosjean, D., Appel, B. R., and Wesolowski, J. J. *The Character and Origins of Smog Aerosols*, Wiley, New York (1980).

Hirschfelder, J. O., Curtiss, C. F., and Bird, R. B. *Molecular Theory of Gases and Liquids*, Wiley, New York (1954).

Judeikis, H. S., and Siegel, S. "Particle Catalyzed Oxidation of Atmospheric Pollutants," *Atmos. Environ.*, **7**, 619–631 (1973).

Kim, C. S., and Liu, B. Y. H. "Experimental Studies of Coagulation of Free Molecule Aerosols," in *Aerosols*, B. Y. H. Liu, D. Y. H. Pui, and H. J. Fissan (Eds.), Elsevier, New York, 923–925 (1984).

Lee, P. S., and Shaw, D. T. "Dynamics of Fibrous-Type Particles: Brownian Coagulation and the Charge Effect," *Aerosol Sci. Technol.*, **3**, 9–16 (1984).

Marlow, W. H. "Size Effects in Aerosol Particle Interactions: The van der Waals Potential and Collision Rates," *Surface Sci.*, **106**, 529–537 (1981).

Marlow, W. H. "Long-Range Attraction in the Collisions of Free-Molecular and Transition Regime Aerosol Particles," 13th International Symposium on Rarified Gas Dynamics (1982).

McMurry, P. H. "Photochemical Aerosol Formation from SO_2: A Theoretical Analysis of Smog Chamber Data," *J. Colloid Interface Sci.*, **78**, 513–527 (1980).

McMurry, P. H. and Wilson, J. C. "Growth Laws for the Formation of Secondary Ambient Aerosols: Implications for Chemical Conversion Mechanisms," *Atmos. Environ.*, **16**, 121–134 (1982).

Mulholland, G. W., and Baum, H. R. "Effect of Initial Size Distribution on Aerosol Coagulation," *Phys. Rev. Letters*, **45**, 761–763 (1980).

Novakov, T., Chang, C. S., and Harker, A. B. "Sulfates as Pollution Particles: Catalytic Formation on Carbon (Soot) Particles," *Science*, **186**, 256–261 (1974).

Okuyama, K., Kousaka, Y. and Hayashi, K. "Change in Size Distribution of Ultrafine Aerosols Undergoing Brownian Coagulation," *J. Colloid Interface Sci.*, **101**, 98–109 (1984).

Peterson, T. W., Gelbard, F., and Seinfeld, J. H. "Dynamics of Source-Reinforced, Coagulating, and Condensing Aerosols," *J. Colloid Interface Sci.*, **63**, 426–445 (1978).

Peterson, T. W., and Seinfeld, J. H. "Calculation of Sulfate and Nitrate Levels in a Growing, Reacting Aerosol," *AIChE J.*, **25**, 831–838 (1979).

Peterson, T. W., and Seinfeld, J. H. "Heterogeneous Condensation and Chemical Reaction in Droplets—Application to the Heterogeneous Atmospheric Oxidation of SO_2," in *Adv. Environ. Sci. Technol.*, **10**, 125–180, (1980).

Phillips, W. F. "Drag on a Small Sphere Moving Through a Gas," *Phys. Fluids*, **18**, 1089–1093 (1975).

Pruppacher, H. R., and Klett, J. O. *Microphysics of Clouds and Precipitation*, D. Reidel, Boston (1978).

Ramabhadran, T. E., Peterson, T. W., and Seinfeld, J. H. "Dynamics of Aerosol Coagulation and Condensation," *AIChE J.*, **22**, 840–851 (1976).

Saffman, P. G. and Turner, J. S. "On the Collision of Drops in Turbulent Clouds," *J. Fluid Mech.*, **1**, 16–30 (1956).

Seinfeld, J. H., *Lectures in Atmospheric Chemistry*, AIChE Monograph Series 12, American Institute of Chemical Engineers, New York (1980).

Seinfeld, J. H., and Bassett, M. "Effect of the Mechanism of Gas-to-Particle Conversion on the Evolution of Aerosol Size Distributions," in *Heterogeneous Atmospheric Chemistry*, D. R. Schryer (Ed.), American Geophysical Union, Washington, D.C., 6–12 (1982).

Seinfeld, J. H., and Ramabhadran, T. E. "Atmospheric Aerosol Growth by Heterogeneous Condensation," *Atmos. Environ.*, **9**, 1091–1097 (1975).

Tambour, Y., and Seinfeld, J. H. "Solution of the Discrete Coagulation Equation," *J. Colloid Interface Sci.*, **74**, 260–272 (1980).

Tennekes, H., and Lumley, J. O. *A First Course in Turbulence*, MIT Press, Cambridge, MA (1972).

Wagner, P. E., and Kerker, M. "Brownian Coagulation of Aerosols in Rarified Gases," *J. Chem. Phys.*, **66**, 638–646 (1977).

Williams, M. M. R. "On Some Exact Solutions of the Space- and Time-Dependent Coagulation Equation for Aerosols," *J. Colloid Interface Sci.*, **101**, 19–26 (1984).

PROBLEMS

10.1. Show that for an aerosol population undergoing growth by condensation only with no sources or sinks:

(a)   the total number of particles is constant;

(b)   the average particle size increases with time;

(c)   the total aerosol volume increases with time.

10.2. Show that the solution of the coagulation equation with a constant coagulation coefficient, including first-order particle removal,

$$\frac{\partial n(v, t)}{\partial t} = \tfrac{1}{2} K \int_0^v n(v - \tilde{v}, t) n(\tilde{v}, t)\, d\tilde{v} - K n(v, t) N(t)$$

$$- R(t) n(v, t)$$

with $n_0(v) = (N_0/v_0)\exp(-v/v_0)$ is (Williams, 1984)

$$n(v, t) = \frac{N_0}{v_0} e^{-v/v_0}$$

$$\times \exp\left[-\int_0^t \left[P(t') - \frac{v N_0 K}{2 v_0} \exp\left(-\int_0^{t'} P(t'')\, dt'' \right) \right] dt' \right]$$

where $P(t) = R(t) + KN(t)$.

10.3. Given particle growth laws expressed in terms of particle diameter for the three modes of gas-to-particle conversion discussed in Section 10.8,

$$\frac{dD_p}{dt} = \begin{cases} h_d D_p^{-1} & \text{diffusion} \\ h_s & \text{surface reaction} \\ h_v D_p & \text{volume reaction} \end{cases}$$

show that an aerosol having an initial size distribution $n_0(D_p)$ evolves under the three growth mechanisms according to

$$n(D_p, t) = \begin{cases} n_0\left[\left(D_p^2 - 2h_d t\right)^{1/2}\right] \dfrac{D_p}{\left(D_p^2 - 2h_d t\right)^{1/2}} \\ n_0(D_p - h_s t) \\ n_0\left(D_p e^{-h_v t}\right) e^{-h_v t} \end{cases}$$

10.4. Consider the steady state size distribution of an aerosol subject to growth by condensation, sources, and first-order removal. The steady state size distribution in this situation is governed by

$$\frac{d}{dv}(I(v)n(v)) = S(v) - R(v)n(v)$$

(a) Show that

$$n(v) = \frac{1}{I(v)} \int_0^v S(v') \exp\left[-\int_{v'}^v \frac{R(v'')}{I(v'')} \, dv''\right] dv'$$

(b) Taking $I(v) = h_a v^a$, $R(v) = R_m v^m$, and $S(v) = S_0 \delta(v - v_0)$, show that

$$n(v) = \frac{S_0}{v^a h_a} \exp\left[-\frac{R_m}{h_a(m + 1 - a)}\left(v^{m+1-a} - v_0^{m+1-a}\right)\right]$$

valid for $v \geq v_0$.

10.5. It is of interest to compare the relative magnitudes of processes that remove or add particles from one size regime to another in an aerosol size spectrum. Let us assume that a "typical" atmospheric aerosol size distribution can be divided into three size ranges $0.01 \ \mu\text{m} < D_p < 0.1 \ \mu\text{m}$, $0.1 < D_p < 1.0 \ \mu\text{m}$, and $1 \ \mu\text{m} < D_p < 10 \ \mu\text{m}$, in which the particle number concentrations are assumed to be

$$\frac{0.01\ \mu m < D_p < 0.1\ \mu m}{10^5\ cm^{-3}} \quad \frac{0.1 < D_p < 1.0\ \mu m}{10^2\ cm^{-3}} \quad \frac{1.0\ \mu m < D_p < 10\ \mu m}{10^{-1}\ cm^{-3}}$$

It is desired to estimate the relative contributions of the processes listed below to the rates of change of the aerosol number concentrations in each of the three size ranges:

1. Coagulation
   a. Brownian
   b. Turbulent shear
   c. Differential sedimentation
2. Heterogeneous condensation

For the conditions of the calculation assume air at $T = 298$ K, $p = 1$ atm. For the purposes of the coagulation calculation assume that the particles in the three size ranges have diameters 0.05 μm, 0.5 μm, and 5 μm. For turbulent shear coagulation assume $\varepsilon_k = 1000$ cm^2 sec^{-3}. In the differential sedimentation calculation assume that the particles with which those in the three size ranges collide have $D_p = 10$ μm with a number concentration of 10^{-1} cm^{-3}. For heterogeneous condensation the flux of particles into and out of the size ranges can be estimated by calculating the rate of change of the diameter, dD_p/dt, assuming zero vapor pressure of the condensing vapor species and assuming that the number con-

TABLE P10.1. Estimated Rates of Change of Aerosol Number Densities (cm^{-3} sec^{-1})

	Size Range		
Process	$0.01\ \mu m < D_{p_i} < 0.1\ \mu m^a$	$0.1 \le D_{p_i} \le 1.0\ \mu m^b$	$1.0\ \mu m < D_{p_i} < 10\ \mu m^c$
1. Coagulation			
Brownian			
Turbulent			
Sedimentation			
2. Heterogeneous condensation			
$S = 1.0$			
$S = 2.0$			
$S = 10.0$			

[a]Assuming that $D_{p_i} = 0.05$ μm for all particles, and $N = 10^5$ cm^{-3}.
[b]Assuming that $D_{p_i} = 0.5$ μm for all particles, and $N = 10^2$ cm^{-3}.
[c]Assuming that $D_{p_i} = 5$ μm for all particles, and $N = 10^{-1}$ cm^{-3}.

centration in each size range is uniform across the range. In addition, assume that the condensing species has the properties of sulfuric acid:

$$D = 0.07 \text{ cm}^2 \text{ sec}^{-1}$$

$$M_A = 98 \text{ g mole}^{-1}$$

$$p_A^0(T) = 1.3 \times 10^{-3} \text{ dynes cm}^{-2}$$

$$\rho_p = 1.87 \text{ g cm}^{-3}$$

Examine saturation ratio values, $S = p_A/p_A^0(T)$, of 1.0, 2.0, and 10.0. Show all calculations and carefully note any assumptions you make. Present your results in Table P10.1:

10.6. We want to explore the dynamics of aerosol size distributions undergoing simultaneous growth by condensation and removal at a rate dependent on the aerosol concentration, with a continuous source of new particles. The size distribution function in such a case is governed by

$$\frac{\partial n(v,t)}{\partial t} + \frac{\partial}{\partial v}(I(v,t)n(v,t)) = S(v,t) - R(v,t)n(v,t)$$

where $R(v,t)$ is the first-order removal constant. Let us assume that $I(v,t) = h_a v^a$, $R(v,t) = R_m v^m$, $S(v,t) = S_0 \delta(v - v_0)$ and $n_0(v) = N_0 \delta(v - v_*)$.

(a) Show that under these conditions

$$n(v,t) = \frac{S_0}{v^a h_a} \exp\left[-\frac{R_m}{h_a(m+1-a)}(v^{m+1-a} - v_0^{m+1-a}) \right]$$

$$+ N_0 \exp\left\{ -\frac{R_m}{h_a(m+1-a)} \right.$$

$$\times \left[[v_*^{1-a} + (1-a)h_a t]^{m+1-a/1-a} - v_*^{m+1-a} \right] \right\}$$

$$\times \delta\left[v - (v_*^{1-a} + (1-a)h_a t)^{1/1-a} \right]$$

Hint: The equation for $n(v, t)$ can be solved by assuming a solution of the form $n(v, t) = n_\infty(v) + n^0(v, t)$, where $n_\infty(v)$ is the steady state solution of the equation (see Problem 10.4) and $n^0(v, t)$ is the transient solution corresponding to the initial condition $n_0(v)$ in the absence of the source $S(v, t)$.

(b) Express the solution determined in part (a) in terms of the following dimensionless groups:

$$\theta = \frac{(1 - a)h_a t}{v_*^{1-a}} \qquad y = v/v_0 \qquad \tilde{n} = n/N$$

$$\chi = \frac{v_*}{v_0} \qquad \lambda = \frac{R_m v_0^{m+1-a}}{h_a(m + 1 - a)} \qquad \rho = \frac{N_0 h_a v_*^a}{S_0}$$

where N is the total number of particles.

(c) Examine the limiting cases of $\rho \to \infty$ and $\rho \to 0$. Show that the proper forms of the solution are obtained in these two cases.

(d) Plot the steady state solution $n_\infty(y)$ for $a = 1/3$ and $2/3$, $m = 2/3$ and $\lambda = 0.001, 0.01, 0.1, 1.0, 10.0$. Discuss the behavior of the solutions.

(e) Plot $\tilde{n}(y, \theta)$ as a function of y for $a = 1/3$, $m = 2/3$, $\lambda = 0.01$, $\rho = 100$, and $\chi = 1.1$ for $\theta = 0.1, 1, 10,$ and 100. Discuss.

PART FOUR

Air Pollution Meteorology

Condensation plumes for a 500 ft. and three 250 ft. stacks in Salem, Massachusetts. The picture, taken on a cold February morning, shows the complex thermal structure and large wind shear in the lower atmosphere. Steaming fog in the foreground is over the Beverly-Salem Harbor. The original photograph was taken by Ralph Turcotte, a staff photographer for the Beverly (MA) Times.

ELEVEN

Air Pollution Meteorology

Meteorology is the study of the dynamics of the atmosphere. Meteorological scales of motion can be categorized as follows:

1. *Macroscale.* Phenomena occurring on scales of thousands of kilometers, such as semipermanent high and low pressure areas that reside over the oceans and continents. (The term *synoptic* is commonly used to denote macroscale.)

2. *Mesoscale.* Phenomena occurring on scales of hundreds of kilometers, such as land–sea breezes, mountain-valley winds, and migratory high and low pressure fronts.

3. *Microscale.* Phenomena occurring on scales of the order of 1 km, such as the meandering and dispersion of a chimney plume and the complicated flow regime in the wake of a large building.

Each of these scales of motion plays a role in air pollution, although over different periods of time. For example, micrometeorological effects take place over scales of the order of minutes to hours, whereas mesoscale phenomena influence transport and dispersal of pollutants over hours to days. Finally, synoptic scales of motion have characteristic times of days to weeks. The term "long-range transport" commonly refers to transport on the synoptic scale.

With respect to urban air pollution, the region of the atmosphere governing transport and dispersion is the so-called planetary boundary layer, roughly the lowest 500 m. The planetary boundary layer represents the extent of influence of the earth's surface on wind structure in the atmosphere. Within the planetary boundary layer, winds are influenced by the prevailing high-level flows and the frictional drag of the surface.

The atmospheric temperature profile (the variation of temperature with altitude) has an important effect on wind structure and turbulence in the lowest 500 m. In the troposphere the temperature normally decreases with increasing altitude because of the decrease in pressure with height. The temperature profile against which all others are judged is that observed for a

441

parcel of dry air as it moves upward in a hydrostatically stable atmosphere and expands slowly to lower pressure with no gain or loss of heat. If such a profile exists in the atmosphere, a parcel of air at any height is in neutral equilibrium; that is, it has no tendency either to rise or fall. The atmosphere is, however, very seldom in such delicate equilibrium; the influence of surface heating and large-scale phenomena usually results in a temperature profile different from this reference profile. If the temperature decreases faster with height than the reference profile, air parcels at any height are unstable; that is, if they are displaced either upward or downward, they will continue their movement in the direction in which they were displaced. Such a condition is referred to as unstable. On the other hand, if the temperature decreases more slowly with height than the reference profile (or even increases), air parcels are inhibited from either upward or downward motion and the situation is referred to as stable. The stability condition of the atmosphere plays an important role in determining the rate of dispersal of pollutants.

The phenomenon of direct interest in predicting the dispersion of air pollutants is turbulent diffusion. Actually, turbulent diffusion is something of a misnomer. The phrase refers to the observed spreading of a cloud of marked particles in a turbulent fluid at a rate many orders of magnitude greater than that from molecular diffusion alone. The spreading is really not due to a "diffusion" phenomenon such as results from molecular collisions but rather is a result of the rapid, irregular motion of macroscopic lumps of fluid (called eddies) in turbulence. Thus, the scales of length in turbulent diffusion are much greater than in molecular diffusion, with the contribution of the latter to the dispersion of pollutants in turbulence being virtually negligible. The level of turbulence in the planetary boundary layer increases with increased wind speed, surface roughness, and instability. Turbulence, therefore, arises from both mechanical forces (shear, surface friction) and thermal forces (buoyancy).

In this chapter we discuss three topics (1) the atmospheric energy balance, (2) temperature profiles in the lower atmosphere, and (3) winds. It is possible that increases in the background concentration of even a minor constituent of the atmosphere may lead to significant changes in atmospheric properties. These changes would most likely be reflected in radiative scattering and absorption processes, and therefore a study of the atmospheric energy balance is essential in understanding potential climatic changes due to air pollutants. Lower atmospheric temperature profiles determine in part the stability of the atmosphere, or, in other words, the degree to which turbulence induced by wind, surface roughness, or buoyancy will propagate through the layer. Under strongly stable conditions, disturbances are highly damped and mixing of species is strongly suppressed. It is under such conditions that the worst air pollution episodes have occurred. Finally, the importance of winds to the atmospheric aspects of air pollution is clearly evident. Our discussion of winds in this chapter will be highly qualitative; in Chapter 12 we shall treat air motion in the lower atmosphere from a quantitative standpoint.

11.1. ATMOSPHERIC ENERGY BALANCE

11.1.1. Radiation

Basically all the energy that reaches the earth comes from the sun. The absorption and loss of radiant energy by the earth and the atmosphere are almost totally responsible for the earth's weather, both on a global and local scale. The average temperature on the earth remains fairly constant, indicating that the earth and the atmosphere on the whole lose as much energy by reradiation back into space as is received by radiation from the sun. The accounting for the incoming and outgoing radiant energy constitutes the earth's energy balance. The atmosphere, although it may appear to be transparent to radiation, plays a very important role in the energy balance of the earth. In fact, the atmosphere controls the amount of solar radiation that actually reaches the surface of the earth and, at the same time, controls the amount of outgoing terrestrial radiation that escapes into space. In this section we consider in particular the role of the atmosphere in the earth's energy balance.

Radiant energy, arranged in order of its wavelengths, is called the *spectrum* of radiation. The so-called electromagnetic spectrum is shown in Fig. 11.1. The sun radiates over the entire electromagnetic spectrum, although, as we will see, most of the energy is concentrated near the visible portion of the spectrum, the narrow band of wavelengths from 400 to 700 nm.

Radiation is emitted when an electron drops to a lower level of energy. The difference in energy between the initial and final level, $\Delta\varepsilon$, is related to the frequency of the emitted radiation by Planck's law,

$$\Delta\varepsilon = h\nu = \frac{hc}{\lambda}$$

where $h = 6.63 \times 10^{-34}$ joule sec. When the energy difference $\Delta\varepsilon$ is large, the frequency of the emitted photon is high (very small wavelength) and the radiation is in the X-ray or gamma-ray region. The Planck condition also applies to the absorption of a photon of energy by a molecule. Thus, a molecule can absorb radiant energy only if the wavelength of the radiation corresponds to the difference between two of its energy levels. Since the spacing between energy levels is, in general, different for molecules of different composition and shape, the absorption of radiant energy by molecules of differing structure occurs in different regions of the electromagnetic spectrum (Recall Table 4.1).

The amount of energy radiated from a body depends largely on the temperature of the body. It has been demonstrated experimentally that at a given temperature there is a maximum amount of radiant energy that can be emitted per unit time per unit area of a body. This maximum amount of radiation for a certain temperature is called the *blackbody radiation*. A body

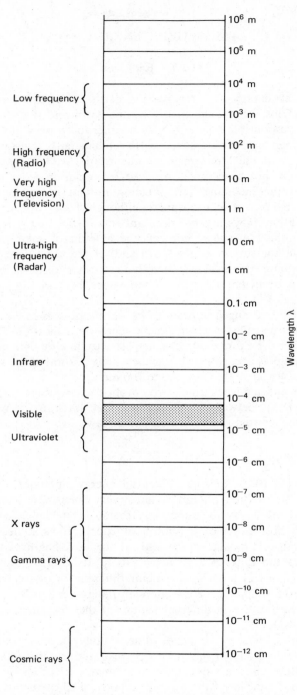

Figure 11.1. Electromagnetic spectrum.

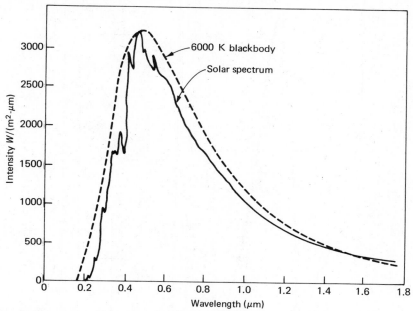

Figure 11.2. Solar spectrum and the monochromatic emissivity of a blackbody at 6000 K.

that radiates for every wavelength the maximum possible intensity of radiation at a certain temperature is called a *blackbody*. This maximum is identical for every blackbody regardless of its constituency. Thus, the intensity of radiation emitted by a blackbody is a function only of the wavelength, absolute temperature, and surface area. The term "blackbody" has no reference to the color of the body. A blackbody can also be characterized by the property that all radiant energy reaching its surface is absorbed.

The energy spectrum of the sun resembles that of a blackbody at 6000 K. (See Fig. 11.2.) The so-called photosphere (the outer layer of the sun) is 400 km thick and varies from 8000 K at the base to about 4000 K at the surface. Thus, it is not in thermodynamic equilibrium as a true blackbody must be, and the sun's spectrum is not exactly a blackbody spectrum. The maximum intensity of incident radiation occurs in the visible spectrum at about 500 nm. In contrast, Fig. 11.3 shows the emission of radiant energy from a blackbody at 300 K, approximating the earth. The peak in radiation intensity occurs at 10,000 nm in the invisible infrared.

Briefly, we can summarize some of the quantities of importance in the study of radiation:

$E =$ total emissive power, the energy radiated from a surface per unit area per unit time in all directions over all wavelengths

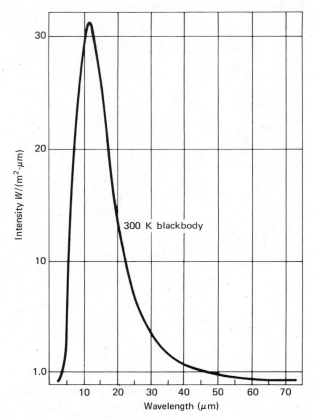

Figure 11.3. Monochromatic emissivity of a blackbody at 300 K.

E_λ = monochromatic emissive power, the energy radiated from a surface per unit area per unit time in all directions in the wavelength range λ to $\lambda + d\lambda$

ε = emissivity, ratio of the total emissive power E to that of a blackbody at the same temperature E_B

ε_λ = monochromatic emissivity, ratio of the monochromatic emissive power E_λ to that of a blackbody at the same temperature

ρ = reflectivity, the fraction of the incident radiation that is reflected by a surface (can also define a monochromatic reflectivity ρ_λ)

τ = transmissivity, the fraction of the incident radiation transmitted through a medium per unit thickness along the path of the mean (can also define a monochromatic transmissivity τ_λ)

α = absorptivity, the fraction of the incident radiation that is absorbed by the surface (can also define a monochromatic absorptivity α_λ). Note that $\rho + \tau + \alpha = 1$

It is important to point out that both absorptivity and reflectivity are properties of the atmosphere. Gases can absorb radiant energy, and particles scatter oncoming radiation back in the direction of its origin.

In order to understand the spectra of Figs. 11.2 and 11.3, we must consider certain of the laws of radiation. *Kirchhoff's law* relates the emission of radiation of a given wavelength at a given temperature to the absorption of radiation of the same wavelength. The law states that every body absorbs radiation of exactly those wavelengths which it is capable of emitting at the same temperature, in other words that the absorptivity by a body of radiant energy of a given wavelength at a given temperature is equal to its emissivity in that wavelength at the same temperature:

$$\varepsilon_\lambda = \alpha_\lambda$$

Planck's law relates the monochromatic emissive power of a blackbody with temperature and wavelength:

$$E_{\lambda B} = \frac{2\pi c^2 h \lambda^{-5}}{e^{ch/k\lambda T} - 1}$$

Planck's law can be seen by examining Figs. 11.2 and 11.3. Figure 11.2 shows the emissive power of a blackbody at 6000 K, the approximate average temperature of the outer layer of the sun. Figure 11.3, on the other hand, shows the emissive power of a blackbody at 300 K, close to the temperature of the earth. Both of these curves obey Planck's law. As can be seen from the curves, the higher the temperature, the greater is the emissive power (at all wavelengths). We also see that, as temperature increases, the maximum value of $E_{\lambda B}$ moves to shorter wavelengths. The wavelength at which the maximum amount of radiation is emitted by a blackbody is found by differentiating Planck's formula with respect to λ, setting the result equal to zero, and solving for λ. The result in terms of nm is

$$\lambda_{max} = \frac{2.897 \times 10^6}{T}$$

where T is in degrees Kelvin. Thus, hot bodies not only radiate more energy than cold ones, they do it at shorter wavelengths. We see that the wavelengths for the maxima of solar and terrestrial radiation are 480 and about 10,000 nm, respectively. The sun, with an effective surface temperature of about 6000 K, radiates about 2×10^5 more energy per square meter than the earth at 300 K.*

*Incoming solar intensity is 1.92 cal cm^{-2} min^{-1}, the so-called solar constant.

If Planck's law is integrated over all wavelengths, the total emissive power of a blackbody is found to be

$$E_B = \int_0^\infty E_{\lambda B}\, d\lambda = \frac{2\pi^5 k^4 T^4}{15 c^2 h^3} = \sigma T^4$$

where $\sigma = 5.673 \times 10^{-8}$ watt m^{-2} K^{-4}, called the Stefan–Boltzmann constant.

The absorption of radiation by gases is one of the most important aspects of both global meteorology and atmospheric chemistry. The solar spectrum is radically altered by absorption as the radiation traverses the atmosphere. The most significant absorbing species in the atmosphere are O_2, O_3, water vapor, CO_2, and dust. Figure 11.4 shows the absorption spectrum for the atmosphere

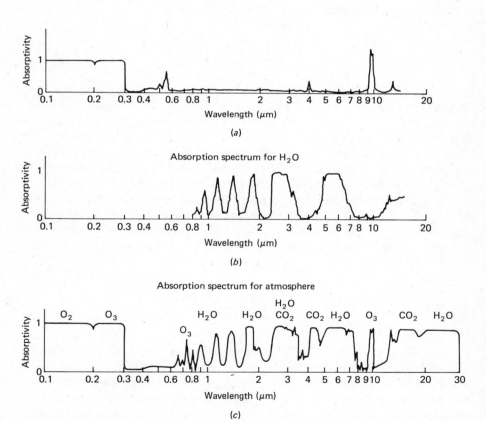

Figure 11.4. Absorption spectra for (a) molecular oxygen and ozone, (b) water, and (c) the atmosphere (Miller, 1966).

as well as the absorption spectra for O_2, O_3, and H_2O. The absorption spectra are quite complex, but they do indicate that only for certain wavelengths may radiation be transmitted through the atmosphere without appreciable loss of energy through absorption. Absorption is so strong in some spectral regions that no solar energy in those regions reaches the surface of the earth. For example, absorption by O_2 and O_3, as discussed earlier in Chapter 4, is responsible for absorption of practically all the incident radiation with wavelengths shorter than 290 nm. However, atmospheric absorption is not strong from 300 to about 800 nm, forming a "window" in the spectrum. About 40 percent of the solar energy is concentrated in the region of 400 to 700 nm. We see that H_2O absorbs in a complicated way, and mostly in the region where the sun's and earth's radiation overlap. Thus, from 300 to 800 nm, the atmosphere is essentially transparent. From 800 to 2000 nm, terrestrial long-wave radiation is moderately absorbed by water vapor in the atmosphere.

Why the molecules in Fig. 11.4 absorb at the particular regions of the spectrum shown can be determined only through elaborate calculations involving the permitted energy levels of the molecules. In general, however, the geometry of the molecule explains why H_2O, CO_2, and O_3 interact strongly with radiation above 400 nm but N_2 and O_2 do not. In H_2O, for example, the center of the negative charge is shifted toward the oxygen nucleus and the center of positive charge toward the hydrogen nuclei, leading to a separation between the centers of positive and negative charge, a so-called electric dipole moment. Molecules with dipole moments interact strongly with electromagnetic radiation because the electric field of the wave causes oppositely directed forces and therefore accelerations on electrons and nuclei at one end of the molecule as compared with the other. Similar arguments hold for ozone; however, nitrogen and oxygen are symmetric and thus are not strongly affected by radiation above 400 nm. The CO_2 molecule is linear but can be easily bent, leading to an induced dipole moment. A transverse vibrational mode exists for CO_2 at 15 μm, just where the earth emits most of its infrared radiation.

It is important to note that the molecules that are responsible for the most pronounced absorption of both solar and terrestrial radiation are the minor constituents of the atmosphere, not nitrogen and oxygen. Thus, ozone in the upper atmosphere effectively absorbs all solar radiation below 290 nm, whereas water vapor and carbon dioxide absorb much of the long-wave terrestrial radiation.

11.1.2. Energy Balance for Earth and Atmosphere

The processes which determine the temperature of the earth and the atmosphere at any location are quite complicated. These processes include absorption and reflection of radiation by gas molecules and particles in the air as well as absorption, reflection, and emission of radiation by the earth's surface. Nevertheless, we can construct a qualitative overall energy balance for the earth and atmosphere.

As the sun's radiation passes through the upper atmosphere, a small amount (about 3 percent) is absorbed by stratospheric ozone. As the radiation traverses the lower atmosphere, it is further reduced by absorption (primarily by water vapor) and by reflection back to space (mainly by clouds but also by dust particles and air molecules). In total, the average absorption by gases, particles, and clouds amounts to about 20 percent of the incoming solar beam. The average reflectivity (called the *albedo*) of the earth and atmosphere together varies from 30 to 50 percent of the incoming radiation, with clouds being responsible for most of this amount. The average value of the albedo, the incoming radiation that is reflected or scattered back to space without absorption, is usually taken to be about 34 percent. It is important to note that the albedo varies considerably, depending on the surface of the earth. For example, in the polar regions, which are covered by ice and snow, the reflectivity of the surface is very high. On the other hand, in the equatorial regions, which are largely covered with oceans, the reflectivity is low, and most of the energy received is absorbed.

In summary, a qualitative balance on incoming radiation yields:

50%	Intercepted by clouds (25% back to space, 23% to earth, 2% absorbed by clouds)
17%	Absorbed by gases and dust in the atmosphere
12%	Scattered by the air (7% back to space, 5% to earth)
19%	Absorbed by the earth
2%	Reflected by the earth back to space
100%	

Thus, on a basis of 100 units of incoming solar energy, 47 units is absorbed by the earth, 34 units is radiated back to space (25 units of reflection by clouds, 7 units of scattering by the atmosphere, and 2 units of reflection by the earth), and 19 units is absorbed by the atmosphere. This is illustrated on the left-hand side of Fig. 11.5.

The surface of the earth also radiates, but since its temperature is only about 285 to 300 K, the radiation is, as we have seen, in the infrared portion of the spectrum with a maximum intensity at 10^4 nm. The atmosphere almost completely absorbs this long-wave radiation from the earth. As is evident from Fig. 11.4, this radiation is effectively absorbed by CO_2 and H_2O. Some of this radiation is reradiated back to earth and some to space. Thus, whereas the short-wave solar radiation penetrates the atmosphere fairly effectively, the reradiated long-wave energy is kept, by and large, in the atmosphere. The long-wave processes are summarized on the right-hand side of Fig. 11.5.

As a result of both the short- and long-wave radiation processes, the atmosphere continually loses energy. This lost energy is replenished in two

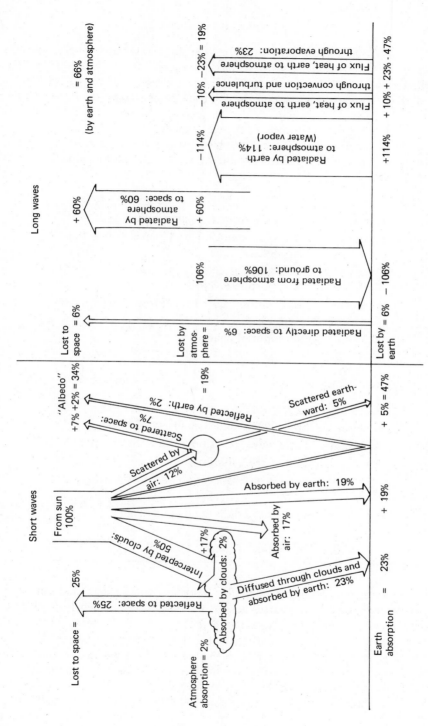

Figure 11.5. Earth's energy balance (Miller, 1966).

451

ways: (1) conduction of heat from the surface to the atmosphere, and (2) evaporation of water from the surface followed by condensation in the atmosphere with its release of latent heat. About two-thirds of the transfer of energy from the earth's surface to the atmosphere occurs by the latter mechanism.

Since the average temperature of the earth remains essentially constant over a long period of time, there is a balance between the incoming solar energy and the outgoing long-wave radiation from the earth. The earth gains and loses energy as follows:

+ 47 units	Absorbed from sun (short-wave)
− 33 units	Lost by evaporation and convection to the atmosphere
− 119 units	Long-wave blackbody radiation (113 absorbed by atmosphere, 6 to space)
+ 105 units	Reradiation back to earth from atmosphere (long-wave)
0 units	Net input of energy

Finally, we can complete the cycle by considering the atmosphere:

+ 19 units	Short-wave radiation absorbed from sun
+ 113 units	Long-wave radiation absorbed from earth
− 105 units	Long-wave radiation reradiated back to earth
+ 33 units	Gained by evaporation and convection from earth
− 60 units	Long-wave radiation back to space
0 units	Net input of energy

As we have seen, the atmosphere, by absorbing such a high fraction of the long-wave radiation of the earth, acts as an insulation to keep heat near the surface of the earth. This is called the *greenhouse effect*. Water in both vapor and droplet form is the principal agent for this effect. From Fig. 11.4 we see that H_2O is strongly absorbing in both the high- and low-energy portion of the infrared spectrum. Carbon dioxide is next in importance in the greenhouse effect. It is not as important as H_2O because its concentration is lower and because its main infrared absorption is localized in a narrow band near 1.5×10^4 nm.

11.2.   TEMPERATURE IN THE LOWER ATMOSPHERE

The layers of the atmosphere can be classified in a number of ways, such as by temperature, density, and chemical composition. From the standpoint of the dispersion of air pollutants, the most important classification is on the basis of temperature, on which the following layers can be identified (see Fig. 11.6):

1. *Troposphere.*   The layer closest to the ground extending to an altitude of 15 km over the equator and 10 km over the poles. Temperature decreases with height at a rate of about 6.5°C km^{-1}. Vertical convection keeps the air relatively well mixed.

2. *Stratosphere.*   Extends from the tropopause to about 50 km in altitude. Temperature is constant in the lower stratosphere and then increases with altitude owing to the absorption of short-wave radiation by ozone. At the stratopause (the top of the stratosphere) the temperature reaches 270 K. There is little vertical mixing in the stratosphere.

3. *Mesosphere.*   Extends from 50 to 85 km, over which temperature decreases with altitude until it reaches 175 K, the coldest point in the atmosphere.

4. *Thermosphere.*   The uppermost layer. Molecular densities are of the order of 10^{13} molecules cm^{-3}, as compared with 2.5×10^{19} at sea level.

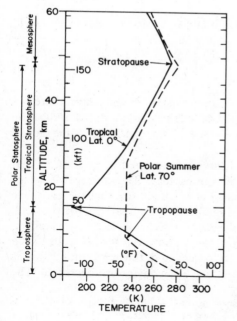

Figure 11.6.   The variation of atmospheric temperature with altitude.

Intense ultraviolet radiation dissociates N_2 and O_2. Temperatures exceed 1000 K.

11.2.1. Pressure and Temperature Relationships in the Lower Atmosphere

Air can be considered an ideal gas, so that at any point in the atmosphere

$$p = \frac{\rho R T}{M_a} \tag{11.1}$$

where ρ is the mass density of air (kg m^{-3}), R is the universal gas constant (8.134 joules K^{-1} mole^{-1}), and M_a is the molecular weight of air (28.97).

The pressure at any height z is due to the weight of air above. Thus, the change of pressure in the vertical direction obeys the relation

$$\frac{dp(z)}{dz} = -\rho g \tag{11.2}$$

Substituting Eq. (11.1) into Eq. (11.2), we obtain the general relation between pressure and temperature at any height z:

$$\frac{dp(z)}{dz} = -\frac{g M_a p}{R T} \tag{11.3}$$

If T were constant with height, Eq. (11.3) could be integrated directly to yield

$$p(z) = p_0 e^{-g M_a z / RT} \tag{11.4}$$

where p_0 is the pressure at ground level.*

As seen in Fig. 11.6, the temperature is not constant in the troposphere but rather decreases with height. Thus, Eq. (11.4) is at best a qualitative indication of the general behavior of $p(z)$. Let us see if we can predict the actual temperature profile in the troposphere.

We shall utilize the concept of an *air parcel*, a hypothetical mass of air that may deform as it moves vertically in the atmosphere. The concept of an air parcel is a tenable one as long as the parcel is of such a size that the exchange of air molecules across its boundary is small when compared with the total number of air molecules in the parcel. As such a parcel rises in the atmosphere, it expands to accommodate the lowering pressure; however, it does so in such a way that exchange of heat between the parcel and the surrounding air is negligible. As the parcel expands upon rising, its temperature decreases. The

---

*The average sea-level pressure is 1.013×10^5 newtons m^{-2} = 1.013×10^6 dynes cm^{-2}. It is customary to use a pressure unit called the *bar* (10^5 newtons m^{-2}) when dealing with atmospheric pressure. Thus, $p_0 = 1.013$ bars = 1013 millibars (mb).

process of vertical mixing in the atmosphere can, for simplicity, be envisioned as one involving a large number of parcels rising and falling. If there is no heat exchange between the parcel and the surrounding air, the parcel and the surrounding air may be at different temperatures (but not different pressures). The relation of the parcel's temperature to that of the air determines whether the parcel will continue rising or falling or whether it will reach a point of equilibrium. Therefore, the variation of temperature with altitude in the atmosphere is a key variable in determining the degree to which pollutant-bearing air parcels will mix vertically.

The variation of temperature with height for a rising parcel of dry air that cools adiabatically, that is, with no exchange of heat with its surroundings, is a basic property of the atmosphere. We now will derive the relation for this temperature change, as it will serve as a reference temperature profile against which to compare all actual profiles. To obtain the desired relation we need only the ideal-gas law and the first law of thermodynamics.

The first law of thermodynamics is expressed as

$$dU = dQ - dW$$

where dU is the increase of internal energy of the system, dQ is the heat input to the system across its boundaries, and dW is the energy lost by the system to the surroundings as a result of work done to alter the volume of the system, namely $p\,dV$. The change in internal energy dU is equal to $C_v\,dT$, where C_v is the heat capacity of the system at constant volume.

Our intent is to apply the first law of thermodynamics to an air parcel whose volume is changing as it either ascends or descends in the atmosphere. Ultimately we will combine our result with Eq. (11.3), and so it is more convenient to work with pressure and temperature as the variables rather than with pressure and volume. Thus, we convert $p\,dV$ to a form involving p and T. To do this, we express the ideal-gas law as $pV = mRT/M_a$ for a mass m of air. Then,

$$d(pV) = \frac{mR\,dT}{M_a}$$

$$= p\,dV + V\,dp$$

Using this result, together with the adiabatic condition of $dQ = 0$, the first law of thermodynamics reduces to

$$C_v\,dT = V\,dp - \frac{mR\,dT}{M_a}$$

$$= \frac{mRT}{M_a}\frac{dp}{p} - \frac{mR\,dT}{M_a} \tag{11.5}$$

Rearranging, we obtain

$$\frac{dT}{dp} = \frac{mRT/M_a p}{C_v + mR/M_a} \tag{11.6}$$

Now we have two equations, Eqs. (11.3) and (11.6), for the relation of T and p with z. Combining these we get

$$\frac{dT}{dz} = -\frac{mg}{C_v + mR/M_a}$$

$$= -\frac{g}{\hat{C}_v + R/M_a}$$

where $\hat{C}_v$ is the heat capacity at constant volume per unit mass of air. We note that $\hat{C}_v + R/M_a = \hat{C}_p$, the heat capacity at constant pressure per unit mass of air. Thus,

$$\frac{dT}{dz} = -\frac{g}{\hat{C}_p} \tag{11.7}$$

which is the rate of temperature change with height for a parcel of dry air rising adiabatically. The quantity $g/\hat{C}_p$ is a constant for dry air, equal to $1°C/102.39$ m or $0.976°C/100$ m. This constant is called the *dry adiabatic lapse rate* and is denoted by Γ. Even though we considered only one parcel, Eq. (11.7) has general applicability to an atmosphere in which a large number of parcels are rising and falling adiabatically, a point which will be demonstrated in Chapter 12.

If the air contains water vapor, the heat capacity $\hat{C}_p$ must be corrected. If ω is the ratio of the mass of water vapor to the mass of dry air in a given volume of air, the corrected $\hat{C}_p$ is given by

$$\hat{C}_p' = (1 - \omega)\hat{C}_{p_{\text{air}}} + \omega\hat{C}_{p_{\text{water vapor}}} \tag{11.8}$$

Since $\hat{C}_{p_w} > \hat{C}_{p_a}$, $\hat{C}_p' > \hat{C}_{p_a}$. Thus, the rate of decrease of T with z is smaller for a water-bearing atmosphere than for dry air. For example, if 3 percent of the atmospheric pressure is due to water vapor, $-dT/dz = 1°C/103$ m.

If the parcel contains water vapor, it may cool upon rising until the partial pressure of the water vapor equals the saturation vapor pressure of water. With sufficient nuclei present, condensation may ensue. Then the process is no longer adiabatic. If ΔH_v is the latent heat of vaporization per gram of water, the release of this heat upon condensation is accounted for by

$$dQ = -\Delta H_v \, d\omega \tag{11.9}$$

Thus,

$$-\Delta H_v \frac{d\omega}{dz} = \hat{C}_p \frac{dT}{dz} - V\frac{dp}{dz} \qquad (11.10)$$

Using Eq. (11.3), we find the lapse rate in a saturated condition to be

$$-\frac{dT}{dz} = \frac{g}{\hat{C}_p} + \frac{\Delta H_v}{\hat{C}_p}\frac{d\omega}{dz} \qquad (11.11)$$

Since $d\omega/dz$, the rate of change of the ratio of the mass of water vapor to the mass of air, is negative for a rising parcel in which water vapor is condensing, the last term in Eq. (11.11) is positive. Thus, the rate of cooling of a rising parcel of moist air is *less* than that for dry air. Since the saturation vapor pressure of water increases very markedly with temperature, the quantity $d\omega/dz$ depends strongly on the temperature. Thus, the wet adiabatic lapse rate is not a constant independent of z. In warm tropical air the wet adiabatic lapse rate is roughly one-third of the dry adiabatic lapse rate, whereas in cold polar regions there is little difference between the two.

11.2.2. Temperature Changes of a Rising (or Falling) Parcel of Air

The relationship between the temperatures and pressures at two heights in an atmosphere with an adiabatic profile is found by integrating Eq. (11.6) between any two points. Employing the ideal-gas relation $\hat{C}_p = \hat{C}_v + R/M_a$, and the definition $\gamma = \hat{C}_p/\hat{C}_v$, the result of this integration is

$$\frac{T(z_2)}{T(z_1)} = \left[\frac{p(z_2)}{p(z_1)}\right]^{(\gamma-1)/\gamma} \qquad (11.12)$$

For example, if z_1 is taken to be ground level, the temperature θ to which dry air originally in the state T, p would come if brought adiabatically to p_0 is given by

$$\theta = T\left(\frac{p}{p_0}\right)^{-(\gamma-1)/\gamma} \qquad (11.13)$$

The temperature θ defined by Eq. (11.13) is called the *potential temperature*. We introduce the potential temperature because an actual atmosphere is seldom adiabatic and we want to relate the actual temperature profile to the adiabatic lapse rate. Adiabatic temperature profiles based on potential temperature are vertical on a plot of z versus θ, thereby facilitating such comparisons.

We can further interpret the potential temperature θ as follows: The gradient of θ with z may be expressed in terms of the gradient of absolute temperature T and the adiabatic lapse rate Γ. From Eq. (11.13) it is easy to see that

$$\frac{1}{\theta}\frac{d\theta}{dz} = \frac{1}{T}\frac{dT}{dz} - \frac{\gamma-1}{\gamma}\frac{1}{p}\frac{dp}{dz} = \frac{1}{T}\left(\frac{dT}{dz} + \Gamma\right) \qquad (11.14)$$

At $z = 0$, $\theta = T$ if p_0 is taken as the surface pressure. Since, in magnitude, θ is quite close to T, Eq. (11.14) is often approximated by

$$\frac{d\theta}{dz} \cong \frac{dT}{dz} + \Gamma \qquad (11.15)$$

Thus, $d\theta/dz$ is a measure of the departure of the actual temperature profile from adiabatic conditions. Integrating Eq. (11.15) with respect to z gives

$$\theta \cong T + \Gamma z \qquad (11.16)$$

One might ask: Why does not the atmosphere always have an adiabatic lapse rate as its actual profile? The reason it does not is that other processes such as winds and solar heating of the earth's surface lead to dynamic temperature behavior in the lowest layers of the atmosphere that is seldom adiabatic. These other processes exert a much stronger influence on the prevailing temperature profile than does the adiabatic rising and falling of air parcels.

Let us compute the temperature change with z of an isolated parcel of air (or possibly other gas) as it rises or falls adiabatically through an atmosphere that is not adiabatic. We assume that conduction or convection of heat across the boundary of the parcel will be slow compared with the rate of vertical motion. Thus, an individual parcel is assumed to rise or fall adiabatically, even when the surrounding air is nonadiabatic.

Let T denote the temperature of the air parcel and T' the temperature of the surrounding air. At any height z, the pressure is the same in the parcel as in the atmosphere. The rate of change of T with p in the parcel is given by Eq. (11.6), and the rate of change of p with z is given by Eq. (11.3). Combining these two relations, we find that

$$\frac{dT}{dz} = -\Gamma\frac{T}{T'} \qquad (11.17)$$

Therefore, the rising air will cool at a greater or lesser rate than the adiabatic, depending on whether its temperature is higher or lower than that of the adjacent atmosphere.

If Λ is the actual lapse rate in the atmosphere, then at any height z

$$T'(z) = T_0' - \Lambda z \qquad (11.18)$$

Then, from Eqs. (11.17) and (11.18),

$$\frac{dT}{dz} = -\Gamma\frac{T(z)}{T_0' - \Lambda z} \qquad (11.19)$$

Integrating Eq. (11.19) with $T(0) = T_0$, the surface temperature of the rising parcel,

$$T(z) = T_0 \left(\frac{T_0' - \Lambda z}{T_0'} \right)^{\Gamma/\Lambda} \tag{11.20}$$

so that, in general,

$$\frac{dT}{dz} = -\Gamma \left(\frac{T_0' - \Lambda z}{T_0'} \right)^{(\Gamma - \Lambda)/\Lambda} \frac{T_0}{T_0'} \tag{11.21}$$

Of course, if $\Lambda = \Gamma$, then

$$\frac{dT}{dz} = -\Gamma \frac{T_0}{T_0'} \tag{11.22}$$

Thus, even if the atmosphere has an adiabatic lapse rate, a parcel of air introduced at the ground at a temperature $T_0 \neq T_0'$ will have a different rate of cooling than the adiabatic.

11.2.3.   Atmospheric Stability

The lapse rate in the lower portion of the atmosphere has a great influence on the vertical motion of air. If the lapse rate is adiabatic, a parcel of air displaced vertically is always at equilibrium with its surroundings. Such a condition, in which vertical displacements are not affected by buoyancy forces, is called *neutral* stability. However, because of surface heating and local weather influences, the atmosphere seldom has an adiabatic temperature profile. The atmosphere is either:

1. *Unstable.*   Buoyancy forces enhance vertical motion.
2. *Stable.*   Buoyancy forces oppose vertical motion.

Let us suppose a warm parcel begins to rise in an atmosphere in which temperature decreases more rapidly with z than the adiabatic rate (its lapse rate exceeds the adiabatic lapse rate). The air parcel cools adiabatically, but the temperature difference between the rising parcel and the surroundings increases with z. If the density of the parcel is ρ and that of the air ρ', the acceleration experienced by the parcel is

$$\text{Acceleration} = g \left(\frac{\rho' - \rho}{\rho} \right)$$

$$= g \left(\frac{T - T'}{T'} \right)$$

Thus, the acceleration increases with z and the parcel continues to rise as long as $T > T'$. We can express the acceleration in terms of the two lapse rates Γ and Λ as follows, if $T_0 \cong T_0'$:

$$\text{Acceleration} = \frac{g(dT/dz - dT'/dz)\, dz}{T'}$$

$$= \frac{g(\Lambda - \Gamma)\, dz}{T'}$$

As long as $\Lambda > \Gamma$, the parcel continues to rise. Similarly, a parcel of air cooler than the surrounding air will continue to descend if its rate of adiabatic heating is less than the lapse rate in the atmosphere. Since vertical motion is enhanced by buoyancy, if $\Lambda > \Gamma$ the atmosphere is called *unstable*. Lapse rates Λ for which $\Lambda > \Gamma$ are called *superadiabatic*.

On the other hand, if $\Lambda < \Gamma$, a rising air parcel will cool more rapidly with height than the surroundings and a point will be reached at which the temperature of the parcel equals that of the surroundings. We see that, if $\Lambda < \Gamma$, the acceleration will oppose the motion of a parcel. Thus, any fluctuations in the temperature of an air parcel will cause it to rise or fall, but only for a short distance. When $\Lambda < \Gamma$, the atmosphere is said to be *stable*. Summarizing, the conditions are:

1. $\Lambda = \Gamma$ neutral stability
2. $\Lambda > \Gamma$ unstable (vertical motions enhanced)
3. $\Lambda < \Gamma$ stable (vertical motions suppressed)

These same arguments may be applied to the case of a moist atmosphere. Because of the release of the latent heat of vaporization, a saturated parcel cools on rising at a slower rate than a dry parcel, since

$$\Gamma_{\text{dry}} > \Gamma_{\text{wet}}$$

Thus, a moist atmosphere is inherently *less* stable than a dry atmosphere, and a stable situation with reference to the dry adiabatic lapse rate may actually be unstable for upward displacements of a saturated air parcel.

Figure 11.7 summarizes the types of temperature profiles found in the lower atmosphere, and Fig. 11.8 shows a typical diurnal variation of temperature near the ground. The air mass near the ground is adiabatic only under special circumstances. Adiabatic conditions are reached usually when the sky is heavy with clouds and there is a moderate to high wind. The clouds prevent radiation from reaching the surface and ensure that the temperature of the ground does not differ greatly from the air just above it. The wind serves to mix the air, thereby smoothing out temperature differences. Vertical movement is then a result of mechanical forces, not buoyancy. From an air pollution standpoint,

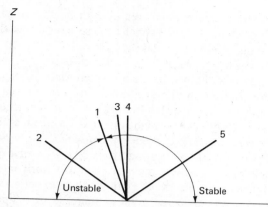

Figure 11.7. Temperature profiles in the atmosphere. (1) Adiabatic lapse rate: T decrease with height such that any vertical movement imparted to an air parcel will result in the parcel maintaining the same T or density as the surrounding air. (Neutral stability) $1°C$ 100 m^{-1}. (2) Superadiabatic: A rising air parcel will be warmer than its environment so it becomes more buoyant and continues rising. (Unstable). (3) Subadiabatic: A rising air parcel is cooler than its surroundings so it becomes less buoyant and returns. (Stable). (4) Isothermal: Temperature constant with height. (Stable). (5) Inversion: Temperature *increases* with height. (Extremely stable).

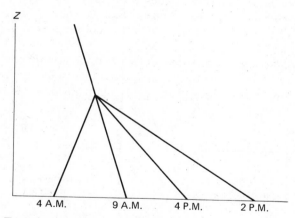

Figure 11.8. Typical diurnal variation of temperatures near the ground. 4 A.M.: Radiation from earth to black sky cools ground lower than air producing a ground-based inversion. 9 A.M.: Ground heated rapidly after sunrise. Slightly subadiabatic. 2 P.M.: Continued heating. Superadiabatic. 4 P.M.: Cooling in the afternoon returns the temperature profile to near adiabatic.

situations in which the temperature increases with height, so-called inversion conditions, are of great importance. Under these conditions the air is very stable, and little mixing of pollutants takes place.

Inversions, as shown in Fig. 11.7, form in one of two ways, through cooling from below or heating from above. Inversions often form, particularly at night, because of radiation cooling at the ground. Horizontal movement of an air mass from above a warm surface (land) to above a cool surface (water) also produces an inversion. (Note that at night the land surface may be cooler than the water.) Such inversions are termed *ground-based* or *surface* inversions. Inversions that are the result of heating from above involve the spreading, sinking, and compression of an air mass as it moves horizontally. As upper layers undergo the greatest elevation change, they experience the greatest degree of compression and thus the greatest increase in temperature. If the temperature increase is sufficient, an inversion will result. The sinking and compression process is termed *subsidence*.

A *frontal inversion* can occur at an interface between two air masses of quite different temperatures, humidity, and pressure. If colder air is advancing, the front is known as a cold front, and vice versa. In each case the warm air overrides the cold air, and in the case of a cold front, the rising warm air leads to condensation and rain following the position of the surface front. An inversion will exist at the interface of both a warm and cold front.

An *advective inversion* is formed when warm air flows over a cold surface or colder air. The inversion can be surface-based, as when warm air flows over cold plains, or elevated, as in the case when a cool sea breeze is overlaid by a warm land breeze.

A *radiational inversion* occurs frequently when the ground cools at night by radiation. The presence of nocturnal radiational inversions prevents the ventilation of emissions during the night in a city. At night in cities, buildings and

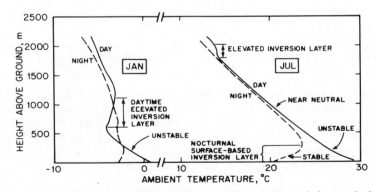

Figure 11.9. Monthly average diurnal and seasonal variations of the vertical thermal structure of the planetary boundary layer at a rural site near St. Louis, MO, based on 1976 data. (Gillani, as reported by National Research Council, 1983).

streets cool slowly, often resulting in an unstable temperature profile for the first hundred meters or so. But this shallow mixing layer is usually topped by a more stable layer.

Figure 11.9 shows the monthly average diurnal and seasonal variations of the vertical thermal structure of the planetary boundary layer at rural site near St. Louis, MO.

11.3.   WINDS

Even though the total input and output of radiant energy to and from the earth are essentially in balance, they are not in balance at every point on the earth. The amount of energy reaching the earth's surface depends, in part, on the nature of the surface (land versus sea, for example) and the degree of cloudiness, as well as on the latitude of the point. For example, at lower solar angles, in the polar regions the same amount of solar energy as radiated to the tropics must pass through more atmosphere and intercept a larger surface area. The uneven distribution of energy resulting from latitudinal variations in insolation and from differences in absorptivity of the earth's surface leads to the large-scale air motions of the earth. In particular, the tendency to transport energy from the tropics toward the polar regions, thereby redistributing energy inequalities on the earth, is the overall factor governing the general circulation of the atmosphere.

In order to visualize the nature of the general circulation of the atmosphere, we can think of the atmosphere over either hemisphere as a fluid enclosed within a long, shallow container, heated at one end and cooled at the other. Because the horizontal dimension of the "container" is so much greater than its vertical dimension, the curvature of the earth can be neglected, and the container can be considered to be rectangular. If such a container were constructed in the laboratory and the ends differentially heated as described above, one would observe a circulation of the fluid, consisting of rising motion along the heated wall and descending motion along the cooled wall, flow in the direction of warm to cold at the top of the box, and flow in the direction of cold to warm along the bottom of the box. The situation we have described is a *thermal circulation*, which is illustrated in Fig. 11.10. (Note, that the vertical scale in Fig. 11.10 is greatly exaggerated in comparison with the horizontal scale.) In the atmosphere, then, the tendency is for warm tropical air to rise and cold polar air to sink, with poleward and equatorward flows to complete the circulation.

However, the general circulation of the atmosphere is not as simple as depicted in Fig. 11.10. Another force arises because of the motion of the earth, the Coriolis force. At the earth's surface an object at the equator has a greater tangential velocity than one in the temperate zones. Air moving toward the south, as in Fig. 11.10, cannot acquire an increased eastward (the earth rotates from west to east) tangential velocity as it moves south and, thus, *to an*

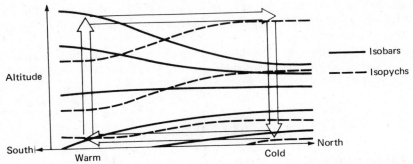

Figure 11.10. Thermal circulation in the atmosphere. At the ground the horizontal pressure gradient causes flow from north to south. At the upper level the flow is reversed.

observer on the earth, appears to acquire a velocity component in the westward direction. Thus, air moving south in the Northern Hemisphere appears to lag behind the earth. To an observer on the earth it appears that the air has been influenced by a force in the westward direction. To an observer in space, it would be clear that the air is merely trying to maintain straight-line motion while the earth turns below it. Friction between the wind and the ground diminishes this effect in the lower atmosphere.

From the standpoint of air motion, the atmosphere can be segmented vertically into two layers. Extending from the ground up to about 500 m is the *planetary boundary layer*, the zone in which the effect of the surface is felt and in which the wind speed and direction are governed by horizontal pressure gradients, shear stresses, and Coriolis forces (Tennekes, 1974; Pielke, 1981; Arya, 1982; Hunt and Simpson, 1982). Above the planetary bound layer is the *geostrophic layer*, in which only horizontal pressure gradients and Coriolis forces influence the flow. Our main interest in this section is with flow in the geostrophic layer. Chapter 12 is devoted to a detailed treatment of wind and temperature behavior in the planetary boundary layer and, in particular, in the surface layer, the lowest 50 m of the atmosphere. Figure 11.11 shows the regions of the atmosphere, defined on the basis of the type of airflow.

To predict the general pattern of macroscale air circulation on the earth we must consider both the tendency for thermal circulation and the influence of Coriolis forces. Figure 11.12 shows the nature of the general circulation of the atmosphere. At either side of the equator is a thermal circulation, in which warm tropical air rises and cool northern air flows toward the equator. The circulation does not extend all the way to the poles because radiative cooling of the upper northward flow causes it to subside (fall) at about 30° N and S latitude. The Coriolis force acting on these cells leads to easterly winds, called the trade winds. The same situation occurs in the polar regions, in which warm air from the temperate zones moves northward in the upper levels, eventually

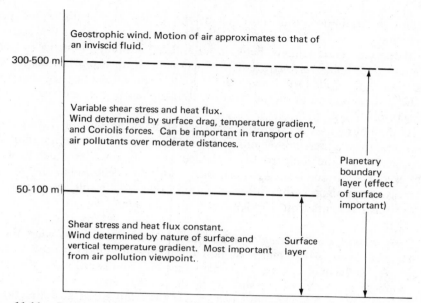

Figure 11.11. Regions of the lower atmosphere classified according to airflow.

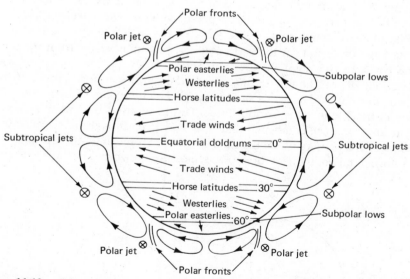

Figure 11.12. Schematic representation of the general circulation of the atmosphere.

cooling by radiation and subsiding at the poles. The result is the polar easterlies.

In the temperate regions, between 40 and 55° latitude, influences of both tropical and polar regions are felt. The major feature of the temperature regions is large-scale turbulence, which results in the circulation shown in Fig. 11.12. The surface winds in the Northern Hemisphere are westerlies because of the Coriolis force.

At the boundaries between thermal circulation at the equator, 30°, and 55° N and S latitude there are regions of calm. The observed net precipitation near the equator and the polar front is explained by rising moist air which cools. At 30° N and S latitude a strong subsidence of dry air occurs, since the air loses its moisture upon ascension in the equatorial zone. As a result net evaporation of the oceans occurs from 10 to 40° N and S latitude.

Derivation of the Geostrophic Wind Speed. The direction of winds in the geostrophic layer is determined by horizontal pressure gradients and Coriolis forces. As we have discussed, an air parcel moving southward in the Northern Hemisphere as a result of pressure gradients is accelerated toward the west by the Coriolis force. We can actually compute the wind speed and direction at any latitude as a function of the prevailing pressure gradient if we assume that only pressure and Coriolis forces influence the flow.

It can be shown that the acceleration experienced by an object on the surface of the earth (or in the atmosphere) moving with a velocity vector $\mathbf{u}$ consists of two components, $-\mathbf{\Omega} \times (\mathbf{\Omega} \times \mathbf{r})$ and $-2(\mathbf{\Omega} \times \mathbf{u})$, where $\mathbf{\Omega}$ is the angular rotation vector for the earth and $\mathbf{r}$ is the radius vector from the center of the earth to the point in question. (For a derivation of these terms see Williamson, 1973.) The first term is simply the centrifugal force, in a direction that acts normal to the earth's surface and is counterbalanced by gravity. The second term, $\mathbf{\Omega} \times \mathbf{u}$, is the Coriolis force. This force arises only when an object, such as an air parcel, is moving, that is, $\mathbf{u} \neq 0$. Even though the Coriolis force is of much smaller magnitude than the centrifugal force, only the Coriolis force has a horizontal component. Since the winds are horizontal in the geostrophic

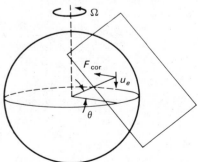

Horizontal plane of velocity u_e

Figure 11.13. Direction of Coriolis force in the Northern Hemisphere.

layer, the Coriolis acceleration is given by the horizontal component of the Coriolis term, namely $2u_G\Omega\sin\beta$, where Ω is the rate of rotation of the earth and β is the latitude. The direction of the Coriolis force is perpendicular to the wind velocity, as shown in Fig. 11.13. Wind speed u_G at latitude β lies in the horizontal plane.

In the geostrophic layer it may be assumed that the atmosphere is inviscid (frictionless) and in laminar flow. The equations of continuity and motion for such a fluid are

$$\frac{\partial u}{\partial x} + \frac{\partial v}{\partial y} + \frac{\partial w}{\partial z} = 0 \tag{11.23}$$

and

$$\frac{\partial u}{\partial t} + u\frac{\partial u}{\partial x} + v\frac{\partial u}{\partial y} + w\frac{\partial u}{\partial z} = -\frac{1}{\rho}\frac{\partial p}{\partial x} + F_x$$

$$\frac{\partial v}{\partial t} + u\frac{\partial v}{\partial x} + v\frac{\partial v}{\partial y} + w\frac{\partial v}{\partial z} = -\frac{1}{\rho}\frac{\partial p}{\partial y} + F_y$$

$$\frac{\partial w}{\partial t} + u\frac{\partial w}{\partial x} + v\frac{\partial w}{\partial y} + w\frac{\partial w}{\partial z} = -\frac{1}{\rho}\frac{\partial p}{\partial z} + F_z \tag{11.24}$$

where u, v, w are the three components of the velocity and F_x, F_y, and F_z are the three components of the external force.

Let the axes be fixed in the earth, with the x axis horizontal and extending to the east, the y axis horizontal and extending to the north, and the z axis normal to the earth's surface. As before, Ω is the angular velocity of rotation of the earth and β the latitude. The components of the Coriolis force in the x, y, and z directions on a particle are the components of $\mathbf{F}_c = -2(\boldsymbol{\Omega} \times \mathbf{u})$.

$$F_{cx} = -2\Omega(w\cos\beta - v\sin\beta)$$

$$F_{cy} = -2\Omega u \sin\beta$$

$$F_{cz} = 2\Omega u \cos\beta \tag{11.25}$$

At great heights, the vertical velocity component w can usually be neglected relative to the horizontal components u and v. Therefore, substituting Eq. (11.25) into Eq. (11.24), we obtain, for steady motion

$$u\frac{\partial u}{\partial x} + v\frac{\partial u}{\partial y} = 2\Omega v \sin\beta - \frac{1}{\rho}\frac{\partial p}{\partial x}$$

$$u\frac{\partial v}{\partial x} + v\frac{\partial v}{\partial y} = -2\Omega u \sin\beta - \frac{1}{\rho}\frac{\partial p}{\partial y} \tag{11.26}$$

We see that the air moves so that a balance is achieved between the pressure gradient and the Coriolis force. Let us consider the situation in which the velocity vector is oriented in the x direction, and so $v = 0$; then

$$u\frac{\partial u}{\partial x} = -\frac{1}{\rho}\frac{\partial p}{\partial x} \tag{11.27}$$

$$0 = -2\Omega u \sin\theta - \frac{1}{\rho}\frac{\partial p}{\partial y} \tag{11.28}$$

We usually denote $2\Omega \sin\beta$ by f, called the Coriolis parameter. From the continuity equation, Eq. (11.23), we see that $\partial u/\partial x = 0$, since $v = w = 0$. Thus, from Eq. (11.27), $\partial p/\partial x = 0$, and the direction of flow is perpendicular to the pressure gradient $\partial p/\partial y$. In addition, from Eq. (11.28), we see that the component of the Coriolis force, $-fu$, is exactly balanced by the pressure gradient, $(1/\rho)\,\partial p/\partial y$. Therefore, the *geostrophic wind speed* u_G is given by

$$u_G = \frac{\partial p/\partial y}{2\rho\Omega\sin\beta} \tag{11.29}$$

The approach to the geostrophic equilibrium for an air parcel starting from rest, accelerated by the pressure gradient and then affected by the Coriolis force, is shown in Fig. 11.14.

The geostrophic balance determines the wind direction at altitudes above about 500 m. In order to describe the air motions at lower levels we must take into account the friction of the earth's surface. The presence of the surface induces a shear in the wind profile, as in a turbulent boundary layer over a flat plate generated in a laboratory wind tunnel. In analyzing the geostrophic wind speed we found that for steady flow a balance exists between the pressure force and the Coriolis force. Consequently, steady flow of air at levels near the ground leads to a balance of three forces: pressure force, Coriolis force, and friction force due to the earth's surface. Thus, as shown in Fig. 11.15a, the net

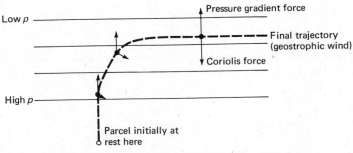

Figure 11.14. Approach to geostrophic equilibrium.

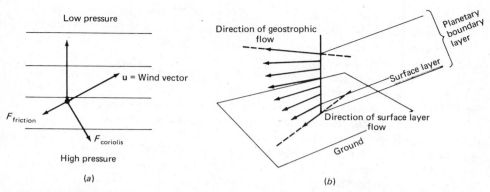

Figure 11.15. Variation of wind direction with altitude. (*a*) Balance of forces among pressure gradient, Coriolis force, and friction. (*b*) The Ekman spiral.

result of these three forces must be zero for a nonaccelerating air parcel. Since the pressure gradient force F_p must be directed from high to low pressure, and the frictional force F_f must be directed opposite to the velocity u, a balance can be achieved only if the wind is directed at some angle toward the region of low pressure. This angle between the wind direction and the isobars increases as the ground is approached since the frictional force increases. At the ground, over open terrain, the angle of the wind to the isobars is usually between 10 and 20°. Because of the relatively smooth boundary existing over this type of terrain, the wind speed at a 10-m height (the height at which the so-called surface wind is usually measured) is already almost 90 percent of the geostrophic wind speed. Over built-up areas, on the other hand, the speed at a 10-m height may be only 50 percent of the geostrophic wind speed, owing to the mixing induced by the surface roughness. In this case the surface wind may be at an angle of 45° to the isobars.

As a result of these frictional effects, the wind direction commonly turns with height, as shown in Fig. 11.15*b*. The variation of wind direction with altitude is known as the *Ekman spiral*. We defer a derivation of the Ekman spiral until Chapter 12, when we have had the opportunity to discuss turbulent transport of momentum.

The pattern of general circulation shown in Fig. 11.12 does not represent the actual state of atmospheric circulation on a given day. The irregularities of land masses and their surface temperatures tend to disrupt the smooth global circulation patterns we have described. Another influence which tends to break up zonal patterns is the Coriolis force. Air which converges at low levels toward regions of low pressure must also execute a circular motion because of Coriolis forces. The effect of friction at the surface is to direct the winds at low levels in part toward the region of low pressure, producing an inward spiraling motion. This vortex-like motion is given the name *cyclone*. The center of a cyclone is usually a rising column of warm air. Similarly, a low-level diverging flow from a high pressure region will spiral outward. Such a region is called an *anticyclone*. In the Northern Hemisphere the motion of a cyclone is counter-clockwise and that of an anticyclone, clockwise. The dimensions of commonly occurring cyclones and anticyclones are from 100 to 1000 km. Most cyclones and anticyclones are born in one part of the world and migrate to another. These are not to be confused with hurricanes or typhoons, which, although they consist of the same type of air motion, are of a smaller scale.

An element of the cyclone-anticyclone phenomenon which has particular importance for air pollution in several parts of the world is the semipermanent subtropical anticyclone, high pressure regions centered over the major oceans. They are called semipermanent because they shift position only slightly in summer and winter. The key feature of the subtropical anticyclone is that the cold subsiding air aloft, which results in the high pressure observed at sea level, is warmed by compression as it descends, often establishing an elevated temperature inversion. The inversion layer generally approaches closer to the ground as the distance from the center of the high pressure increases.

On the eastern side of the subtropical anticyclones the inversion is strengthened by the southerly flow of cool, dry air (recall that in the Northern Hemisphere the rotation in an anticyclone is clockwise). Particularly in coastal areas the low-level air is cooled by contact with the cold ocean, an exchange which tends to strengthen the inversion. Since the air aloft, as well as the southbound low-level flow, is warming, there is little precipitation in these regions. Thus, on the west coasts of continents it is common to find arid, desert-like conditions, such as the deserts of southern California, the Sahara in North Africa, the desert in western Australia, and the coastal plains of South America.

On the other hand, on the western side of the semipermanent anticyclone, inversions are less frequent and the low-level air from the tropics is warm and moist. As it cools on its path to the north, precipitation is heavy. Thus, the eastern coasts of continents in the subtropics are warm and humid, such as the eastern coasts of South America and Africa.

We can now see one of the reasons why Los Angeles is afflicted with air pollution problems. Its location on the west coast of North America in the subtropical region and on the eastern side of the Pacific anticyclone is one in which elevated inversions are frequent and strong. The lowest layer of air (the marine layer) is cooled because of its contact with the ocean. Air pollutants are trapped in the marine layer and prevented from vertically exchanging with upper-level air. Such a situation can lead to serious air pollution problems. The base of a subsidence inversion lies typically at an elevation of about 500 m, with the inversion layer extending another 500 to 1000 m upward. Figure 11.16 shows a cross section of the North Pacific anticyclone.

In addition to the semipermanent anticyclones, there are many migratory cyclones and anticyclones in the temperate zones. Formed by confrontations between arctic and tropical air, they have a lifetime of a few weeks and drift with the westerly winds at about 800 km/day. Precipitation is often associated

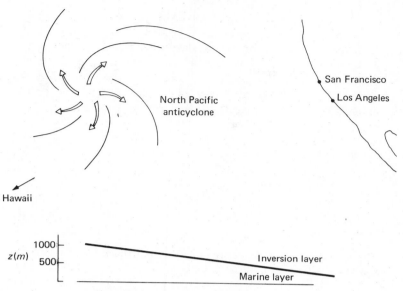

Figure 11.16. North Pacific anticyclone.

with the rising air over the low pressure center of a cyclone. Cyclones are thus usually accompanied by cloudy skies and inclement weather. On the other hand, anticyclones are characterized by clear skies, light winds, and fair weather. Surprisingly enough, anticyclones lead to air pollution problems, particularly when one temporarily ceases its eastward drift and stagnates for a few days. The classic episode in Donora, PA (see Table 2.2) and many in New York occurred under such circumstances. Regions in the United States prone to stagnating anticyclones are the Great Basin between the Rockies and the Sierras, the central basin of California, and the southern Appalachians. In fact, stagnating anticyclones are probably a contributing factor to the haze over the Great Smoky Mountains in eastern Tennessee.

REFERENCES

Arya, S. P. "Atmospheric Boundary Layers Over Homogeneous Terrain," in *Engineering Meteorology*, E. J. Plate (Ed.), Elsevier, Amsterdam, (1982).

Hunt, J. C. R., and Simpson, J. E. "Atmospheric Boundary Layers Over Non-Homogeneous Terrain," in *Engineering Meteorology*, E. J. Plate (Ed.), Elsevier, Amsterdam, (1982).

Miller, A. *Meteorology*, Charles E. Merrill Books, Columbus, Ohio (1966).

National Research Council, *Acid Deposition—Atmospheric Processes in Eastern North America*, National Academy Press, Washington, D.C. (1983).

Pielke, R. A. "Mesoscale Numerical Modeling," *Adv. Geophys.*, **23**, 185–344 (1981).

Tennekes, H. "The Atmospheric Boundary Layer," *Physics Today*, 52–63 (1973).

Williamson, S. J. *Fundamentals of Air Pollution*, Addison-Wesley, Reading, MA (1973).

PROBLEMS

11.1. If the earth-atmosphere system is assumed to be in radiative equilibrium with the sun (that is, it emits as much radiation as it receives), it is possible to estimate a value for the temperature T_e of the earth-atmosphere system. If the planetary albedo is denoted by α and the solar constant by S, show that T_e is given by

$$T_e = \left[\frac{(1 - \alpha)S}{4\sigma} \right]^{1/4}$$

Calculate the value of T_e for $\alpha = 0.34$.

The average surface temperature T_s is considerably higher than the earth-atmosphere radiative equilibrium temperature T_e. Why is this so? How would you attempt to compute an estimate for T_s?

11.2. Show that if the atmosphere is isothermal the temperature change of a parcel of air rising adiabatically is

$$T(z) = T_0 e^{-\Gamma z/T_0'}$$

where T_0 and T_0' are the temperatures of the parcel at the surface and of the air at the surface, respectively.

11.3. A rising parcel of air will come to rest when its temperature T equals that of the surrounding air, T'. Show that the height z where this occurs is given by

$$z = \frac{1}{\Lambda} \left[T_0' - \left(\frac{T_0'^{\Gamma}}{T_0^{\Lambda}} \right)^{1/(\Gamma - \Lambda)} \right]$$

What condition must hold for this result to be valid?

11.4. Show that the condition that the density of the atmosphere does not change with height is

$$\frac{dT}{dz} = -3.42 \times 10^{-2} {}^\circ\text{C m}^{-1}$$

11.5. It has been proposed that air pollution in Los Angeles can be abated by drilling large tunnels in the mountains surrounding the basin and pumping the air out into the surrounding deserts. You are to examine the power requirements in displacing the volume of air over the Los Angeles basin. Assume the basin has an area of 4000 km^2 and that the polluted air is confined below an elevated inversion with a mean height of 400 m. The coefficient of friction for air moving over the basin is assumed to be 0.5, and the minimum energy needed to sustain airflow is equal to the energy dissipated by ground friction. Determine the power required to move the air mass 7 km hr^{-1}. Compare your result with the capacity of Hoover Dam: 1.25×10^6 kW.

11.6. Elevated inversion layers are a prime factor responsible for the incidence of community air pollution problems. It is interesting to consider the feasibility of eliminating an elevated inversion layer. In principle, this could be done either by cooling all the air from the inversion base upward to a temperature below that at the inversion base or by heating all the air below the top of the inversion to a temperature higher than that at the inversion top.

Show that the energy E required to destroy an elevated inversion by heating from below is given by

$$E = \rho C_p \left[\Gamma (H_T - H_B) + (T_T - T_B) \right] \frac{H_T + H_B}{2}$$

where
ρ = average density of air
C_p = heat capacity of air
H_B, H_T = heights of base and top of inversion
T_B, T_T = temperatures of base and top of inversion

Assume that the lapse rate below the base of the inversion is adiabatic and that the rate of temperature increase with height in the inversion is linear.

Estimate the value of E for typical September conditions at Long Beach, California, at 7 A.M. Use

$$H_B = 475 \text{ m} \qquad T_B = 14.1°C$$
$$H_T = 1055 \text{ m} \qquad T_T = 22.4°C$$

If the area of the Los Angeles basin is 4000 km^2 and the energy produced by oil burning with 100 percent efficiency is 1.04×10^7 cal/kg of oil, what is the amount of oil required in order to destroy the inversion over the entire basin?

TWELVE

Micrometeorology

In this chapter we will concentrate on air motion in the lowest layers of the atmosphere. Such air motion, taking place adjacent to a solid boundary of variable temperature and roughness, is virtually always turbulent. This atmospheric turbulence is responsible for the transport of heat, water vapor, and pollutants from the surface to the atmosphere as a whole. Our objective in this chapter will be to understand the basic phenomena that influence atmospheric turbulence.*

12.1. BASIC EQUATIONS OF ATMOSPHERIC FLUID MECHANICS

We wish to derive the equations that govern the fluid density, temperature, and velocities in the lowest layers of the atmosphere. These equations will form the basis from which we can subsequently explore the processes that influence atmospheric turbulence.

The equations of continuity and motion for a compressible, Newtonian fluid in a gravitational field are

$$\frac{\partial \rho}{\partial t} + \frac{\partial}{\partial x_i}(\rho u_i) = 0 \tag{12.1}$$

and

$$\rho\left(\frac{\partial u_i}{\partial t} + u_j \frac{\partial u_i}{\partial x_j}\right) = \frac{\partial}{\partial x_k}\left[\mu\left(\frac{\partial u_i}{\partial x_k} + \frac{\partial u_k}{\partial x_i}\right) - \left(p + \frac{2}{3}\mu\frac{\partial u_j}{\partial x_j}\right)\delta_{ik}\right] - \rho g \delta_{3i} \tag{12.2}$$

---

*The subject of atmospheric turbulence has received a great amount of attention. Our treatment here will, of necessity, be rather limited. The interested reader may pursue this area to greater depth in Monin and Yaglom (1971, 1975), Plate (1971, 1982), Nieuwstadt and van Dop (1982), and Panofsky and Dutton (1984).

where $u_i(x_1, x_2, x_3, t)$ is the fluid velocity component in direction i, μ is the fluid viscosity, and δ_{ij} is the Kronecker delta, defined by $\delta_{ij} = 1$ if $i = j$, and $\delta_{ij} = 0$ if $i \neq j$. In Eq. (12.1) and (12.2) we have taken the x_3 axis as vertically upward. If $\mu = 0$, Eqs. (12.1) and (12.2) reduce to the Euler equations of motion introduced in Chapter 11 in connection with the derivation of the relation for the geostrophic wind speed. We have not included a term accounting for the Coriolis acceleration in Eq. (12.2), since we shall be interested only in processes taking place on limited spatial and temporal scales over which the air motion is not influenced substantially by the rotation of the earth.

The energy equation is

$$\rho\left(\frac{\partial U}{\partial t} + u_j \frac{\partial U}{\partial x_j}\right) = k \frac{\partial^2 T}{\partial x_j \partial x_j} - p \frac{\partial u_j}{\partial x_j} + \Phi + Q \tag{12.3}$$

where U is the internal energy per unit mass ($= \hat{C}_v T$ for a perfect gas), k is the thermal conductivity (assumed constant), Φ is the heat generated per unit volume and time as a result of viscous dissipation, and Q represents the heat generated by any sources in the fluid.

For an ideal gas, p and ρ are related by the equation of state:

$$p = \frac{\rho R T}{M_a} \tag{12.4}$$

Equations (12.1) to (12.4) represent six equations for the six unknowns u_1, u_2, u_3, p, ρ, and T. These equations can therefore be solved, in principle, subject to appropriate boundary and initial conditions to yield velocity, pressure, density, and temperature profiles in an ideal gas. Because of the highly coupled nature of Eq. (12.1) to Eq. (12.4), these equations are virtually impossible to solve analytically. However, we can exploit certain aspects characteristic of the lower atmosphere to simplify them.

When the atmosphere is at rest ($u_i = 0$), Eqs. (12.2) and (12.3) become

$$\frac{\partial p_e}{\partial x_1} = \frac{\partial p_e}{\partial x_2} = 0 \qquad \frac{\partial p_e}{\partial x_3} = -g\rho_e \tag{12.5}$$

$$\frac{\partial^2 T_e}{\partial x_3^2} = 0 \tag{12.6}$$

where the subscript e denotes equilibrium values and where we have assumed there are no heat sources ($Q = 0$). In writing Eq. (12.6), we have also assumed that the atmosphere is horizontally homogeneous. It follows from Eq. (12.6) that at equilibrium in the absence of heat sources, the temperature varies linearly with height,

$$T_e = T_0\left(1 - \frac{x_3}{H}\right)$$

where T_0 is the surface temperature and H is the height at which T_e becomes zero [chosen simply to satisfy the two necessary boundary conditions of Eq. (12.6)]. Therefore, the pressure, density, and temperature in an equilibrium atmosphere are governed by

$$\frac{\partial p_e}{\partial x_3} = -g\rho_e$$

$$p_e = \frac{\rho_e R T_e}{M_a} \tag{12.7}$$

$$T_e = T_0\left(1 - \frac{x_3}{H}\right)$$

Upon integration, we obtain

$$p_e = p_0\left(1 - \frac{x_3}{H}\right)^{gHM_a/RT_0}$$

$$\rho_e = \rho_0\left(1 - \frac{x_3}{H}\right)^{(gHM_a/RT_0)-1} \tag{12.8}$$

where $p_0 = \rho_0 R T_0/M_a$, the surface state. Thus, when the atmosphere is at rest, the ratio of the equilibrium values at any height to the corresponding surface values are related by

$$\frac{p_e}{p_0} = \left(\frac{\rho_e}{\rho_0}\right)^n \tag{12.9}$$

where

$$\frac{n}{n-1} = \frac{gHM_a}{RT_0}$$

The lapse rate Λ, as expressed in $T_e = T_0 - \Lambda x_3$, is given by

$$\Lambda = \frac{T_0}{H} = \frac{gM_a}{R}\frac{n-1}{n}$$

In the special case in which $n = \gamma = \hat{C}_p/\hat{C}_v$, the atmosphere is adiabatic. As we know, in this case (since $R/M_a = \hat{C}_p - \hat{C}_v$ for a perfect gas)

$$\Lambda = \Gamma = \frac{g}{\hat{C}_p} \tag{12.10}$$

We shall now consider the description of the atmosphere when there is motion. In doing so we shall consider only a shallow layer adjacent to the ground, in which case we can make some rather important simplifications in the equations of continuity, motion, and energy. The approximations we make are called the *Boussinesq approximations*. The conditions for their validity have been examined by Spiegel and Veronis (1960), Calder (1968), and Dutton (1976).

We can express the equilibrium profiles of pressure, density, and temperature in terms of functions of x_3 only as follows:

$$p_e = p_0 + p_m(x_3)$$

$$\rho_e = \rho_0 + \rho_m(x_3) \tag{12.11}$$

$$T_e = T_0 + T_m(x_3)$$

We consider only a shallow layer, so that p_m/p_0, ρ_m/ρ_0, and T_m/T_0 are all small compared with unity. When there is motion, we can express the actual pressure, density, and temperature in terms of the sum of the equilibrium values and a small correction due to the motion (denoted by a tilde). Thus, we write

$$p = p_0 + p_m(x_3) + \tilde{p}(x_1, x_2, x_3, t)$$

$$\rho = \rho_0 + \rho_m(x_3) + \tilde{\rho}(x_1, x_2, x_3, t) \tag{12.12}$$

$$T = T_0 + T_m(x_3) + \tilde{T}(x_1, x_2, x_3, t)$$

where we assume that the deviations induced by the motion are sufficiently small that the quantities $\tilde{p}/p_0$, $\tilde{\rho}/\rho_0$, and $\tilde{T}/T_0$ are also small compared with unity.

For the equation of continuity we have

$$\frac{\partial u_i}{\partial x_i} = -\frac{1}{\rho}\left(\frac{\partial \rho}{\partial t} + u_j\frac{\partial \rho}{\partial x_j}\right) \equiv -\frac{1}{\rho}\frac{D\rho}{Dt} = -\frac{D}{Dt}\ln\rho$$

$$= -\frac{D}{Dt}\ln\left[\rho_0\left(1 + \frac{\rho_m + \tilde{\rho}}{\rho_0}\right)\right]$$

$$= -\frac{D}{Dt}\frac{\rho_m + \tilde{\rho}}{\rho_0} \quad {}^* \tag{12.13}$$

---

*D/Dt denotes the substantial derivative and is defined by

$$\frac{D}{Dt} \equiv \frac{\partial}{\partial t} + u_j\frac{\partial}{\partial x_j}$$

where we have employed the Maclaurin series expansion for $\ln(1 + x)$ for $x \ll 1$. However, we see that the right-hand side of Eq. (12.13) is small compared with unity, so that to a first-order approximation the continuity equation can be written as

$$\frac{\partial u_i}{\partial x_i} = 0 \tag{12.14}$$

which, of course, is the continuity equation for an incompressible fluid.

We now subtract the reference equilibrium state, Eq. (12.5) from the equation of motion, Eq. (12.2). Using Eq. (12.14), we obtain

$$\frac{\partial u_i}{\partial t} + u_j \frac{\partial u_i}{\partial x_j} = -\frac{1}{\rho} \frac{\partial \tilde{p}}{\partial x_i} + \frac{\mu}{\rho} \frac{\partial^2 u_i}{\partial x_j \partial x_j} - \frac{g\tilde{\rho}}{\rho} \delta_{i3} \tag{12.15}$$

Let us examine the two terms $-(1/\rho)(\partial \tilde{p}/\partial x_i)$ and $-(g\tilde{\rho}/\rho)\delta_{i3}$ appearing in Eq. (12.15). We can write the first of these terms as

$$\frac{1}{\rho} \frac{\partial \tilde{p}}{\partial x_i} = \frac{\rho_e - \tilde{\rho}}{(\rho_e + \tilde{\rho})(\rho_e - \tilde{\rho})} \frac{\partial \tilde{p}}{\partial x_i}$$

$$= \frac{1}{\rho_e^2 - \tilde{\rho}^2} \left(\rho_e \frac{\partial \tilde{p}}{\partial x_i} - \tilde{\rho} \frac{\partial \tilde{p}}{\partial x_i} \right)$$

$$\cong \frac{1}{\rho_e} \frac{\partial \tilde{p}}{\partial x_i}$$

For a shallow layer, ρ_e may be replaced by ρ_0, and so

$$\frac{1}{\rho} \frac{\partial \tilde{p}}{\partial x_i} \cong \frac{1}{\rho_0} \frac{\partial \tilde{p}}{\partial x_i} \tag{12.16}$$

Next we consider the term $-(g\tilde{\rho}/\rho)\delta_{i3}$, which expresses the vertical acceleration on a fluid element as a result of density fluctuations. Assuming that the fluctuations in density from the surface value are small, we can expand ρ in a Taylor series about ρ_0 as follows:

$$\rho = \rho_0 \left(1 + \frac{p_m}{p_0} - \frac{T_m}{T_0} \right) + \rho_0 \left(\frac{\tilde{p}}{p_0} - \frac{\tilde{T}}{T_0} \right) \tag{12.17}$$

In the atmosphere the relative magnitude of pressure deviations from the reference pressure as a result of motion, that is, $\tilde{p}$, is small compared with temperature fluctuations,

$$\frac{\tilde{p}}{p_0} \ll \frac{\tilde{T}}{T_0}$$

Thus, Eq. (12.17) becomes

$$\tilde{\rho} = -\rho_0 \frac{\tilde{T}}{T_0}$$

that is, the deviations in density from the reference state can be attributed solely to temperature deviations.

The final form of the approximate equation of motion is therefore

$$\frac{\partial u_i}{\partial t} + u_j \frac{\partial u_i}{\partial x_j} = -\frac{1}{\rho_0} \frac{\partial \tilde{p}}{\partial x_i} + \frac{\mu}{\rho_0} \frac{\partial^2 u_i}{\partial x_j \partial x_j} + \frac{g\tilde{T}}{T_0} \delta_{i3} \qquad (12.18)$$

We now consider the energy equation, Eq. (12.3). First, the contribution of viscous dissipation Φ to the energy balance is negligible in the atmosphere. Upon subtracting Eq. (12.6) from Eq. (12.3) we obtain the equation governing the temperature fluctuations,

$$\rho \hat{C}_v \left[\frac{\partial (T_e + \tilde{T})}{\partial t} + u_j \frac{\partial}{\partial x_j} (T_e + \tilde{T}) \right] = k \frac{\partial^2 \tilde{T}}{\partial x_j \partial x_j} - p \frac{\partial u_j}{\partial x_j} + Q \qquad (12.19)$$

where we have retained the term $p(\partial u_j / \partial x_j)$ since, although $\partial u_j / \partial x_j \cong 0$, p is large so that $p(\partial u_j / \partial x_j)$ is the same order of magnitude as the other terms in the equation. In fact, we can determine the order of $p(\partial u_j / \partial x_j)$ as follows: From the continuity equation and the ideal-gas law,

$$p \frac{\partial u_j}{\partial x_j} = -\frac{p}{\rho} \frac{D\rho}{Dt}$$

$$= -\frac{RT}{M_a} \frac{D\rho}{Dt}$$

$$= \frac{\rho_0 R}{M_a} \frac{D}{Dt} (T_e + \tilde{T}) - \frac{Dp_e}{Dt}$$

$$= \frac{\rho_0 R}{M_a} \frac{D}{Dt} (T_e + \tilde{T}) + u_3 g \rho_0 \qquad (12.20)$$

where in the last step we have employed Eq. (12.5). Using the relation $\hat{C}_p - \hat{C}_v = R/M_a$, and upon substituting Eq. (12.20) into Eq. (12.19), we obtain the approximate form of the energy equation:

$$\rho_0 \hat{C}_p \left(\frac{\partial \tilde{T}}{\partial t} + u_j \frac{\partial \tilde{T}}{\partial x_j} \right) + \rho_0 \hat{C}_p u_3 \left(\frac{\partial T_e}{\partial x_3} + \frac{g}{\hat{C}_p} \right) = k \frac{\partial^2 \tilde{T}}{\partial x_j \partial x_j} + Q \qquad (12.21)$$

This equation holds regardless of the choice of reference equilibrium atmosphere. Usually, however, the equilibrium reference condition is chosen to be the adiabatic case, in which

$$\frac{\partial T_e}{\partial x_3} = -\frac{g}{\hat{C}_p}$$

Let us assume that at some initial time $\tilde{T} = 0$ relative to the adiabatic atmosphere. Then, from Eq. (12.21), we see that if $Q = 0$ the condition of $\tilde{T} = 0$ is preserved for $t > 0$ even though there may be motion of the air. Also, the equation of motion Eq. (12.18) reduces to the usual form of the Navier-Stokes equation for the dynamics of an incompressible fluid under the influence of a motion-induced pressure fluctuation $\tilde{p}$ with no contribution from buoyancy forces since $\tilde{T} = 0$. Therefore, for an atmosphere with no sources of heat and initially having an adiabatic lapse rate, the temperature profile is unaltered if the atmosphere is set in motion. As a result, the adiabatic condition can be envisioned as one in which a large number of parcels are rising and falling, a sort of "convective" equilibrium. Thus, we have been able to derive the relation for the adiabatic lapse rate here from the full equations of continuity, motion, and energy, in contrast with the derivation presented in Chapter 11, which was based on thermodynamic arguments.

With the choice of the adiabatic equilibrium condition, Eq. (12.21) becomes

$$\rho_0 \hat{C}_p \left(\frac{\partial \tilde{T}}{\partial t} + u_j \frac{\partial \tilde{T}}{\partial x_j} \right) = k \frac{\partial^2 \tilde{T}}{\partial x_j \partial x_j} + Q \tag{12.22}$$

which is the classic form of the heat conduction equation for an incompressible fluid with constant physical properties.

In summary, the complete set of equations for the lowest layer of the atmosphere is Eqs. (12.14), (12.18), and (12.21) [or (12.22)]. The set consists of five equations for the five unknowns u_1, u_2, u_3, $\tilde{p}$, and $\tilde{T}$. The ideal-gas equation of state is no longer required as it has been incorporated into the equations. The Boussinesq approximations have led to a considerable simplification of the original equations. First of all, the incompressible form of the continuity equation can be used, together with a nearly incompressible form of the equation of motion. In Eq. (12.18) the density enters as ρ_0 in every term except that representing the acceleration due to buoyancy forces.* Finally, the energy equation is just the usual heat conduction equation with T replaced by $\tilde{T}$.

---

*Because of the variation of air density with temperature, motion can arise solely as a result of buoyancy effects induced by temperature nonuniformities. Since the variation of density with temperature leads to the last term on the right-hand side of Eq. (12.18), the equations of motion and energy are not uncoupled, as in the case of forced convection. This situation is called, by contrast, *free convection*, since flow can arise without the imposition of external pressure gradients.

We introduced in Chapter 11 the potential temperature θ and noted that $d\theta/dx_3$ is a measure of the departure of the actual temperature profile from the adiabatic. Thus we expect that a definite relationship should exist between $\tilde{T}$ and θ. From Eq. (11.14) we see that

$$\frac{1}{\theta}\frac{\partial \theta}{\partial x_i} = \frac{1}{T}\left(\frac{\partial T}{\partial x_i} + \frac{g}{\hat{C}_p}\delta_{3i}\right) \tag{12.23}$$

where the quantity in parentheses is the difference between the actual and the adiabatic lapse rates, that is,

$$\frac{1}{\theta}\frac{\partial \theta}{\partial x_i} = \frac{1}{T}\frac{\partial \tilde{T}}{\partial x_i} \tag{12.24}$$

As noted in obtaining Eq. (11.15), since, in magnitude, θ is quite close to T, we can replace Eq. (12.24) by

$$\frac{\partial \theta}{\partial x_i} \cong \frac{\partial \tilde{T}}{\partial x_i} \tag{12.25}$$

Now, using Eq. (12.25), we can rewrite Eq. (12.22) as

$$\rho_0 \hat{C}_p\left(\frac{\partial \theta}{\partial t} + u_j\frac{\partial \theta}{\partial x_j}\right) = k\frac{\partial^2 \theta}{\partial x_j \partial x_j} + Q \tag{12.22'}$$

Although the ρ_0 and T_0 in Eqs. (12.18) and (12.22) refer to the constant surface values, equations of precisely the same form can be derived in which ρ_0 and T_0 are replaced by ρ_e and T_e, the reference profiles. These equations written in that form will be useful later when we consider the dynamics of potential temperature in the atmosphere.

12.2. TURBULENCE

Equations (12.14), (12.18), and (12.22) govern the fluid velocity and temperature in the lower atmosphere. Although these equations are at all times valid, their solution is impeded by the fact that atmospheric flow is turbulent (as opposed to laminar). It is difficult to define turbulence; instead we can cite a number of the characteristics of turbulent flows.* Turbulent flows are irregular and random, so that the velocity components at any location vary randomly with time. Since the velocities are random variables, their exact values can never be predicted precisely. Thus Eqs. (12.14), (12.18), and (12.22) become

---

*Turbulence is a characteristic of flows and not of fluids themselves.

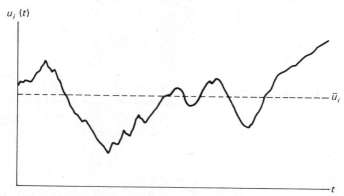

Figure 12.1. Typical record of the velocity in direction i at a point in a turbulent flow.

partial differential equations whose dependent variables are random functions. We cannot, therefore, expect to solve any of these equations exactly; rather, we must be content to determine some convenient statistical properties of the velocities and temperature. The random fluctuations in the velocities result in rates of momentum, heat, and mass transfer in turbulence that are many orders of magnitude greater than the corresponding rates due to pure molecular transport. Turbulent flows are dissipative in the sense that there is a continuous conversion of kinetic to internal energy. Thus, unless energy is continuously supplied, turbulence will decay. The usual source of energy for turbulence is shear in the flow field, although in the atmosphere buoyancy can also be a source of energy.

A particular turbulent flow, say that produced in a laboratory, can be envisioned as one of an infinite ensemble of flows with identical macroscopic boundary conditions. Let us consider a situation of turbulent pipe flow. If the same pipe and pressure drop is used each time the turbulent flow experiment is repeated, the velocity field would always be different no matter how carefully the conditions of the experiment were reproduced. The *mean* or *average* velocity, say as a function of radial position in the pipe, could be determined, in principle, only by averaging the readings made over an infinite ensemble of identical experiments. Figure 12.1 shows a hypothetical record of the ith velocity component at a certain location in a turbulent flow. The specific features of a second velocity record taken under the same conditions would be different but there might well be a decided resemblance in some of the characteristics of the record. In practice it is usually not possible to repeat measurements under identical conditions (particularly in the atmosphere). To compute the mean value of u_i at location $\mathbf{x}$ and time t we would need to average the values of u_i at $\mathbf{x}$ and time t from all the similar velocity records. This ensemble mean is denoted by $\langle u_i(t, \mathbf{x}) \rangle$. If the ensemble mean does not change with time t, we can substitute a time average for the ensemble average.

The time-average velocity is defined by

$$\bar{u}_i = \lim_{T \to \infty} \frac{1}{T} \int_{t_0}^{t_0 + T} u_i(t)\, dt$$

In practice, u_i is usually not a strictly stationary function, that is, one whose statistical properties are independent of time. Rather, the flow may change with time. However, we still wish to define a mean velocity; this is done by defining

$$\bar{u}_i(t) = \frac{1}{T} \int_{t-T/2}^{t+T/2} u_i(t')\, dt'$$

Clearly, $\bar{u}_i(t)$ will depend on the averaging interval T. We need to choose T large enough so that an adequate number of fluctuations are included, but yet not so large that important macroscopic features of the flow would be masked. For example, if T_1 and T_2 are time scales associated with fluctuations and macroscopic changes in the flow, respectively, we would want $T_2 \gg T \gg T_1$.

It is customary to represent the instantaneous value of the wind velocity as the sum of a mean and fluctuating component, $\bar{u}_i + u'_i$. The mean values of the velocities tend to be smooth and slowly varying. The fluctuations $u'_i = u_i - \bar{u}_i$ are characterized by extreme spatial and temporal variations. In spite of the severity of fluctuations, it is observed experimentally that turbulent spatial and temporal inhomogeneities still have considerably greater sizes than molecular scales. The viscosity of the fluid prevents the turbulent fluctuations from becoming too small. Because the smallest scales (or eddies) are still many orders of magnitude larger than molecular dimensions, the turbulent flow of a fluid is described by the basic equations of continuum mechanics in Section 12.1. In general, the largest scales of motion in turbulence (the so-called big eddies) are comparable to the major dimensions of the flow and are responsible for most of the transport of momentum, heat, and mass. Large scales of motion have comparatively long time scales, whereas the small scales have short time scales and are often statistically independent of the large-scale flow. A physical picture that is often used to describe turbulence involves the transfer of energy from the larger to the smaller eddies which ultimately dissipate the energy as heat.

12.3. EQUATIONS FOR THE MEAN QUANTITIES

What we seek, in principle, is a description of a turbulent flow at all points in space and time. Unfortunately, in the equations of motion and energy, the dependent variables u_i, p, and T are random variables, making the equations virtually impossible to solve. To proceed we decompose the velocities, temperature, and pressure into a mean and a fluctuating component,

$$u_i = \bar{u}_i + u_i'$$

$$\theta = \bar{\theta} + \theta'$$

$$p = \bar{p} + p' \qquad (12.26)$$

(Note that $\tilde{T}$ and θ differ only by a constant, and T and $\tilde{T}$ differ only by T_e. Thus, θ' can be regarded as a fluctuation in T, $\tilde{T}$, or θ.) By definition, the mean of a fluctuating quantity is zero, that is,

$$\bar{u}_i' = \bar{\theta}' = \bar{p}' = 0 \qquad (12.27)$$

Thus, a term of the form $\overline{u_i u_j}$ can be written $\bar{u}_i \bar{u}_j + \overline{u_i' u_j'}$, where the mean of the product of two fluctuations is not necessarily (and usually is not) equal to zero. If $\overline{u_i' u_j'} \neq 0$, u_i' and u_j' are said to be correlated.

Our objective is to determine equations for $\bar{u}_i$, $\bar{\theta}$, and $\bar{p}$. To obtain these equations we first substitute Eq. (12.26) into Eqs. (12.14), (12.18), and (12.22). We then average each term in the resulting equations with respect to time. The result, employing Eq. (12.27), is

$$\frac{\partial \bar{u}_i}{\partial x_i} = 0 \qquad (12.28)$$

$$\frac{\partial \bar{u}_i}{\partial t} + \bar{u}_j \frac{\partial \bar{u}_i}{\partial x_j} + \overline{u_j' \frac{\partial u_i'}{\partial x_j}} = -\frac{1}{\rho_0} \frac{\partial \bar{p}}{\partial x_i} + \nu_0 \frac{\partial^2 \bar{u}_i}{\partial x_j \partial x_j} + \frac{g}{T_0} \bar{\theta} \delta_{i3}$$

$$(12.29)$$

$$\rho_0 \hat{C}_p \left(\frac{\partial \bar{\theta}}{\partial t} + \bar{u}_j \frac{\partial \bar{\theta}}{\partial x_j} + \overline{u_j' \frac{\partial \theta'}{\partial x_j}} \right) = k \frac{\partial^2 \bar{\theta}}{\partial x_j \partial x_j} \qquad (12.30)$$

It is customary to employ the relation

$$\frac{\partial u_i'}{\partial x_i} = 0$$

obtained by subtracting Eq. (12.28) from Eq. (12.14), to transform the third terms on the left-hand side of Eqs. (12.29) and (12.30) to $\partial \overline{u_i' u_j'}/\partial x_j$ and

$\partial \overline{u'_j \theta'} / \partial x_j$. Then Eqs. (12.29) and (12.30) are written in the form

$$\frac{\partial}{\partial t}(\rho_0 \bar{u}_i) + \frac{\partial}{\partial x_j}(\rho_0 \bar{u}_i \bar{u}_j) = -\frac{\partial \bar{p}}{\partial x_i} + \frac{\partial}{\partial x_j}\left(\mu \frac{\partial \bar{u}_i}{\partial x_j} - \rho_0 \overline{u'_i u'_j}\right) + \frac{g}{T_0} \bar{\theta} \delta_{i3}$$

(12.31)

$$\rho_0 \hat{C}_p \left(\frac{\partial \bar{\theta}}{\partial t} + \bar{u}_j \frac{\partial \bar{\theta}}{\partial x_j}\right) = \frac{\partial}{\partial x_j}\left(k \frac{\partial \bar{\theta}}{\partial x_j} - \rho_0 \hat{C}_p \overline{u'_j \theta'}\right)$$

(12.32)

These equations, now time-averaged, contain only smoothly varying average quantities, so that the difficulties associated with the stochastic nature of the original equations have been alleviated. However, a new difficulty has arisen. We note the emergence of new dependent variables $\overline{u'_i u'_j}$, $i, j = 1, 2, 3$, and $\overline{u'_j \theta'}$, $j = 1, 2, 3$. When the equations are written in the form of Eqs. (12.31) and (12.32), we can see that $\rho_0 \overline{u'_i u'_j}$ represents a new contribution to the total stress tensor and that $\rho_0 \hat{C}_p \overline{u'_j \theta'}$ is a new contribution to the heat flux vector, that is,

$$\bar{\tau}_{ij} = \left(\mu \frac{\partial \bar{u}_i}{\partial x_j} - \rho_0 \overline{u'_i u'_j}\right)$$

(12.33)

$$\bar{q}_j = -\left(k \frac{\partial \bar{\theta}}{\partial x_j} - \rho_0 \hat{C}_p \overline{u'_j \theta'}\right)$$

(12.34)

Let us consider the terms $-\rho_0 \overline{u'_i u'_j}$. These terms, called the *Reynolds stresses*, indicate that the velocity fluctuations lead to a transport of momentum from one volume of fluid to another. Let us consider the physical interpretation of the Reynolds stresses. To do this, we envision the situation of a steady mean wind in the x_1 direction near the ground. Let the x_2 and x_3 directions be the horizontal direction perpendicular to the mean wind and the vertical direction, respectively. Then, a sudden increase or gust in the mean wind would result in a positive u'_1, whereas a lull would lead to a negative u'_1. Left- and right-hand swings of the wind direction from its mean direction can be described by positive and negative u'_2, respectively, and upward and downward vertical gusts by positive and negative u'_3. If the mean value of a product such as $u'_1 u'_2$ is not to vanish, as we time-average over T, we must find a high frequency of terms of the same sign, either positive or negative, indicating that, say, positive values of u'_1 are more likely to be found with positive values of u'_2 than negative values. Since there is probably no reason to associate gusts or lulls with the wind having a tendency to swing in any particular direction, we would find $\overline{u'_1 u'_2} = 0$. However, since the air needed to sustain a gust must come from faster moving air from above, we would expect positive values of u'_1 to be correlated with negative values of u'_3. Similarly, a lull will result when air is transported upward rather than forward, so that we would expect negative u'_1 to be associated with positive u'_3. As a result of both effects, $\overline{u'_1 u'_3}$ will not vanish and the Reynolds stress $-\rho \overline{u'_1 u'_3}$ will play an important role in the transport of momentum.

Equations (12.28), (12.31), and (12.32) have as dependent variables $\bar{u}_i$, $\bar{p}$, $\bar{\theta}$, $\overline{u'_i u'_j}$, and $\overline{u'_j \theta}$. We thus have 14 dependent variables ($\overline{u'_i u'_j} = \overline{u'_j u'_i}$) and only five equations. In general, one possible means for circumventing this problem is to generate equations which, in essence, are conservation equations for the new dependent variables. We can derive such an equation for the variables $\overline{u'_i u'_j}$, for example by first subtracting Eq. (12.29) from Eq. (12.18), leaving an equation for u'_i. We then multiply this equation by u'_j and average over all terms. Although we can derive the desired equation for $\overline{u'_i u'_j}$, we have unfortunately at the same time generated still more dependent variables $\overline{u'_i u'_j u'_j}$. This problem, arising in the description of turbulence, is called the *closure problem*, for which no general solution has yet been found. At present, we must rely on models and estimates based on intuition and experience to obtain a closed set of equations. Since mathematics by itself will not provide a solution, we must resort to dimensional analysis and quasi-physical models for the Reynolds stresses and the turbulent heat fluxes. The next section is devoted to the most popular empirical models for the turbulent momentum and energy fluxes, the so-called mixing-length models.

12.4. MIXING-LENGTH MODELS FOR TURBULENT TRANSPORT

As we have just seen, the closure problem is the fundamental impediment to obtaining solutions for the mean velocities in turbulent flows. In order to progress at all, from a purely mathematical point of view, we must obtain a closed set of equations. The simplest approach to closing the equations is based on an appeal to a physical picture of the actual nature of turbulent momentum transport.

We can envision the turbulent fluid as comprising lumps of fluid which, for a short time, retain their integrity before being destroyed. These lumps or eddies transfer momentum, heat, and material from one location to another, conceptually in much the same way as molecular motion is responsible for transport in gases. Thus, it is possible to imagine an eddy, originally at one level in the fluid, breaking away and conserving some or all of its momentum until it mixes with the mean flow at another level.

Let us first consider turbulent momentum transport, that is, the Reynolds stresses. We assume a steady turbulent shear flow in which $\bar{u}_1 = \bar{u}_1(x_2)$ and $\bar{u}_2 = \bar{u}_3 = 0$. The equation for $\bar{u}_1$ is

$$\frac{d}{dx_2} \rho \overline{u'_1 u'_2} = \mu \frac{d^2 \bar{u}_1}{dx_2^2} - \frac{\partial \bar{p}}{\partial x_1} \qquad (12.35)$$

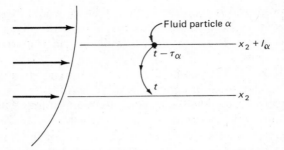

Figure 12.2.   Eddy transfer in a turbulent shear flow.

The mean flux of x_1 momentum in the x_2 direction due to the turbulence is $\rho \overline{u_1' u_2'}$. Let us see if we can derive an estimate for this flux.

We can assume that the fluctuation in u_1 at any level x_2 is due to the arrival at that level of a fluid lump or eddy which originated at some other location where the mean velocity was different from that at x_2. We illustrate this idea in Fig. 12.2, in which a fluid lump which is at $x_2 = x_2 + l_\alpha$ at $t - \tau_\alpha$ arrives at x_2 at t. Let u_{1_α}' be the fluctuation in u_1 at x_2 at time t due to the αth eddy. If the eddy maintains its x_1 momentum during its sojourn, the fluctuation in u_1 at x_2 can be written

$$u_{1_\alpha}' = u_{1_\alpha}(x_2, t) - \bar{u}_1(x_2) \tag{12.36}$$

Suppose that this eddy originated at the level $x_2 + l_\alpha$ at time $t - \tau_\alpha$ with a velocity equal to the mean velocity at that level, namely $\bar{u}_1(x_2 + l_\alpha)$. As long as the x_1 momentum of the eddy is conserved,

$$u_{1_\alpha}(x_2, t) = \bar{u}_1(x_2 + l_\alpha, t - \tau_\alpha) \tag{12.37}$$

Substituting Eq. (12.37) into Eq. (12.36) and expanding $\bar{u}_1(x_2 + l_\alpha, t - \tau_\alpha)$ in a Taylor series about the point (x_2, t), we get

$$u_{1_\alpha}' = l_\alpha \frac{\partial \bar{u}_1}{\partial x_2} - \tau_\alpha \frac{\partial \bar{u}_1}{\partial t} + \frac{1}{2} l_\alpha^2 \frac{\partial^2 \bar{u}_1}{\partial x_2^2} + \frac{1}{2} \tau_\alpha^2 \frac{\partial^2 \bar{u}_1}{\partial t^2} + \cdots \tag{12.38}$$

First, we note that, since the flow has been assumed to be steady, $\bar{u}_1$ does not vary with time. Thus, Eq. (12.38) becomes

$$u_{1_\alpha}' = l_\alpha \frac{d\bar{u}_1}{dx_2} + \frac{1}{2} l_\alpha^2 \frac{d^2 \bar{u}_1}{dx_2^2} + \cdots \tag{12.39}$$

Let L_e be the maximum distance over which an eddy maintains its integrity, that is, $L_e > |l_\alpha|$ for nearly all eddies. Let L be a characteristic length scale of the $\bar{u}_1$ field, say, given by

$$L = \frac{d\bar{u}_1/dx_2}{d^2\bar{u}_1/dx_2^2} \qquad (12.40)$$

Then, as long as

$$L \gg L_e \qquad (12.41)$$

we can truncate second- and higher-order terms in Eq. (12.39), leaving

$$u'_{1_\alpha} = l_\alpha \frac{d\bar{u}_1}{dx_2} \qquad (12.42)$$

We can now consider the turbulent flux $\rho\overline{u'_1u'_2}$. First, we multiply Eq. (12.42) by u'_{2_α}, the velocity fluctuation in the x_2 direction at (x_2, t) associated with the αth eddy, and average the resulting equation over an ensemble of eddies which pass the point x_2, say,

$$\lim_{N\to\infty} \frac{1}{N} \sum_{\alpha=1}^{N} u'_{2_\alpha} l_\alpha$$

Then, assuming that this ensemble eddy average converges to the time average (which it should for a steady flow), we obtain

$$\overline{u'_1u'_2} = \overline{u'_2 l} \frac{d\bar{u}_1}{dx_2} \qquad (12.43)$$

The term $\overline{u'_2 l}$ represents the correlation (negative, if $d\bar{u}_1/dx_2 > 0$) between the fluctuating x_2 velocity at x_2 and the distance of travel of the eddy. As the eddy travels, we expect $\overline{u'_2 l}$ to decrease, since u'_2 is the velocity in the x_2 direction at $x_2 + l$, and the particle is getting farther and farther away from $x_2 + l$ as it moves. Assume l and u'_2 become uncorrelated at L_e, where L_e is a measure of the eddy size. We can then estimate the order of $\overline{u'_2 l}$ as $-L_e\hat{u}_2$, where $\hat{u}_2$ is the turbulent intensity, $(\overline{u'^2_2})^{1/2}$. Employing this relation in Eq. (12.43), we obtain

$$\overline{u'_1u'_2} = -cL_e\hat{u}_2 \frac{d\bar{u}_1}{dx_2} \qquad (12.44)$$

where c is a constant of proportionality.

A reasonable definition of the *mixing length* L_e is the integral length scale

$$L_e = \int_0^\infty \frac{\overline{u'_2(x_2 + l)u'_2(x_2)}}{\overline{u'^2_2}} \, dl \qquad (12.45)$$

The integrand is expected to vanish for sufficiently large l, so that L_e is a measure of the maximum distance in the fluid over which the velocity fluctuations are correlated, or, in some sense, of the eddy size. The experimental determination of L_e simply involves measuring the velocities at two points separated by larger and larger distances.

The turbulent flux can, therefore, be written

$$\rho\overline{u_1'u_2'} = -c\rho L_e \hat{u}_2 \frac{d\bar{u}_1}{dx_2} \tag{12.46}$$

Based on Eq. (12.46) we define an *eddy viscosity* or *turbulent momentum diffusivity* K_M by

$$\rho\overline{u_1'u_2'} = -\rho K_M \frac{d\bar{u}_1}{dx_2} \tag{12.47}$$

where $K_M = cL_e\hat{u}_2$.

We can extend the mixing-length concept to the turbulent heat flux. We consider the same shear flow as above, in which buoyancy effects are, for the moment, neglected. The mean vertical turbulent heat flux is $\rho\hat{C}_p\overline{u_2'\theta'}$. By analogy to the definition of the eddy viscosity, we can define an eddy diffusivity for heat transfer by

$$\rho\hat{C}_p\overline{u_2'\theta'} = -\rho\hat{C}_p K_T \frac{d\bar{\theta}}{dx_2} \tag{12.48}$$

Equations (12.47) and (12.48) provide a solution to the closure problem inasmuch as the turbulent fluxes have been related directly to the mean velocity and potential temperature. However, we have essentially exchanged our lack of knowledge of $\rho\overline{u_1'u_2'}$ and $\rho\hat{C}_p\overline{u_2'\theta'}$ for K_M and K_T, respectively. In general, both K_M and K_T are different for transport in different coordinate directions and are functions of location in the flow field. The variation of these coefficients with flow properties is usually determined from experimental data.

The result of the mixing-length idea used to derive the expressions Eqs. (12.47) and (12.48) is that the turbulent momentum and energy fluxes are related to the gradients of the mean quantities. Substitution of these relations into Eqs. (12.31) and (12.32) leads to closed equations for the mean quantities. Thus, except for the fact that K_M and K_T vary with position and direction, these models for turbulent transport are analogous to those for molecular transport of momentum and energy. The use of a diffusion equation model implies that the length scale of the transport process is much smaller than the characteristic length over which the mean profiles are changing [such as, for example, L, given by Eq. (12.40)]. In molecular diffusion in a gas at normal densities, the length scale of the diffusion process, the mean free path of a molecule, is many orders of magnitude smaller than the distances over which the mean properties of the gas vary. In turbulence, on the other hand, the motions responsible for the transport of momentum, heat, and material are usually roughly the same size as the characteristic length scale for changes in the mean fields of velocity, temperature, and concentration. Thus, in general, a diffusion model for turbulent transport, as exemplified by Eqs. (12.47) and (12.48), is inapplicable in turbulence. In the atmosphere, for example, the characteristic vertical dimension of eddies is of the same order as the distance above the ground as is the characteristic scale of changes in the velocity profile. We must conclude, therefore, that expressions such as Eqs. (12.47) and (12.48) do not possess a firm, rigorous basis, and the success in using them depends on two factors. First, they should ideally be employed in situations in which the length scale for changes in the mean properties is considerably greater than that of the eddies responsible for transport, that is, Eq. (12.41). Second, the values and functional forms of K_M and K_T should be determined from experiments in situations similar to those in which Eqs. (12.47) and (12.48) are to be applied.

12.5. VARIATION OF WIND WITH HEIGHT IN THE ATMOSPHERE

The atmosphere near the surface of the earth can be divided into three layers, as shown in Fig. 11.11; the free atmosphere, the Ekman layer, and the surface layer.* The Ekman layer and the surface layer constitute the so-called planetary boundary layer. The Ekman layer extends to a height of from 300 to 500 m depending on the type of terrain, with the greater thickness corresponding to the more disturbed terrain.

In the Ekman layer, the wind direction tends to turn clockwise with increasing height in the Northern Hemisphere (counterclockwise in the Southern Hemisphere). The wind speed in the Ekman layer generally increases rapidly with height; however, the rate lessens as the free atmosphere is approached. The exact distribution of the wind speed depends on many parameters, particularly the vertical distribution of the horizontal pressure gradient as well as the atmospheric stability.

The layer immediately adjacent to the surface, typically up to 30 to 50 m from the ground, is called the surface layer. Within this layer, the vertical turbulent fluxes of momentum and heat are assumed constant with respect to height, and indeed they define the extent of this region.

In this section we consider the prediction of the variation of wind with height in the surface and Ekman layers. Most of our attention will be devoted to the surface layer, the region in which pollutants are usually first released.

---

*Immediately adjacent to the ground surface, a laminar sublayer can be identified in which molecular viscosities become important. However, the thickness of this layer is typically less than a centimeter. Therefore, for all practical purposes, it can be ignored in the present discussion.

One other item should be discussed before we begin, and that is the question of smooth versus rough surfaces. In meteorological applications, the surface features leading to roughness are usually so closely distributed (for example, grass, crops, bushes, etc.) that only the height of the roughness elements and not their spacing is important. Thus, we characterize a particular rough surface by a single length parameter ε. Whether the surface is "smooth" or "rough" depends on the comparison of ε with the depth of the laminar sublayer. In general, a surface is called *smooth* if the roughness elements are sufficiently small to allow the establishment of a laminar sublayer in which they are submerged. On the other hand, a *rough* surface is one in which the roughness elements are high enough to prevent the formation of a laminar sublayer, so that the flow is turbulent down to the roughness elements. The depth of the laminar sublayer, and hence the classification of the surface as smooth or rough, depends on the Reynolds number of the flow.

12.5.1. Mean Velocity in the Surface Layer in Adiabatic Conditions

Let us consider the steady, two-dimensional turbulent flow of air in the surface layer parallel to the ground at $x_3 = 0$. We assume that $\bar{u}_1 = \bar{u}_1(x_3)$ and $\bar{u}_2 = 0$. Our object is to determine $\bar{u}_1(x_3)$ when the vertical temperature profile is adiabatic. Since in this case $\theta = 0$ we need consider only the x_1 component of the time-averaged equation of motion,

$$\frac{d}{dx_3}\rho\overline{u_1' u_3'} = \mu\frac{d^2\bar{u}_1}{dx_3^2} - \frac{\partial\bar{p}}{\partial x_1} \tag{12.49}$$

which we can write in the more concise form

$$\frac{\partial\bar{\tau}_{13}}{\partial x_3} = \frac{\partial\bar{p}}{\partial x_1} \tag{12.50}$$

where $\bar{\tau}_{13}$ is the total shear stress. If $\partial\bar{p}/\partial x_1$, the pressure gradient in the direction of the mean wind, is independent of x_3, we can integrate Eq. (12.50) to give

$$\bar{\tau}_{13} = \tau_0 + x_3\frac{\partial\bar{p}}{\partial x_1} \tag{12.51}$$

where τ_0 is the value of $\bar{\tau}_{13}$ as $x_3 \to 0$. In most atmospheric situations, and as we shall assume here, $\partial\bar{p}/\partial x_1$ is small, and, provided x_3 is not too large, $\bar{\tau}_{13}$ is approximately equal to τ_0 in the surface layer.

Let us now see what can be determined about the functional dependence of $\bar{u}_1(x_3)$ employing dimensional analysis. The term $\bar{u}_1$ and hence $d\bar{u}_1/dx_3$ should depend on τ_0, ν, ρ, and x_3. We thus have five quantities involving three dimensions (mass, length, and time). We invoke the Buckingham π theorem:

Let $B_1, B_2, \ldots, B_m$ be the m variables in a physical problem. Their functional relationship may be written $F(B_1, B_2, \ldots, B_m) = 0$. If k fundamental dimensions are required to define these variables, then the above relation may be written in terms of $m - k$ dimensionless groups, $F_1(\pi_1, \pi_2, \ldots, \pi_{m-k}) = 0$.

In this case $m = 5$ and $k = 3$, and so there are only two independent dimensionless groups relating the five variables. The π method does not tell us *what* the groups are, only *how many* exist. It will be useful to have a characteristic velocity from among the variables. For this we choose $\sqrt{\tau_0/\rho}$, denote it u_*, and call it the *friction velocity*. As our two groups we select

$$\pi_1 = \frac{d\bar{u}_1}{dx_3}\frac{x_3}{u_*} \qquad \pi_2 = \frac{x_3 u_*}{\nu}$$

The π method tells us that

$$F_1(\pi_1, \pi_2) = 0$$

or, alternatively, that

$$\frac{d\bar{u}_1}{dx_3} = \frac{u_*}{x_3}F_2\left(\frac{x_3 u_*}{\nu}\right) \tag{12.52}$$

This is as far as dimensional analysis will bring us. We now need to add some physical insight. We note first that $x_3 u_*/\nu$ is essentially a Reynolds number. Typical values of u_* and ν for the atmosphere are 100 cm sec^{-1} and 0.1 cm^2 sec^{-1}, respectively. Thus,

$$\frac{x_3 u_*}{\nu} = \begin{cases} 10^5 & x_3 = 1 \text{ m} \\ 10^7 & x_3 = 100 \text{ m} \end{cases}$$

The large values indicate a fully turbulent region. We expect that $d\bar{u}_1/dx_3$ should be independent of ν in this region, since the thickness of the laminar sublayer, proportional to ν/u_*, is of the order of 0.01 cm. Thus, we can set $F_2(x_3 u_*/\nu) = \text{const} = a$, and

$$\frac{d\bar{u}_1}{dx_3} = a\frac{u_*}{x_3} \tag{12.53}$$

Upon integration,

$$\frac{\bar{u}_1(x_3)}{u_*} = a \ln x_3 + \text{const}$$

which may be represented in the dimensionless form

$$\frac{\bar{u}_1(x_3)}{u_*} = a \ln \frac{u_* x_3}{\nu} + \text{const} \qquad (12.54)$$

The constant of integration would in principle be determined by the condition that $\bar{u}_1 = 0$ at $x_3 = 0$. Unfortunately, this boundary condition cannot be satisfied by a finite constant in Eq. (12.54). Thus, we must employ a somewhat different boundary condition. We choose as the condition that the velocity gradient increase without limit as $x_3 \to 0$. This is automatically satisfied by Eq. (12.53). The constant in Eq. (12.54) was evaluated experimentally by Nikuradse for smooth surfaces and he found

$$\frac{\bar{u}_1(x_3)}{u_*} = \frac{1}{\kappa} \ln \frac{u_* x_3}{\nu} + 5.5 \qquad (12.55)$$

where the constant a has been written as $1/\kappa$ with the experimental value of $\kappa = 0.4$. We find from Eq. (12.55) that $\bar{u}_1$ vanishes at $x_3 = \nu/9u_*$, so that Eq. (12.55) holds only for values of x_3 greater than this, approximately 10^{-4} cm.

For a rough surface, there is no laminar sublayer. Thus, $\bar{u}_1$ should depend on τ_0, ρ, ε, and x_3. By dimensional analysis, we reason that

$$\frac{\bar{u}_1(x_3)}{u_*} = \frac{1}{\kappa} \ln \frac{x_3}{\varepsilon} + \text{const} \qquad (12.56)$$

which is usually written

$$\frac{\bar{u}_1(x_3)}{u_*} = \frac{1}{\kappa} \ln \frac{x_3}{z_0} \qquad x_3 \geq z_0 \qquad (12.57)$$

where the integration constant z_0 is called the *roughness* length. Clearly, z_0 should be related to the height of the roughness elements ε. By experiment it has been found that $z_0 \cong \varepsilon/30$. The criteria for smooth or rough flow regimes have been determined experimentally to be

$$\frac{u_* z_0}{\nu} \begin{cases} < 0.13 & \text{smooth flow} \\ > 2.5 & \text{rough flow} \end{cases}$$

Values of z_0 for typical surfaces are given in Table 12.1.

The logarithmic law Eq. (12.57) is determined by the parameters κ, z_0, and u_*. Of the two variables, z_0 is a property of the roughness, whereas u_* must somehow be measured. Commonly, the velocity is measured at some reference height, say 10 m. Substituting this measurement into Eq. (12.57) allows calculation of u_* and subsequent specification of $\bar{u}_1$ at all values of x_3. A better way of obtaining u_* would be a direct measurement of the surface shear

**TABLE 12.1.   Roughness Lengths for
Various Surfaces**[a]

Surface	z_0, m
Very smooth (ice, mud flats)	10^{-5}
Snow	10^{-3}
Smooth sea	10^{-3}
Level desert	10^{-3}
Lawn	10^{-2}
Uncut grass	0.05
Fully grown root crops	0.1
Tree covered	1
Low-density residential	2
Central business district	5–10

[a] McRae et al. (1982).

stress, but this requires elaborate experimental equipment. Thus, in micro-meteorological studies it is usual to infer the shear at the ground from measured profiles of wind velocity distribution, a procedure that works satis-factorily in neutrally stratified boundary layers (Plate, 1971).

12.5.2.   Effects of Temperature on the Surface Layer

In our study of atmospheric turbulence we have to this point neglected any effects of buoyancy. In the atmosphere, however, buoyancy plays an important role in maintaining (or suppressing) the energy of the turbulence. Conse-quently, we must examine the effect of temperature stratification on the nature of turbulence in the surface layer.

The diurnal changes in solar radiation set up a cycle of heating and cooling of the atmospheric boundary layer that is strongly reflected in the wind field (recall Fig. 11.8). At night the air is stably stratified because the ground is colder than the air. As the sun rises, on a clear day, solar radiation heats up the ground faster than the air. Soon after dawn the near laminar flow of the nighttime stable air gives way to turbulent flow. As height increases, the effect of shear stresses at the surface in maintaining turbulence decreases and the effect of buoyancy increases. The warm thermals of air cause vigorous mixing aloft. The thickness of the layer of convective influence increases during the day as surface heating continues. Late in the afternoon the air reaches the same temperature as the ground, and the temperature profile becomes adiabatic since there is no heat flux from the ground. Near evening, the temperature of the air exceeds that of the ground, and the resulting heat flux to the ground causes a stably stratified temperature profile. The stable layer builds in thickness throughout the night just as the unstable layer grew during the day. Wind speed is often very low at night, and under these circumstances shear is virtually nonexistent and stratification becomes dominant.

This typical behavior serves to point out that the atmosphere is seldom adiabatic. Thus, it becomes essential in predicting velocities in the surface layer to consider the effects of temperature on the type of turbulence to be expected.

All that we essentially want to do is to examine the differential equations for the dynamics of the kinetic energy of turbulence and for the dynamics of temperature fluctuations. We will not attempt to derive or discuss in any detail these two equations, as our interest is only in the physical interpretation of the terms in the equations. For complete treatment of the dynamics of atmospheric turbulence we refer the reader to Monin and Yaglom (1971, 1975).

Let us consider a shear flow that is steady and homogeneous in the $x_1 x_2$ plane with the only nonzero mean velocity $\bar{u}_1(x_3)$. The kinetic energy of the turbulence is given by $\frac{1}{2}\overline{u_i' u_i'} = \frac{1}{2}(\overline{u_1' u_1'} + \overline{u_2' u_2'} + \overline{u_3' u_3'})$. A measure of the effect of the turbulence on temperature fluctuations is the mean-square fluctuation $\overline{\theta'^2}$. The dynamic equations governing $\frac{1}{2}\overline{u_i' u_i'}$ and $\overline{\theta'^2}$ in this situation reduce to

$$0 = -\overline{u_1' u_3'}\frac{\partial \bar{u}_1}{\partial x_3} + \frac{g}{T_e}\overline{u_3'\theta'} - \frac{\partial}{\partial x_3}\left(\frac{1}{2}\overline{u_i' u_i' u_3'} + \frac{1}{\rho}\overline{p' u_3'}\right) - \nu\overline{\frac{\partial u_i'}{\partial x_j}\frac{\partial u_i'}{\partial x_j}}$$

$$\quad\quad\quad\quad ① \quad\quad\quad\quad ② \quad\quad\quad\quad\quad\quad\quad ③ \quad\quad\quad ④ \quad\quad (12.58)$$

$$0 = -\overline{u_3'\theta'}\frac{\partial \bar{\theta}}{\partial x_3} - \frac{\partial}{\partial x_3}\left(\frac{1}{2}\overline{\theta'^2 u_3'}\right) - \alpha\overline{\frac{\partial \theta'}{\partial x_j}\frac{\partial \theta'}{\partial x_j}} \quad\quad (12.59)$$

$$\quad\quad\quad\quad ⑤ \quad\quad\quad\quad\quad ⑥ \quad\quad\quad\quad ⑦$$

The terms in these two equations can be interpreted as follows:

① Production of turbulent kinetic energy by shear stresses.
② Production of turbulent kinetic energy by buoyancy (if this term is negative, it represents *loss* of kinetic energy by buoyancy).
③ Turbulent flux of kinetic energy.
④ Dissipation of kinetic energy by molecular viscosity.
⑤ Production of fluctuations by the mean temperature gradient.
⑥ Turbulent flux of mean-square temperature fluctuations.
⑦ Decay of mean-square temperature fluctuations due to molecular conductivity.

These are the basic equations used in the description of atmospheric turbulence. The key feature of interest in this discussion is the buoyant production of turbulent kinetic energy, that is, term ②. In order to have a means of assessing the importance of this term, let us consider the ratio of terms ② and ①,

$$\frac{(g/T_e)\overline{u_3'\theta'}}{\overline{u_1'u_3'}\partial \overline{u}_1/\partial x_3}$$

This ratio is called the *flux Richardson number* and is denoted by Rf. We can then rewrite Eq. (12.58):

$$0 = -\overline{u_1'u_3'}\frac{\partial \overline{u}_1}{\partial x_3}(1 - \text{Rf}) - \frac{\partial}{\partial x_3}\left(\tfrac{1}{2}\overline{u_i'u_i'u_3'} + \frac{1}{\rho}\overline{p'u_3'}\right) - \nu\overline{\frac{\partial u_i'}{\partial x_j}\frac{\partial u_i'}{\partial x_j}}$$

$$(12.60)$$

In our situation $\partial \overline{u}_1/\partial x_3 > 0$, and so $\overline{u_1'u_3'} < 0$ as explained in Section 12.3. Thus, the term $\overline{u_3'\theta'}$ governs the sign of Rf and thus whether kinetic energy is produced or destroyed by the buoyancy. We stress that buoyancy can lead not only to kinetic energy production but also to its destruction. This can be explained readily by the sign of the term $\overline{u_3'\theta'}$.

Case 1. $\overline{u_3'\theta'} > 0$, Rf < 0. Positive values of u_3' occur with positive values of θ'. The actual mean profile is $\overline{\theta}(x_3) = \overline{T}(x_3) - T_e$, as shown in Fig. 12.3. Consider a parcel of air that experiences an upward displacement with $u_3' > 0$. Its temperature will change adiabatically if the fluctuation is rapid. At the new level, the temperature fluctuation θ' is the difference between the parcel's temperature $\overline{\theta}(x_3)$ and that of the surroundings $\overline{\theta}(x_3 + l)$. The parcel's *actual* temperature T decreases in accordance with the adiabatic relation, but its temperature θ, $\theta = T - T_e$, *relative to an adiabatic profile*, remains constant. Thus, in this case, $\theta' > 0$. The production of turbulent kinetic energy is *increased* in Eq. (12.60). Since the actual mean temperature profile must be as shown in Fig. 12.3 (Case 1) we know that this situation occurs under *unstable* conditions ($\partial \overline{\theta}/\partial x_3 < 0$).

Case 2. $\overline{u_3'\theta'} < 0$, Rf > 0. Positive values of u_3' occur with negative values of θ'. Consider a parcel of air which experiences an upward displacement with $u_3' > 0$. Its temperature will change adiabatically and, as noted in Case 1, remain at $\overline{\theta}(x_3)$. Its temperature difference at the new level, θ', will therefore be negative since $\partial \overline{\theta}/\partial x_3 > 0$. Turbulent kinetic energy is lost, since Rf > 0 in Eq. (12.60). This situation occurs under *stable* conditions ($\partial \overline{\theta}/\partial x_3 > 0$).

Case 3. $\overline{u_3'\theta'} = 0$, Rf $= 0$. In this case, there are no contributions to the turbulent kinetic energy from temperature fluctuations. This is recognized as the adiabatic, or *neutral*, case ($\partial \overline{\theta}/\partial x_3 = 0$).

From Eq. (12.60) it is evident that, if Rf $= 1$, turbulent energy is consumed by buoyancy forces as fast as it is generated by shear stresses. Thus, Rf $= 1$

Case 1 $\overline{u_3'\theta'} > 0$, $Rf < 0$

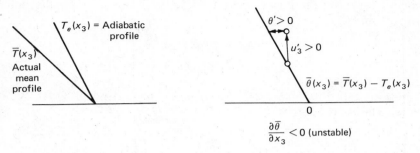

Case 2 $\overline{u_3'\theta'} < 0$, $Rf > 0$

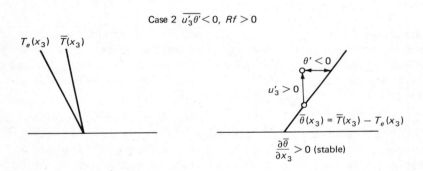

Case 3 $\overline{u_3'\theta'} = 0$, $Rf = 0$

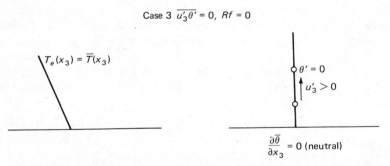

Figure 12.3. Relationship between the sign of Rf and atmospheric stability.

represents a theoretical limit beyond which, that is, Rf > 1, atmospheric turbulence is completely suppressed. (Actually, experimental observations have shown that turbulence cannot be maintained for values of Rf greater than about 0.2. We will discuss this point below.)

The flux Richardson number is a function of the distance from the ground. To illustrate the dependence of Rf on x_3, we consider the case (near-neutral conditions) in which the velocity profile is logarithmic, that is,

$$\frac{\partial \bar{u}_1}{\partial x_3} = \frac{u_*}{\kappa x_3}$$

By definition of the surface layer, the Reynolds stress $-\overline{\rho u_1' u_3'}$ is constant and equal to ρu_*^2, and the vertical mean turbulent heat flux $\bar{q}_3 = \rho \hat{C}_p \overline{u_3' \theta'}$ is constant. We can then write Rf:

$$\text{Rf} = -\frac{\kappa g x_3 \bar{q}_3}{\rho \hat{C}_p T_0 u_*^3} \tag{12.61}$$

We see that Rf is essentially a dimensionless length,

$$\text{Rf} = \frac{x_3}{L} \tag{12.62}$$

where L, called the *Monin-Obukhov* length, is given by*

$$L = \frac{-\rho \hat{C}_p T_0 u_*^3}{\kappa g \bar{q}_3} \tag{12.63}$$

We see that L is simply the height above the ground at which the production of turbulence by both mechanical and buoyancy forces is equal. The Monin-Obukhov length, like Rf, provides a measure of the stability of the surface layer, that is, (see Table 12.2)

$$L > 0 \quad \text{stable } (\bar{q}_3 < 0)$$
$$L < 0 \quad \text{unstable } (\bar{q}_3 > 0)$$
$$L = \infty \quad \text{neutral } (\bar{q}_3 = 0)$$

Although Rf is a convenient measure of the stability condition of the atmosphere, its measurement is difficult since both heat and momentum fluxes

*The Monin-Obukhov length can be obtained directly from dimensional analysis. The turbulence characteristics in the surface layer are governed in general by the following variables: (g/T_0), ρ, ν, k, τ (or u_*), $\bar{q}_3$, z_0, and x_3. We assume that (1) molecular effects can be neglected, that is, ν and k, and (2) variations in the roughness length z_0 only shift the profiles but do not affect their form. Then, the variables are (g/T_0), ρ, τ (or u_*), $\bar{q}_3$ (or $\bar{q}_3/\rho\hat{C}_p$), and x_3. We have five variables in four dimensions (mass, length, time, and temperature), so that by the Buckingham π theorem we have only one dimensionless group from among these variables. That group is

$$\text{Rf} = \frac{x_3}{L}$$

where κ is just a dimensionless proportionality factor.

TABLE 12.2. Interpretation of the Monin-Obukhov Length L with Respect to Atmospheric Stability

L		Stability condition
Small negative	$-100 \text{ m} < L < 0$	Very unstable
Large negative	$-10^5 \text{ m} \leq L \leq -100 \text{ m}$	Unstable
Very large (positive or negative)	$|L| > 10^5 \text{ m}$	Neutral
Large positive	$10 \text{ m} \leq L \leq 10^5 \text{ m}$	Stable
Small positive	$0 < L < 10 \text{ m}$	Very stable

must be determined simultaneously. In order to obtain a more convenient form of Rf from the point of view of measurement, we employ the definitions of an eddy viscosity and thermal conductivity by Eqs. (12.47) and (12.48), so that Rf may be written

$$\text{Rf} = \frac{K_T g}{K_M T_0} \frac{\partial \bar{\theta} / \partial x_3}{(\partial \bar{u}_1 / \partial x_3)^2} \tag{12.64}$$

Aside from K_T and K_M, Rf now involves quantities that can be measured rather easily. In order to isolate the ratio K_T/K_M we define the *gradient Richardson number* Ri by

$$\text{Ri} = \frac{g}{T_0} \frac{\partial \bar{\theta} / \partial x_3}{(\partial \bar{u}_1 / \partial x_3)^2} \tag{12.65}$$

Thus,

$$\text{Rf} = \frac{K_T}{K_M} \text{Ri} \tag{12.66}$$

Both Rf and Ri have significance in determining atmospheric conditions. The stability of the surface layer at any height is described by Rf, which is identically equal to zero in neutral conditions. A small absolute value of Rf indicates that the atmosphere is in a near-neutral condition, where a logarithmic velocity profile is valid. A small absolute value of Rf can arise in either of two ways. First, L can be large, implying that the heat flux $\bar{q}_3$ is small or u_* is large. Second, x_3 can be small. Thus, even in a flow significantly deviating from neutral conditions, these exists a layer close to the ground in which $|\text{Rf}|$ is small and the flow resembles that in neutral stratification. Because the logarithmic law was used in deriving Eq. (12.62), this equation is valid only in the limit of small $|\text{Rf}|$. When $|\text{Rf}|$ is large, we still might expect Rf to depend only on x_3/L, although not in as simple a fashion as Eq. (12.62).

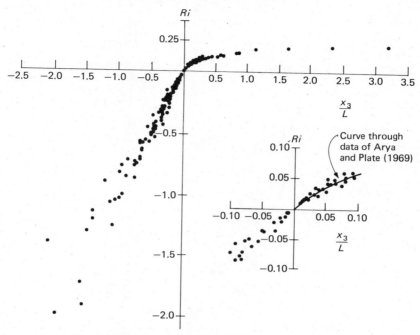

Figure 12.4.   Ri as a function of x_3/L (Plate, 1971).

In unstable conditions, Rf < 0. As Rf becomes more negative (as a result of $\bar{q}_3$ or x_3 increasing), the effect of mechanical generation of turbulence becomes less and less important compared with buoyant production of turbulent energy. A point is reached, at about Rf $\cong$ −0.03, where the flow becomes totally dominated by buoyancy effects and essentially becomes a free convection flow.

Under stable conditions, Rf > 0. As Rf becomes more positive (as a result of $\bar{q}_3$ or x_3 decreasing), the effect of buoyancy is to suppress the mechanically generated turbulence. As Rf increases, a point is reached where the turbulence should be suppressed. A first guess at this critical value of Rf was unity, although experimental data seem to indicate that the critical flux Richardson number is no larger than 0.2 (Plate, 1971).

Theoretically we have obtained Eq. (12.66) relating Rf, Ri, and K_T/K_M. Since Rf is related to x_3/L, it should therefore be possible to correlate both Ri and K_T/K_M with x_3/L. Experimental data on Ri and K_T/K_M versus x_3/L collected by Plate (1971) from many sources are shown in Figs. 12.4 and 12.5. For Ri the x_3/L dependency is well confirmed, and excellent agreement is achieved between field and laboratory data. The correlation of K_T/K_M with x_3/L is less successful. The reason is that K_T and K_M refer to dynamically different quantities, i.e. heat and momentum, and differences in stability lead to different modes of transport of these two quantities.

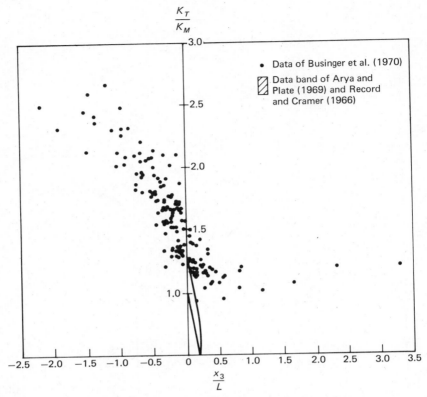

Figure 12.5. K_T/K_M as a function of x_3/L (Plate, 1971).

Measurements of wind velocity components, such as depicted in Fig. 12.1 are important in characterizing atmospheric turbulence. Certain statistical properties of the turbulence can be extracted from such records. The *intensity* of turbulence is related to $\overline{u_i'^2}$, or $\sigma_{u_i}^2$ (no summation), the variance of the velocity distribution of the ith component about its mean value. The σ_{u_i} values bear a direct relation to the diffusing power of the atmosphere. Two other useful properties are the standard deviations of the fluctuations in the horizontal direction of the wind, σ_θ, and the vertical direction of the wind, σ_ϕ. It is important to realize that σ_{u_i}, σ_θ, and σ_ϕ depend on the sampling and averaging times inherent to a velocity record such as that shown in Fig. 12.1.

Figure 12.6 presents a general summary of the vertical variation of the standard deviation of the horizontal and of the vertical wind directions with height and stability. The construction of these figures is based on actual data. Figure 12.6a shows the variation of the horizontal wind direction standard deviation for a sampling time of about 10 min as measured up to about 130 m. For a given stability condition, values of σ_θ for sampling times greater than a

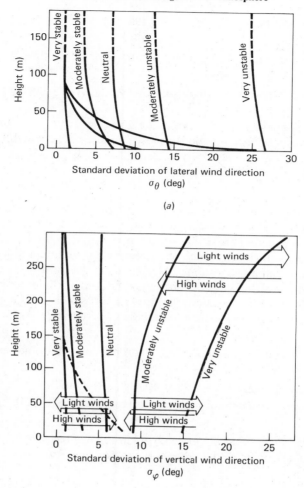

(a)

(b)

Figure 12.6. (a) Vertical variation of the lateral wind direction standard deviation σ_θ as a function of stability. (b) Vertical variation of the vertical wind direction standard deviation σ_ϕ as a function of stability. (Slade, 1968).

minute or so will always be greater when the wind is light then when it is strong. The curve in Fig. 12.6a representing very stable conditions (which by their nature are associated with light winds) exhibits this behavior. The three branches represent limits to σ_θ, with the central curve that for typical inversion conditions. In all cases, the large values of σ_θ at the surface do not decrease very rapidly with height. Often the standard deviation of the crosswind velocity fluctuation σ_{u_2} (if the mean wind is directed along the x_1 axis) can be related to σ_θ. The following are general statements concerning the variation of σ_{u_2} with wind speed, stability, and height (Slade, 1968):

1.   At a given height during neutral conditions, σ_{u_2} is proportional to wind speed.
2.   For a given wind speed and height, σ_{u_2} is greater during unstable than during stable conditions.
3.   For a given stability condition at a given height, σ_{u_2} increases with wind speed and surface roughness, most markedly during stable conditions.
4.   The value of σ_{u_2} does not change appreciably with height during any stability condition.

Figure 12.6b presents vertical profiles of vertical direction fluctuations for averaging times of a few seconds. The effect of wind speed on vertical fluctuations is different from that on the horizontal. Light winds at low levels are associated with large values of σ_{ϕ} during unstable conditions and small values during stable conditions. Mechanically induced vertical turbulence decreases with height whereas buoyancy-induced turbulence increases with height. The standard deviation of the vertical velocity fluctuations σ_{u_3} are related to σ_{ϕ}. General statements regarding σ_{u_3} are (Slade, 1968):

1.   Under neutral conditions, σ_{u_3} is proportional to wind speed and constant with height.
2.   In a stable atmosphere, σ_{u_3} decreases with height.
3.   Under unstable conditions, σ_{u_3} increases markedly with height.

Although the along-wind component of turbulence has not received as much experimental attention as the other two components, some general characteristics of σ_{u_1} are:

1.   At a fixed height, σ_{u_1} is proportional to wind speed.
2.   At a fixed height, σ_{u_1} increases with increasing instability.
3. σ_{u_1} is generally independent of height during neutral and unstable conditions but decreases with height during stable conditions.

12.5.3.   Wind Profiles in the Nonadiabatic Surface Layer

In stable and unstable conditions the velocity profiles of the atmospheric surface layer deviate from the logarithmic law. In this section we will outline briefly the forms of velocity profiles in these conditions. Since the stratified-boundary-layer conservation equations cannot be solved (because of the closure problem), we must resort to empirical profiles, based largely on dimensional analysis.

Suppose we are interested in the height dependence of some mean property $\bar{f}$ (say velocity) in the surface layer. In carrying out a dimensional analysis, six quantities must be considered: (g/T_0), ρ_0, u_*, $(\bar{q}/\rho\hat{C}_p)$, x_3, $\bar{f}$. From the π theorem, we have six quantities involving four fundamental units; two independent dimensionless groups thus result. Let us choose x_3/L and $\bar{f}(x_3)/f_0$ as these two groups, where f_0 is a group with the dimensions of f, formulated from (g/T_0), ρ, u_*, and $(\bar{q}/\rho\hat{C}_p)$. Thus,

$$\frac{\bar{f}(x_3)}{f_0} = F\left(\frac{x_3}{L}\right)$$

where F is some universal function. For example, if $\bar{f}(x_3) = \bar{u}(x_3)$, we choose f_0 as u_*/κ, and if $\bar{f}(x_3) = \bar{\theta}(x_3)$ we choose f_0 as $-(1/\kappa u_*)(\bar{q}/\rho\hat{C}_p) = T_*$. Let us denote the group x_3/L by ζ. Note that $\zeta = \mathrm{Rf}$ only in the surface layer. Therefore, we can in theory, represent the dependence on height of mean velocity and temperature (and their gradients) by universal functions of ζ, for example,

$$\frac{\partial \bar{u}_1}{\partial x_3} = \frac{u_*}{\kappa L} g(\zeta) \tag{12.67}$$

$$\frac{\partial \bar{\theta}}{\partial x_3} = \frac{T_*}{L} g_1(\zeta) \tag{12.68}$$

These equations are generalizations of the logarithmic layer equations to the case of a thermally stratified layer. We remind the reader that the adiabatic temperature profile in a *stagnant* layer is the familiar 1°C/100 m decrease. However, in the presence of a *mean wind* in the x direction with a logarithmic profile, the neutral temperature profile is given by

$$\frac{\partial \bar{\theta}}{\partial x_3} = \frac{T_*}{\gamma x_3}$$

We have not taken the space to derive this result, although it is obtained in the same manner as the logarithmic velocity law.

Substituting Eqs. (12.67) and (12.68) into the defining equations for the eddy coefficients K_M and K_T, we obtain

$$K_M = \frac{\kappa u_* L}{g(\zeta)} \tag{12.69}$$

and

$$K_T = \frac{\kappa u_* L}{g_1(\zeta)} \tag{12.70}$$

In neutral conditions, $g(\zeta) = \zeta^{-1} = L/x_3$ and

$$K_M = \kappa u_* x_3 \qquad (12.71)$$

The basic problem is to determine the forms of $g(\zeta)$ and $g_1(\zeta)$. We know the forms under neutral conditions, and so we look for distinct forms for stable and unstable conditions which will approach each other as $|\zeta| \to 0$. We consider first the velocity profile and rewrite Eq. (12.67):

$$\frac{\partial \bar{u}_1}{\partial x_3} = \frac{u_*}{\kappa L} g(\zeta) = \frac{u_* \zeta}{\kappa x_3} g(\zeta) = \frac{u_*}{\kappa x_3} \phi(\zeta) \qquad (12.72)$$

As $\bar{q} \to 0$, $\zeta \to 0$, we must obtain

$$\frac{\partial \bar{u}_1}{\partial x_3} = \frac{u_*}{\kappa x_3}$$

and so we need $\lim_{\zeta \to 0} \phi(\zeta) = 1$. In effect, for $x_3 \ll |L|$ the layer is essentially adiabatic. Thus, as we noted, L is a measure of the thickness of a layer in which thermal effects are unimportant. When $x_3 \ll |L|$ (near neutral conditions)

$$\frac{x_3}{|L|} \cong |\mathrm{Rf}|$$

At low levels $x_3/|L| \cong 0$ and the effect of buoyancy can be neglected. The level to which the logarithmic law is valid depends on the magnitude of Rf. Over rough ground with strong winds, the so-called dynamic sublayer (adiabatic) may extend to 10 m, whereas over smooth ground with strong surface heating it may extend only up to 1 m.

For ζ close to zero, we can expand $\phi(\zeta)$ in a power series:

$$\phi(\zeta) = 1 + \beta_1 \zeta + \beta_2 \zeta^2 + \cdots \qquad (12.73)$$

Usually the available data permit evaluation only of one coefficient, and so we truncate after the linear term. Substituting Eq. (12.73) into Eq. (12.72) and integrating we obtain

$$\bar{u}_1(x_3) = \frac{u_*}{\kappa} \left(\ln \frac{x_3}{z_0} + \beta \frac{x_3 - z_0}{L} \right) \qquad (12.74)$$

It is important to note that $\zeta \geq 0$ and $\zeta \leq 0$ may correspond to different values of the parameter β. However, although its magnitude must be established from experimental data, the sign of β can be determined. Under stable conditions ($L > 0$, $\zeta > 0$) vertical turbulent momentum exchange is suppressed and the velocity profile increases more rapidly with x_3 than in the adiabatic case. Under unstable conditions ($L < 0$, $\zeta < 0$), on the other hand, intense turbulent mixing leads to equalization of the velocity, and so $\bar{u}_1(x_3)$ increases more slowly with height than in the adiabatic case. Thus, $\beta[(x_3 - z_0)/L]$ must be > 0 for $L > 0$ and < 0 for $L < 0$. Therefore, β must be > 0 for both $\zeta > 0$ and $\zeta < 0$. The value of β yielding the best fit to data depends on the range of ζ values considered. For unstable stratification, values of β from 3 to 6 have been obtained; for stable stratification, typical values range from 5 to 7 (Plate, 1971).

Although Eq. (12.74) holds for fairly small values of $|\zeta|$, the cases of large negative (unstable) or positive (stable) require other formulas. Generally accepted forms of the universal function $\phi(\zeta)$ are those of Businger et al. (1971),

$$
\phi(\zeta) = \begin{cases} 1 + 4.7\zeta & \zeta > 0 \quad \text{stable} \\ 1 & \zeta = 0 \quad \text{neutral} \\ (1 - 15\zeta)^{-1/4} & \zeta < 0 \quad \text{unstable} \end{cases} \tag{12.75}
$$

12.5.4. Determination of the Friction Velocity u_*

An expression for the friction velocity u_* can be obtained from Eq. (12.72) by integrating Eq. (12.72) between x_{3_0} and a reference height x_{3_r} at which a measurement of $\bar{u}_1$ is available,

$$
u_* = \frac{\kappa \bar{u}_1(x_{3_r})}{\displaystyle\int_{x_{3_0}}^{x_{3_r}} \phi\left(\frac{x_3}{L}\right) \frac{dx_3}{x_3}} \tag{12.76}
$$

where we have assumed that $\bar{u}_1(x_{3_0}) = 0$. Using Eq. (12.75), we can evaluate approximately Eq. (12.76) as (Benoit, 1977),

$$
\frac{u_*}{\kappa \bar{u}_1(x_{3_r})} = \begin{cases} \left[\ln\left(\frac{x_{3_r}}{x_{3_0}}\right) + \frac{4.7}{L}(x_{3_r} - x_{3_0}) \right]^{-1} & \zeta > 0 \quad \text{stable} \\[12pt] \left[\ln\left(\frac{x_{3_r}}{x_{3_0}}\right) \right]^{-1} & \zeta = 0 \quad \text{neutral} \\[12pt] \left\{ \ln\left(\frac{x_{3_r}}{x_{3_0}}\right) + \ln\left[\frac{(\eta_0^2 + 1)(\eta_0 + 1)^2}{(\eta_r^2 + 1)(\eta_r + 1)^2} \right] \right. \\[12pt] \left. + 2\left[\tan^{-1}\eta_r - \tan^{-1}\eta_0\right] \right\}^{-1} & \zeta < 0 \quad \text{unstable} \end{cases}
$$

$$\tag{12.77}$$

where

$$
\eta_r \left[1 - 15\frac{x_{3_r}}{L} \right]^{1/4} \qquad \eta_0 = \left[1 - 15\frac{x_{3_0}}{L} \right]^{1/4}
$$

12.5.5. Empirical Formula for the Mean Wind Speed

The mean wind speed is frequently represented empirically as a power law function of height,

$$\frac{\bar{u}_1(x_3)}{\bar{u}_r} = \left(\frac{x_3}{x_{3_r}}\right)^p \tag{12.78}$$

The exponent p is then to be determined on the basis of atmospheric conditions. By differentiating Eq. (12.78) with respect to x_3, p is found from

$$p = \frac{x_3}{\bar{u}_1}\left(\frac{\partial \bar{u}_1}{\partial x_3}\right) \tag{12.79}$$

Using Eq. (12.72) in Eq. (12.79), we obtain

$$p = \frac{u_*}{\kappa \bar{u}_1}\phi(\zeta) \tag{12.80}$$

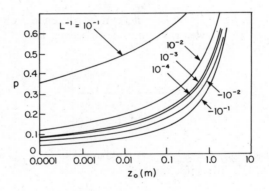

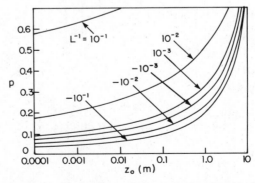

Figure 12.7. Exponent in the power-law expression for wind speed

$$\frac{\bar{u}_1(x_3)}{\bar{u}_r} = \left(\frac{x_3}{x_{3_r}}\right)^p$$

as a function of the roughness length z_0 and the Monin–Obukhov length L.

which can be expressed as a function only of ζ as

$$p = \frac{\phi(\zeta)}{F(\zeta, \zeta_0)} \qquad (12.81)$$

where $\zeta_0 = z_0/L$. Huang (1979) has presented $F(\zeta, \zeta_0)$ as

$$F(\xi, \zeta_0) = \ln\left[\frac{(\xi - 1)(\xi_0 + 1)}{(\xi + 1)(\xi_0 - 1)}\right] + 2\left[\tan^{-1}\xi - \tan^{-1}\xi_0\right] \qquad (12.82)$$

where $\xi = \phi(\zeta)^{-1}$ and $\xi_0 = \phi(\zeta_0)^{-1}$. Huang (1979) has presented values of p from Eq. (12.81), and these values are given in Figure 12.7.

12.6. THE PASQUILL STABILITY CLASSES

The Monin–Obukhov length L is not a parameter that is routinely measured. Recognizing the need for a readily usable way to define atmospheric stability based on routine observations, Pasquill (1961) introduced the concept of

TABLE 12.3. Estimation of Pasquill Stability Classes[a]

Surface Wind Speed at 10 m (m sec^{-1})	Solar Radiation[b]			Night Time Cloud Cover Fraction	
	Strong	Moderate	Slight	$\geq \frac{4}{8}$	$\leq \frac{3}{8}$
< 2	A	A—B	B		
2–3	A—B	B	C	E	F
3–5	B	B—C	C	D	E
5–6	C	C—D	D	D	D
> 6	C	D	D	D	D

A:	extremely unstable	D:	neutral
B:	moderately unstable	E:	slightly stable
C:	slightly unstable	F:	moderately stable

[a] Turner (1969).
[b] Incoming Radiation

(Category)	Solar Insolation	
	(Langley min^{-1})	(W m^{-2})
Strong	I > 1.0	I > 700
Moderate	$0.5 \leq I \leq 1.0$	$350 \leq I \leq 700$
Slight	I < 0.5	I < 350

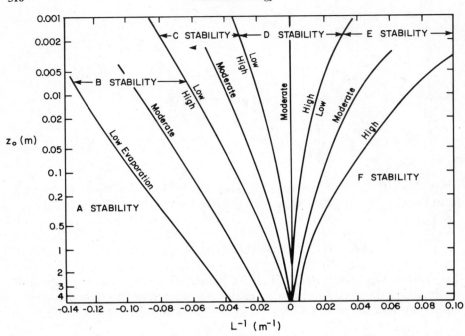

Figure 12.8. A relationship between Monin–Obukhov length L and roughness height z_0 for various Pasquill stability classes (Myrup and Ranzieri, 1976).

TABLE 12.4. Coefficients for Straight Line Approximation to
Figure 12.8 as a Function of Stability Classes[a]

$$\frac{1}{L} = a + b \log z_0$$

	Pasquill Stability Class	Coefficients	
		a	b
Extremely Unstable	A	-0.096	0.029
Moderately Unstable	B	-0.037	0.029
Slightly Unstable	C	-0.002	0.018
Neutral	D	0	0
Slightly Stable	E	$+0.004$	-0.018
Moderately Stable	F	$+0.035$	-0.036

[a]Golder (1972).

stability classes defined in Table 12.3. These classes have proved very useful in atmospheric diffusion calculations, as we will see shortly.

Golder (1972) established a relation between the Pasquill stability classes, the roughness length z_0, and L (Figure 12.8). To simplify calculation of $1/L$, Golder's plot can be approximated by the correlation

$$\frac{1}{L} = a + b \log z_0$$

as shown in Table 12.4.

12.7. THE CONVECTIVE BOUNDARY LAYER

When the turbulence in the atmospheric boundary layer is maintained largely by buoyant production, the boundary layer is said to be in a convective state. The source of buoyancy is the upward heat flux originating from the ground heated by solar radiation. Convective turbulence is relatively vigorous and causes rapid vertical mixing in the atmospheric boundary layer.

The height of the atmospheric or planetary boundary layer under neutral conditions can be estimated from (Blackadar and Tennekes, 1968)

$$z_p = \alpha \frac{u_*}{f} \quad \text{neutral} \tag{12.83}$$

where f is the Coriolis parameter and α is a constant the value of which is about 0.35 (Zilitinkevich, 1972). Under nonneutral conditions the corresponding estimates are (Zilitinkevich, 1972)

$$z_p = \begin{cases} \alpha\left(\dfrac{u_*}{f}\right)\left(\dfrac{u_*}{fL}\right)^{-1/2} & \text{stable} \\[3mm] \alpha\left(\dfrac{u_*}{f}\right)\left(-\dfrac{u_*}{fL}\right)^{1/2} & \text{unstable} \end{cases} \tag{12.84}$$

where the stable value is not allowed to exceed that calculated from Eq. (12.83) and the unstable value is not allowed to be less than that calculated from Eq. (12.83).

The determination of z_p under unstable conditions is usually not critical to performing atmospheric diffusion calculations because a temperature inversion layer, which limits the extent of vertical mixing, is generally present at some height z_i well below z_p.

From the definition of the Monin-Obukhov length, shear production of turbulence is confined to a layer of height the order of $|L|$. Under convective conditions, then, we expect

$$-\frac{L}{z_i} \ll 1 \qquad (12.85)$$

Equation (12.85) can be written as

$$\frac{-L}{z_i} = \left(\frac{u_*}{w_*}\right)^3 \ll 1 \qquad (12.86)$$

where w_* is the *convective velocity scale* given by

$$w_* = \left(\frac{g}{T_0}\frac{\bar{q}_3}{\rho\hat{C}_p}z_i\right)^{1/3} \qquad (12.87)$$

Velocity and temperature gradients are confined to the surface layer defined by $x_3 < |L|$. Above $|L|$ the wind velocity and potential temperature are virtually uniform with height. Venkatram (1978) has presented a method to estimate the value of the convective velocity scale w_*. On the basis of this method, he showed that convective conditions in the planetary boundary layer are a common occurrence (Venkatram, 1980). In particular, the planetary boundary layer is convective during the daytime hours a substantial fraction of a year ($\sim$ 7 months). For example, for a wind speed of 5 m sec^{-1}, a kinematic heat flux $\bar{q}_3/\rho\hat{C}_p$ as small as 0.1°C m sec^{-1} can drive the planetary boundary layer into a convective state.

12.8. METEOROLOGICAL MEASUREMENTS IMPORTANT IN AIR POLLUTION

There are several *primary* meteorological measurements necessary in assessing atmospheric transport and mixing characteristics as related to the dispersion of air pollutants. Those related to the wind are:

1. Wind direction.
2. Wind speed.
3. Wind turbulence.

Surface wind direction is measured by a *wind vane*, essentially a flat plate on a horizontal rod which aligns itself with the wind direction. Wind direction aloft is determined by *pilot balloons* (less than 1 m in diameter, equipped to carry a small radio for tracking) and *tetroons* (a constant-volume balloon in the shape of a tetrahedron, which is ballasted so as to remain at a nearly constant elevation).

Surface wind speed is recorded by a class of instruments called *anemometers*. Typical anemometers are:

1. Rotation anemometer: a small windmill.
2. Cup anemometer: three conical cups on a freely rotating vertical shaft.
3. Hot-wire anemometer: an electrically heated element the temperature of which is related to the velocity of the passing wind.

Wind speed measurements aloft are made by balloons and tetroons.

Figure 12.1 shows a typical record of one wind component which might be obtained by an anemometer. From such a record a mean velocity $\bar{u}_i$ can be obtained. Wind turbulence refers to the properties of the fluctuations about the mean in a record such as the one shown in Fig. 12.1. These fluctuations are primarily responsible for the spreading of a cloud of pollutants in the atmosphere. It is important to measure all three components of the wind velocity, since the vertical fluctuations are often the most important in transporting pollutants. The vertical velocity fluctuations provide a direct measure of the stability of the atmosphere. In order to obtain a record such as the one shown in Fig. 12.1 a sensitive, rapidly responding wind vane and anemometer are required. Vertical fluctuations can be measured by:

1. Bivane: a wind vane constructed so as to measure wind direction fluctuations in vertical as well as horizontal planes.
2. *u-v-w* anemometer (refers to the three wind components): a system of three propellers mounted at the ends of orthogonal shafts.

The standard elevation for wind instruments is 10 m over level, open terrain, where "open terrain" is usually interpreted as that where the distance to any obstacle is 10 times or more the height of the obstacle.

Other primary meteorological measurements are temperature profile and radiation. Temperature profiles are measured by *wiresonde* (a temperature sensor carried aloft by a kite balloon), *dropsonde* (a temperature sensor lowered by a parachute), and *radiosonde* (pressure, temperature, and humidity sensors carried aloft by a balloon). Solar radiation intensity is measured by an *actinometer*, a device in which two metallic strips, one of which is absorbing and one reflecting, lie side by side under a glass dome. The amount of differential bending is an indication of the radiation intensity. Also, the net heating or cooling at or near the surface can be measured by two black metal strips, one facing up, the other down. The differential heating or cooling establishes an emf between the strips.

Other *secondary* measurements often reported include visibility, humidity, and precipitation.

REFERENCES

Arya, S. P. S., and Plate, E. J. "Modeling of the Stably Stratified Atmospheric Boundary Layer," *J. Atmos. Sci.*, **26**, 656–665 (1969).

Benoit, R. "On the Integral of the Surface Layer Profile-Gradient Functions," *J. Appl. Meteorol.*, **16**, 859–860 (1977).

Blackadar, A. K., and Tennekes, H. "Asymptotic Similarity in Neutral Barotropic Planetary Boundary Layers," *J. Atmos. Sci.*, **25**, 1015–1020 (1968).

Businger, J. A., Wyngaard, J. C., Izumi, Y., and Bradley, E. F. "Flux Profile Relationships in the Atmospheric Surface Layer," *J. Atmos. Sci.*, **28**, 181–189 (1971).

Calder, K. L. "In Clarification of the Equations of Shallow-Layer Thermal Convection for a Compressible Fluid Based on the Boussinesq Approximation," *Q. J. Roy. Meteorol. Soc.*, **94**, 88–92 (1968).

Dutton, J. A. *The Ceaseless Wind*, McGraw-Hill, New York (1976).

Golder, D. "Relations among Stability Parameters in the Surface Layer," *Boundary Layer Meteorol.*, **3**, 47–58 (1972).

Huang, C. H. "Theory of Dispersion in Turbulent Shear Flow," *Atmos. Environ.*, **13**, 453–463 (1979).

McRae, G. J., Goodin, W. R., and Seinfeld, J. H. "Development of a Second-Generation Mathematical Model for Urban Air Pollution I. Model Formulation," *Atmos. Environ.*, **16**, 679–696 (1982).

Monin, A. S., and Yaglom, A. M. *Statistical Fluid Mechanics*, Volume 1, MIT Press, Cambridge, MA (1971).

Monin, A. S., and Yaglom, A. M. *Statistical Fluid Mechanics*, Volume 2, MIT Press, Cambridge, MA (1975).

Myrup, L. O., and Ranzieri, A. J. "A Consistent Scheme for Estimating Diffusivities to be Used in Air Quality Models," Report CA-DOT-TL-7169-3-76-32, California Dept. of Transportation, Sacramento (1976).

Nieuwstadt, F. T. M., and van Dop, H. (Eds.) *Atmospheric Turbulence and Air Pollution Modeling*, D. Reidel, Dordrecht, Holland (1982).

Panofsky, H. A., and Dutton, J. A. *Atmospheric Turbulence*, Wiley, New York (1984).

Pasquill, F. "The Estimation of the Dispersion of Windborne Material," *Meteorol. Magazine*, **90**, 33–49 (1961).

Plate, E. J. *Aerodynamic Characteristics of Atmospheric Boundary Layers*, U.S. Atomic Energy Commission, Oak Ridge, Tenn. (1971).

Plate, E. J. (Ed.) *Engineering Meteorology*, Elsevier, New York (1982).

Record, F. A., and Cramer, H. E. "Turbulent Energy Dissipation Rates and Exchange Processes above a Nonhomogeneous Surface," *Q. J. Roy. Meteorol. Soc.*, **92**, 519–532 (1966).

Slade, D. H. (Ed.) *Meteorology and Atomic Energy—1968*, U.S. Atomic Energy Commission, Washington, D.C. (1968).

Spiegel, E. A., and Veronis, G. "On the Boussinesq Approximation for a Compressible Fluid," *Astrophys. J.*, **131**, 442–447 (1960).

Turner, D. B. *Workbook of Atmospheric Diffusion Estimates*, U.S. Environmental Protection Agency Report 999-AP-26, Washington, D.C. (1969).

Venkatram, A. "Estimating the Convective Velocity Scale for Diffusion Applications," *Boundary Layer Meteorol.*, **15**, 447–452 (1978).

Venkatram, A. "The Relationship Between the Convective Boundary Layer and Dispersion from Tall Stacks," *Atmos. Environ.*, **14**, 763–767 (1980).

Zilitinkevich, S. S. "On the Determination of the Height of the Ekman Boundary Layer," *Boundary Layer Meteorol.*, **3**, 141–145 (1972).

PROBLEMS

12.1. An interpretation of the potential temperature θ is afforded by considering an adiabatic process. Changes in entropy can be related to those in temperature and pressure by

$$dS = \left(\frac{\partial S}{\partial T} \right)_p dT + \left(\frac{\partial S}{\partial p} \right)_T dp$$

(a) Show that

$$dS = \frac{\hat{C}_p}{T} dT - \frac{R}{M_a} \frac{dp}{p}$$

(b) From this result, show that in an adiabatic process ($dS = 0$), $d\theta = 0$, and that

$$\theta = \text{const} \times \frac{T}{p^{(\gamma - 1)/\gamma}}$$

12.2. In Chapter 11 we discussed the Ekman spiral, that is, the variation of wind direction with altitude in the planetary boundary layer. The analytical form of the Ekman spiral can be derived by considering a two-dimensional wind field (no vertical component), the two components of which satisfy

$$\frac{\partial}{\partial z} \left(K_M \frac{\partial \bar{u}}{\partial z} \right) - \frac{1}{\rho} \frac{\partial p}{\partial x} + f\bar{v} = 0$$

$$\frac{\partial}{\partial z} \left(K_M \frac{\partial \bar{v}}{\partial z} \right) - \frac{1}{\rho} \frac{\partial p}{\partial y} - f\bar{u} = 0$$

where K_M is a constant eddy viscosity and f is the Coriolis parameter. At some height the first terms in each of these equations are expected to become negligible, leading to the geostrophic wind field. Take the x axis to be oriented in the direction of the geostrophic wind, in which case

$$f\bar{u}_G = - \frac{1}{\rho} \frac{\partial p}{\partial y}$$

Show that the solutions for $\bar{u}(z)$ and $\bar{v}(z)$ are

$$\bar{u}(z) = \bar{u}_G(1 - e^{-\alpha z}\cos\alpha z)$$

$$\bar{v}(z) = \bar{u}_G e^{-\alpha z}\sin\alpha z$$

where $\alpha = \sqrt{f/2K_M}$. In what way is this solution oversimplified?

12.3. The outer boundary of the planetary boundary layer can be defined as the point at which the component in the Ekman spiral disappears. From the solution of Problem 12.2, it is seen that this occurs when $\alpha z_G = \pi$.

    (a)   Using representative values of f and K_M, estimate the depth of the planetary boundary layer.

    (b)   The magnitude of the total turbulent stress at the surface is given by

$$\tau_0 = \frac{\rho K_M}{\sqrt{2}}\left(\left.\frac{\partial\bar{u}}{\partial z}\right|_{z=0} + \left.\frac{\partial\bar{v}}{\partial z}\right|_{z=0}\right)$$

Show that for a planetary boundary layer

$$\tau_0 = \frac{z_G}{\sqrt{2}\,\pi}f\rho\bar{u}_G$$

Estimate the magnitude of τ_0 in dynes per square centimeter.

    (c)   The surface layer can be estimated as that layer in which τ_0 changes by only 10 percent of its value at the surface. In the planetary boundary layer the turbulent stress terms in the equations of motion are of the same order as the Coriolis acceleration terms, both about 0.1 in cgs units. Estimate $\partial\tau/\partial z$, and from this estimate the thickness of the surface layer.

12.4. Consider the prediction of the diurnal atmospheric temperature profile under stagnant conditions. In this circumstance it is necessary to consider spatial variations in temperature in only the vertical direction. If it is assumed that absorption of radiation by the atmosphere can be neglected, the potential temperature θ satisfies

$$\frac{\partial\theta}{\partial t} = \frac{\partial}{\partial z}\left(K\frac{\partial\theta}{\partial z}\right) \tag{A}$$

assuming that K may be taken as constant. It may also be assumed that, at sufficiently high altitudes, the temperature profile should approach the adiabatic lapse rate, that is,

$$\theta \to 0 \quad \text{as } z \to \infty \tag{B}$$

The ground ($z = 0$) temperature is governed by solar heating during the day and radiational cooling during the night. Therefore $\theta(0, t)$ may be expressed as

$$\theta(0, t) = A \cos \omega t \tag{C}$$

where A is the amplitude of the diurnal surface temperature variation and $\omega = 7.29 \times 10^{-5}$ sec^{-1}.

(a) Show that a solution which satisfies Eqs. (A) to (C) is

$$\theta(z, t) = A e^{-\beta z} \cos(\omega t - \beta z)$$

where $\beta = \sqrt{\omega/2K}$. This is the so-called long-time solution or steady-state solution which represents the temperature dynamics corresponding to the influence of the surface forcing function (C).

(b) Show that the elevation H which marks either the base or top of an inversion is found from

$$\sin(\omega t - \beta H) - \cos(\omega t - \beta H) = \frac{g}{A\beta \hat{C}_p} e^{\beta H}$$

Can there be more than one inversion layer?

(c) Consider the evolution of the temperature profile from an initial profile

$$\theta(z, 0) = f(z) \tag{D}$$

Show that the solution of (A) to (D) is

$$\theta = A e^{-\beta z} \cos(\omega t - \beta z) - \frac{A}{\pi} \int_0^\infty e^{-\eta t} \sin\left(z \sqrt{\frac{\eta}{K}}\right) \frac{\eta}{\eta^2 + \omega^2} \, d\eta$$

$$+ \frac{1}{2\sqrt{\pi K t}} \int_0^\infty f(\eta) \left[e^{-(z-\eta)^2/4Kt} - e^{-(z+\eta)^2/4Kt} \right] d\eta$$

(d) Plot the steady-state solution for $K = 10^4$ cm^2 sec^{-1} and $A = 4°$C. Note that a surface inversion is predicted at night (take $t = 0$ to be midnight), followed by weak, elevated, probably multiple inversions during the day.

PART FIVE

Atmospheric Diffusion

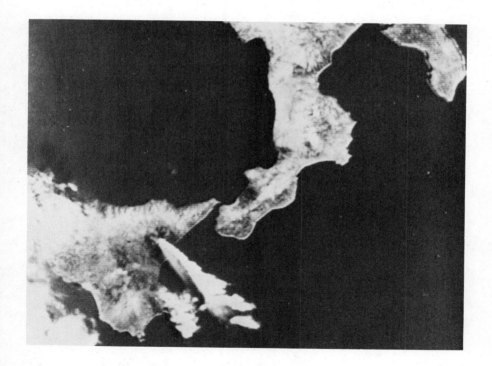

Satellite picture of Mt. Etna volcano eruption on the Italian island of Sicily taken by the American National Oceanic and Atmospheric Administration NOAA7 satellite, May 17, 1983. The dust cloud from the volcano, on island at left, drifts toward the southeast in this view received by the Bochum Observatory in West Germany.

THIRTEEN

Atmospheric Diffusion Theories

A major goal of our study of the atmospheric aspects of air pollution is to be able to describe mathematically the spatial and temporal distribution of contaminants released into the atmosphere. The next three chapters are devoted to the subject of atmospheric diffusion and its description. It is common to refer to the behavior of gases and particles in turbulent flow as turbulent "diffusion" or, in this case, as atmospheric "diffusion," although the processes responsible for the observed spreading or dispersion in turbulence are not the same as those acting in ordinary molecular diffusion. A more precise term would perhaps be atmospheric dispersion, but to conform to common terminology we will use atmospheric diffusion. This chapter is devoted primarily to developing the two basic ways of describing turbulent diffusion. The first is the *Eulerian* approach in which the behavior of species is described relative to a fixed coordinate system. The Eulerian description is the common way of treating heat and mass transfer phenomena. The second approach is the *Lagrangian* in which concentration changes are described relative to the moving fluid. As we will see, the two approaches yield different types of mathematical relationships for the species concentrations that can, ultimately, be related. Each of the two modes of expression is a valid description of turbulent diffusion; the choice of which approach to adopt in a given situation will be seen to depend on the specific features of the situation.

13.1. EULERIAN APPROACH

Let us consider N species in a fluid. The concentration of each must, at each instant, satisfy a material balance taken over a volume element. Thus, any accumulation of material over time, when added to the net amount of material convected into the volume element, must be balanced by an equivalent amount of material that is produced by chemical reaction in the element, that is emitted into it by sources, and that enters by molecular diffusion. Expressed mathematically, the concentration of each species, c_i, must satisfy the continuity equation

$$\frac{\partial c_i}{\partial t} + \frac{\partial}{\partial x_j} u_j c_i = D_i \frac{\partial^2 c_i}{\partial x_j \partial x_j} + R_i(c_1, \ldots, c_N, T) + S_i(\mathbf{x}, t)$$

$$i = 1, 2, \ldots, N \quad (13.1)$$

where u_j is the jth component of the fluid velocity, D_i is the molecular diffusivity of species i in the carrier fluid, R_i is the rate of generation of species i by chemical reaction (which depends in general on the fluid temperature T), and S_i is the rate of addition of species i at location $\mathbf{x} = (x_1, x_2, x_3)$ and time t.[*]

In addition to the requirement that the c_i satisfy Eq. (13.1), the fluid velocities u_j and the temperature T, in turn, must satisfy the Navier–Stokes and energy equations, Eqs. (12.18) and (12.22), which themselves are coupled through the u_j, c_i, and T with the total continuity equation and the ideal-gas law (we restrict our attention to gaseous systems). In general, it is necessary to carry out a simultaneous solution of the coupled equations of mass, momentum, and energy conservation to account properly for the changes in u_j, T, and c_i and the effects of the changes of each of these on each other. In dealing with atmospheric pollutants, however, since species occur at parts-per-million concentrations, it is quite justifiable to assume that the presence of pollutants does not affect the meteorology to any detectable extent; thus, the equation of continuity Eq. (13.1) can be solved independently of the coupled momentum and energy equations.[†] Consequently, the fluid velocities u_j and the temperature T can be considered independent of the c_i. From this point on we will not explicitly indicate the dependence of R_i on T.

The complete description of pollutant behavior rests with the solution of Eq. (13.1). Unfortunately, because the flows of interest are turbulent, the fluid velocities u_j are random functions of space and time. As was done in Chapter 12, it is customary to represent the wind velocities u_j as the sum of a deterministic and stochastic component, $\bar{u}_j + u_j'$.

To illustrate the importance of the definition of the deterministic and stochastic velocity components $\bar{u}_j$ and u_j', let us suppose a puff of pollutant of known concentration distribution $c(\mathbf{x}, t_0)$ at time t_0. In the absence of chemical reaction and other sources, and assuming molecular diffusion to be

---

[*] As in Chapter 12, we will continue to use the convention of (x_1, x_2, x_3) as coordinate axes and (u_1, u_2, u_3) as fluid velocity components when dealing with the transport equations in their most general form. Eventually it will be easier to use an (x, y, z), (u, v, w) system when dealing with specific problems and we will do so at that time.

[†] Two effects could, in principle, serve to invalidate this assumption. Less likely is that sufficient heat would be generated by chemical reactions to influence the temperature. More likely, however, is that a polluted layer would become so concentrated that absorption, reflection, and scattering of radiation by the pollutants would result in alterations of the fluid behavior. We will not consider either of these effects here.

negligible, the concentration distribution at some later time is described by the *advection equation*,

$$\frac{\partial c}{\partial t} + \frac{\partial}{\partial x_j}(u_j c) = 0 \tag{13.2}$$

If we solve this equation with $u_j = \bar{u}_j$ and compare the solution with observations we would find in reality that the material spreads out more than predicted. This extra spreading is, in fact, what is referred to as turbulent diffusion and results from the influence of the random component u'_j which we have ignored. Now let us solve this equation with the precise velocity field u_j. We should then find that the solution agrees exactly with the observations (assuming, of course, that molecular diffusion is negligible), implying that if we knew the velocity field precisely at all locations and times there would be no such phenomenon as turbulent diffusion. Thus, turbulent diffusion is an artifact of our lack of complete knowledge of the true velocity field. Consequently, one of the fundamental tasks in turbulent diffusion theory is to define the deterministic and stochastic components of the velocity field.

Replacing u_j by $\bar{u}_j + u'_j$ in Eq. (13.1) gives

$$\frac{\partial c_i}{\partial t} + \frac{\partial}{\partial x_j}\left[(\bar{u}_j + u'_j)c_i\right] = D_i \frac{\partial^2 c_i}{\partial x_j \partial x_j} + R_i(c_1, \ldots, c_N) + S_i(\mathbf{x}, t)$$

$$\tag{13.3}$$

Since the u'_j are random variables, the c_i resulting from the solution of Eq. (13.3) must also be random variables; that is, because the wind velocities are random functions of space and time, the airborne pollutant concentrations are themselves random variables in space and time. Thus, the determination of the c_i, in the sense of being a specified function of space and time, is not possible, just as it is not possible to determine precisely the value of any random variable in an experiment. We can at best derive the probability that at some location and time the concentration of species i will lie between two closely spaced values. Unfortunately, the specification of the probability density function for a random process as complex as atmospheric diffusion is almost never possible. Instead, we must adopt a less desirable but more feasible approach, the determination of certain statistical properties of the c_i, most notably the *mean* $\langle c_i \rangle$.

The mean concentration can be interpreted in the following way. Let us suppose an experiment in which a puff of material is released at a certain time and concentrations are measured downwind at subsequent times. We would measure $c_i(\mathbf{x}, t)$, which would exhibit random characteristics because of the wind. If it were possible to repeat this experiment under identical conditions, we would again measure $c_i(\mathbf{x}, t)$, but because of the randomness in the wind field we could not reproduce the first $c_i(\mathbf{x}, t)$. Theoretically we could repeat this experiment an infinite number of times. We would then have a so-called ensemble of experiments. If at every location $\mathbf{x}$ and time t we averaged all the concentration values over the infinite number of experiments, we would have computed the theoretical mean concentration $\langle c_i(\mathbf{x}, t) \rangle$.* Experiments like this cannot, of course, be repeated under identical conditions, and so it is virtually impossible to measure $\langle c_i \rangle$. Thus, a measurement of the concentration of species i at a particular location and time is more suitably envisioned as one sample from a hypothetically infinite ensemble of possible concentrations. Clearly, an individual measurement may differ considerably from the mean $\langle c_i \rangle$.

It is convenient to express c_i as $\langle c_i \rangle + c_i'$, where, by definition, $\langle c_i' \rangle = 0$. Averaging Eq. (13.3) over an infinite ensemble of realizations of the turbulence yields the equation governing $\langle c_i \rangle$, namely

$$\frac{\partial \langle c_i \rangle}{\partial t} + \frac{\partial}{\partial x_j} \left(\bar{u}_j \langle c_i \rangle \right) + \frac{\partial}{\partial x_j} \langle u_j' c_i' \rangle$$

$$= D_i \frac{\partial^2 \langle c_i \rangle}{\partial x_j \, \partial x_j} + \langle R_i (\langle c_1 \rangle + c_1', \ldots, \langle c_N \rangle + c_N') \rangle + S_i(\mathbf{x}, t) \quad (13.4)$$

Let us consider the case of a single inert species, that is $R = 0$. We note that Eq. (13.4) contains dependent variables $\langle c \rangle$ and $\langle u_j' c' \rangle$, $j = 1, 2, 3$. We thus have more dependent variables than equations. Again, this is the closure problem of turbulence. For example, if we were to derive an equation for the $\langle u_j' c' \rangle$ by subtracting Eq. (13.4) from Eq. (13.3), multiplying the resulting equation by u_j' and then averaging, we would obtain

$$\frac{\partial}{\partial t} \langle u_j' c' \rangle + \frac{\partial}{\partial x_k} \left(\bar{u}_k \langle u_j' c' \rangle \right) + \langle u_j' u_k' \rangle \frac{\partial \langle c \rangle}{\partial x_k} = \frac{\partial}{\partial x_k} \left(D \frac{\partial}{\partial x_k} \langle u_j' c' \rangle - \langle u_j' u_k' c' \rangle \right)$$

$$j = 1, 2, 3 \quad (13.5)$$

Although we have derived the desired equations, we have at the same time generated new dependent variables $\langle u_j' u_k' c' \rangle$, $j, k = 1, 2, 3$. If we generate additional equations for these variables, we find that still more dependent variables appear. The closure problem becomes even worse if a nonlinear chemical reaction is occurring. If the single species decays by a second-order reaction, then the term $\langle R \rangle$ in Eq. (13.4) becomes $-k(\langle c \rangle^2 + \langle c'^2 \rangle)$, where $\langle c'^2 \rangle$ is a new dependent variable. If we were to derive an equation for $\langle c'^2 \rangle$ we would find the emergence of new dependent variables $\langle u_j' c'^2 \rangle$, $\langle c'^3 \rangle$, and $\langle \partial c' / \partial x_j \, \partial c' / \partial x_j \rangle$. It is because of the closure problem that an Eulerian

---

*We have used different notation for the mean values of the velocities and the concentrations, that is $\bar{u}_j$ versus $\langle c_i \rangle$, in order to emphasize the fact that the mean fluid velocities are normally determined by a process involving temporal and spatial averaging, whereas the $\langle c_i \rangle$ always represent the theoretical ensemble average.

description of turbulent diffusion will not permit exact solution even for the mean concentration $\langle c \rangle$.

13.2. LAGRANGIAN APPROACH

The Lagrangian approach to turbulent diffusion is concerned with the behavior of representative fluid particles.* We therefore begin by considering a single particle which is at location $\mathbf{x}'$ at time t' in a turbulent fluid. The subsequent motion of the particle can be described by its trajectory, $\mathbf{X}[\mathbf{x}', t'; t]$, that is, its position at any later time t. Let $\psi(x_1, x_2, x_3, t) \, dx_1, dx_2 \, dx_3 = \psi(\mathbf{x}, t) \, d\mathbf{x} =$ probability that the particle at time t will be in volume element x_1 to $x_1 + dx_1$, x_2 to $x_2 + dx_2$, and x_3 to $x_3 + dx_3$, that is, that $x_1 \le X_1 < x_1 + dx_1$, and so on. Thus, $\psi(\mathbf{x}, t)$ is the probability density function (pdf) for the particle's location at time t. By the definition of a probability density function

$$\int_{-\infty}^{\infty} \int_{-\infty}^{\infty} \int_{-\infty}^{\infty} \psi(\mathbf{x}, t) \, d\mathbf{x} = 1$$

The probability density of finding the particle at $\mathbf{x}$ at t can be expressed as the product of two other probability densities:

1. The probability density that if the particle is at $\mathbf{x}'$ at t' it will undergo a displacement to $\mathbf{x}$ at t. Denote this probability density $Q(\mathbf{x}, t|\mathbf{x}', t')$ and call it the *transition probability density* for the particle.

2. The probability density that the particle was at $\mathbf{x}'$ at t', $(\mathbf{x}', t')$, integrated over all possible starting points $\mathbf{x}'$. Thus,

$$\psi(\mathbf{x}, t) = \int_{-\infty}^{\infty} \int_{-\infty}^{\infty} \int_{-\infty}^{\infty} Q(\mathbf{x}, t|\mathbf{x}', t')\psi(\mathbf{x}', t') \, d\mathbf{x}' \qquad (13.6)$$

The density function $\psi(\mathbf{x}, t)$ has been defined with respect to a single particle. If, however, an arbitrary number m of particles are initially present and the position of the ith particle is given by the density function $\psi_i(\mathbf{x}, t)$, it can be shown that the ensemble mean concentration at the point $\mathbf{x}$ is given by

$$\langle c(\mathbf{x}, t) \rangle = \sum_{i=1}^{m} \psi_i(\mathbf{x}, t) \qquad (13.7)$$

By expressing the pdf $\psi_i(\mathbf{x}, t)$ in Eq. (13.7) in terms of the initial particle distribution and the spatial-temporal distribution of particle sources $S(\mathbf{x}, t)$, say in units of particles per volume per time, and then substituting the resulting expression into Eq. (13.6), we obtain the following general formula

*By a "fluid particle" we mean a volume of fluid large compared with molecular dimensions but small enough to act as a point that exactly follows the fluid. The "particle" may contain fluid of a different composition than the carrier fluid, in which case the particle is referred to as a "marked particle."

for the mean concentration:

$$\langle c(\mathbf{x}, t) \rangle = \int_{-\infty}^{\infty} \int_{-\infty}^{\infty} \int_{-\infty}^{\infty} Q(\mathbf{x}, t | \mathbf{x}_0, t_0) \langle c(\mathbf{x}_0, t_0) \rangle \, d\mathbf{x}_0$$

$$+ \int_{-\infty}^{\infty} \int_{-\infty}^{\infty} \int_{-\infty}^{\infty} \int_{t_0}^{t} Q(\mathbf{x}, t | \mathbf{x}', t') S(\mathbf{x}', t') \, dt' \, d\mathbf{x}' \qquad (13.8)$$

The first term on the right-hand side represents those particles present at t_0, and the second term on the right-hand side accounts for particles added from sources between t' and t.

Equation (13.8) is the fundamental Lagrangian relation for the mean concentration of a species in turbulent fluid. The determination of $\langle c(\mathbf{x}, t) \rangle$, given $\langle c(\mathbf{x}_0, t_0) \rangle$ and $S(\mathbf{x}', t)$, rests with the evaluation of the transition probability $Q(\mathbf{x}, t | \mathbf{x}', t')$. If Q were known for $\mathbf{x}$, $\mathbf{x}'$, t, and t', the mean concentration $\langle c(\mathbf{x}, t) \rangle$ could be computed by simply evaluating Eq. (13.8). However, there are two substantial problems with using Eq. (13.8). First, it holds only when the particles are not undergoing chemical reactions. Second, such complete knowledge of the turbulence properties as would be needed to know Q is generally unavailable except in the simplest of circumstances.

13.3. COMPARISON OF EULERIAN AND LAGRANGIAN APPROACHES

The techniques for describing the statistical properties of the concentrations of marked particles, such as air pollutants, in a turbulent fluid can be divided into two categories: Eulerian and Lagrangian. The Eulerian methods attempt to formulate the concentration statistics in terms of the statistical properties of the Eulerian fluid velocities, that is, the velocities measured at fixed points in the fluid. A formulation of this type is very useful not only because the Eulerian statistics are readily measurable (as determined from continuous time recordings of the wind velocities by a fixed network of anemometers) but also because the mathematical expressions are directly applicable to situations in which chemical reactions are taking place. Unfortunately, the Eulerian approaches lead to a serious mathematical obstacle known as the closure problem, for which no generally valid solution has yet been found.

By contrast, the Lagrangian techniques attempt to describe the concentration statistics in terms of the statistical properties of the displacements of groups of particles released in the fluid. The mathematics of this approach is more tractable than that of the Eulerian methods, in that no closure problem is encountered, but the applicability of the resulting equations is limited because of the difficulty of accurately determining the required particle statistics. Moreover, the equations are not directly applicable to problems involving nonlinear chemical reactions.

Having demonstrated that exact solution for the mean concentrations $\langle c_i(\mathbf{x}, t) \rangle$ even of inert species in a turbulent fluid is not possible in general by either the Eulerian or Lagrangian approaches, we now consider what assumptions and approximations can be invoked to obtain practical descriptions of atmospheric diffusion. In Section 13.4 we shall proceed from the two basic equations for $\langle c_i \rangle$, Eqs. (13.4) and (13.8), to obtain the equations commonly used for atmospheric diffusion. A particularly important aspect is the delineation of the assumptions and limitations inherent in each description.

13.4.   EQUATIONS GOVERNING THE MEAN CONCENTRATION OF SPECIES IN TURBULENCE

13.4.1.   Eulerian Approaches

As we have seen, the Eulerian description of turbulent diffusion leads to the so-called closure problem, as illustrated in Eq. (13.4) by the new dependent variables $\langle u'_j c'_i \rangle$, $j = 1, 2, 3$, as well as any that might arise in $\langle R_i \rangle$ if nonlinear chemical reactions are occurring. Let us first consider only the case of chemically inert species, that is, $R_i = 0$. The problem is to relate the variables $\langle u'_j c' \rangle$ if we wish not to introduce additional differential equations.

The most common means of relating the turbulent fluxes $\langle u'_j c' \rangle$ to the $\langle c \rangle$ is based on the mixing-length model of Section 12.4. In particular, it is assumed that (summation implied over k)

$$\langle u'_j c' \rangle = -K_{jk} \frac{\partial \langle c \rangle}{\partial x_k} \qquad j = 1, 2, 3 \tag{13.9}$$

where K_{jk} is called the eddy diffusivity. Equation (13.9) is called both mixing-length theory and K theory. Since Eq. (13.9) is essentially only a definition of the K_{jk}, which are, in general, functions of location and time, we have, by means of Eq. (13.9), replaced the three unknowns $\langle u'_j c' \rangle$, $j = 1, 2, 3$, with the six unknowns K_{jk}, $j, k = 1, 2, 3$ ($K_{jk} = K_{kj}$). If the coordinate axes coincide with the principal axes of the eddy diffusivity tensor $\{ K_{jk} \}$, then only the three diagonal elements K_{11}, K_{22}, and K_{33} are nonzero, and Eq. (13.9) becomes*

$$\langle u'_j c' \rangle = -K_{jj} \frac{\partial \langle c \rangle}{\partial x_j} \tag{13.10}$$

*No summation is implied in this term, for example,

$$\langle u'_1 c' \rangle = -K_{11} \frac{\partial \langle c \rangle}{\partial x_1}$$

It is beyond our scope to consider the conditions under which $\{ K_{jk} \}$ may be taken as diagonal. For our purposes we note that ordinarily there is insufficient information to assume that $\{ K_{jk} \}$ is not diagonal.

In using Eq. (13.4), two other assumptions are ordinarily invoked, namely:

1. Molecular diffusion is negligible compared with turbulent diffusion,

$$D_i \frac{\partial^2 \langle c \rangle}{\partial x_j \, \partial x_j} \ll \frac{\partial}{\partial x_j} \langle u_j' c' \rangle$$

2. The atmosphere is incompressible,

$$\frac{\partial \bar{u}_j}{\partial x_j} = 0$$

With these assumptions and Eq. (13.10), Eq. (13.4) becomes

$$\frac{\partial \langle c \rangle}{\partial t} + \bar{u}_j \frac{\partial \langle c \rangle}{\partial x_j} = \frac{\partial}{\partial x_j} \left(K_{jj} \frac{\partial \langle c \rangle}{\partial x_j} \right) + S(\mathbf{x}, t) \qquad (13.11)$$

This equation is termed the semiempirical equation of atmospheric diffusion, or just the *atmospheric diffusion equation*, and will play a very important role in what is to follow.

Let us return to the case in which chemical reactions are occurring, for which we refer to Eq. (13.4). Since R_i is almost always a nonlinear function of the c_i, we have already seen that additional terms of the type $\langle c_i' c_j' \rangle$ will arise from $\langle R_i \rangle$. The crudest approximations we can make regarding $\langle R_i \rangle$ is to replace $\langle R_i(c_1, \ldots, c_N) \rangle$ by $R_i(\langle c_1 \rangle, \ldots, \langle c_N \rangle)$, thereby neglecting the effect of concentration fluctuations on the rate of reaction. Invoking this approximation, as well as those inherent in Eq. (13.11), we obtain for each species i,

$$\frac{\partial \langle c_i \rangle}{\partial t} + \bar{u}_j \frac{\partial \langle c_i \rangle}{\partial x_j} = \frac{\partial}{\partial x_j} \left(K_{jj} \frac{\partial \langle c_i \rangle}{\partial x_j} \right) + R_i(\langle c_1 \rangle, \ldots, \langle c_N \rangle) + S_i(\mathbf{x}, t)$$

$$(13.12)$$

A key question is: Can we develop the conditions under which Eq. (13.12) is a valid description of atmospheric diffusion and chemical reaction?

13.4.2. Conditions for Validity of the Atmospheric Diffusion Equation

Let us consider a two-dimensional flow containing a single species that decays by a second-order reaction (Lamb, 1973). Assuming $\bar{u}_1 = \bar{u} = \text{const}$, $\bar{u}_2 = \bar{v} = 0$, and molecular diffusion can be neglected, the exact equation for $\langle c \rangle$ is, using (x, y, z) coordinates,

$$\frac{\partial \langle c \rangle}{\partial t} + \bar{u} \frac{\partial \langle c \rangle}{\partial x} + \frac{\partial}{\partial y} \langle v' c' \rangle = -k(\langle c \rangle^2 + \langle c'^2 \rangle) \qquad (13.13)$$

where we have ignored the term $(\partial/\partial x)\langle u'c' \rangle$ as small compared with $\bar{u}$ $\partial\langle c \rangle/\partial x$. Our objective is to develop the conditions under which Eq. (13.13) can be approximated by

$$\frac{\partial\langle c \rangle}{\partial t} + \bar{u}\frac{\partial\langle c \rangle}{\partial x} = \frac{\partial}{\partial y}\left(K_{yy}\frac{\partial\langle c \rangle}{\partial y} \right) - k\langle c \rangle^2 \tag{13.14}$$

In doing so we will be able to see the conditions under which the mixing-length concept might be expected to apply in turbulent diffusion.

In the context of the two-dimensional problem considered here, the mixing-length hypothesis holds that the concentration fluctuation at any point (x, y, t) is due to the arrival at that point of a fluid eddy that originated at some other location where the mean concentration $\langle c \rangle$ was different from that at (x, y, t). Let c'_j be the fluctuation at (x, y, t) due to the jth eddy. Then

$$c'_j = \underset{\text{arriving eddy}}{c_j(x, y, t)} - \underset{\text{mean concentration}}{\langle c(x, y, t) \rangle} \tag{13.15}$$

Let us suppose that this eddy originated on the level $y + l_j$ at time $t - \tau_j$, where the mean concentration was $\langle c(x, y + l_j, t - \tau_j) \rangle$. During the time τ_j required to traverse the distance l_j, the concentration of the diffusing material in the eddy changes because of chemical decay according to (neglecting entrainment effects)

$$\frac{dc_j}{dt} = -kc_j^2 \tag{13.16}$$

Therefore, the concentration in the eddy on arrival at (x, y, t) is

$$c_j(x, y, t) = \frac{\langle c(x, t + l_j, t - \tau_j) \rangle}{1 + k\tau_j\langle c(x, y + l_j, t - \tau_j) \rangle} \tag{13.17}$$

Let τ_e be the maximum time over which an eddy maintains its integrity, that is, so that $\tau_e > \tau_j$ for nearly all eddies. Also, let τ_c be a characteristic time scale for the second-order chemical reaction,

$$\tau_c = (k\langle c \rangle_{\text{max}})^{-1} \tag{13.18}$$

Then, for cases in which the chemical decay takes place much more slowly than the turbulent transport, that is, $\tau_c \gg \tau_e$, Eq. (13.17) reduces to

$$c_j(x, y, t) = \langle c(x, y + l_j, t - \tau_j) \rangle \tag{13.19}$$

Indeed this is the exact form employed in the usual mixing-length hypothesis for an inert species. Substituting Eq. (13.19) into Eq. (13.15) and expanding

$\langle c(x, y + l_j, t - \tau_j) \rangle$ in a first-order Taylor series about the point (x, y, t) we get

$$c'_j = l_j \frac{\partial \langle c \rangle}{\partial y} - \tau_j \frac{\partial \langle c \rangle}{\partial t} \tag{13.20}$$

Having determined an expression for c'_j, we can now consider $\langle u'c' \rangle$ and $\langle c'^2 \rangle$ in Eq. (13.13). Multiplying Eq. (13.20) by v'_j, the velocity fluctuation in the y component of the velocity associated with the jth eddy, and averaging the resulting equation over a large number of eddies that pass the point (x, y), we get

$$\langle v'c' \rangle = \langle v'l \rangle \frac{\partial \langle c \rangle}{\partial y} - \langle v'_j \tau_j \rangle \frac{\partial \langle c \rangle}{\partial t} \tag{13.21}$$

where l is the "mixing length" defined so that $\langle v'l \rangle = \langle v'_j l_j \rangle$. Similarly, the expression for $\langle c'^2 \rangle$ is obtained by squaring Eq. (13.20) and averaging:

$$\langle c'^2 \rangle = \langle l^2 \rangle \left(\frac{\partial \langle c \rangle}{\partial y} \right)^2 - 2\langle l_j \tau_j \rangle \frac{\partial \langle c \rangle}{\partial y} \frac{\partial \langle c \rangle}{\partial t} + \langle \tau_j^2 \rangle \left(\frac{\partial \langle c \rangle}{\partial t} \right)^2 \tag{13.22}$$

Since the quantities $\langle v'l \rangle$, $\langle v'_j \tau_j \rangle$, $\langle l_j \tau_j \rangle$, $\langle l^2 \rangle$, and $\langle \tau_j^2 \rangle$ involve hypothetical parameters, there is no chance to obtain rigorous analytical expressions for these quantities; rather, it is possible only to estimate their order of magnitude. We consider first $\langle v'_j \tau_j \rangle$ and $\langle l_j \tau_j \rangle$. Although the variables in each of these two terms are not statistically independent, we expect them to be uncorrelated in each case since τ_j is always positive and l_j and v'_j are equally likely to be either positive or negative. Thus

$$\langle v'_j \tau_j \rangle = \langle l_j \tau_j \rangle = 0 \tag{13.23}$$

Next we consider $\langle v'l \rangle$. We expect this term to be negative since negative values of l_j are correlated with positive values of v'_j in a shear flow in which $\bar{u}$ increases with y. It is reasonable to approximate $\langle v'l \rangle$ by

$$\langle v'l \rangle = -\langle v'^2 \rangle \tau_e \tag{13.24}$$

Similarly, we find

$$\langle l^2 \rangle = \langle v'^2 \rangle \tau_e^2 \tag{13.25}$$

Considering $\langle \tau_j^2 \rangle$, it seems reasonable to assume that the square root of this quantity is roughly equal to the time scale of the energy-containing eddies since it is those eddies that are primarily responsible for the turbulent flux of material. Since τ_e is a good measure of such a time scale,

$$\langle \tau_j^2 \rangle = \tau_e^2 \tag{13.26}$$

The basic restrictions leading to Eq. (13.20) can be expressed as

$$k\langle c\rangle_{\max}\tau_e \ll 1 \tag{13.27}$$

$$\frac{\langle v'^2\rangle^{1/2}\tau_e}{L_c} \ll 1 \tag{13.28}$$

$$\frac{\tau_e}{T_c} \ll 1 \tag{13.29}$$

where L_c and T_c are characteristic length and time scales of the flow. If Eqs. (13.27) to (13.29) are satisfied, we can substitute Eqs. (13.21) to (13.26) into Eq. (13.13) to obtain

$$\frac{\partial\langle c\rangle}{\partial t} + \bar{u}\frac{\partial\langle c\rangle}{\partial x} = \frac{\partial}{\partial y}\left(K_{yy}\frac{\partial\langle c\rangle}{\partial y}\right) - k\left[\langle c\rangle^2 + K_{yy}\tau_e\left(\frac{\partial\langle c\rangle}{\partial y}\right)^2 + \tau_e^2\left(\frac{\partial\langle c\rangle}{\partial t}\right)^2\right] \tag{13.30}$$

where $K_{yy} = \langle v'^2\rangle^{1/2}\tau_e$.

Let us now compare Eqs. (13.30) and (13.14), the only difference being the last two terms on the right-hand side of Eq. (13.30). First, we rewrite all four terms on the right-hand side of Eq. (13.30) and below each its order of magnitude:

$$\frac{\partial}{\partial y}\left(K_{yy}\frac{\partial\langle c\rangle}{\partial y}\right) - k\langle c\rangle^2 - kK_{yy}\tau_e\left(\frac{\partial\langle c\rangle}{\partial y}\right)^2 - k\tau_e^2\left(\frac{\partial\langle c\rangle}{\partial t}\right)^2$$

$$\frac{K_{yy}\langle c\rangle}{L_c^2} \qquad k\langle c\rangle^2 \qquad \frac{kK_{yy}\tau_e\langle c\rangle^2}{L_c^2} \qquad \frac{k\tau_e^2\langle c\rangle^2}{T_c^2}$$

From Eq. (13.29), the last term is negligible. Furthermore, since the first and second terms are automatically assumed to be of the same order of magnitude, we must have $K_{yy}\langle c\rangle/L_c^2 \approx k\langle c\rangle^2$. Using this fact, we may express the third term as $k\tau_e\langle c\rangle(k\langle c\rangle^2)$, which by Eq. (13.27) is negligible compared with $k\langle c\rangle^2$.

We may conclude from the above that Eq. (13.14) is a valid description of turbulent diffusion and chemical reaction as long as Eqs. (13.27) to (13.29) hold, namely that the reaction processes are slow compared with turbulent transport and the characteristic length and time scales for changes in the mean concentration field are large compared with the corresponding scales for turbulent transport.

Because the eddy time scale τ_e and the length scale $\langle v'^2\rangle^{1/2}\tau_e$ are often quite large in the atmosphere, the above conditions are violated near strong isolated sources. For example, for the lateral turbulent velocity, component τ_e may be about 1 min and $\langle v'^2 \rangle^{1/2} \cong 1$ m sec^{-1}. Thus, to satisfy the condition that the characteristic length scale of the concentration field be much greater than that of the turbulence, the spatial scale for variations in $\langle c \rangle$, and hence S, must be of the order of 100 to 1000 m. In addition, under these conditions the time scale of the fastest reactions must be no smaller than of the order of about 10 min.

The conclusion we draw at this point is that Eq. (13.12) is a valid model *provided it is applied to situations in which chemical reactions are "slow" and the distribution of sources is "smooth."*

13.4.3. Lagrangian Approaches

We now wish to consider the derivation of usable expressions for $\langle c_i(\mathbf{x}, t) \rangle$ based on the fundamental Lagrangian expression Eq. (13.8). As we have seen, the utility of Eq. (13.8) rests on the ability to evaluate the transition probability $Q(\mathbf{x}, t | \mathbf{x}', t')$. The first question, then, is: Are there any circumstances under which the form of Q is known?

To attempt to answer this question let us go back to the advection equation, Eq. (13.2), for a one-dimensional flow with a general source term $S(x, t)$,

$$\frac{\partial c}{\partial t} + \frac{\partial}{\partial x}(uc) = S(x, t) \tag{13.31}$$

Since the velocity u is a random quantity, the concentration c that results from the solution of Eq. (13.31) is also random. What we want to do is to solve Eq. (13.31) for a particular choice of the velocity u and find the concentration c corresponding to that choice of u. For simplicity, let us assume that u is independent of x and depends only on time t. Thus, the velocity $u(t)$ is a random variable depending on time. Since $u(t)$ is a random variable, we need to specify the probability density for $u(t)$. A reasonable assumption for the probability distribution of $u(t)$ is that it is Gaussian,

$$p_u(u) = \frac{1}{(2\pi)^{1/2}\sigma_u} \exp\left[-\frac{(u - \bar{u})^2}{2\sigma_u^2}\right] \tag{13.32}$$

where the mean value is $\langle u(t) \rangle = \bar{u}$, and the variance is σ_u^2. In the process of solving Eq. (13.31) we will need an expression for the term, $\langle (u(t) - \bar{u})(u(\tau) - \bar{u}) \rangle$. We will assume that $u(t)$ is a stationary random process with the correlation,

$$\langle (u(t) - \bar{u})(u(\tau) - \bar{u}) \rangle = \sigma_u^2 \exp(-b|t - \tau|) \tag{13.33}$$

This expression says that the maximum correlation between the velocities at two times occurs when those times are equal, and is equal to σ_u^2. As the time separation between $u(t)$ and $u(\tau)$ increases, the correlation decays exponentially with a characteristic decay time of $1/b$. Stationarity implies that the statistical properties of u at two different times t and τ depend only on $t - \tau$ and not on t and τ individually.

Let us now solve Eq. (13.31) for a time-varying source of strength $S(t)$ at $x = 0$. The solution, obtained by the method of characteristics, is

$$c(x, t) = \int_0^t \delta(x - X(t, \tau)) S(\tau) \, d\tau \qquad (13.34)$$

where

$$X(t, \tau) = \int_\tau^t u(t') \, dt' \qquad (13.35)$$

is just the distance a fluid particle travels between times τ and t. Since $X(t, \tau)$ is a random variable, so is $c(x, t)$. We are really interested in the mean, $\langle c(x, t) \rangle$. Thus, taking the expected value of Eq. (13.34), we obtain

$$\langle c(x, t) \rangle = \int_0^t \langle \delta(x - X(t, \tau)) \rangle S(\tau) \, d\tau \qquad (13.36)$$

Since the pdf of $u(t)$ is Gaussian, that for $X(t, \tau)$ is also Gaussian,

$$p_X(X; t, \tau) = \frac{1}{(2\pi)^{1/2} \sigma_x} \exp\left[-\frac{(X - \bar{X})^2}{2\sigma_x^2} \right] \qquad (13.37)$$

where $\bar{X}(t, \tau)$ and $\sigma_x^2(t, \tau)$ are the mean and variance, respectively, of $X(t, \tau)$. The expression for $\langle c(x, t) \rangle$ can be written in terms of p_X as

$$\langle c(x, t) \rangle = \int_0^t S(t') \int_{-\infty}^\infty \delta(x - X(t, t')) p_X(X; t, t') \, dX \, dt'$$

$$= \int_0^t S(t') p_X(x; t, t') \, dt' \qquad (13.38)$$

By comparing Eq. (13.38) with Eq. (13.8), we see that $p_X(x; t, t')$ is precisely $Q(x, t | x', t')$, except that there is no dependence on x' in this case. Let us compute $\bar{X}(t, \tau)$ and $\sigma_x^2(t, \tau)$ based on the definition of $X(t, \tau)$ and the properties of u. We note that

$$\bar{X}(t, \tau) = (t - \tau)\bar{u} \qquad (13.39)$$

and

$$\sigma_x^2(t, \tau) = \langle (X(t, \tau) - \bar{X})^2 \rangle$$

$$= \langle X(t, \tau)^2 \rangle - \bar{X}^2 \qquad (13.40)$$

Since

$$\langle X(t,\tau)^2 \rangle = \left\langle \int_\tau^t u(t')\, dt' \int_\tau^t u(t'')\, dt'' \right\rangle$$

$$= \int_\tau^t \int_\tau^t \langle u(t')u(t'') \rangle\, dt'\, dt'' \qquad (13.41)$$

using Eqs. (13.33), (13.39), (13.40), and (13.41), we obtain

$$\sigma_x^2(t,\tau) = \frac{2\sigma_u^2}{b^2}\left[b(t-\tau) + e^{-b(t-\tau)} - 1 \right] \qquad (13.42)$$

so $\sigma_x^2(t,\tau) = \sigma_x^2(t-\tau)$.

If the source is just a pulse of unit strength at $t = 0$, that is, $S(t) = \delta(t)$, then Eq. (13.38) becomes

$$\langle c(x,t) \rangle = \frac{1}{(2\pi)^{1/2}\sigma_x(t)} \exp\left[-\frac{(x-\bar{u}t)^2}{2\sigma_x^2(t)} \right] \qquad (13.43)$$

Thus, we have found that the mean concentration of a tracer released in a flow where the velocity is a stationary, Gaussian random process has a distribution that is, itself, Gaussian. This is an important result.

The mean position of the distribution at time t is $\bar{u}t$, just the distance a tracer molecule has travelled over a time t at the mean fluid velocity $\bar{u}$. The variance of the mean concentration distribution, $\sigma_x^2(t)$, is just the variance of $X(t,\tau)$. This result makes sense since $X(t,\tau)$ is just the random distance that a fluid particle travels between times τ and t, and this distance is precisely that which a tracer molecule travels.

Let us examine the limits of Eq. (13.42) for large and small values of t. For large t, that is, $t \gg b^{-1}$, the characteristic time for velocity correlations, Eq. (13.42) reduces to

$$\sigma_x^2 = \frac{2\sigma_u^2 t}{b} \qquad (13.44)$$

For $t \ll b^{-1}$, $\exp(-bt) \cong 1 - bt + (bt)^2/2$, and

$$\sigma_x^2 = \sigma_u^2 t^2 \qquad (13.45)$$

Thus, we find that the variance of the mean concentration distribution varies with time according to

$$\sigma_x^2 \approx \begin{cases} t^2 & \text{small } t \\ t & \text{large } t \end{cases}$$

This example can be readily generalized to three dimensions. If we continue to assume that there is a mean flow only in the x-direction, then the expression for the mean concentration resulting from an instantaneous point source of unit strength at the origin is

$$\langle c(x, y, z, t)\rangle = \frac{1}{(2\pi)^{3/2}\sigma_x(t)\sigma_y(t)\sigma_z(t)}$$

$$\times \exp\left[-\frac{(x - \bar{u}t)^2}{2\sigma_x^2(t)} - \frac{y^2}{2\sigma_y^2(t)} - \frac{z^2}{2\sigma_z^2(t)}\right] \quad (13.46)$$

where σ_y^2 and σ_z^2 are given by equations analogous to that for σ_x^2.

To summarize again, we have shown through a highly idealized example that the mean concentration in a stationary, homogeneous Gaussian flow field is itself Gaussian. If the turbulence is stationary and homogeneous, the transition probability density Q of a particle depends only upon the displacements in time and space and not on where or when the particle was introduced into the flow. Thus, in that case, $Q(\mathbf{x}, t|\mathbf{x}', t') = Q(\mathbf{x} - \mathbf{x}'; t - t')$. The Gaussian form of Q turns out to play an extremely important role in atmospheric diffusion theory, as we will see.

13.5. SOLUTION OF THE ATMOSPHERIC DIFFUSION EQUATION FOR AN INSTANTANEOUS SOURCE

We begin in this section to obtain solutions for atmospheric diffusion problems. Let us consider, as we did in the previous section, an instantaneous point source of strength S at the origin in an infinite fluid with a velocity $\bar{u}$ in the x-direction. We desire to solve the atmospheric diffusion equation, Eq. (13.11), in this situation. Let us assume, for lack of anything better at the moment, that K_{xx}, K_{yy} and K_{zz} are constant. Then Eq. (13.11) becomes

$$\frac{\partial\langle c\rangle}{\partial t} + \bar{u}\frac{\partial\langle c\rangle}{\partial x} = K_{xx}\frac{\partial^2\langle c\rangle}{\partial x^2} + K_{yy}\frac{\partial^2\langle c\rangle}{\partial y^2} + K_{zz}\frac{\partial^2\langle c\rangle}{\partial z^2} \quad (13.47)$$

to be solved subject to

$$\langle c(x, y, z, 0)\rangle = S\delta(x)\delta(y)\delta(z) \quad (13.48)$$

$$\langle c(x, y, z, t)\rangle = 0 \quad x, y, z \to \pm\infty \quad (13.49)$$

The solution of Eqs. (13.47) to (13.49) is given in Appendix 13.A.1. It is

$$\langle c(x, y, z, t)\rangle = \frac{S}{8(\pi t)^{3/2}(K_{xx}K_{yy}K_{zz})^{1/2}}$$

$$\times \exp\left[-\frac{(x-\bar{u}t)^2}{4K_{xx}t} - \frac{y^2}{4K_{yy}t} - \frac{z^2}{4K_{zz}t}\right] \quad (13.50)$$

Note the similarity of Eqs. (13.50) and (13.46). In fact, if we define $\sigma_x^2 = 2K_{xx}t$, $\sigma_y^2 = 2K_{yy}t$, and $\sigma_z^2 = 2K_{zz}t$, the two expressions are identical. There is, we conclude, evidently a connection between the Eulerian and Lagrangian approaches embodied in a relation between the variances of spread that arise in a Gaussian distribution and the eddy diffusivities in the atmospheric diffusion equation. We will explore this relationship further as we proceed.

13.6.   MEAN CONCENTRATION FROM CONTINUOUS SOURCES

We just obtained expressions Eqs. (13.46) and (13.50) for the mean concentration resulting from an instantaneous release of a quantity S of material at the origin in an infinite fluid with stationary, homogeneous turbulence and a mean velocity $\bar{u}$ in the x-direction. We now wish to consider a continuously emitting source under the same conditions. The source strength is q (g sec^{-1}).

13.6.1.   Lagrangian Approach

A continuous source is viewed conceptually as one that began emitting at $t = 0$ and continues as $t \to \infty$. The mean concentration achieves a steady state, independent of time, and $S(x, y, z, t) = q\delta(x)\delta(y)\delta(z)$. The basic Lagrangian expression Eq. (13.8) becomes

$$\langle c(x, y, z, t)\rangle = \int_0^t Q(x, y, z, t|0, 0, 0, t')q\, dt' \quad (13.51)$$

The steady state concentration is given by

$$\langle c(x, y, z)\rangle = \lim_{t \to \infty} \langle c(x, y, z, t)\rangle = \lim_{t \to \infty} \int_0^t Q(x, y, z, t|0, 0, 0, t')q\, dt'$$

$$(13.52)$$

The transition probability density Q has the general Gaussian form of Eq.

(13.46),

$$Q(x, y, z, t|0,0,0,t') = (2\pi)^{-3/2}\left[\sigma_x(t - t')\sigma_y(t - t')\sigma_z(t - t')\right]^{-1}$$

$$\times \exp\left[-\frac{(x - \bar{u}(t - t'))^2}{2\sigma_x^2(t - t')} - \frac{y^2}{2\sigma_y^2(t - t')} - \frac{z^2}{2\sigma_z^2(t - t')}\right]$$

$$(13.53)$$

which can be expressed as $Q(x, y, z, t - t'|0,0,0,0)$. Thus,

$$\langle c(x, y, z)\rangle = \lim_{t \to \infty} \int_0^t Q(x, y, z, \tau|0,0,0,0)q\,d\tau \qquad (13.54)$$

Thus, the steady state concentration resulting from a continuous source is obtained by integrating the unsteady state concentration over all time from 0 to ∞,

$$\langle c(x, y, z)\rangle = \int_0^\infty \frac{q}{(2\pi)^{3/2}\sigma_x\sigma_y\sigma_z}\exp\left[-\frac{(x - \bar{u}t)^2}{2\sigma_x^2} - \frac{y^2}{2\sigma_y^2} - \frac{z^2}{2\sigma_z^2}\right]dt$$

$$(13.55)$$

We need to evaluate the integral in Eq. (13.55). To do so we need to specify $\sigma_x(t)$, $\sigma_y(t)$ and $\sigma_z(t)$. For the moment let us assume simply that $\sigma_x(t) = \sigma_y(t) = \sigma_z(t) = \sigma(t)$, where we do not specify how σ depends on t. We note that the term $\exp\{(x - \bar{u}t)^2/2\sigma_x^2]\}$ is peaked at $t = x/\bar{u}$ and falls off exponentially for longer or shorter values of t. Thus, the major contribution of this term to the integral comes from values of t close to $x/\bar{u}$. Thus, let us perform a Taylor series expansion of

$$G(t) = \exp\left[-\frac{(x - \bar{u}t)^2 + y^2 + z^2}{2\sigma^2(t)}\right]$$

about $t = x/\bar{u}$. Using

$$G(t) = G(x/\bar{u}) + \left(\frac{dG}{dt}\right)_{t=x/\bar{u}}(t - x/\bar{u})$$

we find

$$\left(\frac{dG}{dt}\right)_{t=x/\bar{u}} = -\exp\left[-\frac{y^2 + z^2}{2\sigma^2(t)}\right]\left\{\frac{1}{\sigma^3(t)}\frac{d\sigma}{dt}(y^2 + z^2)\right\}_{t=x/\bar{u}}$$

If we let $E = (y^2 + z^2)/2\sigma^2(t)$, then

$$\left(\frac{dG}{dt}\right)_{t=x/\bar{u}} = -\exp(-E)\left[\frac{2}{\sigma}\frac{d\sigma}{dt}E\right]_{t=x/\bar{u}}$$

Thus the Taylor series approximation of the exponential is

$$\exp\left[-\frac{(x - \bar{u}t)^2 + y^2 + z^2}{2\sigma^2(t)}\right] = e^{-E}\left\{1 - \left(t - \frac{x}{\bar{u}}\right)\left(E\frac{2}{\sigma}\frac{d\sigma}{dt}\right)_{t=x/\bar{u}}\right\}$$

$$(13.56)$$

Now, assume that the major contribution to the integral comes from values of t in the range,

$$\frac{x}{\bar{u}} - a\frac{\sigma}{\bar{u}} \le t \le \frac{x}{\bar{u}} + a\frac{\sigma}{\bar{u}}$$

Substituting Eq. (13.56) into Eq. (13.55) yields

$$\langle c(x, y, z)\rangle = \int_{(x-a\sigma)/\bar{u}}^{(x+a\sigma)/\bar{u}} \frac{q}{(2\pi)^{3/2}\sigma^3(t)}e^{-E}\left[1 - \left(t - \frac{x}{\bar{u}}\right)\left(\frac{2}{\sigma}\frac{d\sigma}{dt}E\right)_{t=x/\bar{u}}\right]dt$$

$$(13.57)$$

If we now neglect the $(t - x/\bar{u})$ term as being of order $a\sigma/\bar{u}$ and assume that within the limits of integration $\sigma(t) \cong \sigma(x/\bar{u})$, we get

$$\langle c(x, y, z)\rangle = \frac{2qe^{-E}(a\sigma/\bar{u})}{(2\pi)^{3/2}\sigma^3} \tag{13.58}$$

To obtain a, if we impose the condition of conservation of mass, that is, that the total flow of material through the plane at any x is q, we obtain $a = (\pi/2)^{1/2}$. Thus, Eq. (13.58) becomes

$$\langle c(x, y, z)\rangle = \frac{q}{2\pi\bar{u}\sigma^2(x/\bar{u})}\exp\left[-\frac{y^2 + z^2}{2\sigma^2(x/\bar{u})}\right] \tag{13.59}$$

The assumptions made in deriving Eq. (13.59) require that $a\sigma/\bar{u} \ll x/\bar{u}$. Thus, the condition for validity of the result is

$$\frac{\sigma(x/\bar{u})}{x} \ll 1$$

Physically, the mean concentration emanating from a point source is a plume that can be visualized to be comprised of many puffs each of whose concentration distributions is sharply peaked about its centroid at all travel distances. Thus, the spread of each puff is small compared to the downwind distance it has travelled. This assumption is called the *slender plume approximation*.

The procedure we have followed to obtain Eq. (13.59) can be readily generalized to $\sigma_x \neq \sigma_y \neq \sigma_z$. The result is

$$\langle c(x, y, z) \rangle = \frac{q}{2\pi\bar{u}\sigma_y\sigma_z} \exp\left[-\frac{y^2}{2\sigma_y^2} - \frac{z^2}{2\sigma_z^2} \right] \tag{13.60}$$

This equation for the mean concentration from a continuous point source occupies a key position in atmospheric diffusion theory and we will have occasion to refer to it again and again.

An Alternate Derivation of Eq. (13.60). Our derivation of Eq. (13.60) was based on physical reasoning concerning the amount of spreading of a puff compared to its downwind distance. We can obtain Eq. (13.60) in slightly different manner by assuming specific functional forms for σ_x, σ_y, and σ_z. Specifically, let us select the "long-time" form (recall Eq. (13.44)),

$$\sigma_x^2 = a_x t \qquad \sigma_y^2 = a_y t \qquad \sigma_z^2 = a_z t \tag{13.61}$$

Thus, it is desired to evaluate

$$\langle c(x, y, z) \rangle = \int_0^\infty \frac{q}{(2\pi)^{3/2}(a_x a_y a_z)^{1/2} t^{3/2}}$$

$$\times \exp\left[-\frac{(x - \bar{u}t)^2}{2a_x t} - \frac{y^2}{2a_y t} - \frac{z^2}{2a_z t} \right] dt$$

This integral can be expressed as

$$\langle c(x, y, z) \rangle = \frac{q}{(2\pi)^{3/2}(a_x a_y a_z)^{1/2}} \int_0^\infty t^{-3/2} \exp\left[-\frac{(r^2 - 2\bar{u}xt + \bar{u}^2 t^2)}{2a_x t} \right] dt$$

where $r^2 = x^2 + (a_x/a_y)y^2 + (a_x/a_z)z^2$. Thus

$$\langle c(x, y, z) \rangle = \frac{q}{(2\pi)^{3/2}(a_x a_y a_z)^{1/2}} e^{\bar{u}x/a_x} \int_0^\infty t^{-3/2} \exp\left[-\left(\frac{r^2}{2a_x t} + \frac{\bar{u}^2 t}{2a_x}\right)\right] dt$$

Let $\eta = t^{-1/2}$ and

$$\langle c(x, y, z) \rangle = \frac{2q}{(2\pi)^{3/2}(a_x a_y a_z)^{1/2}} e^{\bar{u}x/a_x} \int_0^\infty \exp\left[-\left(\frac{r^2\eta^2}{2a_x} + \frac{\bar{u}^2}{2a_x\eta^2}\right)\right] d\eta$$

The integral is of the general form,

$$\int_0^\infty e^{-(a\eta^2 + b/\eta^2)} \, d\eta = \frac{1}{2}\left(\frac{\pi}{a}\right)^{1/2} e^{-2(ab)^{1/2}}$$

so finally

$$\langle c(x, y, z) \rangle = \frac{q}{2\pi(a_y a_z)^{1/2} r} \exp\left[-\frac{\bar{u}}{a_x}(r - x)\right] \tag{13.62}$$

is the expression for the mean concentration from a continuous point source of strength q at the origin in an infinite fluid with the variances given by Eq. (13.61). If advection dominates plume dispersion so that only the concentrations close to the plume centerline are of importance, we will be interested in the solution only for values of x, y, and z that satisfy

$$\frac{\left(\frac{a_x}{a_y}\right)y^2 + \left(\frac{a_x}{a_z}\right)z^2}{x^2} \ll 1$$

which can be viewed as the result of two assumptions, that

$$\frac{y^2 + z^2}{x^2} \ll 1$$

and that

$$\frac{a_x}{a_y} = 0(1); \qquad \frac{a_x}{a_z} = 0(1)$$

The latter assumption implies that the variances of the wind speeds are of the same order of magnitude. Since

$$r = x\left\{1 + \left[(a_x/a_y)y^2 + (a_x/a_z)z^2\right]/x^2\right\}^{1/2} \tag{13.63}$$

using $(1 + \zeta)^p = 1 + \zeta p + \dots$, Eq. (13.63) can be approximated by*

$$r = x\left\{1 + \frac{(a_x/a_y)y^2 + (a_x/a_z)z^2}{2x^2}\right\} \tag{13.64}$$

In Eq. (13.62) we approximate r by x and $r - x$ by the above expression. Thus Eq. (13.62) becomes

$$\langle c(x, y, z)\rangle = \frac{q}{2\pi(a_y a_z)^{1/2}x}\exp\left\{-\frac{\bar{u}}{2a_x x}\left[(a_x/a_y)y^2 + (a_x/a_z)z^2\right]\right\}$$

$$\tag{13.65}$$

If we relate time and distance from the source x by $t = x/\bar{u}$, then we can use Eq. (13.61) to write

$$\sigma_y^2 = \frac{a_y x}{\bar{u}} \qquad \sigma_z^2 = \frac{a_z x}{\bar{u}} \tag{13.66}$$

Then Eq. (13.65) becomes identical to Eq. (13.60).

Still Another Derivation of Eq. (13.60). We can use the following relation

$$\lim_{\sigma \to 0} \frac{1}{(2\pi)^{1/2}\sigma}\exp\left(-\frac{(x - x')^2}{2\sigma^2}\right) = \delta(x - x') \tag{13.67}$$

to take the limit of the x-term in Eq. (13.56) as $\sigma_x \to 0$. Using Eq. (13.67) and letting $\xi = \bar{u}t$ we get

$$\langle c(x, y, z)\rangle = \lim_{\xi \to \infty} \int_0^{\xi/\bar{u}} \frac{q}{2\pi\bar{u}\sigma_y\sigma_z}\exp\left[-\frac{y^2}{2\sigma_y^2} - \frac{z^2}{2\sigma_z^2}\right]\delta(x - \xi)\,d\xi$$

*The expression

$$(1 + \zeta)^p = 1 + \binom{p}{1}\zeta + \binom{p}{2}\zeta^2 + \dots$$

is valid for all p if $-1 < \zeta < 1$. Thus,

$$(1 + \zeta)^{1/2} = 1 + \tfrac{1}{2}\zeta + \tfrac{1}{8}\zeta^2 + \dots$$

for $-1 < \zeta < 1$. Note that

$$\binom{p}{\nu} = \frac{p!}{\nu!(p - \nu)!}$$

where for noninteger p, $p! = \Gamma(p + 1)$.

where σ_y and σ_z are now functions of $\xi/\bar{u}$. This derivation is the shortest, but we delayed it after those that more clearly illustrate the physical assumptions.

13.6.2. Eulerian Approach

The problem of determining the concentration distribution resulting from a continuous source of strength q at the origin in an infinite isotropic fluid with a velocity $\bar{u}$ in the x-direction can be formulated by the Eulerian approach as:

$$\bar{u}\frac{\partial \langle c \rangle}{\partial x} = K\left(\frac{\partial^2 \langle c \rangle}{\partial x^2} + \frac{\partial^2 \langle c \rangle}{\partial y^2} + \frac{\partial^2 \langle c \rangle}{\partial z^2} \right) + q\delta(x)\delta(y)\delta(z) \quad (13.68)$$

$$\langle c(x, y, z) \rangle = 0 \qquad x, y, z \to \pm\infty \qquad (13.69)$$

The solution of Eqs. (13.68) and (13.69) is given in Appendix 13.A.2. It is

$$\langle c(x, y, z) \rangle = \frac{q}{4\pi Kr} \exp\left[-\frac{\bar{u}(r - x)}{2K} \right] \qquad (13.70)$$

where $r^2 = x^2 + y^2 + z^2$, or

$$r = x\left(1 + \frac{y^2 + z^2}{x^2} \right)^{1/2} \qquad (13.71)$$

If we invoke the slender plume approximation, we are interested only in the solution close to the plume centerline. Thus, as in Eq. (13.63), Eq. (13.71) can be approximated by

$$r \cong x\left(1 + \frac{y^2 + z^2}{2x^2} \right) \qquad (13.72)$$

If in Eq. (13.70) r is approximated by x and $r - x$ by $(y^2 + z^2)/2x$, Eq. (13.70) becomes

$$\langle c(x, y, z) \rangle = \frac{q}{4\pi Kx} \exp\left[-\left(\frac{\bar{u}}{4Kx} \right)(y^2 + z^2) \right] \qquad (13.73)$$

An Alternate Derivation of Eq. (13.73). Equation (13.73) is based on the slender plume approximation as expressed by Eq. (13.72). We will now show that the slender plume approximation is equivalent to neglecting diffusion in the direction of the mean flow in the atmospheric diffusion equation. Thus, $\langle c \rangle$

is governed by

$$\bar{u}\frac{\partial\langle c\rangle}{\partial x} = K\left(\frac{\partial^2\langle c\rangle}{\partial y^2} + \frac{\partial^2\langle c\rangle}{\partial z^2}\right) + q\delta(x)\delta(y)\delta(z) \tag{13.74}$$

$$\langle c(0, y, z)\rangle = 0 \tag{13.75}$$

$$\langle c(x, y, z)\rangle = 0 \qquad y, z \to \pm\infty \tag{13.76}$$

Before we proceed to solve Eq. (13.74) a few comments about the boundary conditions are useful. When the x-diffusion term is dropped in the atmospheric diffusion equation, the equation becomes first-order in x, and the natural point for the single boundary condition on x is at $x = 0$. Since the source is also at $x = 0$ we have an option of whether to place the source on the R.H.S. of the equation, as in Eq. (13.74), or in the $x = 0$ boundary condition. If we follow the latter course, then the $x = 0$ boundary condition is obtained by equating material fluxes across the plane at $x = 0$. The result is

$$\bar{u}\frac{\partial\langle c\rangle}{\partial x} = K\left(\frac{\partial^2\langle c\rangle}{\partial y^2} + \frac{\partial^2\langle c\rangle}{\partial z^2}\right) \tag{13.77}$$

$$\langle c(0, y, z)\rangle = \frac{q}{\bar{u}}\delta(y)\delta(z) \tag{13.78}$$

$$\langle c(x, y, z)\rangle = 0 \qquad y, z \to \pm\infty \tag{13.79}$$

The sets of Eqs. (13.74) to (13.76) and (13.77) to (13.79) are entirely equivalent. We present the solution of Eq. (13.77) in Appendix 13.A.3. The solution is

$$\langle c(x, y, z)\rangle = \frac{q}{4\pi Kx}\exp\left[-\frac{\bar{u}}{4Kx}(y^2 + z^2)\right] \tag{13.80}$$

If we allow K_{yy} to be different from K_{zz}, the analogous result is

$$\langle c(x, y, z)\rangle = \frac{q}{4\pi(K_{yy}K_{zz})^{1/2}x}\exp\left[-\frac{\bar{u}}{4x}\left(\frac{y^2}{K_{yy}} + \frac{z^2}{K_{zz}}\right)\right] \tag{13.81}$$

13.6.3. Summary of Continuous Point Source Solutions

Table 13.1 presents a summary of the solutions obtained in this section. Of primary interest at this point is a comparison of the forms of the Lagrangian and Eulerian expressions, in particular the relationships between eddy diffusivities and the plume dispersion variances. For the slender plume cases, for

TABLE 13.1.   **Expressions for the Mean Concentration from a Continuous Point Source in an Infinite Fluid in Stationary, Homogeneous Turbulence**

Approach	Full Solution	Solution Employing Slender Plume Approximation
Lagrangian		

$$\sigma_x^2 = a_x t \qquad \frac{q}{2\pi(a_y a_z)^{1/2}r}\exp\left[-\frac{\bar{u}}{a_x}(r-x)\right] \qquad \frac{q}{2\pi\bar{u}\sigma_y\sigma_z}\exp\left[-\left(\frac{y^2}{2\sigma_y^2}+\frac{z^2}{2\sigma_z^2}\right)\right]$$

$$\sigma_y^2 = a_y t$$

$$\sigma_z^2 = a_z t \qquad r^2 = x^2 + (a_x/a_y)y^2 + (a_x/a_z)z^2$$

Eulerian

$$\frac{q}{4\pi\left(K_{yy}K_{zz}x^2 + K_{xx}K_{zz}y^2 + K_{xx}K_{yy}z^2\right)^{1/2}} \qquad \frac{q}{4\pi\left(K_{yy}K_{zz}\right)^{1/2}x}$$

$$\times\exp\left\{-\frac{\bar{u}}{2K_{xx}}\left[\left(\frac{x^2}{K_{xx}}+\frac{y^2}{K_{yy}}+\frac{z^2}{K_{zz}}\right)^{1/2}-x\right]\right\} \qquad \times\exp\left[-\frac{\bar{u}}{4x}\left(\frac{y^2}{K_{yy}}+\frac{z^2}{K_{zz}}\right)\right]$$

example, the Lagrangian and Eulerian expressions are identical if

$$\sigma_y^2 = \frac{2K_{yy}x}{\bar{u}} \qquad \sigma_z^2 = \frac{2K_{zz}x}{\bar{u}} \tag{13.82}$$

In most applications of the Lagrangian formulas, the dependence of σ_y^2 and σ_z^2 on x are determined empirically rather than as indicated in Eq. (13.82). Thus, the main purpose of the formulas in Table 13.1 is to provide a comparison between the two approaches to atmospheric diffusion theory.

13.7. STATISTICAL THEORY OF TURBULENT DIFFUSION

Up to this point in this chapter we have developed the common theories of turbulent diffusion in a purely formal manner. We have done this so that the relationship of the approximate models for turbulent diffusion, such as the K-theory and the Gaussian formulas, to the basic underlying theory is clearly evident. When such relationships are clear, the limitations inherent in each model can be appreciated. We have in some cases applied the models obtained to the prediction of the mean concentration resulting from an instantaneous or continuous source in idealized stationary, homogeneous turbulence. However we have not discussed the physical processes responsible for the dispersion of a cloud or a plume other than to attribute the phenomenon to velocity fluctuations. A great deal of insight into the actual nature of turbulent diffusion can be gained by considering, in turn, the dispersion of an instantaneous puff and a continuous plume of pollutants. Such a consideration will also enable us to

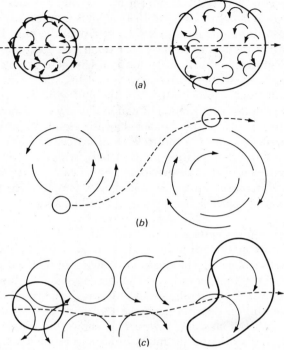

Figure 13.1. Dispersion of a puff of material under three turbulence conditions: (*a*) Puff embedded in a field in which the turbulent eddies are smaller than the puff. (*b*) Puff embedded in a field in which the turbulent eddies are larger than the puff. (*c*) Puff embedded in a field in which the turbulent eddies are comparable in size to the puff.

predict the statistical parameters of cloud and plume dispersion, such as the variances $\sigma_i^2(t)$, which are needed in the actual use of the Gaussian dispersion formulas.

13.7.1. Qualitative Features of Atmospheric Diffusion

The two idealized source types commonly used in atmospheric turbulent diffusion are the instantaneous point source and the continuous point source. An instantaneous point source is the conventional approximation to a rapid release of a quantity of material. Obviously, an "instantaneous point" is a mathematical idealization since any rapid release has finite spatial dimensions. As the puff is carried away from its source by the wind, it will disperse under the action of turbulent velocity fluctuations. Figure 13.1 shows the dispersion of a puff under three different turbulence conditions. Figure 13.1*a* shows a puff embedded in a turbulent field in which all the turbulent eddies are smaller than the puff. The puff will disperse uniformly as the turbulent eddies at its boundary entrain fresh air. In Figure 13.1*b*, a puff is embedded in a turbulent field all of whose eddies are considerably larger than the puff. In this case the puff will appear to the turbulent field as a small patch of fluid which will be convected through the field with little dilution. Ultimately, molecular diffusion will dissipate the puff. Figure 13.1*c* shows a puff in a turbulent field of eddies of size comparable to the puff. In this case the puff will be both dispersed and distorted. In the atmosphere, a cloud of material is always dispersed since there are almost always eddies of size smaller than the cloud. From Figure 13.1 we can see that the dispersion of a puff relative to its center of mass depends on the initial size of the puff relative to the length scales of the turbulence. In order to describe such relative dispersion, we must consider the statistics of the separation of two representative fluid particles in the puff. The analysis of the wandering of a single particle is insufficient to tell us about the dispersion of a cloud (Csanady, 1973).

A continuous source emits a plume that might be envisioned, as we have noted, as an infinite number of puffs released sequentially with an infinitesimal time interval between them. The quantity of material released is expressed in terms of a rate, say grams per minute. The dimensions of a plume perpendicular to the plume axis are generally given in terms of the standard deviation of the mean concentration distribution since the mean cross-sectional distributions are often nearly Gaussian. Figure 13.2 shows the plume "boundaries" and concentration distributions as might be seen in an instantaneous snapshot and exposures of a few minutes and several hours. An instantaneous picture of a plume reveals a meandering behavior with the width of the plume gradually growing downwind of the source. Longer-time averages give a more regular appearance to the plume and a smoother concentration distribution.

If we were to take a time exposure of the plume at large distances from the source, we would find that the boundaries of the time-averaged plume would

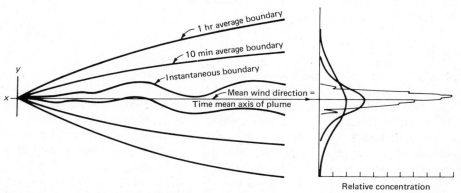

Figure 13.2. Plume boundaries and concentration distributions of a plume at different averaging times.

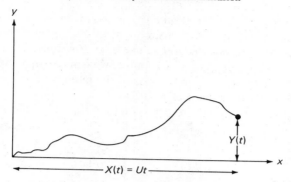

Figure 13.3. Motion of a single marked particle in a turbulent flow.

begin to meander, because the plume would come under the influences of larger and larger eddies, and the averaging time, say several hours, would still be too brief to time-average adequately the effect of these larger eddies. Eddies larger in size than the plume dimension tend to transport the plume intact whereas those that are smaller tend to disperse it. As the plume becomes wider, larger and larger eddies become effective in dispersing the plume and the smaller eddies become increasingly ineffective.

The theoretical analysis of the spread of a plume from a continuous point source can be achieved by considering the statistics of the diffusion of a single fluid particle relative to a fixed axis. The actual plume would then consist of a very large number of such identical particles, the average over the behavior of which yields the ensemble statistics of the plume.

13.7.2. Motion of a Single Particle Relative to a Fixed Axis

Let us consider, as shown in Figure 13.3, a single particle that is at position $\mathbf{x}_0$ at time t_0 and is at position $\mathbf{x}$ at some later time t in a turbulent field. The complete statistical properties of the particle's motion are embodied in the transition probability density $Q(\mathbf{x}, t|\mathbf{x}', t')$. An analysis of this problem for stationary, homogeneous turbulence was presented by Taylor (1921) in one of the classic papers in the field of turbulence. If the turbulence is stationary and homogeneous, $Q(\mathbf{x}, t|\mathbf{x}', t') = Q(\mathbf{x} - \mathbf{x}'; t - t')$; that is, Q depends only on the displacements in space and time and not on the initial position or time. The single particle may be envisioned as one of a very large number of particles that are emitted sequentially from a source located at $\mathbf{x}_0$. The distribution of the concentration of marked particles in the fluid is known once the statistical behavior of one representative marked particle is known. For convenience we assume that the particle is released at the origin at $t = 0$, so that its displacement corresponds to its coordinate location at time t.

The most important statistical quantity is the mean-square displacement of the particle from the source after a time t, since the mean displacement from the axis parallel to the flow direction will be zero. If we envision this particle as one being emitted from a continuous source, we can see that the mean-square displacement of the particle from the axis of the plume will tell us the width of the plume and hence the variances $\sigma_i^2(t)$.

The mean displacement of the particle along the ith coordinate is defined by

$$\langle X_i(t) \rangle = \int_0^t x_i Q(\mathbf{x}; t) \, d\mathbf{x} \tag{13.83}$$

where the braces ($\langle \ \rangle$) indicate an ensemble average over an infinite number of identical marked particles. If the velocity of the particle in the ith direction at any time is $v_i(t)$, the position of the particle at time t is given by (recall Eq. (13.35))

$$X_i(t) = \int_0^t v_i(t') \, dt' \tag{13.84}$$

where the velocity of the particle at any instant is equal, by definition, to the fluid velocity at the spot where the particle happens to be at that instant,

$$v_i(t) = u_i[\mathbf{X}(t), t] \tag{13.85}$$

Let us consider a situation in which there is no mean velocity, so that $v_i(t) = u_i'[\mathbf{X}(t), t]$. If there is a mean velocity, say in the x_i direction, we will be interested in the dispersion about a point moving with the mean velocity. Therefore, the influence of the fluctuating Eulerian velocities on the wanderings of the marked particle from its axis is the key issue here, not its translation in the mean flow. We might also note that, in discussing the statistics of particle motion, all averages are conceptually ensemble averages, carried out over a very large number of similar particle releases. For this reason, we denote mean quantities by braces, as in Eq. (13.83), as opposed to overbars, which have been reserved for time averages. It is understood, however, that when discussing mean properties of the velocity field itself, due to the condition of stationarity, the ensemble average and the time average are identical. The mean displacement can also be computed by ensemble averaging of Eq. (13.84),

$$\langle X_i(t) \rangle = \int_0^t \langle v_i(t') \rangle \, dt' \tag{13.86}$$

where the averaging can be taken inside the integral.

The variance of the displacements is the expected value of the product of X_i and X_j, which is expressed in terms of Q by

$$P_{ij}(t) = \langle X_i(t) X_j(t) \rangle = \int_{-\infty}^{\infty} x_i x_j Q(\mathbf{x}; t) \, d\mathbf{x} \tag{13.87}$$

The diagonal elements $\langle X_i^2(t) \rangle$ are of principal interest since they describe the rate of spreading along each axis. $P_{ii}(t)$ is just $\sigma_i^2(t)$. Using Eq. (13.84) in Eq. (13.87), we obtain (recall Eq. (13.41))

$$P_{ij}(t) = \left\langle \int_0^t v_i(t') \, dt' \int_0^t v_j(t'') \, dt'' \right\rangle$$

$$= \int_0^t \int_0^t \langle v_i(t') v_j(t'') \rangle \, dt' \, dt'' \tag{13.88}$$

The integrand of Eq. (13.88) is defined as the Lagrangian correlation function $R_{ij}(t' - t'')$, so that Eq. (13.88) may be rewritten

$$P_{ij}(t) = \int_0^t \int_0^t R_{ij}(t' - t'') \, dt' \, dt''$$

$$= \int_0^t \int_0^{t-t'} R_{ij}(\zeta) \, d\zeta \, dt' \tag{13.89}$$

By definition $R_{ij}(\zeta) = R_{ji}(-\zeta)$, so that

$$P_{ij}(t) = \int_0^t (t - \zeta) \left[R_{ij}(\zeta) + R_{ji}(\zeta) \right] d\zeta \tag{13.90}$$

We now consider the form of $P_{ij}(t)$ in the two limiting situations, $t \to 0$ and $t \to \infty$. First, for $t \to 0$, $R_{ij}(\zeta) \cong R_{ij}(0) = \langle u_i' u_j' \rangle = \overline{u_i' u_j'}$. Thus,

$$P_{ij}(t) = \overline{u_i' u_j'} t^2 \qquad t \to 0 \tag{13.91}$$

and the dispersion increases as t^2. Next, as $t \to \infty$ we expect the Lagrangian correlation function $R_{ij}(t)$ to approach zero as the motion of the particle becomes uncorrelated with its original velocity. We expect convergence of the following two integrals,

$$\int_0^{\infty} \left[R_{ij}(\zeta) + R_{ji}(\zeta) \right] d\zeta = I_{ij}$$

$$\int_0^{\infty} \zeta \left[R_{ij}(\zeta) + R_{ji}(\zeta) \right] d\zeta = J_{ij}$$

where I_{ij} is proportional to the Lagrangian time scale of the turbulence. Thus, as $t \to \infty$, $P_{ij}(t)$ becomes proportional to t,

$$P_{ij}(t) = I_{ij}t - J_{ij} \tag{13.92}$$

We can obtain these results by a slightly different route. Let us, for example, compute the rate of change of the dispersion $\langle X_i^2(t) \rangle$:

$$
\begin{aligned}
\frac{d}{dt}\langle X_i^2(t) \rangle &= 2\langle X_i(t)v_i(t) \rangle \\
&= 2\left\langle v_i(t)\int_0^t v_i(t')\,dt' \right\rangle \\
&= 2\int_0^t \langle v_i(t)v_i(t') \rangle\,dt' \\
&= 2\int_0^t R_{ii}(t - t')\,dt' \tag{13.93}
\end{aligned}
$$

Integration of Eq. (13.93) with respect to t gives Eq. (13.89).

In summary, we have found that mean-square dispersion of a particle in stationary, homogeneous turbulence has the following dependence on time:

$$
P_{ii}(t) = \begin{cases} \overline{u_i'^2}t^2 & t \to 0 \\ 2K_{ii}t & t \to \infty \end{cases} \tag{13.94}
$$

as we had anticipated by Eqs. (13.44) and (13.45) where

$$K_{ii} = \lim_{t \to \infty} \int_0^t R_{ii}(t - t')\,dt' \tag{13.95}$$

Since $\overline{u_i'^2}$ is proportional to the total turbulent kinetic energy, the total energy of the turbulence is important in the early dispersion. After long times the largest eddies will contribute to R_{ii} and R_{ii} will not go to zero until the particle can escape the influence of the largest eddies. From its definition, K_{ii} has the dimensions of a diffusivity, since as $t \to \infty$,

$$\frac{1}{2}\frac{d\langle X_i^2(t) \rangle}{dt} = K_{ii} \tag{13.96}$$

Now, if we return to Section 13.5 we see that this K_{ii} is precisely the constant eddy diffusivity used in the atmospheric diffusion equation for stationary, homogeneous turbulence. Since the Lagrangian time scale is defined by

$$T_L = \max_i \left[\frac{1}{\overline{u_i'^2}} \int_0^\infty R_{ii}(t)\, dt \right] \tag{13.97}$$

it becomes clear that K theory, with constant K's, should apply only when the diffusion time t is much greater than T_L. Because of large atmospheric eddies, T_L might be quite large. In general, large eddies dominate atmospheric diffusion when diffusion is measured relative to a fixed coordinate system.

It has been recognized that the simple exponential function, $\exp(-t/T_L)$, where t is travel time from the source, appears to approximate $R_{ii}(t)$ rather well (Neumann, 1978; Tennekes, 1979). If

$$R_{ii}(t) = \overline{u_i^2} \exp(-t/T_L) \tag{13.98}$$

then the mean square particle displacement is given by

$$\langle X_i^2(t) \rangle = 2\overline{u_i^2} \int_0^t (t - t') e^{-t'/T_L}\, dt'$$

$$= 2\overline{u_i^2} T_L^2 \left[\frac{t}{T_L} - (1 - e^{-t/T_L}) \right] \tag{13.99}$$

This result is identical to Eq. (13.43) if $b = T_L^{-1}$, which provides a nice connection between the statistical theory of turbulent diffusion and the simple example considered earlier.

13.8. SUMMARY OF ATMOSPHERIC DIFFUSION THEORIES

Turbulent diffusion is concerned with the behavior of individual particles that are supposed to follow faithfully the airflow or, in principle, are simply marked minute elements of the air itself. Because of the inherently random character of atmospheric motions, one can never predict with certainty the distribution of concentration of marked particles emitted from a source. Although the basic equations describing turbulent diffusion are available, there does not exist a single mathematical model that can be used as a practical means of computing atmospheric concentrations over all ranges of conditions.

There are two basic ways of considering the problem of turbulent diffusion, the so-called Eulerian and Lagrangian approaches. The Eulerian method is based on carrying out a material balance over an infinitesimal region fixed in space, whereas the Lagrangian approach is based on considering the meandering of marked fluid particles in the flow. Each approach can be shown to have certain inherent difficulties that render impossible an exact solution for the mean concentration of particles in turbulent flow. For the purposes of practical computation, several approximate theories have been used for calculating mean concentrations of species in turbulence. Two are the K-theory, based on the atmospheric diffusion equation, and the statistical theory, based on the behavior of individual particles in stationary, homogeneous turbulence.

The basic issues of interest with respect to the K-theory are (1) under what conditions on the source configuration and the turbulent field can this theory be applied, and (2) to what extent can the eddy diffusivities be specified in an a priori manner from measured properties of the turbulence. The first question has been addressed in Section 13.4.2. In summary, the spatial and temporal scales of the turbulence should be small in comparison with the corresponding scales of the concentration field.

The statistical theory is concerned with the actual velocities of individual particles in stationary, homogeneous turbulence. Under this assumption the statistics of the motion of one typical particle provides a statistical estimate of the behavior of all particles, and that of two particles an estimate of the behavior of a cluster of particles. In the atmosphere one may expect the cross-wind component (v) of turbulence to be nearly homogeneous since the variations in the scale and intensity of v with height are often small. On the other hand, the vertical velocity component (w) is decidedly inhomogeneous, since characteristically w increases with height above the ground. Thus, the statistical theory should be suitable for describing the spread of a plume in the cross-wind direction regardless of the height but for vertical spread only in the early stages of travel from a source considerably elevated above the ground.

The basic parameter of the statistical theory is the Lagrangian time scale of the turbulence, that is, the time integral of the Lagrangian autocorrelation function. Unfortunately, the Lagrangian time scale is difficult to measure directly, and therefore it would be desirable to determine T_L from the usual fixed-point (Eulerian) turbulence data, a problem which has yet to be solved theoretically. Thus, a rigorous relationship between the Lagrangian and Eulerian time scales of the turbulence, T_L and T_E, is unknown. Several approximate theories lead to the conclusion that T_L/T_E is inversely proportional to the intensity of the turbulence. The relationship $T_L = \beta T_E$, is often used as a rough guide to T_L (Pasquill, 1974).

The deciding factor in judging the validity of a theory for atmospheric diffusion is the comparison of its predictions with experimental data. It must be kept in mind, however, that the theories we have discussed are based on predicting the ensemble mean concentration $\langle c \rangle$, whereas a single experimental observation constitutes only one sample from the hypothetically infinite ensemble of observations from that identical experiment. Thus, it is not to be expected that any one realization should agree precisely with the predicted mean concentration even if the theory used is applicable to the set of conditions under which the experiment has been carried out. Nevertheless, because it is practically impossible to repeat an experiment more than a few times under identical conditions in the atmosphere, one must be content with at most a few experimental realizations when testing any available theory.

APPENDIX

13.A.1. Solution of Eqs. (13.47) to (13.49)

To solve this problem we let $\langle c(x, y, z, t) \rangle = c_x(x, t)c_y(y, t)c_z(z, t)$ with $c_x(x, 0) = S^{1/3}\delta(x)$, $c_y(y, 0) = S^{1/3}\delta(y)$, and $c_z(z, 0) = S^{1/3}\delta(z)$. Then Eq. (13.47) becomes

$$\frac{\partial c_x}{\partial t} + \bar{u}\frac{\partial c_x}{\partial x} = K_{xx}\frac{\partial^2 c_x}{\partial x^2} \tag{13.A.1}$$

$$\frac{\partial c_y}{\partial t} = K_{yy}\frac{\partial^2 c_y}{\partial y^2} \tag{13.A.2}$$

$$\frac{\partial c_z}{\partial t} = K_{zz}\frac{\partial^2 c_z}{\partial z^2} \tag{13.A.3}$$

Each of these equations may be solved by the Fourier transform. We illustrate with Eq. (13.A.1). The Fourier transform of $c_x(x, t)$ is

$$C(\alpha, t) = F\{c_x(x, t)\} = \frac{1}{(2\pi)^{1/2}} \int_{-\infty}^{\infty} c_x(x, t)e^{-i\alpha x}\, dx$$

and thus transforming we obtain

$$\frac{\partial C}{\partial t} + i\alpha\bar{u}C = -\alpha^2 K_{xx}C$$

$$C(\alpha, 0) = \frac{S^{1/3}}{(2\pi)^{1/2}} \tag{13.A.4}$$

The solution of Eq. (13.A.1) is

$$C(\alpha, t) = \frac{S^{1/3}}{(2\pi)^{1/2}} \exp\left[-\left(\alpha^2 K_{xx} + i\alpha\bar{u}\right)t\right]$$

The inverse transform is

$$c_x(x, t) = \frac{1}{(2\pi)^{1/2}} \int_{-\infty}^{\infty} C(\alpha, t)e^{i\alpha x}\, d\alpha$$

Thus,

$$c_x(x,t) = \frac{S^{1/3}}{2\pi} \int_{-\infty}^{\infty} \exp\left[-\left(\alpha^2 K_{xx}t - i\alpha(x - \bar{u}t)\right)\right] d\alpha$$

Completing the square in the exponent,

$$\alpha^2 K_{xx}t - i\alpha(x - \bar{u}t) - \frac{(x - \bar{u}t)^2}{4K_{xx}t} + \frac{(x - \bar{u}t)^2}{4K_{xx}t}$$

$$= \left[\alpha(K_{xx}t)^{1/2} - \frac{i(x - \bar{u}t)}{2(K_{xx}t)^{1/2}}\right]^2 - \frac{(x - \bar{u}t)^2}{4K_{xx}t}$$

Let $\eta = \alpha(K_{xx}t)^{1/2} - i(x - \bar{u}t)/2(K_{xx}t)^{1/2}$ and $d\eta = (K_{xx}t)^{1/2} d\alpha$. Then

$$c_x(x,t) = \frac{S^{1/3}}{2\pi(K_{xx}t)^{1/2}} \exp\left[-\frac{(x - \bar{u}t)^2}{4K_{xx}t}\right] \int_{-\infty}^{\infty} e^{-\eta^2} d\eta$$

the integral equals $\pi^{1/2}$, so

$$c_x(x,t) = \frac{S^{1/3}}{2(\pi K_{xx}t)^{1/2}} \exp\left[-\frac{(x - \bar{u}t)^2}{4K_{xx}t}\right]$$

By the same method

$$c_y(y,t) = \frac{S^{1/3}}{2(\pi K_{yy}t)^{1/2}} \exp\left[-\frac{y^2}{4K_{yy}t}\right]$$

$$c_z(z,t) = \frac{S^{1/3}}{2(\pi K_{zz}t)^{1/2}} \exp\left[-\frac{z^2}{4K_{zz}t}\right]$$

and thus the mean concentration is given by

$$\langle c(x,y,z,t)\rangle = \frac{S}{8(\pi t)^{3/2}(K_{xx}K_{yy}K_{zz})^{1/2}}$$

$$\times \exp\left[-\frac{(x - \bar{u}t)^2}{4K_{xx}t} - \frac{y^2}{4K_{yy}t} - \frac{z^2}{4K_{zz}t}\right] \quad (13.A.5)$$

13.A.2. Solution of Eqs. (13.68)–(13.69)

To solve Eq. (13.68) we begin with the transformation

$$f(x, y, z) = \langle c(x, y, z) \rangle e^{-kx}$$

where $k = \bar{u}/2K$, and Eq. (13.68) becomes

$$\nabla^2 f - k^2 f = \frac{-q}{K} e^{-kx} \delta(x) \delta(y) \delta(z)$$

$$f(x, y, z) = 0 \qquad x, y, z \to \pm\infty$$

First we will solve

$$\nabla_r^2 f - k^2 f = 0$$

where $r^2 = x^2 + y^2 + z^2$. To do so, let $f(r) = g(r)/r$ and

$$\nabla_r^2 f = \frac{1}{r^2} \frac{d}{dr}\left(r^2 \frac{df}{dr}\right) = \frac{1}{r} \frac{d^2 g}{dr^2}$$

so that the equation to be solved is

$$\frac{d^2 g}{dr^2} - k^2 g = 0$$

The solution is

$$g(r) = A_1 e^{kr} + A_2 e^{-kr}$$

Then $A_1 = 0$ satisfies the condition that g is finite as $r \to \infty$, and

$$f(r) = \frac{A}{r} e^{kr}$$

To determine A, we will evaluate

$$\int_V (\nabla_r^2 f - k^2 f)\, dV = -\int_V \frac{q}{K} e^{-kx} \delta(x) \delta(y) \delta(z)\, dV$$

on the sphere with unit radius. The right-hand side is simply $-q/K$. The left-hand side is, using Green's theorem,

$$\int_V (\nabla_r^2 f - k^2 f)\, dV = \int_S \frac{\partial f}{\partial n}\, dS - k^2 \int_V f\, dV$$

On a sphere of unit radius,

$$\int_S \frac{\partial f}{\partial n}\, dS = \int_0^{2\pi} \int_{-\pi}^{\pi} \cos\theta \left(\frac{\partial f}{\partial r}\right)_{r=1} d\theta\, d\phi$$

$$= -4\pi A e^{-k}(k+1)$$

and

$$-\int_V f\, dV = \int_0^1 4\pi r^2 f\, dr = 4\pi A \left[e^{-k}(k+1) - 1 \right]$$

Thus, we obtain $4\pi A = q/K$. Finally,

$$\langle c(x, y, z)\rangle = \frac{q}{4\pi K r} \exp\left[-\frac{\bar{u}(r-x)}{2K} \right]$$

13.A.3. Solution of Eqs. (13.77) to (13.79)

The solution can be carried out by Fourier transform, first with respect to the y-direction and then with respect to the z-direction. If $C(x, \alpha, z) = F_y\{\langle c(x, y, z)\rangle\}$ and $C'(x, \alpha, \beta) = F_z\{C(x, \alpha, z)\}$, then Eq. (13.77) becomes

$$\bar{u}\frac{\partial C'}{\partial x} = -K(\alpha^2 + \beta^2)C'(x, \alpha, \beta) \qquad (13.A.6)$$

The $x = 0$ boundary condition, when transformed doubly, is

$$C'(0, \alpha, \beta) = \frac{q}{2\pi\bar{u}} \qquad (13.A.7)$$

The solution of Eq. (13.A.6) subject to Eq. (13.A.7) is

$$C'(x, \alpha, \beta) = \frac{q}{2\pi\bar{u}} \exp\left[-\frac{Kx}{\bar{u}}(\alpha^2 + \beta^2) \right] \qquad (13.A.8)$$

We must now invert Eq. (13.A.8) twice to return to $\langle c(x, y, z)\rangle$. First

$$C(x, \alpha, z) = \frac{1}{(2\pi)^{1/2}} \int_{-\infty}^{\infty} C'(x, \alpha, \beta)e^{i\beta z}\, d\beta$$

Thus,

$$C(x, \alpha, z) = \frac{q}{(2\pi)^{3/2}\bar{u}} e^{-\alpha^2 Kx/\bar{u}} \int_{-\infty}^{\infty} \exp\left[i\beta z - \frac{Kx\beta^2}{\bar{u}} \right] d\beta \quad (13.A.9)$$

It is now necessary to express the exponential in the integrand as

$$-\left(Kx\beta^2/\bar{u} - i\beta z\right) = -\left[(Kx/\bar{u})^{1/2}\beta - (iz/2)(\bar{u}/Kx)^{1/2}\right]^2 - z^2\bar{u}/4Kx$$

and let $\eta = (Kx/\bar{u})^{1/2}\beta - (iz/2)(\bar{u}/Kx)^{1/2}$. Then Eq. (13.A.9) becomes

$$C(x, \alpha, z) = \frac{q}{(2\pi)^{3/2}\bar{u}}\left(\frac{\bar{u}}{Kx}\right)^{1/2}\exp\left[-\frac{\alpha^2 Kx}{\bar{u}} - \frac{z^2\bar{u}}{4Kx}\right]\int_{-\infty}^{\infty} e^{-\eta^2}\,d\eta$$

Proceeding through identical steps to invert $C(x, \alpha, z)$ to $\langle c(x, y, z)\rangle$, we obtain

$$\langle c(x, y, z)\rangle = \frac{q}{4\pi Kx}\exp\left[-\frac{\bar{u}}{4Kx}(y^2 + z^2)\right] \qquad (13.A.10)$$

REFERENCES

Csanady, G. T. *Turbulent Diffusion in the Environment*, D. Reidel, Dordrecht, Holland (1973).

Lamb, R. G. "Note on Application of K-Theory to Turbulent Diffusion Problems Involving Chemical Reaction," *Atmos. Environ.*, **7**, 257–263 (1973).

Neumann, J. "Some Observations on the Simple Exponential Function as a Lagrangian Velocity Correlation Function in Turbulent Diffusion," *Atmos. Environ.*, **12**, 1965–1968 (1978).

Pasquill, F. *Atmospheric Diffusion*, Second edition, Halsted Press: Wiley, New York (1974).

Taylor, G. I. "Diffusion by Continuous Movements," *Proc. London Math. Soc. Ser. 2*, **20**, 196 (1921).

Tennekes, H. "The Exponential Lagrangian Correlation Function and Turbulent Diffusion in the Inertial Subrange," *Atmos. Environ.*, **13**, 1565–1567 (1979).

PROBLEMS

13.1. As a generalization of Eq. (13.8) we can assume that the particles decay by a first-order reaction. In the presence of first-order decay the probability of finding a given particle at location $\mathbf{x}$ at time t, given that it was at $\mathbf{x}'$ at t', is just the product of two probabilities:

The probability $Q(\mathbf{x}, t|\mathbf{x}', t')$ that the particle will undergo a displacement from $\mathbf{x}'$ to $\mathbf{x}$ from t' to t.

The probability that the particle will not lose its identity by chemical decay during the time interval $t - t'$.

These two events are independent as long as the marked particles in no way influence the fluid motion. Let us now compute the second probability.

First-order decay is equivalent to the condition that the probability that a particle will decay in a time interval dt is proportional to dt. Thus, the probability that a particle will not decay in the small time interval dt is $1 - k\,dt$, where k is the first-order decay constant. To include the case in which k may change with time, we first transform the time coordinate t into the dimensionless value

$$\xi(t) = \int_0^t k(t'')\,dt''$$

The probability that the particle will not decay in a small time interval is then $1 - d\xi(t)$. If we now divide the interval $\xi(t) - \xi(t')$ into n subintervals of length $d\xi$, the probability that the particle will not decay in any of these subintervals is $(1 - d\xi)$. Taking the limit as $d\xi \to 0$, show that Eq. (13.8) becomes

$$\langle c(\mathbf{x}, t) \rangle = \int_{-\infty}^{\infty} \int_{-\infty}^{\infty} \int_{-\infty}^{\infty} Q(\mathbf{x}, t | \mathbf{x}_0, 0) \langle c(\mathbf{x}_0, 0) \rangle$$

$$\times \exp \left[-\int_0^t k(t'')\,dt'' \right] d\mathbf{x}_0 + \int_{-\infty}^{\infty} \int_{-\infty}^{\infty} \int_{-\infty}^{\infty} \int_0^t$$

$$\times Q(\mathbf{x}, t | \mathbf{x}', t') S(\mathbf{x}', t') \exp \left[-\int_{t'}^t k(t'')\,dt'' \right] dt'\,d\mathbf{x}'$$

13.2. Show that Eqs. (13.74)–(13.76) and (13.77)–(13.79) lead to the same solution of the diffusion problem they represent.

13.3. When a cloud of pollutant is deep enough to occupy a substantial fraction of the Ekman layer, its lateral spread will be influenced or possibly dominated by variations in the direction of the mean velocity with height. The mean vertical position of a cloud released at ground level increases at a velocity proportional to the friction velocity u_*. If the thickness of the Ekman layer can be estimated as $0.2u_*/f$, where f is the Coriolis parameter, estimate the distance that a cloud must travel from its source in mid-latitudes for crosswind shear effects to become important.

13.4. Consider a continuous, ground-level crosswind line source of finite length b and strength $S(\mathrm{g\ km^{-1}\ sec^{-1}})$. Assume that conditions are such that the slender plume approximation is applicable.

(a) Taking the origin of the coordinate system as the center of the line, show that the mean ground-level concentration of pollutant at any point downwind of the source is given by

$$\langle c(x, y, 0) \rangle = \frac{S}{(2\pi)^{1/2} \sigma_z \bar{u}} \left[\mathrm{erf} \left(\frac{b/2 - y}{\sqrt{2}\,\sigma_y} \right) + \mathrm{erf} \left(\frac{b/2 + y}{\sqrt{2}\,\sigma_y} \right) \right]$$

(b) For large distances from the source, show that the ground-level concentration along the axis of the plume ($y = 0$) may be approximated by

$$\langle c(x,0,0)\rangle = \frac{Sb}{\pi \sigma_y \sigma_z \bar{u}}$$

(c) The width w of a diffusing plume is often defined as the distance between the two points where the concentration drops to 10 percent of the axial value. For the finite line source, at large enough distances from the source, the line source can be considered a point source. Show that under these conditions σ_y may be determined from a measurement of w from

$$\sigma_y = \frac{w}{4.3}$$

13.5. In this problem we wish to examine two aspects of atmospheric diffusion theory: (1) the slender plume approximation, and (2) surface deposition. To do so, consider an infinitely long, continuously emitting, ground-level crosswind line source of strength q_l. We will assume that the mean concentration is described by the atmospheric diffusion equation,

$$\bar{u}\frac{\partial \langle c\rangle}{\partial x} = K\left(\frac{\partial^2 \langle c\rangle}{\partial x^2} + \frac{\partial^2 \langle c\rangle}{\partial z^2}\right) + q_l \delta(x)\delta(z)$$

$$K\frac{\partial \langle c\rangle}{\partial z} = v_d\langle c\rangle \qquad z = 0$$

$$\langle c(x,z)\rangle = 0 \qquad z \to +\infty \; x = \pm L$$

where the mean velocity $\bar{u}$ and eddy diffusivity K are independent of the height, v_d is a parameter that is proportional to the degree of absorptivity of the surface, the so-called deposition velocity, and L is an arbitrary distance from the source at which the concentration may be assumed to be at background levels. (L is a convenience in the solution and can be made as large as desired to approximate the condition $\langle c\rangle = 0$ as $x \to \pm\infty$.)

(a) It is convenient to place this problem in dimensionless form by defining $X = x/L$, $Z = z/L$, $C(X, Z) = \langle c(x,z)\rangle K/q_l$, $\mathrm{Pe} = \bar{u}L/K$ and $\mathrm{Sh} = v_d L/K$. Show that the dimensionless solution is

$$C(X, Z) = e^{\mathrm{Pe}\,X/2} \sum_{n=1}^{\infty} \left[(\theta_n + \mathrm{Sh})\left(1 + \frac{\sin 2\lambda_n}{2\lambda_n}\right)\right]^{-1} e^{-\theta_n Z}\cos\lambda_n X$$

where $\theta_n^2 = \lambda_n^2 + \mathrm{Pe}^2/4$ and $\lambda_n = [(2n-1)/2]\pi$.

(b)   To explore the slender plume approximation, let us now consider

$$\bar{u}\frac{\partial\langle c\rangle}{\partial x} = K\frac{\partial^2\langle c\rangle}{\partial z^2} + q_l\delta(x)\delta(z)$$

$$K\frac{\partial\langle c\rangle}{\partial z} = v_d\langle c\rangle \qquad z = 0$$

$$\langle c(x,z)\rangle = 0 \qquad z \to +\infty$$

$$\langle c(0,z)\rangle = 0$$

First, express this problem with the source q_l in the $x = 0$ boundary condition and then in the $z = 0$ boundary condition. Solve any one of the three formulations to obtain

$$C(X,Z) = \frac{1}{Pe}\left[\left(\frac{Pe}{\pi X}\right)^{1/2}\exp\left(-\frac{PeZ^2}{4X}\right) - Sh\,\exp\left(Sh\,Z + \frac{Sh^2 X}{Pe}\right)\right.$$

$$\left.\times\,\text{erfc}\left[\left(\frac{X}{Pe}\right)^{1/2}\left(Sh + \frac{PeZ}{2X}\right)\right]\right]$$

(Note that even though the length L does not enter into this problem, we can use it merely to obtain the same dimensionless variables as in the previous problem.)

(c)   We want to compare the two solutions numerically for parameters of interest in air pollution to explore: (1) the effect of diffusion in the X-direction; and (2) the effect of surface deposition. Thus, evaluate the two solutions for the following parameter values:

$$\bar{u} = 1 \text{ m sec}^{-1} \text{ and } 5 \text{ m sec}^{-1}$$

$$K = 1 \text{ m}^2 \text{ sec}^{-1} \text{ and } 10 \text{ m}^2 \text{ sec}^{-1}$$

$$v_d = 0 \text{ and } 1 \text{ cm sec}^{-1}$$

$$L = 1000 \text{ m}$$

Plot $C(X, Z)$ versus Z at a couple of values of X to examine the two effects. Discuss your results.

13.6.   Derive Equation (13.34).

13.7.   Show that Equation (13.37) holds.

FOURTEEN

The Gaussian Plume Equation

We have seen that under certain idealized conditions the mean concentration of a species emitted from a point source has a Gaussian distribution. This fact, although strictly true only in the case of stationary, homogeneous turbulence, serves as the basis for a large class of atmospheric diffusion formulas in common use. The collection of Gaussian-based formulas is sufficiently important in practical application that we devote this chapter to them. The focus of these formulas is the expression for the mean concentration of a species emitted from a continuous, elevated point source, the so-called Gaussian plume equation.

14.1. GAUSSIAN CONCENTRATION DISTRIBUTIONS

The basic Lagrangian expression for the mean concentration is Eq. (13.8),

$$\langle c(x, y, z, t)\rangle = \int_{-\infty}^{\infty} \int_{-\infty}^{\infty} \int_{-\infty}^{\infty} Q(x, y, z, t|x_0, y_0, z_0, t_0)\langle c(x_0, y_0, z_0, t_0)\rangle$$

$$\times dx_0\, dy_0\, dz_0 + \int_{-\infty}^{\infty} \int_{-\infty}^{\infty} \int_{-\infty}^{\infty} \int_{t_0}^{t} Q(x, y, z, t|x', y', z', t')$$

$$\times S(x', y', z', t')\, dt'\, dx'\, dy'\, dz' \tag{14.1}$$

The transition probability density Q expresses physically the probability that a tracer particle that is at x', y', z' at t' will be at x, y, z at t. We showed in Chapter 13 that under conditions of stationary, homogeneous turbulence Q has a Gaussian form. For example, in the case of a mean wind directed along the x-axis, that is, $\bar{v} = \bar{w} = 0$, and an infinite domain, Q is

$$Q(x, y, z, t|x', y', z', t')$$

$$= \frac{1}{(2\pi)^{3/2}\sigma_x\sigma_y\sigma_z}$$

$$\times \exp\left[-\frac{(x - x' - \bar{u}(t - t'))^2}{2\sigma_x^2} - \frac{(y - y')^2}{2\sigma_y^2} - \frac{(z - z')^2}{2\sigma_z^2} \right]$$

$$\tag{14.2}$$

where the variances σ_x^2, σ_y^2, and σ_z^2 are functions of the travel time, $t - t'$.

Up to this point we have considered an infinite domain. For atmospheric applications a boundary at $z = 0$, the earth, is present. Because of the barrier to diffusion at $z = 0$ it is necessary to modify the z-dependence of Q to account for this fact. We can separate out the z-dependence in Eq. (14.2) by writing

$$Q(x, y, z, t|x', y', z', t')$$

$$= \frac{1}{2\pi\sigma_x\sigma_y} \exp\left[-\frac{(x - x' - \bar{u}(t - t'))^2}{2\sigma_x^2} - \frac{(y - y')^2}{2\sigma_y^2} \right] Q_z(z, t|z', t')$$

$$(14.3)$$

To determine the form of $Q_z(z, t|z', t')$, we enumerate the following possibilities:

1. Form of upper boundary condition on z
    (a) $0 \leq z \leq \infty$
    (b) $0 \leq z \leq H$ with no diffusion across $z = H$ (i.e., inversion layer)
2. Type of interaction between the diffusing material and the surface
    (a) Total reflection
    (b) Total absorption
    (c) Partial absorption

For the moment let us continue to consider the vertical domain to be $0 \leq z \leq \infty$.

Total Reflection at $z = 0$. We assume that the presence of the surface at $z = 0$ can be accounted for by adding the concentration resulting from a hypothetical source at $z = -z'$ to that from the source at $z = z'$ in the region $z \geq 0$. Then Q_z assumes the form

$$Q_z(z, t|z', t') = \frac{1}{(2\pi)^{1/2}\sigma_z} \left[\exp\left(-\frac{(z - z')^2}{2\sigma_z^2} \right) + \exp\left(-\frac{(z + z')^2}{2\sigma_z^2} \right) \right]$$

$$(14.4)$$

Total Absorption at $z = 0$. If the earth is a perfect absorber, the concentration of material at $z = 0$ is zero. The form of Q_z can be obtained by the same method of an image source at $-z'$, with the change that we now *subtract* the distribution from the source at $-z'$ from that for the source at $+z'$. The result is

$$Q_z(z, t|z', t') = \frac{1}{(2\pi)^{1/2}\sigma_z}\left[\exp\left(-\frac{(z-z')^2}{2\sigma_z^2}\right) - \exp\left(-\frac{(z+z')^2}{2\sigma_z^2}\right)\right]$$

(14.5)

The case of partial absorption at $z = 0$ cannot be treated by the same image source approach since some particles are reflected and some are absorbed. We will consider this case shortly.

We now turn to the case of a continuous source. The mean concentration from a continuous point source of strength q at height h above the (totally reflecting) earth is given by (it is conventional to let h denote the source height, and we do so henceforth),

$$\langle c(x, y, z)\rangle = \lim_{t \to \infty} \int_0^t \frac{q}{(2\pi)^{3/2}\sigma_x\sigma_y\sigma_z}\exp\left[-\frac{(x-\bar{u}t')^2}{2\sigma_x^2} - \frac{y^2}{2\sigma_y^2}\right]$$

$$\times\left[\exp\left(-\frac{(z-h)^2}{2\sigma_z^2}\right) + \exp\left(-\frac{(z+h)^2}{2\sigma_z^2}\right)\right]dt' \quad (14.6)$$

As usual, we will be interested in the slender plume case, so we evaluate the integral in the limit of $\sigma_x \to 0$. (Recall Eq. (13.67).) The result is:

$$\langle c(x, y, z)\rangle = \frac{q}{2\pi\bar{u}\sigma_y\sigma_z}\exp\left(-\frac{y^2}{2\sigma_y^2}\right)$$

$$\times\left[\exp\left(-\frac{(z-h)^2}{2\sigma_z^2}\right) + \exp\left(-\frac{(z+h)^2}{2\sigma_z^2}\right)\right] \quad (14.7)$$

the so-called *Gaussian plume equation*.

For a totally absorbing surface at $z = 0$,

$$\langle c(x, y, z)\rangle = \frac{q}{2\pi\bar{u}\sigma_y\sigma_z}\exp\left(-\frac{y^2}{2\sigma_y^2}\right)$$

$$\times\left[\exp\left(-\frac{(z-h)^2}{2\sigma_z^2}\right) - \exp\left(-\frac{(z+h)^2}{2\sigma_z^2}\right)\right] \quad (14.8)$$

14.2. DERIVATION OF THE GAUSSIAN PLUME EQUATION AS A SOLUTION OF THE ATMOSPHERIC DIFFUSION EQUATION

We saw in the previous chapter that by assuming constant eddy diffusivities K_{xx}, K_{yy}, and K_{zz}, the solution of the atmospheric diffusion equation has a Gaussian form. Thus, it should be possible to obtain Eqs. (14.7) or (14.8) as a solution of an appropriate form of the atmospheric diffusion equation. More importantly, because of the ease in specifying different physical situations in the boundary conditions for the atmospheric diffusion equation, we want to include those situations that we were unable to handle easily in Section 14.1, namely the existence of an inversion layer at height H and partial absorption at the surface. Readers not concerned with this solution may skip directly to Section 14.3.

Let us begin with the atmospheric diffusion equation with constant eddy diffusivities,

$$\frac{\partial \langle c \rangle}{\partial t} + \bar{u} \frac{\partial \langle c \rangle}{\partial x} = K_{xx} \frac{\partial^2 \langle c \rangle}{\partial x^2} + K_{yy} \frac{\partial^2 \langle c \rangle}{\partial y^2} + K_{zz} \frac{\partial^2 \langle c \rangle}{\partial z^2} + S(x, y, z, t)$$

$$\langle c(x, y, z, 0) \rangle = 0 \tag{14.9}$$

$$\langle c(x, y, z, t) \rangle = 0 \qquad x, y \to \pm\infty$$

For the boundary conditions on z we assume that an impermeable barrier exists at $z = H$,

$$\frac{\partial \langle c \rangle}{\partial z} = 0 \qquad z = H \tag{14.10}$$

The case of an unbounded region $z \geq 0$ is simply obtained by letting $H \to \infty$. To include the case of partial absorption at the surface, we write the $z = 0$ boundary condition as

$$K_{zz} \frac{\partial \langle c \rangle}{\partial z} = v_d \langle c \rangle \qquad z = 0 \tag{14.11}$$

where v_d is a parameter that is proportional to the degree of absorptivity of the surface, the so-called deposition velocity. We will study the properties and specification of v_d in Chapter 16; for now let us treat it merely as a parameter. For total reflection, $v_d = 0$, and for total absorption, $v_d = \infty$.

Solution of Eqs. (14.9) to (14.11). The solution of Eq. (14.9) can be expressed in terms of the Green's function $G(x, y, z, t | x', y', z', t')$ as

$$\langle c(x, y, z, t) \rangle = \int_0^H \int_{-\infty}^{\infty} \int_{-\infty}^{\infty} \int_0^t G(x, y, z, t | x', y', z', t')$$

$$\times S(x', y', z', t) \, dt' \, dx' \, dy' \, dz' \tag{14.12}$$

where Eq. (14.12) is identical to Eq. (14.1) and where G satisfies

$$\frac{\partial G}{\partial t} + \bar{u}\frac{\partial G}{\partial x} = K_{xx}\frac{\partial^2 G}{\partial x^2} + K_{yy}\frac{\partial^2 G}{\partial y^2} + K_{zz}\frac{\partial^2 G}{\partial z^2} \tag{14.13}$$

$$G(x, y, z, 0|x', y', z', 0) = \delta(x - x')\delta(y - y')\delta(z - z')$$

$$G = 0 \qquad x, y \to \pm\infty$$

$$\frac{\partial G}{\partial z} = \beta G \qquad z = 0$$

$$\frac{\partial G}{\partial z} = 0 \qquad z = H$$

where $\beta = v_d/K_{zz}$. Physically, G represents the mean concentration at (x, y, z) at time t resulting from a unit source at (x', y', z') at time t'. First we remove the convection term by the coordinate transformation, $\xi = x - \bar{u}(t - t')$, which converts Eq. (14.13) to

$$\frac{\partial G}{\partial t} = K_{xx}\frac{\partial^2 G}{\partial \xi^2} + K_{yy}\frac{\partial^2 G}{\partial y^2} + K_{zz}\frac{\partial^2 G}{\partial z^2}$$

To obtain G we let

$$G(\xi, y, z, t|\xi', y', z', t') = A(\xi, y, t|\xi', y', t')B(z, t|z', t')$$

where

$$\frac{\partial A}{\partial t} = K_{xx}\frac{\partial^2 A}{\partial \xi^2} + K_{yy}\frac{\partial^2 A}{\partial y^2} \tag{14.14}$$

$$A(\xi, y, 0|\xi', y', 0) = \delta(\xi - \xi')\delta(y - y')$$

$$A(\xi, y, t|\xi', y', t') = 0 \qquad \xi, y \to \pm\infty$$

$$\frac{\partial B}{\partial t} = K_{zz}\frac{\partial^2 B}{\partial z^2} \tag{14.15}$$

$$B(z, 0|z', 0) = \delta(z - z')$$

$$\frac{\partial B}{\partial z} = \beta B \qquad z = 0$$

$$\frac{\partial B}{\partial z} = 0 \qquad z = H$$

We begin with the solution of Eq. (14.14). Using separation of variables, $A(\xi, y, t|\xi', y', t') = A_x(\xi, t|\xi', t')A_y(y, t|y', t')$. The solutions are symmetric,

$$A_x(\xi, t|\xi', t') = \frac{a}{(K_{xx}(t - t'))^{1/2}} \exp\left[-\frac{(\xi - \xi')^2}{4K_{xx}(t - t')} \right]$$

$$A_y(y, t|y', t') = \frac{b}{(K_{yy}(t - t'))^{1/2}} \exp\left[-\frac{(y - y')^2}{4K_{yy}(t - t')} \right]$$

Thus,

$$A(\xi, y, t|\xi', y', t') = \frac{a'}{(K_{xx}K_{yy})^{1/2}(t - t')}$$

$$\times \exp\left[-\frac{(\xi - \xi')^2}{4K_{xx}(t - t')} - \frac{(y - y')^2}{4K_{yy}(t - t')} \right]$$

We determine a' from the initial condition,

$$A(\xi, y, 0|\xi', y', 0) = \delta(\xi - \xi')\delta(y - y')$$

or

$$\frac{a'}{(K_{xx}K_{yy})^{1/2}(t - t')} \int_{-\infty}^{\infty}\int_{-\infty}^{\infty} \exp\left[-\frac{(\xi - \xi')^2}{4K_{xx}(t - t')} \right]$$

$$\times \exp\left[-\frac{(y - y')^2}{4K_{yy}(t - t')} \right] d\xi\, dy$$

$$= \int_{-\infty}^{\infty}\int_{-\infty}^{\infty} \delta(\xi - \xi')\delta(y - y')\, d\xi\, dy$$

which reduces to $a' = 1/4\pi$. Thus,

$$A(\xi, y, t|\xi', y', t') = \frac{1}{4\pi(K_{xx}K_{yy})^{1/2}(t - t')}$$

$$\times \exp\left[-\frac{(\xi - \xi')^2}{4K_{xx}(t - t')} - \frac{(y - y')^2}{4K_{yy}(t - t')} \right] \quad (14.16)$$

Now we proceed to solve Eq. (14.15) to obtain

$$B(z,t|z',t') = \frac{2}{H} \sum_{n=1}^{\infty} \frac{(\lambda_n^2 + \beta^2)\cos[\lambda_n(H-z')]\cos[\lambda_n(H-z)]}{(\lambda_n^2 + \beta^2) + \beta}$$

$$\times \exp[-\lambda_n^2 K_{zz}(t-t')] \tag{14.17}$$

where the λ_n are the roots of

$$\lambda_n \tan \lambda_n H = \beta$$

In the case of a perfectly reflecting surface, $\beta = 0$, and

$$B(z,t|z',t') = \frac{2}{H} \sum_{n=1}^{\infty} \cos[\lambda_n(H-z')]\cos[\lambda_n(H-z)]\exp[-\lambda_n^2 K_{zz}(t-t')]$$

where $\sin \lambda_n H = 0$. This result can be simplified somewhat to

$$B(z,t|z',t') = \frac{2}{H} \sum_{n=0}^{\infty} \cos\left(\frac{n\pi z}{H}\right)\cos\left(\frac{n\pi z'}{H}\right)\exp\left[-\left(\frac{n\pi}{H}\right)^2 K_{zz}(t-t')\right]$$

$$\tag{14.18}$$

The desired solution for $G(x,y,z,t|x',y',z',t')$ is obtained by combining the expressions for $A(\xi,y,t|\xi',y',t')$ and $B(z,t|z',t')$. In the case of a totally reflecting earth, we have

$$G(\xi,y,z,t|\xi',y',z',t') = \frac{1}{2\pi H(K_{xx}K_{yy})^{1/2}(t-t')}$$

$$\times \sum_{n=0}^{\infty} \cos\left(\frac{n\pi z}{H}\right)\cos\left(\frac{n\pi z'}{H}\right)$$

$$\times \exp\left[-\left(\frac{n\pi}{H}\right)^2 K_{zz}(t-t')\right]$$

$$\times \exp\left[-\frac{(\xi-\xi')^2}{4K_{xx}(t-t')} - \frac{(y-y')^2}{4K_{yy}(t-t')}\right]$$

$$\tag{14.19}$$

As usual, we are interested in neglecting diffusion in the x-direction as compared with convection, that is, the slender plume approximation. We could return to the original problem neglecting the term $\partial^2 \langle c \rangle / \partial x^2$ in Eq. (14.9) and repeat the solution. We can also work with Eq. (14.19) and let $K_{xx} \to 0$. To do so return to Eq. (14.16), and let $\sigma_x^2 = 2K_{xx}(t - t')$. Using Eq. (13.67) to take the limit of the x-term as $\sigma_x \to 0$,

$$
\begin{aligned}
G(x, y, z, t|x', y', z', t') = \sum_{n=0}^{\infty} & \left\{ \frac{2}{H} \cos\left(\frac{n\pi z}{H} \right) \cos\left(\frac{n\pi z'}{H} \right) \right. \\
& \left. \times \exp\left[-\left(\frac{n\pi}{H} \right)^2 K_{zz}(t - t') \right] \right\} \\
& \times \frac{1}{2\left(\pi K_{yy}(t - t') \right)^{1/2}} \exp\left[-\frac{(y - y')^2}{4K_{yy}(t - t')} \right] \\
& \times \delta(x - x' - \bar{u}(t - t'))
\end{aligned}
\tag{14.20}
$$

Now we consider a continuous point source of strength q at $(0, 0, h)$. The continuous source solution is obtained from the unsteady solution from

$$
\begin{aligned}
\langle c(x, y, z) \rangle = \lim_{t \to \infty} \int_0^H \int_{-\infty}^{\infty} \int_{-\infty}^{\infty} \int_0^t G(x, y, z, t|x', y', z', t') \\
\times q\delta(x')\,\delta(y')\,\delta(z' - h)\,dt'\,dx'\,dy'\,dz'
\end{aligned}
$$

The solution is illustrated for the case of a totally reflecting earth. Using Eq. (14.20) and carrying out the integration, we obtain

$$
\begin{aligned}
\langle c(x, y, z) \rangle = \frac{q}{\left(\pi K_{yy} \right)^{1/2} H} \sum_{n=0}^{\infty} \cos\left(\frac{n\pi z}{H} \right) \cos\left(\frac{n\pi h}{H} \right) \int_0^{\infty} \frac{1}{(t - t')^{1/2}} \\
\times \exp\left[-\frac{y^2}{4K_{yy}(t - t')} -\left(\frac{n\pi}{H} \right)^2 K_{zz}(t - t') \right] \\
\times \delta(x - \bar{u}(t - t'))\,dt'
\end{aligned}
$$

Evaluating the integral,

$$
\begin{aligned}
\langle c(x, y, z) \rangle = \frac{q}{\left(\pi K_{yy} \right)^{1/2} H\bar{u}} \sum_{n=0}^{\infty} \cos\left(\frac{n\pi z}{H} \right) \cos\left(\frac{n\pi h}{H} \right) \\
\times \left\{ \frac{1}{(x/\bar{u})^{1/2}} \exp\left[-\frac{y^2}{4K_{yy}x/\bar{u}} -\left(\frac{n\pi}{H} \right)^2 K_{zz}x/\bar{u} \right] \right\}
\end{aligned}
\tag{14.21}
$$

This is the expression for the steady state concentration resulting from a continuous point source located at $(0, 0, h)$ between impermeable, nonabsorbing boundaries separated by a distance H when diffusion in the direction of the mean flow is neglected.

Finally, we wish to obtain the result when $H \rightarrow \infty$, that is, only one bounding surface at a distance h from the source. Let

$$\sigma_y^2 = 2K_{yy}x/\bar{u} \qquad \sigma_z^2 = 2K_{zz}x/\bar{u}$$

and Eq. (14.21) can be expressed as

$$\langle c(x, y, z) \rangle = \frac{2q}{(2\pi)^{1/2}\bar{u}\sigma_y H} \sum_{n=0}^{\infty} \cos\left(\frac{n\pi z}{H}\right)$$

$$\times \cos\left(\frac{n\pi h}{H}\right) \exp\left[-\frac{y^2}{2\sigma_y^2} - \left(\frac{n\pi}{H}\right)^2 \frac{\sigma_z^2}{2}\right]$$

Now let $H \rightarrow \infty$.

$$\langle c(x, y, z) \rangle = \frac{2q}{(2\pi)^{1/2}\bar{u}\sigma_y} \exp\left[-\frac{y^2}{2\sigma_y^2}\right]$$

$$\times \int_0^{\infty} \cos(\pi z/H)\cos(\pi h/H)\exp\left[-\frac{(\pi\sigma_x)^2}{2H^2}\right] d(1/H)$$

Now,

$$\cos(\pi z/H)\cos(\pi h/H) = 1/2[\cos(\pi(z+h)/H) + \cos(\pi(z-h)/H)]$$

and

$$\langle c(x, y, z) \rangle = \frac{q}{(2\pi)^{1/2}\bar{u}\sigma_y} \exp\left[-\frac{y^2}{2\sigma_y^2}\right]$$

$$\times \left\{ \int_0^{\infty} \cos[\pi(z+h)/H]\exp\left[-\frac{(\pi\sigma_z)^2}{2H^2}\right] d(1/H) \right.$$

$$\left. + \int_0^{\infty} \cos[\pi(z-h)/H]\exp\left[-\frac{(\pi\sigma_z)^2}{2H^2}\right] d(1/H) \right\}$$

The integrals can be evaluated with the aid of tables* to produce Eq. (14.7).

14.3. SUMMARY OF GAUSSIAN POINT SOURCE DIFFUSION FORMULAS

The various point source diffusion formulas we have derived are summarized in Table 14.1.

*Note that

$$\int_0^{\infty} e^{-\alpha x^2}\cos\beta x\, dx = 1/2(\pi/\alpha)^{1/2}\exp(-\beta^2/4\alpha)$$

TABLE 14.1. Point Source Gaussian Diffusion Formulas

Mean Concentration	Assumptions

Gaussian puff formula

$$\langle c(x,y,z,t)\rangle = \frac{S}{(2\pi)^{3/2}\sigma_x\sigma_y\sigma_z}\exp\left[-\frac{(x-x'-\bar{u}(t-t'))^2}{2\sigma_x^2} - \frac{(y-y')^2}{2\sigma_y^2}\right]$$

$$\times\left[\exp\left(-\frac{(z-z')^2}{2\sigma_z^2}\right) + \exp\left(-\frac{(z+z')^2}{2\sigma_z^2}\right)\right]$$

Total reflection at $z = 0$

$\bar{\mathbf{u}} = (\bar{u},0,0)$

$S = S\delta(x-x')\,\delta(y-y')\,\delta(z-z')\,\delta(t-t')$

$0 \leq z \leq \infty$

Gaussian puff formula

$$\langle c(x,y,z,t)\rangle = \frac{S}{(2\pi)^{3/2}\sigma_x\sigma_y\sigma_z}\exp\left[-\frac{(x-x'-u(t-t'))^2}{2\sigma_x^2} - \frac{(y-y')^2}{2\sigma_y^2}\right]$$

$$\times\left[\exp\left(-\frac{(z-z')^2}{2\sigma_z^2}\right) - \exp\left(-\frac{(z+z')^2}{2\sigma_z^2}\right)\right]$$

Total absorption at $z = 0$

$\bar{\mathbf{u}} = (\bar{u},0,0)$

$S = S\delta(x-x')\,\delta(y-y')\,\delta(z-z')\,\delta(t-t')$

$0 \leq z \leq \infty$

Gaussian puff formula

$$\langle c(x,y,z,t)\rangle = \frac{S}{4\pi\sqrt{K_{xx}K_{yy}}\,(t-t')}\exp\left[-\frac{(x-x'-\bar{u}(t-t'))^2}{4K_{xx}(t-t')} - \frac{(y-y')^2}{4K_{yy}(t-t')}\right]$$

$$\times\frac{2}{H}\sum_{n=0}^{\infty}\cos\lambda_n z\cos\lambda_n z'\exp[-\lambda_n^2 K_{zz}(t-t')]$$

Total reflection at $z = 0$

$\bar{\mathbf{u}} = (\bar{u},0,0)$

$S = S\delta(x-x')\,\delta(y-y')\,\delta(z-z')\,\delta(t-t')$

$0 \leq z \leq H$

$$\lambda_n = \frac{n\pi}{H} \qquad \sigma_y^2 = 2K_{yy}(t-t') \qquad \sigma_z^2 = 2K_{zz}(t-t')$$

$$\sigma_x^2 = 2K_{xx}(t-t')$$

Gaussian puff formula

$$\langle c(x,y,z,t)\rangle = \frac{S}{4\sqrt{K_{xx}K_{yy}}(t-t')}\exp\left[-\frac{(x-x'-\bar{u}(t-t'))^2}{4K_{xx}(t-t')} - \frac{(y-y')^2}{4K_{yy}(t-t')}\right]$$

$$\times \frac{2}{H}\sum_{n=1}^{\infty}\frac{(\lambda_n^2+\beta^2)\cos[\lambda_n(H-z')]\cos[\lambda_n(H-z)]}{(\lambda_n^2+\beta^2)+\beta}$$

$$\times \exp[-\lambda_n^2 K_{zz}(t-t')]$$

$$\lambda_n\tan\lambda_n H = \beta$$

$$\beta = v_d/K_{zz}$$

$$\sigma_x^2 = 2K_{xx}(t-t')$$

$$\sigma_y^2 = 2K_{yy}(t-t')$$

$$\sigma_z^2 = 2K_{zz}(t-t')$$

Partial absorption at $z = 0$

$\bar{\mathbf{u}} = (u,0,0)$

$S = S\delta(x-x')\,\delta(y-y')\,\delta(z-z')\,\delta(t-t')$

$0 \leq z \leq H$

Gaussian plume formula

$$\langle c(x,y,z)\rangle = \frac{q}{2\pi\bar{u}\sigma_y\sigma_z}\exp\left(-\frac{y^2}{2\sigma_y^2}\right)\left[\exp\left(-\frac{(z-h)^2}{2\sigma_z^2}\right)+\exp\left(-\frac{(z+h)^2}{2\sigma_z^2}\right)\right]$$

Total reflection at $z = 0$

$\bar{\mathbf{u}} = (u,0,0)$

$S = q\delta(x)\,\delta(y)\,\delta(z-h)$

Slender plume approximation

$0 \leq z \leq \infty$

Gaussian plume formula

$$\langle c(x,y,z)\rangle = \frac{q}{2\pi\bar{u}\sigma_y\sigma_z}\exp\left(-\frac{y^2}{2\sigma_y^2}\right)\left[\exp\left(-\frac{(z-h)^2}{2\sigma_z^2}\right)-\exp\left(-\frac{(z+h)^2}{2\sigma_z^2}\right)\right]$$

Total absorption at $z = 0$

$\bar{\mathbf{u}} = (\bar{u},0,0)$

$S = q\delta(x)\,\delta(y)\,\delta(z-h)$

Slender plume approximation

$0 \leq z \leq \infty$

Gaussian plume formula

$$\langle c(x,y,z)\rangle = \frac{q}{\sqrt{2\pi}\,\bar{u}\sigma_y H}\sum_{n=0}^{\infty}\exp\left(\frac{n\pi z}{H}\right)\cos\left(\frac{n\pi h}{H}\right)$$

$$\times \exp\left[-\left(\frac{y^2}{2\sigma_y^2}\right)-\left(\frac{n\pi}{H}\right)^2\frac{\sigma_z^2}{2}\right]$$

Total reflection at $z = 0$

$\bar{\mathbf{u}} = (\bar{u},0,0)$

$S = q\delta(x)\,\delta(y)\,\delta(z-h)$

$0 \leq z \leq H$

571

14.4. DISPERSION PARAMETERS IN GAUSSIAN MODELS

We have derived several Gaussian-based models for estimating the mean concentration resulting from point source releases of material. We have noted that the conditions under which the equation is valid are highly idealized and therefore that it should not be expected to be applicable to very many actual ambient situations. Because of its simplicity, however, the Gaussian plume equation has been applied widely (U.S. Environmental Protection Agency, 1980). The justification for these applications is that the dispersion parameters σ_y and σ_z used have been derived from concentrations measured in actual atmospheric diffusion experiments under conditions approximating those of the application. This section is devoted to a summary of several results available for estimating Gaussian dispersion coefficients.

14.4.1. Correlations for σ_y and σ_z Based on Similarity Theory

As we noted in Section 13.7, the variances of the mean plume dimensions can be expressed in terms of the motion of single particles released from the source. (At a *particular instant* the plume outline is defined by the statistics of the trajectories of two particles released simultaneously at the source. We have not considered the two-particle problem here.) In an effort to overcome the practical difficulties associated with using Eq. (13.90) to obtain results for σ_y and σ_z, Pasquill (1971) suggested an alternate definition that retained the essential features of Taylor's statistical theory but which is more amenable to parameterization in terms of readily measured Eulerian quantities. As adopted by Draxler (1976), American Meteorological Society (1977), and Irwin (1979), the Pasquill representation leads to

$$\sigma_y = \sigma_v t F_y \tag{14.22}$$

$$\sigma_z = \sigma_w t F_z \tag{14.23}$$

where σ_v and σ_w are the standard deviations of the wind velocity fluctuations in the y- and z-directions, respectively, and F_y and F_z are universal functions of a set of parameters that specify the characteristics of the atmospheric boundary layer. The exact forms of F_y and F_z are to be determined from data.

The variables on which F_y and F_z are assumed to depend are the friction velocity u_*, the Monin-Obukhov length L, the Coriolis parameter f, the mixed layer depth z_i, the convective velocity scale w_*, the surface roughness z_0, and the height of pollutant release above the ground h.*

---

*As in Section 12.7, it is conventional when referring to unstable conditions to represent the depth of the unstable, or mixed, layer by z_i. From a mathematical point of view in terms of the equations for mean concentration z_i is identical to H, the height of an elevated layer impermeable to diffusion.

The variances σ_y^2 and σ_z^2 are therefore treated as empirical dispersion coefficients, the functional forms of which are determined by matching the Gaussian solution to data. In that way, σ_y and σ_z actually compensate for deviations from stationary, homogeneous conditions that are inherent in the assumed Gaussian distribution.

Of the two standard deviations, σ_y and σ_z, more is known about σ_y. First, most of the experiments from which σ_y and σ_z values are inferred involve ground level measurements. Such measurements provide an adequate indication of σ_y, whereas vertical concentration distributions are needed to determine σ_z. Also, the Gaussian expression for vertical concentration distribution is known not to be obeyed for ground-level releases, so the fitting of a measured vertical distribution to a Gaussian form is considerably more difficult than that for the horizontal distribution where lateral symmetry and an approximate Gaussian form are good assumptions.

For lateral dispersion Irwin (1979) developed expressions for σ_v based on the work of Deardorff and Willis (1975), Draxler (1976), and Nieuwstadt and van Duuren (1979),

$$\sigma_v = \begin{cases} 1.78u_*[1 + 0.059(-z_i/L)]^{1/3} & z_i/L < 0 \\ 1.78u_* & z_i/L \geq 0 \end{cases} \qquad (14.24)$$

Irwin (1979), based on the work of Panofsky et al. (1977) and Nieuwstadt (1980), proposed the following form for F_y

$$F_y = \begin{cases} [1 + (t/T_i)^{1/2}]^{-1}; \ T_i^{-1} = \dfrac{2.5u_*}{z_i}[1 + 0.0013(-z_i/L)]^{1/3} & \dfrac{z_i}{L} \leq 0 \\ [1 + 0.9(t/T_0)]^{-1}; \ T_0^{-1} = 1.001 & \dfrac{z_i}{L} > 0 \end{cases}$$

$$(14.25)$$

We note that Eq. (14.22) when combined with Eqs. (14.24)–(14.25) possess the same limiting behavior as the statistical theory; that is, $\sigma_y \approx t$ as $t \to 0$ and $\sigma_y \approx t^{1/2}$ as $t \to \infty$.

The case of unstable or convective conditions is a special one in determining atmospheric dispersion. Since under convective conditions the most energetic eddies in the mixed layer scale with z_i, the time scale relevant to dispersion is z_i/w_*. This time scale is therefore roughly the time needed after release for material to become well mixed through the depth of the mixed layer.

A wide range of field and laboratory measurements on vertical wind velocity fluctuations under unstable conditions can be represented by $\sigma_w = w_* G(z/z_i)$ (Irwin, 1979) where

$$G(z/z_i) = \begin{cases} 1.342(z/z_i)^{0.333} & z/z_i < 0.03 \\ 0.763(z/z_i)^{0.175} & 0.03 < z/z_i < 0.40 \\ 0.722(1 - z/z_i)^{0.207} & 0.40 < z/z_i < 0.96 \\ 0.37 & z/z_i > 0.96 \end{cases} \qquad (14.26)$$

Under neutral and stable conditions the formulation for σ_w developed by Binkowski (1979) can be used,

$$\sigma_w = u_* \left[\frac{\phi_m(z/L) - z/L}{3kf_m} \right]^{1/3} \qquad z/L \geq 0 \qquad (14.27)$$

where from Eq. (12.75)

$$\phi_m(z/L) = 1 + 4.7z/L \qquad (14.28)$$

and where

$$f_m = \begin{cases} 0.4\left[1 + 3.9z/L - 0.25(z/L)^2\right] & z/L \leq 2 \\ 0.4[6.78 + 2.39(z/L - 2)] & z/L > 2 \end{cases} \qquad (14.29)$$

The next step to complete parameterization of the vertical dispersion coefficients is to specify F_z. Between neutral conditions and $-z_i/L < 0$, Irwin (1979) gives an interpolation formula that we do not reproduce here. Draxler (1976) developed the following results for F_z under neutral and stable conditions,

$$F_z = \begin{cases} \left[1 + 0.9(t/T_0)^{1/2}\right]^{-1} & z < 50 \text{ m} \\ \left[1 + 0.945(t/T_0)^{0.8}\right]^{-1} & z \geq 50 \text{ m} \end{cases} \qquad (14.30)$$

Both expressions require specification of the characteristic time T_0. While an initial estimate of 50 seconds was given by Draxler, Irwin (1979) proposed additional values of T_0.

14.4.2. Correlations for σ_y and σ_z Based on Pasquill Stability Classes

The correlations for σ_y and σ_z in the previous subsection require knowledge of atmospheric variables that may not be available. In that case, one needs correlations for σ_y and σ_z based on readily available ambient data. The Pasquill stability categories A through F introduced in Section 12.6 provide a basis for such correlations.

The most widely used σ_y and σ_z correlations based on the Pasquill stability classes have been those developed by Gifford (1961). The correlations, commonly referred to as the Pasquill–Gifford curves, appear in Figures 14.1 and 14.2.

For use in dispersion formulas it is convenient to have analytical expressions for σ_y and σ_z as functions of x. Many of the empirically determined

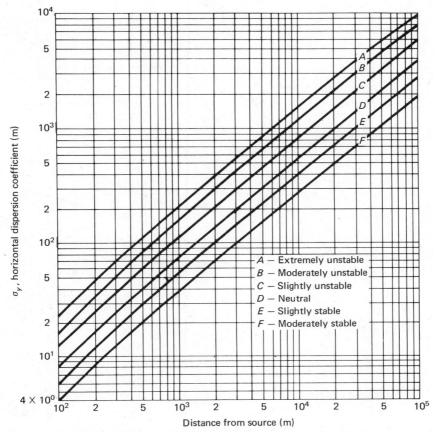

Figure 14.1. Correlations for σ_y based on the Pasquill stability classes A–F (Gifford, 1961). These are the so-called Pasquill-Gifford curves.

forms can be represented by the power-law expressions,

$$\sigma_y = R_y x^{r_y} \tag{14.31}$$

$$\sigma_z = R_z x^{r_z} \tag{14.32}$$

where R_y, R_z, r_y, and r_z depend on the stability class and the averaging time. Some commonly used dispersion coefficients, including those of Pasquill–Gifford (P–G), are summarized in Table 14.2. Both the ASME and Klug dispersion coefficients are expressible by Eqs. (14.31) and (14.32). Although the σ_y correlation for the P–G coefficients is expressible in the form Eq. (14.31),

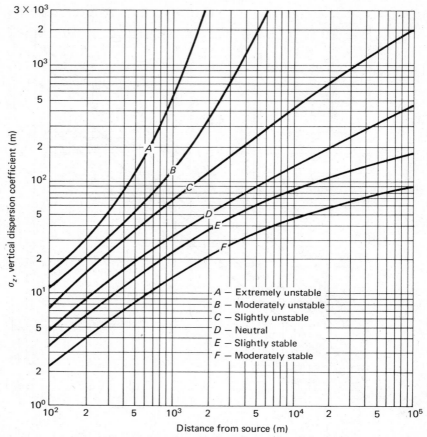

Figure 14.2. Correlations for σ_z based on the Pasquill stability classes A–F (Gifford, 1961). These are the so-called Pasquill-Gifford curves.

that for σ_z requires a three-parameter form,*

$$\sigma_z = \exp\left[I_z + J_z \ln x + K_z (\ln x)^2\right] \qquad (14.33)$$

For completeness we also give σ_y in this form in Table 14.2 for the P–G correlations. The three sets of coefficients in Table 14.2 are based on different data. In choosing a set for a particular application, one should attempt to use

*There are points of controversy surrounding the P–G coefficients, including the stack heights at which they apply and the downwind distances to which they extend. Regardless of their technical merits, the P–G coefficients have been incorporated (with and without modifications) into computer programs developed by and endorsed by the U.S. Environmental Protection Agency. Note that some of these programs conservatively assume that the P–G coefficients are for an averaging time of one hour despite the fact that the true P–G averaging time is about ten minutes.

TABLE 14.2. Coefficients in Gaussian Plume Dispersion Parameter Correlations[a]

$$\sigma_y(x) = R_y x^{r_y} \qquad \sigma_z(x) = R_x x^{r_z}$$

$$\sigma_y(x) = \exp\left[I_y + J_y \ln x + K_y(\ln x)^2\right]$$

$$\sigma_z(x) = \exp\left[I_z + J_z \ln x + K_z(\ln x)^2\right]$$

Source	Averaging Time Min	Coefficient	Stability Class					
			A	B	C	D	E	F
Pasquill–Gifford (Turner, 1969; (Martin, 1976)	10	R_y	0.443	0.324	0.216	0.141	0.105	0.071
		r_y	0.894	0.894	0.894	0.894	0.894	0.894
ASME (1973)	60	R_y	0.40	0.36		0.32		0.31
		r_y	0.91	0.86		0.78		0.71
		R_z	0.40	0.33		0.22		0.06
		r_z	0.91	0.86		0.78		0.71
Klug (1969)	10	R_y	0.469	0.306	0.230	0.219	0.237	0.273
		r_y	0.903	0.885	0.855	0.764	0.691	0.594
		R_z	0.017	0.072	0.076	0.140	0.217	0.262
		r_z	1.380	1.021	0.879	0.727	0.610	0.500
Pasquill–Gifford (Turner, 1969)	10	I_y	−1.104	−1.634	−2.054	−2.555	−2.754	−3.143
		J_y	0.9878	1.0350	1.0231	1.0423	1.0106	1.0148
		K_y	−0.0076	−0.0096	−0.0076	−0.0087	−0.0064	−0.0070
		I_z	4.679	−1.999	−2.341	−3.186	−3.783	−4.490
		J_z	−1.7172	0.8752	0.9477	1.1737	1.3010	1.4024
		K_z	0.2770	0.0136	−0.0020	−0.0316	−0.0450	−0.0540

[a]Application restricted to downwind distances not exceeding 10 km (Hanna et al., 1982).

577

that set most representative of the conditions of interest. (See Gifford (1976), Weber (1976), AMS Workshop (1977), Doran et al. (1978), Sedefian and Bennett (1980), and Hanna et al. (1982).)

14.5. PLUME RISE

In order to ensure that waste gases emitted from stacks will rise above the top of the chimney, the gases are usually released at temperatures hotter than the ambient air and are emitted with considerable initial momentum. Since the maximum mean ground-level concentration of effluents from an elevated point source depends roughly on the inverse square of the effective stack height, the amount of plume rise obtained is an important factor in reducing ground-level concentrations. The effective stack height is taken to be the sum of the actual stack height h_s and the plume rise Δh, defined as the height at which the plume becomes passive and subsequently follows the ambient air motion,

$$h = h_s + \Delta h \tag{14.34}$$

The behavior of a plume is affected by a number of parameters, including the initial source conditions (exit velocity and difference between the plume temperature and that of the air), the stratification of the atmosphere, and the wind speed. Based on the initial source conditions, plumes can be categorized in the following manner:

Buoyant plume:	Initial buoyancy $\gg$ initial momentum
Forced plume:	Initial buoyancy $\simeq$ initial momentum
Jet:	Initial buoyancy $\ll$ initial momentum

We shall deal here with buoyant and forced plumes only. Our interest is in predicting the rise of both buoyant and forced plumes in calm and windy, thermally stratified atmospheres.

Characterization of plume rise in terms of the exhaust gas properties and the ambient atmospheric state is a complex problem. The most detailed approach involves solving the coupled mass, momentum, and energy conservation equations. This approach is generally not used in routine calculations because of its complexity. An alternate approach, introduced by Morton et al. (1956), is to consider the integrated form of the conservation equations across a section normal to the plume trajectory. (See, for example, Schatzmann (1979) and Fischer et al. (1979).)

Table 14.3 presents a summary of several available plume rise formulas expressed in the form,

$$\Delta h = \frac{E x^b}{\bar{u}^a} \tag{14.35}$$

TABLE 14.3. Summary of Several Plume Rise Formulas Expressed in the Form[d]

$$\Delta h = \frac{Ex^b}{\bar{u}^a}$$

Reference	Atmospheric Stability	a	b	E	Conditions
Plumes dominated by buoyancy forces					
ASME (1973)	Neutral and unstable	1	0	$7.4(Fh_s^2)^{1/3}$	
	Stable	1/3	0	$2.9(F/S_1)^{1/3}$	
Briggs (1969, 1971, 1974)	Neutral and unstable	1	2/3	$1.6F^{1/3}$	$F < 55,\ x < 49F^{5/8}$
		1	0	$21.4F^{3/4}$	$F < 55,\ x \geq 49F^{5/8}$
		1	2/3	$1.6F^{1/3}$	$F \geq 55,\ x < 119F^{2/5}$
		1	0	$38.7F^{3/5}$	$F \geq 55,\ x \geq 119F^{2/5}$
	Stable[a]	1/3	0	$2.4(F/S_2)^{1/3}$	
		0	0	$5F^{1/4}S_2^{-3/8}$	
		1	2/3	$1.6F^{1/3}$	
Plumes dominated by momentum forces					
ASME (1973)	All	1.4	0	$dV_s^{1.4}$	$V_s > 10\text{ m sec}^{-1}$
					$V_s > \bar{u}$
					$\Delta T < 50\text{ K}$
Briggs (1969)	Neutral[b]	2/3	1/3	$1.44(dV_s)^{2/3}$	$V_s/\bar{u} \geq 4$
		1	0	$3dV_s$	$V_s/\bar{u} \geq 4$

Nomenclature for Table 14.3

d = stack diameter, m
F = buoyancy flux parameter, $gd^2V_s(T_s - T_a)/4T_s$, $\text{m}^4\text{ sec}^{-3}$
g = acceleration of gravity, 9.807 m sec^{-2}
p = atmospheric pressure, kPa
p_0 = 101.3 kPa
$S_1 = (g\,\partial\theta/\partial z/T_a)(p/p_0)^{0.29}$, sec^{-2}
$S_2 = (g\,\partial\theta/\partial z)/T_a$, sec$^{-2 c}$
T_a = ambient temperature at stack height, K
T_s = stack exit temperature at stack height, K
$\Delta T = T_s - T_a$
V_s = stack exist velocity, m sec^{-1}

[a] Of these formulas for stable conditions, use the one that predicts the least plume rise.
[b] Of the two formulas for neutral conditions, use the one that predicts the least plume rise.
[c] If the appropriate field data are not available to estimate S_1 and S_2, Table 14.4 can be used.
[d] For further information we refer the reader to Hanna et at. (1982).

TABLE 14.4. Relationship Between Pasquill–Gifford Stability Classes and Temperature Stratification

Stability Class	Ambient Temperature Gradient $\partial T/\partial z$ (°C/100 m)	Potential Temperature Gradient[a] $\partial\theta/\partial z$ (°C/100 m)
A (extremely unstable)	< −1.9	< −0.9
B (moderately unstable)	−1.9 to −1.7	−0.9 to −0.7
C (slightly unstable)	−1.7 to −1.5	−0.7 to −0.5
D (neutral	−1.5 to −0.5	−0.5 to 0.5
E (slightly stable)	−0.5 to 1.5	0.5 to 2.5
F (moderately stable)	> 1.5	> 2.5

[a]Calculated by assuming $\partial\theta/\partial z = \partial T/\partial z + \Gamma$, where Γ is the adiabatic lapse rate, 0.986°C/100 m.

14.6. ANALYTICAL PROPERTIES OF THE GAUSSIAN PLUME EQUATION

When material is emitted from a single elevated stack, the resulting ground-level concentration exhibits maxima with respect to both downwind distance and wind speed. Both directly below the stack, where the plume has not yet touched the ground, and far downwind, where the plume has become very dilute, the concentrations approach zero; therefore, a maximum ground-level concentration occurs at some intermediate distance. Both at very high wind speeds, when the plume is rapidly diluted, and at very low wind speeds, when plume rise proceeds relatively unimpeded, the contribution to the ground-level concentration is essentially zero; therefore, a maximum occurs at some intermediate wind speed.

To investigate the properties of the maximum ground-level concentration with respect to distance from the source and wind speed, we begin with the Gaussian plume equation evaluated along the plume centerline ($y = 0$) at the ground ($z = 0$),

$$\langle c(x,0,0)\rangle = \frac{q}{\pi \bar{u}\sigma_y\sigma_z}\exp\left(-\frac{h^2}{2\sigma_z^2}\right) \tag{14.36}$$

The maximum in $\langle c(x,0,0)\rangle$ arises because of the x-dependence of σ_y, σ_z, and h, as parameterized for example by Eqs. (14.31), (14.32), (14.34), and (14.35). As a buoyant plume rises from its source, the effect of the wind is to bend it over until it becomes level at some distance x_f from the source. Wind speed $\bar{u}$ enters the expression for the ground-level concentration through two terms having opposite effects. First, $\langle c(x,0,0)\rangle$ is proportional to $\bar{u}^{-1}$, such that the lighter the wind the larger is the ground-level concentration. Second, the plume rise Δh is inversely proportional to $\bar{u}^a$, such that the lighter the wind, the higher the plume rise and the smaller is the ground-level concentration. Thus a "worst" wind speed exists at which the ground-level concentration is a maximum at any downwind location. This maximum is different from the largest ground-level concentration that is achieved as a function of downwind distance for any given wind speed. The fact that $\langle c(x, 0, 0) \rangle$ depends on both x and $\bar{u}$ suggests that one may find simultaneously the wind speed and distance at which the highest possible ground-level concentration may occur, the so-called critical concentration. In computing these various maxima, there are two regimes of interest. The first is the region of $x < x_f$ where the plume has not reached its final height, and the second is $x \geq x_f$ when the plume has reached its final height. The latter case corresponds to $b = 0$ in the formula for the plume rise.

We want to calculate the location x_m of the maximum ground-level concentration for any given wind speed. By differentiating Eq. (14.36) with respect to x and setting the resulting equation equal to zero we find

$$-\frac{1}{\sigma_y}\frac{d\sigma_y}{dx} - \frac{1}{\sigma_z}\frac{d\sigma_z}{dx} + \frac{h^2}{\sigma_z^3}\frac{d\sigma_z}{dx} - \frac{h}{\sigma_z^2}\left(\frac{dh}{dx}\right) = 0 \qquad (14.37)$$

Now using the expressions Eqs. (14.31), (14.32), (14.34), and (14.35) for h and σ_y and σ_z as a function of x, we obtain the following implicit equation for x_m,

$$\sigma_z^2(x_m) = \frac{-hb\Delta h + h^2 r_z}{r_y + r_z} \qquad (14.38)$$

where if Eq. (14.33) and its analogous relation for σ_y are used, r_y and r_z in Eq. (14.38) are replaced by $J_y + 2K_y \ln x_m$ and $J_z + 2K_z \ln x_m$, respectively.

In the special case in which $\Delta h = 0$ and σ_y and σ_z are given by Eqs. (14.31) and (14.32), the expression for x_m reduces to (Ragland, 1976)

$$x_m = \left[\frac{h_s^2 r_z}{R_z^2(r_y + r_z)}\right]^{1/2r_z} \qquad (14.39)$$

The value of the maximum ground-level concentration at x_m in the case of σ_y and σ_z given by Eqs. (14.31) and (14.32) and when $b = 0$ is

$$\langle c \rangle_m = \frac{q\gamma^{\gamma/2} R_z^{\gamma-1}}{\pi e^{\gamma/2} R_y h^\gamma \bar{u}} \qquad (14.40)$$

where $\gamma = 1 + r_y/r_z$.

Now we consider the effect of wind speed $\bar{u}$ on the maximum ground-level concentration. The highest concentration at any downwind distance can be determined as a function of $\bar{u}$. Differentiating Eq. (14.36) with respect to $\bar{u}$ we obtain

$$\bar{u}^{2a} - \frac{h_s a E x^b}{\sigma_z^2}\bar{u}^a - \frac{a E^2 x^{2b}}{\sigma_z^2} = 0 \tag{14.41}$$

from which we find that the "worst" wind speed, $\bar{u}_w$, is

$$\bar{u}_w = \left[\frac{2 E x^b}{h_s(\zeta - 1)}\right]^{1/a} \tag{14.42}$$

where $\zeta = (1 + 4\sigma_z^2/ah_s^2)^{1/2}$.

The value of the ground-level concentration at this wind speed is

$$\langle c(x)\rangle_w = \frac{q 2^{-1/a} h_s^{1/a}(\zeta - 1)^{1/a}}{\pi \sigma_y \sigma_z E^{1/a} x^{b/a}} \exp\left[-\frac{h_s^2(\zeta + 1)^2}{8\sigma_z^2}\right] \tag{14.43}$$

When the plume has reached its final height, h becomes independent of x, and the effective plume height can be written as

$$h = h_s + \frac{E'}{\bar{u}^a} \tag{14.44}$$

In that case the "worst" wind speed is (Roberts, 1980; Bowman, 1983)

$$\bar{u}_w = \left[\frac{2 E'}{h_s(\zeta - 1)}\right]^{1/a} \tag{14.45}$$

Finally we can find the combination of location and wind speed that produces the highest possible ground-level concentration, the so-called critical concentration. Considering σ_y and σ_z given by Eqs. (14.31) and (14.32), the critical downwind distance x_c is given by

$$x_c = \left[\left(\frac{h_s}{R_z}\right)\left(\frac{r}{r - 1/a}\right)\left(\frac{1}{r}\right)^{1/2}\right]^{1/r_z} \tag{14.46}$$

where $r = (r_y + r_z + b/a)/r_z$. The critical wind speed $\bar{u}_c$ is

$$\bar{u}_c = (aE)^{1/a}\left(\frac{r^{1/2}}{R_z}\right)^{b/ar_z}\left(\frac{r - 1/a}{h_s}\right)^{(1/a - b/ar_z)} \tag{14.47}$$

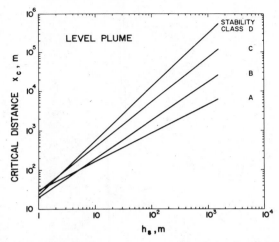

Figure 14.3. Critical downwind distance x_c as a function of source height h_s and stability class for the level plume.

and the critical concentration $\langle c \rangle_c$ is

$$\langle c \rangle_c = \frac{q R_z^{r-1} (r - 1/a)^{r-1/a}}{\pi (aE)^{1/a} R_y h_s^{r-1/a} e^{r/2} r^{r/2}} \tag{14.48}$$

All terms in Eq. (14.48), other than exponents, are positive except for $r - 1/a$. If this term is zero or negative, a critical concentration does not exist. Thus, for a critical concentration to exist it is necessary that $r > 1/a$, or

$$a > \frac{r_z - b}{r_y + r_z} \tag{14.49}$$

Once the plume has reached its final height, $b = 0$, and Eq. (14.49) becomes simply $a > r_z/(r_y + r_z)$.

Let us now apply these general results to some specific cases. Figures 14.3 and 14.4 show the critical distance x_c as a function of the source height h_s and stability class for the level plume and the bent-over plume, respectively. For the level plume, that is, one that has reached its final height, the critical downwind distance is

$$x_c = \left[\frac{a^2 r_z (r_y + r_z)}{R_z^2 \left(a (r_y + r_z) - r_z \right)^2} \right]^{1/2r_z} h_s^{1/r_z} \tag{14.50}$$

For a bent-over plume, that is, one that has not yet reached its final height,

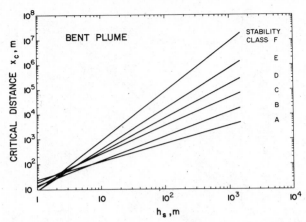

Figure 14.4. Critical downwind distance x_c as a function of source height h_s and stability class for the bent-over plume.

$a = 1$, and

$$x_c = \left[\frac{3r_z(3r_z + 3r_y + 2)}{R_z^2(3r_y + 2)^2} \right]^{1/2r_z} h_s^{1/r_z} \qquad (14.51)$$

For the level plume, $a = 1$ in neutral and unstable conditions and $a = 1/3$ under stable conditions. Coefficients for different stability conditions are given in Table 14.2.

We see that as h_s increases, the downwind distance at which the critical concentration occurs increases. The distance also increases as the atmosphere becomes more stable. When $a = 1$, Eq. (14.49) holds regardless of r_y and r_z (neutral and unstable conditions); for stability classes E and F, however, $a = 1/3$, and from the r_y and r_z values in Table 14.2, we see that Eq. (14.49) is not satisfied. Thus, for a level plume a critical concentration does not exist for stability classes E and F.

REFERENCES

American Meteorological Society Workshop on Stability Classification Schemes and Sigma Curves —Summary of Recommendations, *Bull. Am. Meteorol. Soc.*, **58**, 1305–1309 (1977).

American Society of Mechanical Engineers, "Recommended Guide for the Prediction of the Dispersion of Airbone Effluents," 2nd ed., ASME, New York (1973).

Binokowski, F. S. "A Simple Semi-Empirical Theory for Turbulence in the Atmospheric Surface Layer," *Atmos. Environ.*, **13**, 247–253 (1979).

Bowman, W. A. "Characteristics of Maximum Concentrations," *J. Air Pollution Control Assoc.*, **33**, 29–31 (1983).

Briggs, G. A. *Plume Rise*, U.S. Atomic Energy Commission Critical Review Series T/D 25075 (1969).

Briggs, G. A. "Some Recent Analyses of Plume Rise Observations," in *Proceedings of the Second International Clean Air Congress*, H. M. Englund and W. T. Beery (Eds.), Academic Press, New York, 1029–1032 (1971).

Briggs, G. A. "Diffusion Estimation for Small Emissions," in *Environmental Research Laboratories Air Resources Atmospheric Turbulence and Diffusion Laboratory 1973 Annual Report*, USAEC Rep ATDL-106 Natl. Oceanic Atmos. Admin., Washington, D.C. (1974).

Deardorff, J. W., and Willis, G. E. "A Parameterization of Diffusion Into the Mixed Layer," *J. Appl. Meteorol.*, **14**, 1451–1458 (1975).

Doran, J. C., Horst, T. W., and Nickola, P. W. "Experiment Observations of the Dependence of Lateral and Vertical Dispersion Characteristics on Source Height," *Atmos. Environ.*, **12**, 2259–2263 (1978).

Draxler, R. R. "Determination of Atmospheric Diffusion Parameters," *Atmos. Environ.*, **10**, 99–105 (1976).

Fisher, H. B., List, E. J., Koh, R. C. Y., Imberger, J., and Brooks, N. H. *Mixing in Inland and Coastal Waters*, Academic Press, New York (1979).

Gifford, F. A. "Use of Routine Meteorological Observations for Estimating Atmospheric Dispersion," *Nucl. Safety*, **2**, 47–51 (1961).

Gifford, F. A. "An Outline of Theories of Diffusion in the Lower Layers of the Atmosphere," in *Meteorology and Atomic Energy*, D. Slade (Ed.), USAEC TID-24190, Chapter 3, U.S. Atomic Energy Commission, Oak Ridge, Tennessee (1968).

Gifford, F. A. "Turbulent Diffusion-Typing Schemes: A Review," *Nucl. Safety*, **17**, 68–86 (1976).

Gifford, F. A. "Smoke as a Quantitative Atmospheric Diffusion Tracer," *Atmos. Environ.*, **14**, 1119–1121 (1980).

Hanna, S. R., Briggs, G. A., and Hosker, R. P., Jr. *Handbook on Atmospheric Diffusion*, U.S. Dept. of Energy report DOE/TIC-11223, Washington, DC (1982).

Irwin, J. S. "Scheme for Estimating Dispersion Parameters as a Function of Release Height," EPA-600/4-79-062. U.S. Environmental Protection Agency, Washington, D.C. (1979).

Klug, W. "A Method for Determining Diffusion Conditions from Synoptic Observations," *Staub-Reinhalt. Luft*, **29**, 14–20 (1969).

Martin, D. O. "Comment on the Change of Concentration Standard Deviations with Distance," *J. Air Pollution Control Assoc.*, **26**, 145–146 (1976).

Morton, B. R., Taylor, G. I., and Turner, J. S. "Turbulent Gravitational Convection from Maintained and Instantaneous Sources," *Proceedings of the Royal Society*, London, Series A, **234**, 1–23 (1956).

Murphy, B. D., and Nelson, C. B. "The Treatment of Ground Deposition, Species Decay and Growth and Source Height Effects in a Lagrangian Trajectory Model," *Atmos. Environ.*, **17**, 2545–2547 (1983).

Nieuwstadt, F. T. M., and van Duuren, H. "Dispersion Experiments with SF_6 from the 213m High Meteorological Mast at Cabau in the Netherlands," *Proceedings of the Fourth Symposium on Turbulence, Diffusion and Air Pollution*, Reno, Nevada, American Meteorological Society, Boston, Mass., 34–40 (1979).

Nieuwstadt, F. T. M., "Application of Mixed Layer Similarity to the Observed Dispersion from a Ground Level Source," *J. Appl. Meteorol.*, **19**, 157–162 (1980).

Palazzi, E., DeFaveri, M., Fumarola, G., and Ferraiolo, G. "Diffusion from a Steady Source of Short Duration," *Atmos. Environ.*, **16**, 2785–2790 (1982).

Panofsky, H. A., Tennekes, H., Lenschow, D. H., and Wyngaard, J. C. "The Characteristics of Turbulent Velocity Components in the Surface Layer Under Convective Conditions," *Boundary Layer Meteorol.*, **11**, 355–361 (1977).

Pasquill, F. "Atmospheric Diffusion of Pollution," *Q. J. Roy. Meteorol. Soc.*, **97**, 369–395 (1971).

Ragland, K. W. "Worst Case Ambient Air Concentrations from Point Sources Using the Gaussian Plume Model," *Atmos. Environ.*, **10**, 371–374 (1976).

Roberts, E. M. "Conditions for Maximum Concentration," *J. Air Pollution Control Assoc.*, **30**, 274–275 (1980).

Schatzmann, M. "An Integral Model of Plume Rise," *Atmos. Environ.*, **13**, 721–731 (1979).

Sedefian, L., and Bennett, E. "A Comparison of Turbulence Classification Schemes," *Atmos. Environ.*, **14**, 741–750 (1980).

Turner, D. B. "Workbook of Atmospheric Diffusion Estimates," USEPA 999-AP-26. U.S. Environmental Protection Agency, Washington, D.C. (1969).

U.S. Environmental Protection Agency, "OAQPS Guideline Series, Guidelines on Air Quality Models," Research Triangle Park, North Carolina (1980).

Weber, A. H. "Atmospheric Dispersion Parameters in Gaussian Plume Modeling," EPA-600/4-76-030A, U.S. Environmental Protection Agency, Washington, D.C. (1976).

PROBLEMS

14.1. A power plant burns 10^4 kg hr^{-1} of coal containing 2.5 percent sulfur. The effluent is released from a single stack of height 70 m. The plume rise is normally about 30 m, so that the effective height of emission is 100 m. The wind on the day of interest which is a sunny summer day is blowing at 4 m sec^{-1}. There is no inversion layer. Use the Pasquill–Gifford dispersion parameters from Table 14.2.

(a) Plot the ground-level SO_2 concentration at the plume centerline over distances from 100 m to 10 km. (Use log–log coordinates).

(b) Plot the ground-level SO_2 concentration versus crosswind distance at downwind distances of 200 m and 1 km.

(c) Plot the vertical centerline SO_2 concentration profile from ground level to 500 m at distances of 200 m, 1 km, and 5 km.

14.2. Repeat the calculation of Problem 14.1 for an overcast day with the same wind speed.

14.3. Repeat the calculation of Problem 14.1 if an inversion layer is present at a height of 300 m.

14.4. A power plant continuously releases from a 70 m stack a plume into the ambient atmosphere of temperature 298 K. The stack has diameter 5 m, the exit velocity is 25 m sec^{-1}, and the exit temperature is 398 K.

(a) For neutral conditions and a 20 km hr^{-1} wind, how high above the stack is the plume 200 m downwind?

(b) If a ground-based inversion layer 150 m thick is present through which the temperature increases 0.3°C and if the wind is blowing at 10 km hr^{-1}, will the plume penetrate the inversion layer?

14.5. Mathematical models for atmospheric diffusion are generally derived for either instantaneous or continuous releases. Short-term releases of material sometimes occur and it is of interest to develop the appropriate diffusion formulas to deal with them (Palazzi et al., 1982). The mean concentration resulting from a release of strength q at height h that commenced at $t = 0$ is given by

$$\langle c(x, y, z, t) \rangle = \int_0^t \frac{q}{(2\pi)^{3/2} \sigma_x \sigma_y \sigma_z} \exp\left\{ -\frac{(x - \bar{u}(t - t'))^2}{2\sigma_x^2} - \frac{y^2}{2\sigma_y^2} \right\}$$

$$\times \left\{ \exp\left[-\frac{(z - h)^2}{2\sigma_z^2} \right] + \exp\left[-\frac{(z + h)^2}{2\sigma_z^2} \right] \right\} dt' \quad \text{(A)}$$

The duration of the release will be t_r.

(a) Show that if the slender plume approximation is invoked, the mean concentration resulting from the release is

$\langle c(x, y, z, t) \rangle$

$$= \begin{cases} \langle c_G(x, y, z) \rangle \int_0^t \dfrac{\bar{u}}{(2\pi)^{1/2} \sigma_x} \exp\left[-\dfrac{(x - \bar{u}(t - t'))^2}{2\sigma_x^2} \right] dt' & t \leq t_r \\[3em] \langle c_G(x, y, z) \rangle \int_0^{t_r} \dfrac{\bar{u}}{(2\pi)^{1/2} \sigma_x} \exp\left[-\dfrac{(x - \bar{u}(t - t'))^2}{2\sigma_x^2} \right] dt' & t > t_r \end{cases}$$

where $\langle c_G(x, y, z) \rangle$ is the steady state Gaussian plume result. Show that this reduces to

$\langle c(x, y, z, t) \rangle$

$$= \begin{cases} 1/2 \langle c_G(x, y, z) \rangle \left[\text{erf}(x/\sqrt{2}\,\sigma_x) - \text{erf}\left(\dfrac{x - \bar{u}t}{\sqrt{2}\,\sigma_x} \right) \right] & t \leq t_r \\[3em] 1/2 \langle c_G(x, y, z) \rangle \left[\text{erf}\left(\dfrac{x - \bar{u}(t - t_r)}{\sqrt{2}\,\sigma_x} \right) - \text{erf}\left(\dfrac{x - \bar{u}t}{\sqrt{2}\,\sigma_x} \right) \right] & t > t_r \end{cases}$$

(b) For $t < t_r$ show that $\langle c \rangle$ reaches its maximum at $t = t_r$. After $t = t_r$, the puff continues to flow downwind. Show that at locations where $x \leq \bar{u}t_r/2$, the concentration decreases with increasing t and the maximum concentration is given by that at $t = t_r$. For $x > \bar{u}t_r/2$, show that the maximum concentration occurs when $\partial \langle c \rangle / \partial t = 0$, which gives $t = t_r/2 + x/\bar{u}$ and is

$$\langle c(x, y, z, t) \rangle_{\max} = \langle c_G(x, y, z) \rangle \text{erf}\left(\frac{\bar{u}t_r}{2\sqrt{2}\,\sigma_x} \right) \qquad \begin{array}{l} t > t_r \\ x > \bar{u}t_r/2 \end{array}$$

(c)   Compare $\langle c \rangle_{max}$ and $\langle c_G \rangle$ as a function of $\bar{u}t_r/2\sqrt{2}\,\sigma_x$. What do you conclude?

(d)   We can define the *dosage* over a time interval from t to $t_0 + t_e$ as

$$\bar{c}(x, y, z) = 1/t_e \int_{t_0}^{t_0+t_e} \langle c(x, y, z, t) \rangle \, dt \qquad \text{(B)}$$

Three different situations can be visualized, according to when the release stops:

$$t_r \le t_0 \qquad \text{release stops before exposure period begins}$$
$$t_0 \le t_r \le t_0 + t_e \qquad \text{release stops during exposure period}$$
$$t_r \ge t_0 + t_e \qquad \text{release stops after the exposure period}$$

Show that substituting the appropriate form of $\langle c(x, y, z, t) \rangle$ into (B) leads to the following formulas for the concentration dosage:

$$\bar{c}(x, y, z) = \begin{cases} \begin{aligned} &\frac{\langle c_G(x, y, z) \rangle \sqrt{2}\,\sigma_x}{2t_e\bar{u}} \Bigg\{ F\left[\frac{x - \bar{u}(t_0 - t_r)}{\sqrt{2}\,\sigma_x}\right] \\ &\quad - F\left[\frac{x - \bar{u}(t_0 + t_e - t_r)}{\sqrt{2}\,\sigma_x}\right] \\ &\quad + F\left[\frac{x - \bar{u}(t_0 + t_e)}{\sqrt{2}\,\sigma_x}\right] - F\left[\frac{x - \bar{u}t_0}{\sqrt{2}\,\sigma_x}\right] \Bigg\} \qquad t_r \le t_0 \\[2ex] &\frac{\langle c_G(x, y, z) \rangle \sqrt{2}\,\sigma_x}{2t_e\bar{u}} \Bigg\{ F\left[\frac{x}{\sqrt{2}\,\sigma_x}\right] - F\left[\frac{x - \bar{u}(t_0 + t_e - t_r)}{\sqrt{2}\,\sigma_x}\right] \\ &\quad + F\left[\frac{x - \bar{u}(t_0 + t_e)}{\sqrt{2}\,\sigma_x}\right] - F\left[\frac{x - \bar{u}t_0}{\sqrt{2}\,\sigma_x}\right] \\ &\quad - \frac{\bar{u}(t_r - t_0)}{\sqrt{2}\,\sigma_x}\operatorname{erfc}\left(\frac{x}{\sqrt{2}\,\sigma_x}\right) \Bigg\} \qquad t_0 \le t_r \le t_0 + t_e \\[2ex] &\frac{\langle c_G(x, y, z) \rangle \sqrt{2}\,\sigma_x}{2t_e\bar{u}} \Bigg\{ F\left[\frac{x - \bar{u}(t_0 + t_e)}{\sqrt{2}\,\sigma_x}\right] \\ &\quad - F\left[\frac{x - \bar{u}t_0}{\sqrt{2}\,\sigma_x}\right] - \frac{\bar{u}t_e}{\sqrt{2}\,\sigma_x}\operatorname{erfc}\left(\frac{x}{\sqrt{2}\,\sigma_x}\right) \Bigg\} \qquad t_r \ge t_0 + t_e \end{aligned} \end{cases}$$

where $F(x) = \int_x^\infty \operatorname{erfc}(\xi) \, d\xi$.

(e)   The dosage reaches its maximum value in the interval defined by $t_0 > t_r - t_e$. Show that when $x \ge \bar{u}(t_r + t_e)/2$, the maximum dosage corresponds to

$$t_0 = \frac{x}{\bar{u}} + \frac{t_r - t_e}{2}$$

and that it can be found from

$$c_{max} = \frac{\langle c_G(x, y, z) \rangle \sqrt{2}\,\sigma_x}{2 t_e \bar{u}} \left\{ \bar{u}\frac{t_r + t_e}{\sqrt{2}\,\sigma_x} - \bar{u}\frac{|t_e - t_r|}{\sqrt{2}\,\sigma_x} \right.$$

$$\left. + 2F\left[\frac{\bar{u}(t_r + t_e)}{2\sqrt{2}\,\sigma_x}\right] - 2F\left[\frac{\bar{u}|t_e - t_r|}{2\sqrt{2}\,\sigma_x}\right] \right\}$$

14.6. Chlorine is released at a rate of 30 kg sec^{-1} from an emergency valve at a height of 20 m. We need to evaluate the maximum ground-level dosage of Cl_2 for different durations of release and exposure. Assume a 5 m sec^{-1} wind speed and neutral stability. We may use the dispersion parameters for a continuous emission (they are a good approximation for exposure times exceeding about 2 min). Plot the Cl_2 dosage in ppm versus exposure time in min on a log–log scale over a range of 1 to 100 min exposure time for release durations of 2, 10, and 30 min. (The results needed to solve this problem were obtained in Problem 14.5.)

14.7. SO_2 is emitted from a stack under the following conditions:

$$\text{Stack diameter} = 3 \text{ m}$$
$$\text{Exit velocity} = 10 \text{ m sec}^{-1}$$
$$\text{Exit temperature} = 430 \text{ K}$$
$$\text{Emission rate} = 10^3 \text{ g sec}^{-1}$$
$$\text{Stack height} = 100 \text{ m}$$

For Pasquill stability categories A, B, C, and D, calculate:
(a) The distance from the source at which the maximum ground-level concentration is achieved as a function of wind speed.
(b) The wind speed at which the ground-level concentration is a maximum as a function of downwind distance.
(c) The plume rise at the wind speed in part (b).
(d) The critical downwind distance, wind speed, and concentration.

14.8. Gifford (1968, 1980) has discussed the determination of lateral and vertical dispersion parameters σ_y and σ_z from smoke plume photographs. Let us consider a single plume emanating from a continuous

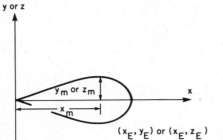

y or z

y_m or z_m

x_m

(x_E, y_E) or (x_E, z_E) **Figure P14.1.**   Plume boundaries.

point source that will be assumed to be at ground level. Thus, the mean concentration divided by the source strength is given by the Gaussian plume equation with $h = 0$,

$$\chi(x, y, z) = \frac{\langle c(x, y, z)\rangle}{q} = (\pi\sigma_y\sigma_z\bar{u})^{-1}\exp\left(-\frac{y^2}{2\sigma_y^2} - \frac{z^2}{2\sigma_z^2}\right) \quad \text{(A)}$$

A view of the plume from either above or the side is sketched in Figure P14.1, where y_E and z_E represent the coordinates of the visible edge of the plume, and y_m and z_m denote the maximum values of y_E and z_E with respect to downwind distance x. Let us consider the visible edge in the y-direction, that is the plume as observed from above.

Integrating (A) over z from 0 to ∞ and evaluating y at y_E gives

$$\chi_E(x) = \int_0^\infty \chi(x, y_E, z)\, dz$$

$$= (\pi\sigma_y\bar{u})^{-1}\exp\left(-\frac{y_E}{2\sigma_y^2}\right)\int_0^\infty \frac{1}{\sigma_z}e^{-z^2/2\sigma_z^2}\, dz$$

$$= (2\pi)^{-1/2}(\sigma_y\bar{u})^{-1}\exp\left(-\frac{y_E}{2\sigma_y^2}\right) \quad \text{(B)}$$

$\chi_E(x)$ represents the mean concentration normalized by the source strength, evaluated at the value of y corresponding to the visible edge of the plume and integrated through the depth of the plume.

(a)   Because the visible edge of the plume is presumably characterized by a constant integrated concentration, $\chi_E(x)$ is a constant χ_E. Show that at $y = y_m$,

$$y_m^2 = \sigma_y^2(x_m) = \sigma_{y_m}^2 \quad \text{(C)}$$

(b) Since χ_E is a constant, (B) is invariant whether evaluated at any x or at x_m. Thus, show that at any x

$$\chi_E = (2\pi)^{-1/2}(\sigma_y\bar{u})^{-1}\exp\left(-\frac{y_E^2}{2\sigma_y^2}\right)$$

and at x_m

$$\chi_E = (2\pi e)^{-1/2}(y_m\bar{u})^{-1}$$

Thus, show that

$$\sigma_y^2 = y_E^2\left[\ln\left(\frac{ey_m^2}{\sigma_y^2}\right)\right]^{-1}$$

(c) Apply this technique to the satellite photograph of the Mt. Etna plume at the beginning of Chapter 13.

14.9. Derive Equation (14.8) as a solution of the atmospheric diffusion equation.

14.10. Murphy and Nelson (1983) have shown that the Gaussian plume equation can be modified to include dry deposition with a deposition velocity v_d by replacing the source strength q, usually taken as constant, with the depleted source strength $q(t)$ as a function of travel time t, where

$$q(t) = q_0\exp\left\{-(2/\pi)^{1/2}v_d\int_0^t\frac{1}{\sigma_z(t')}\exp\left[-\frac{h^2}{2\sigma_z^2(t')}\right]dt'\right\}$$

Verify this result. Show that, if $\sigma_z = (2K_{zz}t)^{1/2}$,

$$q(t) = q_0\exp\left[-\frac{2v_dt^{1/2}}{(\pi K_{zz})^{1/2}}\right]$$

FIFTEEN

The Atmospheric Diffusion
Equation and
Air Quality Models

While the Gaussian equations of Chapter 14 have been widely used for atmospheric diffusion calculations, the lack of ability to include changes in wind speed with height and nonlinear chemical reactions limits the situations in which they may be used. The atmospheric diffusion equation provides a more general approach to atmospheric diffusion calculations than the Gaussian models, since the Gaussian models have been shown to be special cases of that equation when the wind speed is uniform and the eddy diffusivities are constant. The atmospheric diffusion equation in the absence of chemical reaction is

$$
\frac{\partial \langle c \rangle}{\partial t} + \bar{u} \frac{\partial \langle c \rangle}{\partial x} + \bar{v} \frac{\partial \langle c \rangle}{\partial y} + \bar{w} \frac{\partial \langle c \rangle}{\partial z}
$$

$$
= \frac{\partial}{\partial x} \left(K_{xx} \frac{\partial \langle c \rangle}{\partial x} \right) + \frac{\partial}{\partial y} \left(K_{yy} \frac{\partial \langle c \rangle}{\partial y} \right) + \frac{\partial}{\partial z} \left(K_{zz} \frac{\partial \langle c \rangle}{\partial z} \right)
$$

$$\tag{15.1}$$

The key problem in the use of Eq. (15.1) is to choose the functional forms of the wind speeds, $\bar{u}$, $\bar{v}$, and $\bar{w}$, and the eddy diffusivities, K_{xx}, K_{yy}, and K_{zz}, for the particular situation of interest.

15.1. MEAN WIND SPEED

The mean wind speed, usually taken as that coinciding with the x-direction, is often represented as a power-law function of height by Eq. (12.78),

$$
\frac{\bar{u}}{\bar{u}_r} = \left(\frac{z}{z_r} \right)^p
$$

$$\tag{15.2}$$

where p depends on atmospheric stability and surface roughness (Section 12.5.5).

593

15.2. VERTICAL EDDY DIFFUSION COEFFICIENT K_{zz}

The expressions available for K_{zz} are based on Monin–Obukhov similarity theory coupled with observational or computationally-generated data. It is best to organize the expressions according to the type of stability.

In the surface layer K_{zz} can be expressed as

$$K_{zz} = \frac{\kappa u_* z}{\phi(z/L)} \tag{15.3}$$

where $\phi(z/L)$ is given by

$$\phi(z/L) = \begin{cases} 1 + 4.7z/L & z/L > 0 \quad \text{stable} \\ 1 & z/L = 0 \quad \text{neutral} \\ [1 - 15z/L]^{-1/2} & z/L < 0 \quad \text{unstable} \end{cases} \tag{15.4}$$

We note that for stable and neutral conditions, $\phi(z/L)$ is identical to that for momentum transfer, $\phi_m(z/L)$, given by Eq. (12.75). For unstable conditions, $\phi(z/L) = \phi_m(z/L)^2$ (Galbally, 1971; Crane et al., 1977).

Since we generally need expressions for K_{zz} that extend vertically beyond the surface layer, we now consider some available correlations for the entire Ekman layer.

15.2.1. Unstable Conditions

In unstable conditions there is usually an inversion base height at $z = z_i$ that defines the extent of the mixed layer. The two parameters that are key in determining K_{zz} are the convective velocity scale w_* and z_i. We expect that a dimensionless profile $\tilde{K}_{zz} = K_{zz}/w_* z_i$, which is a function only of z/z_i, should be applicable. This form should be valid as long as $\tilde{K}_{zz}$ is independent of the nature of the source distribution. Lamb and Duran (1977) determined that $\tilde{K}_{zz}$ does depend on the source height. With the proviso that the result be applied when emissions are at or near ground level, Lamb et al. (1975) and Lamb and Duran (1977) derived an empirical expression for $\tilde{K}_{zz}$ under unstable conditions, using the numerical turbulence model of Deardorff (1970),

$$\frac{K_{zz}}{w_* z_i} = \begin{cases} 2.5\left(\kappa\dfrac{z}{z_i}\right)^{4/3}[1 - 15(z/L)]^{1/4} & 0 \leq \dfrac{z}{z_i} < 0.05 \\[2ex] 0.021 + 0.408\left(\dfrac{z}{z_i}\right) + 1.351\left(\dfrac{z}{z_i}\right)^2 \\ \quad - 4.096\left(\dfrac{z}{z_i}\right)^3 + 2.560\left(\dfrac{z}{z_i}\right)^4 & 0.05 \leq \dfrac{z}{z_i} \leq 0.6 \\[2ex] 0.2\exp\left[6 - 10\left(\dfrac{z}{z_i}\right)\right] & 0.6 < \dfrac{z}{z_i} \leq 1.1 \\[2ex] 0.0013 & \dfrac{z}{z_i} > 1.1 \end{cases} \tag{15.5}$$

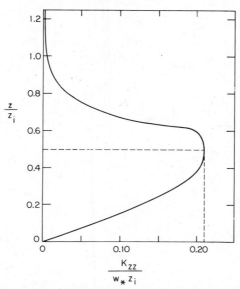

Figure 15.1. Vertical turbulent eddy diffusivity K_{zz} under unstable conditions derived by Lamb and Duran (1977).

Equation (15.5) is shown in Figure 15.1. The maximum value of K_{zz} occurs at $z/z_i \cong 0.5$ and has a magnitude $\cong 0.21 w_* z_i$. For typical meteorological conditions this corresponds to a magnitude of $O(100 \text{ m}^2 \text{ sec}^{-1})$ and a characteristic vertical diffusion time, z_i^2/K_{zz}, of $O(5 z_i/w_*)$.

Other expressions for K_{zz} in unstable conditions exist, notably those of O'Brien (1970) and Myrup and Ranzieri (1976), that are similar in nature to Eq. (15.5).

15.2.2. Neutral Conditions

Under neutral conditions $K_{zz} = \kappa u_* z$ in the surface layer. Since K_{zz} will not continue to increase without limit above the surface layer, it is necessary to specify its behavior at the higher elevations. Myrup and Ranzieri (1976) proposed the following empirical form for K_{zz} under neutral conditions,

$$K_{zz} = \begin{cases} \kappa u_* z & z/z_i < 0.1 \\ \kappa u_* z(1.1 - z/z_i) & 0.1 \le z/z_i \le 1.1 \\ 0 & z/z_i > 1.1 \end{cases} \qquad (15.6)$$

Shir (1973) developed the following relationship for K_{zz} under neutral conditions from a one-dimensional turbulent transport model,

$$K_{zz} = \kappa u_* z \exp\left(-\frac{8fz}{u_*} \right) \qquad (15.7)$$

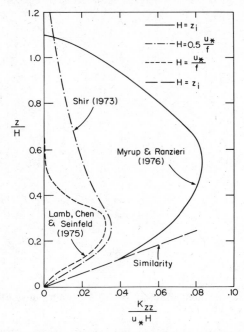

Figure 15.2. Comparison of vertical profiles of vertical turbulent eddy diffusivity K_{zz}.

We note that Myrup and Ranzieri chose the mixed layer depth z_i as the characteristic vertical length scale, whereas Shir uses the Ekman layer height, u_*/f. (Since $L = \infty$ under neutral conditions, the Monin–Obukhov length cannot be used as a characteristic length scale.)

Lamb et al. (1975) calculated K_{zz} under neutral conditions from a numerical turbulence model and obtained

$$K_{zz} = \begin{cases} \dfrac{u_*^2}{f}\left[7.396 \times 10^{-4} + 6.082 \times 10^{-2}\left(\dfrac{zf}{u_*}\right) + 2.532\left(\dfrac{zf}{u_*}\right)^2 \right. \\ \left. \quad - 12.72\left(\dfrac{zf}{u_*}\right)^3 + 15.17\left(\dfrac{zf}{u_*}\right)^4\right]; \qquad 0 \le \left(\dfrac{zf}{u_*}\right) \le 0.45 \\[2ex] \cong 0; \qquad\qquad\qquad\qquad\qquad\qquad\qquad \left(\dfrac{zf}{u_*}\right) > 0.45 \end{cases}$$

(15.8)

The predictions of the three expressions Eqs. (15.6) to (15.8) are compared in Figure 15.2. Note that the scale height H in the figure differs for each equation, in particular

$$H = \begin{cases} z_i & \text{for Eq. (15.6)} \\ 0.5u_*/f & \text{for Eq. (15.7)} \\ u_*/f & \text{for Eq. (15.8)} \end{cases}$$

It is clear that substantial differences exist in the magnitude of K_{zz} predicted by the three expressions. This is due to the lack of knowledge of the form of K_{zz} above the surface layer.

15.2.3.   Stable Conditions

Under stable conditions the appropriate characteristic vertical length scale is L. Businger and Arya (1974) proposed a modification of surface layer similarity theory to extend its vertical range of applicability,

$$K_{zz} = \frac{\kappa u_* z}{0.74 + 4.7(z/L)} \exp\left(-\frac{8fz}{u_*}\right) \tag{15.9}$$

For typical meteorological conditions the maximum value of K_{zz} under stable conditions is in the range 0.5 to 5 m^2 sec^{-1}.

15.3.   HORIZONTAL EDDY DIFFUSION COEFFICIENTS K_{xx} AND K_{yy}

We have seen that when σ^2 varies as t the crosswind eddy diffusion coefficient K_{yy} is related to the variance of plume spread by

$$K_{yy} = \frac{1}{2}\frac{d\sigma_y^2}{dt} = \frac{1}{2}\bar{u}\frac{d\sigma_y^2}{dx} \tag{15.10}$$

for $t \gg T_L$.

Measurements of T_L in the atmosphere are extremely difficult to perform and it is difficult to establish whether the condition $t \gg T_L$ holds for urban scale flows. Csanady (1973) indicates that a typical eddy that is generated by shear flow near the ground has a Lagrangian time scale of the order of 100 sec. Lamb and Neiburger (1971), in a series of measurements in the Los Angeles Basin, estimated the Eulerian time scale T_E to be about 50 sec. In a discussion of some field experiments, Lumley and Panofsky (1964) suggested that $T_L < 4T_E$. If the averaging interval is selected to be equal to the travel time, then an approximate value for K_{yy} can be deduced from the measurements of Willis and Deardorff (1976). Their data indicate that for unstable conditions ($L > 0$)

and a travel time $t = 3z_i/w_*$,

$$\frac{\sigma_y^2}{z_i^2} \simeq 0.64 \qquad (15.11)$$

Employing the previous travel time estimate and combining this result with Eq. (15.10) gives

$$K_{yy} = \frac{1}{6}\frac{\sigma_y^2}{z_i^2}w_* z_i \simeq 0.1 w_* z_i \qquad (15.12)$$

This latter result can be expressed in terms of the friction velocity, u_* and the Monin–Obukhov length L as

$$K_{yy} \simeq 0.1 z_i^{3/4}(-\kappa L)^{-1/3} u_* \qquad (15.13)$$

For a range of typical meteorological conditions this formulation results in diffusivities under unstable conditions of $O(50\text{--}100 \text{ m}^2 \text{ sec}^{-1})$. In practical applications it is usually assumed that $K_{xx} = K_{yy}$.

15.4. SOLUTIONS OF THE STEADY-STATE ATMOSPHERIC DIFFUSION EQUATION

The Gaussian expressions are not expected to be valid descriptions of turbulent diffusion close to the surface because of spatial inhomogeneities in the mean wind and the turbulence. To deal with diffusion in layers near the surface, recourse is generally made to the atmospheric diffusion equation, in which, as we have noted, the key problem is proper specification of the spatial dependence of the mean velocity and eddy diffusivities. Under steady-state conditions, turbulent diffusion in the direction of the mean wind is usually neglected (the slender plume approximation), and if the wind direction coincides with the x-axis, then $K_{xx} = 0$. Thus, it is necessary to specify only the lateral, K_{yy}, and vertical, K_{zz}, coefficients. It is generally assumed that horizontal homogeneity exists so that $\bar{u}$, K_{yy} are independent of y. Hence, Eq. (15.1) becomes

$$\bar{u}\frac{\partial\langle c\rangle}{\partial x} = \frac{\partial}{\partial y}\left(K_{yy}\frac{\partial\langle c\rangle}{\partial y}\right) + \frac{\partial}{\partial z}\left(K_{zz}\frac{\partial\langle c\rangle}{\partial z}\right) \qquad (15.14)$$

Sections 15.1 to 15.3 have been devoted to expressions for $\bar{u}$, K_{zz} and K_{yy} based on atmospheric boundary layer theory. Because of the rather complicated dependence of $\bar{u}$ and K_{zz} on z, Eq. (15.14) must generally be solved numerically. However, if they can be found, analytical solutions are advantageous for studying the behavior of the predicted mean concentration.

15.4.1. Diffusion from a Point Source

A solution of Eq. (15.14) has been obtained by Huang (1979) in the case when the mean wind speed and vertical eddy diffusivity can be represented by the power-law expressions,

$$\bar{u}(z) = az^p \tag{15.15}$$

$$K_{zz}(z) = bz^n \tag{15.16}$$

and when the horizontal eddy diffusivity is related to σ_y^2 by Eq. (15.10).

For a point source of strength q at height h above the ground, the solution of Eq. (15.14) subject to Eqs. (15.10), (15.15), and (15.16) is

$$\langle c(x, y, z) \rangle = \frac{q}{(2\pi)^{1/2}\sigma_y} \exp\left[-\frac{y^2}{2\sigma_y^2}\right] \frac{(zh)^{(1-n)/2}}{b\alpha x}$$

$$\times \exp\left[-\frac{a(z^\alpha + h^\alpha)}{b\alpha^2 x}\right] I_{-\nu}\left[\frac{2a(zh)^{\alpha/2}}{b\alpha^2 x}\right] \tag{15.17}$$

where $\alpha = 2 + p - n$, $\nu = (1 - n)/\alpha$, and $I_{-\nu}$ is the modified Bessel function of the first kind of order $-\nu$.

Equation (15.17) can be used to obtain some special cases of interest. If it is assumed that $p = n = 0$, then Eq. (15.17) reduces to

$$\langle c(x, y, z) \rangle = \frac{q}{(2\pi)^{1/2}\sigma_y} \exp\left[-\frac{y^2}{2\sigma_y^2}\right] \frac{(zh)^{1/2}}{\sigma_z^2 \bar{u}} \exp\left[-\frac{z^2 + h^2}{2\sigma_z^2}\right] I_{-1/2}\left(\frac{zh}{\sigma_z^2}\right)$$

$$\tag{15.18}$$

where

$$\sigma_y^2 = 2K_{yy}x/\bar{u} \qquad \sigma_z^2 = 2K_{zz}x/\bar{u} \tag{15.19}$$

Using the asymptotic form,

$$I_{-1/2}(x) = \left(\frac{2}{\pi x}\right)^{1/2} \cosh x \qquad x \to \infty \tag{15.20}$$

Eq. (15.18) reduces to the Gaussian plume equation. Note that the asymptotic condition in Eq. (15.20) corresponds to $zh \gg \sigma_z^2$.

The case of a point source at or near the ground can also be examined. We can take the limit of Eq. (15.17) as $h \to 0$ using the asymptotic form of $I_\nu(x)$

as $x \to 0$,

$$I_\nu(x) = \frac{x^\nu}{2^\nu \Gamma(1+\nu)} \qquad x \to 0 \tag{15.21}$$

to obtain

$$\langle c(x,y,z)\rangle = \frac{q}{(2\pi)^{1/2}\sigma_y x^{(1+p)/\alpha}} \frac{\alpha}{a^\nu(ba^2)^{(1+p)/\alpha}\Gamma((1+p)/\alpha)}$$

$$\times \exp\left[-\frac{y^2}{2\sigma_y^2}\right]\exp\left[-\frac{a(z^\alpha + h^\alpha)}{ba^2 x}\right] \tag{15.22}$$

15.4.2.   Diffusion from a Line Source

The mean concentration downwind of a continuous, crosswind line source at a height h emitting at a rate q_l (g m^{-1} sec^{-1}) is governed by

$$\bar{u}\frac{\partial\langle c\rangle}{\partial x} = \frac{\partial}{\partial z}\left(K_{zz}\frac{\partial\langle c\rangle}{\partial z}\right)$$

$$\langle c(0,z)\rangle = (q_l/\bar{u}(h))\delta(z-h) \tag{15.23}$$

$$-K_{zz}(0)\left(\frac{\partial\langle c\rangle}{\partial z}\right)_{z=0} = 0 \qquad z = 0$$

$$\langle c(x,z)\rangle = 0 \qquad z \to \infty$$

The solution of Eq. (15.23) for the power-law profiles Eqs. (15.15) and (15.16) is

$$\langle c(x,z)\rangle = \frac{q_l(zh)^{(1-n)/2}}{bax}\exp\left[-\frac{a(z^\alpha + h^\alpha)}{ba^2 x}\right]I_{-\nu}\left[\frac{2a(zh)^{\alpha/2}}{ba^2 x}\right]$$

$$\tag{15.24}$$

For a ground-level line source, $h = 0$, and

$$\langle c(x,z)\rangle = \frac{\alpha q_l}{a\Gamma((p+1)/\alpha)}\left(\frac{a}{\alpha^2 bx}\right)^{(p+1)/\alpha}\exp\left(-\frac{az^\alpha}{\alpha^2 bx}\right) \tag{15.25}$$

15.5.   AIR QUALITY MODELS

An ambient air quality model is a means whereby pollutant emissions can be related to atmospheric pollutant concentrations. Such a model provides, therefore, a link between emission changes from source control measures and the

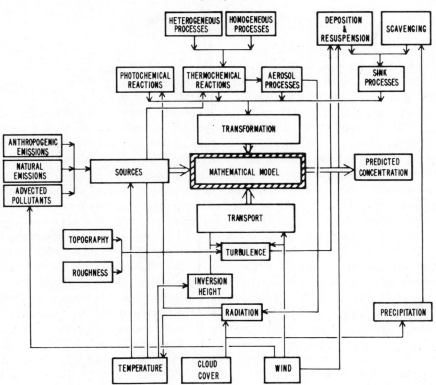

Figure 15.3. Components of a comprehensive air quality model (Seinfeld, 1983).

changes in airborne pollutant concentration levels that can be expected to result. The model will involve considerations of emission patterns, meteorology, chemical transformations, and removal processes. (See Figure 15.3.)

Many difficult questions and complex issues arise in planning for the abatement and control of air pollution in an urban area. Certain key aspects of abatement planning are best addressed through the use of an ambient air quality model; in some cases there are no alternative means of examining the critical issues. Included among those topics for which an ambient air quality model may be particularly useful as an analytical tool are:

1. Establishment of emission control legislation.
2. Evaluation of proposed emission control techniques and strategies.
3. Planning of locations of future sources of air contaminants.
4. Planning for the control of air pollution episodes.
5. Assessment of responsibility for existing levels of air pollution.

15.5.1. Types of Models

Ambient air quality models can be divided, broadly speaking, into two types: physical and mathematical.

Physical models are intended to simulate the atmospheric processes affecting pollutants by means of a small-scale representation of the actual air pollution problem. A physical model sometimes employed to study the dispersion of pollutants consists of a small-scale replica of the urban area or a portion thereof in a wind tunnel. The problems associated with properly duplicating the actual atmospheric scales of turbulent motion make physical models of this variety of limited usefulness. While useful for isolating certain elements of atmospheric behavior and invaluable for studying certain critical details, physical models cannot serve the needs of ambient air quality models capable of relating emissions to air quality under a variety of meteorological and source emission conditions over an urban area. Recourse must be had to mathematical models, which can broadly be classified under two types: (1) models based on statistical analysis of past air monitoring data, and (2) models based on the fundamental description of atmospheric transport and chemical processes.

The first class of mathematical ambient air quality models consists of those based on statistical analysis of past air monitoring data. All large urban airsheds contain a number of air monitoring stations operated under the auspices of air pollution control authorities, at which 15-min to 1-hr average pollutant concentration levels are reported. A great deal of information is potentially available from these enormous data bases, and the statistical analysis of air quality data is the subject of Chapter 17. Models based on the fundamental description of atmospheric physics have been the subject of this and the preceeding two chapters.

15.5.2. Temporal Resolution of Models

The temporal resolution of an ambient air quality model (that is, the time period over which the predicted concentrations are averaged) may vary from several minutes to one year. For example, a model may predict the 15-min average pollutant concentration as a function of location. The requirements in implementing a model will be strongly governed by its temporal resolution.

Models based on statistical analysis of past air monitoring data are generally derived from several years of measurements at one or more stations in an airshed. The concentration actually correlated with emission levels may range from a several minute to a yearly average value. Thus, the model may predict, for example, the probability that the 1-hr average concentration at a certain station will exceed a given level if total source emission levels in the region are at a prescribed value. Since data are generally available on time periods as short as from 15 min to 1 hr, the choice of the time period for averaging of the data for the statistical model is dictated solely by the purposes for which the model is to be used. The input data requirements for a statistical model generally consist only of estimates of source emission levels since meteorology and atmospheric transformation and removal processes are implicit in the reported data.

Models based on the fundamental description of atmospheric transport and chemical processes may have temporal resolution ranging from the order of several minutes to a year. In general, the basis of these models is the equation of continuity for an individual species. Those models that require the solution in time of a differential equation based on the continuity equation can be called *dynamic* models, since they describe the evolution of pollutant concentrations with time at different locations in the airshed. Thus, dynamic models simulate the actual real-time temporal behavior of air pollutants in the atmosphere. These models require as inputs the spatial and temporal distribution of emissions over the region of interest, the spatial and temporal distribution of pertinent meteorological variables, and information on the time rate of change of concentrations at a point resulting from transformation and removal processes.

If certain simplifying assumptions are invoked in dealing with the equation of continuity, such as steady source rates and meteorology, then the equation can be integrated over a long time period to yield a *steady-state* model. A steady-state model is then capable of predicting the spatial distribution of airborne pollutant concentrations under conditions of time-invariant meteorology and source emission rates.

15.5.3. Spatial Resolution of Models

The spatial resolution of an ambient air quality model (that is, the area over which the predicted concentrations are averaged) may vary from several meters to several thousand kilometers. (See Table 15.1.)

A model based on statistical analysis of past air monitoring data might predict concentrations at one or more stations (essentially "point" measurements) or the average of the readings at a number of stations, intended to represent the average pollutant concentrations in the region. In a model based on the solution of the species continuity equations, the concentrations appear-

TABLE 15.1. Air Quality Models Defined According to Their Spatial Scale

Model	Typical Domain Size	Typical Spatial Resolution
Microscale	200 m × 200 m × 100 m	5 m
Mesoscale		
(urban scale)	100 km × 100 km × 5 km	2 km
Regional Scale	1000 km × 1000 km × 10 km	20 km
Synoptic Scale		
(continental scale)	3000 km × 3000 km × 20 km	80 km

ing in those equations are essentially point concentrations. The partial differential equation(s) comprising the model are normally solved numerically by a process that requires the continuous concentration field to be approximated by a discrete grid of points. The choice of the spatial grid on which the equations are solved is governed by the degree of spatial detail in the emissions inventory and the meteorological variables are available with a spatial resolution of 5 km, then the spatial resolution of the predicted concentrations can be no smaller than 5 km. Sometimes it is desired to predict pollutant concentrations in the immediate vicinity of sources, such as a highway. In such a case, the spatial resolution of the concentrations might be as small as a few meters.

Different pollutants pose different needs relative to the spatial scales of modeling. For example, carbon monoxide poses a local problem in the vicinity of heavily traveled highways and intersections. Thus, to assess the effectiveness of motor vehicle emission controls on CO levels requires a model with spatial resolution the order of the width of a city street. On the other hand, photochemical ozone is usually a region-wide problem, caused by area-wide emissions of hydrocarbons and oxides of nitrogen. A model capable of relating emission changes to air quality for photochemical oxidant might only require a minimum spatial resolution of several square kilometers.

15.6.   THE GENERAL STRUCTURE OF MULTIPLE SOURCE PLUME MODELS   (Calder, 1977)

Multiple-source plume (and particularly Gaussian-plume) models are commonly used for predicting concentrations of inert pollutants over urban areas. Although there are many special-purpose computational algorithms currently in use, the basic element that is common to most is the single point-source release. The spatial concentration distribution from such a source is the underlying component and the multiple-source model is then developed by simple superposition of the individual plumes from each of the sources.

The starting point for predicting the mean concentration resulting from a single point source is the assumption of a quasi-steady state. In spite of the obvious long-term variability of emissions, and of the meteorological conditions affecting transport and dispersion, it is assumed as a working approximation that the pollutant concentrations can be treated as though they resulted from a time sequence of different steady states. In urban modeling the time interval is normally relatively short and of the order of 1 hr. The time sequence of steady-state concentrations is regarded as leading to a random series of (1 hr) concentration values, from which the frequency distribution and long-term average can be calculated as a function of receptor location. An assumption normally made is that the dispersion of pollutant is "horizontally homogeneous" and independent of the horizontal location of the source—that is, the source–receptor relation is invariant under arbitrary horizontal translation of the source–receptor pair. Further, the dispersion in a simple point-source plume is assumed to be "isotropic" as regards direction, and independent of the actual direction of the wind transport over the urban area. In principle, the short-term multiple-source plume model then only involves simple summation or integration over all point, line, and area sources and for the different meteorological conditions of plume dispersion.

In most short-term plume models in use at the present time, it is assumed that for each time interval of the quasi-steady state sequence, transport by the wind over the urban area can be characterized in terms of a single "wind-direction." Also for each time interval the three meteorological variables that influence the transport and dispersion are taken to be the mean wind speed, the atmospheric stability category, and the mixing depth. Although the wind direction θ is evidently a continuous variable that may assume any value $(0 < \theta < 360°)$, for reasons of practical simplicity the three dispersion variables are usually considered as discrete, with a relatively small number of possible values for each. The short-term, steady-state, three-dimensional spatial distribution of mean concentration for an individual point-source plume must then be expressed in terms of a plume dispersion equation of fixed functional form, such as the Gaussian plume equation, although the dispersion parameters that appear in its arguments will, of course, depend on actual conditions. Many models assume the well-known Gaussian form, and the horizontal and vertical standard deviation functions, σ_y and σ_z, are expressed as functions of the downwind distance in the plume and of the stability category only.

To illustrate these ideas we consider a fixed rectangular coordinate system with the plane $z = 0$ at ground level, and also assume that the pollutant transport by the wind over the urban area can be characterized in terms of a single horizontal direction that makes an angle, say θ, with the positive x-axis of the coordinate system. We thus explicitly separate the wind-direction variable from all other meteorological variables that influence transport and dispersion, for example, wind speed, atmospheric stability category, and mixing depth. These latter variables may be regarded as defining a meteorological-dispersion index j $(j = 1, 2, \ldots)$ that will be a function of t_n, the interval of time over which meteorological conditions are constant; that is, $j = j(t_n)$. The index number j simply designates a given meteorological state out of the totality of possible combinations, that is, a specified combination of wind speed, stability, and mixing depth. Then from the additive property of concentration it follows that the mean concentration $\langle c(x, y, z; t_n) \rangle$ for the time interval t_n that results from the superposition can be written as a summation (actually representing a three-dimensional integral)

$$\langle c(x, y, z; t_n) \rangle = \sum_{(x', y', z')} Q\{x, y, z; x', y', z', \theta_n, j(t_n)\} S(x', y', z'; t_n) \Delta V$$

$$(15.26)$$

where $S(x', y', z'; t_n) = $ steady emission rate per unit volume and unit time at position (x', y', z') for time interval $t = t_n$, $Q\{x, y, z; x', y', z'; \theta_n, j(t_n)\} =$ mean concentration at (x, y, z) produced by a steady point-source of unit strength located at (x', y', z'), and for time interval t_n when $\theta = \theta_n$, and the summation is taken over all the elemental source locations of the entire region. The function Q is a meteorological-dispersion function that is explicitly dependent on the wind direction θ_n and implicitly dependent on the other meteorological variables that will be determined by the time-sequence t_n. In all simple urban models now in use the function Q is taken to be a deterministic function, although its variables θ_n and $j(t_n)$ may be regarded as random. It is usually assumed that the dispersion function Q is independent of the horizontal location of the source, so that Q is invariant under arbitrary horizontal translations of the source–receptor pair, reducing Q to a function of only two independent horizontal spatial variables, so that Eq. (15.26) may be rewritten as

$$\langle c(z, y, z; t_n) \rangle = \sum_{(X, Y, z')} Q\{X, Y, z, z'; \theta_n, j(t_n)\}$$

$$\times S(x - X, y - Y, z'; t_n) \, \Delta V \qquad (15.27)$$

where $X = x - x'$ and $Y = y - y'$, and the summation extends over the entire source distribution. Finally, it is normally assumed that the dispersion function Q only depends on θ through a simple rotation of the horizontal axes, and that it is independent of the actual value of the single horizontal wind direction that is assumed to characterize the pollutant transport over the urban area, provided the x-axis of the coordinate system is taken along this direction. If this is done then the dispersion function is directionally isotropic.

The long-term average concentration which we note by an uppercase C, is given by

$$C(x, y, z) = \frac{1}{N} \sum_{n=1}^{N} \langle c(x, y, z; t_n) \rangle \qquad (15.28)$$

When the emission intensities S and the dispersion functions Q, that is, the meteorological conditions, can be assumed to be independent or uncorrelated, the average value of the product of S and Q is equal to the product of their average values, and we thus have from Eq. (15.28)

$$C(x, y, z) = \sum_{(X, Y, z')} \overline{Q}(X, Y, z, z') \overline{S}(x - X, y - Y, z') \, \Delta V \qquad (15.29)$$

where $\overline{S}$ denotes the time-average source strength and $\overline{Q}$ the average value of the meteorological dispersion function. Thus if $P(\theta, j)$ denotes the joint-frequency function for wind direction θ and dispersion index j, so that

$$\sum_{\theta} \sum_{j} P(\theta, j) = 1 \qquad (15.30)$$

then

$$\overline{Q}(X, Y, z, z') = \sum_\theta \sum_j Q\{X, Y, z, z'; \theta, j\} P(\theta, j) \qquad (15.31)$$

15.7. NUMERICAL SOLUTION OF THE ATMOSPHERIC DIFFUSION EQUATION

In this section we will discuss some of the aspects of the numerical solution of the atmospheric diffusion equation. We do not attempt to specify which numerical method is best; rather we point out some of the considerations in assessing the adequacy and appropriateness of numerical methods for the atmospheric diffusion equation. Our treatment is, by necessity, brief. We refer the reader to Peyret and Taylor (1983) for more study in this area.

The atmospheric diffusion equation is characterized by three operators:

$\nabla \cdot \mathbf{K} \cdot \nabla c_i$	The diffusion operator
$\boldsymbol{u} \cdot \nabla c_i$	The advection operator
$R_i(\mathbf{c})$	The chemical kinetics operator

These three operators that comprise the equation are distinctly different in basic character, each usually requiring quite different numerical techniques to obtain reasonable numerical solutions. The diffusion operator is parabolic in nature, whereas the advection operator is hyperbolic. The kinetics operator is usually highly nonlinear and exhibits the property of *stiffness*, which results when chemical reactions with widely varying associated time constants are present (Lapidus and Seinfeld, 1971). We should note that no one numerical method is uniformly best for all atmospheric diffusion equation problems. The relative contributions of each of the operators to the overall solution as well as other considerations such as boundary conditions, wind fields, etc., can easily change significantly from problem to problem leading to different numerical requirements.

15.7.1. Finite Difference Methods

Most of the numerical techniques for solving the atmospheric diffusion equation are based on finite difference approximations. That is, a grid, or mesh is defined over the spatial domain and partial derivatives of functions are approximated by divided difference quotients; for example,

$$\frac{\partial c}{\partial x} = \frac{c_i - c_{i-1}}{\Delta x}$$

$$\frac{\partial^2 c}{\partial x^2} = \frac{c_{i+1} - 2c_i + c_{i-1}}{(\Delta x)^2}$$

where Δx is the grid spacing in the x-direction.

Finite difference approximations lead to a set of difference equations that are then solved to obtain the desired approximate solutions. A family of finite difference approximations to solve the simple diffusion equation $\partial c / \partial t = \partial^2 c / \partial x^2$ is

$$\frac{c_i^{n+1} - c_i^n}{\Delta t} = \gamma \left(\frac{c_{i+1}^{n+1} - 2c_i^{n+1} + c_{i-1}^{n+1}}{(\Delta x)^2} \right) + (1 - \gamma) \left(\frac{c_{i+1}^n - 2c_i^n + c_{i-1}^n}{(\Delta x)^2} \right)$$

(15.32)

where γ is a constant satisfying $0 \leq \gamma \leq 1$ and c_i^n is meant to approximate the solution $c(x, t)$ at $t = n \Delta t$, and $x = i \Delta x$.

When $\gamma = 0$, the set of difference equations Eq. (15.32) is said to be *explicit*, since if approximate solution values are known at time $t^n = n \Delta t$, then the approximate values at time $t^{n+1} = (n + 1) \Delta t$ may be explicitly and immediately calculated using Eq. (15.32). If $\gamma = 1$, then one must solve a set of simultaneous linear equations to obtain the values at t^{n+1} and the difference approximations is said to be *implicit*. In general, *implicit* methods will require more computational effort per time step taken than will *explicit* methods of the same basic type.

The concept of *stability* always plays an important role in the choice of a numerical method. In a stable method, unavoidable errors in the solution are suppressed with time. Typically explicit techniques require that constraints be placed on the size of Δt that may be used relative to the size of the spatial grid size Δx in order to maintain stability. The explicit form of Eq. (15.32), that is, $\gamma = 0$, is stable if one requires that $\Delta t < (\Delta x)^2 / 2$.

Generally, implicit techniques have better stability properties than explicit methods. They may often be unconditionally stable and any choice of Δt and Δx may be used (the choice being ultimately based on accuracy considerations alone).

15.7.2. Finite Element Methods

In using a finite element method, one typically divides the spatial domain into zones or "elements" and then requires that the approximate solution have the form of a specified polynomial over each of the elements. For the Galerkin finite element method, the discrete equations are then derived by requiring that the error in this piecewise polynomial approximate solution (i.e., the residual, when the polynomial is substituted into the basic partial differential equation) be orthogonal to the piecewise polynomial space itself. Other finite element methods for determining the discrete equations exist but are less popular than the Galerkin approach.

Characteristically, finite element methods lead to implicit approximation equations to be solved, which are usually more complicated than analogous finite difference equations (hence more costly to solve).

15.7.3. Splitting Methods

Splitting methods, alternating direction implicit (ADI) techniques, and locally one-dimensional (LOD) methods have been developed because fully implicit difference methods for problems in higher space dimensions (2 or 3) can lead to systems of linear equations that are simply too large and/or time consuming to solve. The basic idea is that a large multidimensional problem is approximated locally by a sequence of one-dimensional problems. To illustrate the concept of a splitting method consider the three-dimensional diffusion equation using a standard fully implicit finite difference method on a region having the shape of a cube. We divide the cube up with a uniform grid with N divisions in each direction, that is, we divide it up into N^3 smaller cubes. A fully implicit technique would require the solution of a linear system of equations with N^3 unknowns involving a matrix with a bandwidth of about N^2 at each time step. The cost of solving the linear system using conventional banded Gaussian elimination would be proportional to $(N^2)^2 N^3 = N^7$. Using a splitting technique, for each time step one would solve discrete versions of a series of one-dimensional problems as follows:

$$\frac{c_i^{n+1/3} - c_i^n}{\Delta t} = \frac{c_{i+1}^{n+1/3} - 2c_i^{n+1/3} + c_{i-1}^{n+1/3}}{(\Delta x)^2}$$

$$\frac{c_j^{n+2/3} - c_j^{n+1/3}}{\Delta t} = \frac{c_{j+1}^{n+2/3} - 2c_j^{n+2/3} + c_{j-1}^{n+2/3}}{(\Delta y)^2}$$

$$\frac{c_k^{n+1} - c_k^{n+2/3}}{\Delta t} = \frac{c_{k+1}^{n+1} - 2c_k^{n+1} + c_{k-1}^{n+1}}{(\Delta z)^2}$$

where c^n are the values at $t^n = n\,\Delta t$ and c^{n+1} are the values of $t^{n+1} = (n + 1)\,\Delta t$. To accomplish this on the above $N \times N \times N$ grid would require N^2 solutions of each of the above three equations and the cost of each solution would be proportional to N. So, the total cost to advance one time step using splitting would be proportional to $2N^3$, which is less than the N^7 cost for the fully implicit case. If each one-dimensional method is stable, then the overall technique using splitting is usually also stable. Splitting does not require the exclusive use of finite difference methods; that is, finite element techniques could be used to solve the one-dimensional problems.

15.7.4. Techniques for Specific Operators

Diffusion. From a numerical point of view the diffusion operator is probably the simplest to deal with. Because of its physical nature, diffusion tends to smooth out gradients and lend overall stability to the physical process. Most typical finite difference or finite element procedures are quite adequate for solving diffusion-type operator problems. The primary constraint imposed by the diffusion operator is that explicit numerical techniques cannot be efficiently used because stability considerations dictate excessively small time steps. Thus, implicit methods should be used for the diffusion aspect of a problem. In higher dimensions this requirement implies that splitting will almost certainly have to be used.

Advection. Advection problems tend to be more difficult to solve numerically than are diffusion problems. The advection operator does not smooth or damp out gradients or solutions, but simply transports them about intact. Good numerical methods must accurately reproduce this type of behavior. However, most numerical techniques are incapable of doing this exactly, and produce errors in two ways: first, they may transport the material at the wrong speed (so-called phase errors); second, they tend to disperse the material improperly as it is transported along (dispersion errors). There exist many techniques to treat advection numerically, for which we refer the reader to McRae et al. (1982).

Kinetics. Until recently, the solution of stiff systems of chemical reaction rate equations was a formidable task. However, the development of fully implicit stiffly stable integration techniques has made the solution of purely kinetics problems virtually routine. (See, for example, Hindmarsh (1980).)

15.7.5. Summary

The real challenge that exists is designing adequate techniques to solve effectively and efficiently the atmospheric diffusion equation in higher dimensions. The individual demands of each distinct operator in the equation must be sufficiently satisfied to maintain its proper character, and yet the entire process must be compact and efficient enough so as to be solvable on available computers.

Problems involving only one space dimension can be satisfactorily handled in reasonable time by almost any set of techniques. Fully implicit time integration methods that can satisfactorily handle the stiffness of the nonlinear kinetics operator can be used even when the number of chemical species is fairly large. The discretization can be accomplished using almost any reasonable technique: finite differences, finite elements, etc.

The size of the computational problem can become significant in two dimensions. A 50×50 grid with 10 chemical species produces 25,000 unknowns, a quantity that is very large if one is considering using fully implicit methods. In general, beginning with two dimensions, some form of operator splitting will have to be used to keep storage and computing time within reasonable bounds. Typically, one would split the kinetics operator from advection–diffusion and then split the advection–diffusion operators between the two dimensions.

It is necessary that the total numerical solution process be stable. With splitting processes, it is usually, but unfortunately not always, the case that the overall process is stable if the individual (split) solution techniques are stable. One must examine and test each of the separate solution techniques thoroughly for adequate stability. Assuring stability may require restrictions on maximum permissible time step sizes. For nonlinear problems it is usually not possible to ascertain definitely the stability of a method without knowing the solution being calculated.

The most important quality that any numerical technique should possess is that of being accurate in that it reproduces the basic physical phenomenon that is being approximated. Rigorously establishing the accuracy characteristics of an overall numerical method for solving the atmospheric diffusion equation is usually quite difficult, if not impossible. One of the best techniques for assessing accuracy is to construct a problem for which the exact solution is known and then use the numerical methods to obtain an approximate solution. Comparison with the known exact solution will then give indications of how reliable and accurate a given method may be.

REFERENCES

Businger, J. A., and Ayra, S. P. S. "Height of the Mixed Layer in the Stably Stratified Planetary Boundary Layer," *Adv. Geophys.*, **18A**, 73–92 (1974).

Calder, K. L. "Multiple-Source Plume Models of Urban Air Pollution—Their General Structure," *Atmos. Environ.*, **11**, 403–414 (1977).

Crane, G., Panofsky, H., and Zeman, O. "A Model for Dispersion from Area Sources in Convective Turbulence," *Atmos. Environ.*, **11**, 893–900 (1977).

Csanady, G. I. *Turbulent Diffusion in the Environment*, Reidel Publ., Dordrecht, The Netherlands (1973).

Deardorff, J. W. "A Three-Dimensional Numerical Investigation of the Idealized Planetary Boundary Layer," *Geophys. Fluid Dyn.*, **1**, 377–410 (1970).

Galbally, I. E. "Ozone Profiles and Ozone Fluxes in the Atmospheric Surface Layer," *Q.J.Roy. Meteorol. Soc.*, **97**, 18–29 (1971).

Hindmarsh, A. C. "LSODE and LSODI, Two Initial Value Ordinary Differential Equation Solvers," *ACM SIGNUM Newsletter*, **15**, 10–11 (1980).

Huang, C. H. "Theory of Dispersion in Turbulent Shear Flow," *Atmos. Environ.*, **13**, 453–463 (1979).

Lamb, R. G., and Duran, D. R. "Eddy Diffusivities Derived from a Numerical Model of the Convective Boundary Layer," *Nuov. Cimento*, **1C**, 1–17 (1977).

Lamb, R. G., and Neiburger, M. "An Interim Version of a Generalized Air Pollution Model," *Atmos. Environ.*, **5**, 239–264 (1971).

Lamb, R. G., Chen, W. H., and Seinfeld, J. H. "Numerico-Empirical Analyses of Atmospheric Diffusion Theories," *J. Atmos. Sci.*, **32**, 1794–1807 (1975).

Lapidus, L., and Seinfeld, J. H. *Numerical Solution of Ordinary Differential Equations*, Academic Press, New York (1971).

Lumley, J. L., and Panofsky, H. A. *The Structure of Atmospheric Turbulence*, Wiley, New York (1964).

McRae, G. J., Goodin, W. R., and Seinfeld, J. H. "Numerical Solution of the Atmospheric Diffusion Equation for Chemically Reacting Flows," *J. Comput. Phys.*, **45**, 1–42 (1982).

Myrup, L. O., and Ranzieri, A. J. "A Consistent Scheme for Estimating Diffusivities to be Used in Air Quality Models," Rep. CA-DOT-TL-7169-3-76-32, California Department of Transportation, Sacramento (1976).

O'Brien, J. "On the Vertical Structure of the Eddy Exchange Coefficient in the Planetary Boundary Layer," *J. Atmos. Sci.*, **27**, 1213–1215 (1970).

Peyret, R., and Taylor, T. D. *Computational Methods for Fluid Flow*, Springer-Verlag, New York (1983).

Seinfeld, J. H. "Atmospheric Diffusion Theory," in *Advances in Chemical Engineering*, **12**, J. Wei, K. B. Bischoff, T. B. Drew, and J. H. Seinfeld (Eds.), Academic Press, New York, 209–299 (1983).

Shir, C. C. "A Preliminary Numerical Study of Atmospheric Turbulent Flows in the Idealized Planetary Boundary Layer," *J. Atmos. Sci.*, **30**, 1327–1339 (1973).

Szwarc, A., and Branco, G. M. "Automotive Use of Alcohol in Brazil and Air Pollution Related Aspects," 1985 SAE Congress, SAE Paper 850390, Society of Automotive Engineers, Warrendale, PA (1985).

Willis, G. E., and Deardorff, J. W. "A Laboratory Model of Diffusion into the Convective Boundary Layer," *Q.J.Roy. Meteorol. Soc.*, **102**, 427–447 (1976).

PROBLEMS

15.1. An eight-lane freeway is oriented so that the prevailing wind direction is usually normal to the freeway. During a typical day the average traffic flow rate per lane is 30 cars per minute, and the average speed of vehicles in both directions is 80 km hr^{-1}. The emission rate of CO from an average vehicle is 90 g km^{-1} traveled.

(a) Assuming a 5 km hr^{-1} wind and conditions of neutral stability, with no elevated inversion layer present, determine the average ground-level CO concentration as a function of downwind distance, using the appropriate Gaussian plume formula.

(b) A more accurate estimate of downwind concentrations can be obtained by taking into account the variation of wind velocity and turbulent mixing with height. For neutral conditions we have seen that

$$\bar{u}(z) = u_0 z^{1/7}$$

and

$$K_{zz} = \kappa u_* z = 0.4 u_* z$$

should be used. Assume that the 5 km hr^{-1} wind reading was taken at a 10 m height and that for the surface downwind of the freeway $u_* = 0.6$ km hr^{-1} (grassy field). Repeat the calculation of (a). Discuss your result.

15.2. It is desired to estimate the ground-level, centerline concentration of a contaminant downwind of a continuous, elevated point source. The source height including plume rise is 100 m. The wind speed at a reference height of 10 m is 4 m sec^{-1}. The atmospheric diffusion equation with the power-law correlations Eqs. (15.15) and (15.16) is to be used. The roughness length is 0.1 m.

(a) Calculate the ground-level, centerline mean concentration under the following conditions:

1. Stable (Pasquill stability class F)
2. Neutral (Pasquill stability class D)
3. Unstable (Pasquill stability class B)

(b) Compare your predictions to those of the Gaussian plume equation assuming that $\bar{u} = 4$ m sec^{-1} at all heights. Discuss the reasons for any differences in the two results.

15.3. To account properly for terrain variations in a region over which the transport and diffusion of pollutants are to be predicted, the following dimensionless coordinate transformation is used:

$$\rho = \frac{z - h(x, y)}{Z} \qquad Z = H - h(x, y)$$

where $h(x, y)$ is the ground elevation at point (x, y) and H is the assumed extent of vertical mixing. Likewise, a similar change of variables for the horizontal coordinates may be performed:

$$\xi = \frac{x - x_S}{X} \qquad X = x_N - x_S$$

$$\eta = \frac{y - y_W}{Y} \qquad Y = y_E - y_W$$

where x_N, x_S, y_E, and y_W are the coordinates of the horizontal boundaries of the region. Show that the form of Eq. (15.1) in ξ, η, ρ, t coordinates is

$$\frac{\partial \langle c \rangle}{\partial t} + \frac{\bar{u}}{X} \frac{\partial \langle c \rangle}{\partial \xi} + \frac{\bar{v}}{Y} \frac{\partial \langle c \rangle}{\partial \eta} + \frac{W}{Z} \frac{\partial \langle c \rangle}{\partial \rho}$$

$$= \frac{1}{X^2} \frac{\partial}{\partial \xi} \left[K_{xx} \left(\frac{\partial \langle c \rangle}{\partial \xi} - \Lambda_\xi \frac{\partial \langle c \rangle}{\partial \rho} \right) \right]$$

$$- \frac{\Lambda_\xi}{X} \frac{\partial}{\partial \rho} \left[\frac{K_{xx}}{X} \left(\frac{\partial \langle c \rangle}{\partial \xi} - \Lambda_\xi \frac{\partial \langle c \rangle}{\partial \rho} \right) \right]$$

$$+ \frac{1}{Y^2} \frac{\partial}{\partial \eta} \left[K_{yy} \left(\frac{\partial \langle c \rangle}{\partial \eta} - \Lambda_\eta \frac{\partial \langle c \rangle}{\partial \rho} \right) \right]$$

$$- \frac{\Lambda_\eta}{Y} \frac{\partial}{\partial \rho} \left[\frac{K_{yy}}{Y} \left(\frac{\partial \langle c \rangle}{\partial \eta} - \Lambda_\eta \frac{\partial \langle c \rangle}{\partial \rho} \right) \right]$$

$$+ \frac{1}{Z^2} \frac{\partial}{\partial \rho} \left(K_{zz} \frac{\partial \langle c \rangle}{\partial \rho} \right)$$

where $W = \bar{w} - (\bar{u}/X)\Lambda_\xi Z - (\bar{v}/Y)\Lambda_\eta Z$ and where

$$\Lambda_\xi = \frac{1}{Z}\left(\frac{\partial h}{\partial \xi} + \rho\frac{\partial Z}{\partial \xi}\right) \quad \Lambda_\eta = \frac{1}{Z}\left(\frac{\partial h}{\partial \eta} + \rho\frac{\partial Z}{\partial \eta}\right)$$

15.4. You have been asked to formulate the problem of determining the best location for a new power plant from the standpoint of minimizing the average yearly exposure of the population to its emissions of SO_2. Assume that the long-term average concentration of SO_2 downwind of the plant can be fairly accurately represented by the Gaussian plume equation. Let (X', Y', Z') be the location of the source in the (x', y', z') coordinate system. Assume that

$$\sigma_y^2 = a\bar{u}^\alpha (x' - X')^\beta$$

$$\sigma_z^2 = b\bar{u}^\alpha (x' - X')^\beta \tag{A}$$

where a, b, α, and β depend on the atmospheric stability. The wind $\bar{u}$ is assumed to be in the x' direction. A conventional fixed (x, y, z) coordinate system with x and y pointing in the east and north directions, respectively, will not necessarily coincide with the (x', y', z') system which is always chosen so that the wind direction is parallel to x'. The vertical coordinate is the same in each system, that is, $z = z'$. If the (x', y') coordinate system is at an angle θ to the fixed (x, y) system, show that

$$x' = x\cos\theta + y\sin\theta$$

$$y' = -x\sin\theta + y\cos\theta \tag{B}$$

It is necessary to convert the ground-level concentration $\langle c(x', y', 0)\rangle$ to $\langle c(x, y, 0)\rangle$, the average concentration at $(x, y, 0)$ from a point source at (X, Y, Z) with the wind in a direction at an angle of θ to the x axis. Show that the result is

$$\langle c(x, y, 0)\rangle = \frac{q}{\pi(ab)^{1/2}\bar{u}^{1+\alpha}[(x - X)\cos\theta + (y - Y)\sin\theta]^\beta}$$

$$\times \exp\left\{-\frac{b[(X - x)\sin\theta + (y - Y)\cos\theta]^2 + aZ^2}{2\bar{u}^\alpha ab[(x - X)\cos\theta + (y - Y)\sin\theta]^\beta}\right\}$$

$$\tag{C}$$

and that this equation is valid as long as

$$(x - X)\cos\theta + (y - Y)\sin\theta > 0 \tag{D}$$

Now let $P(\bar{u}_j, \theta_k)$ be the fraction of the time over a year that the wind blows with speed $\bar{u}_j$ in direction θ_k. Thus, if you consider J discrete wind speed classes and K directions,

$$\sum_{j=1}^{J} \sum_{k=1}^{K} P(\bar{u}_j, \theta_k) = 1 \qquad (E)$$

The yearly average concentration at location $(x, y, 0)$ from the source at (X, Y, Z) is given by

$$c(x, y, 0) = \sum_{j=1}^{J} \sum_{k=1}^{K} \langle c(x, y, 0)\rangle P(\bar{u}_j, \theta_k) \qquad (F)$$

where $\langle c(x, y, 0)\rangle$ is given by (C). The total exposure of the region is defined by

$$E = \int\int C(x, y, 0)\, dx\, dy \qquad (H)$$

The optimal source location problem is then: Choose (X, Y) (assuming the stack height Z is fixed) to minimize E subject to the constraint that (X, Y) lies in the region.

Carry through the solution for the optimal location X of a ground-level crosswind line source (parallel to the y axis) on a region $0 \le x \le L$. Let $P_0(\bar{u}_j)$ and $P_1(\bar{u}_j)$ be the fractions of the time that the wind blows in the $+x$ and $-x$ directions, respectively. Show that the value of X to minimize E subject to $0 \le X \le L$ is

$$X_{opt} = \begin{cases} 0 & \alpha_0 < \alpha_1 \\ L & \alpha_0 > \alpha_1 \end{cases}$$

$$\alpha_i = \frac{q}{\pi^{1/2} a} \frac{L^{(1-\beta/2)}}{1 - \beta/2} \sum_{j=1}^{J} \bar{u}_j^{-\alpha/2} P_i(\bar{u}_j) \qquad i = 0, 1$$

15.5. When considering diffusion of species in the atmospheric boundary layer changes in air density with height are not taken into account. However, when treating diffusion up to the tropopause and beyond the effect of decreasing air density must be considered. Starting with the continuity equation for species i expressed in terms of its density ρ_i ($g\,m^{-3}$) show that the form of the atmospheric diffusion equation appropriate for vertical diffusion in the troposphere is

$$\frac{\partial \langle c_i \rangle}{\partial t} = \frac{\partial}{\partial z}\left[K_{zz}\left(\frac{\partial \langle c_i \rangle}{\partial z} - \frac{\langle c_i \rangle}{\rho} \frac{\partial \rho}{\partial z} \right) \right]$$

15.6. In Brazil ethanol is used as a replacement for gasoline as a fuel for internal combustion engines (Szwarc and Branco, 1985). In 1981 Sao Paulo had 1.8×10^6 light-duty vehicles, of which 4.6 percent were ethanol fueled and the remainder were fueled with a mixture of 80 percent gasoline/20 percent ethanol. Average exhaust emissions for Brazilian new light-duty vehicles built from 1981 through 1983 were:

Emission (g km^{-1})

Fuel	CO	HC	NO$_x$	RCHO
Pure ethanol	17.6	1.5	1.1	0.18
20/80 gasohol	28.6	2.5	1.3	0.05

Test results on the aldehyde emissions from several gasoline engines converted to ethanol gave:

Acetaldehyde	32.5 ppm
Formaldehyde	2.1
Others	3.6
Total	38.2 ppm

Assuming the airshed volume over Sao Paulo to be 1600 km^3 and that every vehicle travels 10 km day^{-1}, you have been asked to perform a "box model" simulation of the atmospheric chemistry over Sao Paulo. You may assume that the other aldehyde emissions have the properties of propionaldehyde. The hydrocarbon emissions may be assumed to have the properties of *n*-butane. We are interested in the concentration-time histories of CO, HC, NO$_x$, RCHO, and O$_3$. Assume that the NO$_2$ photolysis profile is that given in Figure 4.4. (This will underestimate the photolysis rate since Sao Paulo is closer to the equator than Los Angeles.) Discuss the information needed and the assumptions you would make in order to carry out this simulation.

SIXTEEN

Atmospheric Removal Processes
and Residence Times

Air pollutants are ultimately removed from the atmosphere by one of two mechanisms:*

1. Wet deposition—absorption into droplets followed by droplet removal by precipitation.
2. Dry deposition—uptake at the earth's surface by soil, water, or vegetation.

Figure 16.1 shows a simplified schematic of gaseous and particulate pollutant pathways indicating both wet and dry deposition processes. A number of different terms are used more or less synomously with wet deposition, including precipitation scavenging, wet removal, washout, and rainout. These terms refer to the removal of material from the atmosphere by various types of precipitation, rain, snow, etc. Washout is sometimes used specifically to refer to in-cloud scavenging and rainout to refer to below-cloud scavenging by falling rain, snow, or hail. Droplets in clouds or falling rain drops are often referred to as hydrometeors.

16.1. GENERAL REPRESENTATION OF ATMOSPHERIC REMOVAL PROCESSES

Let the mean concentration of a gaseous pollutant at (x, y, z) at time t be given by $c(x, y, z, t)$ and the mean aerosol size distribution function by $n(D_p; x, y, z, t)$. (In this chapter we will omit the braces, $\langle \ \rangle$, to indicate mean values, but all concentrations and size distribution functions are understood to represent means as predicted in atmospheric diffusion theories.) In many

---

*Chemical reaction is, of course, a mechanism whereby one species is transformed into another and thus is a removal mechanism for the original species.

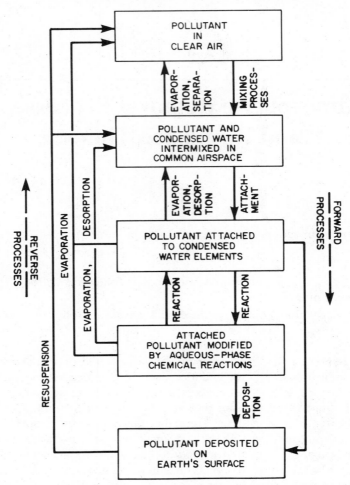

Figure 16.1. Gaseous and particulate pollutant interconversion and removal pathways.

cases it is possible to represent the local rate of removal of the gas and particles by wet deposition as first-order processes, $\Lambda(z, t)c(x, y, z, t)$ and $\Lambda(D_p; z, t)n(D_p; x, y, z, t)$. $\Lambda(z, t)$ and $\Lambda(D_p; z, t)$ are gaseous and particulate *washout coefficients*, respectively, which we have indicated to be dependent in general on height above the surface and time. This first-order representation can be used when the scavenging is irreversible, such as for aerosol particles or highly soluble gases, in which case the rate of removal depends linearly on the airborne concentration of the material and is independent of the quantity of material scavenged previously.

Dry deposition is the name given to the process by which species are removed at the earth's surface. The vertical flux downward of a species is represented in terms of an empirical parameter called the *deposition velocity* v_d multiplied by the concentration of the material at some height z_1 just above the surface,

$$\text{Flux} = v_d c(x, y, z_1, t) \tag{16.1}$$

If the concentration c is that predicted by the atmospheric diffusion equation, then the above expression can be used to equate fluxes at $z = z_1$, to produce a boundary condition to the equation at $z = z_1$ (recall Eq. (14.11)):

$$K_{zz}\left(\frac{\partial c}{\partial z}\right)_{z=z_1} = v_d c(x, y, z_1, t) \tag{16.2}$$

The deposition velocity v_d depends on the particular species or material that is being removed, on the meteorological parameters characterizing the state of the surface layer, and on the nature of the surface itself.

The *wet flux* to the surface is the sum of wet removal from all volume elements aloft, assuming that the scavenged material comes down as precipitation,

$$W_g = \int_0^\infty \Lambda(z, t) c(x, y, z, t)\, dz \tag{16.3}$$

$$W_p = \int_0^\infty \Lambda(D_p; z, t) n(D_p; x, y, z, t)\, dz \tag{16.4}$$

Based on W_g and W_p, we can define the *wet deposition velocity*,

$$v_w = \frac{W_g}{c(x, y, 0, t)} \tag{16.5}$$

Thus, if the material being scavenged is uniformly distributed vertically in a layer of depth H, then the wet deposition velocity is just

$$v_w = \int_0^H \Lambda(z, t)\, dz = \overline{\Lambda} H \tag{16.6}$$

For $H = 1$ km, $\Lambda = 10^{-4}$ sec^{-1}, $v_w = 10$ cm sec^{-1}.

We define the *washout ratio* as

$$w_r = \frac{\text{concentration of material in surface-level precipitation}}{\text{concentration of material in surface-level air}}$$

$$= \frac{c(\text{aq})}{c(x, y, 0, t)} \tag{16.7}$$

The wet flux can be expressed in terms of $c(aq)$ by

$$W = c(aq) p_0 \tag{16.8}$$

where p_0 is the precipitation intensity, usually reported in mm hr^{-1}. Typical values of p_0 are:

$$0.5 \text{ mm hr}^{-1} \quad \text{drizzle}$$
$$25 \text{ mm hr}^{-1} \quad \text{heavy rain}$$

Slinn (1983) has estimated the order of magnitude of w_r. Say a 1 mm (1000 μm) diameter raindrop is the result of the coalescence of 10^6, 10 μm cloud droplets. If each cloud droplet formed as a result of water condensation on an aerosol particle, then each drop contains 10^6 particles. If the typical number concentration of aerosol particles is 10^2 cm^{-3}, then $w_r \cong 10^7$.

The relation between the wet deposition velocity v_w and the washout ratio w_r is

$$v_w = \frac{W}{c(x, y, 0, t)} = \frac{c(aq) p_0}{c(x, y, 0, t)} = w_r p_0 \tag{16.9}$$

For example, if $w_r = 10^6$ and $p_0 = 1$ mm hr^{-1}, then $v_w = 28$ cm sec^{-1}.

To calculate the rates of wet and dry deposition it is necessary to determine the washout coefficient Λ and the deposition velocity v_d, respectively. In the sections following we consider these determinations.

16.2.   PRECIPITATION SCAVENGING OF PARTICLES

We begin our analysis of atmospheric removal processes with the precipitation scavenging of particles by falling drops. As a drop falls through the air it collides with aerosol particles and collects them. We let the diameter of the falling drop be $\tilde{D}_p$ and that of the particles being collected be D_p. Let $V_t(\tilde{D}_p)$ and $v_t(D_p)$ be the fall velocities of the drop and the particles, respectively. The "collision volume" swept out by the falling drop in time dt is $(\pi/4)(\tilde{D}_p + D_p)^2(V_t(\tilde{D}_p) - v_t(D_p)) \, dt$. This collision volume can be visualized as the volume of space within which a collision will occur if a particle of diameter D_p is contained within it. The number of particles of diameter D_p collected in time dt is then just the product of the collision volume and $n(D_p) \, dD_p$. This product would give us the number of particles of diameter D_p collected in time dt if the trajectories of the particles being collected did not depend on the airflow characteristics around the falling drop. However, because the flow streamlines must diverge to go around the falling drop, some of the particles in the collision volume actually get carried by the air flow around the falling drop. Whether a collision will occur or not depends on the fall velocity of the drop, its size, the size of the particle, and its mass. Predicting the trajectory of a particle in the flow around a sphere is a complicated undertaking and beyond our scope (Pruppacher and Klett, 1978). Rather than attempt to model the process fundamentally we will introduce an empirical collision efficiency $E(D_p, \tilde{D}_p)$ which is just the fraction of the particles of diameter D_p contained within the collision volume of a drop of diameter $\tilde{D}_p$ that are collected. Thus, the number of collisions per unit time between particles of diameter D_p and a drop of diameter $\tilde{D}_p$ is

$$\frac{\pi}{4}(D_p + \tilde{D}_p)^2(V_t(\tilde{D}_p) - v_t(D_p))E(D_p, \tilde{D}_p)n(D_p)\,dD_p \qquad (16.10)$$

The rate of accumulation of particle mass experienced by a single collector droplet is

$$\frac{\pi}{4}(D_p + \tilde{D}_p)^2(V_t(\tilde{D}_p) - v_t(D_p))E(D_p, \tilde{D}_p)n_m(D_p)\,dD_p \qquad (16.11)$$

The total rate of collection of mass of all particles of diameter D_p is obtained by integrating Eq. (16.11) over the size distribution of collector droplets,

$$n_m(D_p)\,dD_p\int_0^\infty \frac{\pi}{4}(D_p + \tilde{D}_p)^2(V_t(\tilde{D}_p) - v_t(D_p))E(D_p, \tilde{D}_p)N(\tilde{D}_p)\,d\tilde{D}_p$$

$$(16.12)$$

where $N(\tilde{D}_p)$ is the size distribution function of collector droplets. The integral in Eq. (16.12) is, in fact, the scavenging coefficient $\Lambda(D_p)$,

$$\Lambda(D_p) = \int_0^\infty \frac{\pi}{4}(D_p + \tilde{D}_p)^2(V_t(\tilde{D}_p) - v_t(D_p))E(D_p, \tilde{D}_p)N(\tilde{D}_p)\,d\tilde{D}_p$$

$$(16.13)$$

Two approximations can generally be made in the expression Eq. (16.13):

1. $V_t(\tilde{D}_p) \gg v_t(D_p)$
2. $(D_p + \tilde{D}_p)^2 \cong \tilde{D}_p^2$

With these approximations, Eq. (16.13) becomes

$$\Lambda(D_p) = \int_0^\infty \frac{\pi}{4}\tilde{D}_p^2 V_t(\tilde{D}_p)E(D_p, \tilde{D}_p)N(\tilde{D}_p)\,d\tilde{D}_p \qquad (16.14)$$

The collecting droplet size distribution $N(\tilde{D}_p)$ is not usually known with much certainty. The rainfall rate (mm hr^{-1}) can be measured easily and is related to the raindrop size distribution by

$$p_0 = \int_0^\infty \frac{\pi}{6}\tilde{D}_p^3 V_t(\tilde{D}_p)N(\tilde{D}_p)\,d\tilde{D}_p \qquad (16.15)$$

Thus, one can propose a form for the raindrop size distribution and determine its parameters so that the observed rainfall rate is matched.

16.2.1. Collision Efficiency

The collision efficiency $E(D_p, \tilde{D}_p)$ is equal to the ratio of the total number of collisions occurring between droplets and particles to the total number of particles in an area equal to the droplet's effective cross-sectional area. A value of $E = 1$ implies that all particles in the geometric volume swept out by a falling drop will be collected by the drop. Usually $E < 1$, although E can exceed unity if electrical effects are present. If not all particles that hit a hydrometeor stick, then E must be multiplied by a retention efficiency factor. We assume here that all particles that strike the surface of a droplet are retained by it.

Three distinct mechanisms can be identified whereby particles in the air reach the surface of the falling drop. Particles undergo *Brownian diffusion* that will bring some particles in contact with the drop due to their random motion as they are carried past the sphere by the flow. Because the Brownian diffusivity of particles increases as particle size decreases, we expect that this removal mechanism will be most important for small particles. When analyzing collection by Brownian diffusion, we treat the particles as diffusing massless points. *Interception* takes place when a particle, following the streamlines of flow around an obstacle, is of a size sufficiently large that its surface and that of the obstacle come into contact. Thus, if the streamline on which the particle center lies is within a distance $D_p/2$ of the drop, interception occurs. *Inertial impaction* occurs when a particle is unable to follow the rapidly curving streamlines around an obstacle and, because of its inertia, continues to move toward the obstacle along a path of less curvature than the flow streamlines. Note that the mechanism of inertial impaction is based on the premise that the particle has mass but no size, whereas interception is based on the notion that the particle has size but no mass.

Prediction of the form of E by solving the Navier–Stokes equations around a sphere, followed by solution of the particle equation of motion in that flow field, is an extremely difficult undertaking. An alternative is to rely on dimensional analysis coupled with experimental data. To formulate a correlation for E based on dimensional analysis we must identify the dimensionless groups that arise in the dimensionless equations for capture of a particle by a falling sphere. In doing so, we find that E depends on eight variables: $D_p, \tilde{D}_p, V_t, v_t, \mu_w, \mu_a, D, \rho_a$. The viscosity of water μ_w appears because if internal circulations are established in the drop, they will affect the flow field around it and thus the capture efficiency. These eight variables have three dimensions. Thus, by the Buckingham pi theorem, there are five independent dimensionless groups. The actual groups can be obtained by nondimensionalizing the equations of motion for air and for the particles. The five dimensionless groups and the correlation for E given by Slinn (1983) are:

$$\mathrm{Re} = \frac{\tilde{D}_p V_t \rho_a}{2\mu_a}$$ Reynolds number of collector droplet (defined here on the basis of droplet radius)

$$\mathrm{Sc} = \frac{\mu_a}{\rho_a D}$$ Schmidt number of collected particle

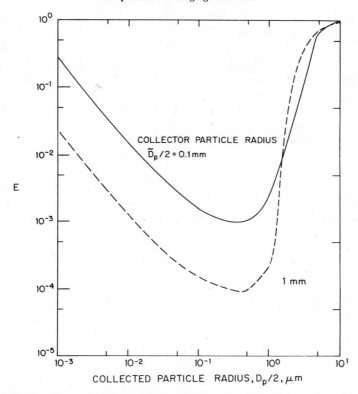

Figure 16.2. Semi-empirical correlation for the collection efficiency E of two drops (Slinn, 1983). The collected particle is assumed to have unit density. For particles of density different from 1.0, the last term in Eq. (16.16) should be scaled by $(\rho_w/\rho_p)^{1/2}$.

$St = 2\tau(V_t - v_t)/\tilde{D}_p$ Stokes number of collected particle (See Eq. (8.40) for definition of τ.)

$\mathcal{K} = D_p/\tilde{D}_p$ Ratio of diameters of collected particle and collector drop

$\omega = \mu_w/\mu_a$ Viscosity ratio

$$E = \frac{4}{\text{Re Sc}}[1 + 0.4\,\text{Re}^{1/2}\text{Sc}^{1/3} + 0.16\,\text{Re}^{1/2}\text{Sc}^{1/2}]$$

$$+ 4\mathcal{K}\left[\omega^{-1} + (1 + 2\,\text{Re}^{1/2})\mathcal{K}\right] + \left[\frac{St - S_*}{St - S_* + 2/3}\right]^{3/2} \quad (16.16)$$

where

$$S_* = \frac{1.2 + (1/12)\ln(1 + \text{Re})}{1 + \ln(1 + \text{Re})} \quad (16.17)$$

The first term in Eq. (16.16) is the contribution from Brownian diffusion, the second is due to interception, and the third represents impaction.

Figure 16.2 shows E calculated from Eq. (16.16) as a function of $D_p/2$ for $\tilde{D}_p/2 = 0.1$ mm and 1.0 mm. Diffusion dominates the collection for small D_p, whereas impaction and interception control removal for large D_p. The characteristic minimum in E occurs in the regime where the particles are too large to have an appreciable Brownian diffusivity yet too small to be collected effectively by either impaction or interception.

16.2.2. Scavenging Rates

We formulated the scavenging coefficient $\Lambda(D_p)$ in terms of the removal of particles of size D_p. We are generally interested in the removal of particles of all sizes. If $\tilde{n}(D_p)$ is the normalized size distribution function,

$$\tilde{n}(D_p) = \frac{n(D_p)}{\int_0^\infty n(D_p)\, dD_p} \tag{16.18}$$

then the normalized, particle average removal rates for the qth moment of the size distribution is

$$\overline{\Lambda}_q = \frac{\int_0^\infty \Lambda(D_p) D_p^q \tilde{n}(D_p)\, dD_p}{\int_0^\infty D_p^q \tilde{n}(D_p)\, dD_p} \tag{16.19}$$

For example, when $q = 2$, $\overline{\Lambda}_2$ is the mean scavenging coefficient for particle surface area and when $q = 3$, $\overline{\Lambda}_3$ is that for particle volume or mass.

Let us illustrate some calculations of particle scavenging rates. To do so let us assume that the falling drops are monodisperse and that the collected particles have the log–normal distribution,

$$\tilde{n}(D_p) = \frac{1}{(2\pi)^{1/2} D_p \log \sigma_g} \exp\left[-\frac{(\log D_p - \log \overline{D}_{pg})^2}{2(\log \sigma_g)^2} \right] \tag{16.20}$$

Figure 16.3 shows the mean scavenging coefficient for particle mass, $\overline{\Lambda}_3/p_0$, normalized by the rainfall rate as a function of the geometric mean particle size $\overline{D}_{pg}$ of the collected particles for $\tilde{D}_p = 0.04$ cm for several values of the geometric standard deviation σ_g. When the geometric mean particle size is less than 0.01 μm, the scavenging rate increases with decreasing σ_g. For geometric mean particle sizes exceeding about 0.1 μm, the scavenging rate increases with increasing σ_g. Past $\overline{D}_{pg}$ about 10 μm, the scavenging coefficient becomes only weakly dependent on σ_g. These trends can be explained by considering the nature of the collection efficiency $E(D_p, \tilde{D}_p)$. For $D_p < 0.01$ μm, E decreases as D_p increases. For a given value of $\overline{D}_{pg}$ an increase in σ_g means that more

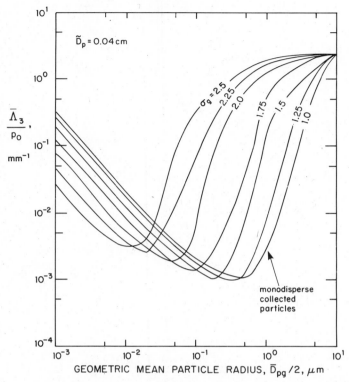

Figure 16.3. Mean scavenging coefficient for particle mass normalized by the rainfall rate as a function of the geometric mean particle radius, $\overline{D}_{pg}/2$, of the collected particles for various values of the geometric standard deviation σ_g of the collected particles. Collector particle diameter is $\tilde{D}_p = 0.04$ cm.

particles are larger than the average particle size than when σ_g is smaller. Since we are considering here the mean scavenging coefficient for particle mass, larger particles contribute proportionately more to the scavenging rate than do the smaller particles. Since the larger particles have a lower collection efficiency in this particle size range, a larger σ_g results in a lower overall mass collection efficiency and hence a lower scavenging rate. In the region of $D_p > 0.1$ μm, E increases with increasing D_p. Thus, an increasing σ_g at a fixed value of $\overline{D}_{pg}$ leads to proportionately more particle mass in the larger size range and thus to a larger overall mass collection efficiency due to the preferential weighting of larger particles inherent in $\overline{\Lambda}_3$. At about $\overline{D}_{pg} = 5$ μm, E approaches 1.0, so the number of particles larger than the geometric mean particle size no longer influences the scavenging rate.

Figure 16.4 shows $\overline{\Lambda}_q/p_0$, for $q = 0, 1, 2, 3$ as a function of $\overline{D}_{pg}$ for $\sigma_g = 2.0$ and $\tilde{D}_p = 0.04$ cm. Thus, we examine here how the choice of the moment q of the distribution influences the normalized mean scavenging coefficient. For

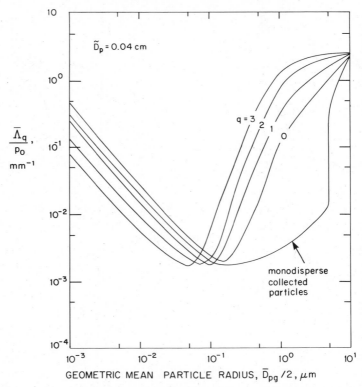

Figure 16.4. Mean scavenging coefficient for the qth moment of particle size normalized by the rainfall rate, $\overline{\Lambda}_q/p_0$ as a function of the geometric mean particle radius, $\overline{D}_{pg}/2$ of the collected particles for a geometric standard deviation $\sigma_g = 2.0$. Collector particle diameter $\tilde{D}_p = 0.04$ cm.

particles between 0.001 and 0.005 μm, the smaller the moment, the higher the scavenging rate. As q is increased, the influence of larger particles on the scavenging rate increases because for a given particle size distribution the average of the qth moment of the distribution increases with q. For example, the mass average particle diameter is larger than the surface area average particle diameter. Since in this small particle size range larger particles have lower collection efficiencies than smaller particles, the higher the moment q, the lower the overall collection efficiency and hence the lower the overall scavenging rate. For particles larger than about 0.1 μm, E increases with increasing D_p and thus the larger moment q, the higher the scavenging rate. As $\overline{D}_{pg}$ approaches 10 μm, E becomes constant, and the scavenging rate becomes independent of the moment q.

Figures 16.5 and 16.6 are the same as Figures 16.3 and 16.4 except that $\tilde{D}_p = 0.4$ cm instead of 0.04 cm. The shapes of the curves are similar to those

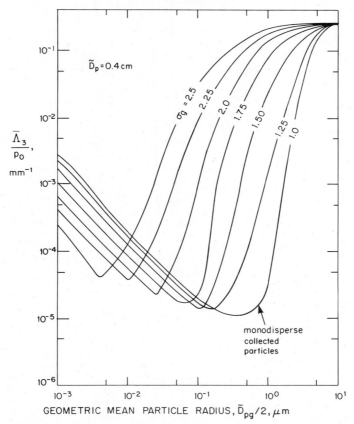

$\dfrac{\bar{\Lambda}_3}{p_0},$

mm^{-1}

GEOMETRIC MEAN PARTICLE RADIUS, $\bar{D}_{pg}/2,\,\mu m$

Figure 16.5. Mean scavenging coefficient for particle mass normalized by the rainfall rate as a function of the geometric mean particle radius, $\bar{D}_{pg}/2$, of the collected particles for various values of the geometric standard deviation σ_g of the collected particles. Collector particle diameter is $\tilde{D}_p = 0.4$ cm.

in Figures 16.3 and 16.4 and are explainable by the same arguments as given above. The scavenging rates are lower for the larger droplets because the larger $\tilde{D}_p$, the smaller is E, and also because the scavenging rate normalized by p_0 is inversely proportional to $\tilde{D}_p$.

Although we do not show calculations here in which both the collected and collector particles have size distributions, such results are given by Slinn (1983). The scavenging coefficient for a monodisperse droplet distribution is larger than that for a polydisperse one since E decreases as $\tilde{D}_p$ increases for an identical distribution of collected particles. Scavenging rates for large aerosol particles ($D_p > 5\ \mu m$) are roughly independent of the collecting drop size distributions since at the large particle end of the collected particle size spectrum E is not a strong function of $\tilde{D}_p$.

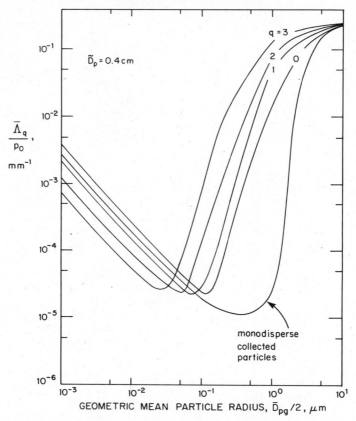

Figure 16.6. Mean scavenging coefficient for the qth moment of particle size normalized by the rainfall rate, $\overline{\Lambda}_q/p_0$ as a function of the geometric mean particle radius, $\overline{D}_{pg}/2$, of the collected particles for a geometric standard deviation $\sigma_g = 2.0$. Collector particle diameter $\tilde{D}_p = 0.4$ cm.

16.3.   PRECIPITATION SCAVENGING OF GASES

The difficult aspect of the precipitation scavenging of particles lies in predicting the collection efficiency. Although there is some uncertainty about the retention efficiency once a particle intercepts a droplet, it is generally assumed, and there is no strong evidence not to assume, that once a particle comes into contact with a droplet it is irreversibly captured. In the precipitation scavenging of gases the rate of transfer of gas molecules to the surface of a stationary or falling droplet can be very accurately predicted; difficulties in predicting gas scavenging rates arise when the scavenged gas has an appreciable vapor pressure over the surface of the drop and thus the composition of the drop must be known in order to predict the net rate of transfer of material to the drop.

The flux of a gaseous species to a cloud or rain drop can be expressed as $k_c(c - c_s)$, where k_c is the species' mass transfer coefficient (cm sec^{-1}), c is the bulk concentration of the species, and c_s is the concentration of the species just at the droplet surface, that is, in equilibrium with the aqueous-phase concentration of the dissolved gas. (Recall Section 6.7.) The mass transfer coefficient for a sphere was given by Eq. (6.62),

$$k_c = D/\tilde{D}_p(2 + 0.6\,\mathrm{Re}^{1/2}\mathrm{Sc}^{1/3}) \qquad (16.21)$$

where the Reynolds number is defined on the basis of the droplet diameter, $\mathrm{Re} = \tilde{D}_p V_t \rho_a / \mu_a$.

16.3.1. Scavenging of an Irreversibly Soluble Gas

Let us begin our study of the precipitation scavenging of gases with a gas that is, for all practical purposes, irreversibly soluble, namely nitric acid (HNO_3) (Levine and Schwartz, 1982). For an irreversibly soluble gas $c_s = 0$. Nitric acid/water equilibria are

$$HNO_3(g) + H_2O \rightleftarrows HNO_3(aq)$$

$$HNO_3(aq) \rightleftarrows H^+ + NO_3^-$$

Since HNO_3 is virtually entirely ionized in aqueous solution, these two equilibria can be combined to

$$HNO_3(g) \rightleftarrows H^+ + NO_3^-$$

with an equilibrium constant of

$$K = \frac{[H^+][NO_3^-]}{p_{HNO_3}} = 1.59 \times 10^{19}\exp(-8710/T)\ \mathrm{M}^2\ \mathrm{atm}^{-1} \quad (16.22)$$

From the value of K at 298 K, $3.26 \times 10^6\ \mathrm{M}^2\ \mathrm{atm}^{-1}$, we see that the assumption that $c_s = 0$ is quite valid in this case.

In simulating gas scavenging by precipitation one may calculate the rate of increase with time or fall distance of the concentration of dissolved gas as a function of droplet size or one may calculate the rate of decrease of the gas-phase concentration. The former approach requires that one specify the gas-phase concentration of the gas being scavenged, whereas calculating the decrease in the gas concentration requires specification of the droplet size spectrum.

The rate of increase of the concentration of irreversibly scavenged gas in a droplet is given by

$$\left(\frac{\pi \tilde{D}_p^3}{6}\right) \frac{dc(\text{aq})}{dt} = \left(\pi \tilde{D}_p^2\right) \times (\text{Flux of species to the drop}) \qquad (16.23)$$

or, using the flux expression, $k_c c$,

$$\frac{dc(\text{aq})}{dt} = \frac{6k_c c}{\tilde{D}_p} \qquad (16.24)$$

For a raindrop falling at its terminal velocity V_t,

$$\frac{dc(\text{aq})}{dz} = \frac{1}{V_t} \frac{dc(\text{aq})}{dt} \qquad (16.25)$$

where z is the fall distance. For constant c, we can substitute Eq. (16.24) into Eq. (16.25) and integrate to obtain

$$c(\text{aq}) = \frac{6k_c}{\tilde{D}_p V_t} cz \qquad (16.26)$$

Thus, when the scavenged gas has a uniform vertical concentration, the quantity of a dissolved, irreversibly scavenged gas increases linearly with fall distance of the drop. The quantity $6k_c / \tilde{D}_p V_t RT$ represents the concentration of dissolved gas achieved per unit fall distance and per unit partial pressure of the gas.

To calculate the rate of decrease of the gas concentration as a result of scavenging, one represents the rate of removal as Λc. Given the droplet size distribution $N(\tilde{D}_p)$, the local rate of removal of an irreversibly soluble gas like HNO_3 is

$$\int_0^\infty k_c \left(\pi \tilde{D}_p^2\right) c N\left(\tilde{D}_p\right) d\tilde{D}_p$$

from which the scavenging coefficient is

$$\Lambda = \int_0^\infty \pi \tilde{D}_p^2 k_c N\left(\tilde{D}_p\right) d\tilde{D}_p \qquad (16.27)$$

TABLE 16.1. Parameters and Calculated Values of Λ for Cloud Savenging of HNO_3[a]

$\tilde{D}_p$, cm	5×10^{-4} to 40×10^{-4}
a, cm^{-4}	2.87
b, cm^{-1}	2.65
N_0, cm^{-3}	288
L, g cm^{-3}	0.17
Λ	0.19

[a]Levine and Schwartz (1982).

Let us first consider in-cloud scavenging and then below-cloud scavenging of an irreversibly soluble gas like HNO_3. We will calculate Λ by Eq. (16.27) assuming a cloud droplet size distribution $N(\tilde{D}_p)$. Levine and Schwartz (1982) used the cloud droplet size distribution of Battan and Reitan (1957),

$$N(\tilde{D}_p) = ae^{-b\tilde{D}_p} \tag{16.28}$$

Table 16.1 gives the parameters and the resulting calculated value of Λ for

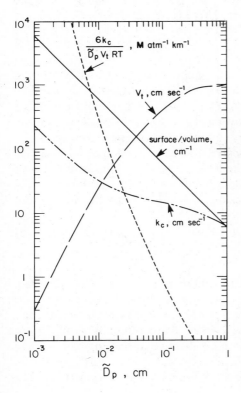

Figure 16.7. Mass transfer coefficient k_c, terminal fall velocity V_t, surface to volume ratio, and group $6k_c/\tilde{D}_p V_t RT$ as a function of droplet diameter $\tilde{D}_p$ (Levine and Schwartz, 1982).

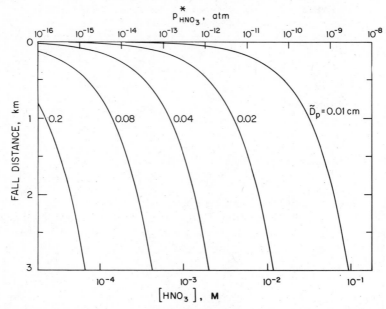

Figure 16.8. Concentration of dissolved HNO_3 and corresponding equilibrium vapor pressure over drops of different diameters as a function of fall distance for $p_{HNO_3} = 10^{-8}$ atm (10 ppb) (Levine and Schwartz, 1982).

cloud scavenging of HNO_3. The value of Λ, approximately 0.2 sec^{-1}, gives a characteristic time of 5 sec for the scavenging of a highly soluble gas like HNO_3 in a cloud. Thus, the uptake process in the cloud is rapid compared with the characteristic times of air movement through the cloud and of the change of cloud liquid water amounts by condensation and precipitation.

To calculate the concentration of dissolved gas as a function of fall distance for a drop we need an expression for the terminal velocity V_t as a function of drop size $\tilde{D}_p$. There are several expressions available for $V_t(\tilde{D}_p)$ (Beard, 1976; Pruppacher and Klett, 1978). For our calculations we will use the correlation,

$$V_t = 958\left[1 - \exp\left(-\left(\tilde{D}_p/0.1710\right)^{1.147}\right)\right] (cm\ sec^{-1}) \qquad (16.29)$$

where $\tilde{D}_p$ is in cm.

Figure 16.7 shows k_c, V_t, the surface to volume ratio, and $6k_c/\tilde{D}_p V_t RT$ as a function of $\tilde{D}_p$, and Figure 16.8 gives the concentrations of dissolved HNO_3 and corresponding equilibrium vapor pressures over drops of different diameters as a function of fall distance for $p_{HNO_3} = 10^{-8}$ atm (10 ppb). From Figure 16.7 it is evident that smaller drops are more effective in scavenging a soluble gas due to their lower fall velocity and increased mass transfer rate for dissolution and larger surface to volume ratio. We note from Figure 16.8 that a

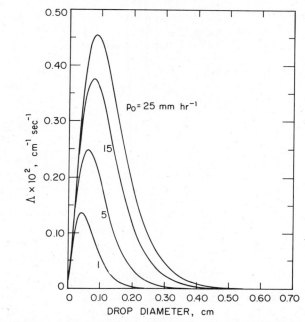

Figure 16.9. Differential scavenging coefficient for the Marshall–Palmer raindrop size distribution (Levine and Schwartz, 1982).

very strong dependence of dissolved HNO_3 on drop size exists. Finally, we see that, except for the very smallest drops, the assumption that $c \gg c_s$ is well justified.

To calculate the scavenging coefficient Λ for rain scavenging we need to specify a raindrop size distribution $N(\tilde{D}_p)$. A frequently used raindrop size distribution is that of Marshall and Palmer (1948),

$$N(\tilde{D}_p) = 0.08 \exp\left(-41\tilde{D}_p p_0^{-0.21}\right) \qquad \tilde{D}_p \geq 0.12 \text{ cm} \qquad (16.30)$$

Figure 16.9 shows the scavenging coefficient,

$$\Lambda(\tilde{D}_p) = \pi \tilde{D}_p^2 k_c N(\tilde{D}_p) \qquad (16.31)$$

for the Marshall-Palmer raindrop size distribution. We note that as rain intensity p_0 increases, $\Lambda(\tilde{D}_p)$ increases. $\Lambda(\tilde{D}_p)$ drops off sharply with $\tilde{D}_p$ for drops larger than 0.1 cm diameter. Table 16.2 gives values of Λ integrated over the entire drop size distribution for various values of p_0. Note the dependence of Λ on the assumed lower limit of the drop size distribution. The difficulty in specifying the lower limit of the drop size distribution is a serious drawback in estimating the overall scavenging coefficient Λ. The cutoff limit of 0.12 cm

TABLE 16.2.   Scavenging Coefficients Λ (sec^{-1}) for
Below-Cloud Scavenging of Nitric Acid Vapor Based on
Marshall–Palmer Raindrop Size Distribution

Rainfall Intensity, p_0 mm hr^{-1}	Minimum Assumed Drop Diameter, $\tilde{D}_p$, cm		
	10^{-10}	0.02	0.12
1	1.2×10^{-4}	1.09×10^{-4}	1.24×10^{-5}
5	3.01×10^{-4}	2.89×10^{-4}	8.08×10^{-5}
15	5.67×10^{-4}	5.54×10^{-4}	2.34×10^{-4}
25	7.61×10^{-4}	7.47×10^{-4}	3.65×10^{-4}
	Λ/p_0 (mm^{-1})		
1	0.431	0.394	0.045
5	0.217	0.208	0.058
15	0.136	0.133	0.056
25	0.110	0.108	0.053

excludes from consideration a large number of small drops that could be responsible for an appreciable fraction of the overall scavenging. Because Marshall and Palmer indicated that Eq. (16.30) may overestimate by as much as 50 percent the number of drops in the 0.02–0.12 cm drop diameter range, the actual value of Λ probably falls somewhere between those for the 0.02 and 0.12 cm cutoffs.

The scavenging rates calculated are in the range of 1 to 3 percent min^{-1} and indicate that below-cloud HNO$_3$ vapor can be significantly depleted during a typical 10 to 30 minute rainfall.

16.3.2.   Scavenging of Reversibly Soluble Gases

Let us now consider a raindrop falling through a layer containing CO_2, SO_2, HNO$_3$, NH$_3$, O_3, and H_2O_2. To illustrate the basic approach to dealing with the scavenging of reversibly soluble gases let us return for a moment to HNO$_3$, which is one of the gases we assume to be present here. Denote the dissolved HNO$_3$ in the drop by

$$[HNO_3(\text{total})] = [HNO_3(\text{aq})] + [NO_3^-]$$

(Previously we neglected HNO$_3$(aq) in Eq. (16.22).) The rate of change of total dissolved HNO$_3$ due to absorption by the falling drop is

$$\left(\frac{\pi \tilde{D}_p^3}{6}\right) V_t \frac{d[HNO_3(\text{total})]}{dz} = (\pi \tilde{D}_p^2) k_{c_{HNO_3}} \left(\frac{p_{HNO_3}}{RT} - \frac{[HNO_3(\text{aq})]}{H_{HNO_3}RT}\right)$$

$$(16.32)$$

Thus, the total dissolved nitric acid changes due to mass transfer, as described by the product of the mass transfer coefficient for HNO_3 transport to a falling sphere of diameter $\tilde{D}_p$ in air, $k_{c_{HNO_3}}$, and the "driving force," which is the difference between the ambient HNO_3 concentration, p_{HNO_3}/RT, and the vapor pressure of HNO_3 just above the drop surface corresponding to $[HNO_3(aq)]$. In the previous section we assumed that all the dissolved HNO_3 went to H^+ and NO_3^- so that $[NHO_3(aq)] \cong 0$. Setting $[HNO_3(aq)] = 0$ in Eq. (16.32) reduces Eq. (16.32) to Eq. (16.24). We showed in fact that for all but the smallest of drops this is a good assumption for HNO_3.* Nevertheless, let us retain the $[HNO_3(aq)]$ term in Eq. (16.32) as a means of showing how to treat the general reversibly soluble gas.

Using the HNO_3 dissociation equilibrium,

$$K_{n1} = \frac{[H^+][NO_3^-]}{[HNO_3(aq)]} \tag{16.33}$$

Eq. (16.32) can be written as

$$V_t \frac{d}{dz} \left\{ \frac{[H^+][NO_3^-]}{K_{n1}} + [NO_3^-] \right\} = \frac{6k_{c_{HNO_3}}}{\tilde{D}_p RT} \left(p_{HNO_3} - \frac{[H^+][NO_3^-]}{H_{HNO_3} K_{n1}} \right) \tag{16.34}$$

Equation (16.34) is an example of a material balance obtained on a drop for a gas that dissociates upon absorption but does not participate in further aqueous-phase chemistry.

Consider now H_2O_2 and O_3, gases that do not dissociate upon absorption but which do participate in aqueous-phase chemistry. For H_2O_2, for example, the material balance on the drop is

$$V_t \frac{d[H_2O_2(aq)]}{dz} = \frac{6k_{c_{H_2O_2}}}{\tilde{D}_p RT} \left(p_{H_2O_2} - \frac{[H_2O_2(aq)]}{H_{H_2O_2}} \right) + \left(\frac{d[H_2O_2(aq)]}{dt} \right)_{reaction} \tag{16.35}$$

A similar equation holds for O_3.

Finally, consider the sulfur balances. First for [S(IV)]

$$V_t \frac{d[S(IV)]}{dz} = \frac{6k_{c_{SO_2}}}{\tilde{D}_p RT} \left(p_{SO_2} - \frac{[SO_2(aq)]}{H_{SO_2}} \right) + \left(\frac{d[S(IV)]}{dt} \right)_{reaction} \tag{16.36}$$

---

*In the case of HNO_3, at the beginning of the drop's fall, if the pH of the drop is relatively high, any HNO_3 absorbed more or less totally dissociates leading to irreversible absorption. Later on, if the pH falls substantially, some of the dissolved HNO_3 may exist as $HNO_3(aq)$, providing some resistance to further absorption.

and for S(VI),

$$V_t \frac{d\,[S(VI)]}{dz} = -\left(\frac{d\,[S(IV)]}{dt}\right)_{\text{reaction}} \qquad (16.37)$$

The differential equations for $[H^+]$, $[NO_3^-]$, $[S(IV)]$, and $[S(VI)]$ are coupled through the electroneutrality relation,

$$[H^+] + [NH_4^+] = [OH^-] + [HCO_3^-] + 2[CO_3^{2-}]$$

$$+ [HSO_3^-] + 2[SO_3^{2-}] + [NO_3^-] + 2[SO_4^{2-}] \qquad (16.38)$$

(We have neglected the sulfate/bisulfate equilibrium.) We assume that prior to its fall the drop is already equilibrated with the ambient levels of CO_2 and NH_3. Every term in Eq. (16.38) except $[NO_3^-]$ and $[SO_4^{2-}]$ can be related to $[H^+]$ and gas-phase partial pressures.

The unknown dependent variables in the problem are $[H^+]$, $[NO_3^-]$, $[S(VI)]$, $[H_2O_2]$, and $[O_3]$, for which we have four differential equations and the electroneutrality relation. When we proceed to solve this problem numerically, we find that O_3 and SO_2 reach gas-aqueous equilibrium very quickly, so that differential equations for $[O_3]$ and $[S(IV)]$ become

$$V_t \frac{d\,[O_3(aq)]}{dz} = \left(\frac{d\,[O_3(aq)]}{dt}\right)_{\text{reaction}} \qquad (16.39)$$

$$V_t \frac{d\,[S(IV)]}{dz} = \left(\frac{d\,[S(IV)]}{dt}\right)_{\text{reaction}} \qquad (16.40)$$

Thus, the more or less slightly soluble gases O_3 and SO_2 reach gas-aqueous equilibrium quickly since the drop can become readily saturated with a small quantity of solute. The highly soluble gases such as H_2O_2 and HNO_3 require a much longer time to reach equilibrium.

We consider the following four cases (all values in ppb):

Case	$p_{H_2O_2}$	p_{O_3}	p_{HNO_3}	p_{NH_3}	p_{SO_2}	p_{CO_2}
A	10	50	10	5	20	300
B	10	50	0	5	20	300
C	0	0	10	5	20	300
D	10	50	10	0	20	300

A fall distance of 1 km is assumed, and two drop sizes $\tilde{D}_p = 5$ mm and 0.2 mm are studied. Case A is the base case. In case B we remove the HNO_3, so between cases A and B we can examine the effect of nitric acid on droplet pH. There are no oxidants present in case C, so between cases A and C we can study the effect of S(IV) oxidation on the composition of the drop. Finally,

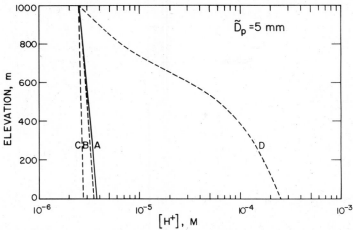

Figure 16.10. Fall of a drop through a layer containing CO_2, SO_2, HNO_3, NH_3, O_3, and H_2O_2. [H^+] as a function of fall distance in Cases A–D in the text. Drop size $\tilde{D}_p = 5$ mm.

case D has no NH_3 present, so comparing cases A and D we can see the effect of neutralization by ammonia.

Figure 16.10 shows [H^+] as a function of fall distance in cases A, B, C, and D for a $\tilde{D}_p = 5$ mm drop. As expected, the pH is lowest in case D in the absence of NH_3. The removal of HNO_3 in case B relative to case A leads to only a slight increase in pH, primarily because the large drop does not absorb

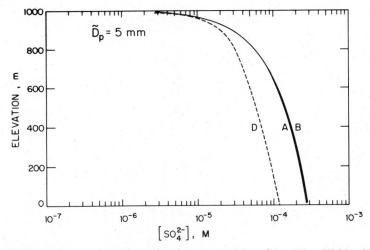

Figure 16.11. Fall of a drop through a layer containing CO_2, SO_2, HNO_3, NH_3, O_3, and H_2O_2. [SO_4^{2-}] as a function of fall distance in cases A, B, and D in the text. Drop size $\tilde{D}_p = 5$ mm.

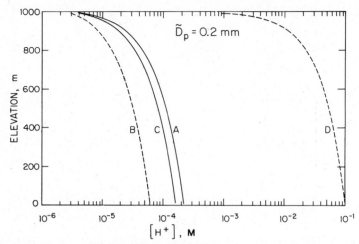

Figure 16.12. Fall of a drop through a layer containing CO_2, SO_2, HNO_3, NH_3, O_3, and H_2O_2. [H^+] as a function of fall distance in Cases A–D in the text. Drop size $\tilde{D}_p = 0.2$ mm.

an appreciable amount of HNO_3 during its fall. The corresponding sulfate profiles are given in Figure 16.11. The quantity of sulfate produced in cases A and B is virtually identical since the absence of HNO_3 for the 5 mm drop was seen in the previous figure to have only a negligible effect on pH. The higher pH in case D leads to lower sulfate formation because of the oxidation by H_2O_2.

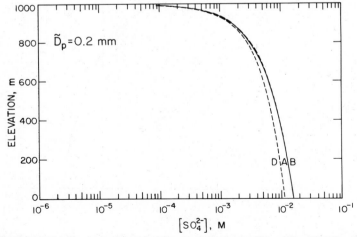

Figure 16.13. Fall of a drop through a layer containing CO_2, SO_2, HNO_3, NH_3, O_3, and H_2O_2. [SO_4^{2-}] as a function of fall distance in cases A, B, and D in the text. Drop size $\tilde{D}_p = 0.2$ mm.

TABLE 16.3.   Physical Parameters for Rain Scavenging Calculation

	$\tilde{D}_p$, mm	
	5	0.2
Time of fall, min.	1.81	22.1
V_t, m sec^{-1}	9.22	0.754
$k_{c_{HNO_3}}$, cm sec^{-1}	275	522
$k_{c_{H_2O_2}}$, cm sec^{-1}	306	588

Figures 16.12 and 16.13 show [H$^+$] and [SO$_4^{2-}$] for the 0.2 mm drop. To understand the differences between the 5 mm and 0.2 mm diameter cases it is useful to compare the physical parameters in Table 16.3. Because the smaller drop spends a much longer time in its fall, there is more time available to absorb HNO$_3$ and thus the differences between cases A and B are more pronounced than for the 5 mm droplet. As a result, the differences between cases B and C are greater than in the case of the larger droplet. The general pH attained in the 0.2 mm drop is much lower for all cases than for the 5 mm drop. Because of the pH range involved the effect of NH$_3$ on sulfate formation is less pronounced than for the larger drop.

16.4.   DRY DEPOSITION

Dry deposition refers to the transfer of airborne material, both gaseous and particulate, to the earth's surface, including soil, water, and vegetation, where it is removed. The dry deposition process can be viewed as consisting of three distinct steps. The first step involves the transport of the material through the surface layer to the immediate vicinity of the surface. This step is controlled by turbulent diffusion in the surface layer and is sometimes referred to as the *aerodynamic* component of the transfer. The second step involves the diffusion of the material through the laminar sublayer just adjacent to the surface to the ultimate absorbing substrate. This step is called the *surface* component of the transport. Although the laminar sublayer is typically only the order of 10^{-1} to 10^{-2} cm thick, the diffusion through this layer can be critically important in the overall rate of deposition. The solubility or absorptivity of species at the surface determines how much of the species that diffuses through the laminar sublayer actually is removed, and this final process, called the *transfer* component, constitutes the third step. A nonreactive species such as argon or helium is not removed at all by dry deposition, since once it has diffused to the surface it is not absorbed.

The mechanisms of transport leading to dry deposition are complex, and thus in describing the rate of removal of a species by dry deposition one does not attempt to represent the processes at their most fundamental level of detail.

The dry deposition process is represented in terms of a *deposition velocity* v_d defined in Eq. (16.1). Thus, the deposition velocity is best viewed as a proportionality constant between vertical flux and concentration whose magnitude is empirically established.

The dry deposition process can be viewed conceptually by analogy to electrical or heat flow through a series of resistances. The transfer of material from the atmosphere to the surface takes place through three resistances, the aerodynamic resistance, the surface layer resistance, and the transfer resistance. These resistances are denoted r_a, r_s, and r_t, and they have units of sec cm^{-1}. Their relation to v_d is

$$v_d = (r_a + r_s + r_t)^{-1} \qquad (16.41)$$

The aerodynamic resistance r_a accounts for the turbulent diffusion of material from the free atmosphere to the surface laminar sublayer. Thus, r_a depends on the usual meteorological parameters, such as wind speed, atmospheric stability, and surface roughness. The surface layer resistance depends on parameters characterizing diffusion across a laminar sublayer and thus on molecular rather than turbulent properties. The transfer resistance depends on the physico-chemical interaction between the material and the surface.

For dry deposition of particles it is necessary to modify Eq. (16.41) in two respects. First, the transfer resistance r_t is absent, since once the particle encounters the surface it is considered to have deposited. Second, if the particle has an appreciable settling velocity v_s, that settling velocity contributes to the deposition rate. The modified form of Eq. (16.41) for particles is then

$$v_d = (r_a + r_s + r_a r_s v_s)^{-1} + v_s \qquad (16.42)$$

Various experimental methods are used to measure deposition velocities: (1) box methods, (2) profile analysis, and (3) eddy correlation measurements. The box method consists of placing an enclosure over a surface and measuring the rate of decay of the concentration in the enclosure. Although the method is easy to use, it must be established that the presence of the enclosure does not alter the surface removal rate from that in its absence in order for data from this method to be meaningful.

The profile analysis method involves measuring the mean concentration profile to establish the downward flux. To obtain the profile, accurate concentration differences must be measured (on the order of 1 percent of the mean concentration).* To correlate the flux data with atmospheric parameters, micrometeorological measurements to establish stability, etc., are required.

---

*When sensors suitable for direct measurement of fluxes are not available, assumptions regarding the eddy diffusivity are made to provide a method for estimating fluxes from measurements of vertical concentration gradients. Hicks and Wesely (1978) and Droppo (1980) have summarized a number of critical considerations. In particular, with a typical value of $u_* = 40$ cm s^{-1} and neutral stability, the concentration difference between adjacent levels differing in height by a factor of two is about 9 percent, for a 1 cm s^{-1} deposition velocity. In unstable (daytime) conditions, smaller gradients would be expected for the same v_d; in stable conditions, they would be greater.

The eddy correlation technique is based on a direct measurement of the turbulent flux at a given level. Within the surface layer, which is typically of order 10 m deep, the flux of a species that is not being removed by rapid chemical reaction is assumed to be uniform throughout the layer. Thus, the downward flux within the surface layer is a measure of the rate of removal at the surface. The vertical flux of a species is obtained by averaging the product of the fluctuating velocity and concentration of the species, $\langle w'c' \rangle$. The sensor time response must be short enough to resolve the significant contributions to the turbulent flux. Eddy-correlation methods have been used in experiments addressing the fluxes of ozone (Eastman and Stedman 1977), sulfur (Galbally et al., 1979; Hicks and Wesely 1980), nitrogen oxides (Wesely et al., 1982), carbon dioxide (Jones and Smith, 1977), and small particles (Wesely et al., 1977).

16.4.1. Aerodynamic Resistance

As we have noted, the overall resistance to transport from the bulk atmosphere to the earth's surface can be considered to be the result of three resistances in series, the first of which is the aerodynamic resistance. Since the overall rate of dry deposition is represented by the deposition velocity, the overall resistance is expressed as the inverse of a velocity. Thus, for the aerodynamic resistance we seek an expression that is the inverse of a characteristic velocity. The aerodynamic resistance r_a is a function of the wind speed, atmospheric stability, and surface roughness and is independent of the species being transferred. This resistance can be viewed as characteristic of the resistance to momentum transfer to the surface. We will derive the expression for r_a under neutral conditions; the appropriate results for other stability conditions can be obtained from the material in Chapter 12.

Let us define a momentum transfer velocity $v_M(z_1, z_0)$ by $v_M(z_1, z_0) = u^2_*/(\bar{u}(z_1) - \bar{u}(z_0))$, which, with $\bar{u}(z_0) = 0$, becomes

$$v_M(z_1, z_0) = \frac{u_*^2}{\bar{u}(z_1)} \tag{16.43}$$

Combining Eqs. (12.57), (16.14) and (16.44) in order to eliminate u_* in favor of $\bar{u}(z_1)$ which is measurable yields

$$v_M(z_1, z_0) = \frac{\kappa^2 \bar{u}(z_1)}{(\ln(z_1/z_0))^2} \tag{16.44}$$

The momentum transfer resistance $r_a(z_1, z_0)$ is then just the inverse of $v_M(z_1, z_0)$,

$$r_a(z_1, z_0) = \frac{(\ln(z_1/z_0))^2}{\kappa^2 \bar{u}(z_1)} \tag{16.45}$$

If the aerodynamic resistance were the only resistance to dry deposition, then $v_d = r_a(z_1, z_0)^{-1} = v_M(z_1, z_0)$.

16.4.2. Surface Layer Resistance

The surface layer resistance expresses the transport step across the laminar sublayer just adjacent to the receptor surface. Although transfer across such a layer is a molecular phenomenon and thus is described in terms of the Schmidt number of the material, the structure and thickness of the layer are unknown, so we must resort to empirical analysis. The actual thickness of the laminar sub-layer depends on the value of u_*, so we write the transfer resistance across the layer as

$$r_s = A\,Sc^\alpha/u_* \tag{16.46}$$

where A and α are determined experimentally. A commonly accepted value for α is $2/3$. The wind-water tunnel results of Moller and Schumann (1970) appear to require $A \cong 1.7$, whereas Wesely and Hicks (1977) recommend $A = 5$ for SO_2 transfer to vegetated surfaces.

The surface layer resistance r_s can be related to the usual micrometeorological variables as follows. We define a height z_v below that of the roughness length z_0. The surface resistance is then represented as*

$$r_s(z_0, z_v) = \frac{1}{\kappa u_*}\ln\left(\frac{z_0}{z_v}\right) \tag{16.47}$$

Shephard (1974) recommended using the constant value

$$\ln\left(\frac{z_0}{z_v}\right) = 2.0 \tag{16.48}$$

for transfer to vegetation on the basis of data obtained over rough, vegetated surfaces. Wesely and Hicks (1977) suggested $\ln(z_0/z_v) = 2.6$ for SO_2 transfer. Using the value of 2.6, the resistance is then

$$r_s(z_0, z_v) = \frac{2.6}{\kappa u_*} \tag{16.49}$$

and eliminating u_* we have

$$r_s(z_0, z_v) = \frac{2.6}{\kappa^2 \bar{u}(z_1)}\ln\left(\frac{z_1}{z_0}\right) \tag{16.50}$$

These expressions based on a constant value for $\ln(z_0/z_v)$ do not explicitly include the Schmidt number dependence of the surface transport process.

---

*This expression is sometimes written as $r_s = (u_* B)^{-1}$, where B represents a dimensionless limiting deposition velocity for the case of concentrations measured sufficiently close to a receptor surface that the resistance to momentum transfer is negligible.

We thus have two models for the surface layer resistance to gases in dry deposition. The model having Schmidt number dependence is based essentially on laboratory studies, whereas Eq. (16.50) is an attempt to cast the surface resistance in a form similar to the aerodynamic resistance.

Small particles are transferred through the surface layer by Brownian diffusion in much the same way as gases. For larger particles both gravitational and inertial effects become important, the former characterized by the settling velocity v_s, Eq. (8.41), and the latter by the characteristic relaxation time τ of the particle, as given in Eq. (8.40). The characteristic time τ is a measure of the tendency of a particle to continue its trajectory when the air flow curves. Because of its inertia, a particle will continue along its prior path for a time the order of τ, and the larger the value of τ the greater the chance that the particle will impact on a surface. To incorporate both Brownian diffusion and inertial effects in particle motion in the surface layer, the following correlation for the surface layer has been used:

$$r_s = \left(Sc^{-2/3} + 10^{-3/St}\right)^{-1} u_*^{-1} \tag{16.51}$$

where St is the Stokes number, $St = \tau u_*^2/\nu$.

16.4.3. Transfer Resistance

The efficiency with which a surface captures molecules or particles that impact upon it is influenced considerably by its chemical composition as well as its physical structure. Uptake rates of many gases by vegetation are essentially determined by biological factors, such as the stomatal resistance. In daytime, this is known to be the case for SO_2 (Wesely and Hicks, 1977) and for O_3 in most situations (Wesely et al., 1978). The similarity between SO_2 and O_3 is not complete, however, because the presence of liquid water promotes SO_2 uptake relative to O_3 due to their differences in solubility. Surface wetness plays a role in controlling the rate of deposition of almost all airborne materials. Although this factor is difficult to quantify, we expect that hygroscopic materials will be more strongly retained than hydrophobic ones. If the surface is not a perfect sink, an additional resistance r_t exists for the final transfer of the material to the surface since not all of the impinging molecules or particles adhere to the surface.

16.4.4. Total Resistance

The dry deposition velocity for transfer to the surface is related to the individual resistances by Eq. (16.41) for gases and by Eq. (16.42) for particles, and can be expressed simply as $v_d = r_{total}^{-1}$, where r_{total} is the sum of the resistances. We would like to examine how the overall deposition velocity v_d depends on the three resistances for dry deposition of a gas. In performing this

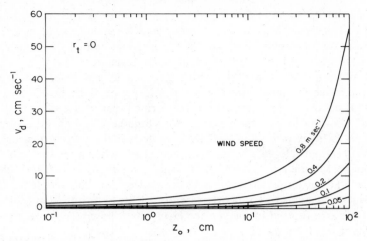

Figure 16.14. Deposition velocity as a function of roughness length z_0 for various wind speeds at $z_1 = 2m$. Transfer resistance $r_t = 0$.

analysis it is useful to employ the surface resistance model of Eq. (16.50) so that we need not specify the Schmidt number of the transferring species. The total resistance for transfer from a height z_1 to adherence to the surface is

$$r_{\text{total}} = r_a(z_1, z_0) + r_s(z_0, z_v) + r_t(z_v, 0) \qquad (16.52)$$

Using Eqs. (16.45) and (16.50) in Eq. (16.52) we have

$$r_{\text{total}} = \frac{\ln(z_1/z_0)}{\kappa^2 \bar{u}(z_1)} \left\{ \ln\left(\frac{z_1}{z_0}\right) + 2.6 \right\} + v_t^{-1} \qquad (16.53)$$

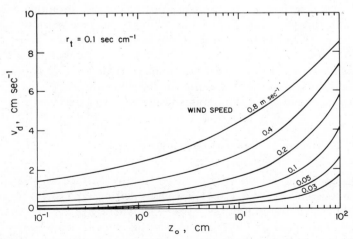

Figure 16.15. Deposition velocity as a function of roughness length z_0 for various wind speeds at $z_1 = 2m$. Transfer resistance $r_t = 0.1$ sec cm^{-1}.

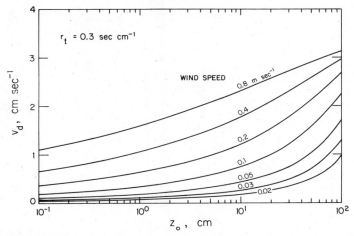

Figure 16.16. Deposition velocity as a function of roughness length z_0 for various wind speeds at $z_1 = 2m$. Transfer resistance $r_t = 0.3$ sec cm^{-1}.

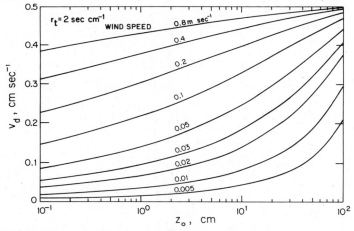

Figure 16.17. Deposition velocity as a function of roughness length z_0 for various wind speeds at $z_1 = 2m$. Transfer resistance $r_t = 2$ sec cm^{-1}.

Let us evaluate the relative importance of these three resistances by calculating the overall deposition velocity v_d as a function of the wind speed $\bar{u}(z_1)$ and the roughness length z_0 for a range of typical values. In the evaluation we have chosen $z_1 = 2$ m and varied z_0 from 0.1 to 100 cm, so as to cover all types of surfaces. Wind velocities ranging from 0.5 cm sec^{-1} to 8 m sec^{-1} will be considered. Figure 16.14 shows the variation of v_d when $r_t = 0$, whereas Figures 16.15 to 16.18 depict v_d for progressively increasing transfer resistances of 0.1, 0.3, 2.0, and 20.0 sec cm^{-1}. Figure 16.19 shows the effect of the transfer resistance on v_d at a wind speed of 8 m sec^{-1}.

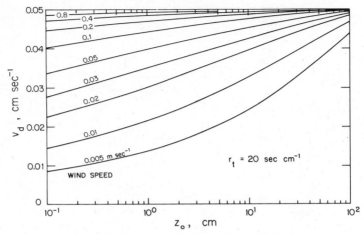

Figure 16.18. Deposition velocity as a function of roughness length z_0 for various wind speeds at $z_1 = 2m$. Transfer resistance $r_t = 20$ sec cm^{-1}.

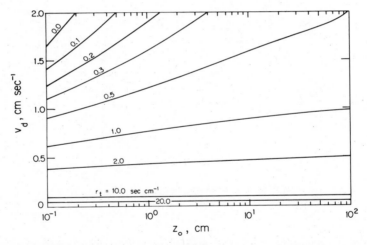

Figure 16.19. Deposition velocity as a function of surface roughness for various transfer resistances at wind speed of 8 m sec^{-1} at $z_1 = 2m$.

We see from Figure 16.14 that even with zero transfer resistance the overall deposition velocity v_d can be small if the wind speed is low. As the transfer resistance is progressively increased, the overall deposition velocity decreases rapidly, and for transfer resistances greater than 1 sec cm^{-1}, v_d is less than 1 cm sec^{-1} regardless of the wind speed. In addition, for transfer resistances exceeding 1 sec cm^{-1}, the deposition velocity is almost constant and independent of the roughness length z_0. We see thus that the final transfer resistance is

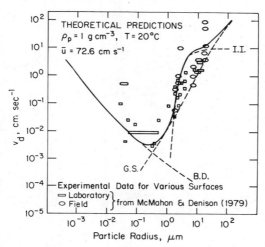

Figure 16.20. Experimental data on particle dry deposition velocities shown together with the solid curve representing the net deposition velocity as predicted by considering the mechanisms of Brownian diffusion (B.D.), gravitational settling (G.S.), and inertial impaction (I.I.) (National Center for Atmospheric Research, 1982).

a key parameter determining the magnitude of the overall deposition velocity. If, in spite of high wind speeds, low overall deposition velocities are measured, then it can be concluded that a major part of the resistance in the overall dry deposition process is due to the final transfer onto the surface of the receptor.

For a rapidly (essentially irreversibly) depositing gas such as HNO_3 every molecule that hits the surface sticks, and the atmospheric transport processes control the rate of deposition. At the other extreme a slowly depositing gas will have a negligible atmospheric concentration gradient, and its rate of deposition is controlled by the final transfer resistance.

16.5. EXPERIMENTAL OBSERVATIONS OF DRY DEPOSITION

Figure 16.20 shows experimental data on particle deposition velocities plotted in a format showing the physical processes involved. Large particles ($D_p > 20$ μm) deposit mainly by gravitational settling, whereas very small particles ($D_p < 0.1$ μm) behave much like gases. The limiting process for the deposition of small particles is usually Brownian diffusion through the laminar surface layer. Particles in the 0.1 to 1.0 μm diameter range deposit the least rapidly since they are not large enough for gravitational settling to be important nor are they small enough to have an appreciable Brownian diffusivity. Considerable uncertainty exists concerning the deposition velocities of particles in the

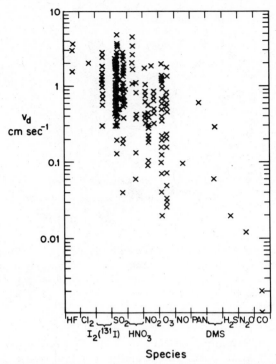

Species

Figure 16.21. Experimental data on gas dry deposition velocities ranked approximately in order of reactivity (National Center for Atmospheric Research, 1982). DMS = dimethyl sulfide.

0.1 to 1.0 μm diameter size range. The key question is whether the deposition velocity of particles in this size range exceeds 0.1 cm sec^{-1}. Wind tunnel studies generally yield the lowest values of v_d, usually less than 0.1 cm sec^{-1}, a result usually attributed to the absence of surface roughness and the increased surface area of vegetation. Field measurements of v_d for particles show significant variations, and although the bulk of the evidence from field data indicates v_d values of order 0.1 cm sec^{-1}, the existence of a number of studies giving v_d values approaching or exceeding 1.0 cm sec^{-1} makes it difficult at this time to prescribe a specific value.

Figure 16.21 shows an assemblage of deposition velocity data for gases ranked approximately in terms of reactivity. The bulk of the experiments on dry deposition of gases have involved SO$_2$, O$_3$, or NO$_x$. Examination of Figure 16.21 indicates both broad agreement and large variation among the measurements. There are indeed many factors that influence the dry deposition process for gases, including seasonal effects, diurnal effects (sunlight, atmospheric stability), and meteorological effects (temperature, humidity, wind speed).

TABLE 16.4. SO_2 and Sulfate Average Deposition Velocities Used in Atmospheric Transport and Removal Calculations

Source	Material	v_d, cm sec^{-1}	
Henmi (1980)	SO_4^{2-}	0.4	
	SO_2	2.0	
Eliassen (1978)	SO_4^{2-}	0.2	
	SO_2	0.8	
Shannon (1981)	SO_4^{-2}, SO_2	summer $\begin{cases} 0.1 & \text{night} \\ 0.9 & \text{noon} \end{cases}$	
		winter $\begin{cases} 0.1 & \text{night} \\ 0.6 & \text{noon} \end{cases}$	

There are several paths for gaseous species to transfer into the interior of leaves. One is directly through the epidermis of the leaf, involving the so-called cuticular resistance. An alternate route is via the pores of leaves, involving a stomatal resistance that controls transfer to within stomatal cavities, and a subsequent mesophyllic resistance that parameterizes transfer from substomatal cavities to leaf tissue. Comparison between resistances to transfer for water vapor, ozone, sulfur dioxide, and gases that are similarly soluble and/or chemically reactive, shows that in general such species are transferred via the stomatal route, whenever stomates are open. Otherwise, cuticular resistance appears to play a significant role. Cuticular uptake of ozone and of species like NO and NO_2 appears to be quite significant, whereas for SO_2 this appears to be less important. When leaves are wet, such as after heavy dewfall, uptake of SO_2 is exceedingly efficient until the pH of the surface water becomes sufficiently acidic to impose a chemical limit on the rate of absorption of gaseous SO_2. However, the insolubility of ozone causes dewfall to inhibit ozone dry deposition.

Table 16.4 gives some suggested values of average deposition velocities for use in atmospheric transport and removal calculations. In summary, $v_d = 1$ cm sec^{-1} is a good overall estimate for SO_2. v_d values for sulfate particles have been measured in the range from 0.01 to 1.0 cm sec^{-1}. Extrapolation of empirical formulas by Sehmel (1980) suggests a value of 0.5 cm sec^{-1}. Wesely and Shannon (1984) have evaluated available data on sulfate dry deposition velocities and determined an estimated 24-hr daily average sulfate deposition velocity during summer over North America of 0.25 cm sec^{-1} with a large diurnal variation. Shannon (1981) has set v_d values for SO_2 and sulfate as equal. This appears to be a good strategy at present.

16.6.   AIR TRAJECTORY LONG-RANGE TRANSPORT MODELING

The entire transport and removal phenomenon was depicted in a general way in Figure 16.1. The competitive nature of the processes can be depicted simply as follows with reference to the sulfur system.

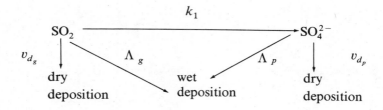

In spite perhaps of an overly simplified treatment of SO_2 to sulfate conversion chemistry, linear models such as that depicted above capture the essence of the competition between conversion and wet and dry deposition as removal mechanisms.

The simplest long-range transport model one can envision consists of a moving box or column of air that is well-mixed from the ground up to a specified upper boundary and which follows an air trajectory from its point of inception. The box is assumed to have a constant volume, and from a mathematical point of view the box behaves merely as a chemical reactor having continuous injection of fresh emissions, chemical transformation, and removal. If M_{SO_2} and M_{SO_4} represent the masses of SO_2 and sulfate in the box at time t, these quantities are governed by

$$\frac{dM_{SO_2}}{dt} = -\left(k_1 + \Lambda_g + v_{d_g}/H\right)M_{SO_2} + Q_{SO_2} \qquad (16.54)$$

$$\frac{dM_{SO_4}}{dt} = -\left(\Lambda_p + v_{d_p}/H\right)M_{SO_4} + k_1 M_{SO_2} + Q_{SO_4} \qquad (16.55)$$

$$M_{SO_2}(0) = M_{SO_2}^0 \qquad M_{SO_4}(0) = M_{SO_4}^0 \qquad (16.56)$$

where H is the mixing height and Q is the source rate. To make this model slightly more realistic, one can allow the box size to increase in accord with expected turbulent mixing and the mixing height H can be varied in accord with observations. For a discussion of the air trajectory long-range transport model we refer the reader to Gislason and Prahm (1983).

16.7. ATMOSPHERIC RESIDENCE TIMES AND GLOBAL BUDGETS

The global chemical cycle of a substance was referred to in Chapter 1 as a description of all significant sources and loss mechanisms to achieve a material balance. In Chapter 1 we presented estimates of the fluxes in the global sulfur and nitrogen cycles.

16.7.1. General Definitions

If M is the total quantity of material in a reservoir, then a material balance yields (Slinn, 1980)

$$\frac{dM}{dt} = P + I - R - O \tag{16.57}$$

where

$$P = \text{total mass production rate}$$
$$I = \text{total mass inflow rate}$$
$$R = \text{total mass removal rate}$$
$$O = \text{total mass outflow rate}$$

A characteristic time constant τ_r for the species in the reservoir can be defined from Eq. (16.58) as

$$\frac{1}{\tau_r} = \frac{1}{M}\frac{dM}{dt} = \frac{P+I}{M} - \frac{R+O}{M} \tag{16.58}$$

We can define, in addition, characteristic times for:

$$\tau_P = \frac{M}{P} \qquad \text{production}$$

$$\tau_I = \frac{M}{I} \qquad \text{inflow}$$

$$\tau_R = \frac{M}{R} \qquad \text{removal}$$

$$\tau_O = \frac{M}{O} \qquad \text{outflow}$$

and the total growth rate

$$\tau_S^{-1} = \tau_P^{-1} + \tau_I^{-1} \tag{16.59}$$

and the total decay rate

$$\tau_L^{-1} = \tau_R^{-1} + \tau_O^{-1} \qquad (16.60)$$

Thus,

$$\frac{1}{\tau_r} = \frac{1}{\tau_S} - \frac{1}{\tau_L} \qquad (16.61)$$

Under steady-state conditions, $dM/dt = 0$, and $P + I = R + O$. Thus, $\tau_S = \tau_L$, and $\tau_r \to \infty$. The mean residence time of the species in the reservoir is then

$$\frac{M}{P + I} = \frac{M}{R + O} = \tau \qquad (16.62)$$

Although we will deal in more detail with sulfur residence times shortly, consider, as an illustration of Eq. (16.63), the mean residence time of all sulfur compounds in the troposphere (Slinn, 1980). If the average concentration of sulfur species in the troposphere is 1 ppb, then since the mass of the troposphere is about 4×10^{21} g, $M \cong 4$ Tg. Natural and anthropogenic sources of sulfur contribute to give a total of about 200 Tg yr^{-1}. Thus, the mean residence time of sulfur compounds in the troposphere is estimated as

$$\tau \cong \frac{4 \text{ Tg}}{200 \text{ Tg yr}^{-1}} \cong 1 \text{ week}$$

Consider a species in steady state in a reservoir in which the loss rate is first-order in the concentration, with a first-order coefficient k that is uniform throughout the reservoir. Then $R = kM$ and if there is no outflow, $\tau^{-1} = k$. More generally, if there are several first-order removal processes, then

$$\frac{1}{\tau} \sum_i k_i \qquad (16.63)$$

We see that, as in the case of dry deposition, separate removal paths add together to give a total residence time like electrical resistances in parallel add to give a total resistance. If the characteristic time associated with removal path i is τ_i then $\tau_i^{-1} = k_i$. For two paths

$$\frac{1}{\tau} = \frac{1}{\tau_1} + \frac{1}{\tau_2} \qquad (16.64)$$

and

$$\tau = \frac{\tau_1 \tau_2}{\tau_1 + \tau_2} \qquad (16.65)$$

If $\tau_1 \gg \tau_2$, $\tau \cong \tau_2$. Thus, the overall residence time is controlled by the process with the shortest characteristic time or the fastest removal rate.

In addition to the net growth rate τ_r^{-1}, the total rates of growth and decay, τ_S^{-1} and τ_L^{-1}, the rates of production, inflow, removal, and outflow, τ_P^{-1}, τ_I^{-1}, τ_R^{-1}, and τ_O^{-1}, and the residence time, τ, there are characteristic mixing times (Slinn, 1980). These mixing times are independent of the other characteristic times since they depend on different physical processes. Let the characteristic mixing times in the x, y, and z directions be $\tau_{M,x}$, $\tau_{M,y}$, and $\tau_{M,z}$. For a reservoir to be "well-mixed" it is necessary that

$$\tau_{M,i} \ll (\tau_P, \tau_R)$$

$$\tau_{M,i} \ll (\tau_I, \tau_O)$$

A well-mixed steady state reservoir will have

$$\frac{1}{\tau_{M,i}} \gg \frac{1}{\tau_S} = \frac{1}{\tau_L} = \frac{1}{\tau} \gg \frac{1}{\tau_r}$$

According to this condition a reservoir is poorly mixed if at least one of the characteristic mixing times is not small compared with the species residence time τ. Thus, a reservoir can be well-mixed for some species and poorly mixed for others depending on their residence times τ. Mixing times in the atmosphere are different for different directions. For the entire troposphere, for example,

$$\tau_{M,z} \approx 1 \text{ week}$$

$$\tau_{M,x} \quad \text{and} \quad \tau_{M,y} \approx 1 \text{ year}$$

Thus, for Kr^{85} which has $\tau = 10$ yr, the troposphere can be considered to be well mixed, whereas for sulfur, where $\tau \cong 1$ week, the troposphere is clearly not well mixed.

For the purpose of calculating the global chemical cycle of a species, it is customary to treat the troposphere as a large well-mixed vessel, or perhaps as two communicating, well-mixed vessels, corresponding to the northern and southern hemispheres. The troposphere–stratosphere division is a natural one because the characteristic time for mixing in the troposphere is short relative to that for troposphere–stratosphere exchange. Likewise, mixing between the two hemispheres is slow compared to that within each hemisphere.

Let us develop the equations governing the total moles of a species in the troposphere, M_i. The dynamic material balance on the reservoir can be written as

$$\frac{dM_i}{dt} = S_i - L_i \tag{16.66}$$

where S_i and L_i represent the source and loss rates.* The terms S_i and L_i consist of the following contributions:

$$S_i \begin{cases} S_i^n & \text{natural emissions} \\ S_i^a & \text{anthropogenic emissions} \\ S_i^c & \text{chemical reactions} \end{cases}$$

$$L_i \begin{cases} L_i^d & \text{dry deposition} \\ L_i^w & \text{wet deposition} \\ L_i^c & \text{chemical reactions} \\ L_i^t & \text{transport to the stratosphere} \end{cases}$$

The loss processes are usually represented as first order, for example, $L_i^d = k_i^d M_i$, where the first-order rate constants which we will denote by k's must be specified. Thus Eq. (16.66) becomes

$$\frac{dM_i}{dt} = S_i^n + S_i^a + S_i^c - \left(k_i^d + k_i^w + k_i^c + k_i^t \right) M_i \qquad (16.67)$$

If the concentration of the species is not changing, then a steady state may be presumed in which

$$S_i^n + S_i^a + S_i^c - \left(k_i^d + k_i^w + k_i^c + k_i^t \right) M_i = 0 \qquad (16.68)$$

The mean residence time of species i can be calculated by either

$$\tau_i = \frac{1}{k_i^d + k_i^w + k_i^c + k_i^t} \qquad (16.69)$$

or

$$\tau_i = \frac{M_i}{S_i^n + S_i^a + S_i^c} \qquad (16.70)$$

To use Eq. (16.69) the individual first-order rate constants for removal must be estimated, whereas in Eq. (16.70), estimates for the total number of moles in the troposphere, which can be derived from a concentration measurement, and for the source strength terms are needed. Because of the difficulty in specifying the k_i values, mean residence times are often estimated from Eq. (16.70).

Let us consider for a moment how the rate constant k_i^d might be estimated. The rate of removal of a species at the surface of the earth can be written as $v_{d_i} c_i A_e$. c_i is the molar concentration, assumed uniform in the troposphere, and

*Thus, $S = P + I$ and $L = R + O$.

A_e is the surface area of the earth. Thus, $v_{d_i} c_i A_e = k_i^d M_i$ and so $k_i^d = v_{d_i} A_e / V_{\text{trop}}$, where V_{trop} is the volume of the troposphere.

16.7.2. Atmospheric Sulfur Residence Times

Let us use the foregoing ideas to analyze the atmospheric sulfur budget, which is shown schematically in Figure 16.22. Natural and anthropogenic emissions occur as SO_2 (or as H_2S and other reduced sulfur species that are rapidly oxidized to SO_2), which may be removed by wet or dry deposition or oxidized to sulfate, which may also be removed by the two processes. Transport to the stratosphere is not an important process for sulfur species. Note that the residence time of a molecule of SO_2 is generally different from the residence time of a sulfur atom. Writing Eq. (16.68) for both SO_2 and SO_4^{2-}, we obtain

$$S_{SO_2}^n + S_{SO_2}^a - \left(k_{SO_2}^d + k_{SO_2}^w + k_{SO_2}^c \right) M_{SO_2} = 0 \qquad (16.71)$$

$$k_{SO_2}^c M_{SO_2} - \left(k_{SO_4}^d + k_{SO_4}^w \right) M_{SO_4} = 0 \qquad (16.72)$$

The mean residence time of SO_2 is

$$\tau_{SO_2} = \frac{M_{SO_2}}{S_{SO_2}^n + S_{SO_2}^a}$$

$$= \frac{1}{k_{SO_2}^d + k_{SO_2}^w + k_{SO_2}^c} \qquad (16.73)$$

whereas that for sulfate is

$$\tau_{SO_4} = \frac{M_{SO_4}}{k_{SO_2}^c M_{SO_2}}$$

$$= \frac{1}{k_{SO_4}^d + k_{SO_4}^w} \qquad (16.74)$$

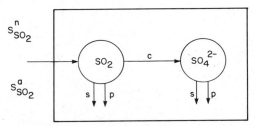

Figure 16.22. Atmospheric sulfur budget.

The mean residence time of a sulfur atom is

$$\tau_S = \frac{M_{SO_2} + M_{SO_4}}{S_{SO_2}^n + S_{SO_2}^a} \tag{16.75}$$

which can be expressed in terms of the two previous mean residence times as

$$\tau_S = \tau_{SO_2} + b\tau_{SO_4} \tag{16.76}$$

where

$$b = \frac{k_{SO_2}^c M_{SO_2}}{S_{SO_2}^n + S_{SO_2}^a} \tag{16.77}$$

the fraction of S converted to SO_4^{2-} before being removed.

We can also define individual characteristic times such as

$$\tau_{SO_2}^d = k_{SO_2}^d{}^{-1}, \qquad \tau_{SO_2}^w = k_{SO_2}^w{}^{-1}, \qquad \tau_{SO_4}^d = k_{SO_4}^d{}^{-1}$$

so that

$$\frac{1}{\tau_{SO_2}} = \frac{1}{\tau_{SO_2}^d} + \frac{1}{\tau_{SO_2}^w} + \frac{1}{\tau_{SO_2}^c} \tag{16.78}$$

$$\frac{1}{\tau_{SO_4}} = \frac{1}{\tau_{SO_4}^d} + \frac{1}{\tau_{SO_4}^w} \tag{16.79}$$

We can also define the mean residence time of a sulfur atom before surface removal or precipitation scavenging by

$$\tau_S^{d,w} = \frac{M_{SO_2} + M_{SO_4}}{k_{SO_2}^{d,w} M_{SO_2} + k_{SO_4}^{d,w} M_{SO_2}} \tag{16.80}$$

so that using

$$\frac{S_{SO_2}^n + S_{SO_2}^a}{M_{SO_2} + M_{SO_4}} = \left(k_{SO_2}^d + k_{SO_2}^w\right) \frac{M_{SO_2}}{M_{SO_2} + M_{SO_4}} + \left(k_{SO_4}^d + k_{SO_4}^w\right) \frac{M_{SO_4}}{M_{SO_2} + M_{SO_4}} \tag{16.81}$$

we get

$$\frac{1}{\tau_S} = \frac{1}{\tau_S^d} + \frac{1}{\tau_S^w} \tag{16.82}$$

The mean residence times for a sulfur atom before surface removal (or precipitation scavenging) can be related to the mean surface removal residence times for SO_2 and SO_4^{2-} as follows. Noting that

$$\tau_S^d = \frac{M_{SO_2} + M_{SO_4}}{k_{SO_2}^d M_{SO_2} + k_{SO_4}^d M_{SO_4}}$$

$$= \frac{M_{SO_2} + M_{SO_4}}{\dfrac{M_{SO_2}}{\tau_{SO_2}^d} + \dfrac{M_{SO_4}}{\tau_{SO_4}^d}}$$

$$= \frac{1}{\dfrac{M_{SO_2}}{M_{SO_2} + M_{SO_4}}\dfrac{1}{\tau_{SO_2}^d} + \dfrac{M_{SO_4}}{M_{SO_2} + M_{SO_4}}\dfrac{1}{\tau_{SO_4}^d}} \qquad (16.83)$$

we have

$$\frac{1}{\tau_S^d} = \frac{c}{\tau_{SO_2}^d} + \frac{(1-c)}{\tau_{SO_4}^d} \qquad (16.84)$$

where

$$c = \left[1 + \frac{b\left(k_{SO_2}^d + k_{SO_2}^w + k_{SO_2}^c\right)}{k_{SO_4}^d + k_{SO_4}^w}\right]^{-1} \qquad (16.85)$$

Rodhe (1978) has estimated values of the sulfur residence times (in hours):

$\tau_{SO_2}^d$	$\tau_{SO_2}^w$	$\tau_{SO_2}^c$	τ_{SO_2}	$\tau_{SO_4}^d$	$\tau_{SO_4}^w$	τ_{SO_4}
60	100	80	25	> 400	80	80

Assuming $c = 0.5$, the sulfur atom residence times are ($c = SO_2$ fraction of total sulfur)

τ_S^d	τ_S^w	τ_S
120	90	50

Based on Eq. (16.85) then, the assumption of $c = 0.5$ is consistent with that of $b = \frac{1}{3}$. Because of the uneven spatial distribution of anthropogenic sources and the relatively short residence time of sulfur in the atmosphere, global averages do not provide an accurate description of man's influence on the sulfur cycle in populated parts of the world.

REFERENCES

Battan, L. J., and Reitan, C. H. "Droplet Size Measurements in Convective Clouds," in *Artificial Stimulation of Rain*, Pergamon Press, New York, 184–191 (1957).

Baulch, D. L., Cox, R. A., Crutzen, P. J., Hampson, R. F., Jr., Kerr, F. A., Troe, J., and Watson, R. P. "Evaluated Kinetic and Photochemical Data for Atmospheric Chemistry: Supplement 1." CODATA Task Group on Chemical Kinetics, *J. Phys. Chem. Ref. Data*, **11**, 327–496 (1982).

Beard, K. V. "Terminal Velocity and Shape of Cloud and Precipitation Drops Aloft," *J. Atmos. Sci.*, **33**, 851–864 (1976).

Bolin, B., Aspling, G., and Persson, C. "Residence Time of Atmospheric Pollutants as Dependent on Source Characteristics, Atmospheric Diffusion Processes, and Sink Mechanisms," *Tellus*, **26**, 185–194 (1974).

Droppo, J. G. "Experimental Techniques for Dry Deposition Measurements," in *Atmospheric Sulfur Deposition*, D. S. Shriner, C. R. Richmond, and S. E. Lindberg (Eds.), Ann Arbor Press, Ann Arbor, 209–221 (1980).

Eastman, J. A., and Stedman, D. H. "A Fast Response Sensor for Ozone Eddy Correlation Measurements," *Atmos. Environ.*, **11**, 1209–1212 (1977).

Eliassen, A. "The OECD Study of Long-Range Transport of Air Pollutants: Long-Range Transport Modeling," *Atmos. Environ.*, **12**, 479–487 (1978).

Galbally, I. E., Garland, J. A., and Wilson, M. J. G. "Sulfur Uptake from the Atmosphere by Forest and Farmland," *Nature*, **280**, 49–50 (1979).

Gislason, K. B., and Prahm, L. P. "Sensitivity Study of Air Trajectory Long-Range Transport Modeling," *Atmos. Environ.*, **17**, 2463–2472 (1983).

Grasslands, "The CHON Photochemistry of the Troposphere," NCAR/CQ-7-1980-ASP. Boulder, CO, 161–172 (1980).

Heicklen, J. "Atmospheric Lifetimes of Pollutants," *Atmos. Environ.*, **16**, 821–823 (1982).

Henmi, T. "Long-Range Transport Model of SO_2 and Sulfate, and its Application to the Eastern United States," *J. Geophys. Res.*, **85**, 4436–4442 (1980).

Hicks, B. B., and Wesely, M. L. "An Examination of Some Micrometeorological Methods for Measuring Dry Deposition," U.S. Environmental Protection Agency Report, EPA-600/7-78-160 (1978).

Hicks, B. B., and Wesely, M. L. "Turbulent Transfer Processes to a Surface and Interaction with Vegetation," in *Atmospheric Sulfur Deposition*, D. S. Shriner, C. R. Richmond, and S. E. Lindberg (Eds.), Ann Arbor Press, Ann Arbor, 199–207 (1980).

Jones, E. P., and Smith, S. D. "A First Measurement of Sea-Air CO_2 Flux by Eddy Correlation," *J. Geophys. Res.*, **82**, 5990–5992 (1977).

Lenschow, D. H., Delany, A. C., Stankov, B. B., and Stedman, D. H. "Airborne Measurements of the Vertical Flux of Ozone in the Boundary Layer," *Boundary-Layer Meteorol.*, **19**, 249–265 (1980).

Lenschow, D. H., Pearson, R., and Stankov, B. B. "Estimating the Ozone Budget in the Boundary Layer by Use of Aircraft Measurements of Ozone Eddy Flux and Mean Concentration," *J. Geophys. Res.*, **86**, 7291–7297 (1981).

Levine, S. Z., and Schwartz, S. E. "In-Cloud and Below-Cloud Scavenging of Nitric Acid Vapor," *Atmos. Environ.*, **16**, 1725–1734 (1982).

Marshall, J. S., and Palmer, M. W. M. "The Distribution of Raindrops with Size," *J. Meteorol.*, **5**, 165–166 (1948).

McMahon, T. A., and Denison, P. J. "Empirical Atmospheric Deposition Parameters—A Survey," *Atmos. Environ.*, **13**, 571–585 (1979).

Moller, U., and Schumann, G. "Mechanisms of Transport from the Atmosphere to the Earth's Surface," *J. Geophys. Res.*, **75**, 3013–3019 (1970).

National Center for Atmospheric Research, *Regional Acid Deposition: Models and Physical Processes*, Boulder, CO (1982).

Pruppacher, H. R., and Klett, J. D. *Microphysics of Clouds and Precipitation*, D. Reidel, Boston (1978).

Rodhe, H. "Budgets and Turn-Over Times of Atmospheric Sulfur Compounds," *Atmos. Environ.*, **12**, 671–680 (1978).

Sehmel, G. A. "Particle and Gas Dry Deposition. A Review," *Atmos. Environ.*, **14**, 983–1012 (1980).

Shannon, J. D. "A Model of Regional Long-Term Average Sulfur Atmospheric Pollution, Surface Removal and Net Horizontal Flux," *Atmos. Environ.*, **15**, 689–701 (1981).

Shephard, J. G. "Measurements of the Direct Deposition of Sulfur Dioxide onto Grass and Water by Profile Method," *Atmos. Environ.*, **8**, 69–74 (1974).

Slinn, W. G. N. "Relationships Between Removal Processes and Residence Times for Atmospheric Pollutants," *AIChE Symposium Series*, #196, Vol. 76, Air Pollution: 1. The Clean Air Act, 2. Energy Needs, 185–203 (1980).

Slinn, W. G. N. "Precipitation Scavenging," in *Atmospheric Sciences and Power Production—1979*, Chapter 11, Div. of Biomedical Environmental Research, U.S. Dept. of Energy (1983).

Wesely, M. L., and Hicks, B. B. "Some Factors that Affect the Deposition Rates of Sulfur Dioxide and Similar Gases on Vegetation," *J. Air Pollution Control Assoc.*, **27**, 1110–1116 (1977).

Wesely, M. L., Hicks, B. B., Dannevik, W. P., Frisella, S., and Husar, R. B. "An Eddy Correlation Measurement of Particulate Deposition from the Atmosphere," *Atmos. Environ.*, **11**, 561–563 (1977).

Wesely, M. L., Eastman, J. A., Cook, D. R., and Hicks, B. B. "Daytime Variation of Ozone Eddy Fluxes to Maize," *Boundary Layer Meteorol.* **15**, 361–373 (1978).

Wesely, M. L., Eastman, J. A., Stedman, D. H., and Yalvac, E. D. "An Eddy-Correlation Measurement of NO_2 Flux to Vegetation and Comparison to O_3 Flux," *Atmos. Environ.*, **16**, 815–820 (1982).

Wesely, M. L., and Shannon, J. D. "Improved Estimates of Sulfate Dry Deposition in Eastern North America," *Environ. Progress*, **3**, 78–81 (1984).

PROBLEMS

16.1. When a species is being removed by precipitation scavenging, the process is often represented as a first-order loss with the coefficient being the scavenging coefficient Λ.

(a) If Λ depends on time, show that the atmospheric diffusion equation can be transformed into a form not involving the first-order loss term by defining a new variable,

$$\tilde{c} = c \exp\left[\int_0^t \Lambda \, dt' \right]$$

(b) Show that for constant Λ the Gaussian plume equation is

$$c(x, y, z) = \frac{q}{2\pi \bar{u}\sigma_y\sigma_z} \exp\left(-\frac{y^2}{2\sigma_y^2} \right) \exp\left(-\frac{\Lambda x}{\bar{u}} \right)$$

$$\times \left[\exp\left(-\frac{(z - h)^2}{2\sigma_z^2} \right) + \exp\left(-\frac{(z + h)^2}{2\sigma_z^2} \right) \right]$$

16.2. Calculate the aerosol scavenging coefficient $\Lambda(D_p)/N$ as a function of the diameter D_p of the scavenged particle over a size range of 0.01 to 0.1 μm diameter for drops of diameter $\tilde{D}_p = 5$ mm falling at their terminal velocity in air at 25°C.

16.3. Calculate the mean aerosol scavenging coefficient,

$$\frac{\overline{\Lambda}}{N} = \frac{\int_0^\infty \Lambda(D_p) n(D_p)\, dD_p}{\int_0^\infty n(D_p)\, dD_p}$$

for the same conditions as Problem 16.2 where the aerosol being scavenged has a log–normal size distribution with $\overline{D}_{pg} = 0.01$ μm and 1.0 μm, each case having $\sigma_g = 2.0$.

16.4. Verify the calculation presented in Table 16.1.

16.5. Prepare a plot analogous to Figure 16.8 for the scavenging of NH_3 for $p_{NH_3} = 10^{-8}$ atm (10 ppb).

16.6. Calculate the scavenging coefficient for below-cloud scavenging of NH_3 based on the Marshall–Palmer raindrop size distribution for rainfall intensities of $p_0 = 1$, 5, 15, and 25 mm hr^{-1}. Assume a minimum raindrop diameter of $\tilde{D}_p = 0.02$ cm.

16.7. Consider a raindrop falling through a layer containing a uniform concentration of SO_2. Show how to calculate the rate of approach of the dissolved S(IV) to its equilibrium value as a function of time of fall. Apply your result to the case of $\tilde{D}_p = 5$ mm, $T = 25°C$, $p_{SO_2} = 10^{-8}$ atm (10 ppb) to compute how long it takes for the drop to reach equilibrium with the surrounding gas phase. Repeat the calculation for H_2O_2 at the same background concentration.

16.8. Bolin et al. (1974) have presented a one-dimensional steady state model based on the atmospheric diffusion equation to be able to estimate the effect of dry deposition on vertical pollutant concentrations. In the model the mean concentration is governed by

$$\frac{d}{dz}\left(K_{zz}\frac{dc}{dz}\right) + q\delta(z - h) = 0$$

$$\left(K_{zz}\frac{dc}{dz}\right)_{z=z_v} = v_d c \qquad z = z_v$$

$$c = 0 \qquad z \to \infty$$

with

$$K_{zz} = \begin{cases} \kappa u_* z & z_v \le z \le H \\ \kappa u_* H & z > H \end{cases}$$

Thus, the source is taken at a height h and of strength q. Horizontal effects are neglected, and neutral stability is assumed up to a layer at height H, thereafter remaining constant. The object of the model is to be able to study the effect of v_d on the vertical concentration profiles and thereby to assess the degree of importance of dry deposition.

(a) When the source height is in the constant diffusivity layer, that is, $h > H$, show that

$$c(z) = \begin{cases} \dfrac{1 + \dfrac{v_d}{\kappa u_*} \ln(z/z_v)}{1 + \dfrac{v_d}{\kappa u_*}\left[\dfrac{h-H}{H} + \ln\left(\dfrac{H}{z_v}\right)\right]} & z_v \leq z \leq H \\[4ex] 1 - \dfrac{v_d(h-z)}{\kappa u_* H\left[1 + \dfrac{v_d}{\kappa u_*}\left(\dfrac{h-H}{H} + \ln\left(\dfrac{H}{z_v}\right)\right)\right]} & H \leq z < h \end{cases}$$

(b) When the source height $h < H$, show that

$$c(z) = \frac{1 + \dfrac{v_d}{\kappa u_*} \ln\left(\dfrac{z}{z_v}\right)}{1 + \dfrac{v_d}{\kappa u_*} \ln\left(\dfrac{h}{z_v}\right)}$$

(c) Calculate and plot the vertical concentration distribution for the following conditions:

$$h = 50, 200 \text{ m}$$

$$v_d = 0.1, 10, 10^7 \text{cm sec}^{-1}$$

$$z_v = 0.5 \text{ cm}$$

$$\bar{u} = 1, 4, 8 \text{ m sec}^{-1}$$

Discuss your results.

16.9. Calculate the dry deposition velocity of SO_2 to the earth's surface as a function of the transfer resistance under the following conditions: neutral stability, $u_* = 1$ m sec^{-1}, $\bar{u}(10 \text{ m}) = 1.5$ m sec^{-1}. Consider transfer resistances r_t of 0, 0.3, and 2.0 sec cm^{-1}. Discuss your results.

16.10. Prepare a plot of particle dry deposition velocity as a function of particle diameter. For atmospheric conditions assume a Monin–Obukhov length of $L = 15$, $z_0 = 10$ cm, and $u_* = 15$ cm sec^{-1}. Consider a particle size range of 0.001 μm to 10 μm diameter, and assume that the particles have a density of 2 g cm^{-3}.

16.11. Consider a species that is totally man-made and which was first emitted to the atmosphere at a time say $t = 0$. If the fractional rate of removal from the atmosphere by all processes is p yr^{-1}, let us calculate the fraction f of the total amount of the compound produced up to time t still remaining in the atmosphere at any time t. Let us assume that mixing between the northern and southern hemispheres is fast enough to provide a homogeneous concentration in the troposphere.

(a) Let the emission rate of the species be given by $P(t) = P_0 e^{rt}$. If $M(t)$ is the total mass in the atmosphere at time t, show that M is governed by

$$\frac{dM}{dt} = P_0 e^{rt} - pM \qquad M(0) = 0$$

and that the solution is

$$M(t) = \frac{P_0}{r + p}\left(e^{rt} - e^{-pt}\right)$$

Show that the total quantity produced in time t is

$$Q(t) = \frac{P_0}{r}\left(e^{rt} - 1\right)$$

so the fraction f still in the atmosphere at time t is

$$f = \frac{M(t)}{Q(t)} = \frac{r}{r + p}\left[\frac{e^{rt} - e^{-pt}}{e^{rt} - 1}\right]$$

The mean residence time, $\tau = p^{-1}$, can be estimated from the relation for f. A value of f can be estimated from the measured atmospheric concentration of the compound and the total quantity emitted. Knowing f and r, τ can be calculated as $1/p$. For $rt \gg 1$, $f \cong r/(r + p)$.

(b) Let us now assume that the troposphere can be divided into northern and southern hemispheres with an inter-hemispheric fractional mixing rate of m yr^{-1}. The rate of removal from the atmosphere, p yr^{-1}, is assumed to be the same in both hemispheres. If all the manufacture and release of the compound is assumed to occur in the northern hemisphere, then let us find the ratio of concentrations, R, between the northern and southern hemispheres at any time t.

Let

$$M_N = \text{mass of species in northern hemisphere}$$

$$M_S = \text{mass of species in southern hemisphere}$$

Show that the hemispheric material balances are

$$\frac{dM_N}{dt} = P_0 e^{rt} - pM_N + m(M_S - M_N)$$

$$\frac{dM_S}{dt} = m(M_N - M_S) - pM_S$$

$$M_N(0) = M_S(0) = 0$$

Using

$$M_N + M_S = \frac{P_0}{r+p}(e^{rt} - e^{-pt})$$

show that

$$M_S(t) = \frac{mP_0}{r+p}$$

$$\times \left[\frac{e^{rt}}{r+p+2m} - \frac{e^{-pt}}{2m} + \left(\frac{1}{2m} - \frac{1}{r+p+2m} \right) e^{-(p+2m)t} \right]$$

and

$$R = \frac{M_N(t)}{M_S(t)}$$

$$= \frac{2(r+p+m)e^{rt} - (r+p+2m)e^{-pt} - (r+p)e^{-(2m+p)t}}{2me^{rt} - (r+p+2m)e^{-pt} + (r+p)e^{-(2m+p)t}}$$

TABLE P16.1. Atmospheric Concentrations of Three Species

| | Atmospheric Concentrations, ppt | | | |
| | Hemisphere | | | |
Species	N	S	Avg	f
A	80 ± 5	57	69	0.87
B	65 ± 17	20 ± 5	43	0.37
C	15 ± 12	1.5	8	0.07

For $e^{rt} \gg 1$,

$$R \cong 1 + \frac{r + p}{m}$$

(c) As an application of the foregoing theory, let us estimate the atmospheric residence times of the three species in Table P16.1, which presents atmospheric concentrations, together with values of f estimated from total production data (assuming that each species is of anthropogenic origin only). As noted above, the atmospheric residence time $\tau = p^{-1}$. Given values of f and r, p can be calculated from $f = r/(r + p)$ since these species have been emitted long enough so that $rt \gg 1$. Plot f versus p (and τ) for $r = 0.15$ yr^{-1} showing points corresponding to the three compounds.

(d) An independent calculation of atmospheric residence times can be made by performing the global balance over both northern and southern hemispheres. Using the data in Table P16.1 as rough estimates of the thoroughly mixed background concentration in each hemisphere, estimate the values of p yr^{-1} by preparing a plot of R versus p for $r = 0.15$ yr^{-1} and $m = 0.2$, 0.4, and 0.7.

Using the value $R = 1.4$ from Table P16.1 for A, and $r = 0.15$ yr^{-1} with $p = 0.02$ yr^{-1}, the most appropriate value for m is 0.4 yr^{-1}. For the error ranges given by $R = 1.4 \pm 0.2$, $r = 0.13 \pm 0.03$, and $p = 0.03 \pm 0.01$, the extreme range in m values can be determined. The estimates of p are independent of the approximations of relative production rates used in the first calculation. On the other hand, the direct release of compounds in the southern hemisphere systematically leads to lower measured values of R, a high estimate of m from A data, and low estimates of p for a given choice of r.

Assuming a reasonable approximate value of $r = 0.15$ yr^{-1}, show that satisfactory agreement between both methods of calculation can be obtained for $m \sim 0.4$ yr^{-1}, $p_B = 0.3$ yr^{-1}, and $p_C = 2$

yr^{-1}. While these estimates could readily be in error by a factor of 2 or 3, it is clear that the atmospheric residence time of C is less than one year, and that of B is not more than about five or six years.

16.12. Once released at the earth's surface, a molecule diffuses upward into the troposphere and at any time may be removed by chemical reaction with other species, by absorption into particles and droplets, or by photodissociation. If the removal processes are rapid relative to the rate of diffusion, the species will not get mixed uniformly in the troposphere before it is removed. If, on the other hand, removal is slow relative to the rate of diffusion, the species may have a uniform tropospheric concentration. In this problem we wish to calculate the characteristic lifetime of tropospheric species (Heicklen, 1982).

Consider a species A whose removal from the atmosphere can be expressed as a first-order reaction, that is, $R_A = -k_A c_A$. If the removal of A is the result of reaction with background species B, then k_A can be a pseudo-first-order rate constant that includes the concentration of B in it. The intrinsic rate constant is given by the Arrhenius expression, $k_A = A_0 \exp(-E_a/RT)$. In the case of reaction with B, $A_0' = A_0 c_B$.

Let us assume that the vertical concentration distribution of A can be represented generally as $c_A = c_{A_0} \exp(-\xi_A z)$ by analogy to the exponential decrease of pressure with altitude, $p = p_0 \exp(-\xi z)$. Show that the tropospheric lifetime of A over the tropospheric height H_T is given by

$$\tau_T = \frac{1 - e^{-\xi_A H_T}}{\xi_A \int_0^{H_T} k_A(T, z) \exp(-\xi_A z) \, dz}$$

TABLE P16.2. Rate Constants for OH— Reactions of Atmospheric Species[a]

Species	$k = A_0 \exp(-E_a/RT)$ A_0, cm³ molecule^{-1} sec	$E_a/R, K$
HCl	3.0×10^{-12}	-425
CH_3Cl	1.9×10^{-12}	-1120
CHF_2Cl	1.3×10^{-12}	-1670
CH_3SCH_3	5.5×10^{-12}	150
CH_4	2.4×10^{-12}	-1710
H_2S	1.1×10^{-11}	-225

[a] Baulch et al. (1982).

The tropospheric temperature profile can be approximated by $T(z) = T_0 - \alpha z$, where $T_0 = 293$ K and $\alpha = 5.5$ K km^{-1}. Show that the ratio of the lifetime of species A to that at the earth's surface is

$$\frac{\tau_T}{\tau_0} = \frac{[1 - \exp(-\xi_A H_T)]\exp(-E_a/RT_0)}{\xi_A \int_0^{H_T}\exp(-E_a/R(T_0 - \alpha z))\exp(-\xi_A z)\, dz}$$

Let us apply the foregoing theory to some atmospheric constituents whose principal removal reactions are with the OH radical. Place the computed values of τ_T/τ_0 for the species in Table P16.2 on a plot of τ_T/τ_0 versus k_A at surface conditions. Discuss.

PART SIX

Special Topics

SEVENTEEN

Air Pollution Statistics

Air pollutant concentrations are inherently random variables because of their dependence on the fluctuations of meteorological and emission variables. We already have seen from Chapter 13 that the concentration predicted by atmospheric diffusion theories is the mean concentration $\langle c \rangle$. The randomness of atmospheric concentrations is evident in Figure 17.1, which shows a continuous, 16-hr record of SO_2 concentrations measured at a location in Philadelphia in 1964. There are important instances in analyzing air pollution where the ability simply to predict the theoretical mean concentration $\langle c \rangle$ is not enough. Perhaps the most important situation in this regard is in ascertaining compliance with ambient air quality standards. We recall from Chapter 1 that air quality standards are frequently stated in terms of the number of times per year that a particular concentration level can be exceeded. In order to estimate whether such an exceedance will occur, or how many times it will occur, it is necessary to consider the statistical properties of the concentration. The object of this chapter is to develop the tools needed to analyze the statistical character of air quality data.

As noted, Figure 17.1 shows a continuous 16-hr record of SO_2 concentrations measured at a location in Philadelphia. The presumption behind such a data record is that the instrument used to carry out the measurements was able to measure SO_2 continuously. Other instruments will require a period of time τ over which to accumulate a sample sufficient to produce a measurement. If the measurement is truly continuous, then the random concentration can simply be represented as $c(t)$, whereas if an averaging time τ is inherent in the data, then the concentrations can be denoted by $c_\tau(t_1), c_\tau(t_2), \ldots, c_\tau(t_n)$, $t_1 < t_2 < \cdots < t_n$, where $\tau = t_2 - t_1 = t_3 - t_2 = \ldots$, and t_i is the beginning of the time period over which the averaging is done. The averaging can actually be carried out by the measuring instrument itself or can be done on the continuous data record. In the latter case, Figure 17.1 shows the two 8-hr average concentrations, one from 0 to 8 hrs and the second from 8 to 16 hrs. Also shown are the

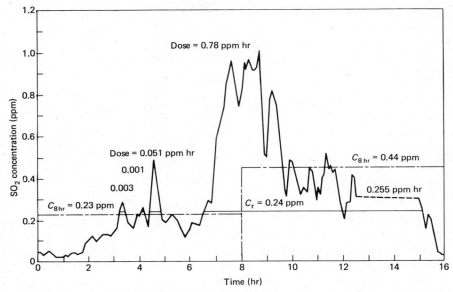

Figure 17.1. Record of SO$_2$ concentrations measured at a point in Philadelphia on January 26, 1964 (Larsen et al., 1967).

dosages (time integral of the concentration) over those periods when the concentration exceeded 0.24 ppm.

Hourly average concentrations are the most common way in which urban air pollutant data are reported. These hourly average concentrations may be obtained from an instrument that actually requires a one-hour sample in order to produce a data point or by averaging data taken by an instrument having a sampling time shorter than one hour. If we deal with one-hour average concentrations, those concentrations would be denoted by $c_\tau(t_i)$, where $\tau = 1$ hr. For convenience we will omit the subscript τ henceforth; however it should be kept in mind that concentrations are usually based on a fixed averaging time. There are 8760 hr in a year, so that if we are interested in the statistical distribution of the 1 hr average concentrations measured at a particular location in a region, we will deal with a sample of 8760 values of the random variable c.

The random variable is characterized by a probability density function $p(c)$, such that $p(c)\,dc$ is the probability that the concentration c of a particular species at a particular location will lie between c and $c + dc$. Our first task will be to identify probability density functions (pdf's) that are appropriate for representing air pollutant concentrations. Once we have determined a form for $p(c)$ we can proceed to calculate the desired statistical properties of c.

17.1. PROBABILITY DISTRIBUTIONS FOR AIR POLLUTANT CONCENTRATIONS

If we plot the frequency of occurrence of a concentration versus concentration we would expect to obtain a histogram like that sketched in Figure 17.2(a). As the number of data increases, the histogram should tend to a smooth curve such as that in Figure 17.2(b). Note that very low and very high concentrations occur only rarely. We recall that aerosol size distributions exhibited a similar overall behavior; there are no particles of zero size and no particles of infinite size. Thus, a probability distribution that is zero for $c = 0$ and as $c \to \infty$ is also desired for air pollutant concentrations.

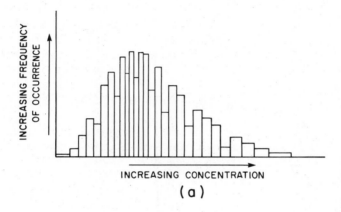

(a)

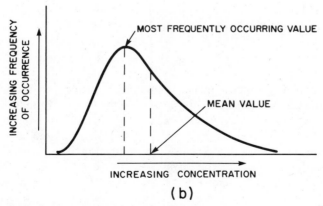

(b)

Figure 17.2. Hypothetical distributions of air pollutant concentrations. (a) Histogram. (b) Continuous distribution.

Although there has been speculation as to what probability distribution is optimum in representing air pollutant concentrations from a physical point of view (Bencala and Seinfeld, 1976), it is largely agreed that there is no *a priori* reason to expect that air pollutant concentrations should adhere to a specific probability distribution. Moreover, it has been demonstrated that a number of pdf's are useful in representing air quality data. Each of these distributions has the general features of the curve shown in Figure 17.2(b); they represent the distribution of a nonnegative random variable c that has probabilities of occurrence approaching zero as $c \to 0$ and as $c \to \infty$. Georgopoulos and Seinfeld (1982) summarize the functional forms of many of the pdf's that have been proposed for air pollutant concentrations. (See also Tsukatami and Shigemitsu, 1980.) In addition, Holland and Fitz-Simons (1982) have developed a computer program for fitting statistical distributions to air quality data.

Which probability distribution actually best fits a particular set of data depends on the characteristics of the set. The two distributions that have been most widely used for representing air pollutant concentrations are the log–normal and the Weibull, and we will focus on these two distributions here.

17.1.1.   The Log–Normal Distribution

We have already dealt extensively with the log–normal distribution in Chapter 7 for representing aerosol size distribution data. If a concentration c is log–normally distributed, its pdf is given by Eq. (7.29),

$$p_L(c) = \frac{1}{(2\pi)^{1/2} c \ln \sigma_g} \exp\left[-\frac{(\ln c - \ln \mu_g)^2}{2 \ln^2 \sigma_g} \right] \tag{17.1}$$

where μ_g and σ_g are the geometric mean and standard deviation of c.

Figure 17.3 shows sample points of the distribution of one-hour average SO_2 concentrations equal to or in excess of the stated values for Washington, D.C, for the seven-year period December 1, 1961 to December 1, 1968. A log–normal distribution has been fitted to the high-concentration region of these data.

We recall that the geometric mean, or median, is the concentration at which the straight line plot crosses the 50th percentile. The slope of the line is related to the standard geometric deviation, which can be calculated from the plot by dividing the 16th percentile concentration (which is one standard deviation from the mean) by the 50th percentile concentration (the geometric mean). (This is the 16th percentile of the *complementary* distribution function $\bar{F}(c)$; equivalently it is the 84th percentile of the cumulative distribution function $F(c)$.) For the distribution of Figure 17.3, $\mu_g = 0.042$ ppm and $\sigma_g = 1.96$. Plots such as Figure 17.3 are widely used in air quality analysis because it is important to know the probability that concentrations will equal or exceed certain values.

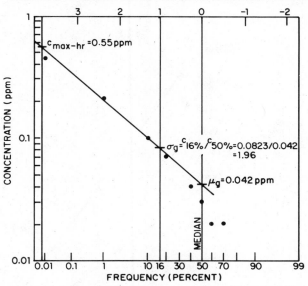

Figure 17.3. Frequency of 1-hour average SO_2 concentrations equal to, or in excess of, stated values at Washington, D.C., Dec. 1, 1961–Dec. 1, 1968 (Larsen, 1971).

17.1.2. The Weibull Distribution

The pdf of a Weibull distribution is

$$p_W(c) = (\lambda/\sigma)(c/\sigma)^{\lambda-1}\exp\left[-(c/\sigma)^{\lambda}\right] \tag{17.2}$$

$$\sigma, \lambda > 0$$

As was done with the log–normal distribution, it is desired to devise a set of coordinates for graph paper on which a set of data that conforms to a Weibull distribution will plot as a straight line. To do so we can work with the complementary distribution function, $\bar{F}_W(c)$. The complementary distribution function of the Weibull distribution is

$$\bar{F}_W(c) = \exp\left[-(c/\sigma)^{\lambda}\right] \tag{17.3}$$

Taking the natural logarithm of Eq. (17.3) and changing sign,

$$\ln\left(\frac{1}{\bar{F}_W(c)}\right) = \left(\frac{c}{\sigma}\right)^{\lambda} \tag{17.4}$$

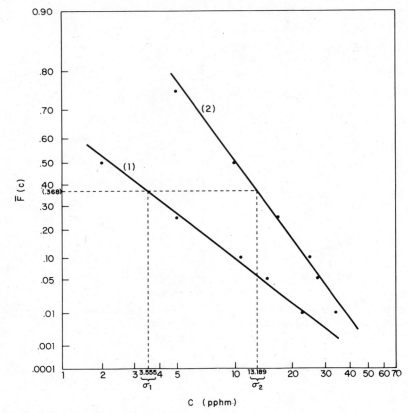

Figure 17.4. Weibull distribution fits of the 1971 hourly-average (1), and daily maximum hourly-average (2) oxidant concentration at Pasadena, CA (Georgopoulos and Seinfeld, 1982).

Now take the logarithm (base 10) of both sides of Eq. (17.4),

$$\log\left[\ln\left(\frac{1}{\overline{F}_W(c)}\right)\right] = \lambda[\log c - \log \sigma] \qquad (17.5)$$

Therefore, if we plot $\log[\ln(1/\overline{F}_W(c))]$ versus $\log c$, data from a Weibull distribution will plot as a straight line. The values $\log[\ln(1/\overline{F}_W(c))]$ are the values on the ordinate scale of Figure 17.4, so-called extreme value probability paper. The scale is constructed so that a computation of $\log[\ln(1/\overline{F}_W(c))]$ of each value of $\overline{F}_W(c)$ yields a linear scale.

By setting $\log c = \log \sigma$ in Eq. (17.5), we obtain $\overline{F}_W(c) = e^{-1} = 0.368$. This point is shown on Figure 17.4. The parameter λ, which is the slope of the straight line, can be found by using any other point on the line and solving Eq.

(17.5) for λ:

$$\lambda = \frac{\log\left[\ln\left(\frac{1}{\overline{F}_W(c)}\right)\right]}{\log c - \log \sigma} \qquad (17.6)$$

Suppose we use, for a second point, that point on the line that crosses $\overline{F}_W(c) = 0.01$. Then

$$\lambda = \frac{0.663}{\log c_{0.01} - \log \sigma} \qquad (17.7)$$

17.2.   ESTIMATION OF PARAMETERS IN THE DISTRIBUTIONS

Each of the two distributions we have presented is characterized by two parameters. The fitting of a set of data to a distribution involves determining the values of the parameters of the distribution so that the distribution fits the data in an optimal manner. Ideally, this fitting is best carried out using a systematic optimization routine that estimates the parameters for several distributions from the given set of data and then selects that distribution that best fits the data, using a criterion of "goodness of fit" (Holland and Fitz-Simons, 1982). We present two methods here that do not require a computer optimization routine. The first method has, in effect, already been described. It is formally called the method of quantiles. The second is the method of moments, which requires the computation of the first (as many as the parameters of the distribution) sample moments of the "raw data." The procedure suggested should start with the construction of a plot of the available data on the appropriate graph paper (that gives a straight line for the theoretical distribution), in order to get a preliminary notion of the goodness of fit. Then one would apply one of the following methods to evaluate the parameters of the "best" distribution.

17.2.1.   Method of Quantiles

We have seen that the parameters μ_g and σ_g of the log–normal distribution can be estimated by using the 50th percentile and 16th percentile values (Section 7.3). These percentiles are called quantiles. Also, Eqs. (17.6) and (17.7) indicate how this approach can be used to determine the two parameters of the Weibull distribution.

For the log–normal distribution, for example, we have already illustrated how μ_g and σ_g are estimated from the concentrations at the 50 percent and 84 percent quantiles; that is

$$\ln c_{0.50} - \ln \mu_g = 0$$

$$\ln c_{0.84} - \ln \mu_g = \ln \sigma_g$$

Choosing as a further illustration the 95 percent and 99 percent quantiles, we obtain

$$\ln c_{0.95} - \ln \mu_g = 1.645 \ln \sigma_g$$

$$\ln c_{0.99} - \ln \mu_g = 2.326 \ln \sigma_g$$

For the Weibull distribution, the quantile concentration is given by

$$c_{q_i} = \sigma \left[\ln \left(\frac{1}{1 - q_i} \right) \right]^{1/\lambda}$$

Using the 0.80 and 0.98 quantiles, for example, we obtain the estimates for the parameters λ and σ as

$$\lambda = \frac{0.88817}{\ln c_{0.98} - \ln c_{0.80}}$$

$$\sigma = \exp(1.53580 \ln c_{0.80} - 0.53580 \ln c_{0.98})$$

17.2.2. Method of Moments

To estimate the parameters of a distribution by the method of moments, the moments of the distribution are expressed in terms of the parameters. Estimates for the values of the moments are obtained from the data, and the equations for the moments are solved for the parameters. For a two-parameter distribution, values for the first two moments are needed.

The rth noncentral moment of a random variable c with a pdf $p(c)$ is defined by

$$\mu'_r = \int_0^\infty c^r p(c) \, dc \tag{17.8}$$

and the rth central moment (moment about the mean) is

$$\mu_r = \int_0^\infty (c - \mu'_1)^r p(c) \, dc \tag{17.9}$$

The mean value of c is μ'_1, and the variance is μ_2, which is commonly denoted by σ^2, or sometimes Var$\{c\}$.

Consider first the estimation of μ_g and σ_g for the log–normal distribution. Let $\mu = \ln \mu_g$ and $\sigma = \ln \sigma_g$. The first and second noncentral moments of the log–normal distribution are

$$\mu_1' = \exp\left[\mu + \frac{\sigma^2}{2}\right] \tag{17.10}$$

$$\mu_2' = \exp(2\mu + 2\sigma^2) \tag{17.11}$$

After solving Eqs. (17.10) and (17.11) for μ and σ^2, we have

$$\mu = 2 \ln \mu_1' - (1/2) \ln \mu_2' \tag{17.12}$$

$$\sigma^2 = \ln \mu_2' - 2 \ln \mu_1' \tag{17.13}$$

μ_1', μ_2', and μ_2 are related through $\mu_2 = \mu_2' - \mu_1'^2$ and are estimated from the data by

$$M_1' = \frac{1}{n} \sum_{i=1}^{n} c_i \tag{17.14}$$

and

$$M_2' = \frac{1}{n} \sum_{i=1}^{n} c_i^2, \tag{17.15}$$

$$M_2 = \frac{1}{n-1} \sum_{i=1}^{n} (c_i - M_1')^2 \tag{17.16}$$

where n is the number of data points. Thus, the moment estimates of the parameters of the log–normal distribution are given by

$$\mu = 2 \ln M_1' - (1/2) \ln M_2' \tag{17.17}$$

$$\sigma^2 = \ln M_2' - 2 \ln M_1' \tag{17.18}$$

For the Weibull distribution, the mean and variance are given by

$$\mu_1' = \sigma \Gamma(1 + 1/\lambda) \tag{17.19}$$

where Γ is the gamma function and

$$\mu^2 = \sigma^2 [\Gamma(1 + 2/\lambda) - \Gamma^2(1 + 1/\lambda)] \tag{17.20}$$

In solving these equations for σ and λ, we can conveniently use the coefficient of variation given by $(\mu_2)^{1/2}/\mu_1'$. Then the moment estimators of the sample

correspond to λ so that

$$\left[\frac{\Gamma(1 + 2/\lambda)}{\Gamma^2(1 + 1/\lambda)} - 1\right]^{1/2} = \frac{(M_2)^{1/2}}{M_1'} \tag{17.21}$$

$$\sigma = \frac{M_1'}{\Gamma(1 + 1/\lambda)} \tag{17.22}$$

To aid in the determination of λ in fitting a set of data to the Weibull distribution, one can use Figure 17.5, in which the left hand side of Eq. (17.21) is shown as a function of λ for $0 < \lambda < 9$.

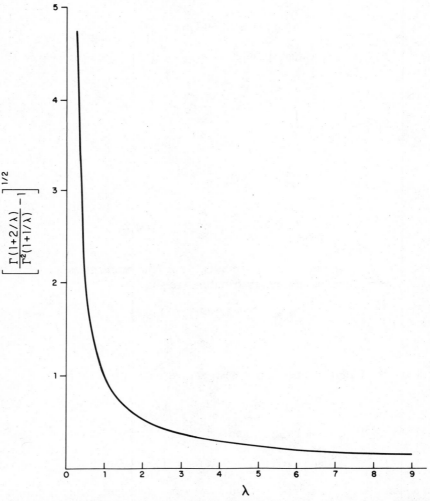

Figure 17.5. Calculation of parameter λ in fitting a set of data to a Weibull distribution by the method of moments (Georgopoulos and Seinfeld, 1982).

TABLE 17.1.   1971 Hourly-Average Pasadena, California, Ozone Data Fitted to a Weibull Distribution

| | Concentration (pphm) Equalled or Exceeded by the Stated Percent of Observations | | | | | | | | |
	1%	2%	3%	4%	5%	10%	25%	50%	75%
Data (hourly-average)	24	20	18	16	15	11	5	2	1
Weibull distribution	23.5	19.2	16.8	15.1	13.8	10	5.3	2.3	0.76
Data (daily max)	34	33	32	30	28	25	17	10	5
Weibull distribution	38.8	34.6	32	30.1	28.6	24.8	16.6	10.2	5.5

As an example, we consider the fitting of a Weibull distribution to 1971 hourly average ozone data from Pasadena, California. The data consist of 8303 hourly values (there are 8760 hours in a year). The maximum hourly value reported was 53 pphm. The arithmetic mean and standard deviation of the data are $M_1' = 4.0$ pphm and $M_2^{1/2} = 5.0$ pphm, and the geometric mean and geometric standard deviation are 2.4 and 2.6 pphm, respectively.

If one assumes that the hourly average ozone concentrations fit a Weibull distribution, the parameters of the distribution can be estimated from Eqs. (17.21) and (17.22) to give $\lambda = 0.808$ and $\sigma = 3.555$ pphm.

It is interesting also to fit only the daily maximum hourly average ozone values to a Weibull distribution. For these data there exist 365 data points, the maximum value of which is, as already noted, 53 pphm. The arithmetic mean and standard deviation of the data are $M_1' = 12.0$ pphm and $M_2^{1/2} = 8.6$ pphm; the geometric mean and geometric standard deviation are 9.1 and 2.2 pphm, respectively. Table 17.1 gives a comparison of the data and the Weibull distribution concentration frequencies in the two cases. Both fits are very good, the fit to the daily maximum values being slightly better. Figure 17.4 shows the two distributions plotted on extreme-value probability paper.

17.3.   ORDER STATISTICS OF AIR QUALITY DATA

One of the major uses of statistical distributions of pollutant concentrations is to assess the degree of compliance of a region with ambient air quality standards. These standards define acceptable upper limits of pollutant concentrations and acceptable frequencies with which such concentrations can be exceeded. The probability that a particular concentration level, x, will be exceeded in a single observation is given by the complementary distribution function $\bar{F}(x) = \text{Prob}\{c > x\} = 1 - F(x)$.

When treating sets of air quality data, available as successive observations, we may be interested in certain random variables, as, for example:

the highest (or, in general, the rth highest) concentration in a finite sample of size m;

the number of exceedances of a given concentration level in a number of measurements or in a given time period;

the number of observations (waiting time or "return period") between exceedances of a given concentration level.

The distributions and pdf's, as well as certain statistical properties of these random variables, can be determined by applying the methods and results of *order statistics* (or statistics of extremes) (Gumbel, 1958; Sarhan and Greenberg, 1962; David, 1981).

17.3.1. Basic Notions and Terminology of Order Statistics

Consider the m random unordered variates $c(t_1)$, $c(t_2), \ldots, c(t_m)$, that are members of the stochastic process $\{c(t_i)\}$ that generates the time series of available air quality data. If we arrange the data points by order of magnitude, then a "new" random sequence of ordered variates $c_{1;m} \geq c_{2;m} \geq \cdots \geq c_{m;m}$ is formed. We call $c_{i;m}$ the ith *highest order statistic* or ith *extreme statistic* of this random sequence of size m.

In the exposition that follows we assume in general that:

The concentration levels measured in successive nonoverlapping periods— and hence the unordered random variates $c(t_i)$—are independent of one another.

The random variables $c(t_i)$ are identically distributed.

17.3.2. Extreme Values

Assume that the distribution function $F(x)$, as well as the pdf $p(x)$, corresponding to the total number of available measurements, are known. They are called the *parent* (or initial) distribution and pdf respectively. The probability density function $p_{r,m}(x)$ and the distribution function $F_{r,m}(x)$ of the rth highest concentration out of samples of size m are evaluated directly from the parent pdf $p(x)$ and the parent distribution function $F(x)$ as follows.

The probability that $c_{r,m} = x$ equals the probability of $m - r$ trials producing concentration levels lower than x, times the probability of $r - 1$ trials producing concentrations above x, times the probability density of attaining a concentration equal to x, multiplied by the total number of combinations of arranging these events (assuming complete independence of the data). In other words, the pdf of the rth highest concentration has the trinomial form.

$$p_{r;\,m}(x) = \frac{m!}{(r-1)!(m-r)!}[F(x)]^{m-r}[1-F(x)]^{r-1}p(x)$$

$$= \frac{1}{B(r,m-r+1)}[F(x)]^{m-r}[1-F(x)]^{r-1}p(x) \quad (17.23)$$

where B is the beta function (Pearson, 1934). In particular, for the highest and second highest concentration values ($r = 1, 2$) we have

$$p_{1;\,m}(x) = m[F(x)]^{m-1}p(x) \quad (17.24)$$

and

$$p_{2;\,m}(x) = m(m-1)[F(x)]^{m-2}[1-F(x)]\,p(x) \quad (17.25)$$

The probability $F_{r;\,m}(x)$ that $c_{r;\,m} \leq x$ is identical to the probability that no more than $r-1$ measurements out of m result in $c_{r;\,m} > x$. Every observation is considered as a Bernoulli trial with probabilities of "success" and "failure" $F(x)$ and $1 - F(x)$, respectively. Thus,

$$F_{r;\,m}(x) = \sum_{k=0}^{r-1} \binom{m}{k}[1-F(x)]^k[F(x)]^{m-k} \quad (17.26)$$

For the particular cases of the highest and the second highest values ($r = 1, 2$), Eq. (17.26) becomes

$$F_{1;\,m}(x) = [F(x)]^m \quad (17.27)$$

$$F_{2;\,m}(x) = m[F(x)]^{m-1} - (m-1)[F(x)]^m \quad (17.28)$$

It is worthwhile to note the dependence of the probability of the largest values on the sample size. From Eq. (17.27) we obtain

$$F_{1;\,n}(x) = [F_{1;\,m}(x)]^{n/m} \quad (17.29)$$

Thus, if the distribution of the extreme value is known for one sample size, it is known for all sample sizes.

Let the pdf of the rth highest concentration out of a sample of m values be denoted $p_{r;\,m}(c)$. Once this pdf is known, all the statistical properties of the random variable $c_{r;\,m}$ can be determined. However, the integrals involved in the expressions for the expectation and higher order moments are not always easily evaluated, and thus there arises the need for techniques of approximation. The most important result concerns the evaluation of the expected value of $c_{r;\,m}$. In fact, for sufficiently large m, an approximation for $E\{c_{r;\,m}\}$ is provided by the value of x satisfying (David, 1981)

$$F(x) = \frac{m - r + 1}{m + 1} \qquad (17.30)$$

In terms of the inverse function of $F(x)$, $F^{-1}(x)$ (that is $F^{-1}[F(x)] = x$), we have the asymptotic relation

$$E\{c_{r;\,m}\} \cong F^{-1}\!\left(\frac{m - r + 1}{m + 1}\right),$$

$$\text{as} \quad m \to \infty \qquad (17.31)$$

17.4. EXCEEDANCES OF CRITICAL LEVELS

The number of exceedances (episodes), $N_x(m)$ of a given concentration level x in a set of m successive observations $c(t_i)$, is itself a random function. Similarly, the number of averaging periods (or observations) between exceedances of the concentration level x, another random function called the *waiting time*, *passage time*, or *return period*, is of crucial interest in the study of pollution episodes.

17.4.1. Distribution of Exceedances

In the case of independent, identically distributed variates, each one of the observations is a Bernoulli trial; therefore, the probability density function of $N_x(m)$ is, in terms of the parent distribution $F(x)$:

$$p_N(N_x;\, m,\, x) = \binom{m}{N_x}[1 - F(x)]^{N_x} F(x)^{m - N_x} \qquad (17.32)$$

Thus, the expected number of exceedances $\overline{N}_x(m)$ of the level x in a sample of m measurements is

$$\overline{N}_x(m) = m(1 - F(x)) = m\overline{F}(x) \qquad (17.33)$$

The expected percentage of exceedances of a given concentration level x is just $100\overline{F}(x)$.

17.4.2. Expected Return Period or Waiting Time

The expected return period is defined as the average number of averaging periods (or observations) between exceedances of a given level x. The probability that the concentration will exceed x for the first time at observation n is

$$f_n = \Pr\{c \le x\}^{n-1}\Pr\{c > x\}$$

$$= [F(x)]^{n-1}[1 - F(x)] \qquad (17.34)$$

By definition the expected value of the return period is

$$E\{n\} = \sum_{n=1}^{\infty} nf_n \qquad (17.35)$$

and

$$\sum_{n=1}^{\infty} n[F(x)]^{n-1}[1 - F(x)] = [1 - F(x)] \sum_{n=1}^{\infty} n[F(x)]^{n-1}$$

Since $F(x) < 1$, we can write

$$\sum_{n=1}^{\infty} n[F(x)]^{n-1} = 1 + 2F + 3F^2 + \cdots = \frac{1}{[1 - F(x)]^2} \qquad (17.36)$$

Combining Eqs. (17.35) and (17.36), we obtain

$$E\{n\} = \frac{1}{1 - F(x)} = [\bar{F}(x)]^{-1} \qquad (17.37)$$

The variance of the number of observations between exceedances of a given level x is

$$\mathrm{Var}\{n\} = \sum_{n=1}^{\infty} (n - E\{n\})^2 f_n$$

$$= \sum_{n=1}^{\infty} \left[n - \frac{1}{1 - F} \right]^2 F^{n-1}(1 - F)$$

$$= (1 - F) \sum_{n=1}^{\infty} n^2 F^{n-1} - 2 \sum_{n=1}^{\infty} nF^{n-1} + \frac{1}{1 - F} \sum_{n=1}^{\infty} F^{n-1}$$

$$(17.38)$$

Using the relations

$$\sum_{n=0}^{\infty} F^n = 1/(1 - F)$$

$$\sum_{n=0}^{\infty} nF^{n-1} = 1/(1 - F)^2$$

$$\sum_{n=1}^{\infty} n(n - 1)F^{n-2} = 2/(1 - F)^3$$

we obtain from Eq. (17.38)

$$\text{Var}\{n\} = \frac{F}{(1 - F)^2} \qquad (17.39)$$

17.5. ALTERNATIVE FORMS OF AIR QUALITY STANDARDS

In the evaluation of whether ambient air quality standards are satisfied in a region, aerometric data are used to estimate expected concentrations and their frequency of occurrence. If it is assumed that a certain probability distribution can be used to represent the air quality data, the distribution is fit to the current years' data by estimating the parameters of the distribution. It is then assumed that the probability distribution will hold for data in future years; only the parameters of the distribution will change as the source emissions change from year to year. If the parameters of the distribution can be estimated for future years, then the expected number of exceedances of given concentration levels, such as the ambient air quality standard, can be assessed.

Table 17.2 gives four possible forms for an ambient air quality standard. We have used ozone as the example air pollutant in the table. The ambient air

TABLE 17.2. Alternative Statistical Forms of the Ozone Air Quality Standard[a]

No.	Form
1	0.12 ppm hourly average with expected number of exceedances per year less than or equal to one
2	0.12 ppm hourly average not to be exceeded on the average by more than 0.01% of the hours in one year
3	0.12 ppm annual expected maximum hourly average
4	0.12 ppm annual expected second-highest hourly average

[a] For most practical purposes forms 1 and 3 can be considered equivalent.

quality standards involve a concentration level and a frequency of occurrence of that level. In this section we want to examine the implications of the form of the standard on the degree of compliance of a region. The choice of one form of the standard over another can be based on the impact that each form implies for the concentration distribution as a whole (Curran and Hunt, 1975; Mage, 1980).

The first step in the evaluation of an air quality standard is to select the statistical distribution that supposedly best fits the data. We will assume that the frequency distribution that best fits hourly-averaged ozone concentration data is the Weibull distribution. Since the standards are expressed in terms of expected events during a one-year period of one-hour average concentrations, we will always use the number of trials m equal to the number of hours in a year, 8760. We would use $m < 8760$ only to evaluate the parameters of the distribution if some of the 8760 hourly values are missing from the data set.

Let us now analyze each of the four forms of the ozone air quality standard given in Table 17.2 from the point of view that ozone concentrations can be represented by a Weibull distribution.

1. Expected Number of Exceedances of 0.12 ppm Hourly Average Concentration Less than or Equal to One per Year. The expected number of exceedances $\overline{N}_x(m)$ of a given concentration level in m measurements is given by Eq. (17.33), which, in the case of the Weibull distribution, becomes

$$\overline{N}_x = m \exp\left[-(x/\sigma)^\lambda\right] \tag{17.40}$$

If we desire the expected exceedance to be once out of m hours, that is, $\overline{N}_{x_1} = 1$, the concentration corresponding to that choice is

$$x_1 = \sigma(\ln m)^{1/\lambda} \tag{17.41}$$

For $m = 8760$, Eq. (17.41) becomes

$$x_1 = (9.08)^{1/\lambda} \tag{17.42}$$

2. The 0.12 ppm Hourly Average Concentration Not to Be Exceeded on the Average by More than 0.01 Percent of the Hours in One Year. The expected percentage of exceedance of a given concentration, x, is given by $100\ \overline{F}(x)$, which, for the Weibull distribution, is

$$\overline{\Pi}(x) = 100 \exp\left[-(x/\sigma)^\lambda\right] \tag{17.43}$$

Equation (17.43) can be rearranged to determine the concentration level that is expected to be exceeded $\overline{\Pi}(x)$ percent of the time,

$$x = \sigma\left[\ln(100/\overline{\Pi}(x))\right]^{1/\lambda} \tag{17.44}$$

Therefore, we can calculate the concentration that is expected to be exceeded 0.01 percent of the hours in one year as

$$x_{0.01} = \sigma(9.21)^{1/\lambda} \tag{17.45}$$

3, 4. The 0.12 ppm Annual Expected Maximum Hourly Average Concentration and 0.12 ppm Annual Expected Second-Highest Hourly Average Concentration. The expected value of the rth highest concentration for a Weibull distribution is

$$E\{c_{r;\,m}\} = \frac{m!}{(r-1)!(m-r)!} \int_0^\infty (x/\sigma)^\lambda$$

$$\times \left\{1 - \exp\left[-(x/\sigma)^\lambda\right]\right\}^{m-r} \left\{\exp\left[-(x/\sigma)^\lambda\right]\right\}^r dx \tag{17.46}$$

We wish to evaluate this equation for $r = 1$ and $r = 2$, corresponding to standards 3 and 4, respectively, in Table 17.2, to obtain $E\{c_{1;\,m}\}$ and $E\{c_{2;\,m}\}$, the expected highest and second highest hourly concentrations, respectively, in the year, with $m = 8760$. Unfortunately, the integral in Eq. (17.46) cannot be evaluated easily. Even numerical techniques fail to give consistent results, because of the singularity at $x = 0$. Thus, the asymptotic relation for large m, Eq. (17.31), must be used in this case. For the Weibull distribution we have

$$1 - \exp\left[-\left(\frac{E\{c_{r;\,m}\}}{\sigma}\right)^\lambda\right] = \frac{m-r+1}{m+1} \tag{17.47}$$

For $m = 8760$ and $r = 1, 2$ we must solve, respectively, the equations

$$1 - \exp\left[-\left(\frac{E\{c_{1;\,m}\}}{\sigma}\right)^\lambda\right] = \frac{8760}{8761} \tag{17.48}$$

and

$$1 - \exp\left[-\left(\frac{E\{c_{2;\,m}\}}{\sigma}\right)^\lambda\right] = \frac{8759}{8761} \tag{17.49}$$

to obtain

$$E\{c_{1;\,m}\} = \sigma(9.08)^{1/\lambda} \tag{17.50}$$

and

$$E\{c_{2;\,m}\} = \sigma(8.38)^{1/\lambda} \tag{17.51}$$

17.5.1.   Evaluation of Alternative Forms of the Ozone Air Quality Standard with 1971 Pasadena, California Data

Earlier, 1971 hourly-average and maximum daily hourly-average ozone concentrations at Pasadena, California, were fit to Weibull distributions. We now wish to evaluate the four forms of the ozone air quality standard with these data. For convenience all concentration values will be given as pphm rather than ppm.

1.   Expected Number of Exceedances of 12 pphm Hourly Average Concentration Less than or Equal to One per Year.   The expected number of exceedances of 12 pphm, based on the Weibull fit of the 1971 Pasadena, California, hourly-average data, is from Eq. (17.40)

$$N_{12} = 8760 \exp\left[-\left(\frac{12}{3.555}\right)^{0.808}\right] = 605.2$$

The hourly-average ozone concentration that is exceeded at most once per year is from Eq. (17.41)

$$x_1 = 3.555(\ln 8.760)^{1/0.808}$$

$$= 54.41 \text{ pphm}$$

which agrees well with the actual measured value of 52 pphm.

If, instead of the complete hourly-average Weibull distribution, we use the distribution of daily maximum hourly-average values, the expected number of exceedances of a daily maximum of 12 pphm is

$$\overline{N}_{12} = 365 \exp\left[-\left(\frac{12}{13.189}\right)^{1.416}\right] = 152.2$$

and the daily maximum 1 hr concentration that is exceeded once per year, at most, is

$$x_1 = 13.189 \,(\ln 365)^{1/1.416}$$

$$= 46.2 \text{ pphm}$$

It is interesting to note that this value is underpredicted if we use the distribution of daily maxima instead of the distribution based on the complete set of data.

2.   The 12-pphm Hourly Average Concentration Not to Be Exceeded on the Average by More than 0.01 Percent of the Hours in One Year.   The expected percentage of exceedances of 12 pphm is, from Eq. (17.43),

$$\Pi(12) = 100 \exp\left[-\left(\frac{12}{3.555}\right)^{0.808}\right] = 6.91 \text{ percent}$$

The concentration that is expected to be exceeded 0.01 percent of the hours in the year is, from Eq. (17.44)

$$x_{0.01} = 3.555\left(\ln\frac{100}{0.01}\right)^{1/0.808} = 55.5 \text{ pphm}$$

This form of the standard cannot be evaluated from the distribution of daily maxima since it is stated based on a percentage of all the hours of the year.

3, 4.   The 12-pphm Annual Expected Maximum Hourly Average Concentration and 12-pphm Annual Expected Second-Highest Average Concentration. The annual expected maximum hourly average concentration is obtained from Eq. (17.50) for $E\{c_{1;m}\}$, and for $\sigma = 3.555$, $\lambda = 0.808$. We have

$$E\{c_1\} = 54.41 \text{ pphm}$$

(whereas the observed (sample) maximum hourly average value was 53 pphm). Similarly, for the annual expected second highest hourly average concentration we have from Eq. (17.51),

$$E\{c_2\} = 49.40 \text{ pphm}$$

17.5.2.   Selection of the Averaging Time

An interesting question of interpretation arises when an ambient air quality standard involves a several-hour averaging period. For example, the 8-hr National Ambient Air Quality Standard for carbon monoxide is 9 ppm, not to be exceeded more than once per year. Two principal interpretations of the 8-hr standard have been proposed (McMullin, 1975). One approach is to examine all possible 8-hr intervals by calculating a moving 8-hr average (24 8-hr averages each day). The other approach is to examine three consecutive non-overlapping 8-hr intervals per day, usually beginning, for sake of convenience, at midnight, 8:00 a.m., and 4 p.m. The principal appeal of the moving average is that it approximates the body's integrating response to cumulative CO exposure. A disadvantage is that the moving 8-hr average affords no reduction in the number of data points to be examined compared with the input of 1-hr values. The consecutive interval approach offers the convenience of reducing a year's 8760 hourly values to a set of 1095 consecutive 8-hr periods. McMullin (1975) examined 1972 data for three sites (Newark, New Jersey; Camden, New Jersey; and Spokane, Washington) and found that the maximum and second-highest concentration values derived from moving averages can be at least 20 percent higher than corresponding values detected by the consecutive 8-hr intervals. He found that the natural fluctuation in the time of day when the maximum occurs and the variability and episode length make it doubtful that any framework of consecutive 8-hr intervals can adequately portray the essential characteristics of CO exposure. He therefore recommended the moving 8-hr average as more sensitive to actual maximum levels and to short episodes.

17.6.   RELATING CURRENT AND FUTURE AIR POLLUTANT STATISTICAL DISTRIBUTIONS

The reduction R in current emission source strength to meet an air quality goal is often calculated by the so-called rollback equation,

$$R = \frac{E\{c\} - E\{c\}_s}{E\{c\} - c_b} \tag{17.52}$$

where $E\{c\}$ is the current annual mean of the pollutant concentration, $E\{c\}_s$ is the annual mean corresponding to the air quality standard c_s, and c_b is the background concentration assumed to be constant. Since, as we have seen, the air quality standard c_s is usually stated in terms of an extreme statistic, such as the concentration level that may be exceeded only once per year, it is necessary to have a probability distribution to relate the extreme concentration c_s to the annual mean $E\{c\}_s$. We assume that if, in the future, the emission level is halved, the annual mean concentration will also be halved. The key question is: if the emission level is halved, what happens to the predicted extreme concentration in the future year; is it correspondingly halved or does it change by more or less than that amount?

To address this question, assume that the concentration in question can be represented by a log–normal distribution (under present as well as future conditions). If a current emission rate changes by a factor $\kappa (\kappa > 0)$, while the source distribution remains the same (if meteorological conditions are unchanged, and if background concentrations are negligible), the expected total quantity of inert pollutants having an impact on a given site over the same time period should also change by the factor κ. The expected concentration level for the future period is therefore given, for a log–normally distributed variable, by (recall $\mu = \ln \mu_g$ and $\sigma = \ln \sigma_g$)

$$E\{c'\} = e^{\mu' + \sigma'^2/2} = \kappa e^{\mu + \sigma^2/2} \tag{17.53}$$

where the primed quantities of c', μ', σ' apply to the future period, and the unprimed quantities apply to the present. On an intuitive basis if meteorological conditions remain unchanged, the standard geometric deviation of the log–normal pollutant distribution should remain unchanged; that is, $e^{\sigma'} = e^{\sigma}$. Thus, $e^{\mu'} = \kappa e^{\mu}$, or

$$\mu' = \mu + \ln \kappa \tag{17.54}$$

The probability that future concentration level c' will exceed a level x is

$$\bar{F}_{c'}(x) = 1 - \frac{1}{\sqrt{2\pi}} \int_{-\infty}^{(\ln x - \mu')/\sigma'} e^{-\eta^2} \, d\eta$$

$$= \bar{F}_c(x/\kappa) \tag{17.55}$$

using Eq. (17.54). Similarly,

$$\bar{F}_{c'}(\kappa x) = 1 - \frac{1}{\sqrt{2\pi}} \int_{-\infty}^{(\ln x - \mu')/\sigma'} e^{-\eta^2} \, d\eta$$

$$= \bar{F}_c(x) \tag{17.56}$$

Thus, the probability that the future level κx will be exceeded just equals the probability that with current emission sources the level x will be exceeded. Therefore, with equal σ, all frequency points of the distribution shift according to the factor κ. This results in a parallel translation of the graph of $F(x)$ or $\bar{F}(x)$, when plotted against $\ln x$.

Figure 17.6 shows two log–normal distributions with the same standard geometric deviation but with different geometric mean values. The geometric mean concentrations of the two distributions are 0.05 ppm and 0.10 ppm, and the standard geometric deviations are both 1.4. The mean concentrations can be calculated with the aid of $\ln E\{c\} = \ln \mu_g + 1/2 \ln^2 \sigma_g$ and the material presented above. We find that $E_1\{c\} = 0.053$ ppm, and $E_2\{c\} = 0.106$ ppm for the two distributions, respectively. The variances can likewise be calculated with the aid of $\mathrm{Var}\{c\} = [\exp(2\mu + \sigma^2)][e^{\sigma^2} - 1]$ to obtain $\mathrm{Var}_1\{c\} = 0.00034$ ppm^2 and $\mathrm{Var}_2\{c\} = 0.00134$ ppm^2.

Suppose that distribution No. 1 represents current conditions, and therefore, that the current probability of exceeding a concentration of 0.13 ppm is about 0.0027 (which corresponds to about one day per year if the distribution is of 24-hr averages). If the emission rate were doubled, the new distribution function would be given by distribution No. 2. The new distribution has a median value twice that of the old one, since total loadings attributable to emissions have doubled. In the new case, a concentration of 0.13 ppm will be exceeded 22 percent of the time, or about 80 days a year, and the concentration that is exceeded only one day per year rises to 0.26 ppm.

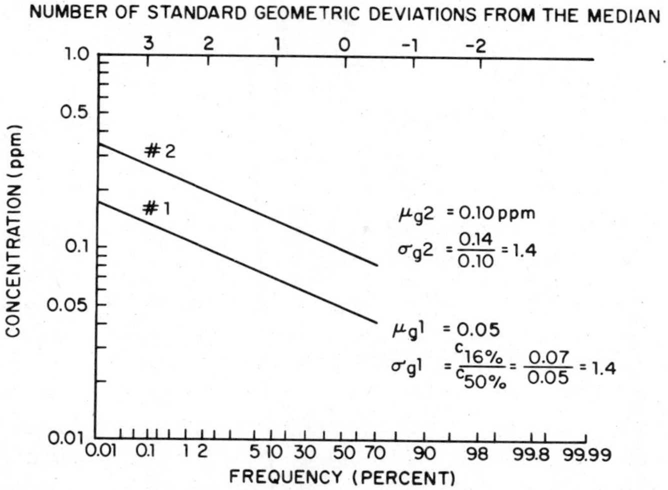

NUMBER OF STANDARD GEOMETRIC DEVIATIONS FROM THE MEDIAN

Figure 17.6. Two log–normal distributions with the same standard geometric deviation.

REFERENCES

Bencala, K., and Seinfeld, J. H. "On Frequency Distributions of Air Pollutant Concentrations," *Atmos. Environ.*, **10**, 941–950 (1976).

Curran, T. C., and Hunt, W. F., Jr. "Interpretation of Air Quality Data with Respect to the National Ambient Air Quality Standards," *J. Air Pollution Control Assoc.*, **25**, 711–714 (1975).

David, H. A. *Order Statistics*, 2nd ed., Wiley, New York (1981).

Feller, W. *An Introduction to Probability Theory and Its Applications*, Vol. 1, 3rd ed., Wiley, New York (1968).

Georgopoulos, P. G., and Seinfeld, J. H. "Statistical Distributions of Air Pollutant Concentrations," *Environ. Sci. Technol.*, **16**, 401A–416A (1982).

Gumbel, E. J. *Statistics of Extremes*, Columbia University Press, New York (1958).

Holland, D. M., and Fitz-Simons, T. "Fitting Statistical Distributions to Air Quality Data by the Maximum Likelihood Method," *Atmos. Environ.*, **16**, 1071–1076 (1982).

Larsen, R. I., Zimmer, C. E., Lynn, D. A., and Blemel, K. G. "Analyzing Air Pollutant Concentration and Dosage Data," *J. Air Pollution Control Assoc.*, **17**, 85–93 (1967).

Larsen, R. I. *A Mathematical Model for Relating Air Quality Measurements to Air Quality Standards*, EPA Publication No. A-89, Research Triangle Park, North Carolina (1971).

Larsen, R. I. "A New Mathematical Model of Air Pollutant Concentration Averaging Time and Frequency," *J. Air Pollution Control Assoc.*, **19**, 24–30 (1969).

Mage, D. T. "The Statistical Form for the Ambient Particulate Standard Annual Arithmetic Mean versus Annual Geometric Mean," *J. Air Pollution Control Assoc.*, **30**, 796–798 (1980).

McMullin, T. B. "Interpreting the Eight-Hour National Ambient Air Quality Standard for Carbon Monoxide," *J. Air Pollution Control Assoc.*, **25**, 1009–1014 (1975).

Pearson, K. *Tables of the Incomplete Beta Function*, Biometrika Office, London (1934).

Sarhan, A. E., and Greenburg, B. G. (Eds.), *Contributions to Order Statistics*, Wiley, New York
    (1962).

Tsukatami, T., and Shigemitsu, K. "Simplified Pearson Distributions Applied to Air Pollutant
    Concentration," *Atmos. Environ.*, **14**, 245–253 (1980).

PROBLEMS

17.1. Show how to construct the axes of extreme value probability paper on
which a Weibull distribution will plot as a straight line.

17.2. Figure 1.7 showed the frequency distributions of SO_2 and sulfate at
nine locations in the eastern U.S. from August 1977 to July 1978. Using
the data points on the two figures, fit log–normal distributions to the
SO_2 concentrations at Duncan Falls, Ohio and to the sulfate concentrations at Montague, Massachusetts. If the data points do not fall exactly
on the best-fit log–normal lines, comment on possible reasons for
deviations of the measured concentrations from log normality.

17.3. Figure 1.8 showed the frequency distributions of CO concentrations
measured inside and outside an automobile traveling a Los Angeles
commuter route. Fit log–normal distributions to the exterior 1-min and
30-min averaging time data. If the data points do not fall exactly on the
best-fit log–normal lines, comment on possible reasons for deviations of
the measured concentrations from log normality. What can be said
about the relationship of the best-fit parameters for the log–normal
distributions at 1-min and 30-min averaging times.

TABLE P17.1.   **Carbon Monoxide Concentrations at Pasadena, California, for 1982.
Some Statistics of 1 hr-Average Concentrations (ppm)**

Month	Weekly 1 Hr-Avg Maxima	Highest 1 Hr-Avg Value	Mean of Daily 1 Hr-Avg Maxima
January	17, 12, 8, 10	17	7.2
February	10, 8, 9, 7	10	5.3
March	5, 7, 6, 6	7	4.0
April	3, 5, 4, 5, 2	5	2.9
May	3, 4, 3, 3	4	3.2
June	5, 4, 3, 4	5	2.5
July	2, 3, 3, 4, 3	4	2.4
August	6, 3, 5, 4	6	2.8
September	7, 6, 4, 8	8	3.8
October[a]	8, 12, 11, —, 11	(12)	(7.2)
November	13, 10, 10, 11	13	6.9
December	15, 14, 20, 8, 13	20	8.9

[a] No data were available for the fourth week of October.

17.4. Table P17.1 gives CO concentrations at Pasadena, California, for 1982, in particular the weekly maximum 1-hr average concentrations, and the monthly mean of the daily 1-hr average maximum concentrations.

(a) Plot the weekly 1-hr average maximum values on log–probability paper and extreme-value probability paper.

(b) Determine the two parameters of both the log–normal and Weibull distributions by the method of moments and the method of quantiles. Based on your results select one of the two distributions as representing the best fit to the data.

(c) What was the expected number of exceedances of the weekly 1-hr average maximum CO concentration at Pasadena of the National Ambient Air Quality Standard for CO of 35 ppm?

(d) What is the expected number of weekly 1-hr average maximum observations between successive exceedances of 35 ppm?

(e) What is the variance of the number of weekly 1-hr average maximum observations between successive exceedances of 35 ppm?

(f) For the expected exceedance of 35 ppm to be once in 52 weeks, how must the parameters of the distribution change?

17.5. Consider a single elevated continuous point source at a height h of strength q. Assume that the wind blows with a speed that is log–normally distributed with parameters μ_{ug} and σ_{ug} and with a direction that is uniformly distributed over 360°. No inversion layer exists.

(a) Determine the form of the statistical distribution of $\langle c(x, y, 0) \rangle$ in terms of the known quantities of the problem.

(b) If the source strength changes from q to κq, determine the form of the new distribution of $\langle c(x, y, 0) \rangle$.

(c) If the air quality standard is related to the value that is exceeded only once a year, derive an expression for the change in this value as a function of location resulting from the source strength change.

17.6. If the CO emission level from the entire motor vehicle population is reduced to one-half its value at the time the data in Figure 1.8 were obtained, calculate the expected changes in the three CO frequency distributions. (Note that in order to calculate this change one needs the results of Problem 17.3.) How does the frequency at which a level of 50 ppm occurs change due to a halving of the emission rate? How does the expected return period and its variance change for the 50 ppm level from the old to the new emission level?

EIGHTEEN

Acid Rain

18.1. OVERVIEW OF ACID PRECIPITATION

In Chapters 4 and 5 we found that, once emitted to the atmosphere, SO_2 and NO_x become oxidized to sulfate and nitrate through both gas- and aqueous-phase processes. Moreover, from Chapters 9 and 16, we also found that ambient gases and particles can be scavenged by atmospheric liquid water and, in the case of particles, serve as condensation nuclei for cloud droplets. Thus, on the basis of what we have already learned, we expect that a possible fate of atmospheric SO_2 and NO_x will be incorporation into liquid water as sulfates and nitrates, respectively. These solutions containing sulfate and nitrate are likely to be acidic. The alternative to scavenging by liquid water or ice of atmospheric species is dry deposition at the earth's surface. We can imagine that SO_2 and NO_x, over the course of transport from their sources, can be converted chemically to acidic sulfate and nitrate and ultimately be removed by wet or dry deposition to the earth's surface. The point where the deposition occurs can be either close to or quite distant from the source, depending on the height of the source, the chemical nature of the atmosphere, the abundance of liquid water, and so forth. Although dry deposition is generally not monitored, the chemical nature of rainfall, at least its pH, is frequently measured, so that when the process described above is occurring, its existence is frequently inferred from rainfall that is unusually acidic and/or contains sulfates and nitrates at levels exceeding those of "clean" rain.

The phenomenon we have just described is commonly identified by the term *acid rain*. As we have just noted, the removal of sulfates and nitrates from the atmosphere occurs by both wet and dry processes. Consequently, the overall process is more properly termed *acid deposition*, consisting of both wet acid deposition (i.e., acid precipitation) and dry acid deposition. Because of the focus on the composition of rainwater, this entire process is usually called simply acid rain. Even though the term acid rain implies removal only by wet deposition, it is important to keep in mind that dry deposition of the acidic substances also occurs when such substances are in the atmosphere and that the effects attributable to acid rain are in fact a result of a combination of wet and dry deposition.

18.1.1. Historical Perspective

The phenomenon of acid rain appears to have been discovered first by an English chemist, Robert Angus Smith, in the middle of the nineteenth century. In 1853 Smith published a report on the chemistry of rain in and around the city of Manchester. Little attention was paid to acid rain for almost a century. In 1961, a Swedish soil scientist named Svante Odin established a Scandinavian network to measure surface water chemistry. On the basis of his measurements Odin showed that acid precipitation was a large-scale regional phenomenon in much of Europe with well-defined source and sink regions, that precipitation and surface waters were becoming more acidic, that long-distance (100 to 2000 km) transport of sulfur- and nitrogen-containing species was taking place over Europe, and that there were marked seasonal trends in the deposition of major ions and acidity. Odin also hypothesized long-term ecological effects of acid rain, including decline of fish populations, leaching of toxic metals from soils into surface waters, and decreased forest growth.

   The major foundations for our present understanding of acid rain and its effects were laid by Eville Gorham. On the basis of research in England and Canada, Gorham showed as early as 1955 that much of the acidity of precipitation near industrial regions can be attributed to combustion emissions, that progressive acidification of surface waters can be traced to precipitation, and that the free acidity in soils receiving acid precipitation is due primarily to sulfuric acid.

   Concern about acid precipitation in North America developed first in Canada and then later in the United States, although it was perhaps not until the 1970s that the true scope of the problem was appreciated. Both Canada and the United States have instituted long-term programs for the chemical analysis of precipitation. The above brief summary of acid rain historical highlights is based on the review of Cowling (1982), which contains a meticulous account of developments associated with the discovery of and attempts to deal with acid rain.

18.1.2. What is Acid Rain?

Absolutely neutral precipitation would have a pH of 7. Even precipitation in areas totally free of local anthropogenic emissions, however, is presumed to be in equilibrium with atmospheric trace constituents at their background levels. Recognizing this, the "natural" acidity of rainwater is often taken to be pH 5.6, which is that of pure water in equilibrium with the global atmospheric concentration of CO_2 (330 ppm), and this pH value of 5.6 has been used as the demarcation line for acidic precipitation.* Carbon dioxide is not, however, the

---

* Total acidity is the reservoir of hydrogen ions in solution, which constitutes the base neutralizing capacity of the solution. The total acidity consists of both free protons (strong acidity) and undissociated protons (weak acidity). pH is a measure of the strong acidity only.

only background trace constituent of the atmosphere capable of influencing the pH of rainwater. Charlson and Rodhe (1982) have shown that, in the absence of common basic compounds such as NH_3 and $CaCO_3$, rainwater pH values due to natural sulfur compounds alone could be expected to be about 5.0. Galloway et al. (1982) have reported precipitation chemistry data from remote areas of the globe and have found background pH values of 5.0 or greater, with the relative contributions of H_2SO_4, HNO_3, and other acids HX to the acidity of the precipitation varying from site to site. Analyses of 1955–1956 eastern U.S. precipitation data by Stensland and Semonin (1982) indicate background pH values of around 5.0.

We conclude therefore that rain of pH greater than 5.6 has not been influenced by man, or if it has, it has sufficient buffering capacity so that acidification does not occur. Rain with pH between 5.0 and 5.6 may have been influenced by man but not to an extent exceeding that of natural background sulfur species. (Again, anthropogenic influences, if present, are mitigated by natural buffering, since a pH of 5.0 is considered to be that in equilibrium with natural background sulfur compounds.) If the pH of rain is less than 5.0, we can be fairly certain that man-made influences are present. Although the issue of what is acid rain (and who caused it) is not a simple one, it is reasonable to consider precipitation with pH < 5.0 as acid rain.

TABLE 18.1.   Chemical Analyses of Acid Rain[a]

Species	Concentration μeq 1^{-1}		
	Sjoangen, Sweden[b] 1973–1975	Hubbard Brook, New Hampshire[c] 1973–1974	Pasadena California[d] 1978–1979
SO_4^{2-}	69	110	39
NO_3^-	31	50	31
Cl^-	18	12	28
NH_4^+	31	22	21
Na^+	15	6	24
K^+	3	2	2
Ca^{2+}	13	10	7
Mg^{2+}	7	32	7
H^+	52	114	39
pH	4.30	3.94	4.41

[a] Morgan (1982).
[b] Granat (1978).
[c] Likens et al. (1979).
[d] Liljestrand and Morgan (1980).

Table 18.1 gives concentrations of constituents in rain at three locations where acid rain has been reported. It can often be assumed that the predominant ions in acid rain are H^+, NH_4^+, Ca^{2+}, and SO_4^{2-} and NO_3^- (Gorham et al., 1984). Thus, the sum $(H^+ + NH_4^+ + Ca^{2+})$ should equal the sum $(SO_4^{2-} + NO_3^-)$.* We see from Table 18.1 that this assumption is not precisely true, especially for those locations where rain composition is influenced by sea salt and therefore contains appreciable sodium and chloride. In an analysis of precipitation over the eastern United States, Gorham et al. (1984) showed that at the most polluted group of sites H^+ averages 61.7 μeq 1^{-1} (pH 4.21) and is almost twice the concentration of the summed base cations $(NH_4^+ + Ca^{2+})$, whereas at the least polluted group of sites H^+ averages 21.4 μeq 1^{-1} (pH 4.67) and about equals the sum of the two base cations.

18.1.3. Current Data and Historical Trends

In North America, most of the northeastern United States and portions of Ontario, Quebec, Nova Scotia, and Newfoundland, as well as portions of the upper Midwest, the Rocky Mountains, and the West Coast of the United States, now receive acidic precipitation (Glass et al., 1982). Serious symptoms of acidification have been documented in the Adirondack Mountains of New York State (Schofield, 1982). The Adirondack area, in the northeastern part of New York State, has been one of the most widely studied areas with respect to effects of acid precipitation. Many areas of New England and Appalachia characterized by relatively insoluble bedrock and thin soils (see next section), as well as areas in the northern Midwest, show signs of acidification.

Although precipitation is most acidic in the northeastern United States and southeastern Canada, the geographic extent of the problem encompasses all states east of the Mississippi (Likens et al., 1979; Roth et al., 1985). In California precipitation with pH between 4.0 and 5.0 is common (Liljestrand and Morgan, 1981). Similar observations have been made in the Puget Sound basin and on the west slopes of the Cascade Mountains near Seattle-Tacoma (Powers and Rambo, 1981). The data from existing monitoring programs show acid precipitation now embraces about two-thirds of the total land area of North America (Cowling, 1982). Figure 18.1 shows the volume-weighted mean pH of precipitation for North America over the period April 1979 to March 1980, together with estimated SO_2 emissions by U.S. state and Canadian province for the same period.

The volume-weighted mean is computed by multiplying the concentration of a species by either the depth of rainfall or the liquid equivalent depth of snowfall. Summing over all precipitation events and dividing by the total liquid

---

*When representing acidity-related measurements, the unit of equivalents per liter is often used. The equivalent weight of a species is its molecular weight divided by its valence. Thus, concentrations of ions in rainwater are frequently expressed as eq 1^{-1} instead of M, the difference being the factor of the valence of the ion.

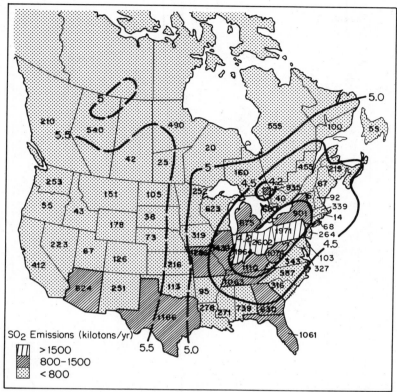

Figure 18.1. Sulfur dioxide emissions in North America in 1980 and precipitation-weighted mean pH in 1980 (U.S./Canada Work Group 2, 1982).

depth for all events gives the volume-weighted mean. For species that do not undergo reactions in the collection device (such as sulfate), the volume-weighted mean is the concentration that would result if the samples from all events were physically mixed and the resulting concentration measured. The volume-weighted pH is computed by first converting the individual pH measurements to concentration units. One then calculates the volume-weighted H^+ concentration and reconverts to pH.

The average pH and SO_4^{2-} concentration at a set of eastern U.S. precipitation monitoring stations during 1977 and 1978 was pH = 4.21 and $[SO_4^{2-}]$ = 25.7×10^{-6} M (Kleinman, 1984). During the summer months, the corresponding figures were 4.07 and 39.4×10^{-6} M and, for the winter months, 4.33 and 13.4×10^{-6} M. Although measurements of the pH of rainfall in southern California have gone as low as 2.9, the acidity of that region's rain is, on the average, one-third less than in the northeast United States. A typical average value of the pH of rain in Pasadena, California, for 1979–1980 was 4.8. In

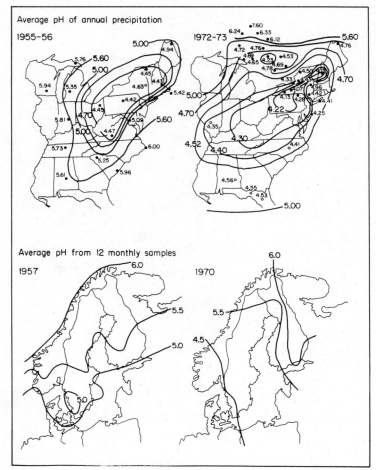

Figure 18.2. Trends in precipitation acidity in eastern North America and northern Europe (Chemical and Engineering News, 1976).

Riverside, California, about 100 km east of Los Angeles, where there are bases such as soil dust and ammonia from cattle feedlots and other agricultural activities, the pH during that time period was about 5.2.

Figure 18.2 shows the temporal trends in precipitation acidity in North America and Europe for the period from the mid-1950s to 1970. Total SO_2 emissions in the eastern United States doubled from 1950 to 1970 and then decreased by about 9 percent from 1970 to 1980.* Estimates of Canadian SO_2 emissions indicate a 20 percent increase from 1955 to 1976. Electric utilities

---

*A good historical inventory of SO_2 and NO_x emissions for the United States is that of Gschwandtner et al. (1983).

constitute the predominant SO_2 source in the eastern United States, whereas copper and nickel smelters represent the major Canadian SO_2 sources (Galloway and Whelpdale, 1980). The major SO_2 source in the western United States is smelters, followed by coal-fired power plants. Total NO_x emissions in the eastern United States increased by a factor of 2.4 from 1950 to 1980 with a peak in 1978, and Canadian NO_x emissions tripled between 1955 and 1976.

Hidy et al. (1984) have presented an analysis of historical bulk deposition data and ambient air quality data for sulfate and nitrate in relation to estimated changes in SO_2 and NO_x emissions in the northeastern United States and southeastern Canada. This analysis indicates that, since 1955, changes in precipitation sulfate and nitrate qualitatively follow patterns of emission change, with declines in sulfate and increases in nitrates. Long-term continuous records of precipitation sulfate show distinct geographical differences, so that no single station can be used to infer regionwide trends. Data records suggest that the changes in precipitation sulfate at rural sites in New York State and New Hampshire were more influenced by SO_2 changes in nearby source regions than by those in more distant source regions. In addressing the question whether sulfate deposition is linearly proportional to SO_2 emissions, Hidy et al. (1984) concluded that a linear proportionality is not uniformly supported and, to the extent it exists, is more applicable to SO_2 emissions from relatively nearby sources in the Northeast. From the results of continuing analysis the extent to which sulfate deposition is linearly proportional to SO_2 emissions has not been conclusively determined. (See, for example, Hidy (1984).)

18.1.4. Effects of Acid Deposition

The effects of acid deposition can be traced to the acidification of lakes and other surface waters. We have only a limited understanding in many cases of the mechanisms of ecosystem damage resulting from acid deposition. Perhaps the most complete understanding relates to the mechanisms of damage to fish. Less is known about the threats to other forms of aquatic life, from algae to amphibians. We are only in the initial stages of elucidating the mechanisms of tree damage.

By definition, lakes acidify when they lose alkalinity (Roth et al., 1985). Total alkalinity or acid neutralizing capacity is the reservoir of bases in solution. In natural clear waters, most of the acid neutralizing capacity consists of bicarbonate ion, HCO_3^-. Carbonate alkalinity is defined by

$$\text{alkalinity} = [HCO_3^-] + 2[CO_3^{2-}] + [OH^-] - [H^+]$$

When strong acids such as sulfuric acid enter bicarbonate waters, the additional hydrogen ions are neutralized by reacting with the bicarbonate, and the alkalinity decreases by the amount of strong acid added:

$$2H^+ + SO_4^{2-} + 2HCO_3^- = CO_2 \cdot H_2O + SO_4^{2-}$$

The acid neutralizing capacity of the lake buffers it against large changes in pH. Acidification occurs when a watershed receives an input of hydrogen ions that exceeds its supply of buffering ions, usually bicarbonate. Many soils take up hydrogen ions from acidic deposition by cation exchange with Ca^{2+}, Mg^{2+}, Na^+, or K^+. Watersheds vary in their ability to exchange base cations. Surface water acidification will not occur if the supply of base cations is sufficient and if precipitation contacts soil long enough before flowing into surface waters.

Available data strongly suggest that lakes surrounded by poorly buffered soil and underlain by granitic bedrock that have been exposed to acid precipitation have become more acidic (Havas et al., 1984). The hydrology and chemistry of lakes and streams are highly individualistic (Havas et al., 1984). For some lakes, direct atmospheric input may predominate; for others, surface or subsurface runoff may provide the major source of water. The type and depth of soil and the bedrock characteristics affect the chemistry of drainage waters. In addition, the lake's size and depth, the area of the drainage basin, and the residence time of water in the lake are all features that influence the response of a lake to acid rain.

The type of acidity in a lake has profound effects both on lake water chemistry and on the biota inhabiting the lake (Havas et al., 1984). As the pH of a lake decreases, the concentrations of several potentially toxic metals, such as aluminum, iron, manganese, copper, nickel, zinc, lead, cadmium, and mercury, increase (Dickson, 1980; Schofield, 1982; Havas and Hutchinson, 1983). Certain lakes, known as dystrophic lakes, are naturally acidic. These lakes usually have brown to yellow water caused by humic-derived organic acids. The organic acids in naturally acidic, brown water lakes reduce metal toxicity over that in clear water lakes (Baker and Schofield, 1980).

Abundant data show a significant correlation between increasing acidity and decreasing fish populations (Schofield, 1982). At first it was thought that acid alone was killing the fish, but it appears that aluminum dissolved from the soil by acid precipitation is primarily responsible. If the buffering capacity of the soil is high enough and the water stays in the soil long enough, bases in the soil react with the aluminum ions released into the water and they do not pass into the lakes and streams. Aluminum ions irritate fishes' gills and cause the gills to produce a protective mucus. This initiates a process that erodes the gill filament until the fish suffocates. Morphological deformities, spawning failure, and changes in blood chemistry have all been linked to acidification both in field observations and laboratory experiments (see references cited in Havas et al., 1984).

As we have noted, acid deposition consists of both wet (precipitation) and dry components.* Because of the difficulty of knowing exactly how much dry

---

*Actually a third type of acid deposition can be identified that is termed *occult* precipitation. As clouds and fog encounter trees, droplets are deposited on the trees and, from the trees, drip down to the earth. It has been estimated that in coastal regions vegetation can receive up to 50 percent of its total moisture from the occult precipitation of impacted cloud and fog water (Hoffmann, 1984).

deposition a region is receiving, measurements of effects of acid deposition have been correlated with the wet component only. Moreover, since sulfate and pH are the quantities most frequently measured, from the point of view of the chemical composition of rain, sulfate and/or H^+ are often used as the chemical indicators when correlating effects, although recent measurements include nitrate and other ionic components. The commonly used unit for representing acid deposition is kg hectare^{-1} yr^{-1}. (1 hectare = 10^4 m^2.) Evidence derived from studies in the eastern United States and Canada indicates that damage to ecosystems has probably not occurred in areas receiving precipitation of pH greater than 4.7 or, correspondingly, wet sulfate deposition of less than 14 to 16 kg hectare^{-1} yr^{-1}. Damage is most probably occurring with wet sulfate loadings exceeding 20 kg hectare^{-1} yr^{-1}, and almost certainly occurs for loadings over 30 kg hectare^{-1} yr^{-1}. It has been estimated that lakes having alkalinities less than 200 μeq l^{-1} are sensitive to acid precipitation. The mean SO_4^{2-} deposition for all sites in the eastern United States is 23.1 kg hectare^{-1} yr^{-1} (Gorham et al., 1984).

It has been estimated that dry deposition contributes approximately 50 percent of the total sulfur deposition in the Adirondack Mountains. The measured wet deposition rate of sulfur in this area is about 10 kg hectare^{-1} yr^{-1}. (This is equivalent to 30 kg SO_4^{2-} hectare^{-1} yr^{-1}). If we assume an SO_2 dry deposition velocity of 1 cm sec^{-1} and an SO_2 concentration of 2.5 ppb, then the dry deposition rate predicted is also 10 kg S hectare^{-1} yr^{-1}. Thus, only a fairly low SO_2 concentration is sufficient to give a dry deposition rate comparable to the wet deposition rate.

In the western United States the ratio of dry to wet deposition and the ratio of NO_x to SO_2 emissions are greater than in the East.* Thus, wet deposition loadings of sulfate may not be an accurate indicator of the potential for ecosystem damage in that area (Roth et al., 1985). In addition, because many of the western lakes susceptible to acidification are at high elevations where snow predominates over rain as a mode of delivery of acidity, that route must be accounted for.

18.2. KEY QUESTIONS IN ACID RAIN

Perhaps the single word that best characterizes the acid rain phenomenon is *competition*. The nature of acid deposition depends on competition between gas-phase and liquid-phase chemistry, competition between airborne transport and removal, and competition between dry and wet deposition. The key

---

*John et al. (1984) have estimated relative amounts of wet and dry deposition in the Los Angeles area. Liljestrand and Morgan (1981) measured the acidity of rainwater in the Los Angeles basin for the 1978-79 season, obtaining approximately 30 μN = 30 neq cm^{-3}. With an annual precipitation of 50 cm yr^{-1}, the net average wet flux of acidity is estimated to be 1500 neq cm^{-2} yr^{-1}. For dry deposition of SO_2 or HNO_3, John et al. (1984) have estimated about 3000 neq cm^{-2} yr^{-1}, about twice the estimated wet flux.

questions in acid rain are related to attempting to understand how the competitive paths interact. The overall objective is to predict, for a particular region, how the quantity and chemical nature of acidic deposition would be affected by changes in source emission rates of primary pollutants. In this section we will define the key questions in acid rain from this viewpoint.

18.2.1. Chemical and Physical Processes

The atmospheric paths leading to acid deposition are depicted in Figure 18.3. The first key question in acid rain is, what are the mechanisms by which precipitation becomes acidified?

There are three major pathways by which sulfate can be incorporated into precipitation: (1) nucleation scavenging of sulfate-containing aerosol particles in cloud formation; (2) aqueous-phase formation of sulfate from absorbed SO_2 in cloud droplets; and (3) below-cloud scavenging of aerosol sulfate by rain. There is actually a fourth route, the aqueous-phase production of sulfate in falling raindrops from SO_2 scavenged between cloud base and the earth. This route need not be considered because the time scale for such oxidation is small when compared to that for in-cloud oxidation. The major paths for incorporation of nitrate are similar: (1) nucleation scavenging of nitrate-containing aerosols in cloud formation; (2) absorption of gaseous nitric acid by cloud droplets; and (3) below-cloud scavenging of nitrate-containing aerosols by rain. Note that aqueous-phase formation of nitrate from absorbed NO and NO_2 was found in Chapter 5 to be too slow to be of atmospheric importance.

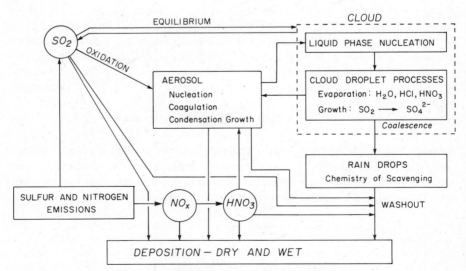

Figure 18.3. Atmospheric paths leading to acid deposition.

If the dominant mechanism for incorporation of sulfate and nitrate into rain were scavenging of pre-existing aerosol particles, either in-cloud or below-cloud, then the acidity of rain would be highly dependent on particle scavenging efficiencies and on those parameters that control the ambient aerosol sulfate and nitrate concentrations. Because aerosol sulfate and nitrate result largely from gas-phase conversion of SO_2 and NO_x to sulfuric and nitric acids, respectively, the controlling variables would be such quantities as solar radiation and hydrocarbon and NO_x concentrations. If, on the other hand, the dominant mode of sulfate inclusion in rain were the oxidation of dissolved SO_2, then the controlling variables would be the concentrations of aqueous-phase oxidizing species such as H_2O_2 and O_3, the levels of certain catalysts in the water such as manganese and iron, the concentration of NH_3, and the concentration of SO_2 itself. Nitrate inclusion, if not occurring by aerosol scavenging, would result from gaseous HNO_3 scavenging. Gaseous nitric acid levels are controlled by the same variables that govern particulate nitrate, so we expect nitrate levels to be dependent on gas-phase photochemical processes. Thus, the key questions are, what are the relative contributions of the possible paths of incorporation of sulfate and nitrate into precipitation, and, as a result, what are the principal variables that affect the degree of incorporation?

These questions have been addressed both experimentally and theoretically. The experimental approach has consisted of comparing measured cloud and rainwater compositions with those of aerosols. The theoretical approach has been based on formulating models of atmospheric transport and wet and dry deposition, including treatments of cloud formation and precipitation.

Several field studies have attempted to elucidate the sulfate-inclusion mechanisms in actual precipitation events (Holt et al., 1981 a, b; Hegg and Hobbs, 1981, 1982; Kallend et al., 1982; Harrison and Pio, 1983; Lazrus et al., 1983; Richards et al., 1983; Daum et al., 1983; Leaitch et al., 1983). In analyzing data from such studies the key comparison is that between the chemical composition of the rainwater and that of the ambient aerosol. If the two compositions are the same, then aerosol scavenging cannot be ruled out as a prime mode of incorporation. If, on the other hand, the compositions differ appreciably, a process other than direct aerosol scavenging is indicated.

A representative field study was that of Daum et al. (1983), in which measurements were made of in situ gaseous NO_x, HNO_3, O_3, NH_3, and SO_2, aerosol sulfur, and cloudwater pH near Charleston, South Carolina, on February 18 and 28, 1982, in an attempt to determine the source of cloudwater acidity. The composition of interstitial aerosol relative to that of cloudwater provides an indication of the source of cloudwater acidity. The $[H^+]/[NH_4^+]$ ratio observed in the interstitial aerosol was much less than that for cloudwater or for typical clear air aerosol. Thus, the amount of acidity present in rainwater sampled was not able to be explained solely on the basis of scavenging of ambient aerosol. Figure 18.4 shows the frequency distribution of the $[H^+]/[NH_4^+]$ ratio measured in clear air aerosol and rainwater by Daum et al.

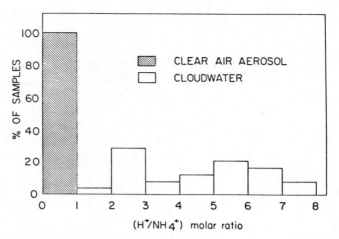

Figure 18.4. Frequency distribution of $[H^+]/[NH_4^+]$ ratio measured in clear air aerosol and rainwater over Charleston, SC, February 1982 (Daum et al., 1983).

(1983). It is clear from these data that the composition of the two samples is markedly different: for aerosols the ratio is substantially less than 1, whereas for cloudwater samples the ratio was always greater than 1. Their results strongly suggest that the enhanced acidity of cloudwater over that of clear air aerosol is attributable to SO_2 or $SO_2 + NO_x$ and are suggestive of the role of aqueous-phase reactions. Similar conclusions were arrived at on the basis of other field data by Hegg and Hobbs (1981, 1982), Kallend et al. (1982), Lazrus et al. (1983), and Harrison and Pio (1983).

The measurements of Daum et al., together with other measurements, suggest that there is simply too little aerosol, even if completely scavenged, to account for the sulfate found in precipitation. Moreover, the molar ratio of ammonium to hydrogen ion is frequently a factor of ten higher in the ambient aerosol than in precipitation. In short, acid rain is generally more acidic than the atmospheric aerosol (Tanner et al., 1981).

Predictions of the relative importance of the various sulfate-inclusion pathways by atmospheric models indicate that, depending on the particular situation, nucleation scavenging, aqueous-phase oxidation, and scavenging of aerosols by raindrops all may contribute to wet sulfate deposition. (See, for example, Hegg et al., 1984; Charlson et al., 1983; Kleinman, 1984; Hegg, 1983.) In all cases, however, aqueous-phase SO_2 oxidation in cloud droplets is predicted to be an important component and, in some cases, the vastly predominant one. Thus, whereas paths of aerosol scavenging by cloud droplet nucleation and by falling hydrometeors cannot be neglected, although largely inferential, the available evidence suggests that in-cloud oxidation is the largest contributor to sulfate formation in acid rain.

18.2.2.   Source–Receptor Relationships

In developing control strategies to deal with acid rain, one seeks to establish whose emissions are deposited where, a so-called source–receptor relationship. For sulfur, for example, it is desired to relate the deposition at site j, as measured in kg hectare^{-1} yr^{-1}, to the strength of source i, as measured, say, also in kg hectare^{-1} yr^{-1}. Clearly, the amount of emitted sulfur from a source that impacts a particular receptor location will vary from day to day depending on the prevailing meteorological conditions, such as the wind speed and direction, the depth of the layer through which mixing occurs, the chemical reactivity of the atmosphere, the presence of clouds and precipitation, and so forth. Such source–receptor relationships, on a day-to-day basis, can only be derived from mathematical models that include transport, chemical reactions, and removal processes.

Actually of greater interest than day-to-day source–receptor relationships is the source–receptor relation over a meaningful averaging time, such as a season or a year. Thus, we would like to know, over the course of a year, say, what fraction of the emissions from a particular source or source region impacts a given receptor location. If the receptor region is, for example, the Adirondack Mountains region of New York State, then a possible specific version of this question is, what fraction of the SO_2 emissions from the State of Ohio is deposited as wet sulfate, on a yearly basis, in the Adirondacks? The development of source–receptor relationships is the second key question associated with acid rain.

18.2.3.   Linearity

The source–receptor relationships we just discussed, if available, tell us the fraction of the emissions from a particular source or source region that is deposited at a particular receptor site over a given averaging time. From the standpoint of designing control strategies, we would like to know by how much deposition of sulfate, say, at a receptor site will be reduced if SO_2 emissions from a source are reduced by a certain amount. Because the source of sulfate in precipitation and dry deposition is anthropogenic emissions of SO_2, it seems reasonable that, over a long-enough averaging time and over a large-enough area, sulfate deposition will decrease on a one-to-one basis as SO_2 emissions are decreased. For example, if SO_2 emissions over eastern North America are reduced by 50 percent, it is reasonable to expect that the sum of wet and dry sulfate deposition over that area averaged over a year would also decrease by 50 percent. In other words, sulfate deposition would be expected to vary *linearly* with changes in SO_2 emissions.

Let us examine this question further. SO_2 is transformed to sulfate by gas- and aqueous-phase chemical reactions in the atmosphere. If the rate of conversion of SO_2 to sulfate depends linearly on the concentration of SO_2, with all other factors being equal, we expect that sulfate deposition will respond proportionately to changes in SO_2 levels. On the other hand, if the chemical reactions producing sulfate depend on the square of the ambient SO_2 concentration, it is conceivable that if SO_2 emissions are reduced, sulfate production could slow down sufficiently that during the residence time of the air over eastern North America sulfate deposition would decrease more than proportionately with the reduction in SO_2. Alternatively, let us suppose that the conversion of SO_2 to sulfate occurs by a reaction between dissolved SO_2 and an oxidant, such that the rate of conversion depends on the concentrations of both SO_2 and the oxidant. If the reaction is stoichiometric between dissolved SO_2 and the oxidant, the component in lower concentration will control the overall rate of conversion. Moreover, if the oxidant is the limiting component, then reduction in the level of SO_2, as long as the oxidant remains limiting, could produce no reduction in the amount of sulfate formed. Thus, we see that, depending on the nature of the sulfate formation process, it is possible to experience either more or less than proportionate reductions in sulfate deposition corresponding to decreases in SO_2 emissions. In such a case the SO_2–sulfate deposition relation can be said to be nonlinear.

Obviously, the question of the degree of linearity between SO_2 emission level changes and sulfate deposition is a key one in control strategy evaluation. And if the relation is nonlinear, the additional question is, what is the effect of changes in other atmospheric constituents on the rate of sulfate formation? It is important to stress that the question of linearity is inextricably tied to the spatial and temporal scales of averaging that are being considered. Whereas the SO_2–sulfate relation may be strongly nonlinear on a particular day when conversion is controlled by an available oxidant, when taking an average of an entire year's conditions over a region the size of eastern North America, the SO_2–sulfate relation may be much closer to linear. Thus, when discussing the linearity of acid rain, we need to delineate whether we are referring to the scientific aspects of the SO_2/sulfate and NO_x/nitrate chemistry or to the more regulatory-focused aspects of the long-time, large-area emission/deposition relationship.

18.3.   CHEMISTRY OF ACID RAIN

The chemical reactions that convert SO_2 to sulfate and NO_x to nitrate are central to the atmospheric processes that determine the relationship between the precursors and acidic deposition of sulfate and nitrate. Both gas- and aqueous-phase processes can be of importance in this step.

The reactions primarily responsible for the conversion of SO_2 and NO_x to H_2SO_4 and HNO_3 in the gas phase both involve the OH radical,

$$SO_2 + OH \xrightarrow[\text{steps}]{\text{several}} H_2SO_4$$

$$NO_2 + OH \longrightarrow HNO_3$$

Thus, the rates of conversion of SO_2 and NO_2 in the gas phase depend on the

OH concentration. Recall Section 4.6 in which we noted that SO_2 conversion rates by the OH–SO_2 reaction have been estimated by Calvert and Stockwell (1984) to vary from 0.7 percent hr^{-1} under summer conditions to 0.12 percent hr^{-1} in winter. Using the same estimated OH levels, NO_x conversion rates to HNO_3 were estimated to vary from 6.2 percent hr^{-1} (summer) to 1.1 percent hr^{-1} (winter). These estimated rates for SO_2 and NO_x conversion are, in fact, consistent with those observed in urban plumes in clear air. Because of the relatively higher rate of the NO_2–OH reaction as compared to the SO_2–OH reaction, one might hypothesize that HNO_3 production will occur more rapidly than H_2SO_4 production in the vicinity of sources. On the basis of gas-phase chemistry alone, therefore, one might expect the ratio of sulfate to nitrate would increase with distance from a source-rich region.

The sulfuric acid formed in the gas-phase will immediately associate with water molecules to form sulfuric acid aerosol. The nitric acid will remain as a vapor until it is absorbed by a cloud or rain drop or reacts with ammonia. The gaseous and particulate species may be removed at the surface by dry deposition any time along the way.

Conversion of SO_2 to H_2SO_4 aerosol in the gas-phase is presumably primarily dependent on the OH concentration, which depends indirectly on levels of NO_x and hydrocarbons as well as sunlight intensity. That rate of conversion is linear with respect to SO_2, but influenced in a complex, and most likely nonlinear way, by concentrations of NO_x and hydrocarbons through their effect on OH levels. Additional sulfate is formed upon absorption of SO_2 by droplets, followed by aqueous-phase oxidation. The amount of SO_2 absorbed depends on both the SO_2 concentration and the solution pH. The rate of oxidation in solution depends on the availability of reactants such as H_2O_2 and O_3. If that rate is controlled by the level of oxidant, then reductions in SO_2 levels will not lead to proportional reductions in sulfate, since there is more SO_2 present than can react with the available oxidant. In such a case, a nonlinear SO_2–sulfate response will occur. Precipitation nitrate levels arise by scavenging of gaseous HNO_3 and nitrate-containing aerosols. The rate of formation of nitric acid is dependent on the general level of photochemical reactivity of the atmosphere, and thus nitrate levels may respond nonlinearly to changes in NO_x emissions depending on how those changes affect OH levels.

To examine the response of the aqueous-phase chemistry to variations in reactant levels let us return to the system considered in Section 5.6, a droplet in an environment of SO_2, NH_3, HNO_3, O_3, and H_2O_2. In Section 5.6 we used this system to show how pH and concentrations evolve in time when an aqueous-phase reaction is occurring. Here we want to study the same system, but our attention will be focused on the concentrations achieved after a fixed amount of time, say one hour, as a function of the starting partial pressures and, in the case of a closed system, the water phase volume ratio L.

We begin with the case of an open system. Concentrations predicted after 1 hr are given in Table 18.2. We examine three SO_2 levels, from moderately (1 ppb) to highly (100 ppb) polluted, and two $[H_2O_2(aq)]$ levels, 10^{-7} and 10^{-5} M. Along the first row, $[H_2O_2(aq)] = 10^{-7}$ M and $p_{HNO_3} = 0$, sulfate produc-

TABLE 18.2. Matrix of Cases to Explore the Effect of Changes in SO_2, HNO_3, and H_2O_2 Levels on Sulfate, Nitrate, and pH Levels in an Open System[a]

p_{HNO_3}, ppb		p_{SO_2}, ppb		
		1	10	100
	pH	5.5	5.2	4.8
$[H_2O_2(aq)] = 10^{-7}$ M	[S(VI)]	0.83×10^{-3} M	0.18×10^{-2} M	0.38×10^{-2} M
0	pH	5.5	5.1	4.6
$[H_2O_2(aq)] = 10^{-5}$ M	[S(VI)]	0.85×10^{-3} M	0.20×10^{-2} M	0.63×10^{-2} M
	pH	3.6	3.6	3.6
$[H_2O_2(aq)] = 10^{-7}$ M	[S(VI)]	0.45×10^{-6} M	0.45×10^{-5} M	0.45×10^{-4} M
0.01	pH	3.6	3.6	3.6
$[H_2O_2(aq)] = 10^{-5}$ M	[S(VI)]	0.36×10^{-4} M	0.36×10^{-3} M	0.36×10^{-2} M

[a] $p_{NH_3} = 5$ ppb; $p_{O_3} = 50$ ppb.

tion is due almost entirely to O_3 due to the high pH. A reduction in p_{SO_2} from 100 to 1 ppb leads to a factor 4 to 5 reduction in sulfate. When $[H_2O_2(aq)] = 10^{-5}$ M, the same change in SO_2 leads to only a factor of 2 decrease in sulfate after 1 hr. At this level of H_2O_2, its oxidation reaction begins to assume importance. In the absence of HNO_3, the pH decreases continuously, acting to retard the sulfate formation. The lower p_{SO_2}, which leads to a lower rate of sulfate formation, is compensated in part by a higher pH and a higher reaction rate by O_3 oxidation, the net effect being a less than proportional decrease in sulfate for a decrease in SO_2.

For $p_{HNO_3} = 0.01$ ppb, assuming an open system, the pH of the aqueous phase is dominated by the nitric acid. At pH 3.6, H_2O_2 oxidation accounts for 80 percent of the sulfate formation at 10^{-7} M H_2O_2 and over 99 percent at 10^{-5} M H_2O_2. At $p_{HNO_3} = 0.01$ ppb in the open system, the amount of sulfate formed varies linearly with p_{SO_2} at both H_2O_2 levels. Since the pH is, in essence, fixed by the HNO_3, the total dissolved S(IV) is fixed and depends linearly on p_{SO_2}. With $[H_2O_2(aq)]$ also fixed, the rate of sulfate formation depends proportionately on the SO_2 concentration. Thus, in this open system, at pH levels below about 4, where H_2O_2 oxidation is expected to be dominant, sulfate yields should vary linearly with SO_2 levels.

The case of an open system is somewhat unrealistic from a practical point of view, since we expect that the highly soluble gases like H_2O_2 and HNO_3 will be depleted from the gas phase in the physical volume of the cloud (Daum et al.,

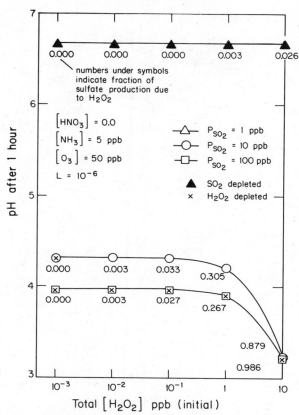

Figure 18.5. Effect of total quantity of H_2O_2 on the pH achieved in a cloud after 1 hr for the concentrations of HNO_3, NH_3, and O_3 shown on the figure, and for the three SO_2 levels indicated. Water phase volume ratio $L = 10^{-6}$.

1983). Thus, we now consider the same situation but assume a closed system. In this case, the initial partial pressures are taken to be the total concentrations in the system. In the case of a closed system it is necessary to specify one additional quantity that is not required in the open system, namely the water phase volume ratio L. We will examine the behavior of the system for three values of L, 10^{-6}, 10^{-8}, and 10^{-10}, spanning the range from typical clouds to urban aerosols.

We consider just the effect of $p_{H_2O_2}$ with $p_{HNO_3} = 0$ (Figure 18.5). When $p_{SO_2} = 1$ ppb, all the SO_2 is depleted in 1 hr for all H_2O_2 levels studied. Since the pH is high in this case, due to the low SO_2 level, virtually all the sulfate formation is due to O_3, and thus we do not expect the H_2O_2 level to be influential. For $p_{SO_2} = 10$ and 100 ppb, the H_2O_2 level does not assume importance as an oxidant until $p_{H_2O_2} \cong 1$ ppb. When $p_{SO_2} = 100$ ppb, the

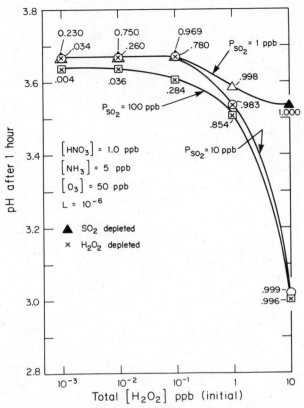

Figure 18.6. Effect of total quantity of H_2O_2 on the pH achieved in a cloud after 1 hr for the concentrations of HNO_3, NH_3, and O_3 shown on the figure, and for the three SO_2 levels indicated. Water phase volume ratio $L = 10^{-6}$.

available H_2O_2 is depleted during the hour at all H_2O_2 levels. The pH reduction at 10 ppb H_2O_2 is due to the substantial amount of sulfate formed. In the absence of HNO_3, therefore, the pH is controlled by the dissolved SO_2 and the amount of sulfate produced.

Figure 18.6 shows exactly the same situation as Figure 18.5 except that $p_{HNO_3} = 1$ ppb. The presence of HNO_3 lowers the initial pH and dominates the establishment of the initial pH. Because the pH is controlled largely by the HNO_3, pH values are close for all three SO_2 levels. Note the increased importance of H_2O_2 for sulfate formation as p_{SO_2} decreases. This is due to the fact that H_2O_2 is depleted at high SO_2 but survives as an effective oxidant for smaller SO_2 levels.

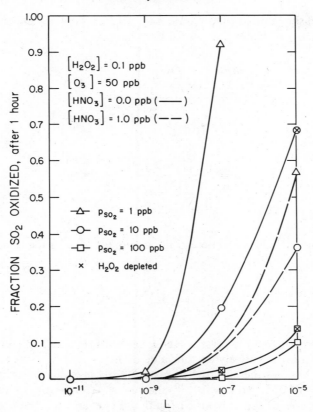

Figure 18.7. Effect of water phase volume ratio L on the fraction of SO_2 oxidized in 1 hr at $[H_2O_2] = 0.1$ ppb and $[O_3] = 50$ ppb and at $[HNO_3]$ levels of 0 and 1.0 ppb, and $[SO_2]$ levels of 1, 10, and 100 ppb.

The effect of water phase volume ratio is shown in Figure 18.7, in terms of the fraction of SO_2 oxidized, for $HNO_3 = 0$ and 1 ppb. First, we note a dramatic increase in the fraction oxidized with increasing L due to the greater liquid capacity. Higher fractions of SO_2 are oxidized at the lower SO_2 levels. The addition of HNO_3 lowers the pH and retards the overall oxidation. With $HNO_3 = 0$, at $L = 10^{-7}$, an increase of p_{SO_2} from 1 to 10 ppb leads to an increase in sulfate formed from 0.9 to 2 ppb. In this case, the pH is controlled by the sulfur system, and the increase in pH accompanying the increase in p_{SO_2} from 1 to 10 acts to retard the sulfate formation and produce less than a proportional increase in sulfate level. When HNO_3 is present, because of its strong control of pH, the fractional conversions become much closer at the three SO_2 levels. Thus, at $L = 10^{-7}$, the fractional conversions after 1 hr at SO_2 levels of 1, 10, and 100 ppb are 0.1, 0.08, and 0.01, respectively.

It can be shown that the nitrate ion, and thereby its effects on $[H^+]$, depends only on L. From Section 5.6.1 we have

$$[NO_3^-] = \frac{\dfrac{K_{n1}}{[H^+]}[HNO_3]_{total}}{\dfrac{1}{H_{HNO_3}RT} + L\left(1 + \dfrac{K_{n1}}{[H^+]}\right)}$$

$$\cong \frac{[HNO_3]_{total}}{\dfrac{[H^+]}{K_{n1}H_{HNO_3}RT} + L}$$

At the pH and L values of interest, the dominant term in the denominator is L,* and thus

$$[NO_3^-] \cong \frac{[HNO_3]_{total}}{L}$$

This result explains why a certain HNO_3 level exerts a strong control on pH and depends most sensitively on the value of L.

Figure 18.8 shows the effect of p_{SO_2} on the pH level achieved after 1 hr at $L = 10^{-10}$ and 10^{-6}. At $L = 10^{-10}$, the pH varies smoothly with p_{SO_2} and remains high due to the very small fractional conversion of SO_2 (see Figure 18.7 for $L = 10^{-10}$). The behavior at $L = 10^{-6}$ is most intriguing. At low SO_2 levels ($p_{SO_2} < 1$ ppb), pH levels remain very high (since HNO_3 is assumed absent) and all the SO_2 is depleted (by O_3 reaction) during the course of the hour. When $p_{SO_2} > 1$ ppb, the pH is lowered dramatically, acting to "turn on" the H_2O_2 mechanism relative to that for O_3. For $p_{SO_2} > 20$ ppb, all the H_2O_2 is depeleted. If HNO_3 is present, we will not see this dramatic effect of SO_2 level on pH, and the HNO_3 level will be low, and H_2O_2 will be the predominant oxidant.

We draw the following conclusions based on our simulation of the closed system:

1. When HNO_3 is present at levels the order of 1 ppb or higher, the pH of the solution is controlled largely by the total HNO_3 and the phase volume ratio L.

2. At pH levels below about 4, H_2O_2 oxidation predominates as the aqueous-phase sulfate forming mechanism. H_2O_2 level influences pH only indirectly through its role in sulfate production.

---

*$K_{n1}H_{HNO_3}RT = 7.093 \times 10^7$ at 298 K.

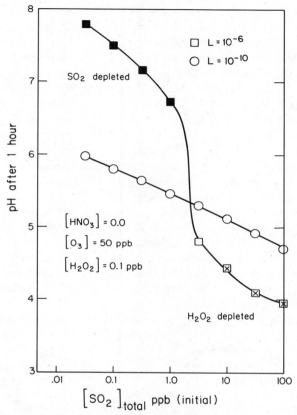

Figure 18.8. Effect of SO_2 concentration on the pH achieved after 1 hr in a cloud at the concentration levels of HNO_3, O_3, and H_2O_2 indicated and at water phase volume ratios $L = 10^{-6}$ and 10^{-10}.

3. At phase volume ratios typical of clouds, $L \cong 10^{-6}$, for p_{SO_2} levels below about 10 ppb, and H_2O_2 about 10 ppb, approximately 100 percent of the available SO_2 will be oxidized in 1 hr. Available H_2O_2, even down to H_2O_2 levels of 0.1 ppb, does not become the limiting reagent until p_{SO_2} values approach 100 ppb.

4. In the region referred to in (3), the amount of sulfate formed varies linearly with p_{SO_2}. Nonlinear effects arise only at p_{SO_2} levels approaching 100 ppb.

The idealized calculation just presented shows what are thought to be the essential elements of the aqueous-phase chemistry of acid rain. It is of interest to compare the results of that calculation with those of other investigators. We found in our hypothetical situation that droplet pH was strongly controlled by the dissolved nitric acid. Gorham et al. (1984) have shown, however, that analysis of mean annual ionic concentrations in wet deposition in the eastern United States indicates that concentrations of H^+ are predicted better by concentrations of SO_4^{2-} than by NO_3^- or the sum $(SO_4^{2-} + NO_3^-)$. An explanation for this correlation is not readily available. Measurements of H_2O_2 in rain and cloud water show a range of concentrations between approximately 10^{-5} and 10^{-4} M (Kok, 1980; Zika et al., 1982). Water with this composition is in equilibrium with between 0.1 and 1.0 ppb gas-phase H_2O_2. Kleinman (1984) has examined the question of whether H_2O_2 can account for the in-cloud oxidation of SO_2 and found that under summertime conditions between 3 and 5 ppb of H_2O_2 would be required to account for estimated in-cloud sulfate formation. Seigneur et al. (1984) presented the results of simulations of atmospheric sulfate and nitrate formation by both gas- and aqueous-phase paths under conditions typical of the midwestern and northeastern United States. Their calculations suggest that the relation between sulfate and SO_2 variations is nearly linear in a cloud-free atmosphere but is nonlinear if clouds are present due to the H_2O_2 and O_3 reactions. A reduction in NO_x concentrations was found to lead to proportional reductions in nitrate. Acid concentrations were found to be rather insensitive to changes in reactive hydrocarbon concentrations.

In conclusion, we see that the acid rain system is a chemically complex one. How acidic sulfate and nitrate levels will vary in response to changes in atmospheric levels of the precursors depends on the prevailing conditions.

18.4.   CLOUD PROCESSES IN ACID RAIN

Pollutants and condensed water can come to occupy common airspace as a result of (1) relative movement of the pollutant and condensed water into the same air volume, and/or (2) in situ phase change of water vapor to produce condensed water. On a global average, it has been estimated that 90 percent of all precipitation scavenging occurs as a consequence of the second process (U.S. Environmental Protection Agency, 1983). Reverse processes such as evaporation also occur, and a single pollutant molecule may be involved in several condensation-evaporation cycles before it is delivered to the earth's surface in precipitation. The pollutant itself can influence the condensation process. For example, if the local aerosol consists of a high concentration of small, nonhygroscopic particles, the corresponding cloud should contain larger numbers of smaller droplets. Unpolluted marine air that contains large sea salt particles is characterized by clouds with large drop sizes, whereas continental clouds are typically composed of larger concentrations of smaller droplets, reflecting the nature of the continental aerosol. Acid-forming particles are chemically competitive for water vapor and thus tend to participate actively as cloud condensation nuclei, an attribute that tends to enhance their propensity to become scavenged early in storm systems. As discussed earlier, the aerosol composition will be reflected in the cloudwater composition.

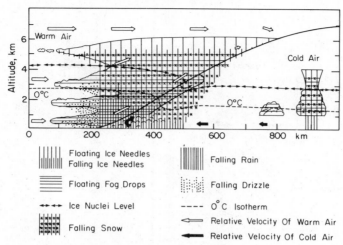

Figure 18.9. Floating Ice Needles / Falling Ice Needles · Floating Fog Drops · Ice Nuclei Level · Falling Snow · Falling Rain · Falling Drizzle · 0°C Isotherm · Relative Velocity Of Warm Air · Relative Velocity Of Cold Air

Figure 18.9. Vertical cross section of a typical warm front.

Once initial nucleation has occurred, cloud droplets may grow by further condensation of water vapor. A competition for water vapor usually exists in an evolving cloud (Pruppacher and Klett, 1978). Suspended cloud droplets also grow by coagulation. Large hydrometeors fall through the cloud and scavenge smaller drops and aerosol.

Scavenging rates and pathways will be dictated to a large extent by the basic nature of the particular storm causing wet removal. All storms are initiated by a cooling of air leading to water condensation. The cooling generally occurs via vertical motion of air at fronts between one or more air masses. For practical purposes it is convenient to divide mid-latitude continental storms into two classes, "frontal" and "convective."

In a frontal storm a cool, northern air mass is separated from a warm, southern air mass by an east-west front. The natural tendency to exchange heat from southern to northern latitudes in the Northern Hemisphere leads to a tongue of warm air intruding into the cold air mass. In the Northern Hemisphere the disturbance will tend to move in an easterly direction. A frontal storm can consist of a warm front or a cold front.

Figure 18.9 shows the vertical structure of a warm front. The warm air aloft inhibits vertical mixing of air between the two air masses. The warm, moist air moves up over the cold air, expanding, cooling and forming clouds and precipitation. Because of the intense cloud formation, warm-front storms can usually be expected to be effective scavengers of pollutants within the warm air mass. Scavenging of pollutants from the underlying cold air mass is less effective due to the absence of clouds in the cold air mass.

The vertical structure of a cold front storm is shown in Figure 18.10. The warm air is forced ahead by the moving cold air, producing a more steeply inclined frontal surface than in the warm-front storm. In both storm types the

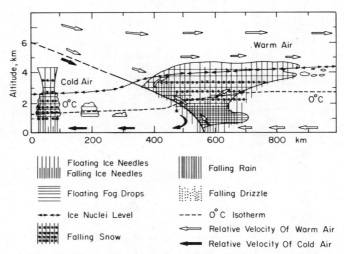

Figure 18.10. Vertical cross section of a typical cold front.

presence of low-level warm air creates a relatively unstable situation leading to convective uplifting and the formation of clouds and precipitation.

An idealized cross section of a typical *convective* storm is shown in Figure 18.11. Such storms develop due to atmospheric instabilities and are characterized by the pumping of low-level air up through the cloud to higher levels through the storm's updraft region. Convective clouds provide a means for

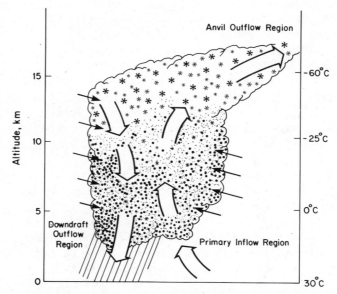

Figure 18.11. Idealized cross section of an isolated convective storm.

quickly transporting boundary layer air into the free troposphere. Updrafts in convective clouds can range from 1 m sec^{-1} to several tens of meters per second. The large water content of convective clouds allow them to be highly effective scavengers of air pollutants.

One meteorological situation in the eastern United States that is particularly conducive to acid deposition is a stagnating summertime high pressure system (Mueller and Hidy, 1980; Altshuller, 1980). In this situation, as a slow-moving high pressure center moves toward the East Coast, clockwise circulation around the high pressure system brings warm, humid air northward from the Gulf of Mexico. Emissions accumulate in the air mass and are slowly transported north and east. With clear skies and a high moisture content, the conditions favoring transformation of SO_2 to sulfates and NO_x to nitrates are present. Under these conditions high sulfate concentrations are often recorded from the eastern Ohio Valley into the Northeast. When thunderstorms break out in this air mass, the pollutants are delivered to the surface as wet deposition.

18.5. SOURCE–RECEPTOR RELATIONSHIPS

Substances emitted into the atmosphere may be deposited on the earth very close to the source, or they may be transported by winds for several days and many hundreds of kilometers, during which they may be chemically converted to other forms. A key issue in acid rain is determining the source of emissions that ultimately impact a given area as acid deposition. If this source–receptor connection can be made, then it is theoretically possible to develop emission control strategies with a particular receptor region in mind.

Determining the source–receptor relationship involves two basic aspects: identifying the trajectories of air parcels that arrived at the receptor location, and predicting the physico-chemical behavior of pollutants along those trajectories.

Both forward and reverse trajectories can be computed. The forward trajectory traces the path of emissions from source to receptor. The reverse trajectory traces the path of air from the receptor backwards to where it originated. Trajectories have to be determined based on wind measurements at various levels in the atmosphere. Because wind measuring stations anywhere above ground level are sparsely distributed and record data at intervals of only every 12 hr or so, trajectory calculations are highly uncertain. The trajectories of emissions are determined by estimating the wind speed and direction for a period of time, say six hr. The effluent released during this period is then assumed to move according to the wind estimate. The wind speed and direction for the second six-hr period are then used to move the parcel from its position at the end of the first six hr to its next position. Any error in judging the wind speed and direction in any period will cause the next estimate to be made for the wrong location. In addition, wind speed and direction vary with altitude, so that material at different heights will generally be carried in different directions at different speeds. Samson and Moody (1980) calculated reverse trajectories using wind data at four different altitudes for a receptor area in the Adirondack Mountains of New York State. They found that emissions from four different regions, ranging from North Carolina to western Kentucky, were predicted to arrive at the receptor site depending on the height assumed for the wind trajectories.

The most prominent advantage of the trajectory concept is that it enables the use of air quality models that are conceptually simple (see Section 16.6). These models consider a hypothetical moving parcel of air that is carried along the air trajectory within which pollutants are transformed and removed. Clearly, a more rigorous approach based on a three-dimensional simulation of the wind field, coupled with an appropriate treatment of diffusion, transformation, and removal, can alleviate the shortcomings of the simpler trajectory model. However, as in the urban case, such models are useful only for simulating certain events. The trajectory model can be used to represent time-averaged phenomena, as long as the wind field used represents the appropriate time-averaged field.

18.6. ACID FOG

Urban fogs can become acidic by the same mechanisms as cloudwater. A number of measurements have been made of fog in southern California (Waldman et al., 1982; Munger et al., 1983; Hoffmann, 1984). The measurements show pH values ranging from 3 to less than 2. The most extreme event observed in southern California was a relatively light evaporation fog at Corona del Mar during which the pH reached a low of 1.7. The nitrate level was roughly three times the sulfate level in that particular fog. In fact, this ratio seems to hold for Los Angeles fogs as a whole (Hoffmann, 1984).

The pH of a fog has been found to be a function of time. At the beginning of the fog, the concentrations of its major chemical components, typically sulfate, nitrate, chloride, ammonium, calcium, and hydrogen ion, are high; as the fog develops, the liquid water content rises, the droplets are diluted, and the acidity drops; and then as the air is heated, evaporation takes place, the relative humidity decreases, and the pH is lowered again.

REFERENCES

Altshuller, A. P. "Seasonal and Episodic Trends in Sulfate Concentrations (1963–1978) in the Eastern U.S.," *Environ. Sci. Technol.*, **14**, 1337–1349 (1980).

Baker, J. P., and Schofield, C. L. in *Proceedings of the International Conference on Ecological Impact of Acid Precipitation*, D. Drablos and A. Tollau (Eds.), Sandefjord, Norway, 292–293 (1980).

Calvert, J. G., and Stockwell, W. R. "The Mechanisms and Rates of the Gas Phase Oxidations of Sulfur Dioxide and the Nitrogen Oxides in the Atmosphere," in SO_2, NO_2, *Oxidation Mechanisms: Atmospheric Considerations*, J. G. Calvert (Ed.), Butterworth, Boston, 1–62 (1984).

Charlson, R. J., and Rodhe, H. "Factors Controlling the Acidity of Natural Rainwater," *Nature*, **295**, 683–685 (1982).

Charlson, R. J., Vong, R., and Hegg, D. A. "The Sources of Sulfate in Precipitation. 2. Sensitivities to Chemical Variables," *J. Geophys. Res.*, **88**, 1375–1377 (1983).

Chemical and Engineering News, Nov. 22, 1976.

Cowling, E. B. "Acid Precipitation in Historical Perspective," *Environ. Sci. Technol.*, **16**, 110A-123A (1982).

Daum, P. H., Schwartz, S. E., and Newman, L. "Acidic and Related Constituents in Liquid Water Stratiform Clouds," *J. Geophys. Res.*, **89**, 1447–1458 (1983).

Dickson, W. in *Proceedings of the International Conference on Ecological Impact of Acid Precipitation*, D. Drablos and A. Tollau (Eds.), Sandefjord, Norway, 75–83 (1980).

Galloway, J. N., and Whelpdale, D. M. "An Atmospheric Sulfur Budget for Eastern North America," *Atmos. Environ.*, **14**, 409–417 (1980).

Galloway, J. N., Likens, G. E., Keene, W. C., and Miller, J. M. "The Composition of Precipitation in Remote Areas of the World," *J. Geophys. Res.*, **87**, 8771–8786 (1982).

Gislason, K. B., and Prahm, L. P. "Sensitivity Study of Air Trajectory Long-Range Transport Modeling," *Atmos. Environ.*, **17**, 2463–2472 (1983).

Glass, N. R., Arnold, D. E., Galloway, J. N., Hendrey, G. R., Lee, J. J., McFee, W. W., Norton, S. A., Powers, C. F., Rambo, D. L., and Schofield, C. L. "Effects of Acid Precipitation," *Environ. Sci. Technol.*, **16**, 162A–169A (1982).

Gorham, E., Martin, F. B., and Litzau, J. T. "Acid Rain: Ionic Correlations in the Eastern United States, 1980–1981," *Science*, **225**, 407–409 (1984).

Granat, L. "Sulfate in Precipitation as Observed by the European Atmospheric Network," *Atmos. Environ.*, **12**, 413–424 (1978).

Gschwandtner, G., Gschwandtner, K. C., and Elridge, K. "Historic Emissions of Sulfur and Nitrogen Oxides in the United States from 1890 to 1980," Report on EPA contract 68-02-3311, prepared by Pacific Environmental Services, Inc., Durham, NC (1983).

Harrison, R. M., and Pio, C. A. "A Comparative Study of the Ionic Composition of Rainwater and Atmospheric Aerosols: Implications for the Mechanism of Acidification of Rainwater," *Atmos. Environ.*, **17**, 2539–2544 (1983).

Havas, M., Hutchinson, T. C., and Likens, G. E. "Red Herrings in Acid Rain Research," *Environ. Sci. Technol.*, **18**, 176A–186A (1984).

Hegg, D. A. "The Sources of Sulfate in Precipitation. 1. Parameterization Scheme and Physical Sensitivities," *J. Geophys. Res.*, **88**, 1369–1374 (1983).

Hegg, D. A., and Hobbs, P. V. "Cloud Water Chemistry and the Production of Sulfates in Clouds," *Atmos. Environ.*, **15**, 1597–1604 (1981).

Hegg, D. A., and Hobbs, P. V. "Measurements of Sulfate Production in Natural Clouds," *Atmos. Environ.*, **16**, 2663–2668 (1982).

Hegg, D. A., Rutledge, S. A., and Hobbs, P. V. "A Numerical Model for Sulfur Chemistry in Warm-Frontal Rainbands," *J. Geophys. Res.*, **89**, 7133–7147 (1984).

Hidy, G. M. "Source-Receptor Relationships for Acid Deposition: Pure and Simple?" *J. Air Pollution Control Assoc.*, **34**, 518–531 (1984). (See also **34**, 905–917 (1984).)

Hidy, G. M., Hansen, D. A., Henry, R. C., Ganesan, K., and Collins, J. "Trends in Historical Acid Precursor Emissions and Their Airborne and Precipitation Products," *J. Air Pollution Control Assoc.*, **34**, 333–354 (1984).

Hoffmann, M. R. "Acid Fog," *Engineering and Science*, 5–11, September 1984.

Holt, B. D., Cunningham, P. T., and Kumar, R. "Oxygen Isotopy of Atmospheric Sulfates," *Environ. Sci. Technol.*, **15**, 804–808 (1981a).

Holt, B. D., Kumar, R., and Cunningham, P. T. "Oxygen-18 Study of the Aqueous Phase Oxidation of Sulfur Dioxide, " *Atmos. Environ.*, **15**, 557–566 (1981b).

Hong, M. S., and Carmichael, G. R. "An Investigation of Sulfate Production in Clouds Using A Flow-Through Chemical Reactor Model Approach," Dept. of Chemical Engineering, Univ. of Iowa (1984).

John, W., Wall, S. M., and Wesolowski, J. J. "Assessment of Dry Acid Deposition in California," Final Report to State of California Air Resources Board, Air and Industrial Hygiene Laboratory, Berkeley, CA, June 1984.

Kallend, A. S., Marsh, A. R. W., Glover, G. M., Webb, A. H., Moore, D. J., Clark, P. A., Fisher, B. E. A., Dear, D. J. A., Lightman, P., and Laird, C. K. "Studies of the Fate of Atmospheric Emissions in Power Plant Plumes Over the North Sea," in *Physico-Chemical Behavior of Atmospheric Pollutants*, B. Versino and H. Ott (Eds.), D. Reidel, Dordrecht, Holland, 482–491 (1982).

Kleinman, L. I. "Oxidant Requirements for the Acidification of Precipitation," *Atmos. Environ.*, **18**, 1453–1457 (1984).

Kok, G. L. "Measurements of Hydrogen Peroxide in Rainwater," *Atmos. Environ.*, **14**, 653–656 (1980).

Lazrus, A. L., Haagenson, P. L., Kok, G. L., Huebert, B. J., Kreitzberg, C. W., Likens, G. E., Mohnen, V. A., Wilson, W. E., and Winchester, J. W. "Acidity in Air and Water in a Case of Warm Frontal Precipitation," *Atmos. Environ.*, **17**, 581–591 (1983).

Leaitch, W. R., Strapp, J. W., Wiebe, H. A., and Isaac, G. A. "Measurements of Scavenging and Transformation of Aerosol inside Cumulus," in *Precipitation Scavenging, Dry Deposition and Resuspension*, H. R. Pruppacher, R. G. Semonin, and W. G. N. Slinn (Eds.), Elsevier, New York, 53–69 (1983).

Likens, G. E., Wright, R. G., Galloway, J. N., and Butler, T. J. "Acid Rain," *Sci. Am.*, **241**, 43–51 (1979).

Liljestrand, H. M., and Morgan, J. J. "Spatial Variations in Acid Precipitation in Southern California," *Environ. Sci. Technol.*, **15**, 333–339 (1981).

Morgan, J. J. "Factors Governing the pH, Availability of H$^+$, and Oxidation Capacity of Rain," in *Atmospheric Chemistry*, E. D. Goldberg (Ed.), Springer-Verlag, 17–40 (1982).

Mueller, P. K., and Hidy, G. M. "The Sulfate Regional Experiment: Report of Findings," Vols. 1–3, EPRI EA-1901, Electric Power Research Institute, Palo Alto, CA (1980).

Munger, J. W., Jacob, D. J., Waldman, J. M., and Hoffmann, M. R. "Fogwater Chemistry in an Urban Atmosphere," *J. Geophys. Res.*, **88**, 5109–5121 (1983).

National Research Council, *Acid Deposition–Atmospheric Processes in Eastern North America*, National Academy Press, Washington, D.C., (1983).

Oppenheimer, M. "The Relationship of Sulfur Emissions to Sulfate in Precipitation," *Atmos. Environ.*, **17**, 451–460 (1983a).

Oppenheimer, M. "The Relationship of Sulfur Emissions to Sulfate in Precipitation—II. Gas Phase Processes," *Atmos. Environ.*, **17**, 1489–1495 (1983b).

Powers, C. F., and Rambo, D. L. "The Occurrence of Acid Precipitation on the West Coast of the United States," *Environ. Monitoring Assessment*, **1**, 93–105 (1981).

Pruppacher, H. R., and Klett, J. D. *Microphysics of Clouds and Precipitation*, D. Reidel, Dordrecht, Holland (1978).

Richards, L. W., Anderson, J. A., Blumenthal, D. L., McDonald, J. A., Kok, G. L., and Lazrus, A. L. "Hydrogen Peroxide and Sulfur (IV) in Los Angeles Cloud Water," *Atmos. Environ.*, **17**, 911–914 (1983).

Roth, P., Blanchard, C., Harte, J., Michaels, H., and El-Ashry, M. T. *The American West's Acid Rain Test*, World Resources Institute, Washington, DC (1985).

Samson, P. J., and Moody, J. L. "Trajectories as Two-Dimensional Probability Fields," 11th International Meeting on Air Pollution Modeling, Amsterdam, The Netherlands, Nov. 24, 1980.

Samson, P. J., and Small, M. J. "The Use of Atmospheric Trajectory Models for Diagnosing the Sources of Acid Precipitation," American Chemical Society, 183rd National Meeting, Las Vegas (1982).

Schofield, C. L., in *Acid Rain/Fisheries*, Proceedings International Symposium on Acidic Precipitation and Fishery Impacts in Northeast North America, R. E. Johnson (Ed.), Ithaca, NY, 57–67 (1982).

Seigneur, C., Saxena, P., and Roth, P. M. "Computer Simulations of the Atmospheric Chemistry of Sulfate and Nitrate Formation," *Science*, **225**, 1028–1029 (1984).

Stensland, G. J., and Semonin, R. G. "Another Interpretation of the pH Trend in the United States," *Bull. Am. Meteorol. Soc.*, **63**, 1277–1284 (1982).

Tanner, R. L., Leaderer, B. P., and Spengler, J. D. "Acidity of Atmospheric Aerosol," *Environ. Sci. Technol.*, **15**, 1150–1153 (1981).

U.S. Environmental Protection Agency, *The Acidic Deposition Phenomenon and Its Effects: Critical Assessment Review Papers*, Vol. I—Atmospheric Sciences, Public Review Draft, Report EPA-600/8-83-016A, Washington, D.C. (1983).

U.S./Canada Work Group #2, "Atmospheric Science and Analysis," Final Report, H. L. Ferguson and L. Machta (Co-chairmen), U.S. Environmental Protection Agency, Washington, D.C. (1982).

Waldman, J. M., Munger, J. W., Jacob, D. J., Flagan, R. C., Morgan, J. J., and Hoffmann, M. R. "Chemical Composition of Acid Fog," *Science*, **218**, 677–680 (1982).

Zika, R., Satzman, E., Chameides, W. L., and Davis, D. D. "H_2O_2 Levels in Rainwater Collected in South Florida and the Bahama Islands," *J. Geophys. Res.*, **87**, 5015–5017 (1982).

PROBLEMS

18.1. Calculate the effect on the pH of atmospheric liquid water of dissolved aerosol SO_4^{2-} and the liquid water content L, assuming that the concentrations of CO_2 and SO_2 are constant and equal to 340 ppm and 100 ppt, respectively. Ammonia is assumed to be absent. In particular, fill in the pH values in the table below:

SO_4^{2-}, $\mu g \, m^{-3}$	L, g m^{-3}		
	0.1	0.5	2.5
0.04			
0.2			
1.0			

18.2. The probability of an SO_2 molecule being transformed to sulfate and wet deposited on land can be expressed as the product of the probabilities of the molecule being processed through precipitating air parcels over land and of being absorbed and deposited (Oppenheimer, 1983a). Show that if t_{SO_2} is the regional mean lifetime of SO_2 and $f(t)$ is the probability of a dry period lasting a time of length t, that is, of a wet event occurring at time t, then the probability of an SO_2 molecule being processed through precipitation is equal to

$$\int_0^\infty f(t)e^{-t/t_{SO_2}}\,dt$$

Assuming that the frequency distribution of rain events is given by

$$f(t) = \frac{1}{T_D}e^{-t/T_D}$$

show that this probability is equal to $t_{SO_2}/(t_{SO_2} + T_D)$.

If we identify t_{SO_2} with the characteristic time for SO_2 removal by dry deposition, we obtain an upper limit on t_{SO_2} because some SO_2 will be lost by gas phase conversion into material that is not wet deposited. Let us use $t_{SO_2} = 60$ hr. A value of T_D typical of the eastern United States is $T_D = 138$ hr. Thus, we see that the probability of an emitted SO_2 molecule being processed through precipitation before dry deposition is about 0.3.

Considering the region of interest to be the eastern United States and Canada, Oppenheimer (1983a) estimated the following sulfur emissions and wet deposition for the 1977–79 period:

$$\text{Emissions} = 10.26 \times 10^9 \text{ kg S yr}^{-1}$$

$$\text{Wet Deposition} = 2.25 \times 10^9 \text{ kg S yr}^{-1}$$

Calculate the probability of an SO_2 molecule being absorbed and deposited in this region. Discuss your result.

18.3. In order to evaluate potential emission control strategies for acid rain one would like to understand the relationship of decreases in SO_2 emissions to changes in precipitation sulfate levels. A lower limit on the change in precipitation sulfate can be obtained by assuming that all sulfate formation occurs in the liquid phase under oxidant limited circumstances. Assume that airborne SO_2 occurs in two streams, a part that is processed through precipitating air parcels during its airborne lifetime and a part that is not, labeled A and B, respectively. The part that is passed through precipitating air parcels, A, is then subdivided into two streams, a portion that is absorbed, oxidized and deposited as sulfate and a part that is not oxidized, labeled A_1 and A_2, respectively. Assume that an emissions reduction is not reflected in A_1, but only in

A_2 and B, until A_2 is exhausted. Thereafter, the emissions reduction reduces A_1 on a proportional basis.

Show that the response of wet deposition to a fractional emissions reduction $X/(A + B)$ is

$$\delta = \left\{ \frac{X}{A + B} - \frac{A_2}{A + B} \right\} / \beta$$

where β = probability of an SO_2 molecule being absorbed and deposited. (Note that if $\beta = 1$, $A_2 = 0$, and $\delta = X/(A + B)$.)

Using the value of β determined in Problem 18.2, evaluate δ for a 50 percent reduction in emissions.

18.4. In this problem, following Oppenheimer (1983b), we wish to explore the scenario that the atmospheric path leading to precipitation sulfate occurs only by gas phase oxidation of SO_2 to sulfate aerosol, followed by either incorporation of the aerosol in droplets or dry deposition.

Let

$g_6(t)$ = probability density that an air parcel is subjected to a dry period of length t, followed by precipitation beginning in the interval $(t, t + dt)$.

p_6 = probability that aerosol processed through a precipitating air parcel is scavenged and deposited.

p_1, p_5 = probabilities that SO_2 or sulfate aerosol, respectively, are not lost from the regional boundary layer before wet or dry deposition.

$f_2(t), f_7(t)$ = probabilities that SO_2 or sulfate aerosol, respectively, escape dry deposition for time t.

$g_4(t)$ = probability density that an SO_2 molecule remains unoxidized for a period of length t, followed by oxidation in the interval $(t, t + dt)$.

Show that the probability of an SO_2 molecule being oxidized to sulfate aerosol in the regional boundary layer before passing through a precipitating air parcel is

$$P_{ox} = p_1 \int_0^\infty g_4(t) f_2(t) \, dt$$

and the probability of sulfate aerosol being wet deposited is

$$P_{wd} = p_5 p_6 \int_0^\infty g_6(t) f_7(t) \, dt$$

and thus that the probability that an SO_2 molecule is both oxidized to sulfate and deposited is

$$P_{dep} = P_{ox} P_{wd}$$

Let us assume that $f_7(t) = e^{-t/\tau_7}$, with $\tau_7 = 280$ hr. (Based on $v_d = 0.1$ cm sec^{-1} and a 1 km boundary layer), $p_1 = p_5 = 0.75$, $g_6(t) = \tau_6^{-1}e^{-t/\tau_6}$, with $\tau_6 = 138$ hr. Also, we take $p_{dep} = 0.22$. Finally, values of p_6 ranging from $1/3$ to 1.0 have been assumed. Essentially, p_6 is very uncertain because the cloud microphysics is unknown. Using the above values show that

$$p_{wd} = 0.5 p_6$$

and consequently that $p_{ox} = 0.44 p_6^{-1}$. Discuss this result.

Assuming that all SO_2 emission reductions reduce the unoxidized SO_2 fraction before any of the oxidized part is reduced, and using $p_6 = 0.5$, determine the percentage reduction in wet sulfate deposition resulting from a 50 percent reduction in SO_2 emissions.

18.5.   To quantify source–receptor relationships, long-range transport models have been developed (see, for example, Gislason and Prahm, 1983). Many of these models are of the so-called trajectory type in which the concentration changes in a parcel of air are computed as the parcel is advected by the wind field. In most of the trajectory models used in the SO_2/sulfate system, all transformations and removal processes are represented as first-order. (The use of trajectory models to describe long-range transport presumes that we can estimate the location of an air parcel as a function of time. It is clearly an approximation to assume that an air parcel maintains its integrity over a period of many hours to days. Nevertheless, the concept of an integral air parcel has been useful in allowing the formulation of the trajectory model.)

The first-order dry deposition rate constants for SO_2 and SO_4^{2-} for use in a trajectory model are $k^d_{SO_2} = v_{d_{SO_2}}/H$ and $k^d_{SO_4} = v_{d_{SO_4}}/H$, where v_d are the deposition velocities and H is the height of the vertical extent of the model. The height of the mixed layer H varies both diurnally and seasonally, although it is common for regional-scale, single-layer trajectory models to consider only the seasonal variation.

Using the following parameter values, characteristic of noontime, summertime conditions in the northeastern United States (Samson and Small, 1982):

$$H = 1500 \text{ m}$$

$$k_c = 0.03 \text{ hr}^{-1}$$

$$v_{d_{SO_2}} = 1 \text{ cm sec}^{-1}$$

$$v_{d_{SO_4}} = 0.4 \text{ cm sec}^{-1}$$

$$k_{w_{SO_2}} = 5 \times 10^4 \, p_0/H \qquad \left. \begin{array}{l} p_0 \text{ in mm hr}^{-1} \\ \\ H \text{ in mm} \end{array} \right.$$

$$k_{w_{SO_4}} = 2.32 \times 10^5 p_0^{0.625}/H$$

carry out a trajectory model simulation of long-range transport of the sulfur species in that area. Note that the model does not include cloud removal of SO_2. Start a trajectory at the Indiana/Ohio/Kentucky three-state intersection and run it on a line to Albany, NY, at a speed of 10 km hr^{-1}. Continue the calculation for 96 hr and record the complete sulfur material balance for the parcel, including airborne SO_2 and SO_4^{2-}, dry deposited SO_2 and SO_4^{2-}, and wet deposited sulfur. The SO_2 emission rates can be taken as those for 1980 (Figure 18.1):

Ohio	2602×10^3 tons yr^{-1}
Pennsylvania	1971×10^3 tons yr^{-1}
New York	901×10^3 tons yr^{-1}

Assume that three emissions are distributed uniformly over each state. The areas of the states are:

Ohio	115,740 km^2
Pennsylvania	119,316 km^2
New York	137,796 km^2

and the distance as the crow flies from the Indiana/Ohio/Kentucky intersection to Albany, NY, is 966 km. Assume that it rains during the last hour of each 24 hr period at a rate of $p_0 = 10$ mm hr^{-1}. Calculate the total quantity of SO_2 emitted along the trajectory, together with the quantity remaining at the end, the quantities lost by wet and dry deposition, and the quantity converted to sulfate. Perform the same material balance on sulfate. For the purpose of calculation assume the moving air parcel to have a base of 10^4 m^2.

18.6. Clouds act like giant pumps through which large quantities of air are processed. Aside from transporting boundary layer air into the free troposphere, clouds act as filters and remove soluble gases and aerosols from that air. Although the physics of the interaction among cloud droplets, gases, and aerosols is very complex, insights can be gained by representing in-cloud processes as a flow-through reactor in which boundary layer air containing SO_2, HNO_3, NO_x, NH_3, O_3, H_2O_2, CO_2, and aerosol flows through the well-mixed region (reactor) representing the cloud (Hong and Carmichael, 1984). We say that the cloud consists of cloud droplets of radius R_c and number concentration N_c. Gases are absorbed and aerosol particles are captured, and inside the droplets chemical reactions occur.

Show that, subject to these assumptions, within the gas phase the concentration of a species i obeys

$$V\frac{dc_i}{dt} = q\left(c_i^0 - c_i\right) - Vk_{ni}c_i - k_{gi}V4\pi R_c^2 N_c\left(c_i - c_i'/H_i RT\right)$$

where V = cloud volume, q = volumetric flow rate of air through the cloud, c_i^0 = concentration of species i in the entrained air, k_{ni} = first-order rate constant for gas-phase conversion of species i, k_{gi} = mass transfer coefficient, and c_i^l is the liquid-phase concentration of species i. Then show that the liquid-phase concentration of species i is governed by:

$$V_l \frac{dc_i^l}{dt} = k_{gi} V 4\pi R_c^2 N_c \left(c_i - c_i^l / H_i RT \right) - q_l c_i^l + V_l R_i$$

where V_l = liquid water volume, q_l = volumetric flow rate of water out by the cloud by rainfall, and R_i = rate of generation of species i by liquid-phase reactions.

The microphysics of the cloud will be represented in terms of the liquid water content L, rainfall intensity p_0, updraft velocity w, cloud depth h_c, and cloud cross-sectional area A.

We wish to use this model to investigate sulfate production in clouds. The conditions to be simulated are as follows. (Take $T = 273$ K.)

Case	$[SO_2]$, ppb	$[O_3]$, ppb	$[NH_3]$, ppb	$[HNO_3]$, ppb	$[H_2O_2]$, ppb	R_c, cm	p_0, mm hr^{-1}	w, m sec^{-1}	h_c, km	L, cm^3 m^{-3}
1	50	100	1	10	10	0.003	1	2.5	5	0.3
2	50	100	1	10	50	0.003	1	2.5	5	0.3
3	50	100	1	10	50	0.003	10	2.5	5	0.3
4	50	100	1	10	50	0.03	1	2.5	5	0.3

The in-cloud S(IV) oxidation reactions to be considered are those involving O_3 and H_2O_2. The necessary equilibrium and kinetic data can be obtained from Chapter 5. The dynamic calculations should be done by numerically integrating the differential equations for c_i and c_i^l together with the relevant electroneutrality relation. The results of the computation should be presented in terms of the ratio of c_i at $t = 25$ min to c_i at $t = 0$. Discuss your results.

Index

729